Perspectives on the
Development of
Memory and Cognition

CONTRIBUTORS

John M. Belmont, *University of Kansas Medical Center, Kansas City, Kansas*
Ann L. Brown, *University of Illinois, Champaign, Illinois*
Earl C. Butterfield, *University of Kansas Medical Center, Kansas City, Kansas*
Joseph C. Campione, *University of Illinois, Champaign, Illinois*
Michael Cole, *The Rockefeller University, New York, New York*
Frank N. Dempster, *University of California, Berkeley, California*
John H. Flavell, *University of Minnesota, Minneapolis, Minnesota*[1]
John W. Hagen, *University of Michigan, Ann Arbor, Michigan*
Robert V. Kail, Jr., *University of Pittsburgh, Pittsburgh, Pennsylvania*
Akira Kobasigawa, *University of Windsor, Windsor, Ontario*
Lynn S. Liben, *University of Rochester, Rochester, New York*[2]
Barbara K. Lindauer, *Purdue University, West Lafayette, Indiana*[3]
John A. Meacham, *State University of New York, Buffalo, New York*
Barbara E. Moely, *Tulane University, New Orleans, Louisiana*
Scott G. Paris, *Purdue University, West Lafayette, Indiana*
Hayne W. Reese, *West Virginia University, Morgantown, West Virginia*
William D. Rohwer, Jr., *University of California, Berkeley, California*
Sylvia Scribner, *The Rockefeller University, New York, New York*
Alexander W. Siegel, *University of Pittsburgh, Pittsburgh, Pennsylvania*
Keith G. Stanovich, *University of Michigan, Ann Arbor, Michigan*
Tom Trabasso, *Princeton University, Princeton, New Jersey*[4]
Henry M. Wellman, *University of Minnesota, Minneapolis, Minnesota*[5]

[1] Present address: Stanford University, Stanford, California
[2] Present address: Pennsylvania State University, University Park, Pennsylvania
[3] Present address: University of Denver, Denver, Colorado
[4] Present address: University of Minnesota, Minneapolis, Minnesota
[5] Present address: Arizona State University, Tempe, Arizona

Perspectives on the Development of Memory and Cognition

Edited by

ROBERT V. KAIL, JR.
University of Pittsburgh

JOHN W. HAGEN
University of Michigan

 LAWRENCE ERLBAUM ASSOCIATES, PUBLISHERS
1977   Hillsdale, New Jersey

DISTRIBUTED BY THE HALSTED PRESS DIVISION OF

JOHN WILEY & SONS

New York   Toronto   London   Sydney

Lawrence Erlbaum Associates, Inc., Publishers
62 Maria Drive
Hillsdale, New Jersey 07642

Distributed solely by Halsted Press Division
John Wiley & Sons, Inc., New York

Library of Congress Cataloging in Publication Data

Main entry under title:

Perspectives on the development of memory and
    cognition.

    Includes bibliographical references and indexes.
    1. Memory in children.   2. Cognition in
children.   I. Kail, Robert V.   II. Hagen, John W.
BF723.M4p47   155.4'13   77-23942
ISBN 0-470-99273-5

Printed in the United States of America

Contents

v

Preface

For most of the twentieth century, interest in children's memory has been restricted mainly to the development of tests of retention that were included in standardized tests of intelligence. Systematic investigations of children's memory were almost nonexistent. For example, in 1965 memory was not included as an entry in the index of *Child Development Abstracts and Bibliography*. The situation has changed, however, during the past decade. The study of developmental changes in children's memory has attracted the attention of many developmental psychologists, with the result that research in the area has flourished. Returning to *Child Development Abstracts and Bibliography,* there were 43 references to memory in 1975, a figure that surely underestimates growth in the literature of children's memory because of the complementary increase in the technical vocabulary now used to describe mnemonic phenomena (e.g., encoding, retrieval).

Why has the study of children's memory drawn the interest of so many researchers? At least three elements seem to have converged in the 1960s to create a Zeitgeist favorable to the study of developmental changes in memory. First, developmental psychologists had long been interested in the role of language in children's learning, an interest that was operationalized in studies of transposition and discrimination shifts during the 1950s and 1960s. Much of the research was guided by a hypothesis developed from stimulus–response psychology that the young, preverbal child responds to absolute characteristics of stimuli, while the older, verbal child produces verbal labels for stimuli, which mediate his response. Dissatisfaction with the verbal mediation hypothesis grew in the late 1960s, as it became apparent that the older child's superior ability to learn and remember could not be reduced to a mere ability to label. Instead, labeling was only one of many skills used by older children to process information. Consequently, the research interests of many child psychologists were diverted from tests of the verbal mediation hypothesis to describing developmental changes in the acquisition and retention of information.

Accompanying the dissatisfaction with S–R approaches to children's learning and memory was renewed interest in Piaget's description of cognitive development. In the S–R atmosphere that had prevailed, the study of memory was limited to investigations of the amount of material that could be retained and rates of forgetting. With such an impoverished conception of memory, it is little wonder that few developmental psychologists were attracted to the area. Piaget provided an alternative perspective on the study of development: a cognitive framework, in which the role of memorial processing plays a critical role in a person's acquisition, organization, and use of knowledge. Thus, renewed interest in Piagetian theory specifically fostered interest in cognitive development generally, which altered the nature of research in children's memory from simple investigations of age-related changes in memory span to more complex studies of the relation of mnemonic development to cognitive development.

A final factor contributing to the focus on the study of children's memory is the emergence of memory as an important area of study within experimental psychology. During the 1960s it became apparent that learning could not be studied in isolation from memory, and attention was focused, for example, on the manner in which information was stored as it was learned. At the same time, information theory, computer simulation, and linguistics began to have an impact on research. The result of these latter forces on experimental psychology was to force attention to a total information-processing system in which memory played a key role. The shift of emphasis from learning to memory in experimental psychology no doubt helped create an atmosphere conducive to research on children's memory and also provided developmental psychologists with several of the methodological tools necessary to conduct that research.

Thus, we can attribute at least some of the current interest in children's memory to dissatisfaction with the verbal mediation description of age differences in children's learning and memory, the impact of Piagetian theory, and increased interest in memory on the part of experimental psychologists. Having described some of the historical roots of contemporary research on the development of memory, it would be most satisfying to provide an integrated picture of that research. Such a characterization is not yet possible, unfortunately. A theoretical account has not yet been offered that encompasses the many developmental changes that occur in memory. What we have instead are several dominant themes that seem to characterize different aspects of memory development. We have organized the volume around two of these broad themes. The first theme is that memory development is not the development of a unitary skill; rather, it represents the development of a diverse assortment of skills and subskills. The development of some of these skills is discussed in Part I, "The Development of Basic Memory Processes." A second theme is that memory develops not in isolation from other cognitive skills but in interaction with them. Consequently, an understanding of memorial processing may be necessary to study other cognitive skills, as can be seen in Part II, "The Role of Memory in Cognitive Development."

We think that the authors of the chapters have skillfully depicted these various aspects of memory development, and that a foundation for a theory of memory development has been laid. We hope that from their efforts such a theory may emerge.

ROBERT V. KAIL, JR.
JOHN W. HAGEN

Part I

THE DEVELOPMENT OF BASIC MEMORY PROCESSES

1

Metamemory

John H. Flavell
Stanford University

Henry M. Wellman
Arizona State University

I. OVERVIEW OF MEMORY DEVELOPMENT

Memory development is not and could not be a unitary process of change and acquisition, progressing toward a single ontogenetic destination. It could not be such a process because memory itself is not a homogeneous psychological domain. For the student of memory development, it may be useful to distinguish four broad, partially overlapping categories of memory-related phenomena.

The first category consists of the most basic operations and processes of the memory system. Examples include the processes by which an object is recognized, the processes of representation underlying recall of absent objects or events, and the process of cueing or associating, by which one thing calls to mind or reminds us of another, related thing. We are not conscious of the actual working of these processes, and while we may be able to set them in motion by a conscious effort to remember, we probably cannot regulate or control their operation once set into motion.

In addition, most of these processes probably undergo no significant development with age (e.g., Brown, 1973). What few may develop appear to have a strongly maturational cast to them. For instance, the ability to recall an absent object, as contrasted with the ability to recognize one that is present, must presuppose the more general capacity to have conscious internal representations. This capacity is widely believed to emerge some time during late infancy, and maturational factors probably play a large role in its development. The more typical instance of this category may undergo no real development at all, however. For example, one is not really surprised to learn that, for 2-year-olds as for their elders, recall of one item can indeed cue recall of another, semantically related item (Goldberg, Perlmutter, & Myers, 1974). In sum, we would echo Morrison, Holmes, and Haith's (1974) conclusion, deleting only the qualifier

3

"visual": "To use a computer metaphor, the basic 'hardware' of visual memory seemed to exist at all age levels [p. 424]."

The second, third, and fourth categories of memory phenomena are reminiscent of Brown's (1975) distinction between "knowing," "knowing how to know," and "knowing about knowing," respectively. They are considerably more interesting to a developmentalist than the first.

The second category has to do with relatively direct, involuntary, and usually unconscious effects of one's attained level of general cognitive development on one's memory behavior. Older individuals presumably store, retain, and retrieve a great many inputs better or differently than younger ones. They will do so simply because developmental advances in the content and structure of their semantic or conceptual systems render these inputs more familiar, meaningful, conceptually interrelated, subject to inference and gap filling, or otherwise more memorable for them. The participation of such content and structure, "knowing" or knowledge, in the mnemonic process can and usually does take place unconsciously and automatically, as do the operations of the first category. Indeed, an organism would be badly adapted to its environment if very much of its remembering required deliberate, voluntary, self-conscious activity.

The third category in this taxonomy of memory phenomena subsumes the enormous variety of potentially conscious behaviors that an individual may voluntarily elect to carry out in the service of any mnemonic end, that is, strategies. It is sometimes distinguishable from the second by its more voluntary, strategic quality. An adult dog has basic memory "hardware" (first category) and has certainly acquired knowledge of its world that powerfully affects its mnemonic activity (second category). We are loath to credit it with much development in the third category, however. This category includes but goes beyond what Atkinson and Shiffrin (1968) probably had in mind when they coined the term *control processes*. Mentally rehearsing someone's number during the brief journey from telephone book to telephone, deliberately trying to fix a name in memory by surrounding it with vivid retrieval cues, consciously attempting to reconstruct the day's events in order to remember when and where you might have mislaid your pen, and purposefully making a note on your calendar so you won't forget to call the plumber tomorrow—these are all familiar, everyday examples.

The fourth category refers to the individual's knowledge of and awareness of memory, or of anything pertinent to information storage and retrieval. One of us has christened it *metamemory* (Flavell, 1971a), in analogy with *metalanguage*. A person has metamemory if he knows that some things are easier for him to remember than others, is aware that one item is on the verge of recall while another item is wholly irretrievable at present, and numerous other things we are about to catalog. Since metamemory refers to cognition about a type of human activity, it is of course a form of social cognition.

In the present chapter the focus in on developments in the fourth category. We first present a model of what the growing child could conceivably acquire in the domain of metamemory, accompanied by brief reviews of existing research evidence on metamnemonic acquisitions (Section II). There follows a discussion of possible relations between metamemory and other psychological phenomena, especially the third area just discussed, strategic memory behavior (Section III). We conclude with some guesses about how metamemory might be acquired (Section IV). We do not attempt to define metamemory very precisely in this chapter, cleanly distinguishing it from processes in the other three categories (the third, especially). We also do not propose a systematic developmental ordering or timetable for the myriad forms of metamemory, indicating which forms might normally be expected to precede which in ontogeny. Such an ordering has been roughly outlined by Kreutzer, Leonard, and Flavell (1975, chap. IV). Anything more than a rough outline would be premature, in our judgment, given the newness of the area and the relative paucity of solid research evidence concerning it.

II. VARIETIES OF METAMEMORY:
A CLASSIFICATION SCHEME AND A SURVEY
OF RELEVANT LITERATURE

The present scheme is an attempt to answer what appears to be a central question concerning metamemory: *What might a person conceivably come to know, or know how to find out, concerning memory as a function of cognitive growth and learning experience?* We want to be able to classify, in other words, *everything* of this sort that might develop. The insertion of the phrase "know how to find out" allows for the likely possibility that some knowledge about memory may be constructed by a subject for the very first time in response to an experimenter's query, for example, by mentally testing out various mnemonic activities appropriate to the query and formulating his response on the basis of feedback from these covert "dry runs." Other knowledge may of course already exist in implicit or explicit form on the basis of previous memory experiences. The assumption, then, is that both mnemonic knowledge and skill at acquiring mnemonic knowledge are likely outcomes of cognitive growth and learning experience. Finally, we do not assume that all such acquired knowledge must be veridical, although most of it probably is.

In brief, the taxonomy we propose is this. First, some situations call for planful memory-related exertions and some do not. A person no doubt comes to know this fact. Second, performance in a memory situation or task is influenced by a number of factors the nature of which a person might know. We see three main classes of such factors: (1) memory-relevant characteristics of the person himself; (2) memory-relevant characteristics of the task; and (3) potential employable strategies.

A. Sensitivity to the Objective Need
for Efforts at Present Retrieval
or at Preparation for Future Retrieval

Among the important things a growing person may learn is to be attuned to and responsive to those occasions when it is adaptive either to try to retrieve something right now or to prepare himself and/or his environment for effective future retrieval. It goes without saying that, like all of us, the young child is constantly learning and recalling things *incidentally,* that is, without any deliberate intention to learn or recall. But what about *intentional* retrieval or preparation for future retrieval? Will he do either when explicitly asked to by someone else (elicited activity)? Will he do either without explicitly being asked to if an "objective need" is present (spontaneous activity)?

We shall take up these two questions presently, but first some comments about terminology are in order. The expression *preparation for retrieval* is preferable here to *storage, study,* or *memorization* because it is more general. Marking one's calendar is preparing the external environment so that it will facilitate future retrieval of something. Rehearsal or verbal elaboration is preparing oneself, or one's "internal environment," for exactly the same purpose. Terms like *storage* and *memorization* primarily connote the latter, internal type of activity and consequently are too limited to cover the wide range of intelligent activities adults routinely use to optimize future retrieval. Similarly, *retrieval* is used instead of, say, *recall,* because it subsumes recognition memory, paraphrase versus rote reproduction of the original input, inspecting one's calendar, and any other form of data recovery not clearly connoted by *recall.* More important, it permits, even though it may not immediately suggest, the interpretation that the search process and the item searched for may themselves also be external as well as internal.

In real, everyday, extralaboratory life our search and "retrieval" activities often alternate unpredictably between the inner world and the outer world. For example, we may first try unsuccessfully to remember exactly where we left that missing pen (internal search), then look for it in various likely places (external search based on internal retrieval), perhaps get cued by what we encounter there to think of still other likely places (more internal search and retrieval), and finally search for and find the pen in one of them (external search and retrieval). Thus, not all preparation for future retrieval entails internal storage or memorization processes, and not all subroutines of all retrieval sequences entail internal retrieval or remembering processes. In fact, what we are calling "knowledge about memory" may itself be too narrow a designation, since some of the "knowledge" one might wish to talk about in this connection may not be about "memory" as conventionally understood. It might, for example, consist of knowledge about how to search the *external* world intelligently, a form of knowledge that also undergoes a marked development with age (Drozdal & Flavell, 1975).

1. Elicited Activities

Let us begin with the question about activities elicited by explicit retrieval and preparation-for-retrieval directives from others. Children will, from a very early age, search the internal and external world in response to another's retrieval directive. For instance, they will try to answer questions like "Where's your dolly?" and "What did you see at the zoo today?" However, we know of no formal studies dealing with the very young child's knowledge, abilities, and dispositions as regards such elicited retrieval. In the case of mnemonic, in-the-head retrieval, for instance, when does the child come to learn that what is not immediately remembered may come to mind with a little more thought and sustained concentration? Our guess is that early in development he automatically gives up if he cannot find the requested item immediately, and only subsequently learns that staying with the retrieval problem a little longer sometimes pays off. We are of course talking here only about simple persistence at this early level in attending to another person's request for retrieval, not about the use of clever retrieval strategies to supplement this nonstrategic retrieval effort.

There does exist some research evidence concerning young children's reactions to explicit instructions to prepare for future retrieval, as contrasted with instructions to retrieve right now. Most of this evidence centers on a developmental hypothesis initially proposed by Russian investigators (e.g., Istomina, cited in Smirnov, 1973; Smirnov & Zinchenko, 1969; Yendovitskaya, 1971) and first tested in the United States by Appel, Cooper, McCarrell, Sims-Knight, Yussen, and Flavell (1972). According to this "differentiation hypothesis," as Appel et al. (1972) called it, the young child does not really understand that an explicit request to memorize a set of items for future recall is an implicit request to do something special with those items. It is an implicit request to scrutinize them very carefully and at length, or to name or rehearse them—in other words, to engage in some sort of intensive intellectual commerce with those items that might facilitate later retrieval. The young child has to acquire the recognition that a memorization instruction is a tacit invitation to be planful and goal directed, to do something now that will only come to fruition later. In particular, he must learn to differentiate a future-oriented memorization instruction from a present-oriented perception instruction. Early in development, both might be treated as requests merely to perceive the items in an idle, essentially purposeless fashion.

Appel et al. (1972) obtained initial support for the differentiation hypothesis in two experiments with 4-, 7-, and 11-year-old children. Comparisons were made between children's study behavior and subsequent recall performance under instructions to memorize items for future recall versus instructions just to look carefully at the items. The 11-year-olds clearly differentiated between the two instructions, both conceptually and behaviorally. They seemed to know that the memorization task called for special study activities (e.g., spontaneous categorization, rehearsal), were more likely to engage in such activities under the memorization instruction than under the look instruction, and consequently achieved better recall results in the memorization condition. Appel et al. (1972) concluded that the 7-year-olds probably differentiated more clearly conceptually than behaviorally. That is, they probably grasped the general meaning and implications of the memorization instructions but typically did not command the study techniques that would behaviorally testify to the presence of that understanding. Finally, it was concluded that the 4-year-olds probably failed to differentiate both conceptually and behaviorally, and had yet to acquire a clear notion of deliberate, intentional memorization.

This picture of the development of intentional preparation for future retrieval has been revised in subsequent research (Wellman, Ritter, & Flavell, 1975; Yussen, 1975). The key idea turns out to have been Appel et al.'s (1972) distinction between conceptual and behavioral differentiation, as used in their characterization of what the 7-year-olds in their study knew versus what they did. First of all, it is now becoming very clear that many 7-year-olds in our society will indeed process items differently and recall them better under a memorization versus look instruction if they "can," that is, if they can think of anything mnemonically beneficial to do with those particular items (Salatas & Flavell, 1976; Yussen, Gagné, Gargiulo, & Kunen, 1974). For instance, they may carefully inspect and name items under a memorization instruction, and that may benefit recall in some task situations. That is, children of this age do seem to distinguish conceptually between an instruction to memorize and a nonmnemonic cognitive processing instruction.

Second, some conception of intentional memorization is detectable in even younger children, according to recent evidence. Yussen (1974) found that 4½- to 5½-year-olds will look at a model more, under conditions of perceptual distraction, if explicitly told to remember the model's behavior in order to reproduce it later. Unlike more sophisticated mnemonics (e.g., cumulative rehearsal, categorical grouping), "looking more" is a simple study behavior that a preschooler is likely to have under good control.

Even 3-year-olds seem to understand something of what it means to remember intentionally a spatial location, according to two recent series of studies (Acredelo, Pick, & Olsen, 1975; Wellman et al., 1975). In the Acredelo et al. (1975) experiment, children were taken on strolls, exposed to an event, and later asked to find the spot where the event had taken place. On one trial the child was told at the time that he would later have to find it; on another trial he was not. Recall was a great deal better when foreknowledge was provided.

In the Wellman et al. (1975) investigation, 3-year-olds experienced a series of trials of this kind: The child saw the experimenter hide a toy under one of a number of identical cups; the experimenter used a pretext to leave the room for 40 to 45 seconds; he asked the child to find the toy as soon as he returned. The toys were central figures in a story narrative that extended over the trials, and different toys were hidden under different identical cups on different trials. Some children were told to "*wait* here with the X (hidden toy)" and others to "*re-*

member where the X is." In two of Wellman et al.'s (1975) studies, the children asked to remember the location of the toys exhibited more behaviors during the delay period that looked like deliberate or semideliberate preparation for future retrieval than did children who merely waited with the toy; examples included touching or looking at the baited box, and making the baited box distinctive early in the delay. In one of these studies, it was easy for almost all the children to remember where the toy was. In another, the recall task was made harder by adding more cups. The children in the "remember" condition recalled better than the children in the "wait" condition in the latter study, and memory-relevant delay period behavior was correlated with recall in the "remember" group.

Wellman et al. (1975) suggested two possible explanations for such precocious-looking intentional storage. One is the availability of simple but task-appropriate strategies in that particular situation, such as looking and touching. This factor is emerging as an important consideration in interpreting data on memory development generally, we believe. The second is the fact that what had to be remembered, in both the Wellman et al. (1975) and Acredelo et al. (1975) studies, was the spatial location of a concrete object, not a series of object names. The young child may get a good deal of reinforced practice at trying to remember where things are in everyday life. Adults often encourage or demand this kind of memory, for example, exhort him to keep track of his toys and clothing. Also, memory for object locations is often a useful means to his own objectives.

2. Spontaneous Activities

Very little is known about the development of spontaneous, as contrasted with elicited or instructed, intentional activities in response to an objective need. Moreover, what little is known concerns preparation for future retrieval rather than present retrieval. Suppose that an adult has just retrieved certain items on a recall test and failed to retrieve others. He will probably be aware that, with a second recall test of those same items imminent, the situation tacitly calls for further study of the latter, missed items in preference to the former, successfully retrieved ones. It turns out that 7-year-olds are considerably less sensitive than adults to the differential-study implications of this particular situation (Masur, McIntrye, & Flavell, 1973).

A study by Siegler and Liebert (1975) entailed the planful use of an external rather than an internal memory store. Ten- and 13-year-olds were given the task of setting four switches into all possible up-down positions, in order to find the unique combination that would make an electric train run. They were supplied with paper and pencil and told, "There are many possibilities and you don't want to repeat the same choices you already made, so you might want to keep a record of which choices you have tried and found not to work." They found that keeping written records was quite strongly associated with the number of distinct combinations generated, and also that many more 13-year-olds than 10-year-olds elected to keep such records. Siegler and Liebert (1975) suggest that the younger children may simply not have anticipated the need or utility of doing so.

On the retrieval side, it has been shown in several studies that providing children with external memory aids, such as visible records of past solution attempts, may facilitate solution of problems (e.g., Eimas, 1970; Roodin & Gruen, 1970; Sieber, Kameya, & Paulson, 1970). Lipsitt and Eimas (1972) conclude from such evidence that "deficiencies in complex problem-solving situations may often be a function of the unavailability of relevant information and not of the absence of the necessary rules or operations, as has often been assumed [p. 31]." While we agree with this conclusion, there is an interesting ambiguity in their term, *unavailability*. First, the child might do poorly without the external memory provided by the experimenter because he is simply incapable of recalling the pertinent information at the appropriate moment or, recalling it, cannot hold it in working memory long enough to use it in solving the problem. Either could of course happen to any problem solver, however sophisticated, under conditions of memory or attentional overload. A second possibility, however, is that the child might be quite capable of recalling the information if he thought to try, but might simply not think to try. There may, in other words, be no spontaneous self-instruction to try to retrieve pertinent information, that is, the retrieval counterpart of the spontaneous preparation-for-retrieval shortcoming seen by Siegler and Liebert (1975) and Masur et al. (1973).

The term *production deficiency* was initially coined to describe a child's failure to use any particular memorization strategy spontaneously when the situation called for it, even though he could and would use that strategy effectively if explicitly directed to do so by someone else (Flavell, 1970). The sense of the present discussion is that the young child may have a far more general and pervasive "production deficiency" than that: He may seldom think of deliberately trying to retrieve at all, or of deliberately trying to prepare for future retrieval at all, in response to situations that commonly elicit precisely these sorts of cognitive efforts in more mature individuals. Part of metamemory development, then, may consist of coming to know when and why one should intentionally store and retrieve information.

B. Knowing What Variables Interact in What Ways to Affect the Quality of Performance on a Retrieval Problem

1. Person Variables

Person variables include all temporary and enduring personal attributes and states that are relevant to data retrieval. There is a great deal that a developing individual could potentially learn, and learn how to find out, about himself as a mnemonic organism. First, he could develop a "mnemonic self-concept" that becomes increasingly elaborated and differentiated with respect to different retrieval tasks and different retrievers. For instance, experience may have taught him that he is only fair at remembering places and dates, but quite good at remembering people. He could also form impressions about how his skills at doing such things compare with those of other people: specific individuals and generalized others of similar and different ages, backgrounds, abilities, and personalities.

There is, moreover, much to learn about the capacities, limitations, and idiosyncracies of the human memory system. The growing person could discover that immediate memory is of small span and limited duration, and that additional processing may be needed to optimize subsequent retrieval. He could also induce from experience the related, sad fact that one cannot always count on retrieving later what was stored earlier, plus the happy fact that what cannot be remembered right now will often be remembered eventually. There is the further knowledge that the memory system can be untrustworthy as well as porous: It is possible to remember what did not happen and to misremember what did, in addition to outright forgetting.

The growing child may gradually learn how to read his own memory states and statuses with fair accuracy, and also to understand the behavioral implications of being in this as opposed to that state. As he becomes more attuned to internal "mnemonic sensations," he might intuit that one datum was never stored and another is in memory somewhere, but absolutely unrecoverable right now. The behavioral implication in both cases is to forgo or abandon efforts at retrieval. In contrast, a third datum might be experienced as right on the threshold of recall (the "tip of the tongue" feeling), and the child could have learned to be more optimistic when he senses his memory to be in that particular state. He may also have discovered that, when learning something, the clear implication of a feeling of poor or uncertain retrievability is to keep on studying until some more satisfactory state of recall readiness is experienced.

A distinction between two related types of metamemory within this general category is suggested by this account. The first two paragraphs of this section refer mainly to general, previously acquired knowledge about the properties of self and others. The third paragraph speaks instead about the ability to monitor and interpret concrete experiences in the here and now. Thus, the one type of metamemory concerns enduring abilities and traits, while the other refers to transient processes and states. Needless to say, present monitoring and interpreting of specific states is informed by acquired knowledge of general properties, and knowledge of these properties must be acquired in part by monitoring and interpreting states.

In the case of general properties, it has been shown in three investigations that older children may have a clearer and more accurate conception of their own memory abilities and limitations than do younger children. Flavell, Friedrichs, and Hoyt (1970) asked children to predict how many depicted objects they would be able to recall in correct serial order, and subsequently assessed the children's actual ability to do so. The predictions were secured by briefly exposing successively longer sequences of pictures, either until the child thought that the series had now become too long for him to recall or until a series of 10 pictures had been presented. Over one-half of the younger children (4–6 years of age) predicted "unrealistically" (the maximum, 10-object series), whereas fewer than one-fourth of the older ones (7–10 years) did so. Moreover, considering only the remaining, "realistic" children, the older ones predicted significantly more accurately than the younger ones.

Markman (1973) essentially replicated this part of Flavell et al.'s (1970) study, using only a 5-year-old sample. The children in her study proved to be just about as inaccurate in predicting their own recall as the younger children in Flavell et al.'s study. By using additional procedures she was also able to show that children of this age (1) can predict their ability to perform certain motor tasks (e.g., the distance they can jump) much more accurately than they can predict their ability to recall; (2) predict others' ability to recall at about the same mean level of accuracy as they do their own, with the two accuracy scores also being positively correlated within individual subjects; and (3) believe that older people can recall more than younger ones (teen-agers > peers > 2-year-olds).

Finally, Yussen and Levy (1975), with 4-, 8-, and 20-year-olds, obtained age trends in accuracy of memory span prediction congruent with those found by Flavell et al. (1970). Mean predicted versus mean actual spans, reading from youngest to oldest groups, were: 8.18 versus 3.34, 6.60 versus 4.71, and a very accurate 5.89 versus 5.52. In a second study, Yussen and Levy (1975) gave 8- and 20-year-old subjects falsely low norm information, that is, indicating that people of the subject's age have smaller spans than is actually the case. The provision of this information reduced the 8-year-olds' predicted spans to their actual spans and reduced the 20-year-olds' to below their actual spans. It seems to us that the adults, especially, in Yussen and Levy's study demonstrated an impressive amount of metamemory. They could predict their memory spans accurately; they were sensibly uncertain about their ability to predict them, in view of the novelty of the task situation; they believed that information about peers' performance on a novel memory task might provide a useful clue.

Preliminary developmental evidence on a number of aspects of metamemory, including Person variables, has been presented in a recent monograph by Kreutzer et al. (1975). Twenty children in each of grades K, 1, 3, and 5 were interviewed individually (approximate ages: 6, 7, 9, and 11 years, respectively). The 14 interview items in the battery each contained one or more questions or problems dealing with information retrieval or preparation for future retrieval. The older children in this study seemed to have a more differentiated self-concept in this area than the younger ones. For example, they appeared more attuned to the fact that memory ability varies from occasion to occasion within the same individual, and differs from individual to individual within the same age group. In addition, while 5-year-olds may believe that older children can *recall* better than younger ones (Markman, 1973), Kreutzer et al. (1975) found that 9- and 11-year-olds may further believe that older children will also *study* differently in preparation for future recall.

At the same time, Kreutzer et al.'s younger subjects did seem to use everyday mnemonic terminology such as *remember, forget,* and the like fairly appropriately. A number of them also sensed that briefly presented rote information is subject to rapid memory loss: If just told a phone number to dial, one had better dial it right away rather than get a drink of water first. They also believed that a child who learned bird names in school last year "and then forgot them" would nonetheless find them "easier to learn" this year than a classmate who had not had them last year.

In the case of here-and-now memory monitoring, there is evidence that young children are liable to have at least some awareness of how well they have just done on a retrieval test. They may be aware, for instance, that they have or have not completed recall of all the items just presented for learning (Neimark, Slotnick, & Ulrich, 1971), although older children are likely to be better at this than younger ones (Geis & Lange, 1975). They can also easily recognize which items they have just recalled and which they have not, when shown the entire set afterwards (Masur et al., 1973). Finally, they show some ability to estimate the accuracy of their own recognition memory judgments (Berch & Evans, 1973). If a 5-year-old child feels certain that an item has been presented previously or has not been presented previously, he is more likely to be correct in fact than if he feels uncertain about his judgment; this relationship between certainty and accuracy is considerably stronger in 8-year-olds, however.

In contrast, younger children do not seem to be as able as older ones to assess or predict their readiness to retrieve in advance, that is, prior to the actual recall test. The children in Flavell et al.'s (1970) study were carefully instructed to study a set of items until they were absolutely sure they could recall them all without error. The size of each child's item set was determined by his previous recall performance. In each of three successive trials he first studied the items, then signaled his readiness to recall them, and immediately thereafter attempted to do so. Children 4–6 years of age were much less proficient at estimating their readiness for recall than children 7–10 years of age. The latter's recall was usually perfect on all three trials. The former's was not, and did not improve significantly over trials. Markman (1973) also repeated and extended this portion of the Flavell et al. (1970) investigation. She concluded that Flavell et al.'s experimental procedures may have actually led them to *overestimate* a 5-year-old's ability to monitor his own preparedness for retrieval. Neimark et al. (1971) also found that a number of their 6-year-old subjects were rather poor at assessing their own readiness to recall. Indeed, there is recent evidence (Denhière, 1974) that adults are by no means perfect at such assessment.

Ongoing or recent mnemonic experiences can sometimes provide clues for other mnemonic judgments and predictions, but the young child's use of them is variable. Immediately prior experience in actually recalling strongly categorized lists may heighten a 6- or 7-year-old's awareness of the greater ease of learning and recall of such lists, but the evidence is not altogether unequivocal on this point (Moynahan, 1973; Salatas & Flavell, 1976). Markman (1973) found that some of the 5-year-olds in her study improved in their ability to predict their own memory span with practice in such prediction, even if given no feedback as to prediction accuracy; others did not, however, even with such feedback. Some of the children in Yussen and Levy's (1975) study tried (and, of course, failed) to recall sequences of 9 and 10 items *before* being asked to predict their ability to recall sequences of this length and shorter. Such actual recall experience had no effect on their predicted spans, even in the 8-year-old group. As for the 4-year-olds, according to Yussen and Levy (1975):

> The authors were amazed by the several preschoolers who actually predicted that they could recall 10 or 9 items after just being shown that they could not recall this many in the . . . practice sequence. The preschoolers were aware of their failure but said things like: "If you gave me a different list like that, I could do it" [p. 507].

Finally, one further study has dealt with here-and-now memory monitoring in children (Wellman, in press). In adults one of the most intriguing examples of memory monitoring is the everyday tip-of-the-tongue experience (Brown & McNeill, 1966) or the related feeling-of-knowing experience (Hart, 1965). In both of these phenomena a person is in the position of failing to recall something but still knowing that he knows it. In such experiences the person not only monitors the state of an item in his own memory, but monitors it even in the item's "absence." In making a feeling-of-knowing judgment, for example, individuals who cannot recall an answer to a question predict whether or not they could recognize the answer among a set of alternatives. Adults can make this kind of prediction accurately (Hart, 1965, 1967), in spite of the fact that, when they make it, the answer cannot be retrieved and there is no present opportunity for it to be recognized.

Wellman (in press) studied feeling-of-knowing and tip-of-the-tongue experiences and their concomitants in 5-, 7-, and 9-year-old children. Each child was presented with a series of depicted items and asked to name them. If he could not name an item he was asked (1) if he felt he knew the name anyway, and would therefore later recognize it among a set of alternatives, and (2) if he had ever seen the item before. He was subsequently tested for actual recognition of the name, as indicated in (1). Accuracy of predicted recognition/nonrecognition increased with age, indicating an increase in the ability to monitor the states of unrecalled items. More interestingly, for the 5-year-olds judgments of whether an item had been seen before proved to be much more accurate predictors of subsequent name recognition than were judgments about recognizability, while judgments of the latter type were the better predictors for the 9-year-olds. Obviously, knowing if you have seen an item before is an important clue to knowing if you will recognize its name. Apparently, the younger children were poor at assessing what was in memory not because the relevant subjective clues were inaccessible to them—accurate feelings of having seen the item before in the present case— but because they may not recognize that they *are* clues. In addition, there was a definite increase with age in overt expressions of apparent tip of the tongue states, for example, "Oh, I *know* that, I just can't remember the name," and related states of incipient recall.

2. Task Variables

There is much to learn about the factors that make some retrieval tasks harder than others. First, some bodies of information (data, items) are harder to store and retrieve than others; and second, for any given body of stored information, some retrieval demands are more taxing than others.

For the first, considerable knowledge could be acquired as to the different properties of the input information that have effects on its subsequent retrievability. A few of these properties can characterize individual units of information considered in isolation from other units (but not, of course, in isolation from the experiential history and cognitive capabilities of the learner). For example, units that are easily encoded (labeled, imaged), meaningful, and familiar will normally be easier to remember than units that are not.

The majority of retrieval-relevant properties, however, have to do with relations among units, and hence with the structure and organization of whole sets or subsets of information units. Like the above-mentioned properties of individual untis, these relations are familiar to all students of human learning and memory. One piece of information may facilitate the recall of another if they are related for the learner in any of a wide variety of ways. The two may frequently co-occur in experience, be members of the same class or parts of the same whole, occupy adjacent positions in some familiar serial structure, or be related by some logical or causal connection. *Any* meaningful link may make one a retrieval cue for the other, and mature learners may have become aware of this fact about memory. They are virtually certain to have become aware of the influence of a more banal property of the data set, namely, its size. Retrieval is more likely to be incomplete as the list of words, prose passage, or whatever body of information the person is supposed to learn becomes longer or more extensive.

People may also acquire the ability to make complex judgments about retrieval difficulty, weighing the probable influence of one property against that of another. They might recognize, for example, that a list of 16 words could be much easier to recall than a list of 10, provided that the latter consisted of randomly selected words and the former consisted of the series "north,"

"north–northeast," "northeast," "east–northeast" . . . "north–northwest." Finally, not all properties of individual information units or groups of units have substantial effects on retrievability. For example, a list of words should not be appreciably easier to remember if double-spaced rather than single-spaced, or if written in red rather than blue ink. Mature learners may also have acquired some ability to distinguish retrieval-irrelevant properties from retrieval-relevant ones.

As for retrieval demands, an experienced learner could come to understand that difficult retrieval problems make different demands on the retriever, even when the input data remain the same. He could know, for example, that it is normally much easier to recognize something he has previously experienced than to recall it outright, with no external stimulus present to help his retrieval. Similarly, there is the learnable generalization that it is easier to recall the gist of a prose passage or a complex visual stimulus than to reproduce it exactly, word for word or line by line. The individual may also discover that items of information are harder to recall or recognize accurately if subject to the interfering effects of similar, confusable items. Retrieval situations differ considerably, both quantitatively and qualitatively, in the demands they place on the retriever. A level or type of data recovery perfectly suitable for one situation may not be at all appropriate for another. This, too, is part of what the developing person could come to know about memory.

At least some developmental evidence exists concerning most of these task variables. Some of the 6- and 7-year-olds in Kreutzer et al.'s (1975) study seemed to believe that such properties of individual items as familiarity and perceptual salience can make them easier to remember. Similarly, 7-year-olds in Moynahan's (1973) study often said that items that are easy to name or identify are easier to remember. Most of the younger children in Kreutzer et al.'s (1975) investigation seemed very much aware that increasing the number of items in a set increases recall difficulty. Of 16 kindergartners who initially judged one set of items to be easier to learn than another, equal-sized set, 10 reversed their judgment as soon as even one item was added to the easier set.

As for relationships among items, metamemory development regarding categorical structure has received the most study so far. In a study by Moynahan (1973), 7-, 9-, and 10-year-old children were asked to predict the relative difficulty of remembering sets of strongly categorized items versus equal-sized and otherwise comparable sets of conceptually unrelated items. The two older groups were significantly more likely than the youngest to predict that the categorized sets would be easier to recall. Moynahan was also able to show that this developmental difference could not be explained away by any correlated age differences in children's ability to detect the categories or to remember categorized sets better than noncategorized ones. Similarly, Salatas and Flavell (1976) found that a number of 6-year-olds were not immediately cognizant of the mnemonic advantages of categorical organization, even when explicitly made aware of its presence. As indicated earlier, there is evidence from both studies that actual experience in learning categorized lists may make some children in this age range more conscious of its advantages.

In a related study by Tenney (1975), children 5, 8, and 11 years of age were given one word by the experimenter and asked to generate three others; given a second word and again asked to produce three others; and so on. For one group at each age level, the child's three words were in each case to be free associates of the experimenter's word. For a second group, they were to be members of the same category, for example, "three other colors" if the experimenter's word was *blue*. For a third group, they were to be "three other words that would be very easy for you to remember along with the word *blue*." Recall and clustering for the resulting lists were assessed in a second session. Tenney's findings were reminiscent of Moynahan's (1973). Five-year-olds had no difficulty in providing other category members on request (subjects in the second group) and showed high clustering and recall for the lists so generated. However, the first and third groups at this age level behaved very similarly in the first session, and showed low clustering and recall in the second session. According to Tenney (1975):

> The discrepancy between the types of structure which the kindergartners would have found useful [i.e., categorical structures] and the relationships which they actually incorporated into their lists was striking. They made up essentially the same kind of list whether they were asked to free associate or to make up lists for recall [p. 112].

In contrast, when older children were asked to compose an easy-to-remember quartet of words that included *blue*, they were very likely to spontaneously provide three more color words, just like children who were actually given categorization instructions.

Finally, Danner (1976) assessed children's metamemory for categorization at the sentence rather than single-word level. Children 8, 10, and 12 years of age listened to and then tried to recall two 12-sentence passages, each containing four sentences on each of three topics. A polar bear was the subject of one passage, for instance, and 4 of the 12 sentences dealt with the topic of the bear's appearance. In one passage, the sentences were grouped or clustered together by topic, for example, all four "bear appearance" sentences adjacent to one another. In the other passage, no two sentences from a given topic ever followed one another. The former, grouped passage was better recalled and showed higher recall clustering than the unorganized one at all age levels. When subsequently shown all the sentences written out on separate cards and spatially organized as originally presented, older children were better able to detect the organizational differences between the passages than younger ones. Children were also tested for their ability to "take good notes" in preparation for future retrieval of the stories. In Danner's task, that meant making an adequately rationalized selection of one sentence card from each topic, if only allowed to "keep" a total of three cards as "notes" to aid future recall of the entire passage. Of the 24 children at each age level, 5 8-year-olds, 15 10-year-olds, and 21 12-year-olds made such rationalized choices.

As for other kinds of organization, Moynahan (1973) found that her 7-year-olds seemed to understand that serial recall of a linear sequence of colored blocks is likely to be easier when blocks of the same colors are adjacent rather than randomly placed in the series. Thus, while they may not have sensed that categorizable objects portrayed in pictures are easier to recall than unrelated ones, they were likely to believe that a red-red-blue-blue-yellow-yellow block sequence would be easier to reproduce from memory than, say, a red-red-blue-yellow-blue-yellow one. Kreutzer et al. (1975) presented a set of object pictures in two ways: in list form, and woven together into a story ("A man gets up out of *bed*, and gets dressed, putting on his best *tie* and *shoes*. . . ."). The child was then asked if the story presentation would make it easier or harder for an imaginary child of his age to remember the pictures, and why. The investigators found significant increases with age in selection of the story mode of presentation as the "easier" choice and in fairly intelligible, appropriate-sounding justifications of this choice.

In another interview item, Kreutzer et al. (1975) first acquainted the child with paired-associate learning task procedures, and then asked if one of two sets of four word pairs on cards would be "easier for you to learn" than the other, and if so, why. The experimenter explained that "these words are opposites, *boy* goes with *girl, hard* goes with *easy, cry* goes with *laugh,* and *black* goes with *white,* and these words are people and things they might do, so *Mary* goes with *walk, Charley* goes with *jump, Joe* goes with *climb,* and *Anne* goes with *sit.*" The experimenter then added pairs of words one by one to the set initially judged easier to learn until the child said the other set was now easier. The developmental trends were dramatic. Most 6- and 7-year-olds apparently failed to recognize the enormously greater ease of learning of the pairs of opposites. In contrast, the 9- and 11-year-olds did recognize it and, in many cases, could also explain why.

Yet the younger children clearly understood that at least one variable does *not* affect ease of learning and recall: They were almost unanimous in asserting that spreading out a set of pictures does not make them any easier or harder to remember than before.

Two items from the Kreutzer et al. (1975) study were devised to test children's sensitivity to differences in retrieval demands and difficulties with respect to a single set of input items. A number of the 9- and 11-year-olds, but almost none of the 6- and 7-year-olds, seemed to understand that it might be harder to recall a set of people's names if you had learned another, potentially confusable set of people's names right afterwards than if you had not. That is, they showed some intuitive understanding of the classical phenomenon of retroactive interference. There were also marked age trends in the recognition that rote, word-for-word retrieval of a story is harder than free, tell-it-in-your-own-words retrieval. Almost all of the older children but only about one-fourth of the younger ones knew both that a requirement of rote as opposed to paraphrased recall would make the retrieval task harder, and also that it would call for more intensive preparation or study prior to retrieval time.

Finally, temporal aspects of memory tasks have been considered in two studies. Kreutzer et al. presented 20 object pictures and asked which of two children would remember the most—a child who studied them for 1 minute or a child who studied them for 5 minutes—and why. About half the 6-year-olds and almost all the 7-year-olds seemed to sense that more study time was likely to result in more objects recalled. In a study by Rogoff, Newcomb, and Kagan (1974), groups of 4-, 6-, and 8-year-olds were first given concrete experience with one of three temporal delays: a few minutes, one day, or seven days. Each child was then shown a pile of 40 pictures and told he had to remember them for a length of time equal to the delay he had experienced previously. The child inspected the pictures at his own pace, and his inspection time was recorded. Children in the one- or seven-day condition studied longer than those in the few-minutes condition at 8 but not at 6 or 4 years of age. Somewhere in the early elementary school years, then, children apparently come to understand that more items to recall and longer retention intervals both call for more study time.

3. Strategy Variables

There is much to say about the development of knowledge of storage and retrieval strategies, but most of it is taken up in other chapters. Thus, we will only mention a few conceptual points and research findings not likely to be described elsewhere in this volume. It is once again convenient to distinguish between strategies that may serve as preparation for future retrieval and strategies that may facilitate present retrieval.

As Reitman (1970) has pointed out, the variety of specific moves a cognitively mature individual might think to make in preparing for future retrieval is virtually limitless. Change the nature of the task, or the state of the person with respect to it, and such an individual is likely to respond with a spontaneous and often adaptive change in preparation strategy. Butterfield and Belmont (1975) posit an "executive function" that initiates these strategic adaptations, selecting new "control processes" to suit new task conditions. It is reasonable to suppose that this executive function is informed by a considerable amount of metamemory.

We would underscore once again the fact that most retrieval problems in real life are in the nature of open-book rather than closed-book exams: The retriever is free to search external sources as well as his memory, and usually does when he can. Correspondingly, the mature information processor is likely to know that preparations for future retrieval can be made in the outer world as well as the inner one. He may mentally rehearse, cluster, or elaborate on the material to be retrieved, but may also store it by making notes, photocopies, photographs, or tape recordings. He may try to assimilate an item into several different semantic networks in hopes of increasing its retrievability, but he may also sow his life space with written reminders, nonverbal prompts, and other external retrieval cues. Some of the internal and external retrieval cues a person may construct intentionally might better be regarded as indirect reminders to retrieve certain information, rather than as direct elicitors of the information itself. A person may write some key words on his calendar as direct retrieval cues to a whole complex of information. If the recovery of that information on a certain day is especially important, however, he may also think it prudent to make a mental or physical note to look at his calendar that day. Deliberate preparation for future retrieval is a form of planning (Flavell, 1970), and could conceivably be as elaborate and variegated as any other form.

Kreutzer et al. (1975) devised two preparation-for-retrieval and two present-retrieval items of the everyday life, "open-book exam" sort. In one of the preparation tasks, the child was asked to imagine that he was going ice skating with a friend after school tomorrow, and hence wanted to be sure to remember to take his skates with him the next morning. He was asked how many ways he could think of, all the things he could do, to be really certain not to forget them. Two major findings emerged: First, older children could think of more different mnemonics than the younger children could, and generally showed a greater sense of planfulness in their answers. Second, "in-the-world" mnemonics were proposed far more often than "in-the-child" mnemonics by children at all grade levels. A child would frequently think of putting his skates where he would be sure to encounter them in the morning, writing himself a note, or asking his mother to remind him. He would much less frequently speak of thinking about the skates the night before or making mental checks of things to do that morning.

In the other preparation task, the child was asked to think of as many things as possible to do to make sure he would remember a birthday party to which he had been invited. Once again, younger as well as older children tended to favor external physical and social resources over internal ones. They talked about writing notes, marking their calendars, putting the party invitation up on the bulletin board, and asking a parent to remind them. No fewer than 19 of the 20 7-year-olds, for example, mentioned an external-to-self information store as their first or only response in both preparation tasks.

Retrieval strategies can be as elaborate and "intelligent" as preparation strategies and can likewise, of course, involve external as well as internal procedures and retrieval targets. The individual's retrieval activities have something of the quality of a Sherlock Holmes tour de force at their most intricate and sophisticated levels (cf. Lindsay & Norman, 1972). Whether the object of his search (X) is in memory, in the external world, or both, the retriever tries to zero in on it by skillfully integrating specific memories, general knowledge, and logical reasoning. When he realizes that X probably will not come to mind by just sitting and waiting (the latter is always a good *first* move), he deliberately searches his memory for related data, in hopes that something recalled will bring him closer to X. In the most elaborate cases of this sort of intelligent, highly indirect and circumlocutious retrieving, the process is virtually one of rational reconstruction of "what must have been," in the light of remembered data, general knowledge, and logical reasoning. As with the most exotic cases of preparation for retrieval, the amount and quality of voluntary, self-initiated intellectual activity involved can be very substantial.

Kreutzer et al. (1975) tested children's knowledge of retrieval strategies in one interview item by asking them to think of all the things they could do to try to find a jacket they had lost while at school. As expected, the older children could think of a greater number of different retrieval strategies than the younger ones. While almost all of the younger children could indeed think of at least one sensible thing to do, such as look in likely places, try the school's Lost and Found, and enlist the help of others, the two most sophisticated strategies were largely confined to the two oldest groups. One strategy consisted of either trying to think of the last place he remembered having his jacket and searching forward from there or retracing his whole day's activities step by step (11 of the 40 9- and 11-year-olds). The other strategy was an explicit temporal ordering of several search plans, presumably from most to least promising, for example, "First I'd do X, and if I didn't find it there, then I'd look in Y" (18 of 40 9- and 11-year-olds). Knowledge about external search akin to the first of these two strategies was investigated in a study by Drozdal and Flavell (1975). If A is the last point in your itinerary where you are sure you possessed a lost item, and if B is the first point where you discovered it is missing, then the $A–B$ segment of your itinerary is the only plausible area to search for it, assuming it could not move or be moved. Children 9 to 10 years of age understand and articulate this line of reasoning very well, according to Drozdal and Flavell's data, but children 5 to 6 years of age do neither.

In the other Kreutzer et al. (1975) retrieval-strategy item the interviewer said to the child:

> Suppose your friend has a dog and you ask him how old his dog is. He tells you he got his dog as a puppy one Christmas but can't remember *which* Christmas. What things could he do to help him remember *which* Christmas he got the dog? Anything else he could do [p. 36]?

The 6-year-olds probably did not understand this rather complex item very well, but the older children generally did. Asking the help of others was a common suggestion at age 7 and older. Especially at age 11, however, other interesting strategies were proposed. Five 11-year-olds suggested looking for naturally occurring external records, for example, the dog's papers or a dog tag. Four proposed searching backwards in memory in a highly methodical, Christmas-by-Christmas fashion, somewhat analogous to searching for the lost jacket by retracing one's steps in the previously mentioned retrieval item. Nine suggested trying to remember things that were temporally associated with the dog's arrival, usually other presents received that Christmas. In one child's words: "Maybe he could remember some of his toys that he got the same Christmas he got his dog and he could tell from the Christmas he got his toys."

This last strategy has that indirect, circumlocutious quality that seems to be the hallmark of much deliberate, strategic remembering. Marked increases with age

in the use of an indirect retrieval procedure were also revealed in a study by Salatas and Flavell (in press). The subjects were 6-, 9-, and 21-year-olds. They first acquired a good strategy *(A)* for remembering all of the items in a set. Their task *(C)* was then to name all of the items in that set that had a certain property (e.g., easily breakable). A good strategy *(B)* to be sure not to miss any items possessing that property would be to recall all of the items in the set, reporting out the breakable items as they were encountered. Many of the 21-year-olds but few of the children spontaneously used *A* to implement *B* and thereby achieve *C*.

4. Interaction Among Variables

It seems certain that an individual who is sophisticated metamnemonically would not think of these previous classes of memory variables as independent of one another, but rather would think of them in complex interaction. He would know, for instance, that a given body of information would be more or less retrievable depending on who was storing it (person × task). He would know that the amount and kinds of strategic preparation he undertakes should be varied in accordance with the mnemonic characteristics of the task (strategy × task). That certain strategies are better suited to him than other strategies are might also be evident (person × strategy). And it is also reasonable to expect the knowledgeable metamnemonic person to appreciate that the fancier, if not the plainer, forms of strategic behavior need to be closely adapted to relevant properties of both person and task (strategy × person × task). Indeed, the adult's ability to generate a seemingly infinite variety of strategies, explicitly tailored to an enormous array of situations and demands (cf. Reitman, 1970), implicates just this interactive sort of knowledge.

It seems to us that much of this interactive mnemonic knowledge is captured by the diagram in Figure 1-1. On the one hand, task variables are represented in this diagram by two subclasses of variables—differences in item characteristics and differences in task demands—and these two sets of variables interact to determine the difficulty of the memory task. On the other hand, personal attributes and employable strategies interact together to determine a person's memory skill on the task. A person whose memory knowledge conformed to this diagram would know, for example, that difficult items offset easy demands, that efficient strategies offset poor memory attributes, and that high ability is needed to ensure adequate performance on difficult tasks.

The knowledge that a person's memory performance is influenced by an interaction of a number of psychological and environmental factors is probably directly related to the more general knowledge that performance of any action is influenced by many similar factors. In fact, Figure 1-1 owes its ancestry to discussions by Heider (1958) of what he called the naive analysis of action. The latter describes a social cognitive understanding of human actions in terms of such commonsense conceptualizations as "ability" and "difficulty."

A reasonable test of children's metamnemonic understanding of the interac-

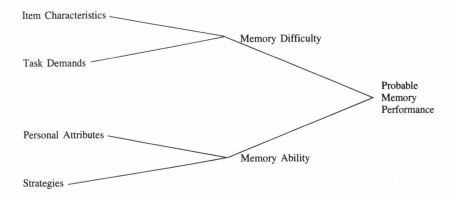

FIGURE 1-1   Metamemory schema of memory variables in interaction.

tions in Figure 1-1 would be to have individuals rate the ease and difficulty of tasks that differ on a combination of variables. For example, a series of memory situations would be presented: (1) some with difficult items and difficult demands; (2) some with difficult items but easy demands (or the reverse); and (3) some with easy items and easy demands. The sophisticated person should know that (3) is easier than (2), and (2) is easier than (1).

In advance of precise data, some tentative evidence about children's developing knowledge of the interaction of memory variables is available. This evidence stems from the spontaneous mention of interaction of variables in the protocols, especially of older children, in the Kreutzer et al. (1975) study. For example, in one item children were shown a list of words and asked if they would choose to study them for one minute or for five. The response, ''There's quite a lot of words here, you know, and it would be kind of hard to learn in just one minute,'' was given by an older child in that study. This response indicates understanding that one task feature, number of words, could offset another, study time. On this item, 16 out of 40 9- and 11-year-olds, but only 3 out of 40 6- and 7-year-olds, spontaneously commented on the number of pictures as a factor justifying their choice of the five-minute study interval.

One other type of memory knowledge seems developmentally important and also indicates an understanding of the interaction of memory variables. This type of metamemory knowledge encompasses an understanding of various memory factors in *means–end interaction*. That is, it consists of knowing that the variables that form a memory problem can be related in a representational scheme consisting of initial state, goal state, and means for transforming the initial state into the goal state. It strikes us that this scheme is a description of a person's knowledge of, and appropriate use of, what Newell and Simon (1972) would call a means–end problem space.

In this type of representation parts of what we have called Person and Task variables go together to characterize the subject's initial state. For example, his initial state might consist of his knowledge of the item characteristics plus knowledge of his own present memory state in relation to those items. Certain aspects of person and strategy variables would then characterize possible transformations that are means to the subject's memory goal or end. These might include, for instance, the subject's knowledge of alternative strategic routes to the goal and his knowledge of his current memory states as related to the desired goal state. Finally, aspects of task and person variables would characterize his knowledge of the goal or end. Examples would be his awareness of task demands and his knowledge of the degree of match between his present memory state and the goal state.

Kreutzer et al. (1975) suggested that children in the middle or late grades of elementary school are much more likely than younger children to represent presented memory information in means–end interaction, speculating that:

> the late elementary school child is much more inclined and able than the kindergartner: to listen to and comprehend the mnemonic problem we present to him; to feel or imagine his way into its various solution steps, including the goal situation where retrieval is finally required . . . ; and then to arrive at one or more adequate-looking means, perhaps after discarding others through feedback from some sort of inner vicarious tryout [p. 53].

Data to support this description are currently only suggestive. For example, Kreutzer et al. (1975) analyzed some of their tasks by tabulating the explicit use of means-end connectives in the children's responses. That is, they looked for statements connected by "so that," "and then," "next," and the like. In one task only 3 out of 20 6-year-olds but 17 out of 20 11-year-olds used such obvious signs of means-end organization of their answers. On another task none of the 6-year-olds but 9 of the 20 11-year-olds proposed a sequence of explicitly connected strategies in response to a posed memory problem.

We have attempted in Section II to categorize the sorts of things the developing child could gradually discover about memory, and to cite research evidence pertinent to each category. According to this classification scheme, the child could learn to identify situations in which it is adaptive to retrieve information or to prepare for future information retrieval. There is also a very great deal that might be learned about the variables that influence mnemonic outcomes: person variables, task variables, strategy variables, and their interactions. We think of this categorization scheme as a preliminary mapping of a new and little-explored area of memory and memory development.

III. RELATIONS BETWEEN METAMEMORY AND OTHER PSYCHOLOGICAL PHENOMENA

In this section we would like to consider metamemory and its development in relation to possible "associated items." One set of associated items is the various other "metas" that also emerge in childhood, and that have recently been receiving study. These "metas" include the child's verbalizable conceptions about language, perception, social interaction, emotions, motor skills, or other domains of interest. Some of these "metas" have been studied under such pseudonyms as "percept inference," "role-taking skills," and "social cognition." In the previous section we talked of the child's metamemory of the factors affecting memory actions and alluded to the conceptual relationship apparent between that and a social cognitive understanding of human actions in general. In fact, much of what was said with regard to person variables and interaction among variables has obvious overlaps with social cognition in its attribution theory and self-attribution forms.

The area of metalanguage has been dealt with in a recent article by Gleitman, Gleitman, and Shipley (1972). They speculate that the various "metas" may be functionally related and emerge more or less synchronously in the child's development. Our own suspicion (see also Markman, 1973) is, first, that any such development of synchronies and functional interrelationships would be extremely difficult to verify, even if they should exist, because of certain very stubborn conceptual and methodological problems that beset all efforts at uncovering developmental synchronies or "stages" (Flavell, 1971b).

Even if a valid reading could be achieved, however, we doubt if all "metas" would in fact prove to emerge synchronously. Rather, it seems plausible that those psychological processes of self and others that tend to be relatively more external and therefore more accessible to perceptual inspection ought to become objects of knowledge earlier than those that are relatively less overt. Recall in this connection Markman's (1973) finding that 5-year-olds are better able to predict their motor performance than their memory performance. Under this argument, knowledge of, say, internal memorization and retrieval ("memory" in the narrower, conventional sense) ought in general to develop later than, say, metalanguage, since speech and writing are external and perceptible. This is, of course, only one variable among the many that may affect the development of all "metas."

A related question has to do with the potential unity or diversity of the various judgments and conceptualizations making up metamemory itself. As we have discussed it, a wide variety of knowledge makes up the domain of metamemory and, empirically, different aspects of this knowledge have been shown to develop at different ages. However, the consistencies and interrelationships that might exist between different pieces of metamnemonic knowledge remain as an interesting and unresearched question. Is the child who is relatively knowledgeable about clustering also relatively knowledgeable about verbal or imaginal elaboration? Does a child who knows something about the interaction of task and strategy variables also usually know something of other interactions, say, person and strategy variables? Few interindividual consistencies in children's metamemory responses were found in the one study in which they have been investigated (Kreutzer et al., 1975). However, as Kreutzer et al. cautioned, their data were not collected with such questions in mind, and their findings in this realm only indicate the need for more careful studies in the future. Very probably, certain classes of metamnemonic knowledge are related, both conceptually and empirically. Discovery of these relationships would certainly add to our knowledge of metamemory and metamemory development.

Finally—the most important question in this section—what can be said of the relationship between metamemory and memory behavior itself? Much of the interest in metamemory has stemmed from the assumption that knowledge of memory plays an important role in the generation and modification of memory-related behavior (Flavell, 1971a; Markman, 1973; Moynahan, 1973). We also endorse the importance of this role, but believe that the metamemory-memory behavior relationship is likely to be quite complex and variable.

Consider any potential memory outcome as reflecting the interrelationship of three factors: the situation, possible behaviors, and the subject's awareness or knowledge—his metamemory. Just this very rough division of factors makes it obvious that any of the following combinations might occur:

1. The situation leads to memory behavior, with no attendant awareness. A case in point would be the incidental, nonintentional storing of some item.

2. The situation leads to memory knowledge, with no attendant memory behavior. An example would be seeing a relationship between items that was not known before and recognizing that it would indeed be mnemonically relevant, but not on that occasion storing or retrieving anything on the basis of that relationship.

3. The situation leads to memory behavior, and the person also becomes aware of the situation-behavior-outcome link. This might occur if an individual incidentally clustered items, say, and then realized that this had had an effect on memory outcome. (This relationship seems reminiscent of Piaget's concept of *reflective abstraction,* as described in the next section.)

4. The situation leads to awareness, and on the basis of this awareness some memory behavior is generated to deal with the situation. The many examples of planful strategic memory behavior would fall here.

Some existing results empirically flesh out these conceptual possibilities. In relation to (1), for example, consider a study of verbal rehearsal by Flavell, Beach, and Chinsky (1966). In that study 31 children in three grades were observed to have verbalized the stimulus names as a mnemonic strategy. Of that number only 23 reported, when questioned, that they had verbalized the items. Fully 25% of the sample were observed to engage in an effective memory behavior but were unable to report that they had.

A study by Salatas and Flavell (1976) is pertinent to (3). Two groups of 6-year-olds were shown a set of categorizable pictures. One group was told to do whatever they wanted to help themselves remember; the other group was instructed merely to inspect the pictures. Both groups were given a recall task after a short interval. Those children instructed to remember were more likely to group the pictures spatially by category during the study interval. Further, children instructed to remember were more likely to subsequently judge that a categorized rather than an uncategorized set of items would be easier to remember. It is possible that practice at studying the items facilitated the metamemory judgemnt. An observation by Ryan, Hegion, and Flavell (1970) in their study of memory behavior in preschool children is also pertinent here. They required children to match a picture of a toy with the appropriate real toy as a strategy for effective recall. Ryan et al. thought that a number of the younger children may have engaged in this picture-object matching simply because picture-object matching is a high-probability response and because they were asked to "use the pictures" in some way. Of interest here is the suggestion that some of the children did seem to engage in the strategy in just this mindless, unaware fashion early in the session, but during the course of the testing, enactment of the strategy in this unknowledgeable manner appeared to lead:

> to the insight that what had just been done constituted an effective mnemonic procedure. Some Ss undoubtedly first enacted the sequence under the aegis of an already formed mediational strategy; but others, we are arguing, may at first only have been engaging in a "false positive" type, mediation-mimicking activity, driven by a low-level matching tendency, and only later have formed this mediational strategy on the basis of feedback from that activity and its mnemonic consequences [Ryan et al., 1970, p. 548].

Finally, let us consider the possible executive, generation-of-behavior role described for metamemory in (4). In discussions of memory behavior in adults it has become apparent that an individual's knowledge of his own memory processes can play an important role in his formulation and employment of strategies for memorization and retrieval (Reitman, 1970; Tulving & Madigan, 1970). Developmentally, it has been shown that children become more and more able to act in an intelligent, planful, task-adaptive manner in an ever-increasing array of tasks (cf. Brown, 1975; Flavell, 1970; Meacham, 1972).

Obviously, this description asserts a (4) type of relation between metamemory and behavior. Given this description, we could expect that a person who intelligently uses a particular memory strategy ought to have some metamemory knowledge of that strategy, and a person who does not use the strategy should be shown to be less knowledgeable. In other words, there ought to be a correlation between appropriate pieces of memory knowledge and pieces of memory behavior.

Having made this prediction, we hasten to point out that any number of factors may attenuate the empirical presence of such an ideal relation. For example, how deterministic, or probable, a link should we expect between a particular metamemory judgment and use of a particular strategy? Suppose a person judges that categorized stimuli are easier to recall than noncategorized ones. Would he inevitably use categorization as a storage strategy, given obviously categorizable stimuli? Not at all. He may know about categorization but think that something else might be better yet in this situation. He may think the list easy enough so that he can use simple inspection for storage. He may have enough knowledge to judge that categorization would be a good strategy, if asked about it, but not enough to think to utilize such a strategy on his own. Lastly, there are undoubtedly gaps between metamemory and memory behavior that have to be chalked up to Original Sin. Moral action does not always accord with moral beliefs, and similarly, we do not always try to retrieve information or prepare for future retrieval in what we believe to be the most effective ways. For example, older children and adults know perfectly well that one "should" concentrate most of one's learning efforts on the least well-mastered segments of whatever is to be acquired (recall Masur et al., 1973). Yet every music student must have at least occasionally succumbed to the temptation to practice those parts he can already play best, for the excellent psychological reasons that it is easier, more fun to do, better for the ego, and less painful to the ears.

Diagnostic factors may also cloud any empirical results. Harking back to our discussion of the Ryan et al. (1970) study, we can ask of any study, Did the child really use the strategy in an intelligent and informed manner or merely in a low-level, habitual manner? Similarly, did the child really answer the metamemory question in an informed way? Lastly, highlighting problems must be accounted for. What are the effects of making an explicit metamemory judgment on subsequent memory behavior, or vice versa?

Given all these problems, we can now indicate some preliminary data in the literature showing a correlation between metamemory judgments and memory behavior. Wellman, Drozdal, Flavell, Salatas, and Ritter (1975) showed in three different instances that children who possessed a particular piece of metamemory knowledge were more likely to engage in a related strategy than those who did not. Two different developmental patterns of metamemory-memory behavior coordination were apparent in these data. In one pattern, even the youngest children tested who could make the metamemory judgment were likely to engage in the related strategic behavior. That is, at all ages, if the child understood certain aspects of the task, then that was reflected in his task-related memory behavior. In the second pattern, metamemory judgments were not related to memory behavior at the younger ages, but were at the older ages. That is, there was a development of metamemory judgment and of memory behavior, and a developing coordination between the two.

The second pattern just discussed implies that the causal chain may be more clearly and exclusively metamemory → memory behavior later in development than it is earlier. At the same time, and paradoxically, metamemory in the sense of present, conscious monitoring of mnemonic means, goals, and variables may actually diminish, as effective storage and retrieval behaviors become progressively automatized and quasi-reflexive through repeated use and overlearning. The metamemory-memory behavior link of the older child is not thereby extinguished, of course. However, the need for it to become clearly conscious may well diminish as the behaviors it once mediated become more self-starting. Clearly, the relationship of knowledge about memory to actual mnemonic behavior, and developmental changes in this relationship, are complicated subjects, but subjects worthy of future research.

IV. HOW METAMEMORY MIGHT DEVELOP: POSSIBLE FORMATIVE EXPERIENCES AND PROCESSES

An important question under this heading would be, What sorts of cognitive skills and concepts might be needed to make possible the attainment of different sorts of knowledge about memory? Each aspect of metamemory undoubtedly has its own list, but a few acquisitions might be important for a wide range of metamemory knowledge. More sophisticated forms of metamemory seem to rely on a multiplication-of-relations type of thinking, for example. Especially, what we have spoken of as the knowledge of the interaction of memory variables implies this type of general cognitive ability, where differing amounts of one factor are systematically related to differing amounts of another. Conceptual developments regarding time and psychological causality should also be generally important. The older child's intentional, means-end view of a variety of memory facts seems to imply some command of temporal order and duration, and also an appreciation of the self's own deliberate actions as effective causes of future effects (see Hagen, 1971, on this point). The child's increasing precision in memory-relevant calculations is probably related to a general ability of older but not younger children to rely on quantitative, metric, and more mathematical-looking cognitive structures.

Assuming, for the moment, the presence of all necessary cognitive prerequisites for any given metamemory acquisition, how is the latter actually acquired? A great deal of what the child comes to know about memory could be acquired through feedback from his own self-initiated experiences, as was suggested in the discussion of the Ryan et al. study in the previous section. A child could learn a great deal by repeatedly noting, for example, interdependencies among the original input data, his own storage and retrieval activities, and what and how much of the original input gets retrieved (Smirnov, 1973). Somewhat like block tower building and somewhat unlike, say, reasoning, mnemonic activities have concrete, semitangible "products" (what is actually remembered), which can be compared to ideal or possible "products" (what had originally been experienced), and variations in the discrepancy between the two are potentially relatable to one's own intervening activities. Much of metamemory development may therefore develop through something analogous to Piaget's *reflective abstraction* process. As we interpret this process, the child abstracts and permanently incorporates into his cognitive structure generalizations or regularities concerning the properties of his own actions vis-à-vis the environment, as contrasted with knowledge about the environment itself that derives from *physical abstraction* (e.g., Piaget, 1970, p. 728). Since metamemory and all other "metas" primarily entail generalizations about people and their actions vis-à-vis objects, a process like reflective abstraction may play an important role in their acquisition.

The child's formation of abstractions about his own behavior is likely to be influenced in a number of ways. As discussed before, from the Russian point of view (Yendovitskaya, 1971), the parents' interaction with the child may greatly influence what the child attends to, and so what abstractions are formed. Parents, teachers, and others may frequently set various types of storage and retrieval tasks to the child, or engage in such efforts themselves under the child's watchful eyes. At times, these significant others may actually provide a model of various memory behaviors, but probably more often they are simply providing "aliments" and demands that shape the child's own thoughts. Along these lines, it seems obvious that a child's experiences in school and with school tasks provide an important set of occasions as well as important "aliments" related to memorizing and retrieving. Cross-cultural studies of the effects of schooling (see the chapter by Cole & Scribner in this volume) provide some indications that the school experience, and its demands, are potent shapers of certain cognitions independent of what subject matter is explicitly and intentionally taught in school. All of this section is of course quite speculative at this point. It is always much harder to specify plausible acquisitional processes than to describe and developmentally order the acquisitions that they generate.

ACKNOWLEDGMENTS

The preparation of this chapter was supported by a National Institute of Child Health and Human Development predoctoral traineeship (HD-00098) to the second author, by a program project grant (HD-05027) to the University of Minnesota's Institute of Child Development, and also by grants to the University's Center for Research in Human Learning from that Institute (HD-01136), from the National Science Foundation (GB-17590), and from the Graduate School.

REFERENCES

Acredelo, L. P., Pick, H. L., Jr., & Olsen, M. G. Environmental differentiation and familiarity as determinants of children's memory for spatial location. *Developmental Psychology,* 1975, *11,* 495–501.

Appel, L. F., Cooper, R. G., McCarrell, N., Sims-Knight, J., Yussen, S. R., & Flavell, J. H. The development of the distinction between perceiving and memorizing. *Child Development,* 1972, *43,* 1365–1381.

Atkinson, R. C., & Shiffrin, R. M. Human memory: A proposed system and its control processes. In K. W. Spence & J. T. Spence (Eds.), *The psychology of learning and motivation: Advances in research and theory* (Vol. 2). New York: Academic Press, 1968.

Berch, D. B., & Evans, R. C. Decision processes in children's recognition memory. *Journal of Experimental Child Psychology*, 1973, *16*, 148–164.

Brown, A. L. Judgments of recency for long sequences of pictures: The absence of a developmental trend. *Journal of Experimental Child Psychology*, 1973, *15*, 473–480.

Brown, A. L. The development of memory: Knowing, knowing about knowing, and knowing how to know. In H. W. Reese (Ed.), *Advances in child development and behavior* (Vol. 10). New York: Academic Press, 1975.

Brown, R., & McNeill, D. The "tip of the tongue" phenomenon. *Journal of Verbal Learning and Verbal Behavior*, 1966, *5*, 325–337.

Butterfield, E. C., & Belmont, J. M. Assessing and improving the executive cognitive functions of mentally retarded people. In I. Bialer & M. Sternlicht (Eds.), *Psychological issues in mentally retarded people*. Chicago: Aldine, 1975.

Danner, F. W. Children's understanding of intersentence organization in the recall of short descriptive passages. *Journal of Educational Psychology*, 1976, *68*, 174–183.

Denhière, G. Apprentissages intentionnels à allure libre: Etude comparative d'enfants normaux et débiles mentaux. *Enfance*, 1974, September–December (3–5), 149–174.

Drozdal, J. G., Jr., & Flavell, J. H. A developmental study of logical search behavior. *Child Development*, 1975, *46*, 389–393.

Eimas, P. D. Effects of memory aids on hypothesis behavior and focusing in young children and adults. *Journal of Experimental Child Psychology*, 1970, *10*, 319–336.

Flavell, J. H. Developmental studies of mediated memory. In H. W. Reese & L. P. Lipsitt (Eds.), *Advances in child development and behavior* (Vol. 5). New York: Academic Press, 1970.

Flavell, J. H. First discussant's comments: What is memory development the development of? *Human Development*, 1971, *14*, 272–278.   (a)

Flavell, J. H. Stage-related properties of cognitive development. *Cognitive Psychology*, 1971, *2*, 421–453.   (b)

Flavell, J. H., Beach, D. R., & Chinsky, J. M. Spontaneous verbal rehearsal in a memory task as a function of age. *Child Development*, 1966, *37*, 283–299.

Flavell, J. H., Friedrichs, A. G., & Hoyt, J. D. Developmental changes in memorization processes. *Cognitive Psychology*, 1970, *1*, 324–340.

Geis, M. F., & Lange, G. Planful storage for planful retrieval: A developmental study of cue utilization in school-aged children. Paper presented at the biennial meeting of the Society for Research in Child Development, Denver, April 1975.

Gleitman, L. R., Gleitman, H., & Shipley, E. F. The emergence of the child as grammarian. *Cognition*, 1972, *1*, 137–164.

Goldberg, S., Perlmutter, M., & Myers, N. Recall of related and unrelated lists by 2-year-olds. *Journal of Experimental Child Psychology*, 1974, *18*, 1–8.

Hagen, J. W. Some thoughts on how children learn to remember. *Human Development*, 1971, *14*, 262–271.

Hart, J. T. Memory and the feeling of knowing experience. *Journal of Educational Psychology*, 1965, *56*, 208–216.

Hart, J. T. Memory and the memory monitoring process. *Journal of Verbal Learning and Verbal Behavior*, 1967, *6*, 685–691.

Heider, F. *The psychology of interpersonal relations*. New York: Wiley, 1968.

Kreutzer, M. A., Leonard, C., & Flavell, J. H. An interview study of children's knowledge about memory. *Monographs of the Society for Research in Child Development*, 1975, *40*(1, Serial No. 159).

Lindsay, P. H., & Norman, D. A. *Human information processing: An introduction to psychology*. New York: Academic Press, 1972.

Lipsitt, L. P., & Eimas, P. D. Developmental Psychology. *Annual Review of Psychology*, 1972, *23*, 1–50.

Markman, E. Factors affecting the young child's ability to monitor his memory. Unpublished doctoral dissertation, University of Pennsylvania, 1973.

Masur, E. F., McIntyre, C. W., & Flavell, J. H. Developmental changes in apportionment of a study time among items in a multitrial free recall task. *Journal of Experimental Child Psychology,* 1973, *15,* 237–246.

Meacham, J. A. The development of memory abilities in the individual and in society. *Human Development,* 1972, *15,* 205–228.

Morrison, F. J., Holmes, D. L., & Haith, M. M. A developmental study of the effect of familiarity on short-term visual memory. *Journal of Experimental Child Psychology,* 1974, *18,* 412–425.

Moynahan, E. D. The development of knowledge concerning the effect of categorization upon free recall. *Child Development,* 1973, *44,* 238–246.

Neimark, E., Slotnick, N. S., & Ulrich, T. The development of memorization strategies. *Developmental Psychology,* 1971, *5,* 427–432.

Newell, A., & Simon, H. A. *Human problem solving.* Englewood Cliffs, N.J.: Prentice-Hall, 1972.

Piaget, J. Piaget's theory. In P. H. Mussen (Ed.), *Carmichael's manual of child psychology* (Vol. 1). New York: Wiley, 1970.

Reitman, W. What does it take to remember? In D. A. Norman (Ed.), *Models of human memory.* New York: Academic Press, 1970.

Rogoff, B., Newcombe, N., & Kagan, J. Planfulness and recognition memory. *Child Development,* 1974, *45,* 972–977.

Roodin, M. L., & Gruen, G. E. The role of memory in making transitive judgments. *Journal of Experimental Child Psychology,* 1970, *10,* 264–275.

Ryan, S. M., Hegion, A. G., & Flavell, J. H. Nonverbal mnemonic mediation in preschool children. *Child Development,* 1970, *41,* 539–550.

Salatas, H., & Flavell, J. H. Behavioral and metamnemonic indicators of strategic behaviors under remember instructions in first grade. *Child Development,* 1976, *47,* 81–89.

Salatas, H., & Flavell, J. H. Retrieval of recently learned information: Development of strategies and control skills. *Child Development,* in press.

Sieber, J. E., Kameya, L. I., & Paulson, F. L. Effect of memory support on the problem-solving ability of test-anxious children. *Journal of Educational Psychology,* 1970, *61,* 159–168.

Siegler, R. S., & Liebert, R. M. Acquisition of formal scientific reasoning by 10- and 13-year-olds: Designing a factorial experiment. *Developmental Psychology,* 1975, *11,* 401–402.

Smirnov, A. A. *Problems of the psychology of memory.* New York: Plenum Press, 1973.

Smirnov, A. A., & Zinchenko, P. I. Problems in the psychology of memory. In M. Cole & L. Maltzman (Eds.), *A handbook of contemporary Soviet psychology.* New York: Basic Books, 1969.

Tenney, Y. J. The child's conception of organization and recall. *Journal of Experimental Child Psychology,* 1975, *19,* 100–114.

Tulving, E., & Madigan, S. A. Memory and verbal learning. *Annual Review of Psychology,* 1970, *21,* 437–484.

Wellman, H. M. Tip of the tongue and feeling of knowing experiences: A developmental study of memory monitoring. *Child Development,* in press.

Wellman, H. M., Drozdal, J. G., Jr., Flavell, J. H., Salatas, H., & Ritter, K. Metamemory development and its possible role in the selection of behavior. In G. A. Hale (Chair), *Development of selective processes in cognition.* Symposium presented at the biennial meeting of the Society for Research in Child Development, Denver, 1975.

Wellman, H. M., Ritter, K., & Flavell, J. H. Deliberate memory behavior in the delayed reactions of very young children. *Developmental Psychology,* 1975, *11,* 780–787.

Yendovitskaya, T. V. Development of memory. In A. V. Zaporozhets & D. B. Elkonin (Eds.), *The psychology of preschool children.* Cambridge, Mass.: M.I.T. Press, 1971.

Yussen, S. R. Determinants of visual attention and recall in observational learning by preschoolers and second graders. *Developmental Psychology,* 1974, *10,* 93–100.

Yussen, S. R. Some reflections on strategic remembering in young children. In G. H. Hale (Chair), *Development of selective processes in cognition.* Symposium presented at the biennial meeting of the Society for Research in Child Development, Denver, 1975.

Yussen, S. R., Gagné, E., Gargiulo, R., & Kunen, S. The distinction between perceiving and memorizing in elementary school children. *Child Development,* 1974, *45,* 547–551.

Yussen, S. R., & Levy, V. M., Jr. Developmental changes in predicting one's own span of short-term memory. *Journal of Experimental Child Psychology,* 1975, *19,* 502–508.

2

Constructive Aspects of Children's Comprehension and Memory

Scott G. Paris
Barbara K. Lindauer

Purdue University

I. INTRODUCTION

> Remembering is not a completely independent function, entirely distinct from perceiving, imaging, or even constructive thinking, but it has intimate relations with them all [Bartlett, 1932, p. 13].

Memory encompasses many cognitive processes and cannot be considered either an isolated mental faculty or a passive storehouse of experience. Consequently, the analysis of children's memory must be embedded in the study of perception, comprehension, and problem solving. As children develop, they acquire complex and creative ways to understand, represent, and remember experiences. The constructive nature of children's comprehension and memory skills is the focus of this chapter.

Much of the renewed interest in constructive processes of cognition (cf. Cofer, 1973; Jenkins, 1974) can be attributed to Sir Frederick Bartlett's (1932) classic research. Bartlett investigated adults' retention of meaningful material, such as pictures and stories, and demonstrated that information is neither remembered nor transmitted by an individual as an exact copy of the original stimulus. Information undergoes blending, condensation, omission, invention, and similar constructive transformations. These changes in remembered information were considered constructive rather than accidental because the distortions usually resulted in memory representations that were simple, easy to label, and consistent with conventional representations of objects.

Constructive processes of memory are often influenced by the individual's "rationalization" and "attitude," according to Bartlett. Although some changes in memory are fortuitous, a great many of the transformations in information are controlled by social, cognitive, and developmental variables, which affect a person's perception and memory of an experience. The individual's attitude, temperament, and character influence the creativity of constructive processing, but this does not mean that people do not share common apperceptions of events. Bartlett postulated that memory is influenced by social "conventionalization" that brings uniformity and conformity to memories shared among people in social groups.

Axiomatic to the constructivist view is the position that new information achieves significance by its correspondence with extant knowledge. For example, adults utilize contextual cues and given information to direct their attention, facilitate comprehension, and make inferential judgments (Bransford & McCarrell, 1974; Haviland & Clark, 1974; Sulin & Dooling, 1974; Wertsch, 1975). However, the process is more than simply mapping new information upon old. As Bartlett (1932) stated:

> To speak as if what is accepted and given a place in mental life is always simply a question of what fits into already formed apperception systems is to miss the obvious point that the process of fitting is an active process, depending directly upon the preformed tendencies and bias which the subject brings to the task [p. 85].

The incorporation of new information into existing cognitive structures is perhaps most accurately described by Piaget as the processes of assimilation and accommodation. Brown (1975a) characterized the interchanging process as "head fitting," and indeed, constructive mechanisms are involved with reciprocal changes in the material to be remembered as well as the cognitive structures to which the information is being assimilated.

Evidence for constructive transformations of information in both comprehension and memory usually has been adduced from studies in which an individual's recall supplements and distorts the original stimulus. For example, adults often automatically comprehend and remember many implied relations in prose (Brockway, Chmielewski, & Cofer, 1974). The constructive quality of adults' memory for sentences and connected discourse has been demonstrated by showing that memory includes amalgamation of information across sentence boundaries, inferential relationships, implied linear orderings, and primarily semantic rather than syntactic information.

The integration, blending, and condensation of semantic relationships in memory give rise to "schemata" in memory. Bartlett did not like the term *schema* because it implied a static arrangement of relations rather than a representation that is continually flexible (cf. Anderson & Ortony, 1975). Bartlett suggested "active, developing patterns" and "organized settings" as alternative labels for "schemata." The operations involved in encoding and retrieval can be characterized as constructive (or reconstructive), and the product of these operations is a mutable representation of experience. This is very similar to Piaget's concept of the operative aspects of memory (Piaget & Inhelder, 1973). The representation includes contextual information and integrated relationships that are influenced by individuals' cognitive abilities and social dispositions.

The central tenets of constructive cognitive processes in memory may be summarized briefly in the following statements:

1. Exact reproduction or recall of an event, especially a meaningful stimulus, is rare; memory usually involves transformations of the input.

2. These transformations can involve either the omission of information and abstractive processing (cf. Zangwill, 1972) or the embellishment of the given information with supplemental and implied relationships. Although memory is characterized as holistic and schematic, particular details and figurative information can be remembered and play an important role in memory.

3. Constructive processes are determined jointly by the immediate context, the cognitive abilities, and the sociohistorical milieu of the individual.

4. Memory schemata are dynamic and changeable. Information can be re-comprehended and transformed during any retrieval of that event or by temporal and structural changes in the schemata to which the event is assimilated. Remembering involves reciprocal interactions between the individual's cognitive schemata and the new information.

The constructive approach appears to be an ideal framework for a developmental analysis of comprehension and memory because the focus is on changes in memory within a person over time as well as the differences among individuals of various ages and abilities. Constructive cognition provides a longitudinal, social, and historical perspective and is conceptually compatible with traditional developmental theorizing. The similarity is apparent in the kinds of experimental paradigms used to investigate constructive memory changes as well as the results of those studies (Piaget & Inhelder, 1973).

Experimental evidence for constructive cognitive processes in children in a variety of research paradigms is reviewed in the following section. This includes an analysis of how children remember related sentences and pictures, with special emphasis on the processes of semantic integration, inference, and elaboration. Although different mechanisms of constructive comprehension and memory are separated in this discussion, they are usually interdependent processes. Following the review, a framework for analyzing constructive cognition based on encoding, storage, and retrieval operations is presented. Throughout the chapter, we shall attempt to elucidate the underlying mechanisms of constructive cognition and the functional utility of these processes for memory and cognitive development.

II. EMPIRICAL EVIDENCE FOR CONSTRUCTIVE PROCESSES IN CHILDREN'S COMPREHENSION AND MEMORY

A. Semantic Integration

That people remember schematic ideas or the semantic integration of elements has long been realized (cf. Binet & Henri, 1894). However, it is only in the 1970s that associationistic and generative syntactic models of language processing have been challenged by findings that adults derive holistic memory representations for sentences and prose (e.g., Bransford & Franks, 1972). Not surprisingly, children, like adults, exhibit the ability to integrate ideas within and across sentence boundaries and derive representations in memory based on the semantic relationships expressed rather than on particular lexical and syntactic features.

At least two types of semantic integration can be distinguished. The first concerns children's ability to amalgamate information expressed in different sentences and was demonstrated in a study by Barclay and Reid (1974) with 5-, 6-, 8-, and 10-year-old children. Short stories were presented that described critical relationships in either (1) full passive sentences; (2) truncated passive sentences with no actor mentioned in the story; or (3) truncated passive sentences with the actor stated in another sentence. Children were told to recall the sentences verbatim; yet sentences were recalled in active or full passive form significantly more often for the truncated passive sentences in which the actor was named than for the truncated passive sentences with no actor. In other words, children integrated information from several sentences and transformed the syntactic style in recall.

It seems intuitive that children, as well as adults, should amalgamate and integrate similar and redundant characteristics of a linguistic message, and indeed, people appear to do this spontaneously and routinely when told to remember contextually related sentences. The purpose of these processes is to "look back" and search through previous knowledge in an effort to add and delete information. The processing depends greatly on noticing redundancies and integrating elements and relationships that are explicitly given albeit in different words, styles, or places.

A second type of semantic integration involves inferences that can be made from the given sentences to derive additional relationships. For example, Paris and Carter (1973) presented sets of three sentences to 7- and 10-year-old children. The first two sentences were premise statements that permitted additional relations to be inferred, while the third sentence was a filler item. A recognition memory task followed in which children were asked to identify the sentences that were exactly like those heard before. Children reported that they had previously heard novel inferences that were semantically consistent with the premises (and did so with a high degree of certainty). The conclusion from this study and a similar investigation with mildly retarded children (Paris, Mahoney, & Buckhalt, 1974) is that children often spontaneously infer relationships among sentences and incorporate these events into an integrated memory representation.

Children can remember a series of related pictures in an integrative fashion also. This process resembles semantic integration with verbal stimuli because it involves the meaningful relationships derived and inferred from a series of related pictures and also because children often label (or can potentially verbally describe and code) the pictorial stimuli. The most direct comparison between verbal and pictorial integration was made in a study by Paris and Mahoney (1974), who asked 8- and 10-year-old children to remember sets of three sentences or pictures that were related thematically. Later, in a recognition memory test with pictures or sentences, children at both age levels responded with a high degree of certainty that new pictures and sentences that were semantically consistent with original premise items had been presented previously. The point of interest here is that children derived inferred relationships among the pictures and integrated them in memory. Integration of pictorial objects and relationships is apparently important for both comprehension and memory. When sets of objects are unitized or conjoined in pictures (or by imagery instructions), children remember them much better than when the objects are seen in static or noninteractive relationships (Hale & Piper, 1974; Horowitz, Lampel, & Takanishi, 1969; Reese, this volume). Organization provided in a picture (Mandler & Stein, 1974) and schematization constructed by the child of his own drawings (Stacey & Ross, 1975) have also been found to facilitate memory.

These integrative processes occur for pictures and imaginal stimuli and appear similar to verbal processes used to construct semantically integrated memory representations. The facts that children sometimes confuse sentences in memory that evoke similar images (Kosslyn & Bower, 1974) and that imagery instructions facilitate semantic integration of sentences (Paris et al., 1974) implicate a constructive process for memory that is common to visual and verbal modalities.

Semantic integration has been obtained on many different tasks with different stimuli and various subject populations. Although the universality of the process is impressive and attests to the robustness of the phenomenon, the semantic relationships being integrated must be specified in greater detail. Perhaps that is one reason why the research continues to be a series of demonstrations that people usually do not remember every sentence, picture, and bit of information that they perceive. Another weakness of the tasks employed to date is the lack of sensitivity to developmental changes in performance. Although semantic integration is important for children's comprehension and memory, no one has devised an adequate task or procedure to assess the cognitive mechanisms that underlie it. For example, the false recognition paradigm is advocated by Tulving and Bower

(1974) as a powerful method for determining the nature of the memory trace. However, it is usually an inappropriate method for developmental analyses when the false alarm rate is used as an index of developmental change. (A false alarm on a recognition memory test refers to a person's response of "Yes, I saw/heard that stimulus before" when, in fact, the item was never presented initially.) The false alarm rate in a recognition memory test will change with age as a function of shifting response biases because young children respond affirmatively on most of the trials. It will change with increased memory capacity for "old" items also. Unfortunately, a sufficient number of trials to perform the proper signal detection analyses usually cannot be administered because of temporal limitations on children's motivation and attention. The lack of clear-cut evidence for developmental improvement in semantic integration is therefore an equivocal finding in research employing the false recognition paradigm.

Barclay and Reid (1974) found no evidence for developmental changes in semantic integration, but this result may be an artifact also. The data of some of the younger children were unanalyzed in that study because of failure to transform passive sentences or to recall the stories, thereby eliminating poor performers from the youngest groups. Free recall skills and facility with active-passive transformations were generally confounded with age in the assessment of the memory representations. The most important problem is the insensitivity of the task to any developmental changes in processing because there are no alternatives to recalling truncated passive sentences with no actors mentioned except as truncated passives. In order for this task to reveal age-related improvement in semantic integration, the youngest children would have had to recall the sentences in passive form. This is an unreasonable expectation for the 5- and 6-year-old children with the least experience and facility with passive sentences. The task revealed no age-related performance differences because successful performance did not depend on any strategy or knowledge that could be expected to change within the age range tested.

With these methodological criticisms in mind, we would like to suggest four important factors regarding comprehension and memory that may result in both qualitative and quantitative changes in semantic integration throughout development: (1) metamorial plans; (2) particular linguistic and cognitive strategies; (3) memory capacity and retrieval abilities; and (4) the task demands. Each is important for all aspects of constructive cognition and will be discussed throughout the chapter.

Initially, semantic integration may be sensitive to children's use of general plans to infer, to look back for redundancies, to add and to delete information intentionally, and to perform other constructive and abstractive processes. These operations may be expected to change developmentally with metamemory development (cf. Flavell & Wellman, this volume) and the increased use of voluntary strategies in memory development (Brown, 1975a; Smirnov & Zinchenko, 1969). The second process involves the specific strategies of semantic integration such as pronominalization rules, syntactic transformational rules, and recognition of semantic identity, paraphrase, and redundancy. The cognitive knowledge on which these processes are expected to operate will also change with age. Certain types of relations may be beyond the comprehension of young children and will prohibit, interfere with, or transform the semantic integration process. Improvements in language skills, the acquisition of reading, and accumulation of knowledge will change the child's schemata and influence the assimilation of information.

The third factor is a general increase in memory capacity that permits better retention of original or premise information, which in turn may facilitate inferential and integrative processes. The retrieval abilities of children also vary with regard to the modality of representation of knowledge and the decreasing dependency on stimulus support for retrieval. The fourth factor involves the task demands and interacts with the other three factors. For example, the ability to integrate information in memory (and subsequently exhibit it) will vary with age and the amount of contextual support given as cues for memory access (Brown, 1975a). Consideration of these factors, the different types of semantic integration, and the methodological problems with children's memory measures will refine the developmental analysis of semantic integration.

B. Memory for Ordered Relations

Closely related to semantic integration of explicit and implicit sentence relationships is children's ability to remember logical, temporal, and causal relations. Memory for structured discourse requires the apprehension and construction of sequential order among a group of elements. For example, if an individual is told that John is taller than Max and Max is taller than Fred, then he may infer that John is taller than Fred. This type of logically ordered relationship with three elements is referred to as a three-term series problem. In a series of experiments, Trabasso (1975) has shown that children can construct linear arrays in memory for transitive inferential relationships among five- and six-term series problems. (See Trabasso, this volume, for a more complete description.) The results of these studies corroborate other investigations with adults (Barclay, 1973; DeSoto, London, & Handel, 1965; Potts, 1972) in which people learn pair-wise comparative relations (e.g., longer, shorter), use them to construct a linear array in an end-point anchoring or ends-inward strategy, and subsequently solve comparative problems based on inferences. Apparently, children derive a semantically integrated memory representation of the linear array (including linguistic and imaginal cues) from the pair-wise comparative sentences.

Children's performance on the five- and six-term series problems and inferential syllogisms investigated by Trabasso revealed no developmental changes in performance. This led Trabasso to assert that children and adults derive similar integrated memory representations and to say, "We are forced to conclude that the cognitive processes of children and adults are very much alike [1975, p. 34]." However, such a conclusion seems premature given the limited methodology. As Trabasso stated, multiple-term series problems are unusual, difficult, and, we might add, very different from customary tasks of natural language processing. Further, Trabasso specifically trained children over *many* trials to a high criterion, and those children who did not learn all the pairs during training were eliminated from the study. In other words, the linear array was induced and overlearned in children, and subsequent comparative judgments and inferences from memory reflected how well children accessed information from the stored array after initial sources of age differences were controlled. The children performed the judgments and inferences as adults do, and Trabasso concluded that all cognitive development is a continuous, quantitative change. This may be a sweeping conclusion for results based on the problem solving of a few transitive comparative terms in a task where all initial age differences in constructive abilities were eliminated by subject selection and criterial training.

Other examples of ordered relationships that require constructive processing are temporal and causal sequences. Brown (1975b) has shown that children as young as 5 years of age can apprehend and reconstruct temporal sequences from pictorial arrangements. The finding is obtained with a reconstructive memory test with the original objects available but not with a free recall test in which memory for the objects is confounded with correct sequential ordering. Brown concluded that even kindergarten children can comprehend temporal relationships: "The superiority of ordered over random sequences suggests that preoperational children, reconstructing logical sequences, are capable of using inferential reasoning to seek and produce the most probable order of events [1975b, p. 160]." In another experimental condition, Brown demonstrated that 5-year-olds could construct logical sequential stories that described the pictures and then could use these self-generated conceptualizations as easily as experimenter-provided stories to comprehend and remember the temporal sequences.

In another series of studies, Brown and Murphy (1975) demonstrated that information about order of events is retained by 4-year-old children when it taps semantic memory and is essential to the story's meaning. Providing an ordered narrative to a sequence of nouns allowed children to generate elaborated relationships within a given story context, and this greatly facilitated reconstructive memory for the sequences.

Integration of logically, temporally, and causally ordered relationships in these studies is solid evidence for young children's ability to schematize events in memory. Some of the tasks described here assess children's spontaneous construction of ordered relationships and can be expected to reveal age-related differences in performance. Tasks that involve extended training in the construction of the orders will not be expected to reveal much change with age, provided that the initial task can be learned at all by the different subject groups. Nonetheless, this area of research is important because of the support it offers for constructive processes of cognition and the integrated schematization of the memory representation.

C. Memory for Stories

Children are able to construct, infer, and integrate semantic relationships among small sets of pictures and sentences. These cognitive processes also appear to be important for children's listening and reading skills in more complex tasks. Although there have been few investigations of children's memory for stories, children seem to organize story relationships in memory by utilizing such constructive processes as inference and integration.

Stein and Glenn (1975) investigated children's recall of narrative stories to determine what structural features of the story would be retained. They classified relationships in the story according to Rumelhart's (1974) system of parsing prose by structural characteristics and identified such units as the setting, activity, goal, and consequences of each story. Two different passages were read to first- and third-grade children, who were asked to free recall the ideas of the stories immediately after presentation as well as one week later. In general, a greater amount of the stories was recalled by older children than by younger children, and more information was recalled immediately than after the delay. The semantic categories of events and consequences were recalled most often by children in both grades, and all children elaborated on the original ideas presented in the story. Stein and Glenn concluded that children's story recall is highly organized and includes many implicit and explicit subunits or ideas.

The derivation and organization of thematic relationships in stories may involve constructive transformations in memory, but the strongest evidence for such changes comes from inferential knowledge that children derive from stories. In the Stein and Glenn study, a great deal of elaborative and inferential recall was observed. These often were statements of inferred consequences and action-oriented goals. Furthermore, there was more constructive processing after one week than immediately, which confirms Bartlett's (1932) observation with adults' recall. Stein and Glenn also found more inferential and elaborative recall by the third graders than by first graders, which suggests a developmental improvement in constructive processing.

An age-related improvement in constructive cognition was also suggested in a study by Paris and Upton (1976). In that study, children in kindergarten through fifth grade were read six stories and immediately after each story were asked a series of yes/no questions pertaining to information that was either explicit or implicit within the passages. Older children remembered the stories better and correctly answered all categories of questions more often than younger children. However, questions concerning inferred presuppositions and consequences of the stories revealed the greatest age-related improvement. Although some of this enhanced ability to derive inferential relationships may be due to a developmental increase in memory capacity, much of the improvement appears to be due to developmental changes in the inferential operations themselves. This interpretation was supported by an analysis of covariance in which an estimate of age-related memory capacity was partialed out of children's performance on inferred presuppositions and consequences. The residual change across age levels was still significant, suggesting developmental improvement in processing of implied semantic relationships.

In a separate experiment, Paris and Upton (1976) investigated the relationship between comprehension of inferred relations and general memory for the story ideas. Each child's performance on the various categories of questions asked immediately after presentation of the story was correlated with the child's free recall of the story half an hour later. The highest correlation was found for the questions regarding inferred presuppositions and consequences, indicating that the best predictor of overall memory for the story ideas was the child's ability to comprehend and remember implied relationships among sentences regarding the beginning and end point of an episode. The predictive value of inferential processing for later recall increased significantly from the 6- to the 10-year-old children, and thus the functional value of constructive processing for subsequent retrieval from memory appears to increase with age.

The processes involved in children's memory for stories may be affected by the same four factors that influence semantic integration. Metamemorial plans, specific strategies and knowledge, memory capacity, and task demands will influence the amount and kind of constructive processing applied to stories. In addition, the acquisition of new information and recurrent retrieval over time will provide new distortions to the schematic information (Bartlett, 1932; Kintsch, 1974; Stein & Glenn, 1975). Each of these factors can potentially change the schemata of the memory representation through addition and deletion of information. Repeated recall of an experience can also distort memory because it allows recursive operations of comprehension and rehearsal to be applied to the memory representation.

D. The Role of Inference

The abilities to comprehend inferred relationships and to blend implicit and explicit information together in memory are fundamental aspects of semantic integration and understanding of stories. Usually, the cognitive skills involved in deriving inferences are studied developmentally as an aspect of problem solving or logical thinking and not as a component of constructive cognition. Inferential processes are important for memory and comprehension, and the retention of implied relations in stories seem to improve developmentally between the ages of 5 and 12 (Paris & Upton, 1976; Stein & Glenn, 1975).

Developmental improvement in inferential processing was illustrated in three studies by Paris and Lindauer (1976). In the first study, 7-, 9-, and 11-year-old children were read eight sentences that contained an instrument that was stated explicitly or implicitly. For example, one sentence was, "The workman dug a hole in the ground (with a shovel)." In a subsequent cued recall test, it was observed that younger children could effectively utilize the instrument (e.g., shovel) as a retrieval cue for the sentence only if it was stated explicitly when the sentence was presented. Older children recalled the sentences easily with instrument cues regardless of implicit or explicit presentation. The effectiveness of implicit instruments as cues for recall was compared to explicit subject, verb, and object cues in a second study. Although 6-year-old children had great difficulty recalling the sentences cued with implicit instrument prompts, 10-year-olds performed equally well with implicit and explicit cues. The significant interactions in both studies between age and type of cue suggest that older but not younger children integrated the inferred information in the memory characterization for the sentence and subsequently used the implied instrument cue to access the entire sentence as effectively as they used other explicit words of the sentence. The ability or inclination to infer additional relationships about sentences apparently increases with age, and the utility of implicit and indirect cues for retrieval from memory shows a corresponding improvement.

It is interesting to note that we eliminated the differences in retrieval effectiveness between implicit and explicit cues in a third study. Young children in the previous studies knew the relationship between the implied instrument and the action described by the sentence yet failed to include the information in the encoded representation. If children process the implied relationship in their efforts to understand the sentence, then the implied instrument should be an effective aid for retrieval. We read a list of ten sentences with explicit and implicit instruments to 7-year-old children, as in the other studies. In addition to repeating the sentences, the children acted out each sentence, which made it necessary to use the imaginary instrument. Implicit and explicit instruments were equally effective as retrieval cues in a subsequent memory test. The procedure apparently forced the children to process the sentences more thoroughly and to construct implied relationships in memory. The procedure also resulted in a higher level of recall than in the first two studies and attests to the functional value of inferential, constructive processes for access to memory.

There is no general framework to define inferential operations or relationships, and that shortcoming may contribute to the variability among investigations and the paucity of studies of inferential processes in children. In spite of the lack of rigorous definitions, we can offer some tentative conclusions regarding inferential processes in comprehension and memory.

1. Inferential operations are directed, constructive acts that synthesize relationships during encoding, retrieval, or problem solving. Inferences may also be drawn spontaneously as automatic "efforts toward understanding." When spontaneous and involuntary (i.e., drawn as part of the goal of the task), inferential relationships are often integrated into memory representations for the event (e.g., the semantic integration tasks). However, implied information can also be derived from memory according to retrieval demands, and this knowledge, although derivable, may not be represented directly in memory.

2. Inferences allow an individual to expand the given information, embellish it with additional idiosyncratic relationships, and process it to a "deeper level" (Craik & Lockhart, 1972). One's knowledge of an event is therefore enriched by inferential processes, and memory for the event is enhanced (Paris & Lindauer, 1976; Paris & Upton, 1976).

3. There is developmental improvement in the production and mediation efficiency of inferential processes on many tasks. Generally, we know that spontaneous inferring improves in some memory tasks where the goal of the task is apprehension of semantic relations within and between sentences (Paris & Lindauer, 1976; Paris & Upton, 1976; Stein & Glenn, 1975). Similarly, the correlation between inferential operations and recall increases with age (Paris & Upton, 1976), as does the effectiveness of implicit retrieval cues. The developmental improvement can be traced to changes in the same four factors that influence semantic integration plus the cognitive processes involved in deducing and inducing probabilistic and logical inferences.

E. The Role of Context and Elaboration

Although all stimuli and behavior are embedded in physical and psychological contexts, experimental evidence suggests that adults' understanding and retention depend on the mapping relationship between the new information and surrounding contextual cues (Bransford & Johnson, 1972; Chafe, 1972; Haviland & Clark, 1974; Jenkins, 1974). The operations involved in mapping implicit and explicit relationships between the context and information to be remembered are often constructive transformations. Specific features of the stimulus are encoded according to an individual's perception of its salient aspects (Anderson & Ortony, 1975; Barclay, Bransford, Franks, McCarrell, & Nitsch, 1974; Tulving & Thompson, 1973).

Granit (1921) demonstrated the importance of generating context for children in the immediate reproduction of visual stimuli. Children ranging from 8 to 13 years of age were shown a series of ambiguous figures that varied in similarity to real objects. Children were subsequently asked to reproduce them. After completing the drawing tasks, questions were asked concerning possible interpretations of the figures. Children tended to draw the ambiguous stimuli as unambiguous familiar objects that were constructed according to the context in which they were encoded. Granit stated, ''Construction can be defined, quite generally, as comprehension of new impressions of form, which by means of associations of similarity, assimilate earlier mental experience. Further, we have found that the associations are chiefly concerned with relational resemblances [1921, p. 240].''

Children also use contextual cues to make decisions about language processing. Klein, Klein, and Bertino (1974) have shown that sixth graders use context to determine word boundaries, whereas fourth graders show less use of contextual cues. Ramanauskas (1972) has shown that retarded adolescents use cues from various sentences within a paragraph to make decisions concerning missing words in the paragraph. It has also been shown that pictorial illustrations accompanying prose that is presented orally can serve as contextual descriptions for the passages and enhance recall (Lesgold, Levin, Shimron, & Guttman, 1975). Although 9- and 10-year-old children can spontaneously map relations and draw inferences from the context, younger children must be directed or taught to use the context.

Despite a limited number of empirical studies regarding children's use of contextual cues to facilitate comprehension and memory, the topic is important for an analysis of constructive cognition. Context cues permit the individual to amalgamate different sources of information about the same event. They also may direct attention to relevant characteristics of the event and promote mapping of correspondence relations between the context and stimulus. The amalgamation, focusing, mapping, and inferring operations are all constructive transformations of the input that allow more complete comprehension. If these operations incorporate the context into the memory representation for the event, then the memory trace itself may undergo constructive transformations.

Many other research findings provide indirect support for the importance of context in children's comprehension and memory. One pertinent example is the finding that elaboration of a stimulus enhances recall. The elaboration phenomenon refers to the operation whereby stimuli to be remembered are associated or linked together by additional relationships in a context. For example, in a paired-associates task two nouns may be elaborated in a sentence (e.g., The ROCK hit the BOTTLE). The provision of elaborative relations by the experimenter dramatically improves memory for the words. When children are directed to construct their own sentence elaborations, they generally remember the words better than when the experimenter provides the elaborations (see Reese, this volume). The semantic relationship is important for both experimenter-provided and subject-generated elaborations. Sentences that describe an active or functional interaction between the two nouns or provide a common contextual theme (e.g., the LADY flew on a BROOM on Halloween) facilitate recall better than sentences that describe the nouns in static positions or noninteractive states (Buckhalt, Mahoney, & Paris, 1976; Mahoney, 1975).

The elaboration phenomenon is clearly within the province of constructive cognition because of the emphasis on generated relationships among stimuli, memory integration of the elaboration, and retrieval mediated through the constructed relationships. Providing or generating a relational context expands the available information of the stimuli and embellishes the events with additional associations, cues, and relationships. These processes whereby a stimulus is embellished may or may not involve inferential operations, but they do elicit idiosyncratic mental representations of the related events. The stimuli become "unitized" and afford parsimonious, semantically integrated contexts as memory representations. The unified representation affords multiple access routes to memory through the various cues that are constructed (e.g., verbal, imaginal, sensory, context of occurrence, idiosyncratic objects, salient relationships). The enhancement in retention that is observed in studies of the elaboration phenomenon can be attributed to the deeper level of processing (cf. Craik & Lockhart, 1972) and comprehension afforded by the construction of a relational context, the semantically integrated memory trace, and the additional access cues available for retrieval.

Developmental trends in elaboration that have been researched extensively concern the gradual spontaneity in producing elaborations during childhood, the decreased reliance with age on explicit retrieval cues, and the greater understanding of complex relationships generated among stimuli. With increasing age children become more proficient in the generation of interactive, semantically based relations between stimuli and employ their own elaborations to enhance recall with greater effectiveness. With adequate systems to evaluate and classify subject-generated elaborations and a conceptual framework for interpreting these constructive changes in cognitive abilities, the elaboration paradigm may be valuable for analyzing age-related changes in the utility of constructive processes for memory.

F. Improvement in Memory over Extended Time Periods

Much of the empirical support for constructive cognition, both historical and contemporary, is derived from evidence of progressive changes in memory over time. Remembering is modified according to the changes in the individual's history, cognitive abilities, and social environment. A typical paradigm for investigating constructive processes of encoding and comprehension involves one memory test and measurement of the correspondence between input and output. In contrast, investigations of longitudinal memory transformations present the individual with several opportunities to retrieve the information (e.g., Bartlett's method of repeated recall) and measure the correspondence between information recalled at each test.

Piaget and Inhelder (1973) summarized a number of pioneering studies investigating improvement in children's long-term memory. In general, memory for an event was shown to be mediated through the child's cognitive systems of organization. A popular example of a Piagetian memory experiment is the seriated-stick problem. Initially, the child is shown an array of seriated sticks ranging from tallest to shortest. A week later, the child is asked to reproduce the array from memory. A similar request is made six months or a year later. The 5- or 6-year-old child typically produces a nonseriated array at the first presentation of the sticks but usually draws the correct seriation of sticks one year later. These findings of "improved" memory over time have been replicated in a number of studies (Altemeyer, Fulton, & Berney, 1969; Furth, Ross, & Youniss, 1974; Liben, 1975).

One explanation of the improvement in long-term memory is that the change occurs in the transformation of the memory representation. Initially, the representation of the seriated array may be assimilated to an incomplete scheme, one that does not contain an appropriate cognitive rule for seriation. As new information is acquired through experience over time, constructive changes take place in the memory representation. These changes are mediated by the acquisition of new cognitive structures related to seriation that reflect the changing operative level of the child. When required to draw the array after the six-month interval, the child can reproduce the seriated array as a result of the constructive changes in his memory representation based on completion of the seriation scheme. This is congruent with Piaget's notion that the operative level of the child determines, in part, the developmental improvement in memory and is based on the belief that incoming information is actively incorporated into the memory representation and causes constructive changes in the stored information. The mechanism for this alteration could be something like recomprehension, whereby the acquisition of new cognitive relations or schemes allows the child to automatically understand the information in a different perspective and perhaps in a more complex manner.

The methodology and interpretation of the results are more complicated than this brief discussion implies, and a detailed analysis of Piagetian memory research is provided by Liben (this volume). In any case, the consistent finding that memory over time changes according to cognitive schematic changes is strong support for constructive transformations in memory and the interaction between memory and other cognitive processes.

III. A FRAMEWORK FOR EVALUATING CONSTRUCTIVE COGNITIVE PROCESSES

The data discussed to this point provide overwhelming evidence that children and adults routinely perform cognitive transformations in attempts to understand and remember meaningful stimuli. Although the amount of research is impressive, a framework is needed for the organization and evaluation of the diverse research regarding constructive cognition.

Research to date has not differentiated comprehension and memory, nor the particular cognitive processes associated with each. The lack of these conceptual distinctions may be attributed to the expository and demonstrative nature of the research. Early studies were devoted to showing that people do not remember all the lexical or syntactic features of language, that people spontaneously amalgamate related information, that people can draw inferences automatically, and that context is important for comprehension. Although these findings are interesting and important, they are primarily demonstrations that some traditional theories (e.g., associationism and generative syntax) are insufficient to account for the results.

Another weakness of the research is the lack of parametric data on the proposed cognitive processes. For example, the demonstration that people semantically integrate related sentences in memory (Bransford & Franks, 1972) is intuitively obvious when the task is structured to prevent rehearsal, to be too lengthy to memorize verbatim, to include a great amount of redundant and identical information, to confound judgments of semantic similarity with probabilistic judgments about sentence identicality (cf. Katz, Atkeson, & Lee, 1974), and to confound responses based on confusion or forgetting of information and the intentional omission of information. Although semantic integration has been demonstrated, this does not mean that people employ the process all of the time, nor that they do not remember specific bits of information. The existence and certainly the importance of the process depend on the task and may vary greatly among many parameters that have yet to be investigated.

We would like to sketch a framework for organizing and interpreting research dealing with constructive cognition that highlights some of the unresolved problems and provides some tentative solutions and proposals for related issues. We shall categorize constructive processes according to the time when the transformation of information might occur, during encoding, storage, or retrieval. Our purposes are (1) to provide a useful and meaningful classification of research now subsumed under the generic label of constructive processes; (2) to differentiate the cognitive acts performed during each stage of processing; and (3) to inquire about the course of development of these various abilities.

A. Constructive Operations Performed during Encoding

Encoding information into memory is similar in many regards to Piaget's notion of assimilation, since both depend heavily on mechanisms of perception and comprehension. Barclay (1973) even labeled his version of constructive cognition as ''assimilation theory'' because operations performed during encoding reflect the idiosyncratic nature of subject-generated units of information. When individuals attempt to remember an event, they must perceive relevant and salient information, choose methods of operating on the information, and subsequently exercise that strategy. These operations necessarily mean that constructive cognition mediates encoding. Even when memory is the involuntary consequence of comprehension, encoding often involves constructive strategies such as the utilization of context, inference, and elaboration.

The numerous strategies for operating on information during encoding may be characterized as processes of information expansion (Paris, 1975). Devices such as chunking, rehearsal, imagery, elaboration, and use of context are different kinds of strategies that the child can apply to the event in order to understand it and relate the experience to an existing cognitive scheme. The original stimulus is enriched by practice and familiarity, by the addition of cues, by additional modes of representing the information, or by interactive relationships among items in the event to be remembered. The enhanced retention that results from contextual provision, verbal elaboration of relationships, and interactive imagery attests to the value of these informationally expansive operations. All of these operations can be regarded as processing changes in the information before it is stored. Information that is presented concurrently (or serially in the case of discourse but within a small time span) undergoes constant monitoring and reorganization. The constructive process is like a recursive mapping of an event onto existing schemata. Continuous reorganization and reinterpretation occurs until the event is terminated and the individual stores the derived representation. Through this dynamic and reciprocal interaction, the information is embellished in many ways (e.g., inferential relations) but also reduced for parsimonious storage (e.g., semantic integration).

The various studies in which children and adults were shown to infer additional relationships spontaneously can also be subsumed under this category of constructive encoding operations. Inferences made in order to understand events will usually be stored with the event, as in the case of semantic integration. However, we should also differentiate these involuntary, goal-oriented inferences from those inferences made ex post facto and directed by retrieval demands. Although additional information synthesized at retrieval may be available, it is likely to be processed and stored differently when constructed during encoding.

The emphasis in the previous discussion on perceptual salience, comprehension, and assimilation fits easily into a developmental model of constructive cognition. It is necessary, however, to clarify the task and subject characteristics further in order to understand the developmental changes. Brown (1975a) has generated a model describing developmental effects on memory tasks that distinguishes (1) those tasks employing episodic from semantic stimuli and (2) those requiring explicit strategies from those that do not. Constructive acts of comprehension may occur for any of these cells formed by the matrix except for episodic tasks, which do not require or permit strategies. Generally, where a particular strategy is called for or necessitated by a task, we find the constructive processes applied in a deliberate fashion. We know, however, that young children seldom use deliberate plans to remember (Kreutzer, Leonard, & Flavell, 1975) and rarely produce and employ efficient strategies. Therefore, on episodic and semantic tasks that require specific strategies we would expect little evidence of constructive abilities by children younger than age 5 and progressively better constructive abilities by older children.

Deliberate strategies may be contrasted with involuntary forms of remembering where those comprehension activities engaged in as part of the goal of the task are remembered better than those aspects that function as a means to solution of the task (Smirnov & Zinchenko, 1969). Tasks such as paragraph comprehension and semantic integration would tap these involuntary memory processes. One would expect developmental differences in constructive abilities if the task were sensitive to differences in cognitive structures and inferences among the children (Paris & Upton, 1976; Paris & Lindauer, 1976). Some semantic integration tasks presumably do not assess different knowledge bases of children and therefore do not exhibit age-related differences (Barclay & Reid, 1974).

In general, we would expect to obtain developmental differences in constructive encoding skills on semantic tasks requiring involuntary information-expansion operations that reflect qualitative differences in the cognitive abilities of the subjects. Another way of saying this is that spontaneous acts of constructive comprehension will be sensitive to age-related differences if they involve cognitive mediational efficiency for correct performance. Deliberate or voluntary transformations of stimuli during encoding will reflect mediational abilities but also include production and selection of appropriate strategies, adoption of metamemorial plans, and efficiency in the use of strategy. These types of mnemonics generally are not integrated into the memory representations for the original stimuli but serve as adjunctive encoding and retrieval cues.

B. Constructive Changes in Memory Representations during Storage

Memory is not static. Information derived and stored from an experience can undergo successive changes. Bartlett's research as well as recent work on memory for prose has shown the dynamic aspects of storage for semantic material. An adequate model of memory must not assume that the input to a memory store is retrieved intact and that the only changes in the trace occur during encoding and retrieval. Memory is not a repository for experiences that are encoded and recalled one time; rather, meaningful material is subject to continuous reorganization in memory. People recall and rehearse events repeatedly, and this recurrent retrieval permits the information to be modified through recursive operations of comprehension. As more information is gathered, existing schemata are modified by deleting or adding relevant facts and relations. This recursive process is common to all phases of constructive cognition, but the phenomenon has been demonstrated with progressive memory changes over extended time periods.

Accomodative changes in the memory representation have been investigated by Piaget and Inhelder (1973), who have shown that memory is dynamic and follows regular transformations that conform to other cognitive rules acquired by the child. Transformations and improvement in memory over time are particularly amenable to developmental investigations because the focus is necessarily on longitudinal changes in memory representations. The representation of an event in memory can be expected to be transformed during storage if the child acquires qualitatively new, different, and efficient ways of interpreting and analyzing the stored information. The change in memory may reflect the acquisition of new knowledge that permits the event to be comprehended in a different manner. It could also reflect the acquisition of a new retrieval rule or even the loss of an old retrieval environment through changes in the sociohistorical context. At any rate, the original memory representation is unavailable and the new trace has incorporated additional information into the old percept such that it is consistent with the child's knowledge.

C. Constructive Operations Performed during Retrieval

Information held in memory can be transformed during retrieval from storage. The demands of the task during retrieval may influence this reconstructive processing. For example, the amount of support given by retrieval cues in a particular task (e.g., recognition, free recall, cued recall) can determine how much and which information is remembered (Brown, 1975a). The retrieval environment directs the child to search memory in particular ways and to derive information consistent with these strategies and cues. In some cases, the retrieval cues elicit spontaneous inferences in the individual's search of memory such that the original information is distorted or reconstructed in accordance with the cues (Loftus & Palmer, 1974). We know that the acquisition with development of new knowledge and retrieval rules permits children to recall events in a manner different from the original understanding and stored representation. More efficient metamemorial plans and mnemonic strategies for retrieval develop with age and may facilitate reconstructive processing as well.

Conceptually, the postulation of transformations performed during retrieval distinguishes between constructive and reconstructive processes. A changed memory representation is the end result in both cases, but the temporal locus of the activity and the processes that motivate the transformations can be different. Of course, many kinds of retrieval may not influence memory representations.

The child can synthesize and generate many relationships from memory when directed to do so at retrieval that were *not* originally intact representations. It is very important to distinguish between knowledge that one can derive from an experience and a person's memory representation for that event. The former involves what is or potentially can be comprehended from the event, and the latter deals with the manner in which that event is stored in memory. This distinction is important for those studies employing free recall or series of questions about a passage because individuals' responses include more than memory for the event: They include knowledge synthesized at retrieval, too. The value of this classification is to help distinguish between constructive and reconstructive processing, comprehension and memory, and information derivable from memory from the specific memory representation (although these are not exclusive dichotomies).

We also want to point out that retrieval demands can function as directed search and inferential operations that may initiate constructive changes in memory. Retrieval and rehearsal operations recreate the experience for the individual and permit additional details to be remembered and new relationships to be synthesized. Cycles of retrieval and recomprehension seem to be common processes involved in recalling past events. This kind of recurrent monitoring of one's knowledge can lead to constructive transformations in memory through the application of recursive strategies of comprehension.

IV. IMPLICATIONS OF THE CONSTRUCTIVE FRAMEWORK

The focus of constructive cognition is on the functional operations of understanding and remembering. Investigators from Gestalt traditions to Bartlett to contemporary researchers have presented persuasive demonstrations that the distortions and modifications imputed on stimuli by children and adults are normal processes of comprehension and memory. Until recently, theories of language and memory did not adequately characterize these processes. For example, the associationistic conceptualization of language that evolved 20 to 30 years ago in the prevailing S–R atmosphere could not be extended very easily to accommodate constructive changes in processing of meaningful stimuli such as sentences and paragraphs. Similarly, structural linguistic theories were often unconcerned about aspects of an individual's performance and did not provide the descriptive or explanatory adequacy required of a psychological theory of language.

One direct implication of constructive processes is the reformulation of theories and models of language and memory. Contemporary conceptualizations of language and memory emphasize psychological referents and context (Bransford & McCarrell, 1974), communicative intentions (Searle, 1969), and inferential processes (Collins, Warnock, Aiello, & Miller, 1975; Winograd, 1972) as critical determinants of the manner by which events are comprehended and remembered. The convergence of diverse fields such as generative semantics, philosophy of language, perception, computer simulation of language processing, and psycholinguistics in similar characterizations of constructive cognition is remarkable and encouraging.

The constructive framework may also enhance our understanding of developmental changes in memory. There is no comprehensive theory or model of the development of memory. This volume and recent reviews of processes in children's memory development (Brown, 1975a; Hagen, Jongeward, & Kail, 1975; Kreutzer et al., 1975) point to the need for a developmental framework. We believe that the functional operations of constructive cognition—contextual mapping, inference, elaboration, semantic integration, and long-term memory modifications—can be readily accommodated to developmental conceptualizations of cognitive organization. Although the global and functional nature of constructive cognition outlined here can reconcile many empirical findings, the framework requires considerable refinement. Terms such as *context* and *inference* must be defined better and grounded in particular operations. Developmental changes in cognitive processes may then be described more rigorously and explicated. The heuristic value of the constructive framework is derived from its emphasis on processes that are readily apparent in many aspects of children's behavior. We shall mention a few examples to illustrate the convergence of operations.

Many of the studies cited previously were concerned with language comprehension and what the child must do in order to understand. Constructive processes of encoding are implicated in studies of children's appreciation of jokes and linguistic ambiguity (Shultz & Horibe, 1974; Shultz & Pilon, 1973). Inability to infer dual readings for ambiguous words or phrases and the failure to relate the punch line to the setting context can make a joke meaningless to a child. Such constructive operations of inference and utilization of context will also be important for the development of the creative usage of figurative language (Pollio & Pollio, 1974). Current views on language acquisition also emphasize constructive cognition. During the first year of life, infants infer intentions of the speaker, infer presuppositions about referents common to the speaker and listener, and construct meaningful relationships about events from many contextual cues (Brown, 1973; Macnamara, 1972; Nelson, 1974).

Perhaps the most obvious area of application for constructive processes is the field of reading. Educators and psychologists have argued that reading is a manifestation of all the skills of thinking. Historically, the field has often been concerned with grapheme-phoneme correspondence skills in decoding the printed word. In more recent approaches, such as that described by Stauffer (1969), it is argued that reading is greatly dependent on semantic and inferential processes. Successful comprehension and memory during reading depend on reorganization, inference, and evaluation of the meaningful relations described. Horn (1937) aptly captured this process in the following quotation:

> The author, moreover, does not really convey ideas to the reader; he merely stimulates him to construct them out of his own experience. If the concept is already in the reader's mind, the task is relatively easy, but if, as is usually the case in school, it is new to the reader, its construction more nearly approaches problem-solving than simple association [p. 154].

The social behavior of children has been neglected in this discussion, but we feel that constructive cognition has much to offer an analysis of social behavior. For example, basic mechanisms of social learning such as imitation involve abstraction of information and inference (Liebert & Swenson, 1971). Even the value imputed on verbal approval and disapproval may be inferred by children from contextual usage of the words (Paris & Cairns, 1972). Mischel's cognitive social learning theory emphasizes cognitive and behavioral *construction competencies* as vital processes in social interactions (Mischel & Mischel, 1975). Shantz (1975) has defined the area of social cognition as "the child's intuitive or logical representation of others, that is, how he characterizes others and makes inferences about their covert, inner psychological experiences [p. 285]." Shantz reviewed many social phenomena that demonstrate constructive processes in comprehension and memory, for example, appreciation of various spatial orientations, role playing, person perception, and inferring of emotional states from facial expressions. Many of these interactions and judgments require inferential processes and appreciation of contextual cues and can be expected to change with age like other aspects of constructive cognition. Flapan (1968), for example, observed that children between 6 and 12 years of age improved in their ability to infer and interpret another person's intentions, feelings, and expectations.

Certainly the constructive framework can be applied to other areas of social cognition like attribution processes, moral development, prejudice, self-concept, and clinical cases of psychopathology where distortion in understanding becomes extreme. Constructive cognition may provide a heuristic framework for investigating similar processes across a broad range of children's behavior, and the converging operations will provide a more complete and detailed view of development.

V. SUMMARY

Constructive cognition represents a social and biological view of human mental faculties that stresses dialectical principles of dynamic interaction between the individual's developmental capacities and the environment. Memory must be regarded as part of a continually changing cognitive representation of the organism's world and never as a static entity, place, or time. Describing memory as a component in a mechanical system that can operate and be studied independently of the individual's perceptual, cognitive, social, and motivational characteristics will lead to underestimations of the complexity of the processes involved in memory as well as produce an incomplete analysis of the integrity of the individual's cognitive processes.

The constructive view of memory implies that a mechanical analogy of storage that does not allow transformations in remembered events is necessarily incomplete. Knowledge that is retained over time undergoes progressive and continuous change from the moment it is first apprehended. The representation is a dynamic integration of constructed meaning. But the information that is retained and the schemata to which it is assimilated both change as a consequence of the incorporation of one into the other. This action of reciprocal, constructive change is identical with the principles of assimilation and accommodation and represents the foundation of developmental growth.

We have described several of the processes involved in constructive cognition such as inference, contextual mapping, elaboration, and integration. These are functional operations applied by children and adults in an effort to understand and remember meaningful stimuli and events. Constructive operations can be distinguished partially on the basis of the temporal locus of the change, that is, encoding, storage, and retrieval. However, information is rarely sequenced in this way only one time. Typically, people retrieve, rehearse, reorganize, and recomprehend previous experiences many times. Recursive operations of constructive cognition provide for flexible and mutable memory representations and continuous refinement in one's knowledge base. Such recursive and constructive changes are adaptive for the individual's acquisition of knowledge and retention of important information.

The framework provided by constructive cognition is ideal for analyzing developmental changes in information processing, the quality of symbolic representations, and the structural nature of acquired knowledge. The focus is on idiosyncratic aspects of comprehension and subsequent memory representation. Constructive processes are sensitive to sociohistorical context variables as well as longitudinal, temporal variables. We have mentioned several areas of cognitive and social research where the model of constructive cognition may be applied. The principles of constructive changes in comprehension and memory have a long history of application across a broad range of behavior and may provide a cohesive framework for the study of cognitive development.

ACKNOWLEDGMENTS

Portions of this work were supported by NIE grant NE-G-00-3-0089 to the first author.

REFERENCES

Altemeyer, R., Fulton, D., & Berney, K. Long-term memory improvement: Confirmation of a finding by Piaget. *Child Development,* 1969, *40,* 845–857.

Anderson, R. C., & Ortony, A. On putting apples into bottles—A problem of polysemy. *Cognitive Psychology,* 1975, *7,* 167–180.

Barclay, J. R. The role of comprehension in remembering sentences. *Cognitive Psychology,* 1973, *4,* 229–254.

Barclay, J. R., Bransford, J. D., Franks, J. J., McCarrell, N. S., & Nitsch, D. Comprehension and semantic flexibility. *Journal of Verbal Learning and Verbal Behavior,* 1974, *13,* 471–481.

Barclay, J. R., & Reid, M. Semantic integration in children's recall of discourse. *Developmental Psychology,* 1974, *10,* 277–281.

Bartlett, F. C. *Remembering.* Cambridge: University Press, 1932.

Binet, A., & Henri, J. La memoire des phrases (Memoire des idees). *L'année Psychologique,* 1894, *1,* 24–59.

Bransford, J. D., & Franks, J. J. The abstraction of linguistic ideas: A review. *Cognition: An International Journal of Cognitive Psychology,* 1972, *2,* 211–249.

Bransford, J. D., & Johnson, M. K. Contextual prerequisites for understanding: Some investigations of comprehension and recall. *Journal of Verbal Learning and Verbal Behavior,* 1972, *11,* 717–726.

Bransford, J. D., & McCarrell, N. S. A sketch of a cognitive approach to comprehension: Some thoughts about what it means to comprehend. In W. B. Weimer & D. S. Palermo (Eds.), *Cognition and symbolic processes.* Hillsdale, N.J.: Lawrence Erlbaum Associates, 1974.

Brockway, J., Chmielewski, D., & Cofer, C. N. Remembering prose: Productivity and accuracy constraints in recognition memory. *Journal of Verbal Learning and Verbal Behavior,* 1974, *13,* 194–208.

Brown, A. L. The development of memory: Knowing, knowing about knowing, and knowing how to know. In H. W. Reese (Ed.), *Advances in child development and behavior* (Vol. 10). New York: Academic Press, 1975.   (a)

Brown, A. L. Recognition, reconstruction, and recall of narrative sequences by preoperational children. *Child Development,* 1975, *46,* 156–166.   (b)

Brown, A. L., & Murphy, M. D. Reconstruction of logical versus arbitrary sequences by preschool children. *Journal of Experimental Child Psychology,* 1975, *20,* 307–326.

Brown, R. *A first language.* Cambridge, Mass.: Harvard University Press, 1973.

Buckhalt, J. A., Mahoney, G. J., & Paris, S. G. Efficiency of self-generated elaborations by EMR and nonretarded children. *American Journal of Mental Deficiency,* 1976, *81,* 93–96.

Chafe, W. L. Discourse structure and human knowledge. In J. B. Carroll & R. O. Freedle (Eds.), *Language comprehension and the acquisition of knowledge.* New York: Wiley, 1972.

Cofer, C. Constructive processes in memory. *American Scientist,* 1973, *61,* 537–543.

Collins, A., Warnock, E. H., Aiello, N., & Miller, M. S. Reasoning from incomplete knowledge. In D. G. Bobrow & A. M. Collins (Eds.), *Representation and understanding.* New York: Academic Press, 1975.

Craik, F. I. M., & Lockhart, R. S. Levels of processing: A framework for memory research. *Journal of Verbal Learning and Verbal Behavior,* 1972, *11,* 671–684.

DeSoto, C. B., London, M., & Handel, S. Social reasoning and spatial paralogic. *Journal of Personality and Social Psychology,* 1965, *2,* 513–521.

Flapan, D. *Children's understanding of social interaction.* New York: Teachers College Press, 1968.

Furth, H., Ross, B., & Youniss, J. Operative understanding in children's immediate and long-term reproductions of drawings. *Child Development,* 1974, *45,* 63–70.

Granit, A. R. A study of the perception of form. *British Journal of Psychology,* 1921, *12,* 223–247.

Hagen, J. W., Jongeward, R. H., & Kail, R. V. Cognitive perspectives on the development of memory. In H. W. Reese (Ed.), *Advances in child development and behavior* (Vol. 10). New York: Academic Press, 1975.

Hale, G. A., & Piper, R. A. Effect of pictorial integration on children's incidental learning. *Developmental Psychology,* 1974, *10,* 847–851.

Haviland, S. E., & Clark, H. H. What's new? Acquiring new information as a process in comprehension. *Journal of Verbal Learning and Verbal Behavior,* 1974, *13,* 512–521.

Horn, E. V. *Methods of instruction in the social studies.* New York: Scribner, 1937.

Horowitz, L. M., Lampel, A. K., & Takanishi, R. N. The child's memory for unitized scenes. *Journal of Experimental Child Psychology,* 1969, *8,* 375–388.

Jenkins, J. J. Remember that old theory of memory? Well, forget it! *American Psychologist,* 1974, *29,* 785–795.

Katz, S., Atkeson, B., & Lee, J. The Bransford-Franks linear effect: Integration or artifact? *Memory & Cognition,* 1974, *2,* 709–713.

Kintsch, W. *The representation of meaning in memory.* Hillsdale, N.J.: Lawrence Erlbaum Associates, 1974.

Klein, H. A., Klein, G. A., & Bertino, M. Utilization of context for word identification decisions in children. *Journal of Experimental Child Psychology,* 1974, *17,* 79–86.

Kosslyn, S. M., & Bower, G. H. The role of imagery in sentence memory: A developmental study. *Child Development,* 1974, *45,* 30–38.

Kreutzer, M. A., Leonard, C., & Flavell, J. H. An interview study of children's knowledge about memory. *Monographs of the Society for Research in Child Development,* 1975, *40*(1, Serial No. 159).

Lesgold, A. M., Levin, J. R., Shimron, J., & Guttman, J. Pictures and young children's learning from oral prose. Paper presented at the biennial meeting of the Society for Research in Child Development, Denver, 1975.

Liben, L. S. Evidence for developmental differences in spontaneous seriation and its implications for past research on long-term memory improvement. *Developmental Psychology,* 1975, *11,* 121–125.

Liebert, R. M., & Swenson, S. A. Abstraction, inference, and the process of imitative learning. *Developmental Psychology,* 1971, *5,* 500–504.

Loftus, E. F., & Palmer, J. C. Reconstruction of automobile destruction: An example of the interaction between language and memory. *Journal of Verbal Learning and Verbal Behavior,* 1974, *13,* 585–589.

Macnamara, J. Cognitive basis of language learning in infants. *Psychological Review,* 1972, *79,* 1–13.

Mahoney, G. J. A developmental study of children's self-generated elaborations in a paired associate recall task. Unpublished doctoral dissertation, George Peabody College, 1975.

Mandler, J. M., & Stein, N. L. Recall and recognition of pictures by children as a function of organization and distractor similarity. *Journal of Experimental Psychology,* 1974, *102,* 657–669.

Mischel, W., & Mischel, H. N. Moral behavior from a cognitive social learning viewpoint. Paper presented at the biennial meeting of the Society for Research in Child Development, Denver, 1975.

Nelson, K. Concept, word, and sentence: Interrelations in acquisition and development. *Psychological Review,* 1974, *81,* 267–285.

Paris, S. G. Integration and inference in children's comprehension and memory. In F. Restle, R. Shiffrin, J. Castellan, H. Lindman, & D. Pisoni (Eds.), *Cognitive theory* (Vol. 1). Hillsdale, N.J.: Lawrence Erlbaum Associates, 1975.

Paris, S. G., & Cairns, R. B. An experimental and ethological analysis of social reinforcement with retarded children. *Child Development,* 1972, *43,* 717–729.

Paris, S. G., & Carter, A. Y. Semantic and constructive aspects of sentence memory in children. *Developmental Psychology,* 1973, *9,* 109–113.

Paris, S. G., & Lindauer, B. K. The role of inference in children's comprehension and memory for sentences. *Cognitive Psychology*, 1976, *8*, 217–227.

Paris, S. G., & Mahoney, G. J. Cognitive integration in children's memory for sentences and pictures. *Child Development*, 1974, *45*, 633–642.

Paris, S. G., Mahoney, G. J., & Buckhalt, J. A. Facilitation of semantic integration in sentence memory of retarded children. *American Journal of Mental Deficiency*, 1974, *78*, 714–720.

Paris, S. G., & Upton, L. R. Children's memory for inferential relationships in prose. *Child Development*, 1976, *47*, 660–668.

Piaget, J., & Inhelder, B. *Memory and intelligence*. New York: Basic Books, 1973.

Pollio, M. R., & Pollio, H. R. The development of figurative language in children. *Journal of Psycholinguistic Research*, 1974, *3*, 185–201.

Potts, G. R. Information processing strategies used in the encoding of linear orderings. *Journal of Verbal Learning and Verbal Behavior*, 1972, *11*, 727–740.

Ramanauskas, S. Contextual constraints beyond a sentence on cloze responses of mentally retarded children. *American Journal of Mental Deficiency*, 1972, *77*, 338–345.

Rumelhart, D. E. Notes on a schema for stories. Paper presented at the Carbonnel Memorial Conference, Pajaro Dunes, California, May 1974.

Searle, J. R. *Speech acts: An essay in the philosophy of language*. London: Cambridge University Press, 1969.

Shantz, C. U. The development of social cognition. In E. M. Hetherington (Ed.), *Review of child development research* (Vol. 5). Chicago: University of Chicago Press, 1975.

Shultz, T. R., & Horibe, F. Development of the appreciation of verbal jokes. *Developmental Psychology*, 1974, *10*, 13–20.

Shultz, T. R., & Pilon, R. Development of the ability to detect linguistic ambiguity. *Child Development*, 1973, *44*, 728–733.

Smirnov, A. A., & Zinchenko, P. I. Problems in the psychology of memory. In M. Cole & I. Maltzman (Eds.), *A handbook of contemporary Soviet psychology*. New York: Basic Books, 1969.

Stacey, J. T., & Ross, B. M. Scheme and schema in children's memory of their own drawings. *Development Psychology*, 1975, *11*, 37–41.

Stauffer, R. *Directing reading maturity as a cognitive process*. New York: Harper & Row, 1969.

Stein, N. L., & Glenn, C. G. A developmental study of children's recall of story material. Paper presented at the biennial meeting of the Society for Research in Child Development, Denver, 1975.

Sulin, R. A., & Dooling, D. J. Intrusion of a thematic idea in retention of prose. *Journal of Experimental Psychology*, 1974, *103*, 255–262.

Trabasso, T. Representation, memory and reasoning: How do we make transitive inferences? In A. D. Pick (Ed.), *Minnesota symposium on child psychology* (Vol. 9). Minneapolis: University of Minnesota Press, 1975.

Tulving, E., & Bower, G. H. The logic of memory representations. In G. Bower (Ed.), *Advances in learning and motivation* (Vol. 8). New York: Academic Press, 1974.

Tulving, E., & Thomson, D. M. Encoding specificity and retrieval processes in episodic memory. *Psychological Review*, 1973, *80*, 352–373.

Wertsch, J. V. The influence of listener perception of the speaker on recognition memory. *Journal of Psycholinguistic Research*, 1975, *4*, 89–98.

Winograd, T. Understanding natural language. *Cognitive Psychology*, 1972, *3*, 1–191.

Zangwill, O. L. *Remembering* revisited. *Quarterly Journal of Experimental Psychology*, 1972, *24*, 123–138.

3

The Development of Mnemonic Encoding in Children: From Perception to Abstraction

Robert V. Kail, Jr.
Alexander W. Siegel
University of Pittsburgh

I. INTRODUCTION

Memory rarely represents experience exactly. Rather, memory results from a complex interaction between an event in the "real world" and an individual's cognitive structures—a process that has come to be known as "encoding." In the present chapter we will selectively review the research on children's encoding, and then provide some general theoretical perspectives for conceptualizing developmental changes in encoding.

We begin with a general description of encoding (Melton & Martin, 1972):

> The core intent of this idea [encoding] is that between the external world and a human's memorial representation of that external world there operate certain processes that translate external information into internal information. These processes may in part be selective, or elaborative, or transformational; some may be optional while others are obligatory [pp. xii–xiii].

Thus codes, coding, and encoding all refer to the fact that an event is somehow transformed when it is represented in memory.

Clearly this definition of encoding is much too broad to be useful in constructing a framework for conceptualizing the development of encoding; some distinction between types of encoding is necessary. Bower's (1972) taxonomy of encoding processes is helpful in this regard. He distinguished four varieties of encoding: stimulus selection, rewriting, elaboration, and componential description. The first three varieties will not be considered here, since they are discussed in other chapters (see, for example, the chapters by Reese and by Hagen and Stanovich). Instead, the present chapter focuses on coding as *componential description*.

We will consider a mnemonic code to be a description of an event in terms of a set of features—a description that occurs automatically (i.e., without the individual's intention or awareness). More specifically, a code may be conceptualized as "an ordered list of attributes with their corresponding values" (Bower, 1967, p. 233). Furthermore, codes typically are not static, but are transformed over time. That is, there seems to be a series of temporally defined levels or stages of encoding. Initial codes reflect primarily the physical or perceptual characteristics of stimuli, such as modality of presentation. Later codes generally reflect conceptual characteristics of stimuli, such as taxonomic class or connotative meaning.

The purpose of the present chapter is to attempt to identify and conceptualize age-related changes that occur in children's encoding of these attributes, features, and characteristics of stimuli. One limitation on the scope of the review should be noted at the outset. While the focus of the chapter is on age-related changes in encoding, the spectrum of development to be considered is limited to childhood, adolescence, and young adulthood. The selection of this age range is not arbitrary but, rather, reflects the nature of much of the extant work and the relative paucity of evidence concerning processes of encoding in individuals outside this age range.[1]

II. DEVELOPMENTAL CHANGES IN CHILDREN'S ENCODING

Given these preliminary considerations, the development of encoding can be discussed in the context of research in which various kinds of codes are, explicitly or implicitly, the focus of study. It is proposed that during the initial stages of encoding, the representation of an event is more or less a reflection of (i.e., isomorphic to) the physical stimulation (e.g., Shepard, 1975), while subsequent encoding seems to be more an abstraction of that event. This abstraction maintains the essential features of the event, most of which are presumed to be conceptually based. We will first consider studies of age-related differences in the initial stages of coding, or "perceptual codes," then examine children's higher-order or "abstractive" coding. As will become apparent, questions concerning developmental changes in rate of encoding and rate of decay of the code have dictated much of the research on initial stages of encoding. In contrast,

---

[1] Recent work on infant memory, described by Cohen and Gelber (1975) and Olson (1976), is a notable exception in this regard.

developmental changes in the format of coding (where format is defined as the type and number of encoded features) have been the usual focus of investigations of children's higher-order coding.

A. Perceptual Codes

Input from a receptor is first processed in a "sensory register," which, because it is capable of storing large amounts of information for very brief periods of time, functions primarily as a temporary repository for minimally processed stimuli. The lion's share of the extant research has been concerned with short-term codes for visual and, to a lesser extent, auditory information. This is particularly true of developmental research. The sensory registers for these two modalities have been called iconic and echoic memory (Neisser, 1967), a terminology that we will adopt here.

1. Iconic Memory

The nature of representation in iconic memory has been described succinctly by Neisser (1967):

> Visual input . . . can be briefly stored in some medium which is subject to very rapid decay. Before it has decayed, information can be read from this medium just as if the stimulus were still active. We can be equally certain that this storage is in some sense a "visual image" . . . [for] the letters appeared to be visually present and legible . . . even when the stimulus had actually been off for 150 msec. That is, although performance was based on "memory" from the experimenter's point of view, it was "perceptual" as far as the experience of the observers was concerned [pp. 18–19].

Thus, visual information can be entered quickly and maintained briefly in iconic memory. Information can be transferred from iconic memory to a more permanent memory store, or it may decay in iconic memory, becoming permanently lost to an individual.

Age-related differences in iconic memory apparently are restricted to ease of accessing (entry) and transfering (output) information that is in iconic memory. Capacity and rate of decay of iconic memory seem to be relatively invariant developmentally. Evidence supporting this conclusion is provided in studies by both Sheingold (1973) and Morrison, Holmes, and Haith (1974). Adults and 5-, 8-, and 11-year-old children first saw an array of seven geometric figures for 100 milliseconds. Then, after a delay ranging from 50 to 1,000 milliseconds, a marker indicated a position where one of the figures had been presented. Finally, individuals selected the stimulus that had been indicated by the pointer from an array of stimuli.

In both studies, when the marker followed presentation of the array of figures by 50 milliseconds, performance was similar at all developmental levels: Using a partial report procedure, estimates of the number of items in iconic memory were comparable for 5-, 8-, and 11-year-olds and adults.[2] Recall declined as the interval between presentation of the array and the marker was increased from 0 to 200 milliseconds, and did so at approximately the same rate for all four age groups. In other words, rate of decay from iconic memory seemed to be very similar for 5-year-olds, older children, and adults.

Interestingly, performance by adults actually improved as the delay interval was increased from 450 to 1,000 milliseconds. Adults apparently used this time to rehearse items in some manner or to transfer information from iconic memory to a less transient memory. For children, however, recall declined during the period from 450 to 1,000 milliseconds, indicating that one source of age-related differences in children's performance on tasks designed to tap iconic memory is the ability to counteract the effects of rapid decay of a memory trace.

Children seem particularly able to encode the spatial locations of stimuli in iconic memory. For example, Finkel (1973) presented a pattern of two to five dots for 150 milliseconds to kindergarten, third-, and sixth-grade children and adults. Following presentation of the pattern, magnetic tokens were used to reconstruct the pattern on a board. Finkel's results are shown in Figure 3-1. To facilitate a comparison between children's encoding of spatial locations and their encoding of the names of the objects seen in those positions, the data from Haith, Morrison, Sheingold, and Mindes (1970) are also shown in Figure 3-1. In the latter study, 5-year-olds and adults were shown one to four line drawings for 150 milliseconds, then selected the drawing(s) that had been presented from an array of ten forms. While the data in Figure 3-1 are only suggestive (the demands of the tasks used in the two experiments were not identical), it appears that 5-year-olds' limited recall of ''name'' information is not accompanied by a limitation on the ability to recall the locations of items. In fact, when asked to recall only the positions of items, young children fared as well as adults.

Thus, pictures and their locations appear to be represented in young children's iconic memory with the same ease and seemingly automatic processing that characterizes adults' storage processes. Children seem particularly able to retain spatial information. A different picture emerges, however, when we consider the

---

[2] Because information decays so rapidly from sensory registers, procedures in which individuals attempt to report everything that was presented (e.g., as in free recall) are inappropriate. In a partial report procedure, a prearranged signal (e.g., a tone), presented after the stimuli, indicates the subset of stimuli to be recalled. Since individuals do not know which subset will be tested until after stimuli have been presented, it is assumed that performance on the subset indicates what might be obtained for the total set if rate of decay were not so rapid. An estimate of the number of items present in iconic memory is then derived by multiplying the percentage accuracy on the subset by the total number of items presented.

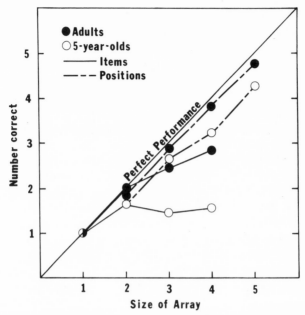

FIGURE 3-1   Item and position recall as a function of array size for 5-year-olds and adults. (After Haith et al., 1970, and Finkel, 1973.)

efficiency with which young children maintain and transfer information in iconic memory, for here young children do not engage spontaneously in the same activities that adults use to ensure subsequent retention of information.

2. Echoic Memory

The auditory analog to iconic memory (i.e., a temporary store in which auditory information is maintained briefly) is echoic memory. Information is lost less rapidly, though, from echoic than from iconic memory, typically decaying in a few seconds rather than the fraction of a second typical of iconic memory.

Research on developmental characteristics of echoic memory is rather sparse, but that which is available yields a relatively consistent picture. Frank and Rabinovitch (1974) used a stimulus suffix paradigm to investigate developmental changes in echoic memory. Strings of six digits were presented auditorily to 8-, 10-, and 12-year-olds. A zero, which was not to be recalled, followed presentation of the final digit in the string by 500, 1,000, 1,500, or 2,000 milliseconds. The presentation of the zero is hypothesized to displace the final digits from echoic memory, thus resulting in decreased recall of these digits in comparison to trials when the zero is not presented (Crowder & Morton, 1969). If the capacity of echoic memory or rate of decay changes developmentally, then the effects of the suffix on recall of final digits should vary with age. For example, if the capacity of echoic memory increases with age, then suffix effects would be greater for younger than for older children. In fact, suffix effects did not differ for children of the three age levels, thus supporting the position that rate of decay from echoic memory is relatively invariant developmentally.[3]

Converging evidence for developmental invariance of echoic memory is found in the results of studies in which children's recall of visually and auditorily presented lists of material is compared. Typically, recall of items from the beginning of a list is unaffected by modality of presentation. For items occurring at the end of the list, however, recall of items presented auditorily exceeds that of items presented visually, presumably owing to the relatively slower rate of decay from echoic memory.

Siegel and Allik (1973), for example, presented series of seven items to 6-, 7-, and 10-year-olds and to adults. When items were presented visually, a series of pictures was shown, one at a time, and each picture was placed face down to form a horizontal row. For auditory presentation, the names of the same pictures were heard through a linear array of speakers (separated by the same distances as were the pictures in the visual condition). In both conditions, after all seven items in a series had been presented, recall was tested by presenting two probes in succession that were identical to two stimuli presented on that trial. The child then pointed to the face-down card (or speaker, following auditory presentation) that matched the probe. Recall of items at the terminal positions in the series was greater following auditory than following visual presentation, when responses to only the first probe on each trial were considered. More important, the difference between recall of items presented auditorily and those presented visually was similar for the three groups of children and for adults.

By the time the second probe on each trial was presented, information apparently had decayed from echoic memory, for retention of items presented auditorily no longer exceeded retention of items presented visually. Again, the effect was similar across all age levels. Thus, the results obtained by Siegel and Allik (1973) converge with those of Frank and Rabinovitch (1974) in suggesting that the temporal parameters of echoic memory codes are similar for children and adults.

---

[3] In an analysis of recall of only the final digit, age differences were found, with the effects of the suffix greatest for 8-year-olds. As Frank and Rabinovitch (1974) point out, problems with the scoring technique used and the presence of a ceiling effect in the older children's recall make interpretations of these data problematic.

3. Summary

Investigations of iconic and echoic memory in children and adults indicate that there are few, if any, developmental differences in the qualitative or quantitative encoding of events at early temporal stages of information processing. Children's initial codes for visual and auditory information do not differ qualitatively from those of adults, nor do they seem to differ quantitatively: Estimates of capacity and decay rates from iconic and echoic memory were found to be similar for 5-year-olds and adults. Thus, perceptual codes of external events that seem to be isomorphic to their referents are common and characteristic from early childhood to adulthood.

B. Abstractive or Transformational Encoding

Representation of information at later stages of processing differs from the initial stages in that the perceptual richness of a literal or isomorphic code is traded off against the cognitive economy and flexibility that is afforded by an abstract feature-based code. Presumably, most of the features of an abstract code identify higher-order, nonisomorphic properties of an event (e.g., Shepard, 1975). Our discussion of these higher order codes is divided into two parts. First, as mentioned previously, information may enter the memorial system through any of several sensory registers, where it is coded in a format associated uniquely with the modality of that register. These distinctive codes might be maintained in subsequent temporal stages of encoding. That is, the nature of temporally later coding may be dependent on the format of the initial perceptual code. Alternatively, all initial codes may be transformed to a common format at some temporal level in processing. We will consider this issue with respect to developmental differences in children's encoding of pictorial and verbal information. Following this, developmental changes in encoding of various features will be considered, with emphasis on encoding of spatial and semantic features.

1. Pictorial and Verbal Encoding: Single Versus Dual Memory Models

Children seem particularly adept at processing pictorial information. For example, 4-month-olds are quite able to recognize a picture that has been shown to them previously (Olson, 1976). For adults as well, memory for pictures is impressive (e.g., Standing, Conezio, & Haber, 1970). For both adults and children, retention of pictures is greater than retention of verbal stimuli, whether the latter is the written or spoken word. Paivio (1971) and others have argued that these results are best conceptualized within a "dual coding system," whereby pictorial stimuli generate simultaneous verbal and nonverbal long-term memory codes. However, if it is assumed that long-term retention depends on encoding an item in terms of semantic attributes, then the locus of the proposed dual-memory codes remains unclear. Verbal and nonverbal codes could be (1) components of a unitary long-term memory system or (2) components of two separate memory systems. Put another way, separate visual and acoustic sensory and short-term processing systems may correspond to different permanent memory systems, or they may be different access routes to a unitary abstract permanent memory system.

An example of a dual-memory model would be that of Paivio (1971), shown in Figure 3-2, in which separate but connected verbal and nonverbal knowledge systems are described. It is assumed that (1) pictures have direct access to the nonverbal system; (2) words have direct access to the verbal system; and (3) transfer from the nonverbal to the verbal system is faster than transfer from the verbal to the nonverbal system. Thus, Paivio's model assumes equivalent access times to the two systems but different transfer times between the two systems.

An alternate approach, suggested by Pellegrino, Rosinski, Chiesi, and Siegel (1976), is to conceptualize memory as a single knowledge system built up of accumulated, organized, perceptual experiences. Concepts in this system have multimodal (or possibly amodal) attributes and can be accessed by a variety of routes, one of which is verbal or linguistic. In such a system it is assumed that pictures access permanent memory faster than words because the acoustic, phonemic, or articulatory processing that may be required for verbal material is bypassed. Of course, transfer time is eliminated since there is only one system.

A choice reaction time task is one paradigm that has been used to evaluate differences between single- and dual-memory models. Individuals are asked to

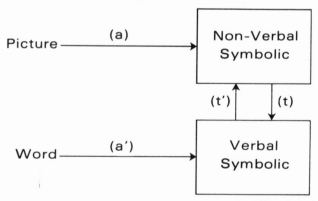

FIGURE 3-2 Simple representation of dual-memory model with separate symbolic systems and access routes for pictorial and verbal input.

determine as rapidly as they can if a pair of stimuli, presented simultaneously, belong to the same or different taxonomic categories. Stimuli consist of two pictures (line drawings of common objects and animals), the corresponding pair of words, or mixed picture-word pairs.

Dual- and single-memory models differ in their predictions concerning the speed with which individuals can make category judgments for the various types of item pairs (see Table 3-1). Several predictions can be made based on a dual-memory model, depending on the initial assumptions. If semantic decisions can be made in either the verbal or the nonverbal system, then reaction times for picture–picture and word–word pairs should not differ, since access times to the nonverbal and verbal systems are equivalent. However, latencies for picture–word pairs should be greater, since both systems would be accessed and transfer of information between systems would be required. An alternate version of the dual-memory model holds that judgments concerning categorical information are made only in the verbal system, while perceptual judgments (e.g., "Which of these two pictures has a larger real-world referent?") are made in the nonverbal system. If this is the case, reaction times should be lowest for the word–word pairs and greatest on picture–picture pairs, with picture–word pairs at the mean of these two extremes.

TABLE 3-1
Single- and Dual-Memory Models—Assumptions and Predictions for
Reaction Time in Semantic Categorization Task

Model	Assumptions	Components of RT	Predictions[a]
Dual memory— semantic categories in both systems	$a = a'$ $t < t'$	$PP = 2a$ $WW = 2a'$ $PW = a + a' + \left(\dfrac{t + t'}{2}\right)$	$PP = WW < PW$
Dual memory— semantic categories in verbal system only	$a = a'$ $t < t'$	$PP = 2a + 2t$ $WW = 2a'$ $PW = a + a' + t$	$WW < PW < PP$ $PW = \left(\dfrac{WW + PP}{2}\right)$
Single semantic memory	$a < a'$	$PP = 2a$ $WW = 2a'$ $PW = a + a'$	$PP < PW < WW$ $PW = \left(\dfrac{WW + PP}{2}\right)$

Note: a = access time for pictures; a' = access time for words; t = transfer time from nonverbal system to verbal system; t' = transfer time from verbal system to nonverbal system; P denotes a picture presented; W denotes a word presented.

[a] The prediction equations and the rationale underlying their derivation are based on Pellegrino et al. (1976).

The alternative single-memory model yields a different set of predictions. Since pictures presumably access semantic memory more rapidly than words, reaction times for semantic categorization should be lower for picture–picture pairs than for word–word pairs. Furthermore, if both pictures and words access the same permanent memory system, then reaction time on picture–word pairs should equal the mean of the reaction times for picture–picture and word–word pairs.

When considered from a developmental perspective, the question of single- versus dual-memory models becomes even more complex, since several possible sequences involving these models are plausible. Thus, there might exist at all points in development only a single-memory system, in which verbal material is accessed more rapidly with development. Alternatively, children's semantic memory could consist initially of two systems that merge to become one system by adulthood (e.g., Gibson, Barron, & Garber, 1972). Finally, there might be two memory systems that develop independently.

The existing data suggest that children's and adult's semantic encoding corresponds to the single-memory rather than to either of the dual-memory descriptions. Thus, for example, Rosinski, Pellegrino, and Siegel (in press) tested 7- and 10-year-olds on a category judgment task of the type described earlier in which picture–picture, word–word, and picture–word pairs were presented.

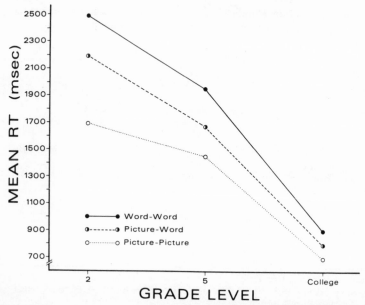

FIGURE 3-3   Mean reaction time (RT) in milliseconds as a function of grade level for three types of word pairs. (From "Developmental changes in the semantic processing of pictures and words" by R. R. Rosinski, J. W. Pellegrino, and A. W. Siegel, *Journal of Experimental Child Psychology*, 1977. Copyright 1977 by Academic Press, Inc. Reprinted by permission.)

The results are presented in Figure 3-3, along with data obtained from college students (from Pellegrino et al., 1976). Overall, 10-year-olds responded more rapidly than did 7-year-olds. More important, latencies of both groups of children and adults differed according to the type of material that was presented. In line with the predictions from the single-memory model, reaction times for picture–picture pairs were faster than those for picture–word pairs, which, in turn, were faster than latencies for word–word pairs. Also in line with the predictions of the single-memory model, picture–word reaction times did not differ from the mean of the picture–picture and word–word latencies.[4]

The pattern of results described by Rosinski et al. seems to be fairly robust: Rader (1975) tested second, third, and sixth graders and graduate students on a similar category judgment task and found the same ordering of latencies across the three conditions at all ages. Thus, these data argue convincingly for the existence, in both children and adults, of a unitary semantic system with differential access routes for verbal and pictorial material. The major developmental change seems to be the rate of access to the single system. Both pictures and words are processed more rapidly with age, and there is a strong suggestion that speed of verbal processing, in particular, increases with age.

In summary, the differences in initial encoding associated with modality of presentation discussed previously do not seem to be maintained in temporally subsequent codes. That is, while information may be coded in iconic memory and echoic memory in a format associated uniquely with those stores, these distinctive initial codes do not seem to correspond to separate long-term memory codes. Instead, long-term memory codes seem to be relatively unaffected by the literal features of the initial perceptual code. In brief, although the form of presentation—auditory, verbal, pictorial—may be a primary determinant of the way in which children and adults initially code information, it is only one of many attributes that may characterize a higher-order mnemonic code.

2. Features of Longer-Term Memory Codes

The list of attributes of an event that a child or adult might encode is virtually without limit. Here we shall focus on two major classes of mnemonic features that have been studied in children and adults: spatial and semantic attributes of events.

---

[4] Other variations of a dual-process model can account for the data obtained by Rosinski et al. (in press) and Rader (1975). For example, by assuming that all decisions concerning semantic categories are made in the nonverbal system, a dual-memory model could predict the results obtained. However, if semantic decisions for verbal material are made in the nonverbal system, why should there be a separate verbal memory system? Such a model appears to be functionally equivalent to a single-memory model (as do other dual-memory models that could explain the data) and thereby is less parsimonious than a single-memory model. For a more detailed discussion of this issue, see Pellegrino et al. (1976).

a. Encoding of spatial information.   Much anecdotal evidence would suggest that spatial location is one readily stored feature of an event. One common example is the ability to remember where a particular word or fact appeared on a printed page. Another would be the experience of remembering where a fellow student sat in a classroom while, at the same time, being unable to remember that individual's name. Both examples suggest that information concerning the spatial location of an object may be part of a long-term mnemonic code.

Experimental evidence confirms that even young children encode spatial information. Von Wright, Gebhard, and Karttunen (1975), for example, showed ten cards, with four pictures on each card, to 5-, 8-, and 12- to 13-year-old children. Then all 40 pictures were presented individually to the children, who were asked to point to the quadrant of the card in which the picture had first appeared. Recall improved with age, but even the youngest children tested were considerably more accurate than would be expected by chance. More important, recall of location was virtually identical under instructions to remember the objects (with no mention made of location) versus instructions to remember only locations. As von Wright et al. (1975) concluded, "location appeared to be coded 'automatically,' at little or no extra cost to the coding of item information, in all age groups [p. 189]."

Serial memory tasks represent a second instance in which children encode spatial information. Here, children are shown a series of pictures of common objects or animals, one at a time; the cards are then placed face down in a horizontal row. Children are then shown a card identical to one of the original stimuli and are asked to turn over the card that matches it. Recall by adults typically is very accurate for those pictures presented last (the "recency" effect), slightly lower for pictures presented first ("primacy" effect), and poorest for pictures presented in the middle of the list. When children younger than 10 years of age are tested, typically only recency effects are found; when older children are tested, both primacy and recency effects appear (Hagen, Jongeward, & Kail, 1975).

A significant primacy effect generally has been taken as evidence that children are cumulatively rehearsing the serially presented items. But is this necessarily the case? Notice that the task described has several components not found in most serial learning paradigms:

1. Each stimulus has a unique spatial location, and it remains in that location during the entire trial.

2. Both the initial and final items are distinctive in that they have adjacent stimuli only on one side.

3. In the typical serial position task, where stimuli are presented one at a time to the child, from left to right, spatial and temporal order of presentation are completely confounded.

Perhaps spatial factors are responsible for the primacy effect. If so, then items in the initial and terminal spatial locations should be recalled accurately regardless of the temporal order of presentation of these items. Siegel, Allik, and Herman (1976) assessed this possibility in a study with 5- to 7-year-olds in which the spatial and temporal components of children's recall were manipulated experimentally. Pictures were placed face down in an eight-room model ranch house for which a unique linear path led from the first room to the last. On each trial pictures were placed in the rooms in one of two ways: (1) from left to right in a linear sequence (thus, as in the standard task, spatial and temporal order were completely confounded), or (2) in a random, nonlinear sequence. In the latter condition, the picture shown first might, for example, be placed in a room in the middle of the house, the second in a room to the far right, the third in the second room from the left, and so on. Recall was tested by presenting a duplicate picture and asking the child to select the matching picture, which was face down in one of the rooms.

Temporal and spatial orders of presentation were independent when pictures were presented in a nonlinear sequence; thus, recall could be analyzed as a function of both the temporal and spatial position in which an item was presented. Performance as a function of temporal position is presented in Figure 3-4. Primacy and recency effects appeared *only* when pictures were presented sequentially; serial position effects were absent when the pictures were presented

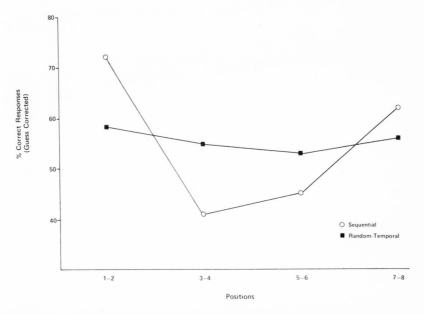

FIGURE 3-4   Percentage of correct responses as a function of temporal order of representation for sequential (i.e., linear) and random presentation. (From ''The primacy effect in young children: Verbal fact or spatial artifact?'' by A. W. Siegel, J. P. Allik, and J. F. Herman, *Child Development,* 1976, *47,* 242–247. Figure 2, p. 246. Copyright 1976 by the Society for Research in Child Development. Reprinted by permission.)

in a random spatial order. When recall was analyzed as a function of spatial position, in Figure 3-5, marked serial position effects were evident, regardless of whether the items were presented in a sequential or random order. Thus, the results of this study provide strong evidence that the spatial component of the typical serial position recall task, rather than the use of rehearsal, is largely responsible for the primacy effect found in young children's serial position curves. Children easily encode the first and last items, that is, those with the distinctive spatial features, from the earliest ages tested. Not only that, they remember these "landmarks" irrespective of their temporal order—significant primacy and recency effects were found both when pictures were presented sequentially and when they were presented in a random order.

To this point, we have discussed young children's encoding of spatial information in experimental situations that, for young children, bear little resemblance to their everyday activities. Only recently have psychologists turned their attention toward children's encoding of spatial information in the large-scale environment (Siegel & White, 1975). Children as young as age 3 seem to be able to encode the spatial location of an event fairly accurately. Acredolo, Pick, and Olsen (1975), for example, took 3-, 4-, and 8-year-old children on strolls during which the experimenter dropped her keys. Later, the children were asked to recall where the keys had been dropped. Eight-year-olds were more accurate than 3-year-olds in an undifferentiated environment, but not in a differentiated envi-

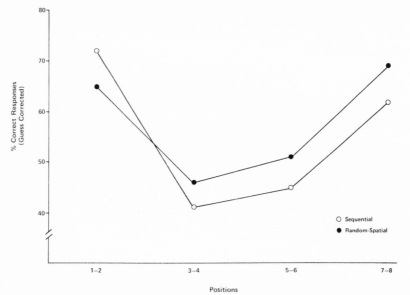

FIGURE 3-5   Percentage of correct responses as a function of spatial order of presentation for sequential (i.e., linear) and random presentation. (From "The primacy effect in young children: Verbal fact or spatial artifact?" by A. W. Siegel, J. P. Allik, and J. F. Herman, *Child Development* 1976, *47*, 242–247. Figure 1, p. 245. Copyright 1976 by the Society for Research in Child Development. Reprinted by permission.)

ronment. For example, when 3-year-olds were tested in a differentiated environment, their mean error of placement was less than 3 feet on a walk of 110 feet. When provided a differentiated environment, even very young children seem to remember the location of real-world events fairly well.

Thus, recent evidence seems to indicate that from a very early age children encode "place" information. This is the case whether the places to be considered represent (1) locations of pictures on a page; (2) end points in a series of items; or (3) places and objects in real-world environments. Such encoding seems to occur automatically, with little active participation necessary on the part of the child. Furthermore, spatial coding seems to place no additional "load" on the memory system; that is, it does not interfere with the encoding of other features, such as semantic ones. Developmental changes in spatial encoding seem to be primarily of a quantitative sort (i.e., accuracy of encoding). We turn now to children's encoding of semantic features, where a more varied pattern of developmental change will appear.

b. Encoding of semantic information.   In addition to information concerning the spatial location of an event, many features of longer-term memory codes refer to semantic characteristics of the event to be remembered. For purposes of our discussion, semantic features have been divided into two general categories: denotative and connotative aspects of meaning. This distinction can be demonstrated easily with a single example. A child might encode "house" as a type of building (encoding of a denotative feature); he might also encode "house" as a place of warmth and security (encoding of connotative features).

When considering encoding of semantic features, it is helpful to keep in mind Tulving's (1972) distinction between episodic and semantic memory:

> Episodic memory receives and stores information about temporally dated episodes or events, and temporal-spatial relations among these events. . . . the specific form in which perceptual input is registered into the episodic memory can at times be strongly influenced by information in semantic memory [which is] a mental thesauraus, [the] organized knowledge a person possesses about words and other verbal symbols, their meaning and referents, about relations among them, and about rules, formulas, and algorithms for the manipulation of these symbols, concepts and relations [pp. 385–386].

Encoding of semantic features, as we have defined it, then refers to the interaction between semantic and episodic memory. In the present section, our concern is with the extent to which the nature of coding in episodic memory is influenced by information that is in semantic memory. That is, when a child processes a word, what features from the "mental thesauraus" comprise the code for that word?

Of particular importance is the possibility that there may be points in development when information from semantic memory does not seem to be a part of the mnemonic code for an event, even though we know that information is in semantic memory. To return to the example given earlier, the child may know (i.e., have in semantic memory) both the denotative and connotative meanings of house, but encode house in episodic memory only in terms of the former. In fact, this turns out to be not merely a possible situation, but one that has been found for several features of encoding.

(1)   Encoding of denotative features.   A principal denotative characteristic of a word—at least of nouns—is its taxonomic class. Experiments in which a release from proactive interference (PI) task (Wickens, 1972) is used have obtained consistent evidence that young children encode taxonomic characteristics of words. In this procedure each of several trials involve (1) presentation of two words to be remembered; (2) a distracting task, such as naming colors, for a brief period; and (3) a period for recall of the two words. Words that share a common feature (e.g., all are animals, all rhyme with *shoe*) are presented on successive trials. Recall typically is nearly perfect on the first trial, but declines on succeeding trials. For example, Kail (1976) found that recall by 7- and 12-year-olds declined on Trials 1 to 3 when names of birds were presented on each trial (see Figure 3-6). Words presented on a later trial to children in an experimental group share a feature that is not shared by words presented on previous trials (e.g., all are pieces of furniture, all rhyme with *rope*). If recall by these children is greater than recall by children in a control group, for whom the feature common to words is not changed on the later trial, then we infer that children encoded the particular feature manipulated in the experiment (here, a taxonomic or acoustic attribute). Thus, recall by children in the experiment just described increased when names

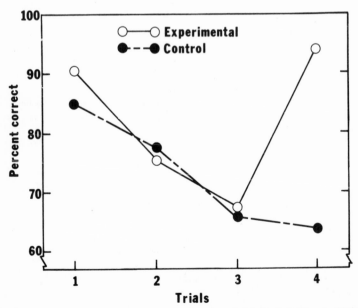

FIGURE 3-6   Percentage of correct responses as a function of trials for 7- to 12-year-olds in control and experimental conditions (After Kail, 1976.)

of mammals were presented on Trial 4 (i.e., "release from PI" was found), indicating that these children apparently encoded the taxonomic class of the words presented.

Even 3- and 4-year-olds demonstrate encoding of several taxonomic categories using the release-from-PI procedure. For example, Esrov, Hall, and LaFaver (1974) tested 3- to 5-year-olds on four trials in a release-from-PI paradigm. For half of the children, the pictures presented on Trials 1 to 3 were from the same category (either animals or clothing), while pictures on Trial 4 were from the alternate category. For the remaining children, pictures presented on all four trials were selected from one of the two conceptual categories. Recall increased from Trial 3 to Trial 4 only when the pictures presented were selected from a new conceptual category, indicating that one attribute of encoding for young children appears to be taxonomic class.

Encoding of taxonomic categories by very young children has also been demonstrated through the use of a habituation paradigm. Faulkender, Wright, and Waldron (1974), for example, presented a series of 36 pictures to 2- and 3-year-olds. Six pictures from one of three conceptual categories (fruits, animals, environmental patterns) were each shown six times. This was followed by a second series of 18 pictures, consisting of six pictures of each of three types: (1) the familiar pictures (i.e., those shown in the series of 36 pictures); (2) pictures that were novel but from the same conceptual category as the familiar pictures; and (3) novel pictures that were from a different category. Children looked longer at the completely novel slides than at the novel slides that were members of the "old" conceptual category; the latter, in turn, were looked at longer than were the familiar pictures. Based on the former result, it would appear that children encoded a picture as belonging to a conceptual category and, based on the latter result, also encoded pictures as particular items within that category.

Choice reaction time is yet another paradigm in which children's encoding of taxonomic features has been investigated. For example, Morin, Hoving, and Konick (1970) first had 6- and 10-year-olds and adults learn the names of drawings from categorized sets that contained either two or four items. Thus, for example, the set of musical instruments included drum and piano, while the set of tools included hammer, saw, pliers, and screwdriver. After individuals had learned the contents of each of four categories, they were asked to judge if two pictures shown successively were members of the same category. The second picture could be either (1) identical to the first (e.g., the same picture of a dog); (2) from the same class as the first (e.g., a dog and a cow); or (3) from a different class than the first (e.g., a dog and a bike).

If a child encodes an item in terms of its membership in a taxonomic category, then reaction time should not differ for categories having two and four instances: A child need only compare the encoded taxonomic classes to see if the pictures match. In contrast, if a child does not encode the taxonomic categories of the first and second pictures as they are presented, then a direct comparison of taxonomic classes is not possible. Instead, the child must retrieve the other pictures that belonged to the same category as the first (or second) picture, then see if that set includes the second (or first) picture. Assuming that items from the set thus retrieved must be processed serially by children (which seems to be what was found by Hoving, Morin, & Konick, 1970), then the time required to decide if pictures are from the same category should depend on the number of elements in the sets to be compared, with larger categories requiring additional time for verification.

Reaction times, in fact, were found to be independent of the category sizes tested in all conditions save one. Six-year-olds required more time to verify that two pictures were from the same category when the pictures presented belonged to four member categories than when they belonged to two member categories. Surprisingly, 6-year-olds' response times were independent of category size when the first and second pictures were from different sets (i.e., "no" responses). Thus, while the older children and adults certainly encoded the taxonomic features of pictures, the data for the younger children are equivocal.

On occasion, children seem to process semantic features even when the words are incidental to the task. This point was demonstrated nicely by Rosinski, Golinkoff, and Kukish (1975) with 7- and 11-year-olds and adults. The time required to label 20 pictures was measured in each of three conditions. In the first, a word unrelated to the picture was superimposed on that picture. A picture of a key, for instance, had *sock* printed across it. In a second condition, nonsense syllables were superimposed on pictures in a similar manner. In a third (control) condition, words and pictures matched (e.g., *hen* printed across a picture of a hen).

Based on previous experimentation, Rosinski et al. expected picture labeling to be slowest in the first two conditions, where pictures and the superimposed materials were unrelated. Of greater importance, however, were possible differences in picture labeling between these two conditions. If, on the one hand, an increase in the time required for labeling (relative to the control group) was due simply to the fact that the conflicting materials present made it more difficult to attend selectively to pictures, then labeling times in the two conditions should not differ. On the other hand, if the increase was due to interference caused by automatic processing of semantic characteristics in a manner akin to the Stroop effect (Stroop, 1935), a different pattern of results would be expected. It should take longer to label the pictures presented with unrelated words than the pictures presented with nonsense syllables, because greater semantic interference should be produced by meaningful words than by nonsense syllables. In fact, a consistent ordering of conditions was found at all age levels. Pictures were labeled most rapidly when they matched the superimposed words. Labeling was slower when nonsense syllables were printed on the pictures, and slower still when unrelated words appeared. Thus, it would seem that coding of denotative characteristics of words may be a relatively automatic process in children as young as age 7.

The class-inclusion relation that exists between many taxonomic categories represents another characteristic that might influence children's encoding of denotative features. For example, a sparrow is a bird, an animal, and a living thing. Children might encode *sparrow* into any or all of these classes, and the encoded classes might change with development. That is, young children might encode words initially only into specific taxonomic categories and, with development, come to encode words into more general classes as well, a hypothesis proposed by Anglin (1970). In fact, in at least one study (Kail, 1976), 7- to 12-year-olds apparently encoded words into two taxonomic categories differing in degree of specificity. Children were tested in a release-from-PI task of the type described previously. Two of the sets of words—birds/mammals and trees/flowers— represented taxonomic classes of greater specificity than had been used in most prior investigations of children's taxonomic encoding. A third set—animals/ plants—was derived from randomly pairing words that were presented in the category of birds with words presented in the category of mammals, and pairing trees with flowers in a like manner. Thus, animals/plants formed superordinate categories to the categories of birds/mammals and trees/flowers. An increase in recall when the category of the words presented changed from animals to plants (or vice versa) would indicate that the child encoded the general taxonomic class to which a word belonged; a similar increase for the birds/mammals and trees/ flowers categories would suggest that children encoded more specific taxonomic information as well. In fact, increases in recall (i.e., release from PI) were found for all sets of words. Thus, 7- to 12-year-olds may encode words like *sparrow* as a member of both the classes of birds and animals.

In certain situations, however, children apparently fail to encode words into taxonomic categories and subcategories. Rosinski et al. (1977) showed children pairs of pictures, pairs of words, or a word and a picture, and asked the children to judge if both stimuli were members of the same taxonomic category. For pairs that were members of the same category (i.e., either animals or articles of clothing), half of the pairs were selected from a common subcategory (e.g., both birds), while the remaining pairs represented different subcategories (e.g., a bird and a fish). For adults, reaction times for pairs from common subcategories are approximately 70 milliseconds less than for pairs from different subcategories (Pellegrino et al., 1976). No differences between the types of subcategories were found for 7- and 10-year-olds. Why children seem to encode subcategories in the release-from-PI task (Kail, 1976) but not in the semantic judgment task used by Rosinski et al. is not immediately apparent. It may be due to the different measures used—one based on accuracy of recall and the other derived from speed of judgment—a point to which we will return in a later section.

In summary, several lines of evidence, derived from studies of release from

PI, habituation, and choice reaction time, converge on the conclusion that taxonomic encoding of a surprisingly sophisticated nature is evident in school-age children and, on occasion, in younger children as well. Children appear to encode taxonomic features routinely and automatically. In effect, representation of words in terms of their taxonomic features appears to be one verbal processing skill at which 6- and 7-year-olds are proficient.

(2)   Encoding of connotative features.   Children's encoding of three con-notative aspects of meaning has been studied: masculine-feminine connotations, values in the semantic space, and sense impressions evoked by words. Each is discussed in the present section.

The masculine or feminine connotation of a word seems to be highly salient for children. Young children can distinguish activities that traditionally are judged sex appropriate from those that are inappropriate, and when asked to select the activities they prefer, show marked preference for sex-appropriate activities (e.g., Nadelman, 1974). In addition to their knowledge of and prefer-ence for sex-appropriate activities, 7- and 10-year-old boys and girls seem to encode the masculine–feminine connotations of words (Kail & Levine, 1976). As shown in Figure 3-7, children's recall declined on Trials 1 to 4 of a release-from-PI task when words connoted activities or objects typically associated with boys (e.g., *hunting, airplane*), but increased on Trial 5 when words connoted girls' activities and objects (e.g., *hopscotch, dolls*). Furthermore, consistent individual differences among girls were apparent. Those girls whose scores on a sex role preference task indicated a high degree of stereotypy encoded the masculine-feminine connotations of words. In contrast, girls whose sex role

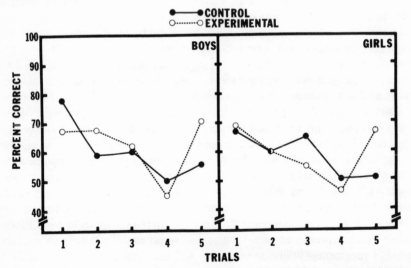

FIGURE 3-7   Percentage of correct responses as a function of trials for 7- to 11-year-old boys and girls in control and experimental conditions. (After Kail & Levine, 1976.)

stereotyping was less extreme failed to encode these connotations. Thus, children's encoding of the masculine-feminine connotations of words seemed to depend, at least in part, on the degree of the child's sex role socialization.

The aspect of connotative meaning that has received the most attention from researchers is Osgood's three-dimensional semantic space, consisting of evaluative, activity, and potency dimensions (Osgood, Suci, & Tannenbaum, 1957). Factor analyses of children's ratings on the semantic differential first reveal an evaluation dimension and a dynamism dimension (DiVesta, 1966). The latter dimension differentiates gradually into the potency and activity dimensions, which seem to be established firmly by age 8. Encoding of words along the evaluation dimension by children aged 10 and older has been demonstrated in experiments in which the release-from-PI methodology was used (e.g., Kail & Schroll, 1974; Pender, 1969). That is, older children seem to encode the positive connotations of words like *fresh* and *save* as well as the negative connotations of words such as *burn* and *hate*. Despite the early emergence of the evaluation dimension in children's ratings, evidence concerning younger children's encoding of words along this dimension is contradictory. Seven- and 8-year-olds encoded the evaluative connotations of words in two studies of release from PI (Corsale, 1974; Pender, 1969); 7- and 8-year-olds apparently failed to encode the evaluative connotations in two other studies (Cermak, Sagotsky, & Moshier, 1972; Kail & Schroll, 1974). There is no obvious difference in methodology between the studies that provide evidence of encoding of evaluative connotations and those that fail to find such evidence. Thus, we conclude that although evaluative connotations of words are present in young children's semantic memory, they are not encoded in episodic memory with the regularity and consistency that was found for children's encoding of taxonomic categories.

School-age children typically fail to encode words along the activity and potency dimensions as well (Pender, 1969), although adults do encode words along these dimensions (Wickens & Clark, 1968). Encoding of these dimensions appears to follow encoding of the evaluative dimension, just as these dimensions appear later in the semantic differential ratings of children.

A final connotative aspect of meaning—one that children typically fail to encode—is the sense impression evoked by a stimulus. That is, words like *barrel, head, balloon* may connote "roundness," while *snow, rice, cigarette* may elicit impressions of "whiteness." Other sense impressions that may be evoked by words include "pointed," "large," "small," "smelly," and "cold." Information concerning the sense impressions of many objects seems to be part of children's semantic memory, for when asked to give sense impressions to words, children's responses are very similar to those of adults (Clark, 1968). Adults, however, seem to encode the sense impressions of words in release-from-PI experiments (Wickens, Reutener, & Eggemeier, 1972), while children between the ages of 6 and 14 typically do not (Kroes, 1973). Children, like adults, know (that is, have in semantic memory) many of the sense impressions that are evoked by a word, but unlike adults, they typically fail to include the sense impression as part of the encoding of a word.

Thus, children's performance on tests of encoding of sense impressions parallels the results for the activity and potency dimensions of the semantic space: Some portion of a child's knowledge concerning a word apparently is not a part of the representation of that word in episodic memory. Why should this be the case? One explanation could be that children have, in reality, encoded the attribute under investigation, but have failed to use this information to facilitate recall. That is, when words presented on a release-from-PI task are from a new category, a new cue for encoding *and retrieval* is available. If a child stored the novel feature, but failed to use it as a cue to retrieve the words, then recall would not be expected to increase. In this situation, however, presenting a cue during the interval for recall should facilitate recall. Kail, Jongeward, Daoust, and Aaron (1976) tested this possibility, but found little increase in recall by 8- and 10-year-olds when such a category cue was given during the recall interval (for example, "Tell me the words, they were both *round* things"). Thus, at least for sense impressions, the failure to find an improvement in recall is not an artifact of the method used to measure encoding; rather it seems to reflect the fact that children did not encode the feature.

(3) Summary. Our understanding of how children come to encode different attributes as they grow older is modest. Nonetheless, the existing data fit a general pattern of increasingly differentiated encoding with development. Denotative characteristics are the essence of a word's meaning and are encoded by very young children. Connotative aspects of meaning, by comparison, are often subtle and contextually determined. We find that connotative aspects of words are encoded rarely by young children and only occasionally by older children.

III. SOME PERSPECTIVES ON THE RESEARCH

In the present chapter we have attempted to provide a general outline of what is known concerning developmental changes in the manner in which an external event is represented in a child's memory. At this point we would like (1) to summarize the picture of developmental changes in encoding depicted in this chapter; (2) to suggest possible processes that may underlie some of the developmental changes that have been observed; and (3) to identify some of the important issues of encoding that await investigation.

Based on the evidence presented in Section II, five general conclusions can be proffered concerning age-related changes in encoding:

1. The initial stages of coding, those in which the code is relatively isomorphic to its referent, are marked by developmental invariance rather than by developmental change.

2. Children's higher-order codes for pictures and words seem to be similar in format; that is, higher-order codes apparently are multimodal (or perhaps amodal) and reflect primarily the conceptual characteristics of the information to be encoded.

3. Even young children encode information related to the spatial location of an event, although there are developmental changes in the absolute level of accuracy of children's encoding of such "place" information.

4. Denotative characteristics of words, those that form the kernel of a word's meaning, also seem to be encoded by very young children.

5. Connotative aspects of meaning, in contrast to spatial and taxonomic features, are encoded only by older children, and in some cases only by adolescents and adults.

This, then, is a descriptive account of at least some of the developmental changes that occur as children construct internal representations of external events. Some of these conclusions are almost forced on us by the consistency with which the evidence supporting them is found in the literature; others are considerably more tentative. Nonetheless, it seems appropriate to speculate on what some of the developmental processes underlying the described age-related changes in mnemonic performance might be.

Almost certainly, part of the development of encoding consists of the development of what might be called applied semantics. That is, age-related differences in encoding reflect the developing child's acquisition of semantic and conceptual knowledge. In particular, the account given here of the acquisition of development of certain features of encoding parallels changes noted by psycholinguists in the child's acquisition of semantic knowledge. Clark (1973), for example, has argued that the meaning of a word for a child (that is, its representation in semantic memory) corresponds to a partial list of the features that characterize that word in an adult's lexicon. Thus, Clark describes how a child's initial definition of *dog* is functionally equivalent to the adult's definition of *animal*. Only later are such features as "four-legged," "barks," and "man's best friend" added to the list of features that constitute the child's knowledge of *dog*. For Clark, "the acquisition of semantic knowledge, then, will consist of adding more features of meaning to the lexical entry of the word until the child's combination of features in the entry for that word corresponds to the adult's [1973, p. 72]." Semantic development thus is a necessary prerequisite for encoding, and we presume that a child's linguistic (i.e., semantic) competence determines those features that a child *may* (as opposed to does) encode.

A second probable factor underlying age-related changes in encoding is a developmental change in the speed or rate of processing of information. It appears that "some irreducible maturational differences in processing are present, along with differences due to nonprocessing features" (Wickens, 1974, p. 739). Faster reaction time with age has been found repeatedly (White, 1970); the evidence abounds in the traditional textbooks and will not be detailed here. Not only simple motor reaction time but reaction speed in all kinds of complex procedures become faster with age. Parallel to these findings have been several studies showing that recognition time also becomes faster with age. These various kinds of quickening may well be associated with an increase in the more rapid EEG waveforms with age (Milner, 1967). The plausibility of this suggestion has been demonstrated in the elegant research of Surwillo (1961, 1963a, b), who has shown a strong correlation between EEG frequency and rate of reaction. It could well be the case that the amount of encoding (for example, number of features) that an individual can handle is related to his speed of reaction (that is, speed in locating, recognizing, meaning, and associating to an event). The gradual age-related increase in the child's speed of reaction might then produce discontinuous changes in encoding ability as various threshold values are reached, permitting more items of information to be encoded in the short temporal span. Pascual-Leone and Smith (1969) have argued in an analogous fashion, and have referred to the discontinuous changes as increases in M space with age.

Thus, given developmental increases in rate of processing, when processing is limited to a fixed, short interval of time, children may appear to encode fewer features of words than adults. It might be postulated that if additional time were allotted for subsequent processing, then developmental differences in encoding might be reduced considerably. A developmental increase in speed of processing might also account for the lack of congruence between data derived from accuracy-based measures and data derived from speed-based measures (for example, studies of children's encoding of taxonomic subcategories).

A third factor underlying age-related changes in encoding might well be what Gibson (1969) has referred to as a trend toward selectivity in attention and perception. The continuity of processing from perception to encoding (of varying degrees of elaboration) and inference is an important component of current models of human information processing (e.g., Craik & Lockhart, 1972). The close relation between perception and encoding is even further emphasized when considered from a developmental frame of reference (Wohlwill, 1962). As Gibson (1969) describes it:

> It is often asserted that the young child is stimulus bound, enslaved by the surrounding milieu, dependent on the present sensory information, and that perceptual development is a process of liberation from the constraints of stimulation. . . . I disagree with this interpretation of perception and perceptual development. Perception is not a process of matching to a representation in the hand, but one of extracting the invariants in stimulus information [pp. 448–449].

This notion of the increasing ability to extract signal from noise has also been discussed in the broad contexts of cognitive development (e.g., Bruner, Wallach, & Galanter's, 1959, notion of cognition as the ability to extract recurrent regularity) and learning (e.g., White & Siegel's, 1976, notion of learning as a process of "becoming unconfused"). We believe that this is an apt characterization of mnemonic encoding as well: Encoding is not a process of matching to a pre-constructed internal representation but, rather, one of extracting salient features from an external event, of extracting signal from noise.

Let us briefly focus, then, on what may be the critical issues for future research on the development of encoding. First, what are the processes of (or underlying) encoding? Throughout this review, we have focused on the consequences of these processes—the code—and have essentially ignored the manner in which that code is constructed. Given the emphasis on encoding as a constructive cognitive operation that occurs over time, it is imperative that models be advanced in which the mechanisms of encoding are delineated. Second, our conclusions with regard to developmental changes in encoding are stated somewhat tentatively because they are derived from a relatively limited data base. Much of the research on semantic encoding, for example, is derived almost solely from studies of release from PI and response latencies in categorical judgment tasks. To what extent are the types of codes and attributes of coding found in laboratory investigations evident in children's encoding during real-world activities, such as conversation, reading, and play? Put another way, what are the boundary conditions of the data reviewed in the present chapter?

IV. A CONCLUDING REMARK

The question of the way in which experience is represented "in the head" has intrigued philosophers for more than two millennia and psychologists for more than a century (Yates, 1966). Yet a chapter on the development of encoding probably could not have been written until a few years ago. This paradox should alert us to the complexities to be encountered in studying mnemonic encoding; at the same time, it should give us some indication of the critical role of encoding in all aspects of mnemonic and cognitive processing.

ACKNOWLEDGMENTS

The authors wish to thank James Pellegrino and Harold Stevenson for their helpful comments on previous drafts of this manuscript.

REFERENCES

Acredolo, L. P., Pick, H. L., Jr., & Olsen, M. G. Environmental differentiation and familiarity as determinants of children's memory for spatial location. *Developmental Psychology,* 1975, *11,* 495–501.
Anglin, J. M. *The growth of word meaning.* Cambridge, Mass.: M.I.T. Press, 1970.
Bower, G. H. A multicomponent theory of the memory trace. In K. W. Spence & J. T. Spence (Eds.), *The psychology of learning and motivation* (Vol. 1). New York: Academic Press, 1967.

Bower, G. H. Stimulus-sampling theory of encoding variability. In A. W. Melton & E. Martin (Eds.), *Coding processes in human memory*. Washington, D.C.: Winston, 1972.

Bruner, J. S., Wallach, M. A., & Galanter, E. H. The identification of recurrent regularity. *American Journal of Psychology*, 1959, *72*, 200–209.

Cermak, L. S., Sagotsky, G., & Moshier, C. Development of the ability to encode within evaluative dimensions. *Journal of Experimental Child Psychology*, 1972, *13*, 210–219.

Clark, D. C. Similarity between children's and adults' adjective responses to noun stimuli. *Journal of Verbal Learning and Verbal Behavior*, 1968, *7*, 705–706.

Clark, E. V. What's in a word? On the child's acquisition of semantics in his first language. In T. E. Moore (Ed.), *Cognitive development and the acquisition of language*. New York: Academic Press, 1973.

Cohen, L. B., & Gelber, E. R. Infant visual memory. In L. Cohen & P. Salapatek (Eds.), *Infant perception: From sensation to cognition* (Vol. 1): *Basic Visual Processes*. New York: Academic Press, 1975.

Corsale, K. The effects of mode of presentation on encoding processes in children's short-term memory. Paper presented at the annual meeting of the American Psychological Association, New Orleans, September 1974.

Craik, F. I. M., & Lockhart, R. S. Levels of processing: A framework for memory research. *Journal of Verbal Learning and Verbal Behavior*, 1972, *11*, 671–684.

Crowder, R. G., & Morton, J. Precategorical acoustic storage (PAS). *Perception and Psychophysics*, 1969, *5*, 365–373.

DiVesta, F. J. A developmental study of the semantic structures of children. *Journal of Verbal Learning and Verbal Behavior*, 1966, *5*, 249–259.

Esrov, L. V., Hall, J. W., & LaFaver, D. K. Preschoolers' conceptual and acoustic encoding as evidenced by release from PI. *Bulletin of the Psychonomic Society*, 1974, *4*, 89–90.

Faulkender, P. J., Wright, J. C., & Waldron, A. Generalized habituation of concept stimuli in toddlers. *Child Development*, 1974, *45*, 1002–1010.

Finkel, D. L. A developmental comparison of the processing of two types of visual information. *Journal of Experimental Child Psychology*, 1973, *16*, 250–266.

Frank, H. S., & Rabinovitch, M. S. Auditory short-term memory: Developmental changes in precategorical acoustic storage. *Child Development*, 1974, *45*, 522–526.

Gibson, E. J. *Principles of perceptual learning and development*. New York: Appleton-Century-Crofts, 1969.

Gibson, E. J., Barron, R. W., & Garber, E. E. The developmental convergence of meaning for words and pictures, Appendix to the final report, *The relationship between perceptual development and the acquisition of reading skill* (Project No. 90046, Grant No. OEG-2-9-420446-1071 (010) between Cornell University and the U.S. Office of Education), 1972.

Hagen, J. W., Jongeward, R. H., & Kail, R. V. Cognitive perspectives on the development of memory. In H. W. Reese (Ed.), *Advances in child development and behavior* (Vol. 10). New York: Academic Press, 1975.

Haith, M. M., Morrison, F. J. Sheingold, K., & Mindes, P. Short-term memory for visual information in children and adults. *Journal of Experimental Child Psychology*, 1970, *9*, 454–469.

Hoving, K. L., Morin, R. E., & Konick, D. S. Recognition reaction time and size of the memory set: A developmental study. *Psychonomic Science*, 1970, *21*, 247–248.

Kail, R. V. Children's encoding of taxonomic classes and subclasses. *Developmental Psychology*, 1976, *12*, 487–488.

Kail, R. V., Jongeward, R. H., Daoust, B. L., & Aaron, D. L. Storage and retrieval components of children's encoding processes. Unpublished manuscript, University of Pittsburgh, 1976.

Kail, R. V., & Levine, L. E. Encoding processes and sex-role preferences. *Journal of Experimental Child Psychology*, 1976, *21*, 256–263.

Kail, R. V., & Schroll, J. T. Evaluative and taxonomic encoding in children's memory. *Journal of Experimental Child Psychology*, 1974, *18*, 426–437.

Kroes, W. H. Conceptual encoding by sense impression. *Perceptual and Motor Skills*, 1973, *37*, 432.

Melton, A. W., & Martin, E. (Eds.), *Coding processes in human memory*. Washington, D.C.: Winston, 1972.

Milner, E. *Human neural and behavioral development*. Springfield, Ill.: Charles C Thomas, 1967.

Morin, R. E., Hoving, K. L., & Konick, D. S. Are these two stimuli from the same set? Response times of children and adults with familiar and arbitrary sets. *Journal of Experimental Child Psychology*, 1970, *10*, 308–318.

Morrison, F. J., Holmes, D. L., & Haith, M. M. A developmental study of the effect of familiarity on short-term visual memory. *Journal of Experimental Child Psychology*, 1974, *18*, 412–425.

Nadelman, L. Sex identity in American children: Memory, knowledge, and preference tests. *Developmental Psychology*, 1974, *10*, 413–417.

Neisser, U. *Cognitive psychology*. New York: Appleton-Century-Crofts, 1967.

Olson, G. M. An information processing analysis of visual memory and habituation in infants. In T. J. Tighe & R. N. Leaton (Eds.), *Habituation: Perspectives from child development, animal behavior, and neurophysiology*. Hillsdale, N.J.: Lawrence Erlbaum Associates, 1976.

Osgood, C. E., Suci, G. J., & Tannenbaum, P. H. *The measurement of meaning*. Urbana: University of Illinois Press, 1957.

Paivio, A. *Imagery and verbal processes*. New York: Holt, Rinehart & Winston, 1971.

Pascual-Leone, J., & Smith, J. The encoding and decoding of symbols by children: A new experimental paradigm and a neo-Piagetian model. *Journal of Experimental Child Psychology*, 1969, *8*, 328–355.

Pellegrino, J. W., Rosinski, R. R., Chiesi, H. L., & Siegel, A. W. Picture-word differences in decision latency: An analysis of single and dual-memory models. Unpublished manuscript, University of Pittsburgh, 1976.

Pender, N. J. A developmental study of conceptual, semantic differential, and acoustic dimensions as encoding categories in short-term memory. Unpublished doctoral dissertation, Northwestern University, 1969.

Rader, N. L. Developmental changes in getting meaning from written words. Paper presented at the biennial meeting of the Society for Research in Child Development, Denver, 1975.

Rosinski, R. R., Golinkoff, R. M., & Kukish, K. S. Automatic semantic processing in a picture-word interference task. *Child Development*, 1975, *46*, 247–253.

Rosinski, R. R., Pellegrino, J. W., & Siegel, A. W. Developmental changes in the semantic processing of pictures and words. *Journal of Experimental Child Psychology*, 1977, *23*, 281–291.

Sheingold, K. Developmental differences in intake and storage of visual information. *Journal of Experimental Child Psychology*, 1973, *16*, 1–11.

Shepard, R. N. Form, formation, and transformation of internal representations. In R. L. Solso (Ed.), *Information processing and cognition: The Loyola symposium*. Hillsdale, N.J.: Lawrence Erlbaum Associates, 1975.

Siegel, A. W., & Allik, J. P. A developmental study of visual and auditory short-term memory. *Journal of Verbal Learning and Verbal Behavior*, 1973, *12*, 409–418.

Siegel, A. W., Allik, J. P., & Herman, J. F. The primacy effect in young children: Verbal fact or spatial artifact? *Child Development*, 1976, *47*, 242–247.

Siegel, A. W., & White, S. H. The development of spatial representations of large-scale environments. In H. W. Reese (Ed.), *Advances in child development and behavior* (Vol. 10). New York: Academic Press, 1975.

Standing, L., Conezio, J., & Haber, R. N. Perception and memory for pictures: Single-trial learning of 2500 visual stimuli. *Psychonomic Science*, 1970, *19*, 73–74.

Stroop, J. R. Studies in interference in serial verbal reactions. *Journal of Experimental Psychology,* 1935, *18,* 643–661.

Surwillo, W. W. Frequency of the "alpha" rhythm, reaction time and age. *Nature,* 1961, *191,* 823–824.

Surwillo, W. W. The relation of simple response time to brain-wave frequency and the effects of age. *Electroencephalography and Clinical Neurophysiology,* 1963, *15,* 105–114. (a)

Surwillo, W. W. The relation of response-time variability to age and the influence of brain wave frequency. *Electroencephalography and Clinical Neurophysiology,* 1963, *15,* 1029–1032. (b)

Tulving, E. Episodic and semantic memory. In E. Tulving & W. Donaldson (Eds.), *Organization of memory.* New York: Academic Press, 1972.

Von Wright, J. M., Gebhard, P., & Karttunen, M. A developmental study of the recall of spatial location. *Journal of Experimental Child Psychology,* 1975, *20,* 181–190.

White, S. H. Some general outlines of the matrix of developmental changes between five and seven years. *Bulletin of the Orton Society,* 1970, *20,* 41–57.

White, S. H., & Siegel, A. W. Cognitive development: The new inquiry. *Young Children,* 1976, *31,* 425–435.

Wickens, C. D. Temporal limits of human information processing: A developmental study. *Psychological Bulletin,* 1974, *81,* 739–755.

Wickens, D. D. Characteristics of word encoding. In A. W. Melton & E. Martin (Eds.) *Coding processes in human memory.* Washington, D.C.: Winston, 1972.

Wickens, D. D., & Clark, S. E. Osgood dimensions as an encoding category in short-term memory. *Journal of Experimental Psychology,* 1968, *78,* 580–584.

Wickens, D. D., Reutener, D. B., & Eggemeier, F. T. Sense impression as an encoding dimension of words. *Journal of Experimental Psychology,* 1972, *96,* 301–306.

Wohlwill, J. F. From perception to inference: A dimension of cognitive development. In W. Kessen & C. Kuhlman (Eds.), *Thought in the young child.* Chicago: University of Chicago Press, 1962.

Yates, F. A. *The art of memory.* Chicago: University of Chicago Press, 1966.

4

Memory: Strategies of Acquisition

John W. Hagen
Keith E. Stanovich
University of Michigan

I. INTRODUCTION

The view that with development children come to employ strategies to facilitate memory has received considerable support in recent years (Hagen, Jongeward, & Kail, 1975). In this chapter, we review evidence on a number of strategies used in acquiring information to be remembered at a later time. These strategies, while differing in age of onset and perfection, all show developmental progressions and appear to be directly linked to improvements in memory. They range from simply naming items to be remembered, to rehearsing fairly large numbers of items, to the deliberate acquisition of certain information at the expense of other available information.

Models of memory that allow for a separation of components in mnemonic processing have proven most useful in synthesizing the developmental research on memory. In particular, the model offered by Atkinson and Shiffrin (1968) introduced a distinction between structural features and control processes of memory. The former refer to the physical limitations and the built-in processes that are invariant features of memory, while the latter concern those processes that are under the direct control of the individual. There are three components to the structure. In the sensory register a literal copy of information is stored, where it decays very quickly. The short-term store provides the individual with a working memory. Information is selected from the sensory register and held here while it is acted on. Information can be maintained in short-term store by rehearsal and may then be transfered to long-term store, the third component. The control processes provide the ways that information is selected, maintained, or deleted, both within and between the structural components. According to Atkinson and Shiffrin (1968), control processes are "transient phenomena under the control of the subject; their appearance depends on such factors as instructional set, the experimental task, and the past history of the subject [p. 106]."

A recent model by Craik and Lockhart (1972) places even greater emphasis on the role of the individual in controlling his memory. Incoming information is analyzed at a number of levels. The more levels a memory trace proceeds through, the better its chances of being retained. At the first levels, information is handled in terms of its physical or sensory features. At the deeper levels, its meaning to the individual comes into play. Rehearsal allows continued attention to specific aspects of information. Maintenance rehearsal is used to retain these aspects temporarily, but does not result in longer-term storage. Elaborative rehearsal, in which information is processed at still deeper levels of analysis, may be used to enhance long-term retention. For example, information may be related to information already in memory or linked mnemonically to something in the individual's immediate environment. The memory trace is strengthened and its likelihood of subsequent recall increased.

We shall now consider developmental research pertinent to acquisition strategies in memory. It should become evident to the reader just how these models that emphasize the role of subject-generated activities to improve memory fit well with this research.

II. REHEARSAL STRATEGIES IN ACQUISITION

A. Verbal Mediation

Mediational mechanisms have been considered by many to be important determiners of cognitive abilities (Kendler & Kendler, 1962; Spiker, 1963). Simply labeling objects in one's environment has been found to improve performance in some tasks. However, below certain age levels children do not, or cannot, provide labels for stimuli, and even if they are induced to do so, their performance is not affected. In order to account for this situation, Reese (1962) formulated the mediational deficiency hypothesis, which postulates a stage in development during which verbal responses to stimuli may occur, but do not serve as mediators. A considerable amount of research has been generated to test this hypothesis.

A memory task was used by Flavell, Beach, and Chinsky (1966) to explore the mediational hypothesis in 5-, 7-, and 10-year-old children. A circular array of pictures of seven common objects was presented, and three were identified on each trial as the ones to be recalled. During a 15-second period between presentation and recall, an observer recorded the child's lip movements to measure any spontaneous verbal activity that might occur. During the delay interval, the child was wearing a space helmet with a visor that covered his eyes but exposed his lips. After the delay, the visor was lifted and the child was asked to point to the three pictures to be remembered. Among the 5-year-olds, only 2 out of 20 children showed verbal naming or rehearsal during the delay. For the 10-year-olds, 17 of the 20 revealed verbal activity in their lip movements. Furthermore, a positive relation was found between the presence of lip movements and the number of items recalled over trials.

The issue of a causal link between this verbal rehearsal and performance in memory was explored by Keeney, Cannizzo, and Flavell (1967). Six- and 7-year-old children were participants, and the procedure was a replication of the study just described. Based on observations made during the delay, children were divided into two groups, those who engaged in verbal activity during the delay and those who did not. The former group recalled significantly better than the latter group did. Then those children who did not rehearse were given additional instructions. During the delay, they were to whisper the names of the pictures to be remembered. The children did so with ease, and their recall improved to the level of recall by children who rehearsed spontaneously. There is a negative note to add, however. When the children were later tested with no demand to whisper the names, they did not do so and their memory also declined.

What can be concluded concerning mediational deficiency? Clearly, children who did not spontaneously use the names were not deficient in mediating, since when instructed to label they did so, and their memory improved. Rather, the authors concluded that these children were characterized by a "production deficiency." The children simply did not use a skill they had available to facilitate recall of the pictures. Of course, the mediational deficiency hypothesis may still apply for younger children who might not show mediation even when instructed to rehearse verbally.

B. The Serial Recall Task

In order to understand more precisely the role of naming of information to be recalled, a serial recall task has been used. Does simply naming the stimuli during acquisition affect recall, and if so, are the effects different at different age levels? Is it also possible that strategies more complex than naming or labeling are invoked during the acquisition phase of the task? These questions are addressed in the research that follows.

The serial recall task was first used by Atkinson, Hansen, and Bernbach (1964). Picture cards are arranged in a horizontal display and shown one at a time to the child. After the first card is shown briefly, it is placed face down in front of the child; the second follows immediately and is placed face down next to the first. The procedure is continued until all cards for that series are lying face down in a row. Typically, four to eight cards are shown on a trial. On subsequent trials, the order of the particular pictures is varied so locations of particular pictures cannot be learned. A cue card is shown immediately after the final card in a series is presented, and the task is to point to the card in the series that matches the cue card. Across trials, a test is made of each of the positions. A child's performance is measured both by the total number of pictures he or she recalled correctly over all trials and by the positional or serial order recall of the pictures. The initial positions in the series are called the *primacy* positions, while the last positions, occupied by those pictures seen just before recall is measured, are called the *recency* postiions.

In a study by Hagen and Kingsley (1968), children 4, 6, 7, 8, and 10 years of age were tested in one of two conditions. In one condition the names of the pictures had to be said aloud by the children, while in the second condition naming was not required. Three predictions were made. First, an increase in overall recall with increasing age was expected. Second, for the younger children, who would not be expected to label spontaneously, required labeling should facilitate recall. Labeling should not affect recall as much for older children, who label spontaneously. Third, findings for serial position recall for

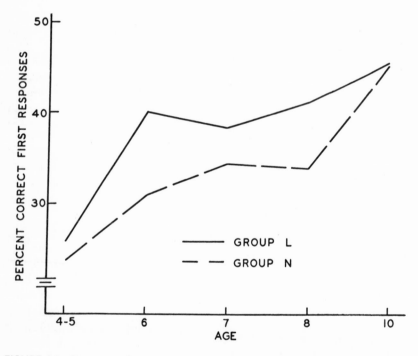

FIGURE 4-1   Percentage of correct responses as a function of experimental group and age level: solid line, label group (L); broken line, no-label group (N). (From Hagen & Kingsley, 1968, p. 120, Fig. 3. Copyright 1968 by the Society for Research in Child Development, Inc.)

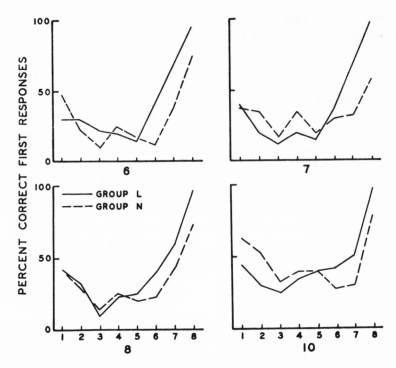

FIGURE 4-2   Percentage correct responses as a function of serial position and experimental condition for four age levels: solid line, label group (L); broken line, no-label group (N). (From Hagen & Kingsley, 1968, p. 117, Fig. 1. Copyright 1968 by the Society for Research in Child Development, Inc.)

the older children should approximate those of adults with elevated performance at the primacy positions as well as at the recency positions.

The predictions proved to be generally correct. Memory did improve with increasing chronological age, as shown in Figure 4-1. Saying the names of the pictures aloud affected retention, but not quite as expected. Facilitation due to labeling was found at the three intermediate age levels, but at the youngest and oldest levels no change in recall occurred. From Figure 4-1, it is evident that there is not a ceiling effect at the oldest age level, since performance did not reach 50% total recall. The results for serial order recall are illustrated in Figure 4-2 for the 6- through 10-year-olds. Three findings are especially obvious. Performance improved as age level increased. At the left-hand portion of each curve, or the primacy positions, recall was not improved by labeling; in fact, at the oldest age level a significant decrement due to labeling was evident. Finally, labeling did facilitate recall at all ages at the right-hand portion, or recency positions, of the serial recall curves. Since this effect was about equal in magnitude to the decrement produced by labeling at the primacy portion of the curve for the 10-year-olds, the net effect was no change in performance, as already seen in Figure 4-1. Hence, verbal labeling appears to faciliate performance in a short-term recall task only under certain circumstances. Quite obviously, the effect is complex and dependent on the developmental level of the individuals involved.

Rehearsal of the sort observed by Flavell et al. (1966) appeared to be a good candidate for a "strategy" engaged in by individuals in the serial recall task. Our task was more difficult than theirs, however, since eight positions had to be retained while waiting for the probe to appear. Cumulative, covert rehearsal of names while additional pictures are being presented could become a cumbersome activity indeed. If one is also trying to say aloud the name of each new picture as it appears, cumulative rehearsal might be disrupted; hence, labeling could lead to poorer performance. Two additional studies were aimed at determining just how verbal labeling and rehearsal affected recall in young children.

Rehearsal induced by the experimenter was the topic of study in the first experiment (Kingsley & Hagen, 1969). In a procedure akin to that of Keeney et al. (1967), 5-year-olds were instructed to rehearse cumulatively the names of the five animals to be recalled in a serial recall task. This age level was selected because no facilitation due to labeling had been found previously, or was there evidence that 5-year-olds rehearsed. In one condition, children were instructed to say aloud the names of the pictures. For example, when the first picture appeared, the child said "bear." When the second was presented, he said, "bear, fish." The name of each new picture was added to the series of overtly rehearsed names. When confusions occurred, the experimenter corrected the error. In another condition, the labeling of the original study was used instead of rehearsal. Children who cumulatively rehearsed the names of pictures recalled more positions correctly than did children who simply labeled. Recall at the primacy portion of the serial position curve was markedly elevated for children in the cumulative rehearsal condition only. The two groups did not differ in recall at the recency positions. Thus, young children who do not typically rehearse can be induced to do so, with the result that recall is enhanced, a finding parallel to that of Keeney et al. (1967).

The second study (Hagen, Hargrave, & Ross, 1973) replicated the induced rehearsal condition just described. In addition, a condition was included in which rehearsal was taught to the child and required during presentation of pictures, but prompting was not given when errors occurred. Under these circumstances, recall was not facilitated; rather, it declined somewhat for 5- and 7-year-olds. On a test for recall given one week later, the performance of the children who had received prompting (and thus had better recall than those who did not receive prompting) was found to have declined. Thus, for children in this age range, induced cumulative rehearsal is effective in aiding recall only when prompts are provided, and it seems to have only a temporary effect.

When the serial recall task was administered to adolescents and college students, the results provided further insight into the rehearsal process (Hagen, Meacham, & Mesibov, 1970). Eight serial positions per trial were used in the task, and when labeling was required, recall was lower at the first six of these positions. Only for the last two, or recency, positions did recall improve due to labeling. For college students, labeling actually produced a *decrement* in overall recall, even though recall was higher for these individuals than for any others tested. Thus, recall in this task continues to improve into adulthood, and labeling imposed experimentally has an increasingly detrimental effect. It seems that as individuals become increasingly proficient in using their own strategies to aid recall, the detriment effect on recall of labeling increases.

How would recall be affected under conditions designed deliberately to interfere with the strategy of cumulative rehearsal? Data relevant to this question came from a study by Hagen and Kail (1973) with 7- and 11-year-olds. A 15-second delay was introduced between the presentation of the final picture in a given trial and the presentation of the cue card on that trial. In one condition, children were instructed to count aloud during this delay; in a second condition, they were simply told to "think about the pictures" during the delay. Both groups were also tested without the delay between presentation and recall.

Under the distraction of counting aloud, recall by older children declined, especially at the primacy positions, while recall by the younger children did not change significantly. In fact, the total recall and serial position curves of both age groups were remarkably similar to the distraction condition. The delay period with no distraction actually resulted in improved recall at the primacy positions for the 11-year-olds, and for these children recall was significantly higher than for the 7-year-olds. In an additional analysis, those 7-year-old children who performed as well as, or better than, the mean performance of the 11-year-olds were looked at as a group. No enhanced primacy effect was found for these "superior 7-year-olds." It was concluded that "children in the seven year age range do not yet characteristically engage in rehearsal to improve recall, but by age eleven years children are proficient in using this strategy" (Hagen & Kail, 1973, p. 835).

Although children at ages 4 to 6 have not typically shown a primacy effect in the serial recall task, some investigators have found evidence for it in young children (Donaldson & Strang, 1969; Keely, 1971). This effect typically is found only at the first position for children at this age level and does not appear to indicate the use of cumulative rehearsal. One possible explanation has been offered by Rosner (1972), who found that young children recalled primacy items accurately only on early trials when stimulus items were repeated, or when new, distinctive items were introduced. She concludes that primacy recall sometimes found at this age level is not attributable to the use of cumulative rehearsal. Another finding of relevance is provided in a study by Siegel, Allik, and Herman (1976) with 5- to 7-year-olds. In the usual administration of the serial recall task, spatial and temporal components are confounded. Pictures are presented one at a time in serial order in a horizontal array. In this study, a condition was included in which the pictures were presented in a random, nonlinear order, thus no longer confounding temporal and spatial orders of presentation. It was found that spatial location was largely responsible for the primacy effect found for children of this age. When the picture presented first did not occupy the first position of the serial array, its probability of recall was no higher than that of pictures presented later in the series. It is apparent, then, that children in this age range are not using the cumulative rehearsal strategy to improve recall.

C. Additional Studies Using a Serial Recall Task

The development of the cumulative rehearsal strategy has been investigated in other studies. Allik and Siegel (1976) used pictures of animals and objects whose names were either one or two syllables long. If the length of time needed for overt rehearsal of an item depends on the amount of time needed for articulating the item, then children using cumulative rehearsal should perform better on a series of one-syllable items than on a series of two-syllable items. Four- 5-, and 6-year-olds were found to recall as many two-syllable as one-syllable items. However, 8- and 11-year-olds recalled more one-syllable than two-syllable items. It appears, then, that cumulative rehearsal was not used spontaneously until after the age of 6, a finding consistent with other studies.

In the studies considered thus far, the stimuli have all been presented visually. However, Siegel and Allik (1973) have compared visual presentation with auditory presentation of the serial list of items to be recalled. In the auditory condition, children were seated before a panel that contained seven small speakers arranged horizontally. On a given trial, the names of the objects to be remembered were heard through these speakers. In the visual condition, pictures were shown by placing them over the speakers used in the auditory condition. Recall of visual stimuli was considerably better than recall of auditory stimuli at all ages tested, from age 6 through college. Further, primacy and recency effects were found for stimuli presented in either mode. Siegel and Allik (1973) speculate that "the pictures themselves had a facilitative effect on performance because a picture can be stored simultaneously in both a visual and an auditory-verbal system [p. 417]."

D. Other Acquisition Strategies

Other strategies for acquiring information to be remembered later have also been identified. No doubt the child learns a complex array of skills to aid his memory in various tasks and situations. The following three studies illustrate what some of these are like.

Children were allowed to control their study time and the number of exposures of pictures to be remembered in a study by Flavell, Friedrichs, and Hoyt (1970). Children were told that their task was to learn the particular pictures that appeared in each of ten windows, and that they could view a picture by pressing a button that provided illumination, thus revealing the picture. The child viewed pictures until he thought he knew them, then called for the experimenter. Accuracy of recall was directly related to chronological age, across the range from age 4 through 10. Further, the amount of time spent in preparation for testing increased dramatically with age. Older children seemed to know what was needed to ensure good performance, as revealed by observations made of the children during study time. Overt naming of the pictures was done primarily by the older children, and rehearsal of names increased during the study period, especially for the oldest children. Testing oneself prior to viewing a picture was another strategy used by the older children. Only at the oldest age level did the children reveal a set of task-appropriate strategies and use them consistently in preparation for recall.

A subsequent investigation of study time also proved revealing (Masur, McIntyre, & Flavell, 1973). A list of pictures to be memorized was given to 7-, 9-, and 20-year-olds. After each trial, they were allowed to choose half of the pictures to study during a 45-second period. Both the 9-year-olds and the adults chose those pictures they had missed on the previous trial significantly more often than did the 7-year-olds. However, using this strategy facilitated recall for the adults but not for the 9-year-olds. Apparently, giving extra time to prepare for recall of material that is not well mastered is a strategy that emerges with age, and is used for a period of time before it is perfected. It would be necessary to test individuals on this task at age levels between age 9 and adulthood to describe accurately just when children become proficient in the use of this strategy.

The rehearsal of lists of nouns to be remembered was studied by Ornstein, Naus, and Liberty (1975). Twenty words from four taxonomic categories were presented to children 8, 11, and 13 years of age in a free recall task. Members of each category were presented either contiguously or randomly. Rehearsal patterns were observed by requiring children to rehearse aloud. When category members were presented contiguously, both 11- and 13-year-old children tended to rehearse taxonomically related items together. When items were presented randomly, only children in the older group did so. Thus, only at this age level did the children adapt their rehearsal to categorical stimuli regardless of the internal structure of the list. While the younger children were found to rehearse, only those at early adolescence applied the strategy to conditions where it was less than obvious to do so.

III. STRATEGIES OF SELECTIVE ATTENTION IN ACQUISITION

A. The Central-Incidental Task

Further insights into the development of acquisition strategies have been gained by adding an incidental learning component to the serial recall task. This paradigm, the central-incidental task, was first introduced by Maccoby and Hagen (1965) and later refined by Hagen (1967). Each of a series of cards contains a picture of an animal and a household object. Children are first told to remember only one of the two classes of objects; then several serial recall trials are administered. The number correct on this part of the task is termed the *central* score. After the serial recall trials, children are given two sets of cards, each comprising the items from one of the two categories used in the central-incidental task. Children are asked to pair the items that had appeared together on the same card during the serial recall trials. The number correct on this part of the task is termed the *incidental* score.

In an initial study (Hagen, 1967), children 6 to 13 years of age were tested. Central memory was found to increase with age, while incidental performance did not vary systematically with age level. A developmental increase in the ability to maintain task performance by excluding irrelevant information is indicated by the fact that the proportion of incidental to total material recalled decreased as chronological age increased. Supporting this general conclusion, central memory scores correlated positively with incidental memory scores at the younger ages, but negatively at the oldest age level. Here again is an indication that older children are more proficient than younger children at selectively excluding information that is incidental to the serial recall task.

In the Hagen (1967) study, several trials were included in which only the central pictures appeared on the cards. Children's central recall was greater here than when central and incidental stimuli were both present. However, adults' central memory performance seems to be relatively unaffected by the presence of incidental stimuli (Hagen et al., 1970). Children, as compared to adults, seem more distracted by irrelevant stimuli due to the lack of a well-developed ability to select relevant information for further processing.

The developmental increase in selecting task-appropriate information for encoding and later recall may be the result of active strategies employed by older individuals. Druker and Hagen (1969) administered a questionnaire after completion of the central-incidental task. Two cognitive strategies—visual scanning of only the central stimuli and verbal labeling of the central stimuli—both showed strong increases with age. Since Druker and Hagen (1969) replicated the developmental increase in the proportion of central material recall to total amount of material recalled, the findings of the questionnaire suggest that older children are better able to employ cognitive skills in order to concentrate exclusively on task-relevant information, as compared to younger children. In addition, the increased tendency to say the names of only the central stimuli is an indication that some form of rehearsal may be mediating performance in the central-incidental task.

Subsequent research with the central-incidental task has implicated processes of somewhat greater complexity. For example, under conditions of distraction, such as requiring individuals to detect the presence of a particular sound, the negative correlation between central and incidental memory observed for the 12- to 13-year-olds is reduced (Hagen, 1967). Labeling produces a similar reduction in this correlation (Hagen et al., 1970). It seems that the strategies used by older individuals to focus attention on central information and ignore incidental information are disrupted when additional cognitive demands are introduced during acquisition. Since labeling has been hypothesized to hinder a cumulative rehearsal process, the results just cited suggest that rehearsal may be one of the strategies used by older children and adults to attend selectively to the relevant material in a task with demands such as the central-incidental task.

Sabo and Hagen (1973) investigated the effect of rehearsal during the retention interval of the central-incidental task with children at ages 8, 10, and 12. A 10-second delay was interposed between the presentation of the last stimulus card and the memory test. Children in one condition were told to "think about the pictures" during the delay; those in a second condition were instructed to count aloud during the delay. The difference between recall of central stimuli in the two conditions increased with age. Allowing rehearsal had a substantial facilitating effect at age 12, a moderate effect at age 10, and no effect at age 8. Incidental memory was unrelated to age level for children who counted during the delay. However, when rehearsal was permitted, incidental performance of 12-year-olds declined. These results point rather strongly to the conclusion that, during an unfilled retention interval, older children make use of a rehearsal process that allows selective retention to task-relevant information. In summary, the research employing the central-incidental paradigm amply documents the developmental progression toward more mature acquisition strategies. Naming of pertinent stimulus items is followed by cumulative rehearsal of the stimuli during their presentation, and finally the child becomes able to rehearse central items when they are absent.

The studies reviewed above all concern central and incidental information as defined with respect to a particular task. It is possible that the increasing selectivity displayed by older children might be specific to the central-incidental task and, thus, may not be a general characteristic of developmental changes in information processing. To date, however, the research that has addressed this issue indicates that the age-related increase in selectivity is a pervasive property of cognitive development. Hagen and Kail (1975) compared the research based on the central-incidental task with that from other tasks in which selective attention is a critical component (e.g., discrimination learning, measures of cognitive style). They concluded that "there appears to be an emerging tendency to employ task-appropriate strategies during this period that certainly involve perceptual processing but also involve a central, cognitive component" (Hagen & Kail, 1975, p. 188).

B. The Role of Stimulus Factors

It is useful to consider what types of stimulus factors effect memory performance and how the influence of these factors changes with age. Studies of this sort serve to increase our understanding of the development of cognitive strategies that can be utilized to aid the acquisition and retention of information.

Hagen and his colleagues have systematically investigated the role of stimulus factors in the central-incidental task. Interest in the manipulation of the stimulus configuration stemmed from the desire to isolate the causes of the developmental increase in the selective retention of the central memory items. An initial hypothesis was that young children have difficulty analyzing stimuli into components. That is, the locus of the developmental increase in selective encoding and retention was in perceptual processing, as opposed to higher-level cognitive processing.

Hagen and Frisch (1968) examined differences in performance attributable to the manner in which central and incidental pictures were paired. In one case, the incidental picture always appeared with the same central picture; in a second case, the pairing was randomized on every trial; and in a third case, the same incidental picture was paired with each central picture on a given trial. The developmental increase in central memory performance was replicated, and central memory was similar in all three conditions. If the younger child's inability to attend selectively is due to difficulty in perceptual analysis, then it would be expected that when the incidental pictures were not always paired with the same central pictures the younger child's central memory would improve. The results were clearly counter to this hypothesis.

Druker and Hagen (1969) conducted another study in which the stimulus configuration was manipulated in an attempt to increase the perceptual salience of the central stimuli for the young children. In one condition, the two pictures were separated spatially from each other, rather than touching as in the standard condition. In a second condition, pictures were presented in a nonalternating fashion, with the central picture always appearing above the incidental picture. (In the standard method of presentation, the central picture appears above the incidental picture on only half of the stimulus pairs.) Central recall was unaffected by either manipulation. Identical memory was unaffected by nonalternation of the stimuli, but decreased when the stimuli were separated spatially. However, incidental memory was reduced equally across age levels (9 through

14 years). The lack of a differential effect of spacing at the lower age levels is further evidence against the idea that younger children display less selectivity because they have difficulty analyzing stimuli into components.

Perceptual discriminability has been improved by using central pictures of one color and incidental pictures of a different color. This manipulation increased central memory performance, but once again the increase was the same at all age levels (Sabo & Hagen, 1973). *Decreasing* the perceptual salience of the central and incidental items by presenting them in action relationships (for example, a bear sweeping with a broom) resulted in increased incidental recall (Hale & Piper, 1974). However, the results mirrored those of other studies described in the present section in that the increase in incidental recall was the same across age levels.

When colored forms are stimuli, with shape designated as the central feature and color as the incidental feature, both central *and* incidental scores have been found to increase between ages 8 and 12 (Hale & Piper, 1973). At first glance, this result appears to be in contradiction with the bulk of the research employing the central-incidental task in that the usual developmental increase in selection of task-relevant information was not evident. However, careful consideration of the nature of the stimulus materials suggests an interpretation that is congruent with previous research. The incidental component of the stimuli (color) was integrally contained within the central stimulus. It is not possible to focus the eyes on only one of the stimulus components as it is with the stimuli commonly used in the central-incidental task. When the components are not easily separable, to attempt to do so is no longer an appropriate task strategy. Thus, Hale and Piper (1973) have convincingly demonstrated that older children display flexibility in employing this strategy. When the stimuli are such that the separation of the components is difficult, older children switch to a strategy of processing both components.

The studies just reviewed have all employed variants of the central-incidental task. Hale, Miller, and Stevenson (1968) investigated selective attention in a naturalistic setting. A film was shown to grade school children, who were then asked questions pertaining either to features central to the main plot or to aspects incidental to the story line. Recall of incidental details increased with age up to 13 years, at which point a decline occurred. Furthermore, various characteristics of the film content appear to interact with age in determining the amount of incidental information recalled (Hawkins, 1973). Considering the extensive differences in the experimental situations, these results bear a marked similarity to those obtained with the central-incidental memory task. However, it remains to be seen whether similar kinds of cognitive strategies are involved in the different situations where selective attention is appropriate.

Taken together, the results of the studies described here indicate rather strongly that the developmental increase in selective encoding and retention of central items is not due to the younger child's inability to discriminate the stimulus components. The selectivity displayed in central-incidental task performances seems to reflect the operation of a stage following initial perceptual discrimination. As Hagen and Kail (1975) conclude, "selectivity in attention of children . . . clearly comes about through the employment of task-appropriate encoding strategies rather than through the use of increasingly finer perceptual discriminations of the stimuli themselves [p. 172]."

IV. SUBJECT AND SOCIOCULTURAL FACTORS

A. Studies of Retardates

One subject variable that has received considerable attention in developmental studies of acquisition strategies is intelligence. Specifically, several research programs have been aimed at investigating the use of acquisition strategies by mentally retarded individuals. This body of research is of much theoretical importance (Brown, 1974) and is increasingly branching out into more naturalistic and applied settings (e.g., Wambold & Hayden, 1975).

Several lines of research suggest that the inferior performance of the mentally retarded on many memory tasks is due to the lack of an efficient rehearsal strategy. Ellis (1970) examined the performance of retarded individuals in a serial recall task. The absence of a primacy effect was interpreted as reflecting the lack of a cumulative rehearsal strategy. In addition, performance was unaffected by rate of presentation, a variable that influences rehearsal in adults. Thus, Ellis' research into serial position effects in the memory performance of retardates suggests that these individuals are unlikely to use rehearsal to facilitate memory.

The research of Belmont and Butterfield (1969, 1971) has led to similar conclusions. These investigators focused on the active acquisition strategies used in a self-paced task in which the participant presents the material to himself at his own pace. Adults often produce a pattern termed *cumulative rehearsal, fast finish* (Belmont & Butterfield, 1971), in which an initial phase of brief pauses between presentations of stimuli is followed by a single long pause, which in turn is followed by a final series of short pauses. Increasing the length of a list serves to increase the number of long pauses interpolating the short series. The interpretation of this pattern has been that individuals are successively filling up a rehearsal buffer. In contrast, retardates' rate of self-presentation remains relatively constant throughout a list. The suggestion here is that mentally retarded individuals were not engaging in any type of organizational or rehearsal strategy. This interpretation is supported by the observation that training retardates in the use of rehearsal resulted in increased recall and pause patterns resembling those of adults (Belmont & Butterfield, 1971; Butterfield, Wambold, & Belmont, 1973). The improvement was most marked at the primacy portion of the curve, where the effects of rehearsal would be most salient. Kellas, Ashcraft, and Johnson (1973) trained groups of mentally retarded adolescents (CAs = 15 to 17 years; IQs = 67 to 72) in a cumulative rehearsal strategy and observed significant effects on interitem pause patterns, overt rehearsal sets, and recall accuracy. In addition, these researchers observed effects of the cumulative rehearsal training on a posttest 13 days later. Taken as a whole, the studies employing variants of the Belmont and Butterfield methodology have provided convincing demonstrations of a rehearsal deficit in the mentally retarded. The paradigm is different enough from those utilized in other studies so that confidence in the generality of the proposed strategy deficit in retarded individuals is increased.

Hagen, Streeter, and Raker (1974) examined the effects of training the retarded to use cognitive strategies in a serial recall task. In one experiment, they examined the effects of a "primitive" cognitive strategy, verbal labeling, on the performance of mentally retarded children (mean CA = 10.6 years; mean MA = 7.9 years). These children performed in a manner similar to nonretarded children of the same mental age. Labeling increased recency performance and decreased primacy performance. In a second experiment, Hagen et al. trained retarded children (Mean CA = 10.8 years; mean MA = 7.8 years) in a cumulative rehearsal strategy and observed an increase in recall, particularly at the primacy positions. The results of Hagen et al. (1974) support the conclusion that the memory performance of mildly retarded children can be improved by training in specific cognitive strategies. In addition, the results are supportive of Zigler's (1969) notion of mental retardation as a developmental lag, in that mildly retarded children performed like nonretarded children of equivalent mental age.

Brown (1974) has reviewed a series of studies from her laboratory where the issue of a cognitive strategy is addressed directly (see also the chapter by Campione and Brown in this volume). The working assumption is as follows: If the retarded are characterized by deficits in certain control processes, then tasks that involve these processes should show differences between retarded and nonretarded individuals; tasks not involving such control processes should yield no performance differences. Brown judiciously chose two tasks that reflected these contrasting outcomes. A picture recognition task was selected on the assumption that efficient performance in such a task does not require sophisticated control processes. In line with Brown's predictions, the performance of mildly retarded adolescents was similar to that of nonretarded individuals. These results were in marked contrast to those obtained from a second task; in which an individual was to remember the last instance of an item seen in one of several possible categories (for example, animals, food, vehicles, clothing). Efficient performance in this "keeping-track" task would seem to result from rehearsing only the last instance of each category. Thus, rehearsal, directed forgetting, and perhaps additional control processes are implicated in this task.

The performance of nonretarded and retarded adolescents on the keeping-track task diverged in a number of ways. In addition to displaying superior accuracy of recall, nonretarded individuals performed just as well regardless of the number of instances per category. For retardates, by contrast, recall declined as the number of instances per category increased. This result suggested that although non-retarded adolescents were selectively rehearsing the last instance of each category, the retarded were not making use of this strategy. Brown, Campione, Bray, and Wilcox (1973) attempted to demonstrate that failure to rehearse selectively contributed to the retardates' poor performance in the keeping-track task. When retarded adolescents were trained to rehearse the last instance of each category, their performance approximated that of nonretarded individuals, and was not dependent on the number of instances per category. Furthermore, retardates trained in the selective rehearsal strategy maintained their performance advantage over a six-month interval (Brown, Campione, & Murphy, 1974).

Brown et al. (1973) provided additional evidence indicating that a selective rehearsal process mediates the performance of adults in the keeping-track task. In a separate experiment, they attempted to disrupt the use of this strategy by requiring a group of nonretarded high school students to repeat each item as it occurred. Recall accuracy under these conditions were reduced markedly. In addition, when rehearsal was disrupted, the performance of nonretarded adolescents was similar to that of the retardates in that it was dependent on the number of instances per category. Thus, the results from studies employing the keeping-track task point rather strongly to a rehearsal deficit in retarded individuals. It seems that retardates do not spontaneously use a selective rehearsal strategy. When trained to use a rehearsal strategy, their performance mirrors that of nonretarded individuals, who, in turn, display a decline in recall when the use of this strategy is prevented. Finally, it is possible to design a situation in which the mentally retarded do not show a deficit by choosing a task (for example, picture recognition) that does not require the spontaneous use of a rehearsal strategy.

It should be noted that successful performance in the keeping-track task requires the spontaneous use of at least two separate strategies, rehearsal and directed forgetting. In the studies just reviewed, it is amply demonstrated that the retarded can be trained to rehearse to improve performance on this task. Bray (1973) demonstrated that, after a rather extensive training procedure, retarded adolescents (CA = 14 to 16; mean IQ approximately 63) could be taught the efficient use of a cue to forget. Additional results of Bray's study are somewhat puzzling. In contrast to a number of other studies, Bray observed spontaneous rehearsal (inferred from persistent primacy effects in the data) by the retarded individuals in this study. At first glance, the discrepancy would seem to result from the extensiveness of Bray's training procedure. However, this explanation is not entirely convincing because individuals were not given explicit training in rehearsal. Rather, Bray's training procedure was concerned with familiarizing individuals with the task and teaching them to use a cue to forget. Thus, the results point to our general ignorance regarding precisely what types of experience or training lead to the use of specific cognitive strategies. Clearly, more research on this important question is warranted.

The performance of retarded individuals on the central-incidental task has also been investigated. Hagen and Huntsman (1971) tested retardates from four MA levels (4, 6, 7, and 9 years) who were attending special education classes, and a group of nonretarded children (age 4 to 8). The pattern of results obtained from the retardates mirrored that obtained from the nonretarded children. Central recall increased with MA level, while incidental recall was relatively constant. Retarded children performed as well as nonretarded children of the same MA level, although their performance was significantly lower than that of children of equivalent CA. However, a group of institutionalized retardates displayed lower central recall and higher incidental recall than nonretarded or noninstitutionalized retardates of equivalent MA. Thus, some performance deficits exhibited by retarded individuals would appear to be due to motivational and emotional factors associated with institutionalization rather than with retardation per se (Zigler, 1966).   Hagen and West (1970) modified the central-incidental task in order to examine the effects of a training procedure on the central recall of retardates (mean IQ = 72). Primary and secondary dimensions were used in place of the central and incidental dimensions. Children at ages 11 and 14 (MAs of 8 and 10.6 years, respectively) were told to remember the pictures of both dimensions and that pennies would be earned for correct recall. However, the payoff for recalling a picture from the primary dimension was five times as great as the payoff for correct recall of a secondary picture. Children at both age levels recalled more pictures from the primary dimension than from the secondary dimension. Clearly, the retarded can benefit from training to encode selectively and retain task-relevant information. However, the mediational role of rehearsal in the retardates' performance on this particular task awaits further investigation.

In summary, the results from a variety of tasks suggest several general conclusions regarding the acquisition strategies of mentally retarded individuals. It seems that in many situations retardates do not employ appropriate cognitive strategies to aid their performance. Specifically, the mentally retarded do not spontaneously rehearse material that is to be retained over time. Although the basic structural features of their memory system appear to be intact, the retarded display inferior performance on memory tasks that are amenable to the use of rehearsal strategies (see the chapter by Campione and Brown for a more complete discussion of the structural/control deficit issue). The memory deficiency shown by retarded individuals appears to stem from deficient control processes. However, as Brown (1974) suggests, deficits in control processes are potentially more remediable than are deficits associated with structural components of the memory system. Training studies appear to support this conjecture in that retarded individuals can be taught to use various rehearsal strategies, with subsequent improvements in memory performance. A few studies have demonstrated fairly long-lasting effects of such training, although this is an area that could benefit from further research.

The research reviewed in this section has direct bearing on a larger theoretical issue in the field of mental retardation. Zigler (1969) has articulated a developmental delay notion that views the retarded individual as undergoing a normal sequence of development at a slower rate. This contrasts with the idea that the retarded are characterized by specific cognitive deficits that remain with them throughout development. The results of the training studies, in addition to other studies indicating that retarded children employ the same cognitive strategies as children of equal MA (Hagen & Huntsman, 1971; Hagen et al., 1974), support Zigler's lag hypothesis concerning the nature of familial retardation. Finally, it should be noted that the majority of the studies reviewed here used mildly retarded children and adults (IQs in the range of 60 to 75). Thus, generalization of the conclusions of the findings to more severely retarded populations is probably not warranted, although clearly this is an area deserving further study.

B. Studies of Children with Reading Disabilities

Another way to study cognitive deficiency is to compare children with specific learning disabilities to children of equivalent chronological age and intelligence levels without such disabilities. This approach was taken by Tarver, Hallahan, and Kaufman (1976), who administered the serial recall task to 8-, 10- and 13-year-old boys with known reading disabilities. Total recall as well as primacy recall increased with increasing age level. At the youngest age level, the primacy effect was found only for boys who were not reading disabled. The authors conclude that the development of efficient encoding strategies occurs at a slower rate in reading-disabled as compared to children without reading disabilities but that reading-disabled children do show the same developmental progression in the growth of these strategies.

Children with reading problems were tested by Pelham and Ross (in press) on measures of central and incidental memory. Children in the first, third, and fifth grades were included. Those who were poor readers scored lower on the central task and higher on the incidental task relative to children reading at grade level at all three grade levels. Performance on these tasks did follow the same developmental course for both groups of children, leading the authors to conclude that selective attention as measured by this task is delayed by two or more years in children with reading disabilities. Thus, the conclusion we reached concerning the development of strategies for recall in the mentally retarded appears to be applicable to children who show a lag in reading ability as well. Whether these lags in performance will be overcome in later adolescence or adulthood is not known at this time.

C. Studies of Sociocultural Factors

Differences in memory attributable to socioeconomic status have received little research attention. However, a few studies have yielded suggestive results. Ellis (1970, study 14) compared the serial recall of 6-year-olds of middle- to upper-class backgrounds with that of similar-aged lower-class children from a Head Start class. Although the mean IQ of the lower-class children was less than that of the middle-class children (85.5 vs. 102.6), overall recall by the two groups of children was similar and did not differ in the primacy and recency portions of the serial position curve. Similarly, McCarver and Ellis (1972) observed no difference in performance for culturally deprived and nondeprived 5-year-olds on a serial recall task. In addition, requiring overt labeling of stimuli resulted in increased recency and decreased primacy performance for both deprived and nondeprived children. Thus, basic memory processes do not seem to vary according to socioeconomic status.

Veroff and McClelland (1974) included the central-incidental task in a battery of tasks given to adults of different social backgrounds. Central memory was found to be related to social status, while incidental memory did not relate to social status. For adults from middle-class groups, incidental memory was unrelated to measures of intelligence. However, incidental memory performance of adults of lower-class backgrounds correlated significantly with measures of intelligence and education. Although based on performance of adults, the results suggest directions for future developmental investigations. Further research on social class differences in the development of the ability to encode selectively and retain task-relevant information seems warranted.

Cross-cultural research using the central-incidental task has been conducted by Wagner (1974) with 7- to 27-year-olds in urban and rural Yucatan. The performance of individuals in the urban sample, who were attending public school, was comparable to that of American subjects. Central memory increased with age, whereas incidental memory decreased after 16 years. Although the decline in incidental memory occurred at a somewhat later age than in American samples, the pattern of results is similar. In contrast, results for individuals from rural areas (where there was little schooling) differed strikingly. Central memory performance was relatively invariant over the entire 20-year age range. Incidental memory increased developmentally until 20 to 21 years of age, then declined at 27. Thus, the rural sample failed to display a tendency to encode selectively and retain task-relevant information. Wagner suggested that certain aspects of formal schooling might possibly aid in the development of mnemonic skills in short-term memory (see also the chapter by Cole and Scribner in this volume).

In a subsequent study, Wagner (1975) investigated the effect of verbal labeling on central and incidental recall of 7- to 21-year-olds from urban Yucatan. When labeling was not required, the pattern of results mirrored that obtained from

American samples: Central memory increased with age, while incidental memory displayed a curvilinear relationship. The effects of labeling were identical to those observed with American subjects. Labeling increased recall at the recency positions across all age levels and decreased primacy recall at the two oldest age levels. The role played by cultural factors in this study may be due to subject characteristics. Specifically, these individuals were in school, as were all the American subjects employed in the previous work on the effects of labeling. The results are thus consistent with the previous study (Wagner, 1974) and point to the conclusion that formal schooling may foster the development of certain cognitive strategies that mediate memory performance in all cultural contexts.

V. CONCLUDING REMARKS

In this chapter, strategies in the acquisition of information to be remembered have been considered. The developmental changes in short-term memory documented here as well as in the other chapters of this volume cannot be attributed solely to improved "memory ability." Rather, the case has been made that these changes occur at least in part because of the increased tendency with increasing age level to invoke task-appropriate strategies to facilitate memory.

Verbal processes and selective attention have both been found to be components in the strategies for facilitating memory that develop with increasing age. Verbal mediators function in ways more complex than simply enhancing information through providing labels. The verbal strategies invoked depend on the demands imposed by the specific recall task. As made clear in the chapter by Flavell and Wellman, the child also becomes increasingly aware and planful when a task requiring memory is put before him. His general strategy is combined with the specific strategies in his repertoire for coping with the task at hand.

The task that incorporates a measure of incidental recall has been found to be useful for inferring changes with age in selective attention to relevant aspects of stimuli. We believe that these are encoding strategies used by the individual to separate out the "most important" information from the mass of information available. What is "most important" is determined by the task demands and the individual's interpretation of these demands. The developmental changes occur across a wide age span. The findings reviewed here for both the central-incidental task and the serial recall task suggest that the developmental course of the strategies for remembering begins early and continues throughout the grade school years.

From the research on children with atypical or delayed cognitive development, it is evident that the mentally retarded do not perform as well as nonretarded children of equivalent age levels on various memory tasks. Further, there seems to be a developmental delay in the use of strategies to help memory in the retarded populations studied as well as in children with reading disabilities. However, the picture is optimistic concerning the potential value of remedial programs for children in either of these categories. The developmental course of memory for these children is very similar to that found in normal children.

REFERENCES

Allik, J. P., & Siegel, A. W. The use of the cumulative rehearsal strategy: A developmental study. *Journal of Experimental Child Psychology,* 1976, *21,* 316–327.

Atkinson, R. C., Hansen, D. N., & Bernbach, H. A. Short-term memory with young children. *Psychonomic Science,* 1964, *1,* 255–256.

Atkinson, R. C., & Shiffrin, R. M. Human memory: A proposed system and its control processes. In K. W. Spence & J. T. Spence (Eds.), *The psychology of learning and motivation* (Vol. 2). New York: Academic Press, 1968.

Belmont, J. M., & Butterfield, E. C. The relations of short-term memory to development and intelligence. In L. P. Lipsett & H. W. Reese (Eds.), *Advances in child development and behavior* (Vol. 4). New York: Academic Press, 1969.

Belmont, J. M., & Butterfield, E. C. Learning strategies as determinants of memory deficiencies. *Cognitive Psychology,* 1971, *2,* 411–420.

Bray, N. W. Controlled forgetting in the retarded. *Cognitive Psychology,* 1973, *5,* 288–309.

Brown, A. L. The role of strategic behavior in retardate memory. In N. R. Ellis (Ed.), *International review of research in mental retardation* (Vol. 7). New York: Academic Press, 1974.

Brown, A. L., Campione, J. C., Bray, N. W., & Wilcox, B. L. Keeping track of changing variables: Effects of rehearsal training and rehearsal prevention in normal and retarded adolescents. *Journal of Experimental Psychology,* 1973, *101,* 123–131.

Brown, A. L., Campione, J. C., & Murphy, M. D. Keeping track of changing variables: Long term retention of a trained rehearsal strategy by retarded adolescents. *American Journal of Mental Deficiency,* 1974, *78,* 446–453.

Butterfield, E. C., Wambold, C., & Belmont, J. M. On the theory and practice of improving short-term memory. *American Journal of Mental Deficiency,* 1973, *77,* 654–669.

Craik, F. I. M., & Lockhart, R. S. Levels of processing: A framework for memory research. *Journal of Verbal Learning and Verbal Behavior,* 1972, *11,* 671–684.

Donaldson, M., & Strang, H. Primacy effect in short-term memory in young children. *Psychonomic Science,* 1969, *16,* 59–60.

Druker, J. F., & Hagen, J. W. Developmental trends in the processing of task-relevant and task-irrelevant information. *Child Development,* 1969, *40,* 371–382.

Ellis, N. R. Memory processes in retardates and normals. In N. R. Ellis (Ed.), *International review of research in mental retardation* (Vol. 4). New York: Academic Press, 1970.

Flavell, J. H., Beach, D. R., & Chinsky, J. M. Spontaneous verbal rehearsal in a memory task as a function of age. *Child Development,* 1966, *37,* 283–299.

Flavell, J. H., Friedrichs, A. G., & Hoyt, J. D. Developmental changes in memorization processes. *Cognitive Psychology,* 1970, *1,* 324–340.

Hagen, J. W. The effect of distraction on selective attention. *Child Development,* 1967, *38,* 685–694.

Hagen, J. W., & Frisch, S. R. *The effect of incidental cues on selective attention* (Report No. 57, USPHS Grand HD 01368). Ann Arbor: University of Michigan, Center for Human Growth and Development, 1968.

Hagen, J. W., Hargrave, S., & Ross, W. Prompting and rehearsal in short-term memory. *Child Development,* 1973, *44,* 201–204.

Hagen, J. W., & Huntsman, N. Selective attention in mental retardates. *Developmental Psychology,* 1971, *5,* 151–160.

Hagen, J. W., Jongeward, R. H., & Kail, R. V. Cognitive perspectives on the development of memory. In H. W. Reese (Ed.), *Advances in child development and behavior* (Vol. 10). New York: Academic Press, 1975.

Hagen, J. W., & Kail, R. V. Facilitation and distraction in short-term memory. *Child Development,* 1973, *44,* 831–836.

Hagen, J. W., & Kail, R. V. The role of attention in perceptual and cognitive development. In W. M. Cruickshank and D. P. Hallahan (Eds.), *Perceptual and learning disabilities in children* (Vol. 2). Syracuse, N.Y.: Syracuse University Press, 1975.

Hagen, J. W., & Kingsley, P. R. Labeling effects in short-term memory. *Child Development,* 1968, *39,* 113–121.

Hagen, J. W., Meacham, J. A., & Mesibov, G. Verbal labeling, rehearsal, and short-term memory. *Cognitive Psychology,* 1970, *1,* 47–58.

Hagen, J. W., Streeter, L. A., & Raker, R. Labeling, rehearsal, and short-term memory in retarded children. *Journal of Experimental Child Psychology,* 1974, *18,* 259–268.

Hagen, J. W., & West, R. F. The effects of a pay-off matrix on selective attention. *Human Development,* 1970, *13,* 43–52.

Hale, G. A., Miller, L. K., & Stevenson, H. W. Incidental learning of film content: A developmental study. *Child Development,* 1968, *39,* 69–77.

Hale, G. A., & Piper, R. A. Developmental trends in children's incidental learning: Some critical stimulus differences. *Developmental Psychology,* 1973, *8,* 327–335.

Hale, G. A., & Piper, R. A. The effect of pictorial integration on children's incidental learning. *Developmental Psychology,* 1974, *10,* 847–851.

Hawkins, R. P. Learning of peripheral content in films: A developmental study. *Child Development,* 1973, *44,* 214–217.

Keely, K. Age and task differences in short-term memory in children. *Perception and Psychophysics,* 1971, *9,* 480–482.

Keeney, T. J., Cannizzo, S. R., & Flavell, J. H. Spontaneous and induced verbal rehearsal in a recall task. *Child Development,* 1967, *38,* 953–966.

Kellas, G., Ashcraft, M. H., & Johnson, N. S. Rehearsal processes in the short-term memory performance of mildly retarded adolescents. *American Journal of Mental Deficiency,* 1973, *77,* 670–679.

Kendler, H. H., & Kendler, T. S. Vertical and horizontal processes in problem solving. *Psychological Review,* 1962, *69,* 1–16.

Kingsley, P. R., & Hagen, J. W. Induced versus spontaneous rehearsal in short-term memory in nursery school children. *Developmental Psychology,* 1969, *1,* 40–46.

Maccoby, E. E., & Hagen, J. W. Effects of distraction upon central versus incidental recall: Developmental trends. *Journal of Experimental Child Psychology,* 1965, *2,* 280–289.

Masur, E. F., McIntyre, C. W., & Flavell, J. H. Developmental changes in apportionment of study time among items in a multitrial free recall task. *Journal of Experimental Child Psychology,* 1973, *15,* 237–246.

McCarver, R. B., & Ellis, N. R. Effect of overt verbal labeling on short-term memory in culturally deprived and nondeprived children. *Developmental Psychology,* 1972, *6,* 38–41.

Ornstein, P. A., Naus, M. J., & Liberty, C. Rehearsal and organizational processes in children's memory. *Child Development,* 1975, *46,* 818–830.

Pelham, W. E., & Ross, A. O. Selective attention in children with reading problems: A developmental study of incidental learning. *Journal of Abnormal Child Psychology,* 1977, *5,* 1–8.

Reese, H. W. Verbal medation as a function of age level. *Psychological Bulletin,* 1962, *59,* 502–509.

Rosner, S. R. Primacy in preschoolers' short-term memory: The effects of repeated tests and shift-trials. *Journal of Experimental Child Psychology,* 1972, *13,* 220–230.

Sabo, R. A., & Hagen, J. W. Color cues and rehearsal in short-term memory. *Child Development,* 1973, *44,* 77–82.

Siegel, A. W., & Allik, J. P. A developmental study of visual and auditory short-term memory. *Journal of Verbal Learning and Verbal Behavior,* 1973, *12,* 409–418.

Siegel, A. W., Allik, J. P., & Herman, J. F. The primacy effect in young children: Verbal fact or spatial artifact? *Child Development,* 1976, *47,* 242–247.

Spiker, C. C. Verbal factors in the discrimination learning of children. In J. C. Wright & J. Kagan (Eds.), Basic cognitive processes in children. *Monographs of the Society for Research in Child Development,* 1963, *21* (Whole No. 2), 53 -68.

Tarver, S. G., Hallahan, D. P., & Kauffman, J. M. Verbal rehearsal and selective attention in children with learning disabilities: A developmental lag. *Journal of Experimental Child Psychology,* 1976, *22,* 375–385.

Veroff, J., & McClelland, L. Incidental learning of adults of different social backgrounds. *Developmental Psychology,* 1974, *10,* 301–302.

Wagner, D. A. The development of short-term and incidental memory: A cross-cultural study. *Child Development,* 1974, *45,* 389–396.

Wagner, D. A. The effects of verbal labeling on short-term and incidental memory: A cross-cultural and developmental study. *Memory & Cognition,* 1975, *3,* 595–598.

Wambold, C. L., & Hayden, C. Training cognitive strategies in the mildly retarded: An applied approach. *Education and Training of the Mentally Retarded,* 1975, *10,* 132–137.

Zigler, E. Mental retardation: Current issues and approaches. In M. L. Hoffman & L. W. Hoffman (Eds.), *Review of child development research* (Vol. 2). New York: Russell Sage Foundation, 1966.

Zigler, E. Developmental versus difference theories of mental retardation and the problem of motivation. *American Journal of Mental Deficiency,* 1969, *73,* 536–555.

5
Imagery and Associative Memory

Hayne W. Reese
West Virginia University

I. INTRODUCTION

In this chapter, the effects of imagery on associative memory are described and interpretations of these effects are discussed. The chapter begins with a general examination of mnemonic imagery and its historical background, continues with an analysis of methodological issues in imagery research, and ends with a review of the relevant research and theoretical interpretations.

A. Functions of Mnemonic Imagery

Images have been assumed to have at least three general functions that can affect memory:

1. One is very direct: The image is simply assumed to be especially memorable (e.g., Berol, 1913). Thus, imaginal encoding is automatically an effective aid to memory.[1] This assumption is rejected in the present chapter because it is both an explanatory principle and a statement of the empirical phenomenon it explains. Such circularity is unacceptable unless all other explanatory attempts fail.

2. Images have been assumed to affect memory through dual coding (e.g., Paivio, 1971). Imaginal memory is apparently independent of verbal memory (Paivio, 1975a, b), and therefore if material to be remembered is encoded in both imaginal and verbal form, there will be two possible ways to gain access to the material when retention is tested. In contrast, if the material is encoded in only

---

[1] Titchener (1909) said of the term *imaginal,* "I wish that we had a better adjective! [p. 7]" It seems superior, however, to *imagistic.*

one form, there will be only one possible way to gain access to it. The probability of successful access is assumed to be greater when there are more possible ways of access.

3. Finally, images have been assumed to provide an effective framework for organizing the material to be remembered, or unitizing it, by representing items as interconnected or associated (e.g., Köhler, 1929). The organization of the material is assumed to increase its memorability. Images that have this function are referred to as *compound images*.

The dual-coding function of images is emphasized in the area of free recall, while the organizing function is emphasized in the area of paired-associate learning and retention. The concern in the present chapter is with associative memory and, hence, with imagery in paired-associate tasks. As noted by several theorists, associations cannot be learned in a paired-associate task until the response items have been learned, and the stimulus items presented as retrieval cues cannot function unless they are recognized as the stimulus items. The inherent memorability of images could aid in stimulus recognition and response learning, and the organizing function could affect the associative component of paired-associate learning.

The dual-coding function of imagery is also relevant to associative memory if it is assumed that acquisition consists of storing two-item clusters (the two items in a cluster would be the stimulus and response items of a pair). According to dual-coding theory, the imaginal and verbal systems are independent, and therefore the retrieval cue must be in the same modality as the item to be remembered. Consequently, dual coding would be more effective than single-modality coding only if (1) the single modality used for storage is not the same as the modality of the retrieval cue and (2) the retrieval cue is not recoded into the required modality.

In later sections, the explanatory power of the assumed memory functions of imagery is examined. As already noted, however, the inherent memorability assumption is rejected as circular; hence, the comparisons are between the organizing function and the dual-coding function. These two assumed functions are not new conceptions but, rather, have a long history of independent development, which is summarized in the next section.

B. Historical Background

Two lines of development in the history of imagery can, with some stretching of the imagination, be related to the three assumed functions of mnemonic imagery. One line was clearly "psychological" even in its inception in the writings of ancient Greek philosophers and also in its later course, and can be related to the inherent memorability and dual-coding assumptions. The other line started with the use of imagery in oratory, first as an aid to the orator and later as an aid to the audience as well. This "mnemotechnic" use of imagery dropped out of scholarly curricula during the Renaissance but continued to be a popular memory art. The mnemotechnic line can be related to the organizing function of mnemonic imagery.

In the "psychological" line the role of imagery in memory was not emphasized, while in the mnemotechnic line imagery was explicitly a memory aid. These historical lines are summarized in the rest of this section. It will be seen that the relations to the modern assumptions about imagery functions are not as clear-cut as implied in the preceding comments; rather, it is a matter of different emphases.

1. The Image in Psychology

Imagery was of interest in classical Greece not only as a memory aid (Aristotle, 1912 ed., p. 67) but also as a theoretical construct used to explain thinking. Imagery was of central interest to psychologists in the classical era of psychology, beginning with John Locke and extending in the twentieth century to Wundt and Titchener. In this era, both *image* and *idea* referred to images, the first term when the sensory character was examined and the second when meaning was examined (see Angell, 1908, p. 201). The interest was in imagery in these senses more than as a memory aid. There was little research on the mnemonic functions of imagery; in fact, some classical psychologists considered the mnemonic systems based on imagery to be of little value, useful only for remembering such things as "a great many unrelated numbers" (Angell, 1908, pp. 242–243; see also Sully, 1891, p. 292 and footnote 1, p. 298; Upham, 1869, pp. 364–365; Quintilian was among the early doubters of the efficacy of mnemonic imagery—see Yates, 1966, p. 24). The mnemonic function of imagery was therefore not emphasized. Nevertheless, images were at least implied to be intrinsically memorable because they were considered to be the source of meanings, and meanings must have a memorable source in order to be readily available to consciousness.

With the advent of behaviorism and its denial that conscious contents are susceptible to scientific study, interest in imagery waned. Meaning became verbal, and the image—when discussed at all—became conditioned sensation. Between (roughly) 1920 and 1960, there was little research on imagery and even less on its mnemonic function. Beginning around 1960, however, interest in imagery, particularly mnemonic imagery, increased greatly. The reasons for this renewal of interest are not yet clear, but it is noteworthy that while the assumption that images are memorable was revived, the memorability of words also continued to be accepted as given.

2. Mnemotechnics

The deliberate use of imagery as a memory aid has a history spanning 25 centuries. The details of this history can be found in Yates' *Art of Memory* (1966), which is the source of the outline given here.

The Greek poet Simonides is credited with having invented a "places and images" memory system in the first quarter of the fifth century B.C. The system had reached the textbook stage in Rome early in the first century B.C., and the textbook—the *Ad Herennium*—had a sustained influence on memory systems through the Renaissance and into the modern era. The system appears, for example, in writings by Cicero, Albertus Magnus, Thomas Aquinas, Francis Bacon, and Leibniz. Toward the end of the Renaissance, however, it developed formally into an occult, heretical art, fell into disrepute, and eventually was dropped from scholarly curricula, although the nonoccult version has remained a popular art, in modified form, even to the present.

In the places and images system, the first step is to select a series of places or locations that produce clear and distinctive memory images in a well-ordered sequence. The second step is to form images for the material to be remembered, such as the main points in a speech or the words in a serial list. Next the latter images are "placed" sequentially into the imagined locations; that is, one imagines the first item in the sequence in the first location, the second item in the second location, and so on. Finally, to remember the material, one takes an imaginary stroll past the memory locations and retrieves from each one the image stored there. When the system works—and there is considerable evidence that it can be highly effective—all of the material is remembered in the correct order. However, according to the *Ad Herennium,* confusion can result from the use of memory locations that are too much like one another. In modern terms, the system involves paired-associate learning; the imagined locations function as stimulus items and the imaginal representations of the material to be remembered function as response items. If the "stimulus" items are similar to one another, there is intralist interference. The implication is that imagery facilitates paired-associate learning, according to the *Ad Herennium,* but does not reduce intralist interference.

In the *Ad Herennium,* it was asserted that the same set of locations can be used again and again for remembering different material. The images placed in the locations need to be rehearsed to be maintained; they fade with disuse, permitting images for new material to be placed with no confusion. In modern terms, use of the system reduces associative interference (interference with second-list acquisition) and reduces proactive interference (interference with delayed recall of the second list), but increases retroactive interference (forgetting of the first list). Later we shall see that these beliefs are only partially supported by research, but the point of immediate relevance is that the image is clearly seen as effective in associative memory. In discussing the system, Albertus Magnus noted that "because reminiscence requires many images, not one, . . . we should figure to ourselves through many similitudes, and unite in figures, that which we wish to retain and remember" (cited in Yates, 1966, p. 68). One could hardly hope for a clearer statement of the utility of unitization through compound imagery.

In the *Ad Herennium,* a distinction was made between memory for ideas and memory for words. (This distinction can be interpreted as a precursor of Tulving's [1972] distinction between "semantic" and "episodic" memory, although the relation between the distinctions is not clear-cut.) According to the *Ad Herennium,* memory for ideas can be based entirely on imagery; but while memory for words is facilitated by imagery, it also requires rote learning. Neither imagery nor rote learning was believed to be strong enough by itself to produce good memory for words, but they were believed to supplement each other to enhance memory for words.

The imagery mnemotechnic is not limited to the use of locations as stimulus items, but can be used with any kind of imaginable material. The key principle is to imagine the material to be remembered as interacting in some way. In a modern application, Atkinson (1975) has used the system to teach Russian vocabulary to college students. The Russian words are presented with their English equivalents in a paired-associate format, and the students are instructed to link each Russian word to an acoustically similar English word and then to link the latter word by compound imagery to the English equivalent of the Russian word. Research on the method is summarized later, in the section on "Practical Implications."

3. Comparison between the Two Lines

1. *Inherent memorability:* In classical psychology, it was believed that images are inherently memorable, but in early mnemotechnics it was believed that rehearsal or repetition is required to maintain images in memory. In modern mnemotechnics, there is generally no mention of a need for repetition (e.g., Berol, 1913; Edwards, 1963), implying an assumption of inherent memorability.

2. *Dual coding:* The history of imagery in psychology seems to reflect the dialectical principle of negation of the negation: The early behaviorists rejected (negated) imagery and relied on the verbal system to explain memory, but imagery was eventually revived as a separate memory system while the verbal system was retained (negation of the negation). The result is the dual-coding conception. In mnemotechnics, the emphasis was on what is now called compound imagery, but in the *Ad Herennium* the treatment of memory for words— requiring rote learning as well as imagery—hints at dual coding. However, the use of imagery for word memory was not considered to have much practical value (see Yates, 1966, pp. 14–15).

3. *Organizing function:* In classical psychology, the use of imagery in associative memory was considered to be artificial and impractical. In mnemotechnics, the practical value of this function was emphasized.

C. Definitions of Imagery

Throughout the preceding discussion, it was asserted that images are effective aids to memory. But what are these "images"? There are several views.

1. General Approaches

If "image" is a primitive predicate, it is incapable of being given a verbal definition, and is definable only by denotation, that is, by pointing at its referents. Obviously, no objective referents can be pointed at, but Skinner (1945) suggested ways in which the definition by denotation could be learned. According to Skinner, verbal behavior is acquired through differential reinforcement supplied by the "verbal community." The reinforcement is given contingently, following occurrences of a particular verbal response in the presence of a particular discriminative stimulus. The discriminative stimulus for appropriate verbalizations about images is a private event, but Skinner suggested that the verbal community can base the reinforcement contingency on *inferences* about occurrences of the private event, using observation of (1) public stimuli that tend to accompany the private event or (2) "collateral" overt responses that tend to be aroused unconditionally by the private event. Skinner suggested as an alternative mechanism the process of transfer or "stimulus induction": The community supplies reinforcement only on the basis of public stimuli, but control of the verbal behavior transfers to private simuli that are partly similar to the public stimuli. Here, according to Skinner, the verbal response refers metaphorically to the private stimulus. Thus, the community attempts, through inference, a direct "denotation" of the appropriate occasions for particular verbalizations, or the "denotation" is metaphorical and occurs spontaneously through transfer. The approach is appealing because of the many problems associated with the other approaches; but it seems to have gained little favor among researchers who study imagery.

If "image" is not a primitive predicate, then it requires a verbal definition in order to be meaningful. The problem of defining imagery verbally is complex (see, e.g., Bugelski, 1971; Pylyshyn, 1973; Richardson, 1969, chap. 1). Part of the complexity is in the number of alternative approaches that can be taken. The mentalistic approach is to define an image as an experience like a sensation but in the absence of the ordinary sensory stimulation (cf. Berlyne, 1965, p. 130). The learning-theory approach is to define it as a conditioned sensation (see Bugelski, 1970). The behavioristic approach is to define "having an image" as "performing as though absent stimuli were present'' (Spiker, personal communication, June 1970). (These definitions are examples; others were offered in each approach.) The operational approach is to define imagery in terms of operations or manipulations used and consequences observed.

Each approach has been criticized by some and extolled by others. For example, Bugelski (1971) has argued that the operational approach is circular. However, it is no more so than for any other intervening variable or inferred entity (see Reese, 1971). Similarly, there is no untoward circularity in behaviorally defining images as "the processes Ss said they followed when instructed to 'picture' the . . . articles'' (Bugelski, Kidd, & Segmen, 1968). Nevertheless, there are problems with a behavioral definition of imagery. The definition quoted from Bugelski et al., for example, refers to *verbal* reports by *instructed* subjects, and does not cover verbal reports given spontaneously by uninstructed subjects or unreported processes in any subjects.

Actually, most researchers—including those who offer behavioral definitions—seem to believe that there is some subjective referent of the term. They write as though the definition they are using implicitly is mentalistic even when their explicit definition is not. Perhaps, however, they have in mind a denotatively learned meaning of *image*.

2. Imagery as Independent Variable

Another problem, about which there has been some controversy, is whether imagery can be an independent variable or must be a dependent variable (Brainerd, 1971; Bugelski, 1972; La Fave, 1972). However, the controversy seems to be based on a failure to distinguish between methodological and theoretical paradigms. The distinction between independent variable and dependent variable is methodological; the distinction between cause and effect is theoretical (Rychlak, 1974). Clearly, imagery cannot be manipulated experimentally in any direct sense; the experimental manipulation involves instructions or materials, and if imagery is affected, it is affected as a dependent variable. However, it can be an "independent variable" in the theoretical sense of "cause." Experimental manipulations can be theorized to affect such variables as processes, states, stages, and other hypothetical constructs, and by this assumption such constructs, including imagery, become "independent variables" (see Bugelski, 1972). Imagery, then, can usefully be treated as an independent variable in experimental studies (see La Fave, 1972). However, caution is required because what is observed is a relation between independent and dependent variables defined in the methodological sense. The inference that the causal variable is imagery can be strong only if alternative causes are ruled out by theoretical analysis of control manipulations.

In nonexperimental studies of imagery, there is no actual manipulation but, rather, selection of persons on the basis of organismic variables that are presumed to be related to imagery. Examples are deafness and self-reports about imagery, which are discussed in a later section. In the methodological sense, independent and dependent variables are clearly identified, but the interpretation of the independent variable is ambiguous (Lindquist, 1956). The problem is theoretical: Although inferences about imagery can be made, their empirical support is tenuous because the independent variable may index other variables in addition to imagery. Note, however, that the problems are the same in kind as in experimental studies. In the logical process generating the inference (see Reese, 1971), imagery may be conceptualized as a dependent variable (e.g., "aphasia results in certain imagery deficits"); nevertheless, in inferences about performance, imagery will be conceptualized as an independent (causal) variable (e.g., "because of imagery deficits, aphasics exhibit certain performance deficits"). The empirical strength of the inference derives from the strength of the tie between the empirical independent variable and the theoretical independent variable.

D. Types of Images

Images are traditionally divided into two general classes: imagination images and memory images (for more elaborate classification schemes, see Horowitz, 1970; Richardson, 1969). Imagination images include hallucinations, dreams, and in general all imagery not related *directly* to phenomena that have been sensed previously. Memory images include afterimages, eidetic images, and in general all imagery related directly to phenomena experienced previously. The concern in this chapter is with memory images, but with the understanding that in some cases the memory image may reflect memory for an imagination image. Two elements may be imagined in a relationship that has not been experienced before—an imagination image—but the imagery will not affect retention unless it is remembered—a memory image.

Although the concern of the chapter is with memory images, two kinds of memory images—afterimages and eidetic images—will not be dealt with in the later sections. As is shown in the rest of the present section, they are severely limited in functional significance with respect to the mainstream of research on memory.

1. Afterimages

Afterimages are formed by prolonged fixation on a target stimulus and then, after the target stimulus is removed, fixation on a blank screen. The afterimage of the target stimulus is experienced as projected on the screen. Several attributes of afterimages are summarized in Table 5-1, to provide contrasts with eidetic images and other memory images. As can be seen, afterimages (1) are experienced as projected, rather than as "in the mind"; (2) move when the eyes move; (3) cannot be controlled (enhanced or suppressed) directly by the person experiencing them; (4) can fuse with sensations to create a new percept; (5) tend to

TABLE 5-1
Attributes of Memory Images

	Type of image		
Attribute	Afterimage	Eidetic image	Other memory images
Projection	Yes	Yes	No
Movement with eyes	Yes	No	No
Controllability	None	Much	Most
Fusion	Yes	Yes	No
Vividness	High	High	Low
Detail	Much	Much	Little
Duration	Brief	Long	Brief
Retrievability	No	No	Yes

Note: Adapted primarily from review by Richardson (1969).

be vivid and detailed; (6) are brief in duration, although they are prolonged by longer fixation and by more intense target stimuli; and (7) cannot be retrieved after they have faded.

The afterimage may be positive but more commonly is negative. In a positive afterimage, the imagined brightness and color relations are the same as in the target stimulus; in a negative afterimage, the brightness relations are reversed, and the colors are the complements of those in the target stimulus. When a positive afterimage is experienced at all, it is typically briefer than negative afterimages.

There are reports of afterimages to imagined stimuli (see Barber, 1971). If imagined stimuli originate in the central nervous system, as is usually assumed, rather than in peripheral receptors, then these reports imply that afterimages also have a central origin. However, Barber (1971) has suggested that demand characteristics were not controlled in the studies yielding these reports. Afterimages are generally believed to have a peripheral origin, specifically continuation of retinal activity. For example, although they move with the eyes, their retinal location is fixed. They are therefore sometimes called aftersensations.

The functional significance of afterimages may be that they prolong the time available for stimulus processing. If so, then it might be important that the afterimage is usually negative, because when negative it is presumably more easily discriminated from actual sensation than when positive.

2. Eidetic Images

An eidetic image is aroused by examination of a target stimulus, and is experienced as a projected reproduction of the target stimulus. Other attributes are summarized in Table 5-1. The relative frequency of eidetikers—persons capable of eidetic imagery—was estimated in the older literature to be as high as 100% in childhood and to decline to zero in adulthood (for review, see Gray & Gummerman, 1975; Haber & Haber, 1964). However, modern estimates are that only 0–11% of children are eidetikers (Gray & Gummerman, 1975; Leask, Haber, & Haber, 1969; Richardson, 1969), and that the relative frequency changes little, if at all, with increasing age.

It has been theorized that eidetic imagery is functionally significant to the extent that abstract modes of representation are restricted (e.g., Paivio, 1971, p. 482). If so, its relative frequency should be enhanced in the young, the illiterate, and the mentally retarded and brain damaged. As noted in the preceding paragraph, it does not seem to occur with enhanced frequency in the young. Furthermore, there is no good evidence relating it to illiteracy (see Gray & Gummerman, 1975; Richardson, 1969). There is, then, reason to question the purported functional significance of eidetic imagery. It may have a high rate of incidence in the mentally retarded and brain damaged, perhaps as much as three times higher than in normal children (see Paivio, 1971, pp. 481–482), but the between-study variability in estimates of relative frequency "has overshadowed any between population differences" (Gray & Gummerman, 1975, p. 395).

Additional evidence against any special functional significance of eidetic imagery is found in studies of its effect on memory. Paivio (1971) suggested that in some persons eidetic imagery produces "astounding accuracy [p. 481]." However, Leask et al. (1969) found that children who used eidetic imagery in a memory task were no more accurate in recall than noneidetikers (see also Gray & Gummerman, 1975). Furthermore, the eidetikers in the Leask et al. study reported that, when left to their own devices in a memory task, they did not rely on their eidetic imagery but suppressed it to allow other types of processing to occur. This strategy is useful especially when the retention interval is long, because although the eidetic image has a long duration relative to some other types of image, it generally begins to fade in a matter of minutes and when gone is not recoverable.

The nature of eidetic imagery and its functional significance are not well established, and Gray and Gummerman (1975) have concluded that the difference between eidetic imagery and ordinary memory imagery is quantitative rather than qualitative. However, this view ignores the general inability to recover the eidetic image once it has faded, in contrast to the relative ease of recovering an ordinary memory image. This difference seems too striking to be classed as quantitative.

II. METHODOLOGICAL PROBLEMS

A. Methods of Manipulating Imagery

Four methods, one nonexperimental and three experimental, have been used to manipulate imagery. Researchers could dispense with the term *imagery* and refer to the method used (a strategy once imposed on the author by the editor of a journal), but because the four methods often yield essentially similar relations to independent and dependent variables, the four terms they operationally define can be "collapsed" (Spiker & McCandless, 1954) for many purposes and replaced by a single term. The single term might as well be imagery, since the researchers believe that this is what is being manipulated anyway. There are, however, some differences among the four terms, and therefore it is sometimes useful to retain the operational distinctions. The four methods are described in this section, and the differential effects they produce are considered in later sections.

1. Individual Differences

The nonexperimental method of manipulating imagery is to select subgroups of individuals who exhibit differences in imagery type or imagery ability as assessed by tests. Relatively standardized tests are available (see, e.g., Forisha, 1975; Richardson, 1969; Sheehan, 1972), but they are not highly correlated (DiVesta, Ingersoll, & Sunshine, 1971; Forisha, 1975). In addition, "pure" imagery types are not found (e.g., Carey, 1915), although "dominant" types are (e.g., Pear, 1924). Perhaps it is not surprising, therefore, that this method of manipulating imagery has seldom been utilized in research on memory. When utilized, however, the results have implied that spontaneous use of compound imagery as a mnemonic aid is more likely in persons who have strong visual imagery than in persons who have weak visual imagery (Ernest & Paivio, 1969; Hollenberg, 1970).

2. Instructions to Use Imagery

One of the two methods used most frequently with older children and adults is to instruct one group to use mnemonic imagery and to omit any reference to mnemonic imagery in the instructions to another group. An example is a paired-associate study with fifth graders (Spiker, 1960, Exp. III).[2] The children in one group were told a "secret" about how to get a good score: "Picture to yourself a boat made of cake, etc." The children in another group were encouraged to learn the pairs, but were not given imagery instructions. Similarly, in a serial-learning study with college students, Bugelski (1968) began by teaching the students a rhyming code for numbers, such as *one—bun* and *two—shoe*. Then students in an experimental condition were instructed to form a mental picture of an

---

[2] Grade is reported here because it was the developmental index variable used by the experimenter. Age may be a better index variable, but characterizing a grade by its mean age can be misleading, and it is cumbersome to use age ranges. Furthermore, age range has seldom been reported in the relevant studies, and sometimes not even the mean age is reported. Throughout the chapter, therefore, the index variable used is the one used by the experimenter. In general, however, a rough age equivalent in years can be obtained by adding 5.5 to the grade level.

interaction between the referent of an item and the referent of the code word for the serial position of the item. Students in a control condition were not told anything about "mental pictures." (For a description of additional control conditions, see Paivio, 1968a.)

Instructions to form a separate image of each item do not facilitate performance (e.g., Bower, 1972; Dempster & Rohwer, 1974), presumably because these instructions do not induce compound imagery.

There has been little research so far in which young children were given imagery instructions. The reason seems to be that investigators in the 1960s did not believe that instructions would be effective with young children because of problems in conveying the notions of "image" and "interaction between items." This belief was supported by research in which instructions were found to be ineffective for young children (Montague, 1970; Rohwer & Eoff, cited in Rohwer, 1973; Wolff & Levin, 1972), but has been disconfirmed by more recent research in which imagery instructions have been used successfully with kindergarten and first-grade children (Danner & Taylor, 1973; Varley, Levin, Severson, & Wolff, 1974; Yuille & Catchpole, 1973). Levin and his co-workers have shown that manipulative activity is an effective, but not necessary, component of imagery instructions for young children (e.g., Varley et al., 1974; Wolff & Levin, 1972; Wolff, Levin, & Longobardi, 1972, 1974).

3. Manipulating Characteristics of Items

The other method used most often with older children and adults is to manipulate the characteristics of the items, without mentioning imagery in the instructions. The two characteristics that have most often been manipulated to control imagery have been rated concreteness and rated image-arousing capacity. The two characteristics are highly correlated (Paivio [1968b] obtained a correlation of .78) and have been used interchangeably. According to Paivio's (1971) theory, the concreteness of an item is related directly to the probability that it will arouse an image. Thus, for example, a concrete word like *house* is assumed to be more likely to arouse an image than a less concrete word like *domicile*. These particular words also differ in meaningfulness and frequency, but neither of these item characteristics is strongly correlated with rated image-arousing capacity (r's = $-.09$, $+.02$, respectively; Paivio, 1968b).

Paivio's assumptions about the probability of imaginal encoding of different types of items are given in Table 5-2. It can be seen that objects and pictures are assumed to have a greater probability of dual coding than words. It might be thought that nonsense syllables would be the lowest in this hierarchy, but the association value of a nonsense syllable apparently reflects the probability of coding the syllable as a noun, and when this coding occurs the noun apparently tends to be concrete (the evidence for this inference is discussed in the section on "Differential Effects of Stimulus and Response Imagery").

When appropriate characteristics of items are manipulated, it is assumed that

TABLE 5-2
Predicted Encoding of Input Items[a]

	Encoding system	
Input Item	Imaginal	Verbal
Object	+ + + +	+ +
Picture	+ + +	+ +
Concrete word	+ +	+ + +
Abstract word	+	+ + +

Note: The greater the number of pluses, the greater the assumed probability of encoding in the system.
[a] Based on Paivio (1971, pp. 179–180 and Fig. 7-1, p. 179).

the probability of using imagery is manipulated even though no instructions to use imagery are given. For example, it is assumed that a group given concrete words will use imagery spontaneously and a group given abstract words will not use imagery. It should be noted that the "imagery" group—the group given concrete words, for example—is the same as the control group used when imagery is manipulated by instructions, in that this control group is also given concrete words and is also given no imagery instructions. Thus, it should not be surprising that somewhat different results are obtained when imagery is manipulated by instructions and when it is manipulated by characteristics of items.

4. Imposed Elaboration

The other experimental method, the one used most often with young children, is called pictorial elaboration. Items are pictured as associated or organized in some way, and the memory image of the picture is assumed to be a compound image. In the control condition, items are pictured side by side but not otherwise associated.

An analogous manipulation is to present verbal items embedded in a phrase or sentence—"imposed verbal elaboration." In the control condition, the words are presented without this kind of verbal context.

B. Distinguishing Compound Imagery from Verbal Elaboration

A problem in research on the functions of imagery is to determine whether the observed effects actually result from compound imagery or result from elaboration of a verbal phrase or sentence. For example, when instructions are used to manipulate imagery, they generally include an example of a compound image, as in Spiker's instruction to "picture a boat made of cake." The phrase "a boat made of cake" is a verbal elaboration of the pair *boat-cake,* and the verbal elaboration could be used as the mnemonic aid rather than an image of a boat made of cake.

Similarly, when pictorial elaboration is used it is possible that the person spontaneously describes the elaborated picture, yielding a verbal elaboration that could serve as the mnemonic aid. The method is similar to Woodworth's (1938, p. 41) method of "learning by the eye or the ear," which is contaminated because persons may verbalize the names of pictured items or visualize the referents of words.

Instructions to generate verbal elaborations have been compared with instructions to generate compound imagery in several studies, and in other studies imposed verbal elaborations have been compared with imposed pictorial elaborations. The typical finding for college students is more facilitation with visual elaboration than with verbal, but because of the contamination problem this finding proves nothing about the nature of the mnemonic mediator actually used. Both elaboration groups could be using imagery, or both could be using verbal elaboration. If details of results are examined, however, the nature of the mediator used can be inferred, provided that a theory is available to serve as a basis for the inference (see Reese, 1971).

Redintegration theory can provide the needed basis for inference. "Redintegration" means that a compound is remembered when an element it contains is presented (e.g., Horowitz & Prytulak, 1969). As Lindworsky (1931) expressed it, "if a *part* of . . . a complex is given, a reproduction does not reinstate the following *part,* but rather the *whole* complex." He suggested, with great foresight, that "perhaps the whole theory of memory will some day have to be reconstructed on this idea [p. 230]."

The subject noun of a sentence usually is more effective as a redintegration cue than any other element in the sentence. However, a compound picture can be redintegrated equally well by any element it contains. Thus, in a paired-associate task forward recall should be greater than backward recall if verbal elaboration is used with the stimulus words as the subject nouns, and forward and backward recall should be equal if compound imagery is used. Research has shown that putative verbal elaboration conditions tend to yield better forward recall than backward recall, and putative compound imagery conditions tend to yield about equal recall in both directions (e.g., Davidson & Dollinger, 1969; Kausler & Gotway, 1969; Lockhart, 1969; Mondani & Battig, 1973; Yarmey & O'Neill, 1969; for review, see Paivio, 1971, pp. 276–285). This research provides relatively clear-cut confirmation of the theoretical predictions, and therefore permits relatively clear-cut inferences about the mediators used. In some studies, however, the evidence about the mediators is inconclusive because the predictions were confirmed only in part rather than in full (e.g., Cole & Kanack, 1972; Yarmey & Ure, 1971).

Another, perhaps less convincing source of evidence about the nature of the mediator is the self-reports of persons questioned about the mediators they used. The mediators reported can be reliably classified into verbal and imaginal types,

but several problems arise when such reports are interpreted to reflect the mediators actually used. First, the reports may indicate only that persons have *beliefs* about the kind of mediators they use, not that they actually use the kind suggested. Second, in groups given imagery instructions there is an implied demand to report imaginal mediators. Finally, experimenter bias may inadvertently influence a person's reports through subtle changes in the questions asked in the postexperimental interview. The problem of bias can be guarded against more effectively than the other two problems, by video taping the session, deleting the person's responses, and having judges rate the imagery demand implied in the interviewer's comments and gestures (for example, the interviewer might be found to express more approval or enthusiasm in response to reports of imagery).

Also relevant to self-report evidence about mediators is research in which instructions and concreteness of items have been manipulated jointly. Paivio, for example, has shown that imagery instructions are more effective with concrete items than with abstract items, and that verbal elaboration instructions are more effective with abstract items than with concrete items. Although this particular interaction has been demonstrated empirically, it is difficult to obtain, since many persons given imagery instructions with abstract items report that they ignored the instructions because of the difficulty of following them and instead used verbal elaboration (for review, see Paivio, 1971). These reports, coupled with failure to obtain the interaction, strongly imply that verbal mediators were used.

Inferences about mediators can sometimes be based on an analysis of errors. When the material to be learned consists of words and persons give synonyms in the recall test, it can be inferred that the mnemonic code was imaginal and that the synonyms reflect decoding errors. For example, Calkins (1898) reported that college students in a free-recall task sometimes made such errors as recalling *mat* when *rug* was the correct word and *light* when *lamp* was correct. This kind of intrusion is not often reported in paired-associate studies (see Paivio, 1972, p. 269), perhaps because synonyms are generally accepted as correct responses. However, it could add to an argument that the mnemonic code was imaginal and not verbal. The argument would not be strong, because an assumption that the mnemonic code is semantic—that is, that *meanings* are stored in memory— would also explain synonymic errors.

Evidence that seemed to support the theory that meanings rather than images are stored was reported by Neisser and Kerr (1973). Imposed sentences with imagery instructions facilitated the performance of college students as much when one of the elements was described as concealed as when it was described as not concealed. However, the "concealed" elements, such as an item in Napoleon's breast pocket, were not concealed in the images reported by the students in a postexperimental interview. These elements were reported as being seen moving into concealment or as being visible by X-ray vision or the like.

Evidence about modality-specific interference can also be used as a basis for inferences about the mediators used. Interference by interpolated tasks generally is greater when the modality in the interpolated task is the same as in the target task than when it is different (e.g., Bigham, 1894; Brooks, 1967; Pellegrino, Siegel, & Dhawan, 1975, in press; Sasson & Fraisse, 1972). This result is predicted by dual-coding theories (e.g., Paivio, 1971); hence, the modality producing more interference implies the modality of coding. For example, if more interference is produced when the items in the interpolated task are visual than when they are verbal, it can be inferred that the target modality is also visual. Regardless of whether the items *presented* in the target task were visual or verbal, the inference would be that the target items were coded in the visual modality; that is, they were coded as images (see Elliott, 1973; Wicker & Holley, 1971).

Still another kind of evidence about the mnemonic mediator used is available in research in which the persons studied were selected to be verbally inept. For example, paired-associate acquisition with imposed pictorial elaboration has been studied in deaf children and in young preschoolers. Neither population is verbally adept, and therefore children from these populations should have a reduced tendency to verbalize descriptions of the pictorial elaborations. Verbal descriptions of pictures by young preschoolers are more likely to be the types that Rohwer (1967) has found to be nonfacilitative than to be the facilitative types (Reese, 1975b). Nevertheless, children of this age exhibit facilitation from pictorial elaboration, implying that the mediator is a compound image.

To summarize, several kinds of evidence can be used to check the possibility of a person's crossing between the verbal and imaginal modes and thus contaminating the experimental conditions. In general, the relevant research suggests that this crossing is uncommon, but the use of such checks is nevertheless still desirable.

III. IMAGERY IN PAIRED-ASSOCIATE TASKS

A. Theoretical Background

In all modern American theories of memory, memory requires cognitive processing of material.[3] The processing transforms the material, and the nature of the

---

[3] Examples are the "information-processing" theory of Shiffrin and Atkinson (1969), the "depth-of-processing" theory of Craik and Lockhart (1972), the "level-of-coding" theory of Paivio (1971), and the "common-code" theories of Anderson and Bower (1973) and Rohwer (1973) (see also Potter & Faulconer, 1975; Tulving & Watkins, 1975). The processes are conceptualized as storage and retrieval operations in the Shiffrin–Atkinson and Craik-Lockhart theories; they are assumed to be hierarchically organized in the Craik-Lockhart and Paivio theories; and they are modality-free propositions (Anderson & Bower, 1973; Attneave, 1974; Pylyshyn, 1973) or modality-free "meanings" (Rohwer, 1973) in the common-code theories. For discussion of information-processing theories, see Reese (1973, 1976b); and for discussion of common-code theories, see Paivio (1975a, b).

transformation depends on the nature of the processing. The processing can be either deliberate or involuntary according to several theorists (see Brown, 1975a), but the kinds or processing involved in associative memory seem to be deliberate (e.g., Rohwer, 1973). Deliberate processing must be induced, either by the demands of the task itself or by some external prompt. Task demands are not as effective for young children as for older individuals, but external prompts can be effective, especially when the processing required is relatively simple.

Rehearsal is a relatively simple processing operation, or "strategy," and it apparently can be induced by instructions even in young children (e.g., Hagen, Jongeward, & Kail, 1975; Millar, 1972). It can also be induced by manipulation of the way material is presented, as demonstrated in the following studies. Reese (1972) and Forbes and Reese (1974) presented four paired-associate lists, all with the same stimulus items. In one condition, the items in a pair were pictured side by side and the lists were presented in the usual way: $A-B$, $A-C$, $A-D$, $A-E$. In another condition, List 1 was presented in the usual way, but for the subsequent lists the new response items were progressively added to form rows of pictures: $A-B$, $A-B-C$, $A-B-C-D$, $A-B-C-D-E$. The latter condition can be interpreted as "imposed rehearsal." If it induced the rehearsal strategy, a person would attend to every item in the row. The most appropriate strategy for acquisition of a single list in the imposed-rehearsal condition is to attend only to the first and last items (the stimulus item and the currently appropriate response item), and therefore rehearsal of all the items presented would interfere with acquisition of the later lists. However, List 4 was followed by a test for retention of all four lists, and rehearsal would enhance retention of the earlier lists by increasing the amount of practice on them. Both of these effects were obtained in preschoolers: the imposed-rehearsal condition yielded slower acquisition but better retention of the "primacy" lists (Reese, 1972). The same primacy effect in retention was obtained in college students (Forbes & Reese, 1974). Thus, the data imply that the rehearsal strategy was induced even in young children.

In the processing theories, images are not inherently memorable but must be processed in order to be retained. The processing that generates the kind of images that facilitate associative memory—compound images—is believed to be more complex than the simple rehearsal strategy just discussed. We have seen that rehearsal can be induced by instructions and by manipulation of materials. The question to be addressed now is whether the more complex processing that produces compound images, "elaboration," can be induced in analogous ways.

Instructions to generate compound images facilitate retention even in kindergarten children (e.g., Wolff & Levin, 1972; Yuille & Catchpole, 1973); consequently, it can be inferred that instructions induce the elaboration strategy. Presenting items high in imagery value (or high in item characteristics related to imagery value) also facilitates retention, even in 4-year-olds (Evertson & Wicker, 1974), and hence can also be inferred to induce elaboration. The remaining question is whether imposed pictorial elaborations induce the elaboration strategy.

According to the processing theories, a pictured elaboration will not be memorable unless it is processed appropriately (e.g., Turvey, 1973). Furthermore, the processing is deliberate, not involuntary. It may seem strange to assume that an elaboration strategy must be induced even when the material presented is already elaborated, but a different version of the assumption may clarify the issue. Reese (1970c) assumed that when a pictorial elaboration is presented, a person must "read" the picture to extract contextual meaning, that is, meaning given by the items in the context of the relation depicted. (The "reading of images" metaphor appears in the *Ad Herennium,* and derives from the older Greek metaphor of memory as a wax tablet. Berlyne [1965] attributed it to Plato in *Theaetetus.* See also Yates, 1966, pp. 7, 35–36.) The "reading" or extraction of meaning requires understanding, and understanding involves conceptualization, which is an elaboration from the picture presented.

Pictorial elaboration facilities retention in college students (e.g., Forbes & Reese, 1974) and in nursery school children (e.g., Reese, 1972) and, hence, can be inferred to induce elaboration. However, the facilitation produced by pictorial elaboration in young children is sometimes relatively less than in older children (see Reese, 1970c). Thus, pictorial elaborations may not always induce the elaboration strategy in young children; young children may be deficient in the "reading" of images.

A problem with the above-mentioned research on the ability of pictorial elaborations to induce compound imagery is that the test is indirect. Maus, Nappe, Trestrail, and Wollen (1972) used a method that provides a somewhat more direct test. They assessed retention in college students after several delay intervals, and found that although imposed elaborations facilitated retention, the effect disappeared when the associations that were correct in long-term retention were deleted from the tests for short-term retention. Thus, pictorial elaborations facilitated retention only if they induced storage in long-term memory, which is the theoretically expected result of using the elaboration strategy.

Kee and White (1975) used a method that provides an even more direct test. They compared the effects of pictorial elaborations and side-by-side control pictures in intentional and incidental memory conditions. In an intentional memory condition, the instructions explicitly refer to the memory requirement; in an incidental memory condition, the memory requirement is not mentioned. The intentional memory instructions are assumed to induce the elaboration process, but the incidental memory instructions should not induce this process. Therefore, if pictorial elaborations facilitate performance equally in the two conditions, it can be inferred that the pictorial elaborations automatically induced the elaboration process. Kee and White tested second graders and obtained equal facilitation from imposed elaborations in the intentional and incidental conditions, but a complication in the design of the study prevented a clear-cut inference. The inference can be clear-cut only if the cognitive activity induced by the incidental memory instructions does not aid memory. Referring to memory in the instructions is not the only way to induce cognitive activities that aid memory (Jenkins, 1974), and unfortunately, the nature of the cognitive activity induced in the incidental memory condition in the Kee and White study is not known.

The validity of the criticism is indicated by research showing that appropriate cognitive activities can be aroused without mentioning memory. Yarmey and Bowen (1972), for example, found that imagery instructions facilitated recall whether or not the memory requirement was mentioned in the instructions. Wolff, Levin, and Longobardi (1974) seem to have obtained a similar effect in kindergarten children, although the results were ambiguous in this respect because the no-elaboration control condition was not included. The children were tested in pairs, in which one child manipulated the objects and the other child passively observed the manipulations. The performers and observers did not differ in immediate recognition memory, but the performers were superior after a 24-hour delay. Memory instructions had no effect.

Hale and Piper (1974) used a variant of the incidental memory design with children 8, 11, and 14 years old. An intentional learning task was given to all children, followed by an incidental memory test. Line drawings of six animal-object pairs were presented in a horizontal array in the intentional learning task, and the children were required to learn the serial positions of the animals. This task was followed by a test for memory of the animal-object pairs, requiring incidental associative learning. The pairs were presented in elaborated pictures or unelaborated pictures. Intentional learning, which involved associations between animals and positions, improved with increasing age; incidental learning did not vary with age, and was inferior to intentional learning. Furthermore, presenting the pairs in elaborated pictures did not influence performance. The pattern of results implies that the elaboration strategy was not automatically induced by the elaborated pictures; otherwise the incidental associative learning would have been facilitated by these pictures. Elaboration of the animal-object pairs would be irrelevant to the intentional learning task; hence, task demands apparently influence the ability of elaborated pictures to induce the elaboration strategy, even in relatively old children.

B. Effects on Acquisition

1. Effects of Source of Images

According to the *Ad Herennium* (Yates, 1966, p. 92), everyone must form his own memory images in order for them to be memorable. In modern terms, self-generated images should be more facilitative than images suggested by someone else. The research evidence does not support the *Ad Herennium*, as shown in Table 5-3. The findings summarized in Table 5-3 may reflect a developmental trend in the relative effectiveness of imagery instructions and im-

TABLE 5-3
Imagery Instructions Versus Imposed Pictorial Elaborations

Study	Kindergarten	1	2	3	4	5	6	College	Elderly
Clarkson et al. (1973)					+		+		
Danner and Taylor (1973)	0		0				+		
Davidson and Levin (1973)			$-^a$		$-^a$				
Jusczyk et al. (1975)	0			0				0	
Kemler and Jusczyk (1975)[b]	−			$-^a$				$-^a$	
Kerst and Levin (1973)					0	0			
Rohwer (1971)[c]	0		0				0		
Rohwer et al. (1971)	−								
Treat and Reese (1976)								0	+
Wolff and Levin (1972, Exp. I)	−		$-^a$						

Note: + means instructions superior; − means imposed elaborations superior; 0 means equal effectiveness.
[a] Difference nonsignificant.
[b] Imagery instructions compared with an imposed elaboration condition in which verbal elaborations were imposed with imagery instructions.
[c] Also, equal effectiveness in Grades 8 and 11.

posed pictorial elaborations, although the evidence for the trend is certainly not strong.

A problem in interpreting such age and condition differences in that the differences obtained must depend in part on how effectively the instructions and elaborations used induce the processing that produces compound imagery, rather than depending only on the relative effectiveness of self-generated images per se. If the instructions are not sufficiently clear to induce a person to generate compound images, then pictorial elaborations may be more effective; and if the pictorial elaborations are poor in quality, instructions may be more effective.

It is possible to get information relevant to the effectiveness of the conditions in inducing compound imagery by asking persons to describe the images they generated. Of course, they could be describing verbal elaborations rather than compound images, but the descriptions are typically detailed, and Bugelski (1968) has suggested that reports of details in purported images imply that the persons are actually describing images. Delin (1968) found that bizarreness and activity in reported images were correlated with accuracy of 15-week retention, which could be interpreted as evidence that his instructions to form bizarre and active images were effective. However, although bizarreness and activity are recommended in the *Ad Herennium* and later treatises (see Yates, 1966), either manipulations of bizarreness have had no effect (e.g., Wollen, Weber, & Lowry, 1972), or bizarreness has interfered with performance. Heinen and Kulhavy (1973) found that college students did better with nonbizarre pictures than with bizarre ones, but the "bizarre" pictures were absurdly bizarre, and Rohwer (1967) has found that analogously bizarre sentences do not facilitate perform-ance. The relevance of these studies is questionable, because the memory treatises refer to bizarreness in self-generated images, and the studies cited have involved bizarreness in imposed elaborations. In a study with bizarreness man-ipulated by instructions (Wood, 1967, Exp. I), bizarreness interfered with col-lege students' performance, and although the interference was not significant, the data contradict the memory treatises.

The effectiveness of pictorial elaborations in inducing compound imagery is more difficult to assess, because relatively few studies have been designed to identify the effective attributes of pictorial elaborations. Bizarreness has been found to be ineffective, as already mentioned, but the amount of detail in the pictures is sometimes effective. Holyoak, Hogeterp, and Yuille (1972) found that performance by kindergarten and third-grade children was better when elaborated pictures used in the study trial were line drawings than when they were color photographs, implying that less detailed pictures are more effective, but line drawings were used in the test trial and therefore the effect may have been on stimulus recognition rather than on associative memory. A similar finding was obtained by Heinen and Kulhavy (1973): Line drawings were more effective than colored drawings as study materials for college students, but since the test items were printed words, stimulus recognition rather than associative memory may have been involved. Consistent with this suggestion, the effect of color was the same for elaborated and unelaborated pictures. Details had no effect in three studies, in which color photographs were as effective as objects for first and third graders (Yuille & Catchpole, 1973, Exp. I), and line drawings were as effective as colored drawings for preschool and kindergarten children (mean ages = 4.5 and 5.5 years) (Emmerich & Ackerman, 1976) and college students (Paivio, Rogers, & Smythe, 1968a). Details facilitated performance in three studies: Iscoe and Semler (1964) found that objects were more effective than color photographs for normal 6-year-olds and for 12-year-old retarded chil-dren; Evertson and Wicker (1974) found that objects and color photographs were more effective than line drawings for nursery school and first-grade children; and Wicker (1970b) found that color photographs were more effective than line drawings for college students, although not significantly so. In general, then, details may or may not aid performance, but they rarely if ever interfere.

Animated cartoons are more effective memory aids than static representations of interactions (Rohwer, 1967). If there is movement in the memory images generated by the cartoons and not in those generated by the static representations, then movement is an effective attribute. The classical treatises recommended "images that move," but this phrase seems to have meant images that move memory, or that move the emotions, mind, or soul (cf. Yates, 1966, pp. 9–10, 206, 248, 299). Active images were also recommended, apparently not in the sense of moving but as opposed to representing passive figures. Yates (p. 12) described an example of an "active" image, from the *Ad Herennium,* that seems to be not moving and not passive, that is, to be a static representation of active figures. The same is true of Yates' example (p. 285) of an "animated" image from Platt, published in 1592, and her examples (pp. 337–338) from Willis, published in 1621 and 1661, in which figures are "standing together with sacks of corne," "pouring wheate out of a sacke," "whetting their sithes." The upshot is that Rohwer's data may indicate that images containing "active" figures are more effective than ones containing passive figures. Activity, in this sense, can be manipulated in pictorial elaborations, as demonstrated by Friedman and Stevenson (1975), and could easily be manipulated in imagery instructions. (However, whether the differential instructions would differentially induce images representing active versus passive figures is another matter.)

The conclusion, then, is that there has been no decisive demonstration of the relative effectiveness of self-generated images versus "imposed" images—as distinguished from the relative effectiveness of imagery instructions versus imposed pictorial elaborations. The research evidence shows that instructions are generally either equal or inferior to imposed elaborations in effectiveness; it is the meaning of this fact that is unclear.

2. Effects of Mode of Elaboration

According to Rohwer (1973), compound imagery should yield the same retention as verbal elaboration, since the effect of both is mediated by the creation of "shared meaning." It should be apparent that the relative effectiveness of the two modes of elaboration cannot be assessed directly, because the experimental manipulations—whether imposed elaboration or instructions—may not be equally effective in inducing the two modes of elaboration. The effects of visual versus verbal *manipulations* can be compared; again, however, the meaning of the comparison is unclear.

The relevant evidence is summarized in Table 5-4. Overall, visual elaborations have been superior to verbal elaborations more often than not, but a developmental trend is apparent in the relative effects of visual and verbal elaboration instructions. The general superiority of visual elaboration is found only after the fourth or fifth grade when elaboration is manipulated by instructions. However, this trend seems more likely to result from the relative effectiveness of the instructions than from the relative effectiveness of the visual and verbal modes of elaboration. The results summarized in Table 5-3 show that imagery instructions are often inferior to imposed pictorial elaborations until the sixth grade, demonstrating that the visual mode of elaboration can be used effectively during the early developmental period and implying that this mode of elaboration is induced more effectively by imposed pictorial elaborations than by imagery instructions.

This interpretation of the developmental trend for instructions is also supported by a comparison with the findings for imposed elaborations. As can be seen in Table 5-4, the general superiority of visual elaborations has been obtained at every developmental level except the nursery school level when imposed elaborations are used. The difference in the transitional age for instructions and for imposed elaborations is most parsimoniously interpreted to be an artifact of the method of manipulation. In addition, it can be seen in Table 5-4 that the *direction* of the difference between visual and verbal elaboration has not been found to reverse between age groups *within* any study. Even the less striking change from positive or negative difference to no difference has been obtained within only three of the studies, one with imposed elaborations (Jusczyk, Kemler, & Bubis, 1975) and two with instructions (Horvitz & Levin, 1972; Levin, McCabe, & Bender, 1975). Thus, the evidence for a developmental trend in the effectiveness of instructions comes more from comparisons between studies than from comparisons within studies. In short, this developmental trend seems not to merit further consideration.

As mentioned earlier, another developmental trend apparent in Table 5-4 is a change in the relative effectiveness of imposed visual and verbal elaborations between the nursery school level and later levels. The summary of results in the table implies that this trend also comes more from between-study comparisons than from within-study comparisons, but within-study findings too fine grained to be represented in the table provide evidence for the trend. In some of the earlier research, two kinds of developmental trend were obtained. The absolute effectiveness of visual elaboration increased with age in some studies; and in some studies its effect relative to verbal elaboration increased with age. That is, the difference between visual elaboration and no-elaboration conditions increased with age, or the difference between visual and verbal elaboration conditions decreased with age (Davidson & Adams, 1970; Milgram, 1967; Reese & Palermo, 1970; Rohwer, 1967; for review, see Rohwer, 1973). These results have not been replicated in more recent studies. For example, Lampel (1973) found that the effectiveness of visual elaboration did not vary with age (3, 4, and 6 years). Reese (1970b) found visual elaboration superior for younger children and verbal elaboration superior for older children, and although the difference between the visual and verbal conditions was not statistically significant at either age the trend is inconsistent with the earlier results.

Some investigators have concluded that the contradictory results indicate that the developmental phenomenon is fragile (e.g., Rohwer, 1973), but it is possible that the discrepancy in results reflects a cohort change such that young children in the later studies were more advanced cognitively than their age peers of the 1960s cohorts (Reese, 1974, 1976a). The nature of the cohort change is that imposed pictorial elaboration is now more effective in inducing young children to form compound images (or "shared meanings," or whatever the relevant process is assumed to be) than it was for young children in the 1960s. Although this statement may seem to be merely a rewording of the empirical phenomenon, the explanation is actually not circular because the cohort change is in cognitive

TABLE 5-4
Visual Versus Verbal Elaboration

Study	N	K	1	2	3	4	5	6	MR	College
				Grade level						
				Imposed elaborations						
Davidson and Adams (1970)				−[a]						
Frederiksen and Rohwer (1974)					+					
Evertson and Wicker (1974)	+	.	+							
Holyoak et al. (1972)		+			+					
Jones (1973)	+									
Juszczyk et al. (1975)										
Recall			+			+				0
Recognition			+[a]			+[a]				0[a]
Kee (1976)				+[a,b]	+[a,b]					
Kee and Rohwer (1970)										
Recall				+						
Recognition				−[a]						
Kee and Rohwer (1973)				+[b]						
Kee and Rohwer (1974)				−[c]	−[c]					
Kemler and Jusczyk (1975)			+			+				+
Kerst and Levin (1973)						−[a,c]	−[a,c]			
Marshall (1965)										+
Means and Rohwer (1974)	0	0				0				
Milgram (1967)	−			−		−				
Odom and Nesbitt (1974)		+[c]					+[c]			
Reese (1965)	−[b]									
Reese (1966)	−[c]									
Reese (1970b)	0									
Rohwer and Ammon (1971)				+						
Rohwer et al. (1967)			+[c]		+[c]			+[c]		
Rohwer et al. (1971)		+	+		+					
Rohwer et al. (1975)	+[b]	+[b]		+[b]						
				Instructions						
Bower and Winzenz (1970)										+
Dempster and Rohwer (1974)										
Exp. I								+		
Exp. III								+[c]		
Horvitz and Levin (1972)[d]					0			+		
Kemler and Jusczyk (1975)			−			−				−
Kerst and Levin (1973)						0[a]	0[a]			
Levin et al. (1973)										
Recall				+[c]		+[c]				
Recognition				+[a,c]		+[a,c]				
Levin et al. (1975)	−	0								
McCabe et al. (1974)[e]	+									

TABLE 5-4 *(continued)*

Study	N	K	1	2	3	4	5	6	MR	College
						Grade level				

Instructions

Study	N	K	1	2	3	4	5	6	MR	College
Paivio et al. (1968b)										+[f]
Paivio and Yuille (1969)										+[f]
Raser and Bartz (1968)										+
Rimm et al. (1969)										+
Taylor (1970, Exp. III)						+				
Taylor and Black (1969)							+			
Taylor et al. (1969)			0	0						
Taylor et al. (1972)								+[c]		
Taylor et al. (1973)								+[c]		
Whitely and Taylor (1974)									0	
Wood (1967)									0	
Yuille and Paivio (1968)										
Abstract										0
Concrete										+[c]

Note: + means visual superior; − means verbal superior; 0 means no difference. N refers to nursery school, K kindergarten, and MR mentally retarded.
[a] Recognition.
[b] Significance not tested.
[c] Nonsignificant.
[d] Combination of imposed and instructed elaboration.
[e] Child manipulates objects in imagery condition.
[f] Reported images versus reported verbal mediators.

abilities of greater scope than the assumed memory processing. One source of the cohort change might be the educational television program *Sesame Street* (Reese, 1974), which accelerates the rate of cognitive development in children who view it (Ball & Bogatz, 1972).

3. Developmental Effects

As already mentioned, deliberate memory processing is less likely to occur in young children than in older individuals. The young child may spontaneously use very simple memory strategies, such as frequent looking or touching in a delayed-reaction test (e.g., Wellman, Ritter, & Flavell, 1975), but these strategies are little if any more advanced than the orienting behaviors of infrahuman species in similar tasks (e.g., Hunter, 1913). When the memory task is more complicated than the delayed-reaction test, young children sometimes do not use an appropriate strategy spontaneously (e.g., Appel, Cooper, McCarrell, Sims-Knight, Yussen, & Flavell, 1972; for review, see Brown, 1975a; Hagen et al.,

1975); sometimes they use an inefficient strategy (e.g., Cuvo, 1975; Siperstein & Budoff, 1975); and sometimes they use a strategy inefficiently (e.g., Friedrich, 1974; Jablonski, 1974; Kobasigawa, 1974). Often a strategy can be induced, as already noted (see also Brown, 1973), but especially when the strategy is complex, more extensive or explicit external prompting is required to induce it than is required for older individuals (Kobasigawa, 1974; Rohwer, 1973; Turnure & Thurlow, 1973). In addition, even when induction is successful, young children sometimes do not continue to use the induced strategy when the prompt is removed (Gruenenfelder & Borkowski, 1975; Hagen, Hargrave, & Ross, 1973; Turnure & Thurlow, 1973), although this transfer is sometimes obtained (Reese, 1970c, pp. 405–406; Yuille & Catchpole, 1974). These findings are consistent with processing theories in which a hierarchy of mnemonic strategies is assumed (see Footnote 3), in that increasingly complex strategies are used spontaneously with increasing age, and induction of complex strategies becomes easier with increasing age (see Reese, 1976a, b).

As noted in the preceding subsection, pictorial elaboration has sometimes been less effective than verbal elaboration for young children, while the two types of elaboration are equally effective for older children or pictorial elaboration is more effective. This developmental trend, as noted, has not been obtained in recent research, perhaps because of a cohort change in the rate of cognitive development. Nevertheless, the trend appears to have been real, and deserves theoretical analysis. An entire symposium was devoted to explanations of the trend (Reese, 1970a), and tests of the hypotheses generated have been reported (e.g., Emmerich & Ackerman, 1976; Rohwer, Kee, & Guy, 1975). One hypothesis was that images must be detailed in order to be effective (Reese, 1970c). The materials used when the developmental trend was obtained were line drawings, which are relatively devoid of details. If young children are less likely or less able than older individuals to construct detailed images from such pictures, the hypothesis explains the developmental trend. The results of relevant studies have been mixed, in that no effect of added details was obtained in one study with preschoolers (Emmerich & Ackerman, 1976) and facilitation was obtained in another (Evertson & Wicker, 1974), but in both studies the findings were the same for older children as for the preschoolers. The lack of a developmental trend, as well as the lack of facilitation for preschoolers, contradicts the hypothesis.

4. Differential Effects of Stimulus and Response Imagery

As mentioned earlier, rated concreteness and image-arousal capacity of items are highly correlated in adults, and manipulating these attributes experimentally has yielded the same pattern of results. Similar results have been obtained with manipulation of other attributes that theoretically are related to imagery (e.g., generality-specificity: Paivio & Olver, 1964). Therefore, these attributes are collectively referred to here as "imagery value."

High imagery value is more facilitative on the stimulus side of paired associates than on the response side (see Paivio, 1971). An effect on the stimulus side could be attributed to an effect on stimulus recognition, and an effect on the response side could be attributed to an effect on response learning. Thus, a possible explanation of the differential effectiveness of imagery on the stimulus and response sides is that it facilitates stimulus recognition more than response learning. The effect on stimulus recognition would presumably result from an effect of imagery on item differentiation (see section on "Effects on Interference"), and although the response items should also become differentiated, they would not necessarily become more available in free recall (the standard measure of response learning). The suggested explanation has experimental support, but as shown later, it nevertheless is weak.

In support of the suggested explanation, Dempster and Rohwer (1974) found that compound-imagery instructions enhanced stimulus recognition (Exp. I, III) and response learning (Exp. II) in sixth graders, but the effect on response learning was relatively weak. Kee and Rohwer (1974) found virtually no effect on response learning in second and third graders, and results obtained by Bender and Taylor (1973) can be interpreted to indicate no effect on response learning in mental retardates. It appears, therefore, that compound imagery facilitates stimulus recognition and has little if any effect on response learning, as assumed in the suggested explanation of the relative effects of imagery value on the stimulus and response sides of paired associates.

This explanation does not require an assumption that imagery affects the associative component of paired-associate acquisition, in that it refers only to the stimulus recognition and response learning components. Therefore, the explanation would be strengthened by evidence that the effects of imagery on the stimulus and response sides are independent of its effect on the associative component. Dempster and Rohwer (1974, Exp. III) have reported relevant data: Instructions to form separate images of the stimulus and response items facilitated stimulus recognition as much as compound-imagery instructions did. Instructions to form separate images of the items do not facilitate associative recall (Bower, 1972; Dempster & Rohwer, 1974), and hence presumably do not affect the associative component of paired-associate acquisition. However, it appears that the effect of imagery on stimulus recognition is less important than its effect on the associative component of paired-associate acquisition (in spite of Wicker's, 1970a, opposite conclusion). Compound-imagery instructions facilitate both associative recall and stimulus recognition, and therefore the effect on associative recall *could* be mediated by the effect on stimulus recognition. In contrast, separate-imagery instructions facilitate stimulus recognition but do not affect associative recall, implying that stimulus recognition does not mediate an effect on associative recall (see also Wicker & Edmonston, 1972).

An alternative, more plausible explanation of the differential effects of imagery value on the stimulus and response sides of paired associates can be derived from redintegration theory. The associative component is assumed in redintegration theory, in that the theory deals with holistic compounds. "Redintegration" means that an element in a compound arouses the whole compound and not merely another element. In the present context, redintegration means that the stimulus item retrieves the stimulus–response association by retrieving the compound image. In contrast, if the stimulus–response association is learned by conditioning, the stimulus item should retrieve only the response item. Items with a high probability of free recall are more effective as stimulus items if retrieval is redintegrative and are more effective as response items if retrieval is based on conditioned association (Horowitz & Prytulak, 1969; see also Horowitz & Manelis, 1972). Items with high imagery value have higher probabilities of free recall than items with low imagery value (e.g., Engel, 1969; Kossuth, Carroll, & Rogers, 1971; see review by Paivio, 1969). Consequently, high-imagery items should be more effective on the stimulus side if retrieval is redintegrative and more effective on the response side if retrieval is based on conditioned association. Assuming that retrieval is redintegrative when imagery is used therefore explains the differential effects of imagery value on the stimulus and response sides of paired associates.

Paivio has suggested a somewhat different explanation based on the concept of redintegration. According to Paivio (1971), imagery value is more important on the stimulus side because of its relation to the probability of dual coding (see Table 5-2): "When the stimulus is presented alone its image-arousal value would be particularly crucial because the stimulus must serve as the cue that redintegrates the compound image from which the response component can be retrieved and recoded as a word [pp. 247–248]." As illustrated symbolically in Figure 5-1, the assumptions are that the mnemonic mediator is a compound image, and that it can be redintegrated only by an image of one of its components, not by a word.

In the redintegration explanations, it is assumed that a compound image is formed when one of the items is high in imagery value, even when the other item is low in imagery value. Yarmey and Paivio (1965) and Paivio and Madigan (1968) found that imagery value had a stronger effect on the stimulus side than on the response side even when words were paired with nonsense syllables. This result, obtained in college students, fits the theory only if it is assumed that the students coded the nonsense syllables as concrete nouns, then recoded the nouns as images and incorporated them in compound images.

In some studies, sets of items rather than pairs have been presented (for review, see Paivio, 1971). Redintegration theory may seem to require recall of all items in the set rather than partial recall. However, after redintegration occurs the unit retrieved must be decoded into elements for output, and nothing in redintegration theory would prevent decoding errors, including errors of omission. Furthermore, complete recall would not by itself rule out the alternative

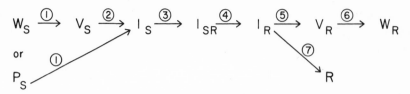

FIGURE 5-1 Symbolic representation of redintegration theory of compound imagery. Symbols: W = word (or nonsense syllable); P = picture; V = code in verbal system; I = code in imagery system. Subscripts: S = stimulus item; R = response item; SR = compound of S and R (a product of Paivio's associative level of processing). Processes: (1) encoding (Paivio's representational level of processing); (2) recoding (Paivio's referential level of processing); (3) redintegration; (4) retrieval; (5) decoding; (6) output of verbal recall response (vocal or written); (7) output of recognition response (e.g., pointing).

possibility, learning by conditioned association, because more than one response can be conditioned to a stimulus, forming a hierarchy of conditioned responses that can be run through in a chainlike fashion. Thus, the occurrence of complete recall is neither necessary nor sufficient to demonstrate retrieval by redintegration as opposed to conditioned association.

5. The Decoding Problem

A theoretical problem is to explain how the correct response is retrieved from a compound image when verbal recall is required. The research surveyed in the present section suggests a solution. According to Paivio (1971), objects are more concrete than pictures, and pictures are more concrete than words. The assumption seems reasonable, in that objects are by definition concrete; pictures are representations of objects and are not as detailed (as noted by Iscoe & Semler, 1964), and words even if highly concrete are still symbolic and therefore always general. Performance with object pairs is generally better than with picture pairs, as already noted, and performance with picture pairs is better than with word pairs (Evertson & Wicker, 1974; Hughes & Walsh, 1971; Rohwer & Ammon, 1971; Rohwer, Ammon, Suzuki, & Levin, 1971; for review, see Paivio, 1971). Exceptions to the trend have been obtained. Yuille and Catchpole (1973, Exp. I) obtained no difference between objects and picture pairs in first and third graders. Similarly, Yarmey and Bowen (1972) tested normal and retarded children 8 to 13 years old, and obtained the usual difference between picture and word pairs when imagery instructions were given but no difference with no-elaboration instructions. However, a floor effect was apparent in the latter condition. Reversals of the difference have also been obtained. Yarmey and Sayer (1972) found that word pairs were more effective for college students than picture pairs, and Cramer (1975) obtained the same effect in children from Grades 2, 4, and 6. However, the pictures in the Yarmey and Sayer study were drawn by the students, and the word pairs in the Cramer study formed commonplace compound words such as *milk-man, cow-boy,* and *cup-cake.*

The effects of pictures and words on the stimulus and response sides of paired associates have been compared in several studies. Here, a typical finding for children (Dilley & Paivio, 1968) is

Picture–Word > Picture–Picture = Word–Word > Word–Picture.

That is, for children pictures are more effective than words on the stimulus side but words are more effective than pictures on the response side. Because pictures have higher imagery value than words, the trend is not consistent with the trends obtained when imagery value of words is manipulated directly.

One interpretation of these findings is that children have difficulty in verbal decoding of pictorial response items (Paivio, 1970; Rohwer, 1970). The superiority of pictures over words on the stimulus side suggests that redintegration is involved. Free recall is better for objects or pictures than for words, especially when the words are abstract but also when they are concrete (e.g., Cole, Frankel, & Sharp, 1971; Kirkpatrick, 1894; Kossuth et al., 1971). Items with a high probability of free recall are more effective on the stimulus side when retrieval is redintegrative (Horowitz & Prytulak, 1969). If it is a compound image that is redintegrated, then the person must retrieve from it the image of the response component and then, because the task requires verbal responses, must decode this image into a verbal response (see Fig. 5-1).

When the response items presented are pictures, the child apparently has trouble decoding the response image retrieved from the compound image. However, when the response items presented are words, they are apparently stored in verbal memory. Data from free-recall and recognition studies support these conclusions (e.g., Davies, 1969, 1972). The assumption is that verbal storage of response items affects the response-learning component of paired-associate acquisition, but compound imagery affects the associative component. Presumably, when the image of the response item is retrieved from the compound image, the child scans the permissible verbal recodings—the list of verbal response codes stored in memory. The verbal storage enhances performance by limiting the choices for verbal coding of the response image. Data obtained by Means and Rohwer (1974) are consistent with this interpretation. They found that experimenter-supplied labels enhanced the effect of imposed pictorial elaboration for preschoolers but not for first and fourth graders, presumably because the older children spontaneously supplied their own labels. The assumption, in full, is based on dual coding. The concrete-word response item is stored in the verbal system with the other response items and is stored in the imaginal system in a compound image. A response list consisting of words is stored either more easily or more accurately than a list consisting of pictures.[4]

---

[4] A theoretical problem is to explain how the response list is retained in verbal memory. If it is retained in short-term memory, an implication is that delay of the associative-recall test should reduce the facilitating effect of compound imagery, because the response list would be less available for use in response selection. The amount of reduction should be less in a recognition test, for which the verbal decoding problem does not arise. There appears to be no study providing relevant data.

The preceding discussion is especially relevant when the subjects are children. When college students are tested, problems associated with decoding are minimized. A typical finding (Paivio & Yarmey, 1966) is

Picture–Word > Picture–Picture > Word–Picture > Word–Word.

The trends obtained when imagery value of words is directly manipulated differ from this trend only in the relation between the first two combinations, implying that the decoding problem is not as important for college students as it is for children.

Evidence that is directly relevant to the decoding hypothesis under consideration has been obtained from comparisons of recall with recognition; the decoding problem does not arise when recognition is required, and therefore pictures should be more effective than words as response items in a recognition test. The evidence is mixed. Supporting the decoding hypothesis, Homzie, Noyes, and Lovelace (1973) obtained the usual superiority of picture–word pairs over picture–picture pairs in *recall* by second graders, but *recognition* was better with picture–picture pairs than with picture–word pairs. Calhoun (1974) obtained the same effects in 4-year-olds and in children from Grades 1, 3, and 5. However, Jones (1973) found that recognition was more accurate in 3- to 4-year-old children when pictures were presented in the test than when words were presented (aurally), even when the study trial items were words. Further evidence that is inconsistent with the decoding hypothesis has been obtained with other procedures. Yuille and Catchpole (1974) found that imagery instructions were equally effective for recall and recognition in first graders, and Jusczyk et al. (1975) found that imposed pictorial elaborations were superior to imposed verbal elaborations for recall as well as recognition. The children tested in the latter study were first and fourth graders. Different results have been obtained with second graders (Kee & Rohwer, 1970): Imposed pictorial elaborations were more effective for recall and imposed verbal elaborations were more effective for recognition. Davidson and Adams (1970) also obtained better recognition in second graders given imposed verbal elaborations.

In summary, the decoding hypothesis explains the differential effects of pictures and words on the stimulus and response sides of paired associates, and the hypothesis is supported by much of the research in which recall and recognition are compared. However, the results of some of this research are inconsistent with the decoding hypothesis. The discrepancies need to be resolved through further research.

C. Effects on Long-Term Retention

Reese (1970c) predicted, on the basis of a cognitive theory, that long-term retention of paired associates will deteriorate more when compound imagery is used in acquisition than when verbal elaboration or rote learning is used. In contrast, the processing theories seem to predict that visual and verbal elaboration will facilitate long-term retention equally. Deeper processing, for example, or "shared meaning," yields longer retention, regardless of whether visual or verbal material is processed. Only a few relevant studies have been reported, and the findings are inconclusive.

Support for Reese's prediction was obtained in an unpublished study (Reese, 1966), in which preschoolers were tested after a 4- to 5-day retention interval. However, the difference obtained between imposed visual and verbal elaboration was nonsignificant. The children were 4 to 6 years old; they learned a 9-pair list and relearned it 4 to 5 days later. There were three treatment groups: imposed verbal elaboration ($N = 7$), imposed pictorial elaboration ($N = 7$), and no elaboration ($N = 4$). On the first relearning trial, the percentages of correct responses were 95.2, 84.1, and 86.1 for the verbal, imagery, and no-elaboration groups, respectively. The trend of these means supports the prediction, but as noted, the means did not differ significantly. Whether or not the null hypothesis is accepted, however, the results fail to support the prediction from the processing theories, in that either verbal elaboration was superior to visual elaboration or neither was superior to no elaboration. The same trend, nonsignificantly poorer retention with imagery than with verbal elaboration, has also been obtained in kindergarteners and first and third graders with a two-day retention interval (Rohwer et al., 1971).

The predicted advantage of verbal elaboration over compound imagery in long-term retention has clearly not been confirmed in other studies. Reese (1965, 1970b) tested preschoolers' retention two weeks after learning under imposed verbal elaboration, imposed pictorial elaboration, and no-elaboration conditions. As shown in Table 5-5, the compound imagery and verbal elaboration conditions did not differ, and both tended to be superior to the no-elaboration conditions. Kerst and Levin (1973) obtained the same effects for one-week retention by fourth and fifth graders, and for instructed elaboration as well as imposed elaboration. These results are consistent with the prediction from the processing theories.

TABLE 5-5
Two-Week Retention of Paired Associates by Preschool
Children

Condition	Retention (% correct)	
	Reese (1965)	Reese (1970b)
Control (original)	68	62
Control (new)	—	75
Imagery	78	87
Verbal	78	88
Combination[a]	74	—

[a] Imposed imagery plus verbal elaboration.

Calhoun (1974) obtained evidence contradicting both Reese's prediction and the prediction from the processing theories. Imagery was manipulated by comparing picture and word combinations in 4-year-olds and children from Grades 1, 3, and 5. The order of effectiveness for recall after one week was

Picture–Picture > Picture–Word > Word–Picture > Word–Word.

However, the statistical significance of the differences was not reported.

Imagery alone has been manipulated in other studies of long-term retention. These studies are not relevant to the null prediction of the processing theories, but are relevant to their prediction that compound imagery will enhance long-term retention. Reese (1970c) predicted that over a *long enough* interval, imagery will yield less retention than rote learning. Therefore, these studies are relevant but cannot be conclusive because "long enough" has not been delimited. The studies are reviewed in the rest of this section.

In a study by Butter (1970), the response items were digits and the stimulus items were nouns with high or low imagery value. Immediate retention was greater with high-imagery stimuli than with low-imagery stimuli, but there was no difference in 20-minute retention, and retention was greater for low-imagery stimuli after two days. Palermo and Shamp (cited in Palermo, 1970) were unable to replicate the reversal, but found that "the effects of imagery are greatly reduced with time [p. 419]." College students were tested in both of these studies. In two other studies with college students and one with first graders, loss in retention after delays of two to seven days was greater in imagery conditions than in control conditions, but the difference in loss probably reflected a floor effect in the control condition in all three studies (Yarmey & Barker, 1971; Yuille, 1971; Yuille & Catchpole, 1974). These studies support Reese's prediction that imagery will be less effective than rote learning for long-term retention, but the support is not impressive. Furthermore, other studies have yielded contradictory evidence.

Delin (1968) instructed college students to form bizarre and active compound images using as many sensory modalities as possible, and to write a description of each image. (The method used to manipulate imagery is hard to classify; it involved instructions, but the relevant attributes of imagery seem to reflect individual differences.) The descriptions were rated by judges on conformity to the instructions. Retention was tested 15 weeks later, and was found to be significantly and positively correlated with the ratings of the images. This result suggests that long-term retention is better when the compound images are better in quality, which would support the processing theories, but since the no-elaboration control condition was not included in this study, the finding can be only suggestive.

Forbes and Reese (1974) gave college students immediate and one-week retention tests and obtained no difference between pictorial elaboration and no-elaboration conditions in retention loss. Retention *loss* was the appropriate measure in this study because the students were given multiple lists, and there were elaboration effects in immediate retention. (Bower & Reitman, 1972, reported a similar study, but without the no-elaboration control.) Schnorr and Atkinson (1969) and Begg and Robertson (1973) also reported loss measures, for college students' retention after six to ten days, and found reduced losses in imagery conditions.

Three other studies with children have been reported. One, with children from kindergarten and Grades 2 and 4 (Brown, 1975b), was like the Forbes and Reese study in that immediate and one-week retention tests were given after multiple-list learning. One-week retention was better in an elaboration condition than in a no-elaboration condition, but there were also differences in immediate retention. The amount of loss is therefore the critical measure, and although it could be estimated from the means reported, performance was at the chance level in the no-elaboration conditions in both retention tests and the relative amount of loss is consequently uninterpretable.

In the other two studies with children (Reese & Parkington, 1973), only a single list was learned, and therefore the loss measure is not required. In one of these studies, with deaf children 6 to 10 years old, retention in pictorial elaboration and no-elaboration conditions did not differ significantly after one week, and the trend of the means was inconsistent with Reese's prediction, favoring the imagery group (51 versus 44% correct retention). In the other study, with hearing children 4 to 5 years old, pictorial elaboration facilitated one-week retention, significantly in some counterbalancing conditions and nonsignificantly in others.

In summary, the long-term mnemonic effectiveness of compound imagery, relative to that of verbal elaboration, has not yet been determined definitively. In four studies with preschoolers and elementary school children the two kinds of elaboration were equally effective after one- or two-week intervals. However, in two other studies with preschoolers and elementary school children verbal elaboration was more effective, though not significantly so, after intervals of two or four to five days. Similarly, the absolute long-term effectiveness of compound imagery is not yet clear. In four studies with college students and one with children, the effect of compound imagery diminished after intervals ranging from two days to one week, suggesting that compound imagery is less effective for long-term retention than for short-term retention. However, in three other studies, two with college students and one with preschoolers, compound imagery tended to facilitate long-term retention; and in two additional studies, one with college students and one with deaf children, compound imagery neither facilitated long-term retention nor reduced it. More research is obviously needed, especially research in which several durations of the retention interval are compared. Among the 17 studies reviewed, none included more than one long duration, and only two included more than one short duration. One additional study with college students, however, included several very short retention intervals—0, 6, and 18 seconds and about 5 minutes (Maus et al., 1972). Imposed elaboration was equally facilitative at all intervals. It would be particularly useful now to have comparisons between compound imagery and verbal elaboration over a range of long retention intervals.

D. Effects on Interference

1. Theoretical Background

Richardson (1972) questioned whether images can really serve a memory function because they are incomplete: "The amount of concrete detail available . . . is relatively slight [p. 121]." Other researchers have also noted the schematic nature of images (e.g., Piaget & Inhelder, 1971; Reed & Johnson, 1975; Rose, Blank, & Bridger, 1972). However, Bugelski (1968) was impressed by the amount of detail reported in mnemonic images, including color, orientation, ownership, and background. Similarly, data obtained by Hollenberg (1970) imply that mnemonic images are relatively detailed. Hollenberg found that imagery ability in children from Grades 1 through 4 facilitated paired-associate acquisition but interfered with concept formation and concept identification. Details in the images could have directed attention to the distinctive attributes of the items and away from the commonalities within the conceptual categories, thus facilitating paired-associate acquisition and interfering with concept acquisition. It appears, therefore, that even if memory images are not as detailed as percepts—just as pictures are not as detailed as actual objects—they still carry details missing from words.[5]

Palermo (1970) noted that the extra details in images might be expected from a strict stimulus-response position to produce interference. Therefore, the fact that images facilitate performance might seem to be a paradox for a strict stimulus-response position. The paradox is easily resolved, however, because in such a position the definition of the image is operational or behavioral and the problem of "details in images" does not arise.

Imagery might affect performance by increasing the strength of the stimulus-response associations, exactly analogous to the effect of extra training trials. If so, then the facilitating effect of imagery on acquisition and retention would be explained, and in addition, it would be expected that associative and proactive interference would be increased but that retroactive interference would be reduced. The experimental designs for these kinds of interference are described in

---

[5] Hollenberg (1970) used the method of individual differences in imagery ability to manipulate imagery. The interference with concept acquisition was not replicated in a study by Saltz and Finkelstein (1974), who manipulated imagery in second graders by comparing pictures and words. For identification of perceptual concepts ("pointed" and "round"), performance with pictures was much better than with words; and for identification of functional concepts ("toys" and "clothing"), performance was the same with pictures and words. Saltz and Finkelstein agreed, however, that pictures carry more details than words.

detail later. Briefly, two lists are presented, both with the same stimulus items but with different response items. "Associative interference" is interference with *acquisition* of the second list; "proactive interference" is interference with *retention* of the second list; and "retroactive interference" is interference with retention of the first list.

Intralist interference should be increased if imagery increases the strength of stimulus-response associations. As detailed later, intralist interference is studied by varying the similarity of stimulus items in a list, and is assumed to result from generalization among these items, increasing with increasing similarity. As the strength of stimulus-response associations increases, generalization also increases. Thus, an imagery group should be superior to a no-imagery group on a noninterference list, with distinctively different stimulus items, and should be inferior on an interference list, with similar stimulus items.

The preceding predictions are based on the assumption that compound imagery increases the strength of stimulus-response associations. An alternative assumption is that it increases the memorability of the associations; that is, it increases the "availability" or "accessibility" of the memory traces (Tulving, 1974). Acquisition would be enhanced because the association between the stimulus and response items in a pair is contained in the compound image, which would be memorable from trial to trial; and retention would obviously be enhanced. In the transfer designs, if compound imagery increases the memorability of the old pair, it should interfere with acquisition and retention of the new pair, because the stimulus should tend to redintegrate the original compound image rather than the new one, thus increasing associative and proactive interference and reducing retroactive interference. All of these expectations are the same as the ones derived from the "strength of association" assumption. However, the expectation about the effects of imagery on intralist interference is not the same. According to the memorability assumption, the pairs—whether in the interference list or in the noninterference list—should be represented by different memory traces. If imagery increases the availability of these traces, intralist interference should not be affected by imagery because the similar stimulus items should not be efficient retrieval cues—a stimulus item should tend to redintegrate not only the appropriate compound image but also the compound images containing similar stimulus items. Furthermore, if imagery increases the accessibility of memory traces, intralist interference should still not be affected because although the similar stimulus items would be *effective* retrieval cues, they should still be *inefficient* retrieval cues.

The "strength of associations" and "memorability" assumptions are different not only because of their different implications about the effect of imagery on intralist interference but also because they are derived from different types of models. Strength of associations is a concept in stimulus-response associationism, which is consistent with the mechanistic paradigm; and availability and accessibility, which define memorability, are concepts in information-processing models, which, depending on details, are consistent with one or another of the nonmechanistic paradigms (see Overton & Reese, 1973; Reese, 1973, 1976b; Reese & Overton, 1970). Thus, although "strength of associations" is the stimulus–response analog of "memorability," these concepts have somewhat different implications within their own paradigms.

Another alternative assumption about the effect of imagery is that it affects performance by reducing effective stimulus similarity, that is, by increasing stimulus differentiation. As will be shown in the concluding section of this chapter, the effect on stimulus differentiation can be explained within either of the above-mentioned paradigms. If imagery increases stimulus differentiation, acquisition would be enhanced by a reduction of intralist errors, and retention would be enhanced because of the reduction of stimulus generalization or because the effective stimuli, being more differentiated, would be more efficient cues for retrieval. Intralist interference would obviously be reduced and associative interference would be overcome rapidly, but retroactive and proactive interference would not be affected.

2. Intralist Interference

Intralist interference is interference with paired-associate acquisition. It results from the use of similar stimulus items in the list, and is usually assumed to result from stimulus generalization. Reese and Parkington (1973) manipulated stimulus similarity between and within lists in two experiments. In the interference list, six pairs were divided into three two-pair sets, or dyads. The stimulus items were line drawings of animals, and within a dyad the stimuli were conceptually the same (for example, two pigs) but differed formally (for example, one pig standing on all fours and a somewhat different pig standing on its hind legs). In the noninterference list, all six stimulus items were different both conceptually and formally (six different animals). The study-test method was used, with recognition required on the test trials. In the first experiment, with deaf children 6 to 10 years old, pictorial elaboration significantly reduced intralist interference. That is, performance on the interference and noninterference lists differed significantly in the no-elaboration control condition, but not in the imagery condition (see top two rows of Table 5-6). In fact, the means in the imagery condition suggest that pictorial elaboration completely eliminated intralist interference.

Consistent with the assumption that intralist interference results from stimulus generalization, imagery reduced within-dyad intrusion errors, which theoretically result from generalization. Only this type of error was affected by imagery in all counterbalancing subconditions. The means are given in the top two rows of Table 5-7.

An unexpected result of this experiment was that imagery did not facilitate performance in the noninterference list, contradicting a vast literature showing facilitation with such lists in children with normal hearing and a smaller literature

TABLE 5-6
Intralist Interference: Speed of Acquisition[a]

Subjects	Condition	List Interference	List Noninterference[b]
Deaf (Exp. I)	Imagery	3.88	4.13
	No-elaboration	6.12	4.25
Hearing (Exp. II)	Imagery	4.94	3.53
	No-elaboration	8.88	5.63

Note: Body of table gives mean trials to criterion.
[a] After Reese and Parkington (1973, Tables 2 and 4).
[b] Mean of two counterbalanced noninterference lists.

TABLE 5-7
Intralist Interference: Mean Errors in Interference List[a]

Subjects	Condition	Type of Error[b] Within dyad	Type of Error[b] Other
Deaf (Exp. I)	Imagery	1.00	4.13
	No-elaboration	3.62	8.12
Hearing (Exp. II)	Imagery	4.12	3.19
	No-elaboration	6.06	10.37

[a] After Reese and Parkington (1973, Tables 3 and 5).
[b] "Within dyad" refers to within-dyad intrusions; "other" refers to the sum of all other types of errors.

TABLE 5-8
Effects of Imagery on Acquisition in Deaf Children[a]

Condition	Sample size	Measure Trials to criterion	Measure Errors to criterion
Imagery	8	6.8	6.0
No-elaboration	7	12.7	20.6

[a] From Reese (1967).

showing facilitation in deaf children. The latter includes a series of experiments by Bugelski (1970) and an unpublished study by the author (Reese, 1967). In the unpublished study, the procedure was the same as in the Reese and Parkington (1973) study and the list was similar to their noninterference list, except that it consisted of five pairs instead of six. Deaf children 4 to 6 years old were tested. The results are presented in Table 5-8. Imagery facilitated performance, and even with the small sample sizes the effect was highly significant: for trials to criterion, $t(13) = 4.41, p < .001$; and for errors to criterion, $t(13) = 4.43, p < .001$.

The age ranges, list lengths, and other procedural details in the relevant studies were comparable, and therefore there is no obvious explanation of the failure of Reese and Parkington to obtain facilitation in the noninterference list. Nevertheless, the results obtained by Reese and Parkington are consistent internally. Pictorial elaboration reduced intralist interference in the deaf children by reducing stimulus generalization, but as noted in the preceding section, it did not significantly affect long-term retention. Apparently, the imposed elaborations did not affect associative memory but increased the differentiation of the stimuli.

Images may increase stimulus differentiation because they direct attention to the distinctive attributes of the stimuli (cf. Davies, 1972; Hollenberg, 1970). In the noninterference list, the nominal stimuli were already clearly differentiated; hence, the imposed elaborations could not increase their differentiation. Elaborations did not affect the strength or memorability of the stimulus-response associations; hence, performance on this list was unaffected by the imagery condition. In the interference list, the nominal stimuli were similar within dyads, and the imposed elaborations increased their differentiation, hence reducing generalization errors and enhancing performance without directly affecting the strength or memorability of the stimulus-response associations.

In a second experiment, Reese and Parkington (1973) tested preschoolers with normal hearing on the same lists and conditions as had been used in the experiment with deaf children. The results are shown in the last two rows of Tables 5-6 and 5-7. In agreement with the results for the deaf children, pictorial elaborations reduced intralist interference, in that the difference between performance on the interference and noninterference lists was smaller in the imagery condition than in the no-elaboration condition. However, contrary to the results for deaf children, interference appeared in the imagery condition as well as in the no-elaboration condition: Performance was significantly worse on the interference list than on the noninterference list in both conditions. Furthermore, unlike the results for deaf children, the amount of interference was not significantly less in the imagery condition than in the no-elaboration condition. Hence, for the hearing children the inference that imagery reduced intralist interference is not justified statistically. The hearing children, like the deaf children, made fewer generalization errors (within-dyad errors) in the imagery condition than in the no-elaboration condition; but unlike the results for the deaf children, the effect of imagery on generalization errors was not significant for the hearing children, although imagery significantly reduced the other types of errors. Finally, imagery tended to facilitate long-term retention in the hearing children, as noted in the preceding section, and this effect was not obtained in the deaf children.

For the hearing children, the statistically justified inferences are that imposed elaborations did not affect stimulus differentiation (hence did not reduce intralist interference) and did not increase the strength of the stimulus-response associations (hence did not increase generalization and intralist interference), but did increase the memorability of the associations (hence reduced general types of errors, increased the speed of acquisition, and increased long-term retention, all without affecting intralist interference.)

A problem with these inferences is that the nonsignificant trends of the means for the hearing children suggest that imagery reduced generalization errors and intralist interference, as it did in the deaf children and as would be expected if imagery increased stimulus differentiation. In other research, imagery did not reduce generalization errors in one study with college students (Dominowski & Gadlin, 1968), but it reduced generalization errors in another study with college students (Wicker, 1970a) and in one with fifth graders (Spiker, 1960). Therefore, the best course at present may be to suggest that more research is needed, but to conclude tentatively that in hearing children imagery increases stimulus differentiation and increases the strength of stimulus–response associations. This combination of effects would be in conflict in an interference list, in that the increased strength of associations would increase generalization but the increased stimulus differentiation would reduce generalization, yielding the pattern of results actually obtained—a relatively small reduction of generalization errors and intralist interference, together with reduction of other errors, increased speed of acquisition, and increased long-term retention. It could also be argued, however, that the effect of imagery was on stimulus differentiation and *memorability* rather than strength of associations. The same pattern of results would be expected, except that the reduction of generalization errors and intralist interference should have been greater than was actually obtained.

Even with either of these tentative conclusions, the effects of imposed elaboration would not be the same for deaf children and hearing children, in that no effect on strength or memorability of associations was evident in the performance of the deaf children. This difference in effects might be attributable to deafness, but the populations tested by Reese and Parkington also differed in age and other demographic variables, and therefore the causes of the difference in effects of imagery remain to be determined.

3. Associative Interference

Associative interference is interference with second-list acquisition in the $A-B$, $A-C$ paradigm. That is, after learning one list there is interference with acquisition of a second list in which the same stimulus items are paired with new response items. The amount of interference is assessed against a control condition with different stimuli and different responses in the two lists ($D-B$, $A-C$).

As already noted, the assumption that compound imagery increases the strength or memorability of stimulus-response associations implies that compound imagery should increase associative interference. The enhanced strength or memorability of the first-list associations would impede the learning of the second-list associations. As also noted, the alternative assumption—that compound imagery increases stimulus differentiation—implies that associative interference would be neither increased nor decreased on the initial trials of the second list, but the associative interference would rapidly disappear because of the reduction of intralist generalization and consequent enhancement of the speed of learning. Another assumption, proposed by Keppel and Zavortink (1969), is that the use of compound imagery encourages recoding of the stimulus items. The nominally identical stimulus items in the two lists would be represented by different images; for example, the stimulus word *shoe* might be imagined as a brogan in the first list and as an overshoe in the second list. The $A-B$, $A-C$ condition would become $D-B$, $A-C$, and little or no associative interference would be expected. According to this "recoding hypothesis," then, compound imagery should reduce associative interference.

Indirect support for the recoding hypothesis was reported by Davidson, Schwenn, and Adams (1970): Associative interference was reduced in sixth graders when noun pairs were embedded in sentences that changed the meanings of the stimulus items from one list to the next. If the sentences were concrete, they may have been encoded imaginally (Begg & Paivio, 1969; Kee, 1967; Kosslyn & Bower, 1974). Additional support for the recoding hypothesis was obtained by Cavoti (1972), who tested college students with concrete–concrete pairs and abstract–concrete pairs, and found significantly less associative interference with the former in the first two transfer trials. However, the effect was not clear-cut, because concreteness interacted significantly with frequency and with two counterbalancing variables, and the effect of concreteness was not consistent across these interactions. Thus, although the main effect obtained by Cavoti supports the recoding hypothesis, the support is not strong.

Bugelski (1968) has also reported data relevant to the recoding hypothesis. He gave 6 ten-item serial lists to college students. Students in an experimental group were taught concrete code-words for the numbers designating the serial positions—for example, *one-bun* and *two-shoe*—and were instructed to form compound images pairing each list-word with its appropriate code-word. In an interview conducted after the learning session, the students were questioned about the use of mnemonic aids. Bugelski reported that "in 95 instances [students in the experimental group] reported the use of the same mnemonic image, i.e., the same shoe, hive, or hen was noted [1968, p. 332]." That is, in 95 instances recoding did not occur. The problem is to convert this frequency into a relative frequency. The experimental group included 18 students, each reporting mnemonics for 10 items in each of 6 lists, yielding a total of 1,080 mnemonics (18 × 10 × 6). Against this base, 9% of the images were repeated (95 ÷ 1080) and the other 91% were recodings. However, if the 95 instances were instances where the same image was used for a particular stimulus in all 6 lists, then the appropriate base is the total number of possible instances, not the total number of mnemonics. This base is 180 (18 persons × the 10 stimulus code-words that appeared in all 6 lists), and against this base the same image was used in all lists 53% of the time (95 ÷ 180), and recoding occurred the other 47% of the time.

Keppel and Zavortnik (1969) interpreted Bugelski's report the first way, but he actually intended the second interpretation (Bugelski, personal communication, July 17, 1972). Thus, Bugelski's data provide little support for the hypothesis that compound imagery encourages recoding of the stimulus items.

Other evidence against the recoding hypothesis has been reported by Davidson and Levin (1973). They used the associative interference paradigm with second and fourth graders, and included a condition designed to encourage imaginal recoding of the stimulus items. For example, a different kind of key was pictured in the two lists. This imposed recoding condition produced the most associative interference.

The assumptions relating imagery to strength or memorability of associations and to stimulus differentiation have experimental support. Spiker (1960, Exp. III) tested fifth-grade children in the associative interference paradigm and manipulated imagery by instructions. The results are shown in Figure 5-2. Note that performance in the interference condition (A–C) was better in the imagery group (Group M) than in the no-elaboration group (Group C). Without the noninterference control condition (D–C), one might interpret this result to reflect a reduction of associative interference by imagery. However, when the performance in the noninterference condition is taken into consideration, it can be seen in Figure 5-2 that during the first few trials on List 2 there was *more* associative interference in

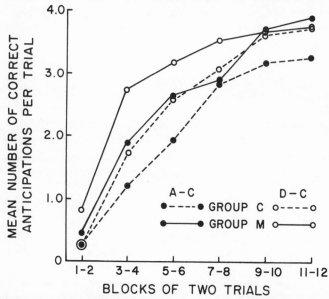

FIGURE 5-2   Associative interference as a function of compound imagery. (From "Associative transfer in verbal paired-associate learning" by C. C. Spiker, *Child Development*, 1960, *31*, 73–87. Figure 3, p. 82. Copyright 1960 by the Society for Research in Child Development. Reprinted by permission.)

the imagery group than in the no-elaboration group. This result clearly demonstrates the necessity to include the noninterference condition in studies of the effects of imagery on associative interference. This control condition was not used in studies by Brown (1975b), Kirk and Johnson (1972), and Reese (1972) with children, nor in studies by Bugelski (1968), Forbes and Reese (1974), Keppel and Zavortnik (1969), and others (see discussion by Paivio, 1971) with college students. Consequently, these studies are ambiguous with respect to possible effects of imagery on associative interference. Wood (1967) included the noninterference control condition in a study with college students, but his results are ambiguous because he did not include a no-elaboration comparison condition. Cheung (1973) included all of the relevant conditions in a study with college students, but no significant associative interference was obtained in any condition; hence, there was no interference to be reduced by imagery.

Spiker had predicted an increase in associative interference in the imagery condition, on the assumption that the use of imagery in List 1 would increase the strength of the List 1 associations. As already noted, however, the same prediction can be derived from the assumption that the use of imagery would increase the *memorability* of the List 1 associations. After Trial 8 of List 2, associative interference disappeared in the imagery group, while there was still interference in the no-elaboration group even in the last block of trials given (Trials 11–12). The facilitative effect of imagery on the strength or memorability of the List 2 associations may have rapidly overcome the interfering effect of the List 1 associations produced by imagery.

Hall (1969) used the associative interference paradigm with kindergarten and second-grade children, and compared picture pairs with aurally presented word pairs. Associative interference was shown with both kinds of items, and more with pictures than with words. This result agrees with Spiker's finding for the early trials of List 2, but the picture–word difference obtained by Hall was not significant.

The major kind of error in all groups in Spiker's study was response omission, but the major effect of imagery was to reduce intralist errors (Hall did not report data on errors). This result implies that imagery increased stimulus differentiation. Therefore, in order to explain all the results of Spiker's study, it is necessary to assume an effect of imagery on both strength or memorability of associations and stimulus differentiation.

Davidson and Levin (1973) found that neither imagery instructions nor pictorial elaboration had any effect on associative interference. The children in their study were younger than in Spiker's study (Grades 2 and 4 vs. Grade 5), and details of procedure differed. The major difference, however, may be that a relatively small, fixed number of trials on List 1 (9 trials) was given in Spiker's study, while children were trained to criterion on List 1 in the Davidson and Levin study. Visual elaboration increased speed of acquisition in the latter study, but if it is assumed that the strength or memorability of the associations was the same in all children who met criterion, there would be no basis for differential associative interference if the effect of imagery was on strength or memorability of associations. That is, imagery would increase the strength or memorability of associations and hence the speed of learning, but the no-elaboration condition would produce equal strength or memorability of associations at the criterion level of performance and hence would produce equal associative interference. Davidson and Levin gave only three trials on the second list, presumably not enough for an effect of imagery on stimulus differentiation to influence performance.

Apparently, compound imagery influences associative memory by affecting the strength or memorability of associations. It can also increase stimulus differentiation. These conclusions are consistent with the conclusions from the work on intralist interference if the trends for preschoolers in this work are accepted rather than only the statistically significant effects.

4. Proactive Interference

One kind of proactive interference is "nonassociative" or "nonspecific." In this kind of proactive interference, material learned earlier interferes with retention of different material learned later. Nonassociative proactive interference can occur within lists or across lists. It has been assumed to be the source of the "primacy" effect—within a serial list, better retention of the first items than of the middle items, and across lists, better retention of the first lists than of middle lists.

Another type of proactive interference is "associative" or "specific." It is assessed in the same paradigm as associative interference, but refers to interference with *retention* of List 2 associations rather than interference with *acquisition* of these associations. The stimulus–response associations acquired in the first list are assumed to be impaired during the acquisition of the second list, but not eliminated. Hence, these old associations interfere with retention of the new, second-list associations to the same specific stimuli. The interference condition can be symbolized as *A–B, A–C,* delay, recall *A–C*. Theoretically, nonassociative proactive interference should also occur, and therefore the best control condition is *D–B, A–C,* delay, recall *A–C,* in which nonassociative proactive interference occurs but associative proactive interference does not. This control condition has not been used in imagery studies.

There have been several studies like Bugelski's (1968), in which a serial list is transformed into a paired-associate list by instructing persons in an experimental condition to use imagery to relate list-words to code-words representing the serial positions (e.g., Bower, 1972; Crovitz, 1970; Johnson, 1970; see also Paivio, 1971). A progressive decline in retention across lists is attributable to proactive interference, and therefore a reduction in the amount of decline can be interpreted as a reduction of proactive interference. However, as noted previously, the associative and nonassociative types are confounded. The studies show that imagery reduces the amount of decline across lists, but the results are somewhat ambiguous because the imagery versus no-elaboration comparison is confounded with a paired-associate versus serial-list distinction. In the no-elaboration condition, standard serial-learning instructions are given, with no mention of imagery, and therefore the list presumably remains a serial list.

Keppel and Zavortnik (1969) avoided this problem by using the serial-position numbers as explicit stimulus items, making the task paired associates for both groups (but confounding the associative and nonassociative types of proactive interference). They obtained some evidence for reduced proactive interference in the imagery condition, in that the groups did not differ in List 1 recall but the imagery group was superior to the no-elaboration group in recall of Lists 2 and 3. However, this effect was obtained only when the stimulus-numbers were in random order, not when they were in serial order.

Forbes and Reese (1974) also avoided the problem of comparing paired-associate tasks with serial tasks by using standard paired-associate lists with and without imposed pictorial elaborations. The results were like those of Keppel and Zavortnik, showing a reduction of proactive interference in the imagery condition.

All of the investigators just cited tested college students. There have been two relevant studies with children, both with designs like the one used by Forbes and Reese. In one of these studies, with preschool children (Reese, 1972), there was no primacy effect, and hence no proactive interference to be reduced. In the other study, with children from kindergarten and Grades 2 and 4 (Brown, 1975b), the relevant analysis (retention as a function of list order) was not reported. Hence, it is not yet known whether imagery affects proactive interference in children.

5. Retroactive Interference

There is a "nonassociative" type of retroactive interference analogous to nonassociative proactive interference. It is generally studied in multilist serial learning or free recall. Sasson (1971) and Sasson and Fraisse (1972) studied this type of retroactive interference in college students, and obtained evidence suggesting that it is reduced by imagery. These investigators presented concrete sentences, then gave an interpolated task involving pictures that were relevant to the sentences (facilitation condition) or irrelevant (retroactive interference condition), or gave a dot estimation task (control condition). Interference was obtained in the retroactive interference condition, but it may have been less than in an analogous condition in which irrelevant *sentences* were presented in the interpolated tasks. Sasson suggested the opposite trend, on the basis of a derived score, and his interpretation is consistent with the data from studies of the specificity of interference with respect to modality of interpolated tasks, discussed earlier, except that the sentences could have been recoded imaginally (e.g., Kee, 1976).

A paired-associate study by Wollen and Lowry (1971) can be interpreted as dealing with nonassociative retroactive interference. They tested college students, and found that imposed pictorial elaboration produced interference, relative to no pictures at all, when the material pictured was not relevant to any of the word pairs presented. The comparison can be interpreted to be between a nonassociative interference condition (*A–B, D–C,* recall *A–B*) with imagery and a noninterference condtion (*A–B,* recall *A–B*) without imagery. Consequently, interference versus noninterference conditions were confounded with imagery versus no-imagery conditions, and therefore the results are ambiguous.

The "associative" type of retroactive interference is measured in the same paradigm as associative interference, but the interference is with retention of List 1. Symbolically, the interference condition is *A–B, A–C,* recall *A–B*. The best control condition is *A–B, D–C,* recall *A–B*. Both conditions involve nonassociative retroactive interference, but only the former involves associative retroactive interference. This design has been used in several studies with college students.

Adams and Montague (1967) included the control condition, but their study dealt with natural language mediators (which reduced retroactive interference). Cavoti (1972) also included the control condition, and manipulated imagery by concreteness of stimulus items. He obtained equal retroactive interference with concrete–concrete and abstract–concrete pairs. In addition, he described a pilot study with words high or low in imagery value as stimulus items and nonsense syllables high in association value as response items. Again, the amount of retroactive interference was the same regardless of the imagery value of the stimulus items.

Cheung (1973) compared *A–B, A–C,* recall *A–B* with *D–B, A–C,* recall *D–B,* and obtained significantly better retention in the latter condition. On the assumption that the *A–B* and *D–B* lists were comparable, retroactive interference was obtained. However, although imagery and verbal elaboration instructions resulted in improved retention, in comparison with no elaboration instructions, they did not significantly reduce retroactive interference (that is, *A–B* and *D–B* retention were facilitated equally by elaboration instructions).

In an unpublished study, the author assessed retroactive interference in 5- to 6-year old children. The results are shown in Table 5-9. It can be seen that

TABLE 5-9
Retroactive Interference in Preschoolers: Percentage
Errors in Recall of List 1[a]

	Condition	
Group	*A–C, A–B*	*A–C, D–B*
Imposed elaboration	30.0	0.0
No-elaboration	75.0	10.0

[a] From Reese (1975a).

retroactive interference was obtained and that imagery facilitated performance in the interference condition. However, the marked floor effect in the noninterference condition makes it impossible to determine whether imagery reduced the amount of retroactive interference. The same kind of floor effect was obtained by Kee and Rohwer (1973), although not in a retroactive interference study. They gave second graders two independent lists and tested for retention of List 1 (equivalent to *A–B, D–C*, recall *A–B*). There was relatively little forgetting, assessed by recall and by recognition, and it was not affected by imposed elaboration.

Another procedure for assessing retroactive interference is to present a series of paired-associate lists, all with the same stimuli, and to test retention at the end. A recency effect (better retention of the last lists) can be interpreted to reflect retroactive interference, but the associative and nonassociative types are confounded. Reese (1972) used this procedure with children 3 to 6 years old. All the children learned four lists. Children in one elaboration group were given elaborations in the standard way: *A–B* elaborations were presented in List 1, *A–C* elaborations in List 2, *A–D* elaborations in List 3, and *A–E* elaborations in List 4. Children in another elaboration group were given the *A–B* elaborations in List 1 and "built-up" or progressive elaborations in Lists 2, 3, and 4: *A–B–C, A–B–C–D, A–B–C–D–E*, each progressively incorporating all the earlier elaborations involving the same stimulus. Two no-elaboration control groups were also included. One was given the standard side-by-side pictures: *A–B* in List 1, *A–C* in List 2, and so on. The other was given the standard side-by-side pictures in List 1, and in each successive list the new response item was added to form a row of pictures, ending with *A–B–C–D–E* in List 4. When the latter control group is compared with the progressive-elaboration group, the amount of repetition of each association is controlled. In the retention test, given after List 4 was learned, a significant recency effect was obtained in the standard conditions but not in the progressive conditions. As shown in Figure 5-3, the reduction in the recency effect in the progressive conditions resulted from improved performance in the first two or three lists. The elaboration conditions were not significantly different from their controls. Thus, retroactive interference was eliminated by the repetitions of responses in the progressive-elaboration and "row" control conditions, but was not affected by imagery.

Forbes and Reese (1974) conducted a similar study with college students, and obtained the same effects except that pictorial elaboration had an effect. As shown in Figure 5-4, the imposed elaborations enhanced retention of the middle lists, thus reducing the recency effect and, according to the present interpretation, reducing retroactive interference.

Brown (1975b) also conducted a similar study, with children from kindergarten and Grades 2 and 4, but she did not report the relevant analysis (retention as a

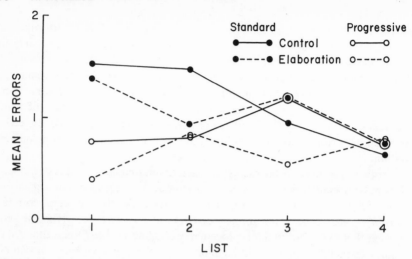

FIGURE 5-3 Retroactive interference in multilist retention by preschoolers. Note that elaboration did not influence the recency effect, and hence did not influence the amount of retroactive interference. However, repetition of response items in progressive-elaboration and progressive-control conditions reduced retroactive interference. (Reese, 1972, previously unreported data.)

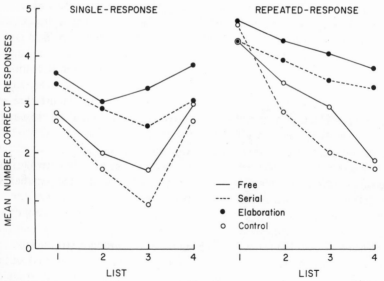

FIGURE 5-4 Retroactive interference in multilist retention by college students. Retroactive interference was reduced by imagery as well as by repetition of response items. (From "Pictorial elaboration and recall of multilist paired associates" by E. J. Forbes and H. W. Reese, *Journal of Experimental Psychology*, 1974, *102*, 836–840. Fig. 1, p. 838. Copyright 1974 by the American Psychological Association. Reprinted by permission.)

function of list order). One retention measure reported was the mean number of stimulus–response sets with all response items in the correct list order. A higher mean would reflect a reduction of interference, but without the specific list information there is no way to determine whether the effect was on primacy or recency, and hence no way to determine whether the effect was on proactive or retroactive interference (as these terms are defined in this chapter). The results nevertheless merit attention, because evidence was obtained that imagery reduces interference, whatever kind it might be, but that this effect varies with age level and treatment condition.

Imagery was manipulated by progressive elaboration. In one condition the sequence of pictures for each stimulus–response set represented a logical progression across the lists, and in another condition the sequence of pictures represented a random progression. The sequence of response items was the same; the experimental variable was the way in which interactions were depicted. In both these conditions, the experimenter also gave descriptions of stimulus-response interactions, but only the ones to be learned in the list being presented. That is, although the child might be shown a picture of the stimulus interacting with two response items, only the part that was immediately relevant was described. Brown also included a no-elaboration condition like Reese's (1972) "row" control condition except that as each item set was presented, the experimenter said, "The _____ goes with the _____," referring to the currently relevant pairing. The children were given immediate and one-week retention tests, but because of floor effects the data on long-term retention are uninterpretable in the present context (see section on "Effects on Long-Term Retention"). Therefore, only the results for the immediate retention test are considered here. Progressive elaboration facilitated retention in the second and fourth graders, especially when the progression was logical, but neither kind of progressive elaboration had any effect in the kindergarteners. Brown then tested two additional groups of kindergarteners, using the same two sets of progressive elaborations but accompanied by a different kind of description. For these two groups, the experimenter described the entire picture and then repeated the part that was immediately relevant. Brown also added a new no-elaboration condition, in which the experimenter named each of the items shown before saying, "The _____ goes with the _____" (referring to the immediately relevant pairing). This naming did not affect performance, but the progressively elaborated sentences did. In fact, when the progressive-elaboration pictures were described progressively, the kindergarten children retained almost as much as the older children did in the initial progressive-elaboration conditions. This finding supports a suggestion by Reese (1970c) that young children may fail to "read" elaborated pictures unless their attention is directed by appropriate verbalizations.

IV. IMPLICATIONS AND FUTURE DIRECTIONS

A. Summary

1. Theoretical Predictions

If the strength of stimulus-response associations is increased by compound imagery, then the following effects should be obtained: (1) acquisition enhanced; (2) long-term retention enhanced; (3) intralist interference increased; (4) associative interference increased; (5) proactive interference increased; and (6) retroactive interference reduced. Alternatively, if compound imagery increases the memorability of stimulus-response associations, then the effects should be the same except that (3) intralist interference should be neither enhanced nor reduced. Finally, if compound imagery increases stimulus differentiation, then the effects should be as follows: (1) acquisition enhanced; (2) long-term retention neither enhanced nor reduced; (3) intralist interference reduced; (4) associative interference neither enhanced nor reduced, but overcome rapidly; (5) and (6) proactive and retroactive interference neither enhanced nor reduced.

2. Effects on Acquisition

Imagery facilitates acquisition, as predicted from all three assumptions about its effects. Visual and verbal elaboration have been compared in several studies with children, and visual elaboration has most often been more effective than verbal elaboration, although the difference has often been nonsignificant. Studies in the 1960s showed a developmental trend in which verbal elaboration was superior to visual elaboration in young children and the two types of elaboration were equally effective in older children. This trend has not been obtained in more recent studies, perhaps because of a "generational" increase in the rate of cognitive development. Research is needed, however, to relate the effectiveness of visual and verbal elaboration to specific cognitive operations.

High imagery value is more facilitative on the stimulus side of paired associates than on the response side. Two plausible explanations are the following: (1) when retrieval is redintegrative, availability in free recall is more important on the stimulus side (high imagery value facilitates free recall); or (2) high-imagery words are likely to be coded as images, and only an image can redintegrate a compound image.

For verbal recall, pictures are better as stimulus items and words are better as response items. The differential effectiveness is especially pronounced in children, and is attributed to difficulty in retrieving the correct verbal response from a compound image. Theoretically, the image of the response item is retrieved from the compound image (redintegrated most effectively by a picture stimulus), but must be decoded into the verbal system for verbal recall. Apparently, storage of the permissible decodings (response learning) is better when the response items presented are words than when they are pictures. It is not clear whether the response list is stored in short-term or long-term memory.

3. Effects on Long-Term Retention

Imagery generally facilitates long-term retention, in agreement with the assumption that it increases the strength or memorability of the associations. Compound imagery and verbal elaboration equally facilitate long-term retention up to two weeks, the longest interval studied. There is some evidence, from studies that did not include a verbal elaboration condition, that the facilitation from compound imagery declines as the retention interval increases. The amount of decline may depend on characteristics such as deafness or age, but more developmental research is needed, especially with the retention interval varied and compound imagery compared with verbal elaboration.

4. Effects on Intralist Interference

In one study, compound imagery reduced intralist interference in deaf children, by increasing stimulus differentiation, and did not affect the strength or memorability of the associations. In the only other study, with hearing preschoolers, compound imagery may have increased the strength of the associations as well as increasing stimulus differentiation. More research is needed to confirm this difference in effects, and to identify its determinants.

5. Effects on Associative Interference

If it is hypothesized that imagery encourages recoding of nominally identical stimulus items in two (or more) lists, then imagery should reduce associative interference. The only support for this hypothesis was dissipated by unexplainable interactions. Contrary to the hypothesis, recoding is not prominent in groups instructed to use imagery. Furthermore, "imposed recoding" *increases* associative interference.

In one study with children, compound imagery increased associative interference early in the transfer list, but the interference quickly disappeared. Thus, it appears that compound imagery affects the strength or memorability of the associations. Compound imagery reduced intralist errors more than other error types; therefore, compound imagery also increases stimulus differentiation. In another study, compound imagery did not affect associative interference, presumably because the no-elaboration group had acquired equally strong or memorable associations and not enough trials were given to assess an effect on stimulus differentiation.

6. Effects on Proactive Interference

Only two studies have dealt with the effects of imagery on proactive interference in children, and the effects were indeterminate in both studies. In college students, imagery seems to reduce proactive interference, although the effect may be fragile. The effect is unexpected if imagery increases the strength or memorability of associations or increases stimulus differentiation—functions demonstrated in the research on intralist and associative interference. However, the expected effect is on the associative type of proactive interference, and in the relevant research the associative and nonassociative types were confounded. Suppose that imagery increases the strength or memorability of associations, and hence increases associative proactive interference, and that imagery increases stimulus differentiation, which has no effect on associative proactive interference but might reduce nonassociative proactive interference. The conflict between these effects would make the overall effect fragile. A problem with this interpretation is the lack of a theoretical basis for an effect of stimulus differentiation on nonassociative proactive interference. An alternative possibility is that the compound images are stored in memory with list markers, and the list markers serve as retrieval cues to reduce proactive interference. This assumption also explains the reduction of associative interference and predicts a reduction of retroactive interference, but it is not parsimonious because effects on strength or memorability of associations and on stimulus differentiation must also be assumed in order to explain the effects of imagery on single-list acquisition and retention, including the effect on intralist interference.

7. Effects on Retroactive Interference

Compound imagery may reduce nonassociative retroactive interference, but the evidence is not strong. It does not affect associative retroactive interference in the traditional paired-associate design, but it reduces retroactive interference in the multilist "recency" designs. The inconsistencies in the results need to be resolved by more research.

B. Implications

1. Theoretical Implications

The evidence strongly implies that compound imagery generally increases the strength or memorability of stimulus–response associations and increases stimulus differentiation. "Strength of associations" is a theoretical concept in stimulus–response theories, and is assumed to be increased by reinforced repetition of the associations. It seems reasonable to assume that imagery increases the strength of associations by facilitating repetition, in that imaginal repetitions can occur in the absence of the external stimulus and overt response. The reinforcer is presumably self-generated but analogous to the usual external reinforcers used in paired-associate studies. A complication is that if an operational definition of imagery is used, the assumption that imagery facilitates repetition loses its "reasonableness" and becomes gratuitous. Gratuitous or not, however, the assumption works and is justified pragmatically.

In processing theories, the memorability of an association depends on the "availability" and "accessibility" of the memory trace that represents the association. A memory trace is *available* if it has not yet faded from storage, but it is *accessible* only if an appropriate retrieval cue is used (e.g., Tulving, 1974). A memory trace may be available only briefly, or it may be available indefinitely. One processing operation that maintains a memory trace is rehearsal. This operation is considered to maintain a trace in short-term memory, because after rehearsal is terminated the trace fades from storage. Another operation that maintains a memory trade is elaboration—imaginal or verbal. It is considered to affect long-term memory; the elaborated trace remains available without continuation of any processing operation. A compound image is produced by imaginal elaboration and is therefore inherently memorable, in that it remains available in long-term memory. It may not remain accessible, and hence may functionally disappear, but the evidence on its continued accessibility is not yet clear-cut. It is worth noting, however, that forgetting seems to result more often from diminished accessibility than from diminished availability (Hultsch, 1975; Reese, 1976a; Tulving, 1974).

The effect of imagery on stimulus differentiation can be attributed to the details contained in images; images contain details missing from words, and hence are automatically more differentiated than words. Again, however, although this explanation is reasonable in processing theories, it is a gratuitous assumption in stimulus–response theories when imagery is defined operationally. More reasonably, the image could be defined in such a way that it functions like a cue-producing response and increases stimulus differentiation by the acquired distinctiveness of cues (cf. Spiker, 1971).

2. Practical Implications

The educational applications of mnemonic imagery have been discussed at length by Rohwer and by Levin (e.g., Levin, 1973; Rohwer, 1970, 1971). Their reports are not reviewed here, but should be consulted for a complete picture of those applications. A report by Atkinson (1975) is especially relevant, however, because of the clear relations of his findings to the findings already summarized in this chapter.

Atkinson has studied mnemonic imagery as an aid to learning Russian and Spanish vocabularies. The vocabulary is presented in a paired-associate format, and Atkinson has found that retention even after six weeks is better in college students after learning with the imagery mnemotechnic than with control instructions. In the mnemotechnic, each foreign-language word is linked to an acoustically similar English word, and the latter word is linked by compound imagery to the English translation of the foreign-language word. The acoustic link is said to be more easily remembered if it is supplied by the experimenter than if it is generated by the student (analogous to the ease of learning and remembering the *one–bun, two–shoe* code for use in serial learning). However, the compound images are more effective if they are generated by the student. Furthermore, compound images are more effective than verbal elaborations. After learning foreign-language-to-English translations with imagery, the English-to-foreign-language translations are easier than when imagery is not used (backward recall is facilitated by imagery). Apparently, then, the principles established by laboratory research can be put to practical use. One final outcome worth special note is that the students enthusiastically endorse the imagery mnemotechnic.

REFERENCES

Adams, J. A., & Montague, W. E. Retroactive inhibition and natural language mediation. *Journal of Verbal Leaning and Verbal Behavior,* 1967, *6,* 528–535.

Anderson, J. R., & Bower, G. H. *Human associative memory.* Washington, D.C.: Winston, 1973.

Angell, J. R. *Psychology: An introductory study of the structure and function of human consciousness* (4th ed.). New York: Holt, 1908.

Appel, L. F., Cooper, R. G., McCarrell, N., Sims-Knight, J., Yussen, S. R., & Flavell, J. H. The development of the distinction between perceiving and memorizing. *Child Development,* 1972, *43,* 1365–1381.

Aristotle. Psychology. In B. Rand (Ed.), *The classical psychologists.* Boston: Houghton Mifflin, 1912.

Atkinson, R. C. Mnemotechnics in second-language learning. *American Psychologist,* 1975, *30,* 821–828.

Attneave. F. How do you know? *American Psychologist,* 1974, *29,* 493–499.

Ball, S., & Bogatz, G. A. Summative research of *Sesame Street:* Implications for the study of preschool children. In A. D. Pick (Ed.), *Minnesota symposia on child psychology* (Vol. 6). Minneapolis: University of Minnesota Press, 1972.

Barber, T. X. Imagery and "hallucinations": Effects of LSD contrasted with the effects of "hypnotic" suggestions. In S. J. Segal (Ed.), *Imagery: Current cognitive approaches.* New York: Academic Press, 1971.

Begg, I., & Paivio, A. Concreteness and imagery in sentence meaning. *Journal of Verbal Learning and Verbal Behavior,* 1969, *8,* 821–827.

Begg, I., & Robertson, R. Imagery and long-term retention. *Journal of Verbal Learning and Verbal Behavior,* 1973, *12,* 689–700.

Bender, N. N., & Taylor, A. M. Instructional treatments based on learning strategies and the recognition memory of retarded children. *American Educational Research Journal,* 1973, *10,* 333–336.

Berlyne, D. E. *Structure and direction in thinking.* New York: Wiley, 1965.

Berol, W. *The Berol system of memory training and mental efficiency.* New York: Funk & Wagnalls, 1913.

Bigham, J. Memory (II). *Psychological Review*, 1894, *1*, 453–461.

Bower. G. H. Mental imagery and associative learning. In L. Gregg (Ed.), *Cognition in learning and memory*. New York: Wiley, 1972.

Bower, G. H., & Reitman, J. S. Mnemonic elaboration in multilist learning. *Journal of Verbal Learning and Verbal Behavior*, 1972, *11*, 478–485.

Bower, G. H., & Winzenz, D. Comparison of associative learning strategies. *Psychonomic Science*, 1970, *20*, 119–120.

Brainerd, C. J. Imagery as a dependent variable. *American Psychologist*, 1971, *26*, 599–600.

Brooks. L. R. The suppression of visualization by reading. *Quarterly Journal of Experimental Psychology*, 1967, *19* (Part 4), 289–299.

Brown, A. L. Mnemonic elaboration and recency judgments in children. *Cognitive Psychology*, 1973, *5*, 233–248.

Brown, A. L. The development of memory: Knowing, knowing about knowing, and knowing how to know. In H. W. Reese (Ed.), *Advances in child development and behavior* (Vol. 10). New York: Academic Press, 1975.   (a)

Brown, A. L. Progressive elaboration and memory for order in children. *Journal of Experimental Child Psychology*, 1975, *19*, 383–400.   (b)

Bugelski, B. R. Images as mediators in one-trial paired-associate learning. II: Self-timing in successive lists. *Journal of Experimental Psychology*, 1968, *77*, 328–334.

Bugelski, B. R. Words and things and images. *American Psychologist*, 1970, *25*, 1002–1012.

Bugelski, B. R. The definition of the image. In S. J. Segal (Ed.), *Imagery: Current cognitive approaches*. New York: Academic Press, 1971.

Bugelski, B. R. Reply to Brainerd. *American Psychologist*, 1972, *27*, 164–165.

Bugelski, B. R., Kidd, E., & Segmen, J. The image as mediator in one-trial paired-associate learning. *Journal of Experimental Psychology*, 1968, *76*, 69–73.

Butter, M. J. Differential recall of paired associates as a function of arousal and concreteness-imagery levels. *Journal of Experimental Psychology*, 1970, *84*, 252–256.

Calhoun, J. P. Developmental and sociocultural aspects of imagery in the picture-word paired-associate learning of children. *Developmental Psychology*, 1974, *10*, 357–366.

Calkins, M. W. Short studies in memory and in association from the Wellesley College Psychological Laboratory. *Psychological Review*, 1898, *5*, 451–462.

Carey, N. Factors in the mental processes of school children. I. Visual and auditory imagery. *British Journal of Psychology*, 1915, *7*, 453–490.

Cavoti, N. J. Rated imagery and the retroactive inhibition paradigm. Unpublished doctoral dissertation, West Virginia University, 1972.

Cheung, R. C. C. Reduction of *A–B, A–C* paired-associate interference through imagery and verbal mediation instructions. Unpublished doctoral dissertation, West Virginia University, 1973.

Clarkson, T. A., Haggith, P. A., Tierney, M. C., & Kobasigawa, A. Relative effectiveness of imagery instructions and pictorial interactions on children's paired-associate learning. *Child Development*, 1973, *44*, 179–181.

Cole, L. E., & Kanack, N. J. Paired-associate learning and bidirectional associative recall in first, third, fifth, and seventh graders. *Journal of Experimental Child Psychology*, 1972, *13*, 129–137.

Cole, M., Frankel, F., & Sharp. D. Development of free recall learning in children. *Developmental Psychology*, 1971, *4*, 109–123.

Craik, F. I. M., & Lockhart, R. S. Levels of processing: A framework for memory research. *Journal of Verbal Learning and Verbal Behavior*, 1972, *11*, 671–684.

Cramer, P. Learning pictures and words: The role of implicit verbal labeling. *Journal of Experimental Child Psychology*, 1975, *19*, 489–501.

Crovitz, H. F. *Galton's walk*. New York: Harper & Row, 1970.

Cuvo, A. J. Developmental differences in rehearsal and free recall. *Journal of Experimental Child Psychology*, 1975, *19*, 265–278.

Danner, F. W., & Taylor, A. M. Integrated pictures and relational imagery training in children's learning. *Journal of Experimental Child Psychology*, 1973, *16*, 47–54.

Davidson, R. E., & Adams, J. F. Verbal and imagery processes in children's paired-associate learning. *Journal of Experimental Child Psychology*, 1970, *9*, 429–435.

Davidson, R. E., & Dollinger, L. E. The effects of deep structure variations in sentences: Free recall and paired-associate learning (Technical Report No. 110). Madison: Wisconsin Research and Development Center for Cognitive Learning, 1969.

Davidson, R. E., & Levin, J. R. Imagery in transfer (Technical Report Draft). Madison: Wisconsin Research and Development Center for Cognitive Learning, 1973.

Davidson, R. E., Schwenn, E. A., & Adams, J. F. Semantic effects in transfer. *Journal of Verbal Learning and Verbal Behavior*, 1970, *9*, 212–217.

Davies, G. M. Recognition memory for pictured and named objects. *Journal of Experimental Child Psychology*, 1969, *7*, 448–458.

Davies, G. M. Quantitative and qualitative aspects of memory for picture stimuli. *Journal of Experimental Child Psychology*, 1972, *13*, 382–393.

Delin, P. S. Success in recall as a function of success in implementation of mnemonic instructions. *Psychonomic Science*, 1968, *12*, 153–154.

Dempster, F. N., & Rohwer, W. D., Jr. Component analysis of the elaborative encoding effect in paired-associate learning. *Journal of Experimental Psychology*, 1974, *103*, 400–408.

Dilley, M. G., & Paivio, A. Pictures and words as stimulus and response items in paired-associate learning of young children. *Journal of Experimental Child Psychology*, 1968, *6*, 231–240.

DiVesta, F. J., Ingersoll, G., & Sunshine, P. A factor analysis of imagery tests. *Journal of Verbal Learning and Verbal Behavior*, 1971, *10*, 471–479.

Dominowski, R. L., & Gadlin, H. Imagery and paired-associate learning. *Canadian Journal of Psychology*, 1968, *22*, 336–348.

Edwards, C. *Perfecting your card memory*. New York: Exposition Press, 1963.

Elliott, L. Imagery versus repetition encoding in short- and long-term memory. *Journal of Experimental Psychology*, 1973, *100*, 270–276.

Emmerich, H. J., & Ackerman, B. P. The effect of pictorial detail and elaboration on children's retention. *Journal of Experimental Child Psychology*, 1976, *21*, 241–248.

Engel, R. High and low imagery words in short-term memory. Unpublished master's thesis, Ohio State University, 1969. (Cited from D. D. Wickens, Encoding categories of words: An empirical approach to meaning. *Psychological Review*, 1970, *77*, 1–15.)

Ernest, C., & Paivio, A. Imagery ability in paired associate and incidental learning. *Psychonomic Science*, 1969, *15*, 181–182.

Evertson, C. M., & Wicker, F. W. Pictorial concreteness and mode of elaboration in children's learning. *Journal of Experimental Child Psychology*, 1974, *17*, 264–270.

Forbes, E. J., & Reese, H. W. Pictorial elaboration and recall of multilist paired associates. *Journal of Experimental Psychology*, 1974, *102*, 836–840.

Forisha, B. D. Mental imagery verbal processes: A developmental study. *Developmental Psychology*, 1975, *11*, 259–267.

Frederiksen, J. D., & Rohwer, W. D., Jr. Elaborative prompt effects in children's paired-associate learning: Design and population comparisons. *Journal of Educational Psychology*, 1974, *66*, 83–89.

Friedman, S. L., & Stevenson, M. B. Developmental changes in the understanding of implied motion in two-dimensional pictures. *Child Development*, 1975, *46*, 773–778.

Friedrich, D. Developmental analysis of memory capacity and information-encoding strategy. *Developmental Psychology*, 1974, *10*, 559–563.

Gray, C. R., & Gummerman, K. The enigmatic eidetic image: A critical examination of methods, data, and theories. *Psychological Bulletin*, 1975, *82*, 383–407.

Gruenenfelder, T. M., & Borkowski, J. G. Transfer of cumulative-rehearsal strategies in children's short-term memory. *Child Development*, 1975, *46*, 1019–1024.

Haber, R. N., & Haber, R. B. Eidetic imagery: I. Frequency. *Perceptual and Motor Skills*, 1964, *19*, 131–138.

Hagen, J. W., Hargrave, S., & Ross, W. Prompting and rehearsal in short-term memory. *Child Development*, 1973, *44*, 201–204.

Hagen, J. W., Jongeward, R. H., & Kail, R. V. Cognitive perspectives on the development of memory. In H. W. Reese (Ed.), *Advances in child development and behavior* (Vol. 10). New York: Academic Press, 1975.

Hale, G. A., & Piper, R. A. Effect on pictorial integration on children's incidental learning. *Developmental Psychology*, 1974, *10*, 847–851.

Hall, V. C. Acquisition and transfer differences between kindergarteners and second-graders on aurally and visually presented paired-associates using an *A–B, A–C* design. *Journal of Experimental Child Psychology*, 1969, *7*, 400–406.

Heinen, J. R. K., & Kulhavy, R. W. Attributes of mediating images in paired-associate learning. Paper presented at the meeting of the American Psychological Association, Montreal, August 1973.

Hollenberg, C. K. Functions of visual memory in the learning and concept formation of children. *Child Development*, 1970, *41*, 1003–1015.

Holyoak, K., Hogeterp, H., & Yuille, J. C. A developmental comparison of verbal and pictorial mnemonics in paired-associate learning. *Journal of Experimental Child Psychology*, 1972, *14*, 53–65.

Homzie, M. J., Noyes, E. J., & Lovelace, E. A. Children's memory for picture versus word responses in paired associates: Recall and recognition tests. *American Journal of Psychology*, 1973, *86*, 567–577.

Horowitz, L. M., & Manelis, L. Towards a theory of redintegrative memory: Adjective-noun phrases. In G. H. Bower & J. T. Spence (Eds.), *The psychology of learning and motivation: Advances in research and theory* (Vol. 6). New York: Academic Press, 1972.

Horowitz, L. M., & Prytulak, L. S. Redintegrative memory. *Psychological Review*, 1969, *76*, 519–531.

Horowitz, M. J. *Image formation and cognition*. New York: Appleton-Century-Crofts, 1970.

Horvitz, J. M., & Levin, J. R. Semantic and imaginal forces in learning as related to age. *Journal of Experimental Child Psychology*, 1972, *14*, 11–20.

Hughes, S. E. D., & Walsh, J. F. Effects of syntactical mediation, age, and modes of representation on paired-associate learning. *Child Development*, 1971, *42*, 1827–1836.

Hultsch, D. F. Adult age differences in retrieval: Trace dependent and cue dependent forgetting. *Developmental Psychology*, 1975, *11*, 197–201.

Hunter, W. S. The delayed reaction in animals and children. *Behavior Monographs*, 1913, 2(1, Whole No. 6).

Iscoe, I., & Semler, I. J. Paired-associate learning in normal and mentally retarded children as a function of four experimental conditions. *Journal of Comparative and Physiological Psychology*, 1964, *57*, 387–392.

Jablonski, E. M. Free recall in children. *Psychological Bulletin*, 1974, *81*, 522–539.

Jenkins, J. J. Remember that old theory of memory? Well, forget it! *American Psychologist*, 1974, *29*, 785–795.

Johnson, R. B. Images as mediators in free recall. *Journal of Experimental Psychology*, 1970, *84*, 523–526.

Jones, H. R. The use of visual and verbal memory processes by three-year-old children. *Journal of Experimental Child Psychology*, 1973, *15*, 340–351.

Jusczyk, P. W., Kemler, D. G., & Bubis, E. A. A developmental comparison of two types of visual mnemonics. *Journal of Experimental Child Psychology*, 1975, *20*, 327–340.

Kausler, D. H., & Gotway, M. A. R-S learning in children. *Journal of Experimental Child Psychology*, 1969, *8*, 190–194.

Kee, D. W. Storage and retrieval of noun-pairs in children's recognition memory: Analysis of presentation mode and elaboration effects. *Journal of Experimental Psychology: Human Learning and Memory,* 1976, *2,* 623–632.

Kee, D. W., & Rohwer, W. D., Jr. Paired-associate learning efficiency as a function of response mode and elaboration. Paper presented at the meeting of the American Educational Research Association, Minneapolis, March 1970.

Kee, D. W., & Rohwer, W. D., Jr. Noun-pair learning in four ethnic groups: Conditions of presentation and response. *Journal of Educational Psychology,* 1973, *65,* 226–232.

Kee, D. W., & Rohwer, W. D., Jr. Response and associative phase components of elaborative prompt effects in children's noun-pair learning. *Journal of Experimental Child Psychology,* 1974, *18,* 62–71.

Kee, D. W., & White, R. B. Noun-pair learning in children: Conditions of pictorial depiction and instructions to learn. Paper presented at the meeting of the American Educational Research Association, 1975.

Kemler, D. G., & Jusczyk, P. W. A developmental study of facilitation by mnemonic instruction. *Journal of Experimental Child Psychology,* 1975, *20,* 400–410.

Keppel, G., & Zavortink, B. Further test of the use of images as mediators. *Journal of Experimental Psychology,* 1969, *82,* 190–192.

Kerst, S., & Levin, J. R. A comparison of experimenter-supplied and subject-generated strategies in children's paired-associate learning. *Journal of Educational Psychology,* 1973, *65,* 300–303.

Kirk, W. J., & Johnson, J. T., Jr. Negative transfer as a function of IQ and mode of presentation in paired-associate learning. *Journal of Experimental Child Psychology,* 1972, *14,* 233–241.

Kirkpatrick, E. A. An experimental study of memory. *Psychological Review,* 1894, *1,* 602–609.

Kobasigawa, A. Utilization of retrieval cues by children in recall. *Child Development,* 1974, *45,* 127–134.

Köhler, W. *Gestalt psychology.* New York: Liveright, 1929.

Kosslyn, S. M., & Bower, G. H. The role of imagery in sentence memory: A developmental study. *Child Development,* 1974, *45,* 30–38.

Kossuth, G. L., Carroll, W. R., & Rogers, C. A. Free recall of words and objects. *Developmental Psychology,* 1971, *4,* 480.

La Fave, L. On Brainerd and his concept of imagery. *American Psychologist,* 1972, *27,* 165–166.

Lampel, A. K. The child's memory for actional, locational, and serial scenes. *Journal of Experimental Child Psychology,* 1973, *15,* 266–277.

Leask, J., Haber, R. N., & Haber, R. B. Eidetic imagery in children: II. Longitudinal and experimental results. *Psychonomic Monograph Supplements,* 1969 *3*(3, Whole No. 35).

Levin, J. R. Inducing comprehension in poor readers: A test of a recent model. *Journal of Educational Psychology,* 1973, *65,* 19–24.

Levin, J. R., Davidson, R. E., Wolff, P., & Citron, M. A comparison of induced imagery and sentence strategies in children's paired-associate learning. *Journal of Educational Psychology,* 1973, *64,* 306–309.

Levin, J. R., McCabe, A. E., & Bender, B. G. A note on imagery-inducing motor activity in young children. *Child Development,* 1975, *46,* 263–266.

Lindquist, E. F. *Design and analysis of experiments in psychology and education.* Boston: Houghton Mifflin, 1956.

Lindworsky, J. *Experimental psychology* (Translated from the 4th German ed. by H. R. DeSilva). New York: Macmillan, 1931.

Lockhart, R. S. Retrieval asymmetry in the recall of adjectives and nouns. *Journal of Experimental Psychology,* 1969, *79,* 12–17.

McCabe, A. E., Levin, J. R., & Wolff, P. The role of overt activity in children's sentence production. *Journal of Experimental Child Psychology,* 1974, *17,* 107–114.

Marshall, G. R. The effect of concrete noun and picture mediation on the paired-associate learning of abstract nouns. Paper presented at the meeting of the Eastern Psychological Association, Atlantic City, April 1965.

Maus, M., Nappe, G., Trestrail, J., & Wollen, K. A. Effects of interacting pictures upon short-term and long-term memory. Paper presented at the meeting of the Western Psychological Association, Portland, Oregon, April 1972.

Means, B. M., & Rohwer, W. D., Jr. A developmental study of the effects of adding verbal analogs to pictured paired associates. Unpublished paper, University of California, Berkeley, 1974.

Milgram, N. A. Verbal context versus visual compound in paired-associate learning by children. *Journal of Experimental Child Psychology*, 1967, *5*, 597–603.

Millar, S. Effects of instructions to visualize stimuli during delay on visual recognition by preschool children. *Child Development*, 1972, *43*, 1073–1075.

Mondani, M. S., & Battig, W. F. Imaginal and verbal mnemonics as related to paired-associate learning and directionality of associations. *Journal of Verbal Learning and Verbal Behavior*, 1973, *12*, 401–408.

Montague, R. B. The effect of mediational instructions on associative skills of first grade innercity children. Paper presented at the meeting of the American Educational Research Association, Minneapolis, March 1970.

Neisser, U., & Kerr, N. Spatial and mnemonic properties of visual images. *Cognitive Psychology*, 1973, *5*, 138–150.

Odom, P. B., & Nesbitt, N. H. Some processes in children's comprehension of linguistically and visually depicted relationships. *Journal of Experimental Child Psychology*, 1974, *17*, 399–408.

Overton, W. F., & Reese, H. W. Models of development: Methodological implications. In J. R. Nesselroade & H. W. Reese (Eds.), *Life-span developmental psychology: Methodological issues*. New York: Academic Press, 1973.

Paivio, A. Effects of imagery instructions and concreteness of memory pegs in a mnemonic system. *Proceedings of the 76th Annual Convention of the American Psychological Association*, 1968, 77–78.   (a)

Paivio, A. A factor-analytic study of word attributes and verbal learning. *Journal of Verbal Learning and Verbal Behavior*, 1968, *7*, 41–49.   (b)

Paivio, A. Mental imagery in associative learning and memory. *Psychological Review*, 1969, *76*, 241–263.

Paivio, A. On the functional significance of imagery. In H. W. Reese (Chair), Imagery in children's learning: A symposium. *Psychological Bulletin*, 1970, *73*, 385–392.

Paivio, A. *Imagery and verbal processes*. New York: Holt, Rinehart & Winston, 1971.

Paivio, A. A theoretical analysis of the role of imagery in learning and memory. In P. W. Sheehan (Ed.), *The function and nature of imagery*. New York: Academic Press, 1972.

Paivio, A. Coding distinctions and repetition effects in memory. In G. H. Bower (Ed.), *The psychology of learning and motivation* (Vol. 9). New York: Academic Press, 1975.   (a)

Paivio, A. Imagery in recall and recognition. In J. Brown (Ed.), *Recall and recognition*. New York: Wiley, 1975.   (b)

Paivio, A., & Madigan, S. A. Imagery and association value in paired-associate learning. *Journal of Experimental Psychology*, 1968, *76*, 35–39.

Paivio, A., & Olver, M. Denotative-generality, imagery, and meaningfulness in paired-associate learning of nouns. *Psychonomic Science*, 1964, *1*, 183–184.

Paivio, A., Rogers, T. B., & Smythe, P. C. Why are pictures easier to recall than words? *Psychonomic Science*, 1968, *11*, 137–138.   (a)

Paivio, A., Smythe, P. C., & Yuille, J. C. Imagery *versus* meaningfulness of nouns in paired-associate learning. *Canadian Journal of Psychology*, 1968, *22*, 427–441.   (b)

Paivio, A., & Yarmey, A. D. Pictures versus words as stimuli and responses in paired-associate learning. *Psychonomic Science*, 1966, *5*, 235–236.

Paivio, A., & Yuille, J. C. Changes in associative strategies and paired-associate learning over trials as a function of word imagery and type of learning set. *Journal of Experimental Psychology*, 1969, *79*, 458–463.

Palermo, D. S. Imagery in children's learning: Discussion. In H. W. Reese (Chair), Imagery in

172   H. W. REESE

children's learning: A symposium. *Psychological Bulletin,* 1970, *73,* 415–421.

Pear. T. H. Imagery and mentality. *British Journal of Psychology,* 1924, *14,* 291–299.

Pellegrino, J. W., Siegel, A. W., & Dhawan, M. Short-term retention of pictures and words: Evidence for dual coding systems. *Journal of Experimental Psychology: Human Learning and Memory,* 1975, *104,* 95–102.

Pellegrino, J. W., Siegel, A. W., & Dhawan, M. Short-term retention of pictures and words as a function of type of distraction and length of delay interval. *Memory & Cognition,* in press.

Piaget, J., & Inhelder, B. *Mental imagery in the child* (Translated by P. A. Chilton). New York: Basic Books, 1971.

Potter, M. C., & Faulconer, B. A. Time to understand pictures and words. *Nature,* 1975, *253,* 437–438.

Pylyshyn, Z. W. What the mind's eye tells the mind's brain: A critique of mental imagery. *Psychological Bulletin,* 1973, *80,* 1–24.

Raser, G. A., & Bartz, W. H. Imagery and paired-associate recognition. *Psychonomic Science,* 1968, *12,* 385–386.

Reed, S. K., & Johnson, J. A. Detection of parts in patterns & images. *Memory & Cognition,* 1975, *3,* 569–575.

Reese, H. W. Imagery in paired-associate learning in children. *Journal of Experimental Child Psychology,* 1965, *2,* 290–296.

Reese, H. W. Associative interference: Pilot study. Unpublished paper, State University of New York at Buffalo, 1966.

Reese, H. W. Deaf study. Unpublished paper, State University of New York at Buffalo, 1967.

Reese, H. W. (Chair) Imagery in children's learning: A symposium. *Psychological Bulletin,* 1970, *73,* 383–421. (a)

Reese, H. W. Imagery in children's paired-associate learning. *Journal of Experimental Child Psychology,* 1970, *9,* 174–178. (b)

Reese, H. W. Imagery and contextual meaning. In H. W. Reese (Chair), Imagery in children's learning: A symposium. *Psychological Bulletin,* 1970, *73,* 404–414. (c)

Reese, H. W. The study of covert verbal and nonverbal mediation. In A. Jacobs & L. B. Sachs (Eds.), *The psychology of private events.* New York: Academic Press, 1971.

Reese, H. W. Imagery and multiple-list paired-associate learning in young children. *Journal of Experimental Child Psychology,* 1972, *13,* 310–323.

Reese, H. W. Models of memory and models of development. *Human Development,* 1973, *16,* 397–416.

Reese, H. W. Cohort, age, and imagery in children's paired-associate learning. *Child Development,* 1974, *45,* 1176–1178.

Reese, H. W. Retroactive interference. Unpublished paper, West Virginia University, 1975. (a)

Reese, H. W. Verbal effects in children's visual recognition memory. *Child Development,* 1975, *46,* 400–407. (b)

Reese, H. W. The development of memory: Life-span perspectives. In P. B. Baltes (Chair), Implications of life-span developmental psychology for child development. In H. W. Reese (Ed.), *Advances in child development and behavior* (Vol. 11). New York: Academic Press, 1976. (a)

Reese, H. W. Models of memory development. *Human Development,* 1976, *19,* 291–303. (b)

Reese, H. W., & Overton, W. F. Models of development and theories of development. In L. R. Goulet & P. B. Baltes (Eds.), *Life-span developmental psychology: Research and theory.* New York: Academic Press, 1970.

Reese, H. W., & Palermo, D. S. Imagery in paired associate learning (Editorial consolidation of separate contributions by the authors). In H. W. Reese & L. P. Lipsitt (Eds.), *Experimental child psychology.* New York: Academic Press, 1970.

Reese, H. W., & Parkington, J. J. Intralist interference and imagery in deaf and hearing children. *Journal of Experimental Child Psychology,* 1973, *16,* 165–183.

Richardson, A. *Mental imagery.* New York: Springer, 1969.

Richardson, A. Voluntary control of the memory image. In P. W. Sheehan (Ed.), *The function and nature of imagery*. New York: Academic Press, 1972.

Rimm, D. C., Alexander, R. A., & Eiles, R. R. Effects of different mediational instructions and sex of subject on paired-associate learning of concrete nouns. *Psychological Reports*, 1969, *25*, 935–940.

Rohwer, W. D., Jr. Social class differences in the role of linguistic structures in paired-associate learning: Elaboration and learning proficiency (Basic Research Project No. 5-0605, Contract Nonr OE 6-10-273). Washington, D.C.: U.S. Office of Education, 1967.

Rohwer, W. D., Jr. Images and pictures in children's learning: Research results and educational implications. In H. W. Reese (Chair), Imagery in children's learning: A symposium. *Psychological Bulletin*, 1970, *73*, 393–403.

Rohwer, W. D., Jr. Prime time for education: Early childhood or adolescence? *Harvard Educational Review*, 1971, *41*, 316–341.

Rohwer, W. D., Jr. Elaboration and learning in childhood and adolescence. In H. W. Reese (Ed.), *Advances in child development and behavior* (Vol. 8). New York: Academic Press, 1973.

Rohwer, W. D., Jr., & Ammon, M. S. Elaboration training and paired-associate learning efficiency in children. *Journal of Educational Psychology*, 1971, *62*, 376–383.

Rohwer, W. D., Jr., Ammon, M. S., Suzuki, N., & Levin, J. R. Population differences and learning proficiency. *Journal of Educational Psychology*, 1971, *62*, 1–14.

Rohwer, W. D., Jr., Kee, D. W., & Guy, K. C. Developmental changes in the effects of presentation media on noun-pair learning. *Journal of Experimental Child Psychology*, 1975, *19*, 137–152.

Rohwer, W. D., Jr., Lynch, S., Suzuki, N., & Levin, J. R. Verbal and pictorial facilitation of paired-associate learning. *Journal of Experimental Child Psychology*, 1967, *5*, 294–302.

Rose, S. A., Blank, M. S., & Bridger, W. H. Intermodel and intramodel retention of visual and tactual information in young children. *Developmental Psychology*, 1972, *6*, 482–486.

Rychlak, J. F. What kind of scientific revolution is called for in psychology? Paper presented at the meeting of the American Psychological Association, New Orleans, September 1974.

Saltz, E., & Finkelstein, C. Does imagery retard conceptual behavior? *Child Development*, 1974, *45*, 1093–1097.

Sasson, R. Interfering images at sentence retrieval. *Journal of Experimental Psychology*, 1971, *89*, 56–62.

Sasson, R. Y., & Fraisse, P. Images in memory for concrete and abstract sentences. *Journal of Experimental Psychology*, 1972, *94*, 149–155.

Schnorr, J. A., & Atkinson, R. C. Repetition versus imagery instructions in the short- and long-term retention of paired-associates. *Psychonomic Science*, 1969, *15*, 183–184.

Sheehan, P. W. (Ed.) *The function and nature of imagery*. New York: Academic Press, 1972.

Shiffrin, R. M., & Atkinson, R. C. Storage and retrieval processes in long-term memory. *Psychological Review*, 1969, *76*, 179–193.

Siperstein, G. N., & Budoff, M. Noun-pair learning at different ages under self-paced and experimenter-paced conditions. Paper presented at the biennial meeting of the Society for Research in Child Development, Denver, April 1975.

Skinner. B. F. The operational analysis of psychological terms. *Psychological Review*, 1945, *52*, 270–277.

Spiker, C. C. Associative transfer in verbal paired-associate learning. *Child Development*, 1960, *31*, 73–87.

Spiker, C. C. Applications of Hull-Spence theory to the discrimination learning of children. In H. W. Reese (Ed.), *Advances in child development and behavior* (Vol. 6). New York: Academic Press, 1971.

Spiker, C. C., & McCandless, B. R. The concept of intelligence and the philosophy of science. *Psychological Review*, 1954, *61*, 255–266.

Sully, J. *Outlines of psychology*. New York: Appleton, 1891.

Taylor, A. M. Visual imagery instruction and non-action versus action situations relative to recall by children (Final Report, Project No. 9-E-030, Grant No. OEG-5-9-245030-0023). Washington, D.C.: U.S. Office of Education, 1970.

Taylor, A. M., & Black, H. B. Variables affecting imagery instruction in children. Paper presented at the meeting of the Midwestern Psychological Association, Chicago, May 1969.

Taylor, A. M., Josberger, M., & Knowlton, J. Q. Mental elaboration and learning in EMR children. *American Journal of Mental Deficiency,* 1972, *77,* 69–76.

Taylor, A. M., Josberger, M., & Whitely, S. E. Elaboration instruction and verbalization as factors facilitating retarded children's recall. *Journal of Educational Psychology,* 1973, *64,* 341–346.

Taylor, A. M., Peloquin, P. V., & Kenworthy, J. Concreteness, verbal context, and imagery, as factors in children's paired associate recall (Research Monograph No. 9, Audio-Visual Research). Bloomington: Indiana University, 1969.

Titchener, E. B. *Lectures on the experimental psychology of the thought processes.* New York: Macmillan, 1909.

Treat, N. J., & Reese, H. W. Age, pacing, and imagery in paired-associate learning. *Developmental Psychology,* 1976, *12,* 119–124.

Tulving, E. Episodic and semantic memory. In E. Tulving & W. Donaldson (Eds.), *Organization of memory.* New York: Academic Press, 1972.

Tulving, E. Cue-dependent forgetting. *American Scientist,* 1974, *62,* 74–82.

Tulving, E., & Watkins, M. J. Structure of memory traces. *Psychological Review,* 1975, *82,* 261–275.

Turnure, J. E., & Thurlow, M. L. Verbal elaboration and the promotion of transfer of training in educable mentally retarded children. *Journal of Experimental Child Psychology,* 1973, *15,* 137–148.

Turvey, M. T. On peripheral and central processes in vision: Inferences from an information-processing analysis of masking with patterned stimuli. *Psychological Review,* 1973, *80,* 1–52.

Upham, T. C. *Mental philosophy,* Vol. 1: *The intellect, with an appendix on language.* New York: Harper, 1869.

Varley, W. H., Levin, J. R., Severson, R. A., & Wolff, P. Training imagery production in young children through motor involvement. *Journal of Educational Psychology,* 1974, *66,* 262–266.

Wellman, H. M., Ritter, K., & Flavell, J. H. Deliberate memory behavior in the delayed reactions of very young children. *Developmental Psychology,* 1975, *11,* 780–787.

Whitely, S. E., & Taylor, A. M. Imagery and verbal elaboration in learning and multiple associates. *Psychological Reports,* 1974, *34,* 859–862.

Wicker, F. W. On the locus of picture-word differences in paired-associate learning. *Journal of Verbal Learning and Verbal Behavior,* 1970, *9,* 52–57. (a)

Wicker, F. W. Photographs, drawings, and nouns as stimuli in paired-associate learning. *Psychonomic Science,* 1970, *18,* 205–206. (b)

Wicker, F. W., & Edmonston, L. P. The effect of several pretraining tasks on picture-word differences in associative learning. Paper presented at the meeting of the Midwestern Psychological Association, Cleveland, May 1972.

Wicker, F. W., & Holley, F. M. Distraction modality and stimulus modality in paired-associate learning. *Psychonomic Science,* 1971, *25,* 218–220.

Wolff, P., & Levin, J. R. The role of overt activity in children's imagery production. *Child Development,* 1972, *43,* 537–547.

Wolff, P., Levin, J. R., & Longobardi, E. T. Motoric mediation in children's paired-associate learning: Effects of visual and tactual contact. *Journal of Experimental Child Psychology,* 1972, *14,* 176–183.

Wolff, P., Levin, J. R., & Longobardi, E. T. Activity and children's learning. *Child Development,* 1974, *45,* 221–223.

Wollen, K. A., & Lowry, D. H. Effects of imagery on paired-associate learning. *Journal of Verbal Learning and Verbal Behavior,* 1971, *10,* 276–284.

Wollen, K. A., Weber, A., & Lowry, D. H. Bizarreness versus interaction of mental images as determinants of learning. *Cognitive Psychology*, 1972, *3*, 518–523.

Wood, G. Mnemonic systems in recall. *Journal of Educational Psychology Monograph*, 1967, *58*(6, Part 2, Whole No. 645).

Woodworth, R. S. *Experimental psychology*. New York: Holt, 1938.

Yarmey, A. D., & Barker, W. J. Repetition versus imagery instructions in the immediate- and delayed-retention of picture and word paired-associates. *Canadian Journal of Psychology*, 1971, *25*, 56–61.

Yarmey, A. D., & Bowen, N. V. The role of imagery in incidental learning of educable retarded and normal children. *Journal of Experimental Child Psychology*, 1972, *14*, 303–312.

Yarmey, A. D., & O'Neill, B. J. S–R and R–S paired-associate learning as a function of concreteness, imagery, specificity, and association value. *Journal of Psychology*, 1969, *71*, 95–109.

Yarmey, A. D., & Paivio, A. Further evidence on the effects of word abstractness and meaningfulness in paired-associate learning. *Psychonomic Science*, 1965, *2*, 307–308.

Yarmey, A. D., & Sayer, L. A. Associative learning of abstract and concrete nouns and their subject-drawn pictorial representations. *Canadian Journal of Psychology*, 1972, *26*, 240–251.

Yarmey, A. D., & Ure, G. Incidental learning, noun imagery-concreteness and direction of associations in paired-associate learning. *Canadian Journal of Psychology*, 1971, *25*, 91–102.

Yates, F. A. *The art of memory*. Chicago: University of Chicago Press, 1966.

Yuille, J. C. Does the concreteness effect reverse with delay? *Journal of Experimental Psychology*, 1971, *88*, 174–148.

Yuille, J. C., & Catchpole, M. J. Associative learning and imagery training in children. *Journal of Experimental Child Psychology*, 1973, *16*, 403–412.

Yuille, J. C., & Catchpole, M. J. The effects of delay and imagery training on the recall and recognition of object pairs. *Journal of Experimental Child Psychology*, 1974, *17*, 474–481.

Yuille, J. C., & Paivio, A. Imagery and verbal mediation instructions in paired-associate learning. *Journal of Experimental Psychology*, 1968, *78*, 436–441.

6
Retrieval Strategies in the Development of Memory

Akira Kobasigawa

University of Windsor

I. INTRODUCTION

Memory may be characterized in terms of three components: encoding, storage, and retrieval. If an event is to be remembered, an individual must (1) properly attend to and interpret that event; (2) store effectively what he has encoded; and (3) be able to gain access to what has been stored. Several developmental psychologists (e.g., Butterfield, Wambold, & Belmont, 1973; Hagen, 1971) have proposed that analyzing memory in terms of separate processes may be useful in isolating components of developmental changes in memory. Age-related improvement in children's performance on memory tasks could be due to the older children's more efficient performance in any one or all of these three components. This argument is examined in this chapter, with a focus on the third component, the retrieval phase of memory performance.

Two major questions concerning children's use of strategies to facilitate retrieval provide the focus for the present chapter. First, does children's use of strategies show age-related changes in the retrieval phase? Second, assuming an affirmative answer to the first question, does children's use of such strategies affect their recall? Section II begins with a brief review of contemporary theoretical work related to the nature of retrieval processes. The conceptual framework discussed in that section will provide the organization for a review of studies investigating developmental changes in retrieval in Section III. The review is based almost entirely on studies conducted with preschool and elementary school children, although older subjects (for example, college students) were included in a few cases. Empirical evidence indicating children's ineffective retrieval of stored information is presented initially. This will be followed by a review of studies that illustrate age-related changes in children's spontaneous and efficient use of some selected skills associated with retrieval process. Then, retrieval situations that do not require deliberate strategies, as well as the relationship between children's storage activities and the effectiveness of retrieval strategies, are examined briefly. It will be argued that the major developmental changes in children's performance on memory tasks are likely to occur mainly when deliberate strategies are needed. Finally, some comments are made on the current status of research on the development of retrieval strategies in Section IV.

II. FRAMEWORK OF RETRIEVAL PROCESSES

A. Conceptual Separation of Storage and Retrieval

The notion that one component of memory is retrieval is not new. Melton (1963) used the term *trace utilization* in his comparison of a theory of memory with a theory of learning. What is important in recent investigation of human memory is that an experimental basis for distinguishing between storage (availability of information in memory) and retrieval (accessibility of stored information to an individual) is provided, and further, the possibility of studying retrieval independently of storage processes is suggested. Prior to the discussion concerning what retrieval processes might consist of, one experimental procedure that illustrates the need for a distinction between storage and retrieval will be described. For our purpose, only one paradigm is presented, one that has been modified and used extensively with children, although other procedures are also available (e.g., Patterson, 1972).

A method used to distinguish between the potential availability of information in memory and its accessibility at a particular time was provided in a study by Tulving and Pearlstone (1966). These investigators asked high school students to remember lists of words that were organized according to conceptual categories (e.g., four-footed animals, weapons). Individuals in a condition of cued recall were given the names of the categories at the time of recall; individuals in a condition of free recall were tested without any cues. The number of words recalled was greater in the cued-recall condition than in the free recall condition. Because individuals in the two conditions were treated identically up to the retrieval phase, one can assume that the amount of information potentially available for recall should have been the same for individuals in both recall conditions. The superiority of cued recall over free recall, therefore, indicates that information may be stored but not accessible under certain retrieval conditions.

Thus, successful remembering depends not only on the availability of information but also on other factors associated with retrieval processes. The presence or absence of retrieval cues has already been identified as one such factor by Tulving and Pearlstone (1966). Undoubtedly, many other factors that occur at retrieval may be responsible for improved or imperfect remembering. A closer examination of retrieval processes, then, is a necessary prerequisite for identifying such additional factors.

B. Stages of Retrieval Processes

The brief sketch of the retrieval process that follows is based heavily on descriptions of these processes in adults (e.g., Lindsay & Norman, 1972; Shiffrin, 1970). The purpose of the present section is to point to several strategies and skills involved in the retrieval process rather than touching on the richness or the scope of any of the existing models.

The retrieval process begins when a question is presented to or raised by an individual, and ends when that person terminates his search of memory. With this definition, the retrieval process may be divided into two major stages: (1) a memory search, in which the individual examines the contents of his memory that may result in the recovery of the desired information, and (2) a decision process, in which he determines whether the information that has been recovered is acceptable as an answer. If the information is not acceptable, the individual may decide to continue the search, in which case the process recycles. Each of these stages will be elaborated in the following discussion.

1. Memory Search

An individual's search of his memory may begin partly under the direction of his overall strategy. The overall strategy determines where he will initiate and how he will proceed with the search, and how exhaustively he should conduct the search. The elaborateness of the overall strategy presumably varies according to the type of information requested and the individual's competence.

The individual's memory search also begins partly directed and restricted by the cues involved in test instructions. Typically, laboratory test instructions have temporal cues that restrict the range of the memory search (for example, "Tell me all the words included in *the list just presented*"). The memory search does not require an elaborate strategy if target items are still in an active state. A telephone number a person just looked up in the directory and the last item he just named are likely to be in his active memory at least for a brief period of time. When a subject is asked to recall a list of items in any order, an overall strategy may be to examine his active memory before searching for those items that are not immediately accessible.

When the test instructions have additional cues, as paired-associate or cued-recall instructions do (for example, "The *dog* jumped over the _____"), a subject can further restrict the search area to associates of a particular referent (that is, *dog*). If a person's task is to indicate simply whether or not a particular item was previously presented on a list, his memory search is greatly controlled by the test instruction, and consequently, the role of his strategy in the memory search may be minimized. Of course, an adult may complicate the task, and use elaborate retrieval strategies even for a recognition test (e.g., Mandler, 1972).

Other cues may be generated from memory in terms of a person's retrieval strategies, some of which are constructed during storage. Consider, for example, an adult's recall of a categorized list. An adult typically detects the categorized nature of the list at the time of learning. During retrieval, he first recalls the category names, then searches for related instances of each of the recalled categories (e.g., Cohen, 1966). Similarly, a list of items may be memorized together with such cues as letters of the alphabet that have an explicit sequence (e.g., Tulving, 1962). An individual notes the first letter of each word on the list during storage, and makes an attempt to associate the word with the letter. At the time of recall, he goes through the letters of the alphabet one at a time and tries to search for the words that went with each letter. The use of such overlearned cues as letters of the alphabet facilitates the search by restricting the search order (alphabetical) as well as the range of search.

The process of memory search may be simple as long as the context of the retrieval situation is consistent with the manner in which items were initially stored. However, when a retrieval question requires reorganization of the stored items, the memory search may become difficult. For example, one of the list items, *sword,* may have been memorized as one of the objects associated with MEDIEVAL KNIGHTS. If the task then is to recall all of the names of the objects that were associated with MEDIEVAL KNIGHTS, an individual can search for and find this particular item (that is, *sword*) using the instruction as a retrieval cue. Retrieval of the same item may become hard, however, if the words to be recalled are all of the objects that were WEAPONS (Funkhouser, 1968; see also Tulving & Thomson, 1973). Under the second retrieval condition, an adult apparently goes through his original classification scheme, instead of using the test instruction as a retrieval cue, to "find" the target items (Salatas & Flavell, 1976). The items may be recalled, but the search process becomes slow.

Finally, a person constantly stores information about events he experiences without any specific plans for future retrieval. If such information is needed later but is not immediately accessible, a person may systematically reconstruct past events by using information he can recall as retrieval cues and clues involved in the question. Lindsay and Norman (1972) illustrated this point with an imaginary individual attempting to answer the question, "What were you doing on Monday afternoon in the third week of September two years ago?" One portion of the question, *two years ago,* initially directs the memory search. Then the next portion of the question, *third week of September,* together with the answer to the first subquestion, directs the subsequent search until the appropriate context is found.

In summary, memory search has been characterized as an individual's attempt to restrict the range of the search by selectively using, in a proper sequence, the clues available in the retrieval instructions and those retrieved as a result of the memory search. The process of memory search can be simple and may not require the use of elaborate strategies when target items are still in an active state or when answers are prepared for anticipated questions. The memory search may become difficult when retrieval questions require reclassification of the stored information or when a person has to construct retrieval plans entirely at the time of recall.

2. Decision Processes

The information found through a memory search may not immediately be given as an answer to the question, but may be evaluated first. A person's decision that the information recovered is sufficient to form acceptable answers may depend on some criterion. A criterion may be how definitely the person should recognize the recovered information as that on a list. The person may examine whether the recovered information fits some required characteristic of the answer (e.g., "Is it a toy used mainly outside the house?") or his information about task requirements (e.g., "Does the task require single or multiple responses?").

How does an individual decide to terminate the memory search? According to Shiffrin (1970), at least three factors are associated with an individual's decision to terminate his search: (1) the extent of the recovery of the desired information mentioned in the preceding paragraph; (2) the expiration of the response time; and (3) the decay of information in memory store. The first factor may be affected by the second and third. For example, if a person finds that the response time is likely to be terminated soon (factor 2) and/or that the recovery process is slow (factor 3), he may lower his criteria for factor 1 and examine fewer items in his memory for each of the questions on a test. The use of this strategy is less likely, however, when response time is unlimited, multiple responses are required, and target items are readily accessible (Shiffrin, 1970).

3. Summary

Remembering depends not only on the content of stored information but also on other factors associated with retrieval processes. Two major types of factors in the retrieval process may affect the amount of information a person can remember. The first type subsumes the individual's various strategies used to find the "locations" of the target information and the presence or absence of effective cues in the test situations. They were discussed in relation to a memory search. Factors of the second type are associated with decision processes used to evaluate the acceptability of information that has been recovered and to terminate a memory search. The distinction between these two types of factors is not meant to be mutually exclusive. Presumably, one type of factor may affect the other. When a quick response is required, an adult may not use an elaborate search strategy. The use of an inefficient search strategy may lead to a slow recovery process. The separation of factors into these two types may be useful at this stage, since the role of factors of the second type in the retrieval process has been largely ignored in developmental studies.

III. RELEVANT STUDIES WITH CHILDREN

While acknowledging that younger children presumably do not store test items as efficiently as older children, some developmental psychologists have argued that poorer performance by younger children on memory tasks may also be due to their inability to retrieve items that have been stored (Eysenck & Baron, 1974; Halperin, 1974). This *retrieval deficit hypothesis* has been examined by using at least two different experimental procedures that suggest limited capacity of the retrieval system in younger children. These studies will be examined in Section III.A.

We have seen (Section II.B) that a person's remembering depends on the use of strategies to locate the target information, the use of appropriate termination rules, and the ability to evaluate the recovered information as to its acceptability. The skills required for such strategies and activities might be expected to show age-related changes. Psychologists interested in developmental changes in retrieval processes have investigated questions related to the development of these skills. At what age will children spontaneously use externally available objects as retrieval cues? Having found a critical retrieval cue, how exhaustively do children search for the associated items with that cue? Studies that are relevant to these questions are also examined in the following Sections III.B and III.C.

A. Availability and Accessibility of Information

1. Free versus Constrained Recall

Learning materials used in the studies to be reviewed are discrete items (pictures or words) that can be grouped into several conceptual categories familiar to children. Children's retrieval difficulties are examined by comparing two types of recall: "constrained" and "free." In the constrained-recall procedure, children are required to recall all the items assigned from a particular category before proceeding to the next category. In the free recall procedure, children are given no category names and are simply asked to recall all of the items they learned in any order they prefer. If younger children are less adept at gaining access to potentially available category information than older children, younger children should benefit more from the constrained recall procedure than older children.

The retrieval deficit hypothesis was examined by Halperin (1974). In this study, 6-, 9-, and 12-year-old children heard a list of 36 words representing 9 categories (e.g., furniture, animals). All of the words from a particular category were presented consecutively, and were preceded by the category name in order to minimize age differences in the encoding of category information. During recall, half of the children were tested under a condition of free recall and the remaining children under a condition of constrained recall. Following two presentation and recall trials, a recognition test was given to all the children. Retrieval or search processes are assumed to be minimized on a recognition test (e.g., Kintsch, 1970), and thus the test provides an additional index of the availability of information in memory.

Providing category names during retrieval facilitated children's recall relative to free recall at all age levels. Thus, children's failure to recall freely some of the words on the list does not necessarily mean that these unrecalled words were not available in memory. At least some of the unrecalled words were available, but for some reason children could not retrieve them under the unaided free recall situation.

In order to examine further how the cuing procedure improved recall by children in the experimental condition, Halperin separated overall recall into two components: (1) category recall, defined as the number of categories recalled by the child, and (2) within-category recall, defined as the average number of words recalled for each category recalled. To illustrate, if a child recalled the words *bed, dresser,* and *bear,* then two categories (furniture and animals) were recalled with a within-category recall score of 1.5. Analysis of these component and recognition scores yielded the following results. The younger children recalled fewer categories than the older children under free recall conditions, but these age differences disappeared under the constrained-recall conditions. Apparently, the same number of higher-order memory units (categories) were available to the children of all ages, although the older children were better able to recall these category units when cues were not provided. Furthermore, older children recalled more items per category regardless of the recall conditions. Finally, the younger children, irrespective of the recall conditions, had lower recognition scores than the older children, suggesting presumably that they were less adept at storing verbal material.

In summary, older children seem to be able to retain information better and also are more able to rely on their own retrieval strategies to gain access to category units available in memory than younger children (Hagen, Jongeward, & Kail, 1975). Research is needed that will tell us precisely what strategies older children did use that younger children did not use. Did older children interrelate some categories so that recall of one category led to recall of additional categories? Did older children simply spend more time than younger children searching for unrecalled categories?

The children at all age levels tested in the Halperin study benefited from the constrained-recall procedures. Similar results were found by other investigators who tested children from kindergarten through adolescents (Eysenck & Baron, 1974; Kobasigawa, 1974; Lange, 1973; Moely, 1968; Scribner & Cole, 1972). With such reliably obtained differences between the two recall conditions, our next question concerns the manner in which the constrained-recall procedure facilitates children's recall. An examination of this question may help to better understand children's difficulties during retrieval.

It has been suggested that cuing by category names improves an individual's reccall by facilitating the retrieval of category units rather than enhancing within-category recall (Tulving & Pearlstone, 1966). This is precisely what Halperin (1974) found. In that study, for all age levels the constrained-recall procedure improved the number of categories recalled, but the average number of words recalled within a recalled category was the same for the two recall conditions.

While the findings in the study by Halperin suggest that children's retrieval limitations in recalling a list of categorizable items is due to their failure to recall category names, in at least three studies (Eysenck & Baron, 1974; Kobasigawa, 1974; Moely, 1968) it was found that the induced category-based recall increased within-category recall as well as category recall scores. In addition, Lange (1973) and Scribner and Cole (1972) found that the constrained procedure facilitated recall even with a list containing only four categories, which children presumably could recall without the assistance of the cuing procedure. Although these investigators did not separate overall recall scores into component scores, in a replication of the Lange study Kobasigawa (unpublished) found that the facilitation was due solely to increased within-category recall.

Constrained recall includes two major components: (1) presenting category names as retrieval cues and (2) requiring a child to conduct an exhaustive category-by-category search (Kobasigawa, 1974). Considering the second component, it should not be surprising that the constrained-recall procedure sometimes improves within-category recall scores. When diffuse category units are formed during presentation either because items are presented in a random order (Scribner & Cole, 1972) or because items within a category are less related (Lange, 1973), children, especially younger ones (Kobasigawa, 1974; Moely, 1968), may fail to exhaustively search each category unless explicitly directed to do so (that is, component 2). The findings suggest, then, that part of the children's failure to retrieve stored information may be due to insufficient memory search as well as failure to gain access to higher-order memory units. The first point, younger children's insufficient memory search, is demonstrated in a study that will be discussed in the next section.

2. Selective Reminding Paradigm

The discrepancy between storage and retrieval of information has also been demonstrated by means of a selective reminding procedure, a modified free recall paradigm (Buschke, 1974). In this paradigm, an entire list is presented only on the first trial. After the first trial, a child is exposed only to those items that he failed to recall on the immediately preceding trial. On each trial, however, the child is asked to recall all of the items on the list.

With this procedure, Buschke (1974) separated retrieval from short-term storage, in which information is retained only briefly, and retrieval from long-term storage, in which information resides for a relatively long period of time. In order to estimate the number of items in long-term storage, Buschke made the following three assumptions: (1) an item recalled on a given trial without presentation indicates retrieval from long-term storage; (2) an item enters long-term storage on the trial immediately before that item is first recalled without presentation; and (3) an item remains in long-term storage once it has been recalled from long-term storage. With these assumptions, the number of items in long-term storage can be estimated by the cumulative number of items that have been retrieved from long-term storage. On the nth trial, for example, a child (1) recalled five items without presentation; (2) recalled two items with presentation and recalled these items on the next trial without presentation; (3) failed to recall two items that he recalled on previous trials without presentation; and (4) recalled one item with presentation but failed to recall that item on the next trial. The child, then, had nine items in long-term storage [(1) + (2) + (3)], seven of which were recalled [(1) + (2)] on the nth trial. One item was recalled from short-term storage (4).

Buschke also separated recall items on each trial into two kinds: Recall of an item was classified as consistent retrieval on trial n if that item was recalled on all of the subsequent trials; recall of an item was defined as random retrieval if that item was not recalled consistently on the remaining trials. It is assumed that the degree of consistent retrieval reflects a person's organized or systematic retrieval search (Buschke, 1974; Patterson, 1972).

In Buschke's study, 5- and 8-year-old children learned to recall a list of 10 animal names under the selective reminding procedure. Recall from short-term storage contributed little to recall at either age level. The number of items available in long-term storage was lower for the younger children than for the older children, suggesting that the 5-year-olds were slower than the 8-year-olds in acquiring information. Important findings for our purpose were (1) that the discrepancy between long-term storage and retrieval from long-term storage was greater for the younger children than for the older children and (2) that this discrepancy tended to become greater with trials for the younger children while becoming smaller for the older children. In addition, consistent retrieval scores were higher than random retrieval scores at the older age level on all trials, whereas this trend was reversed for the younger children, at least during the first four trials. These findings indicate, then, that the lower recall performance of the 5-year-old children was partly due to ineffective retrieval from long-term storage.

In the present section, children's limited capacity to retrieve information has been examined on the basis of two different experimental procedures. Halperin (1974), who used the constrained-recall procedure, was concerned with children's failure to gain access to higher-order memory units and showed that younger children tended to have greater difficulties with this process than older children do. After a child recalls category names either spontaneously or through the constrained-recall procedure, the next problem is to find the available items within each category. Buschke (1974) has shown that younger children are again more inefficient than older children in gaining access to individual items within a category. Thus, we should be concerned in future studies with the question of why older children are better able to conduct a systematic search of recovered categories as well as why older children are better able to retrieve category information. In the next two sections, the development of retrieval skills in children at different age levels will be examined more closely.

B. Use of External Cues by Children

The important role of retrieval cues in children's recall was sufficiently demonstrated in the preceding section, but little attention was paid to the development of spontaneous use of such cues. It was indicated in Section IIB that one important characteristic of an adult who is attempting to recall is that he will often direct his memory search by restricting the range of responses. For this purpose, he uses internal as well as external cues that are likely to remind him of the target information. The child, as he grows older, should presumably become able to recognize the usefulness of a search for retrieval cues when the target information is not accessible directly. The developmental course of the child's use of external cues is examined in the present section. Other processes (e.g., exhaustive search) that may occur as ancillary to the cue utilization will also be discussed.

1. Utilization of External Objects as Retrieval Cues

Do young children look for externally available items that can serve as good retrieval cues when the recovery of the target information is difficult? This question was investigated by Ritter, Kaprove, Fitch, and Flavell (1973) with 3½- to 5½-year-old children. The test materials consisted of six pictures of different persons (e.g., football player) and six small toys (e.g., football), each of which was closely associated with one of the six persons. First, the experimenter showed six "house-toybox" units to the child, who watched each "person" (e.g., football player) go into each of the houses, leaving his toy (football) in the adjacent toybox. While the toy in the toybox was visible from the top, the "person" in the house was no longer visible. The child was then given a duplicate set of the pictures and was asked to find the "friend" of each person. If the child looked at the toys inside the toyboxes, successful recall of each "friend's" location was guaranteed for the child. When the child had matched the six pairs, the experimenter placed one set of the pictures face down on the floor and removed all of the toys and the remaining set of pictures from the room. Then the experimenter asked the child to remember the names of the toys he had just taken from the room. The pictures on the floor could serve as retrieval cues for the recall of the names of toys.

Performance at the different age levels was quite similar when the retrieval cues were visible in the boxes. At least half of the children at each age level used the toys as retrieval cues for recalling the locations of "friends" in the houses. In contrast, distinct developmental changes were observed in children's performance on the second task. Approximately 75% of the older children (4½ to 5½ years of age) used the face-down pictures as retrieval cues without any prompt or with weak prompts ("How can we be sure to name all the toys?"), whereas less than one-quarter of the younger children (3½ to 4½ years of age) used retrieval cues under these prompt conditions. Furthermore, 30% of the younger children still did not use cues even after an explicit demonstration by the experimenter. It appears, then, that some preschool children can think about using external objects as cues for the recall of target information at least in a simple recall situation. This ability seems to increase during preschool years.

Kobasigawa (1974) conducted a similar study with 6-, 8-, and 11-year-old children. The children were shown 24 pictorial items representing 8 categories. Items from a category were presented with the appropriate retrieval cues. For example, each of the three animal pictures (items to be recalled) was presented with the picture of a zoo (cue). During presentation, instructions were given that explicitly indicated the relationships between the cue and each of the three items (for example, "In the zoo you find the bear"). Although only one item was assigned to each cue in the Ritter et al. (1973) study, multiple responses were required for each cue in the Kobasigawa study. Consequently, the role of decision processes or the use of termination rules (e.g., "How long should I search for the related items for each cue?") was relatively more important in the Kobasigawa study than in the Ritter et al. study.

In one of recall conditions of the Kobasigawa study, children were given a duplicate set of cue cards and were allowed to look at the cards if they thought that the cards would be helpful. When this recall procedure was used, many of the 8- and 11-year-old children used the cues spontaneously to recall target items. In contrast, only 4 of the 12 6-year-old children used the cues, and they recalled approximately 45% of the items. Those 6-year-old children who used cues typically moved from one cue to the next, recalling only one item for each cue. Some of the 8-year-old children also did this. Unlike the 6-year-olds, however, the 8-year-olds went through the cue cards several times and recalled 66% of the test items. In contrast, the 11-year-old children used cues to greatly improve their recall; these children recalled about 80% of the items and were more likely than either group of younger children to recall all or most of the items assigned to one category before moving to the next.

Thus, when older children used the cues they tended to recall more items than younger children who also used the cues spontaneously. These observed age changes in the children's spontaneous and efficient use of retrieval cues, however, cannot be attributable simply to the younger children's storage deficit. When the children were shown each cue by the experimenter and asked to recall the three items associated with that cue, age differences in recall disappeared; the children at all age levels could recall approximately 85% of the recall items.

We have seen in the Ritter et al. (1973) study that some preschool children use external objects as retrieval cues. When recall task is made slightly more difficult by assigning additional items to each cue, age-related changes in children's spontaneous and effective use of retrieval cues seem to appear among elementary school children, even though a smiliar amount of information is available in storage at all age levels.

2. Utilization of Category Size Information

In the study just described (Kobasigawa, 1974), 6-year-old children searched for stored information only long enough to recall one item from a given category. Young children might, however, conduct a more exhaustive memory search if the number of items assigned to each cue (that is, category size) was indicated on a retrieval cue card.

This possibility was examined in a subsequent study by Tumolo, Mason, and Kobasigawa (1974) with 6- and 8-year-old children. The recall materials and presentation procedures were identical to those used in the Kobasigawa (1974) study. Children's recall was tested under one of two conditions: Children in an *uninformed* condition were given a deck of cue cards and reminded that some of the recall items went with each of the cue cards; the cue cards given to the children in an *informed* condition had three blue squares on them as reminders of the category size. With these procedures, 6-year-old children recalled 65% of the items when category size information was provided during retrieval, while 6-year-olds in the uninformed condition could recall only 45% of the items. In contrast, the facilitative effect of providing category size information was not observed with the 8-year-old children. Apparently, recall instructions reminding the children that some of the recall items went with each cue, instructions not included in the initial study (Kobasigawa, 1974), were sufficient to produce high recall scores in many of the 8-year-olds in the uninformed condition. Regardless of whether the category size information was present or absent, the 8-year-old children recalled approximately 75% of the recall items. The results also may mean that 8-year-olds are slightly more efficient in the use of retrieval cues than was suggested in the previous study (Kobasigawa, 1974).

The presence of the category size information apparently affected children's search behaviors in one of two ways. Nearly all of the children in the informed condition attempted to recall all three items from a category before they proceeded to the next category (that is, category-based exhaustive search), although they were not always successful in recalling all of the three items. In the uninformed condition, most of the 6-year-olds and approximately one-third of the 8-year-olds went through the deck of cue cards reporting only one item for each cue. About half of these 6-year-old children terminated their recall after looking at each cue once (that is, nonexhaustive search). The remaining 6-year-olds and all of these 8-year-olds went through the cards several times. The latter approach may have represented a strategy of exhaustive search based on the entire list rather than on individual categories. It was, however, an inefficient approach because many of the previously recalled items were repeated each time the child went through the cue cards.

The findings from both the Kobasigawa (1974) and Tumolo et al. (1974) studies are consistent with the hypothesis that children become more proficient with age in the use of an exhaustive search strategy. Provision of category size information appears to be one way to modify younger children's nonexhaustive and nonsystematic search strategies.

Although the information about the size of a set of items to be recalled was more beneficial for younger than for older children in the Tumolo et al. study, this does not preclude the possibility that in other situations such information would also be beneficial to older children who are likely to use a category-based exhaustive search. Adults, for example, may underestimate the size of a particular set ("Tell me the names of the states that begin with the letter M"), or they may overestimate it ("Tell me the names of the states that begin with the letter U"). Individuals in the first situation may terminate their memory search prior to retrieval of all members of the category, while in the second situation they may work longer than is appropriate (Winograd, 1970). Information about set size, then, should be beneficial to older children in terms of allocating an appropriate amount of time for each recall requirement. Set size information, however, probably would not modify their search strategy as it did for the younger children.

Finally, the use of category size information to conduct an exhaustive memory search was an appropriate strategy in the Kobasigawa (1974) and the Tumolo et al. (1974) studies where all or most of the recall items were retrievable from memory by children. The use of the exhaustive search, however, would be quite inappropriate and inefficient when a particular set of items is not definitely in an individual's memory or when quick responses are required. An adult seems to immediately terminate his memory search for a given question by assessing that the required items are not retrieval within the allocated amount of time and decides to move on to more rewarding questions (Lindsay & Norman, 1972; Winograd, 1970). Thus, an interesting avenue for future developmental research would be to determine whether or not children use the exhaustive memory search in a discriminative manner by monitoring the retrievability of the requested information or by considering the amount of time allocated for a recall period.

3. Summary

It has been shown that some preschool children are able to use externally available items as retrieval cues, although it is unclear what proportion of these children use this strategy intentionally. During the elementary school years, children's use of such a strategy becomes more spontaneous, and their memory search more systematic. Young elementary school children typically allocate only a very brief time for retrieval processes, even when additional items are definitely accessible. Do these young children terminate the memory search quickly because (1) they underestimate the magnitude of a required task; (2) they are not sufficiently motivated; or (3) they do not know that retrieval of information sometimes requires additional effort? These questions have not been extensively studied yet. At any rate, when category size information is included in test situations, many young elementary school children are able to use this additional cue to systematically guide their memory search. The presence of category size information apparently has different beneficial effects on strategies during retrieval, depending on the age of the child and task demands.

C. Utilization of Internal Cues (Category Names)

1. Application of Category-Based Recall Procedure to a New List

In studies such as those discussed in the preceding section, objects to guide retrieval may be available in the environment. Such cues were not available in the studies to be reviewed in this section: Children initially had to generate their own retrieval cues from memory and then search for as many associated items as they could with that cue. It was indicated previously (Section III.A) that elementary school children can use a category-by-category retrieval strategy when directed to do so. In this section, the concern is with an associated question: Do more older children than younger children continue to maintain the category-based recall strategy even when explicit instructions referring to the categories are no longer present?

Scribner and Cole (1972) examined this question by presenting, in random order, twenty nouns to 7-, 9-, and 11-year-old children. During the first three practice trials, children in a control condition were reminded, at presentation and recall, of the four categories that were involved in the list; they were, however, allowed to recall items in any order they preferred. Following the same presentation procedure, children in the experimental condition were required to recall, at the experimenter's direction, all of the items for one category before moving on to the next (that is, constrained recall). For all ages, the children in the experimental condition recalled more items than the children in the control condition did, especially on Trials 2 and 3. However, when children's recall was tested under a free recall procedure with a transfer list containing four new categories, differences in recall between experimental and control conditions disappeared at all age levels. The older children in the experimental condition continued to maintain higher clustering scores than those in the control condition on the transfer trial, indicating that older children are more likely than younger children to apply previously practiced strategies to new learning material. The clustering scores of the older children were, however, substantially lower than those obtained during the practice trials. In other words, the older children also failed to use the category-based recall strategy to its full extent.

The difficulties children had in transfering the practiced retrieval skills in the Scribner and Cole (1972) study may be related not solely to a retrieval phase but also to a storage phase. It seems plausible to assume that the effectiveness of a category-based recall strategy depends on whether the items are initially stored in memory according to such category units. Based on this assumption, the findings that many children on the transfer retrieval task discontinued using a category structure as a retrieval aid may be due partly to their failure to organize transfer list items into appropriate category units during the acquisition phase. There are at least two different sources for this failure. First, the children may not have been aware of what storage strategies would be appropriate in order to facilitate the subsequent use of a category-based retrieval strategy. This is more likely to have been the problem for younger children. Second, although the children knew how they should prepare for future retrieval, they did not have sufficient time to organize recall items into category units. The children were exposed to the transfer list only once without receiving any category information. Perhaps Lange (1973) meant to eliminate this second source of difficulty in his study, to which we now turn.

Scribner and Cole presented verbal items successively and used practice and transfer lists containing entirely different categories; Lange used similar procedures but presented pictorial items simultaneously and used the same four sets of categories for both the practice and transfer lists. Thus, category names identified for the practice list were equally applicable for the transfer lists. During a study period for Trial 1, children were required to identify four instances of each of the four categories involved in the list. The recall of half of these children was tested under the constrained procedure, while the recall of the remaining children was tested under the condition of free recall. Each of the two transfer lists was presented to the children on Trials 2 and 3 (transfer trials) without category identification. All of the children were tested for their recall under the free recall procedure. Fifteen-year-olds who received the constrained-recall practice tended to maintain their high clustering in recall during transfer trials. As for the younger children (5½- and 11-year-olds), however, Lange essentially replicated the Scribner and Cole results in terms of both clustering and overall recall scores. Unfortunately, Lange's procedure represents an interference paradigm. A person's recall of the second list is likely to be suppressed when the first and second lists are encoded in the same manner (see, for example, Hagen et al., 1975). While the use of the same categories for both training and transfer lists may be a good idea, the procedure might have introduced different sources of difficulty to children who received the constrained-recall procedures.

As Scribner and Cole (1972) concluded, then, elementary school children apparently need more "extensive training in category retrieval" than simple practice with a constrained-recall procedure in order to use a category structure of a list effectively as a retrieval plan. This training may have to include training children on category grouping during the acquisition phase as well (see Smirnov, Istomina, Mal'tseva, & Samokhvalova, 1971–1972, for such training procedures). In order to determine effective ways to train children, a more detailed examination of the sources of children's difficulties in performing the category-based retrieval strategy is needed.

2. Utilizing a Category Structure as a Retrieval Aid Under Various Situations of Retrieval

Information stored in memory is contained within an organized structure, and adults use this structure to aid them in retrieving information (e.g., Hagen et al., 1975). Studies on children's free recall of categorizable items have indicated that elementary school children do use such retrieval strategies if a strong structure is acquired through presentation procedures (see Jablonski, 1974). When an explicit structure of a recall list is learned during presentation, children as young as 6 years of age even use a hierarchical retrieval plan. For example, they initially search for subcategories of animals (zoo animals, pets, farm animals) before they search for subcategories of household objects during free recall (Worden, 1974). The free recall situation, of course, does not represent all of the test situations children encounter. In some situations, children may be asked to recall only one portion of the learned material. In others, children may be required to reorganize previously stored items according to newly acquired information. An important question, therefore, is how efficiently children can use the organized structure of memory as an aid in locating the required information under various retrieval situations.

Findings relevant to this question were provided in a recent study by Salatas and Flavell (1976). Subjects at the 6-, 9-, and 21-year-old (college student) levels were required to learn a list of words with an explicit category structure (toys, clothes, tools) until they could recall all of the items under the constrained-recall procedure. Consequently, the experimenters were relatively certain that all of the individuals had stored items with their associated retrieval cues and that all of the required items were available in memory. The ability to spontaneously use a category structure as a retrieval plan was assessed by two ''indirect retrieval'' questions, each of which required individuals to reproduce selectively some of the items from each of the original categories. For example, the answers to the question, ''Which ones are small enough to fit in this box (30 × 20 × 13 cm)?'' would include crayons, whistle (toys); belt, ring, bow tie (clothes); needle, scissors (tools). According to Salatas and Flavell, a good retrieval plan that will help determine whether all of the requested items have been recalled would include the following components: (1) retrieve each of the original categories; (2) think about all of the items in that category (an exhaustive search); (3) decide whether each of the recovered items is acceptable as an answer; (4) report verbally items that are accepted; and (5) repeat these processes for the remaining categories. When an individual follows this retrieval plan systematically, his recall scores should be perfect and his verbal responses of ''small'' items and ''outside'' items should be clustered by the original categories (see the example of the answers provided in this paragraph).

Using these two criteria, only one out of 32 6-year-old children and three out of 32 9-year-old children spontaneously used the systematic category search when answering the two ''indirect retrieval'' questions. In contrast, most of the 21-year-olds used this exhaustive category-by-category search. The experimenter then explicitly told the subject how to conduct the systematic category search to answer the two ''indirect retrieval'' questions. Although all of the college students and more than half of the 9-year-olds could follow this explicit instruction, most of the 6-year-olds again failed to meet the category search criteria. When asked to recall all the items in any order they preferred, however, a majority of the 6- and 9-year-old children did use the category organization to structure their nearly perfect recall performance.

At around age 9, then, some children appear to be able to use the category structure to answer the ''indirect retrieval'' questions so long as explicit instructions are provided, but only a few of these children use such skills on a spontaneous basis. It is unlikely, however, that children at this age level planfully used a category-based search. Salatas and Flavell reported that none of the 9-year-old children who were successful on the ''indirect retrieval'' task was aware of his strategy. Most 6- and many 9-year-old children apparently did not have the skills to perform the category-based recall strategy to answer the ''indirect retrieval'' questions; these children failed to perform a systematic category search even when explicit instructions were provided. Unlike the free recall task, in which the individual can simply verbalize all of the items, answering the ''indirect retrieval'' questions requires him (1) to conduct a systematic ''internal'' search and (2) to make a decision as to the acceptability of the recovered information as an answer. These two components may, perhaps, be the major sources of the difficulties for many of the younger children in using successfully the systematic category search in the "indirect retrieval" situation. Do many of the 6-year-old children still fail to conduct an exhaustive "internal" search while making a decision even if such a search is restricted to only one category (e.g., all of the "small" things from the toy category)? It may be that the 6-year-olds were unable to maintain the retrieval plan provided by the experimenter when they had to do (1) and (2) for all of the categories involved in the list.

3. Summary

In a sense, we have reviewed two types of "transfer of training" studies in this section. In both types of studies, children initially practiced using the structural organization of information for the recall of the learned materials. In the first type of study, children were then required to apply this systematic search strategy for the recall of a new list, while children in the second type were to use the practiced strategy for answering new questions about the original material. In the first type, even kindergarten children apparently have the necessary basic skills, although children of a wide age range seem to fail to apply the practiced strategy to a new task. In the second type, however, the required skills involved in the transfer task go beyond a mere category-based search; a child is required to verbally report only some of the items from each of the original categories. Consequently, young children (6-year-olds) could not use the practiced strategy even under explicit instructions. Although some developmental trends were observed in both types, more studies are needed to identify potential sources of difficulties that children of different ages might have in using the organized structure of information as a retrieval plan under various recall situations. It may be worthwhile to point out that the stages of retrieval processes outlined in Section II.B are clearly included in the Salatas and Flavell (1976) study for the purpose of investigation.

D. Cases of No Developmental Differences

The major theme of this chapter is that younger children are more deficient in their use of effective retrieval strategies than older children. This hypothesis has been examined thus far by reviewing the studies in which children's successful performance on memory tasks was assumed to be dependent on the use of elaborate strategies. The hypothesis would also receive support if age differences in remembering are not observed or minimized in experimental situations where successful performance does not require deliberate retrieval strategies (Brown, 1973a). Two such cases will be considered in this section.

1. Recall for Items Presented Recently

It has been suggested previously that the process of memory search can be simple if the target information is still in an active state. Recall for the last item on a list that was just named by a child is such a case. A study by Hagen and Kingsley (1968) serves to illustrate this point. In that study, after eight pictures had been presented one at a time and then placed face down in row, a child was given a cue card and asked to turn over the one presentation card that matched the cue card. Recall for the last-presented items (recency recall) by 6-year-old children was as good as that by 10-year-old children, while recall for the first-presented items was lower for the younger as compared with the older children. In a different experiment by Frank and Rabinovitch (1974), children between the ages of 8 and 12 listened to lists of numbers and were asked to recall as many numbers as they could from the ends of the lists. Recall for recency was high at all age levels, and again age differences in recall were minimized. Thus, when children are asked to recall the last items on lists, those that presumably are still in an active state, age differences in retrieval are likely to be minimal.

2. Judgment of Recency

Which of two events occurred more recently, A or B? If information about events has been stored together with some context cues that suggest dates (e.g., birthday party) or approximate dates (e.g., first semester of my freshman year), one strategy to answer such a question may be to retrieve such contexts in which events took place. Apparently, an 8-year-old child can think about such a strategy (Kreutzer, Leonard, & Flavell, 1975, Retrieval: Event).

In an experimental recency judgment task used by Brown (1973a), the possibility of using such deliberate strategies was eliminated. Test items were presented in no logical sequence and without contextual cues. A child first viewed a long list of pictorial items. Then he was shown two test pictures, both of which had been presented previously, and was asked to indicate which one of the pictures had been presented more recently. Under this testing procedure, Brown (1973a) found that college students' judgments of relative recency were no better than those made by 7-year-olds. In a subsequent study, Brown (1973b) presented inspection items together with background cues to one group of children. The background cues consisted of a house, a garden, and a street that correlated with the temporal order of a child's journey to school. There was again no age difference in the accuracy of children's recency judgments when the background cues were not available. However, when the background cues were provided during presentation, the accuracy of recency judgments by 10-year-olds was greatly improved, while 7-year-olds could not benefit from such cues. Consequently, evidence is available supporting the hypothesis that when a task does not require elaborate retrieval strategies no developmental improvement in performance is likely to appear.

E. Preparation for Future Retrieval

Age-related changes in children's use of retrieval strategies have been discussed independently of encoding and storage processes. This does not mean, however, that facilitative effects on recall of various retrieval strategies are unrelated to the manner in which children initially encode or store information. The relationship between children's storage activities and the effectiveness of retrieval strategies will now be examined briefly.

The notion that children's preparation for future retrieval affects the effectiveness of retrieval cues has been demonstrated by Moely (1968). In this study, pictures from different categories were presented to children of 7 and 10 years of age. Items were either grouped in categories or arranged randomly on presentation cards. Providing subjects with category names at the time of recall increased the number of categories represented in recall following the presentation of items in groups but not following the random presentation of items. Thus, elementary school children's use of category names as retrieval cues may be limited to the extent to which they rehearse the items initially in a conceptually organized manner. When still younger children are used, cuing their recall with category names may interfere with their retrieval if items are not initially organized. Yussen, Kunen, and Buss (1975) have shown that a constrained-recall procedure, as compared with a free recall procedure, significantly decreases rather than increases preschool children's recall following random presentation.

Given that the manner in which children encode and store information affects their future retrieval processes, it seems reasonable to ask whether or not children are aware of such relationships and whether or not they prepare differently during study periods according to the demands of different retrieval situations. In relation to these questions, evidence was found in recent studies that suggests that preschool children apparently begin to realize that remembering requires additional activities besides merely looking at something. Young children become more "attentive" to objects when they anticipate a recall test than when they do not (e.g., Yussen, 1974; Wellman, Ritter, & Flavell, 1975). When preschool children are allowed to "do anything" during storage to facilitate future retrieval, they are able to use external objects as effective retrieval cues for the recall of locations of hidden items (e.g., Ritter, 1975; Ryan, Hegion, & Flavell, 1970).

If future retrieval requires children to conduct an internal rather than an external search, older elementary school children prepare much more efficiently than preschool children do. Appel, Cooper, McCarrell, Sims-Knight, Yussen, and Flavell (1972) examined whether children would inspect items differently when they anticipated a recall test than when they were merely told to look at a set of items. Eleven-year-old children organized pictorial items into conceptual categories and verbally rehearsed the names of the items more frequently when they anticipated the recall test than when they did not. Such rehearsal of related items together should aid these children's future retrieval, since recall of one item would lead to the recall of many other related items. These efficient study activities, however, did not appear even under the memory instruction condition with 4-year-old children.

As a child grows older and experiences different retrieval situations, he may become aware that different retrieval demands (for example, true–false questions versus essay examination; word-by-word recall versus recall of main ideas) require different preparations. Consistent with this expectation, Horowitz and Horowitz (1975) found that 11-year-old children prepared differently when they expected a test of recall than when they expected a recognition test. In contrast, the performance of 5-year-old children did not differ under these two different instructions. Furthermore, older children, as compared to younger, tend to anticipate which groups of items are likely to be more difficult in retrieving than others and, consequently, allocate additional study time for such difficult items (Masur, McIntyre, & Flavell, 1973). An individual beyond the elementary school years may store information with an eye toward those retrieval cues that might be useful later.

From the available evidence, then, we may conclude that storage and retrieval processes are intimately related and that older children are more inclined than younger children to store information with retrieval situations in mind. When age differences in encoding and storage activities are minimized, however, there are also skills unique to retrieval of information at which younger children are less proficient than older children.

IV. CONCLUDING REMARKS

Several conclusions may be tentatively drawn from the studies reviewed in this chapter concerning the use of some selected retrieval strategies. Preschool children appear to have the ability to use an externally available object as a retrieval cue for the recall of directly inaccessible information, even though they may not spontaneously utilize this indirect retrieval strategy. As children grow older, they become able to conduct an exhaustive memory search while using a retrieval cue. During the elementary school years, they acquire skills to perform a systematic memory search as well as skills to make decisions regarding the acceptability of the recovered information. In general, when children make use of the retrieval strategies examined in this chapter, on a spontaneous basis or at the experimenter's direction, their recall performance seems to increase. It has been shown also that such age differences in the efficient use of retrieval strategies are likely to appear when successful performance on memory tasks require deliberate strategies and when test situations are arranged properly so that children can use such strategies to improve recall.

The findings reported in this chapter complement previous research (e.g., Flavell, 1970) concerning children's use of storage strategies in two ways. First, children move from a stage in which they have the required skills to use strategies but do not spontaneously use them to a new stage in which their utilization of strategies is more spontaneous and efficient. Second, such developmental shifts emerge at different ages depending on a particular skill (for example, use of an exhaustive search tends to appear later than use of a simple retrieval cue) and also on a particular situation (for example, use of a category-based recall strategy appears later under a "selective retrieval" task than under a free recall task).

Several comments are made in the remaining section regarding the current status of research. These comments are related to methodological problems as well as to research issues that have been barely investigated.

The first comment is related to a methodological problem. A child's successful use of retrieval strategies is partly affected by how he has encoded information and whether or not that information is available at the time of retrieval. Consequently, a satisfactory demonstration that younger children fail to gain access to the stored information because of difficulties associated with retrieval phase requires an investigator to minimize age differences in encoding and storage problems. Age differences in encoding have been controlled, at least in some studies, by providing children, for example, with category information explicitly at the time of presentation (e.g., Halperin, 1974; Salatas & Flavell, 1976). The availability of information, however, has rarely been equated among children of different ages. Thus, retrieval difficulties observed with younger children may have been associated with storage problems. One unique exception is the study by Salatas and Flavell (1976), in which the experimenters presented items to children until they were relatively certain that all of the required items were stored by both young and old children. This type of procedure should be used more frequently in future for investigating diverse problems of retrieval.

There are many research issues that have been left untouched. Information for the following general questions, however, may be central to our understanding of the development of retrieval processes. These questions are applicable to a wide range of retrieval strategies and situations that have been and will be studied. First, prior to a memory search, what kinds of retrieval plans or overall strategies will or can a child generate? Second, once retrieval plans are generated or given by the experimenter, how efficiently will or can a child follow them? Third, how does a child evaluate various retrieval strategies? Children sometimes fail to use appropriate retrieval strategies on a spontaneous basis although they may possess such skills (the so-called production deficiency). Without information concerning the preceding questions, however, it is impossible to make precise normative statements bearing on different sources of children's deficiency in using particular retrieval strategies under different task conditions. When these questions are included in a research design, we may find that sometimes children are more "planful" than their recall patterns may suggest; they may be using different retrieval strategies than the one the experimenter is interested in. These questions are also related to the cases in which children spontaneously produce effective retrieval strategies. Worden (1974) found that children as young as age 6 ordered their recall by using a hierarchical retrieval plan when recall items were organized explicitly during presentation. Halperin (1974) investigated children's retrieval of categories of different sizes and observed incidentally that children, including 6-year-olds, were inclined to order their memory search by examining the smallest categories (two-item categories) first, before searching the larger categories. While one might want to conclude that young children sometimes use such retrieval strategies as those cited here in order to improve recall, our knowledge of children's "deliberate" or "unintentional" use of retrieval strategies is at this point highly limited.

Because of the newness of the area, the focus of research has been placed on a narrow range of strategies: the use of retrieval cues. In the studies reviewed, all of the available cues, both internal and external, were relevant for directing the memory search and threfore were to be used exhaustively. In addition, the sequence in which children used these cues was immaterial. Children's understanding of the nature of cues (for example, what makes some of the cues more effective than others), their intelligent search strategies, and their understanding of the relationship between retrieval strategies and task demands may be better investigated by observing their flexible and discriminative use of retrieval cues. An important question for future studies is how selectively children can use most critical cues considering the task demands.

The studies reviewed in this chapter were mainly conducted in laboratory situations. We have reason to believe, however, that the children's behaviors observed in these studies are not restricted to the laboratory. Teachers have often observed that young children sometimes fail to give appropriate answers because they do not know how to handle broad questions, that they need very specific questions such as those used in constrained-recall procedures, that they do not use readily accessible recall cues to remind them of the target information, and that they do not spend sufficient time in search of additional unrecalled answers. It is worthwhile to examine what strategies children learn in classrooms for searching for information to form answers. At the same time, conclusions from the laboratory studies need to be examined in situations like those encountered by children in school, as Ceppi (1973) has attempted to do. Experimenters should be aware that there may be retrieval problems that can be best investigated by using school-related materials but not by using discrete items.

It should be apparent, then, that there is a need for much more information on how children search their memory, how they evaluate the recovered information to produce a satisfactory answer, how they terminate the memory search, and how these processes interact with each other. Although there has been a preoccupation with a constrained-free recall paradigm in investigating children's retrieval processes, this paradigm alone will not be sufficient to provide the necessary data for answering these questions. In order to obtain such necessary data, there is also a need for more creative research procedures. It appears that a most appropriate conclusion of the present chapter would be the introductory statement of the Salatas and Flavell (1976) study: "The developmental study of spontaneous retrieval plans and retrieval control skills has barely begun [p. 941]."

REFERENCES

Appel, L. F., Cooper, R. G., McCarrell, N., Sims-Knight, S., Yussen, S. R., & Flavell, J. H. The development of the distinction between perceiving and memorizing. *Child Development*, 1972, *43*, 1365–1381.

Brown, A. L. Judgments of recency for long sequences of pictures: The absence of a developmental trend. *Journal of Experimental Child Psychology*, 1973, *15*, 473–480.   (a)

Brown, A. L. Mnemonic elaboration and recency judgments in children. *Cognitive Psychology*, 1973, *5*, 233–248.   (b)

Buschke, H. Components of verbal learning in children: Analysis by selective reminding. *Journal of Experimental Child Psychology*, 1974, *18*, 488–496.

Butterfield, E. C., Wambold, C., & Belmont, J. M. On the theory and practice of improving short-term memory. *American Journal of Mental Deficiency*, 1973, *77*, 654–699.

Ceppi, C. M. Effects of presented and requested organization of children's recall of semantically-categorized sentences. Unpublished doctoral dissertation, Columbia University, 1973.

Cohen, B. H. Some-or-none characteristics of coding behavior. *Journal of Verbal Learning and Verbal Behavior*, 1966, *5*, 182–187.

Eysenck, M. W., & Baron, C. R. Effects of cuing on recall from categorized word lists. *Developmental Psychology*, 1974, *10*, 665–666.

Flavell, J. H. Developmental studies of mediated memory. In H. W. Reese & L. P. Lipsitt (Eds.), *Advances in Child Development and Behavior* (Vol. 5). New York: Academic Press, 1970.

Frank, H. S., & Rabinovitch, M. S. Auditory short-term memory: Developmental changes in rehearsal, *Child Development*, 1974, *45*, 397–407.

Funkhouser, G. R. Effects of differential encoding on recall. *Journal of Verbal Learning & Verbal Behavior*, 1968, *7*, 1016–1023.

Hagen, J. W. The effects of attention and mediation on children's memory. *Young Children*, 1971, *26*, 290–304.

Hagen, J. W., Jongeward, R. H., Jr., & Kail, R. V., Jr. Cognitive perspective on the development of memory. In H. Reese (Ed.), *Advances in child development and behavior* (Vol. 10). New York: Academic Press, 1975.

Hagen, J. W., & Kingsley, P. R. Labeling effects in short-term memory. *Child Development*, 1968, *39*, 113–121.

Halperin, M. S. Developmental changes in the recall and recognition of categorized word lists. *Child Development*, 1974, *45*, 144–151.

Horowitz, A. V., & Horowitz, V. A. The effects of task-specific instructions on the picture memory of children in recall and recognition tasks. Paper presented at the biennial meeting of the Society for Research in Child Development, Denver, 1975.

Jablonski, E. M. Free recall in children. *Psychological Bulletin*, 1974, *81*, 522–539.

Kintsch, W. Models for free recall and recognition. In D. A. Norman (Ed.), *Models of human memory*. New York: Academic Press, 1970.

Kobasigawa, A. Utilization of retrieval cues by children in recall. *Child Development*, 1974, *45*, 127–134.

Kreutzer, M. A., Leonard, C., & Flavell, J. H. An interview study of children's knowledge about memory. *Monographs of the Society for Research in Child Development*, 1975, *40*(1, Serial No.159).

Lange, G. The development of conceptual and rote recall skills among school age children. *Journal of Experimental Child Psychology*, 1973, *15*, 399–406.

Lindsay, P. H., & Norman, D. A. *Human information processing: An introduction to psychology.* New York: Academic Press, 1972.

Masur, E. F., McIntyre, C. W., & Flavell, J. H. Developmental changes in apportionment of study time among items in a multitrial free recall task. *Journal of Experimental Child Psychology*, 1973, *15*, 237–246.

Mandler, G. Organization and recognition. In E. Tulving & W. Donaldson (Eds), *Organization of memory.* New York: Academic Press, 1972.

Melton, A. W. Implication of short-term memory for a general theory of memory. *Journal of Verbal Learning and Verbal Behavior*, 1963, *2*, 1–21.

Moely, B. E. Children's retention of conceptually related items under varying presentation and recall conditions. Unpublished doctoral dissertation, University of Minnesota, 1968.

Patterson, K. E. Some characteristics of retrieval limitation in long-term memory. *Journal of Verbal Learning and Verbal Behavior*, 1972, *11*, 685–691.

Ritter, K. Development of production and maintenance of a retrieval cue strategy. Unpublished manuscript, University of Western Ontario, 1975.

Ritter, K., Kaprove, B. H., Fitch, J. P., & Flavell, J. H. The development of retrieval strategies in young children. *Cognitive Psychology*, 1973, *5*, 310–321.

Ryan, S. M., Hegion, A. G., & Flavell, J. H. Nonverbal mnemonic mediation in preschool children. *Child Development*, 1970, *41*, 539–550.

Salatas, H., & Flavell, J. H. Retrieval of recently learned information: Development of strategies and control skills. *Child Development*, 1976, *47*, 941–948.

Scribner, S., & Cole, M. Effects of constrained recall training on children's performance in a verbal memory task. *Child Development*, 1972, *43*, 845–857.

Shiffrin, R. M. Memory search. In D. A. Norman (Ed.), *Models of human memory.* New York: Academic Press, 1970.

Smirnov, A. A., Istomina, Z. M., Mal'tseva, K. P., & Samokhvalova, V. I. The development of logical memorization techniques in the preschool and young school child. *Soviet Psychology*, 1971–1972, *10*, 178–195.

Tulving, E. The effect of alphabetical subjective organization on memorizing unrelated words. *Canadian Journal of Psychology*, 1962, *16*, 185–191.

Tulving, E., & Pearlstone, Z. Availability versus accessibility of information in memory for words. *Journal of Verbal Learning and Verbal Behavior*, 1966, *5*, 381–391.

Tulving, E., & Thomson, D. M. Encoding specificity and retrieval processes in episodic memory. *Psychological Review*, 1973, *80*, 352–373.

Tumolo, P. J., Mason, P. L., & Kobasigawa, A. Presenting category size information to facilitate children's recall. Paper presented at the meeting of the Canadian Psychological Association, Windsor, Ontario, 1974.

Wellman, H. M., Ritter, K., & Flavell, J. H. Deliberate memory behavior in the delayed reactions of very young children, *Developmental Psychology*, 1975, *11*, 780–787.

Winograd, E. Effect of knowledge of set size on search termination in long-term memory. *Psychonomic Science*, 1970, *20*, 225.

Worden, P. E. The development of the category-recall function under three retrieval conditions. *Child Development*, 1974, *45*, 1054–1059.

Yussen, S. R. Determinants of visual attention and recall in observational learning by preschoolers and second graders. *Developmental Psychology*, 1974, *10*, 93–100.

Yussen, S. R., Kunen, S., & Buss. R. The distinction between perceiving and memorizing in the presence of category cues. *Child Development*, 1975, *46*, 763–768.

7
Organizational Factors in the Development of Memory

Barbara E. Moely

Tulane University

I. INTRODUCTION

Interest in the relation between memory and cognition has led developmental psychologists to investigate the child's use of knowledge structures in the act of remembering. Extensive research by Piaget and Inhelder (1973) shows that the ability to retain information is very closely related to developmental changes in cognitive skills. Research on the role of stimulus familiarity in information processing (Morrison, Holmes, & Haith, 1974) and on the child's ability to recognize or reproduce free drawings (Stacey & Ross, 1975) has also been concerned with the individual's knowledge system as it affects encoding and reproduction of information.

In the area of verbal memory, the meeting between the individual's cognitive skills and the requirements of a task has been described in terms of the organization that the individual places on discrete verbal items. Organization as a concept has its basis in Gestalt psychology (Postman, 1972), where it was assumed that memory is governed by the laws of perceptual grouping, and that organization is established during initial perception of events in such a way that events are connected by a common relation or property (Bower, 1972). Bartlett (1932) viewed the act of remembering as "built out of the relation of our attitude toward a whole active mass of organized past reactions or experience [p. 213]." According to Mandler (1967), "a set of objects or events is said to be organized when a consistent relation among the members of the set can be specified, and specifically, when membership of the objects or events in subsets (groups, concepts, categories, chunks) is stable and identifiable [p. 330]." It seems to be generally assumed that the grouping of elements into units or sets depends on the perceptual and conceptual skills that an individual applies to the task of remembering.

A. Organization in Free Recall

Organization in children's memory has been most extensively studied using the free recall task, in which the child is presented with a randomly ordered list of items (words, pictures, or objects that can be labeled verbally), and is asked to recall the items orally or in writing. Lists are usually beyond the limits of immediate memory, ranging in length from perhaps 12 to 40 items. The child is told that the items can be recalled in any order; the order used in recall is of major interest. Discrepancies between the ordering of items during presentation and systematic orders shown in recall are taken to reflect the influence of organizational processes. Tulving (1968) identified two varieties of organization that can affect recall order: *Primary organization* is described as resulting from factors independent of an individual's prior familiarity with input items. Superior recall of items that appear at the beginning and at the end of the list during presentation ("primacy" and "recency" effects) may derive from this kind of organization. *Secondary organization*, on the other hand, depends on an individual's prior acquaintance with the items. Secondary organization includes the grouping of items on the basis of common features of form or meaning, where no such grouping was made in presentation.

B. Theoretical Accounts of Recall Organization

Early accounts of the organization shown in free recall reflected an associationist view of verbal learning (e.g., Bousfield, 1953; Deese, 1959), and explained organization on the basis of the similarity between item relationships shown in free association and in recall ordering (Johnson, 1972). Later, Miller's (1956) unitization hypothesis was applied to the free recall task (Tulving, 1962, 1964). Miller proposed that some "chunking" of information is necessary if recall is to exceed the limits of immediate memory span. By recoding discrete input items into larger units, an individual efficiently uses his or her limited memory capacity. During retrieval, the individual accesses higher-order units and "unpacks" them to produce a larger amount of information than he or she could otherwise retain. The notion of recoding has led to an interest in the activity of the individual as he or she prepares for the task of recall (Tulving, 1962).

Keppel (1964) referred to free recall as one of the "simplest" learning situations. Subsequent work toward understanding the processes involved in performing this task have illuminated the complexities in accounting for individuals' behavior. Recent simulation models, when applied to free recall, assume that the items presented for recall are processed through an individual's long-term memory system, which includes very complex and highly structured information "about words and other verbal symbols, their meaning and referents, about relations among them, and about rules, formulas and algorithms for the manipulation of these symbols, concepts and relations'' (Tulving, 1972, p. 386). Models proposed by Anderson (1972) and Bower (1972), by Kintsch (1974), and by Rumelhart, Lindsay, and Norman (1972) differ in the units and relations used to describe semantic memory, but all assume that the individual uses complex stored knowledge in the active processing and grouping of items for free recall.

Craik and Lockhart (1972; Craik, 1973) have suggested that memory for items depends on the manner in which items are processed during presentation. They propose that the persistence of a memory trace is a result of the manner in which the individual analyzes the stimulus to be remembered. Processing of a stimulus involves, at a superficial level, the analysis of physical features such as sounds or visual characteristics and, at deeper levels, the matching of such features against more symbolic, abstract semantic features stored in memory (semantic encoding). At deeper levels, the individual may also generate associations or images to the item, incorporate it into a story, or relate it to similar items, thus producing semantic organization. Persistence of the memory trace can be maintained by a "horizontal" kind of processing, in which aspects of the item are recycled in awareness at a given level. Persistence of the trace can be increased by carrying out deeper levels of analysis, thus increasing the probability that the item will be retrievable at some later time. Characteristics of both the material to be remembered and the individual are assumed to influence the level of processing (and memorability) attained in the following ways:

1. The compatibility of the stimulus with the individual's cognitive structures will affect the ease with which it is encoded and related to other items at a deep level. This is akin to Piaget's notion of assimilation to a knowledge structure as the basis for the child's perceiving and conceptualizing the world (Furth, 1969; Liben, this volume).
2. Attempts to conduct deeper levels of analysis will depend on an individual's biases and expectations in the task, and on the attention given to stimulus materials. Task manipulations that affect an individual's attitude and attention, then, will affect the tendency to employ a semantic memory as a tool for recall.

C. Developmental Changes in Recall

Comparisons of recall by children of varying chronological or mental age levels find, almost invariably, that retention increases with development, from the earliest ages tested (age 2 or 3) through adolescence. Age differences in performance are minimal beyond adolescence, so that individuals 13 to 14 years of age do not differ from college students in amount recalled (Gerjuoy & Spitz, 1966; Wachs, 1969; Willner, 1967). Recall increases with age when lists consist of unrelated items (Rosner, 1971; Wachs, 1969) as well as with lists of items that can be grouped according to semantic relationships (Cole, Frankel, & Sharp,

1971; Neimark, Slotnick, & Ulrich, 1971). For category lists, improvement with age appears both in the number of categories represented in recall and in the number of items recalled from each category that is accessed during recall (Halperin, 1974). In recall of unrelated items, there is an increase with age in the number of items consistently grouped into subjectively constructed "chunks" or units (Rosner, 1971).

Comparisons of institutionalized retardates with normal children matched in mental age have shown superior recall by normals in some instances (Fagan, 1969; Gerjuoy & Alvarez, 1969; Zupnick & Forrester, 1972), although neither Osborn (1960) nor Rossi (1963) found such differences. In general, mental age appears to predict level of recall within both normal and retarded populations (Fagan, 1972; Gerjuoy & Spitz, 1966; Rossi, 1963).

In considering the development of memory skills, changes with age and experience are seen in the amount of material that may be retrieved during recall. It is likely that such developmental changes reflect the nature and extent of information stored in long-term semantic memory. The extent to which the child is able to employ semantic memory appropriately will depend on the "fit" between the materials presented for recall and the child's organized knowledge of the world. A second aspect of development may concern the extent to which the child invokes semantic memory in dealing with a task in which it would be useful. Factors that may influence the use of available skills are not considered in memory models other than that of Craik and Lockhart (1972). Most models assume that semantic knowledge will automatically be employed whenever it is appropriate to the task. However, there is evidence that children may not spontaneously apply their conceptual skills fully in the recall task. Young children will often show less organization of items in recall than they are capable of demonstrating either in other tasks or in variations of the usual recall procedure (Moely, Olson, Halwes, & Flavell, 1969). Appropriate use of existing conceptual skills appears to require additional abilities to plan or select strategies that will be useful for meeting task requirements (Flavell, 1970b). A consideration of the kinds of recall organization used by children may account, at least in part, for the developmental increases in recall just described.

II. THE NATURE OF FREE RECALL ORGANIZATION

A. Primary Organization

Primary organization refers to some consistent ordering of recall that depends on factors other than an individual's knowledge of relations between items. Postman (1972) refers to such orderings as "organization in the weak sense." A common finding, for both children and adults, is that items presented at the end of a list will be recalled first (Hasher & Clifton, 1974). Goldberg, Perlmutter, and Myers (1974) reported that 2-year-olds, when given pairs of items for recall, typically recalled the second item first. The use of a "recency strategy" for ordering recall appears to be very early appearing and automatic, and may result from efforts to maintain items in awareness during the short interval between presentation and recall (Craik & Lockhart, 1972). Serial position curves generally indicate that all age groups show superior recall of recently presented items. Five- and 6-year-olds show facilitation of recall for the last two items on the list (Thurm & Glanzer, 1971), while eighth graders and college students show excellent recall for the last three to five items presented (Cole, Frankel, & Sharp, 1971, Exp. 2; Hasher & Clifton, 1974). With development, there is an increase in the size of the set of recently presented items that can be reported by the individual, but little change in the tendency to employ a recency strategy in ordering recall.

A less common ordering strategy, one that shows some increased use with development, is that of giving priority in recall to items presented in initial list positions (Kellas, McCauley, & McFarland, 1975). Superior recall of items from initial positions over items from middle list positions has been shown by 6-year-old children (and, to a lesser extent, by 5-year-olds) on lists consisting of four to seven items (Thurm & Glanzer, 1971). With longer lists, such a position effect is usually not obtained with children below about the third-grade level (Cole, Frankel, & Sharp, 1971, Exp. 2; Hasher & Clifton, 1974), but becomes more pronounced with increasing chronological or mental age beyond this level (Fagan, 1972; Hasher & Clifton, 1974). These findings are congruent with those reported for serial recall (see chapter by Hagen and Stanovich in this volume), and may be accounted for in terms of age differences in the tendency of children to use rehearsal in preparation for recall. When the child is asked to rehearse aloud during list presentation, increased recall of initial items is likely to occur following frequent rehearsals of those items while new items are being presented (Fagan, 1972; Kellas et al., 1975). Rehearsal appears to be an effective way of preparing to recall items from initial list positions; with age, the individual becomes more likely to engage in such activity.

Another ordering strategy that may result from attempts to rehearse items serially during presentation is that of recalling pairs of list items in the order of presentation. Investigators have reported little use of such a strategy among children below 4 years of age, inconsistent use by 4-year-olds, and frequent use of serial ordering in 5-year-olds (Rossi & Rossi, 1965; Rossi & Wittrock, 1967, 1971). At later developmental levels, children move from organization based on the order of presentation to deliberate reordering of items according to semantic relationships. Moely (1968) and Kobasigawa and Middleton (1972) found evidence for such an age shift between the ages of 5 and 11 years, and also found that the tendency to use presentation order in recall was negatively related to amount recalled. The use of serial ordering may reflect an early attempt by the child to handle information in a systematic fashion. For children beyond the age of about 6, serial ordering is not particularly useful, if the alternative strategy of grouping items semantically is available.

Steinmetz and Battig (1969) reported that children 4 to 13 years of age often produced first in recall those items that had not been recalled on previous trials. Such a strategy might serve to maximize the amount recalled, in that the "weakest" items are mentioned before they can be forgotten. Subsequent work has shown that when presentation is arranged so as to control for the pervasive tendency to report recently presented items first, preschool children do not show a priority strategy for new items (Newman & Edmonston, 1973; Rosner, 1974). Rather, as Newman (1975) has demonstrated, the tendency to adopt this strategy appears by about 8 years of age. Similarly, Masur, McIntyre, and Flavell (1973) found that 9-year-olds and college students were more likely than 7-year-olds to select for study those items which had not been recalled on the immediately preceding trial. Children 8 to 9 years of age and above employ strategies of concentrating study on or giving priority to new items, much as adults do, while younger children typically do not do so.

In summary, some kinds of primary organization are used even by very young children. The major changes with development include tendencies to incorporate more items into the set that is recalled from final list positions, to report first in recall items from initial list positions, and to give priority in recall to new items. The use of serial ordering as a method of primary organization appears to serve some function among preschoolers, but for older children, is not as useful as semantic organization.

B. Measuring Secondary Organization

Two procedures have been developed to investigate the use of recall organization based on relations between items. In the first, the experimenter constructs a list using items that may be grouped into sets on the basis of some semantic or perceptual feature. Items are presented to the individual in a random arrangement, and the recall protocol is examined for grouping or "clustering" of items on the basis of the relevant feature. Organization is evaluated in terms of the number of pairs of items that are clustered relative to some estimate of the number of clustered pairs that would be expected by chance. Either one or several presentation-recall trials may be given. In the second procedure, a list is constructed using words or pictures that bear no obvious semantic or perceptual similarities, and the list is randomly ordered for presentation on each of several presentation-recall trials. Comparisons are made of recall protocols obtained on adjacent trials; similar grouping of items on two consecutive trials, different from the random orders used in presentation, is taken to indicate "subjective organization" of the list.

Various statistical techniques have been developed to measure organization in the recall of words that share common semantic or perceptual features. The relative merits of various measures have been discussed extensively (Dalrymple-Alford, 1971; Frender & Doubilet, 1974; Roenker, Thompson, & Brown, 1971; Shuell, 1969). Shuell (1975) cautions that investigators should familiarize themselves with the assumptions on which clustering measures are based. Moely (1973; Moely & Jeffrey, 1974), in comparisons of various indexes, noted that the Item Clustering Index (Robinson, 1966) was most appropriate for evaluating clustering in category lists, in terms of a rationale of how clustering scores should relate to measures of recall, number of categories represented in recall, and items recalled from each category. However, it may be wise for investigators to follow the suggestion of Colle (1972) that several measures of clustering be employed in summarizing the results of a study, since there is little agreement at present about the nature of assumptions that should be used as the basis for a measure of organization.

A few investigators have measured latency of response during recall as an indicator of organization. Kobasigawa and Orr (1973) recorded the time between successive recalls of two items from the same category (within-category interval) and compared it with the time between successive recalls of any two items from different categories (between-category interval). Kindergarten children showed within-category intervals that were shorter than between-category intervals under conditions that produced a high amount of list organization, but no differences in lengths of intervals when list organization was low. Similarly, Gelfand (1971) reported a relationship between response latencies and clustering scores in adults' free recall. Goldberg et al. (1974), investigating recall of two-item sets by 2-year-olds, noted that the interval between responses was shorter when items were members of the same conceptual category than when items were unrelated. These studies suggest that there is some "psychological reality" to the phenomenon of organization, even for very young children, although its most appropriate measurement may still be a puzzle.

Measures of subjective organization were developed by Tulving (1962) and by Bousfield and Bousfield (1966); modifications have been proposed by Fagan (1968) and by Gorfein, Blair, and Rowland (1968). Measurement of subjective organization is based on the number of pairs of items grouped similarly on adjacent recall trials. Subjective organization is usually found to increase over trials as recall increases, reflecting the organization of items into larger subjective units (Tulving, 1964).

A wide variety of clustering indexes has been employed in research on children's recall. Since the various indexes yield scores that are reasonably well correlated (Moely, 1973), comparisons of age groups or treatments probably are not biased greatly by the use of one measure rather than another. However, there is little agreement concerning appropriate methods by which to determine whether clustering in a given protocol is at an "above-chance" level, owing to differing views concerning estimation of chance performance (Pellegrino, 1975;

Shuell, 1975). In the studies reviewed here, no attempt is made to discuss whether the amount of organization shown exceeds a chance level; instead, the review will focus on relative amounts of clustering produced as a function of age or experimental condition.

C. Developmental Changes in Secondary Organization

Organization of items for recall on the basis of predetermined semantic relations has been found to show regular increases with development across a wide range of ages (e.g., Cole, Frankel, & Sharp, 1971; Moely & Shapiro, 1971; Neimark et al., 1971). Increases appear throughout the age span from about age 2 to college level, although with certain lists and task manipulations an asymptote may be reached at earlier ages. Some comparisons of institutionalized retarded children and normals of matched mental ages have shown normal children to be superior in the use of organization (Gerjuoy & Alvarez, 1969; Zupnick & Forrester, 1972), but others have found inconsistent or nonsignificant differences (Osborn, 1960; Rossi, 1963).

The use of subjective organization increases only slightly during early elementary school years, with the greatest increase appearing between about 10 years of age and adolescence (Laurence, 1966; Rosner, 1971; Shapiro & Moely, 1971). The later developmental improvement shown for subjective organization relative to that shown for category organization suggests that it is more difficult for the child to find ways to group unrelated items than to make use of familiar semantic relations in organizing a list for recall.

D. Relation Between Organization and Recall

It is usually assumed that the use of organization increases the amount of information that will be retrieved. Comparisons of performance on lists that can be organized by conceptual category with that obtained on lists of unrelated words have generally shown superior recall for category lists (Bozinou & Goulet, 1974; Cole, Frankel, & Sharp, 1971; Vaughan, 1968). Cole, Frankel, & Sharp (1971, Exp. 3) found that recall by children from grades 1, 4, 6, and 9 on lists of items that could be organized by category showed different serial position curves than were shown on lists of unrelated items. In particular, recall of items presented in initial and middle list positions was greater for category than for noncategory lists. Manipulations of interitem association strength, a measure that reflects the extent to which list items are interrelated, also affect recall produced by children from grades 2 through 6 (Heckelman & Spear, 1967).

Rosner (1974) found that first-grade children recalled unrelated items even when subjective organization scores were very low. She suggested that young children's recall performance may depend on exposure to items, which increases "response strength" for the items, rather than on organization. Similarly, Laurence (1967) hypothesized that young children might not benefit as much as older children from category organization because of their more limited conceptual skills. Although findings obtained by Laurence (1967, kindergarten group only) and Nelson (1969) support this notion, other studies suggest that young children will use organization when the task is appropriate to their ability level. Tenney (1975) found that kindergarten children's recall was higher for lists of category words than for lists of unrelated words, when lists were made up of words that the child had generated. Goldberg et al. (1974) compared recall of category and unrelated items by children 29–35 months of age. On each trial, two small objects were taken from a box and shown to the child, who attempted to label each item. For half of the trials pairs were members of a single category, while on the remaining trials conceptually unrelated objects were paired. More items and more item pairs were recalled correctly from the related sets than from the unrelated sets, indicating that even very young children can take advantage of conceptual grouping as an aid to recall when the task does not require complex strategies and when the items are familiar to the children. The fact that young children will recall some items without showing subjective organization (Rosner, 1974) does not preclude the possibility that they will find organization helpful under conditions conducive to its use.

Positive correlations have been reported between amount recalled and scores obtained for category organization (Lange & Jackson, 1974; Shultz, Charness, & Berman, 1973) and for subjective organization (Laurence, 1966). Several investigators have found that the magnitude of correlations between organization measures and amount of recalled increases with the age of the individual tested (Gerjuoy & Spitz, 1966; Laurence, 1966; Shapiro & Moely, 1971). Moely (1973) found that the magnitude of correlations will vary with the particular measure of organization used, particularly among young children. With development, the facilitation of recall through organization becomes increasingly apparent.

III. SEMANTIC DEVELOPMENT AND RECALL ORGANIZATION

Developmental changes in the use of the semantic system in recall may be viewed in terms of (1) changes in the features of items that are encoded during presentation and used as a basis for grouping and (2) changes in the structure of semantic categories produced or discovered by the child. Flavell (1970a) refers to these as the "semantics" and "syntax" of classification, respectively. Research bearing on each of these developmental changes will be considered next.

A. Levels of Encoding

Encoding of verbal or visual stimuli can be carried out at superficial perceptual levels or at deeper levels of semantic analysis. Flavell (1970a) notes that studies of classification activity indicate "an ontogenetic shift . . . from equivalences based on the more concrete and immediately given perceptual, situational, and functional attributes of objects to equivalences of a more abstract, verbal-conceptual sort [p. 996]." Underwood (1969) suggested that young children may have difficulty processing verbal items according to semantic features because they are attuned to the phonemic features of spoken words. Research on confusions in word recognition (Bach & Underwood, 1970; Hall & Halperin, 1972), on proactive interference effects (Geis, 1975), and on the generation of responses in free association (Ervin, 1961) all suggest that children do attend to word sounds and use these as a basis for relating items. With age, there is a shift toward processing of semantic features (Bach & Underwood, 1970; Ervin, 1961; Tenney, 1975). Rossi and Wittrock (1971) demonstrated young children's attention to word sounds in a free recall task, using items that could be grouped on the basis of rhyme, syntactic order, or category. Children of mental age 2 clustered chiefly on the basis of sound, while slightly older children used other ways of organizing items. Hasher and Clifton (1974) also demonstrated an ontogenetic shift toward increased salience of semantic categories and decreased salience of phonemic categories as a basis for recall organization.

With age, the extent to which recall is ordered according to phonemic features appears to decrease, although weak clustering on the basis of rhyme has been found with adults (Bousfield & Wicklund, 1969; Dolinsky, 1972). Adults apparently will use rhyme as a basis for grouping if no other means of organization is available (Dolinsky, 1972; Hamill, 1973). Similarly, the 2-year-olds in Rossi and Wittrock's (1971) study may have been taking advantage of the only obvious basis for organization that they identified. Does rhyming aid recall? Again, there appears to be an ontogenetic shift. Children often recall a list of phonemically related words better than lists of unrelated items (Hasher & Clifton, 1974; Heckelman & Spear, 1967; Locke, 1971). Adults, on the other hand, usually do not show such facilitation (Forrester, 1972; Forrester & King, 1971; Laurence & Trotter, 1971).

Another kind of feature that might serve as a cue for relating spoken words is that of syntactic class. Research on children's free associations indicates that there is a shift during the early elementary school years from the use of "syntagmatic" or sentencelike free associations (noun-verb; verb-adverb) to "paradigmatic" associations (noun–noun; verb–verb) (Entwistle, Forsythe, & Muuss, 1964; Ervin, 1961). Rossi and Wittrock (1971) found that children of mental age 3 used some syntactical grouping in recall (similar to syntagmatic responses in free association), but children who were slightly older rarely did so, choosing category organization instead. Among elementary school children and adults, there is no evidence that form class of unrelated words serves as an effective basis for grouping or that such grouping aids recall (Cofer & Bruce, 1965; Tillman & Bradley, 1969).

The same shift from reliance on perceptual features to use of semantic features might be expected with visual stimuli, but this does not appear to be the case. Bousfield, Esterson, and Whitmarsh (1958) investigated the possibility that visual characteristics of pictured items might serve as a basis for recall ordering. The 9- and 10-year-old children in their study did not employ perceptual grouping to a notable extent but, instead, organized items according to conceptual category, as did college students. Moely (1974) found that 4-year-olds made little use of color as a basis for organization, again in a task where alternative grouping by category was possible. Lange and Jackson (1974) reported that children 6 through 16 years of age who sorted pictures of items in preparation for recall rarely did so on the basis of descriptive content (e.g., "They both have wheels"), but relied instead on category or functional relations between items. In general, perceptual cues do not appear to be used in organizing pictures for recall. It may be that pictures allow rapid and automatic processing to a deeper level than words do; with semantic features readily available as a basis for relating items, children would have no need to rely on the more superficial aspects of stimuli.

Thus, there is some evidence that encoding and organization of items on the basis of nonsemantic features occurs more often among young children than among older individuals. Although grouping on the basis of word sounds appears helpful to the young child, it is doubtful that such grouping is as useful as semantic organization, when the child is able to use semantic information. The most common kind of semantic organization studied thus far is category grouping; other semantic features that provide effective bases for organizing items include semantic differential features (Kroes & Libby, 1973), associations between item pairs determined from word association norms (Wicklund, Palermo, & Jenkins, 1965), and interitem associations between all list members (Heckelman & Spear, 1967; Hess & Simon, 1964; Simon & Hess, 1965).

B. Developmental Changes in the Structure of Semantic Categories

Provided that the semantic features of items are processed, developmental changes may still appear in the manner in which such items are grouped or classified. The structure or "syntax" of the child's semantic categories also must be considered in understanding age differences in recall organization.

With development, children in Western cultures begin to conceptualize item classes in terms of superordinate categories, based on the similarity of item attributes (Denney, 1974; Flavell, 1970a). Like young children in Western cultures, individuals in other societies typically group items according to attributes other than similarity of features (Cole, Gay, Glick, & Sharp, 1971). As Denney (1974) suggests, the preference for similarity grouping that develops among members of Western cultures may result from "cognitive socialization" toward a particular kind of abstract thinking.

Characteristics of the young child's organization of information in semantic memory vary considerably. Some investigators find evidence for very early development of category knowledge (Nelson, 1973, 1974a) and knowledge of hierarchical semantic relationships (Steinberg & Anderson, 1975; Worden, 1974). Research on children's classification skills, however, suggests that there will be developmental changes in the structure of the child's classes. Such research appears to be directly relevant to an understanding of recall organization, since the skills required in classification are similar to those employed in organizing a list for recall. Children's semantic groupings of items differ from those made by mature individuals in two ways:

1. The young child may attempt to use similarity as a basis for grouping, but may not do so consistently (changing bases of similarity in the middle of a sort) or may not sort exhaustively (thus forming smaller categories than the older individual) (Flavell, 1970a).

2. Later in development, the child may not rely on similarity attributes but may group items on the basis of interrelationships in his or her own past experience. The child may also form a story or theme to relate the items, rather than searching out a basis for similarity grouping (Denney, 1974; Flavell, 1970a).

Evidence for each of these characteristics also appears in recall task performance. With regard to the first characteristic, Goldberg et al. (1974) and Rossi and Rossi (1965) show perhaps the earliest use of similarity to either facilitate or organize recall, with children between 2 and 3 years of age. However, it has also been suggested that the extent to which a cognitive capacity will be applied in a task is a function of several factors, one of these being the extent to which the capacity has been developed or acquired (Flavell, 1971; Meacham, 1972). A correspondence between developing classification skills and organization in recall was shown by Tomlinson-Keasey, Crawford, and Miser (1975), who found that among 6-year-old children those able to perform class inclusion problems were more likely to use category organization in free recall than were nonclassifiers of the same age. As Meacham (1972) has suggested, the child must achieve a certain level of capability with classification before this skill will be applied to recall.

Nelson (1973, 1974a) has been concerned with early development of the semantic system. She found that 5-year-olds are able to generate instances of categories very capably when asked to respond to category labels such as "animals" or "furniture" (Nelson, 1974b). Although the 5-year-olds produced fewer exemplars for each category than did 8-year-olds, the most frequently given responses for each category label were similar for the two groups. Differences occurred in the boundary conditions of the categories, with the older group showing less diversity of category membership than did the 5-year-olds, who frequently produced inappropriate items largely from related categories. These findings suggested to Nelson that category growth might proceed from a set of focal items taken to represent the category (reported equally well by both age groups) to a broader, but culturally appropriate, definition of the category (shown to an increasing extent with age).

In several studies, sorting tasks, in which individuals are encouraged to group items in preparation for recall, have followed presentation of items. It might be expected that use of such a procedure would allow the young child to maximize use of his or her organizational skills. Lange and Jackson (1974) found that individuals from 6 through 19 years of age showed a substantial relationship between personal organization and subsequent recall ordering, and noted that the amount of recall organization shown by the younger groups was higher than that often obtained in more traditional recall tasks. But even with this personalized sorting procedure, several investigators have concluded that developmentally more mature individuals are better able to make use of sorting task organization as a tool for recall (Lange & Jackson, 1974; Liberty & Ornstein, 1973; Mandler & Stephens, 1967).

In sorting items for recall, the younger child tends to divide a set into more categories, with a smaller number of items in each category, than the older child uses (Lange & Hultsch, 1970; Lange & Jackson, 1974; Worden, 1975). Younger children take a longer time to reach a stable grouping of items than do older individuals, suggesting that their bases for organization are more subject to momentary fluctuations in attention and to the influence of variable task stimuli than are those of older children. Older individuals show more commonality in the way items are assigned to groups, and are better able to explain why they group certain items together (Liberty & Ornstein, 1973; Mandler & Stephens, 1967). Age comparisons typically reveal that children 9 years of age and below differ from 11- and 12-year-olds, as well as from adults, on many of these characteristics. The sorts produced by young children, since they differ in structure and stability from those of adults, may be less useful for recall.

What kinds of built-in list organization will be used most effectively by children? Nelson's view of category development would suggest that the young child's recall should be organized most highly when lists contain items that can be grouped into small categories, especially when those categories are composed of focal or "core" items. As has been indicated, younger children produce smaller categories than do older children in sorting items prior to recall. The use of small categories appears to be a particularly effective organizational technique, in that recall and organization scores are usually higher for lists containing items that are divided into many small categories rather than a few large categories (Mandler, 1967; Mandler & Stephens, 1967; Worden, 1974). It must be noted, however, that in most studies category size has been confounded with the number of categories to be recalled. Also, there is no evidence thus far that the presence of small categories is more helpful to the young child than to the older individual, as would be suggested by Nelson's view of semantic development.

It might also be expected that recall organization would be greater, and developmental changes less notable, when items presented for recall are "core" members of categories. No study has directly investigated this proposal, although attempts to vary category "cohesiveness" or "familiarity" may provide indirect evidence for such an effect. Moely and Jeffrey (1974) compared 6-year-olds' recall of lists constructed to contain highly cohesive or relatively uncohesive members of the same categories, and found better recall and greater organization of cohesive category items. Northrop (1974) found that a list consisting of easy-to-sort items was better recalled and organized by 6-year-olds, and better retained over time, than a list containing items that were relatively difficult to sort into categories. An examination of the items used by Moely and Jeffrey and by Northrop suggests that the more cohesive or easier categories contained items that are close to "core" category exemplars, as reported by Nelson (1974b) and Rosch (1973). Holroyd and Holroyd (1961) found that recall and organization were greater for lists of items that were high-frequency associates of the category name than for lists composed of low-frequency associates. This finding, as well as those of other studies of category cohesiveness (Willner, 1967) or familiarity (Wachs & Gruen, 1971), may be interpreted as demonstrating the importance of category centrality, although the strength of interrelationships between list items may also play a part in determining recall and organization.

A second characteristic of children's organization of items in classification tasks is a tendency to encode items semantically, but to group them on bases other than the similarity of semantic features. Denney (1974) has suggested that although children are capable of using similarity groupings, they may prefer, as a result of experience or training, to categorize items in terms of "complementary" criteria, grouping dissimilar items that share some interrelationship either in one's own past experience or in the experimental situation. For example, a complementary relation between words would be illustrated by the pairs *pipe-tobacco* and *music-piano,* as contrasted with words related according to definitional similarity *(king-ruler* or *ocean-sea).* Denney (1974) reviewed studies of word association, word definition, classification, and memory, and concluded that each of these areas demonstrated a tendency for a change from complementary to similarity grouping between the ages of 6 and 9. Denney and Ziobrowski (1972) constructed lists with pairs of items that could be organized on the basis of similarity or complementary relations, and asked first graders and college students for recall. Although recall and organization scores were unusually low for both age groups, it did appear that the children grouped items on the basis of complementary relations more than on similarity, while the opposite was true for college students. Lange and Jackson (1974), in asking children to sort items prior to recall, found that the pattern of age changes in explanations given for item placement were congruent with Denney's suggestions. In particular, 6-year-olds often produced class-inclusion explanations, indicating the early presence of a capacity for similarity relations; 6-, 9-, and 12-year-olds most often justified groupings according to "functional-contextual" explanations, in which items were related in terms of interdependence in function or context (e.g., "*horse* with *stagecoach* because the horse pulls the stagecoach"). The use of such explanations declined from a peak at age 9 to a minimum at college level as similarity grouping again became common. Although the age levels showing each type of organization differed from Denney's expectations, the pattern of change over development is as she would predict. Finally, Flavell (1970a) notes that in classification tasks children will frequently relate items according to a story or theme, rather than by using similarity relations. Liberty and Ornstein (1973) found that 9-year-olds, more than adults, used story themes to relate items for recall. Thus, findings regarding organization for recall show some support for Denney's suggestions that young children who are able to use similarity as a basis for grouping may prefer, at certain ages, to use other schemes, and that similarity in semantic features becomes more common among older, more highly socialized individuals.

In summary, components of semantic development include changes with age in (1) the tendency to process semantic features of items; (2) the number as well as the size and boundaries of known conceptual categories; and (3) the nature of features that will be used to group items into sets, given that semantic processing has occurred. Level of development will affect the use of organization in recall, in that younger children will organize and recall ineffectively when their abilities do not match the concepts that the experimenter builds into the list for them to use. In order for the child to demonstrate recall organization, it is necessary that the conceptual skills required be congruent with the child's developing semantic system.

C. Production Deficiency in the Use of Semantic Knowledge for Recall

To understand the development of recall organization, it is also necessary to consider factors that determine the child's tendency to employ available skills in performing the task. Flavell (1970b) reviewed a number of studies, encompassing a variety of recall tasks, in which the young child shows a "production deficiency" for the use of relevant mnemonic activities. Although the child may possess the ability to engage in activities to aid recall, such activities may not spontaneously be produced at a time when they would be useful. Moely et al.

(1969) found evidence for a production deficiency in the use of category organization among 5-, 6-, and 8-year-old children. These children were able to sort items into category sets when instructed to do so, but did not spontaneously use this technique as a way to study items for recall or to organize their recalls. With certain instructions, the children were able to invoke categorization skills appropriately. The 8-year-olds showed increased organization during study and recall after the experimenter pointed out that the list was composed of category items. The 5- and 6-year-olds were able to show increased use of organization following a teaching procedure in which they were assisted in forming category groups and instructed to use this procedure in study and recall. Thus, it was possible to help the child use available semantic knowledge in meeting task requirements when such abilities would not have been demonstrated spontaneously.

Similarly, Liberty and Ornstein (1973) found that 9-year-old children did not fully use their abilities to sort items in preparation for recall. When the child was required to match an adult's sorting pattern, use of organization during recall was increased and retention improved. The ease with which the children learned and used adults' sorting patterns suggested that they had some knowledge of the organizational principles used by adults, knowledge that they did not apply when simply given general instructions about preparing for recall.

What factors are responsible for this lag between development and use of abilities? Moynahan (1973) and Tenney (1975) conclude that the young child lacks awareness of the value of organization as a tool for recall. Moynahan (1973) found that 7-year-olds were less able than 9- or 10-year-olds to predict that a set of category items would be easier to recall than a set of unrelated items. The 7-year-olds were, in fact, able to recall categorized lists better, and often were able to detect the categorized nature of the list, but were not aware that organization by category was a helpful recall strategy. Tenney (1975) asked children to compose lists of items that would be easy to remember. She found that 5-year-olds tended to give the first few words that occurred to them upon hearing the cues used to generate items, while older chidlren generated items that followed a category arrangement. Given such a lack of awareness of the usefulness of organization, young children appear to be unable to interpret the instructions to "remember these items" as a suggestion to engage in organizing activity.

A number of studies have been concerned with the effects of task variations that might increase the child's use of recall organization. In designing such studies, it is assumed that the child possesses, in some degree or fashion, relevant knowledge of semantic relationships. Task manipulations are designed not to teach such knowledge, but to assist the child in using it more effectively. It has been demonstrated that the child's use of organization can be increased by certain changes in the task; it is also possible that different manipulations may be effective at different developmental levels. The effects of several manipulations on the recall produced by children of varying age levels are considered next.

IV. EFFECTS OF TASK MANIPULATIONS ON RECALL ORGANIZATION

Modifications of the recall task have included variations in (1) the nature of the activity the child is instructed to carry out during presentation of items; (2) the nature of the stimulus materials to be remembered; and (3) the kinds of pretraining experiences the child receives in preparation for recall. When the child shows a production deficiency for the use of organization, the difficulty may have occurred at any of several levels. The child may not have encoded items in terms of semantic features, thus making relevant organization impossible; he or she may not have discovered the categorized nature of the list, or may not have attempted to rehearse related items in sets in preparation for recall. The task variations described in the following sections attempt to affect one or more of these processes, in order to determine whether age-specific recall and organization patterns can be changed.

A. Instructions and Orienting Tasks

The extent to which the child's study behavior and recall will be affected by instructions has been the topic of a number of studies. If the child is told that the task requires recall (intentional learning), does he or she engage in preparatory behaviors that are different from those used in simply looking at a set of items (incidental learning)? Is the extent or nature of recall affected as a result? Appel, Cooper, McCarrell, Sims-Knight, Yussen, and Flavell (1972) predicted an age difference in children's sensitivity to instructions, such that preschool children would not study or recall differently when instructed to memorize items than when told simply to look at them, while older children, who are aware of the need to engage in relevant activity in preparation for recall, were expected to modify their behaviors according to the instructions given. The two studies reported by Appel et al. (1972) support this hypothesis, in that 11-year-olds showed greater differentiation of study behaviors and subsequent recall performance in response to instructions than did younger children. Appel et al. also noted, however, that the beginnings of differentiation appeared in 7-year-olds, who seemed to be aware that the memory task required some special effort or activity, although they did not differentially engage in relevant activities such as categorization or rehearsal of items prior to recall. Under certain conditions, however, the 7-year-olds did engage in sequential naming of items as a preparation for recall, a finding replicated by Yussen, Gagné, Gargiulo, and Kunen (1974). Flavell and his colleagues (Appel et al., 1972; Flavell & Wellman, this volume) have distinguished between conceptual and behavioral differentiation, noting that children will understand the general implications of instructions to memorize items before they have developed entirely appropriate study techniques to use in preparing for recall.

Horowitz and Horowitz (1975) found that 5-year-olds recalled similarly following instructions that stressed either recall or recognition, while 7- and 11-year-olds recalled better after instructions indicating that the task would require recall rather than recognition. Tversky (1973) has noted that adults encode items differently for recall than for recognition. Recognition depends on the integration of the details of each item, while recall requires the individual to interrelate different list items. Younger children do not interpret instructions so as to make this differentiation. Similarly, Dietrich (1975) found that kindergarten children did not respond differentially to words they were told to "remember" or "forget," while children of second-grade level and above did better on items to be remembered than on those they were instructed to forget.

Vaughan (1968) varied instructions given to first-, fourth-, and seventh-grade students, either telling them to remember pictures for subsequent recall or giving no such instructions. Unlike Appel et al. (1972), Vaughan found no differences at any age level due to intentional or incidental learning set. Clustering of recall occurred in both instruction conditions, and although it increased with age, was present at a fairly high level even in the recalls of first graders. To account for the difference between this and previous studies, it is necessary to consider the nature of the orienting task that Vaughan used in presenting items. Children made up sentences using the name of the object in the picture on each of five presentation trials. It is likely that this orienting task served to focus attention on the meaning of the items presented, so that children were able to make use of semantic similarity as a basis for grouping items during recall.

Other investigators have suggested that the nature of the orienting task used when items are presented is an important determinant of recall and organization. Eagle and Leiter (1964), comparing recall and recognition following intentional or incidental learning instructions, concluded that "intention to learn is crucial for learning only to the extent that it generates adequate learning operations [p. 62]." What sort of "learning operations" are likely to be helpful for recall? Jenkins (1974) describes a series of free recall experiments with adults in which the orienting tasks performed during item presentation were varied. Generally, it was found that tasks requiring the individual to comprehend the meaning of items produced better recall and greater clustering than did orienting tasks that required attention only to the formal characteristics of items. Comprehension tasks, such as rating pleasantness of words or giving appropriate modifiers for list items, led to better recall than did formal tasks that focused attention on word spelling or word sounds. Similar findings have been obtained with children by Russian psychologists (Smirnov & Zinchenko, 1969). Murphy and Brown (1975) measured 4-year-olds' free recall following orienting tasks that required comprehension of items (identifying category membership or evaluative meaning) or attention to formal properties (colors or sounds). They found strong evidence for superior recall following comprehension tasks relative to that shown following formal tasks, while intentional learning instructions did not produce recall different from that obtained in an incidental learning condition. Thus, instructions about the task are important to the extent that they affect the child's attempts to prepare for recall. If a relevant orienting task is used, as was the case in Vaughan's study, incidental or intentional learning instructions will not produce differential effects.

Attention to meaning may be strengthened through the use of a sorting task prior to recall, a manipulation that produces greater recall and organization than are obtained in nonsorting conditions. Lange and Hultsch (1970) asked children to sort pictures into category groups or to simply examine them prior to recall. Children from grades 1, 3, and 5 showed better recall following active sorting than after the nonsorting presentation condition; while for the children from grades 7 and 9 recall was similar for the two conditions. It appears that the older child engages in semantic processing and organization without extra manipulations to encourage it, while the younger child can profit from a condition in which semantic organization is required. Northrop (1974) also found higher recall and greater clustering by first-grade children when they were required to sort items by category before recall, rather than randomly grouping the pictures. The effect of category grouping on recall was maintained when retention was tested after one day or one week, indicating a lasting effect on the storage of items.

In summary, instructions about the goal activity of the recall task are important if they lead the child to attend to semantic features and interelations between items. When such differentiation of behavior is possible, it will be less likely to occur spontaneously among 4- to 6-year-olds than among older children, who are better able to devise strategies to meet the goal stated in the instructions. When orienting tasks are used to focus attention on item meaning and relations between items, no differences between intentional and incidental learning conditions will appear, since all subjects, including young children, will carry out the semantic encoding that is useful for recall.

B. Labeling of Items During Presentation

Overt naming of items by the individual during presentation might be expected to improve recall, because labeling either (1) decreases the difficulty of transforming information from one modality to another (Corsini, 1971); (2) directs the child's attention to each item (Horowitz, Lampel, & Takanishi, 1969); or (3) increases the probability that the child will discover the categorical structure of a list (Furth & Milgram, 1973; Jablonski, 1974).

There is little evidence for any such facilitation. Difficulties involved in translating a picture stimulus to a verbal response usually are circumvented by using easy-to-label pictures. Labeling may have some positive effect on children's attention to list items, but the evidence is mixed. Horowitz (1969) reported better recall but no increased organization by 5- and 8-year-olds who were required to label auditory or visual stimuli during presentation compared with groups who simply looked at or listened to the items. Horowitz et al. (1969), in a task where 3- to 5-year-olds were to identify the missing item in a set of three, found that labeling aided recall of pictures but not of objects. They suggested that labeling directed attention appropriately to each of the pictured items. However, facilitative effects of overt labeling on recall are not seen in other studies (Kossuth, Carroll, & Rogers, 1971; McCarson & Daves, 1972). In fact, labeling may have a detrimental effect on recall, as Rosner (1971) found with ninth graders.

Furth and Milgram (1973) compared recall in a labeling condition with that obtained in a condition in which children traced the outline of each picture as it was presented. Recall and organization were similar in the two conditions for children 4 and 6 years of age, but 9- and 12-year-olds showed better recall and greater organization with labeling than with the tracing task. In light of the findings described earlier concerning different kinds of orienting tasks, it cannot be concluded that labeling facilitated organization. Rather, it is likely that the orienting task required of nonlabelers interfered with the older children's spontaneous semantic processing and organization of items.

C. Objects, Pictures, Words

Pictorial stimuli may be rapidly processed to a deep level, and thus may yield a more persistent memory trace than spoken or printed word stimuli (Craik, 1973). As noted earlier, pictures are infrequently grouped for recall on the basis of superficial nonsemantic features, suggesting that meaning is highly salient for such items. Comparisons of the recall of items presented as pictures or presented as spoken words have generally shown higher recall and organization for pictures, for children between kindergarten and eighth-grade levels (Cole, Frankel, & Sharp, 1971; Horowitz, 1969). Rossi and Rossi (1965) found that modality of presentation (object, picture, word) affected recall, but not organization of items by children 2 to 5 years of age. Bevan and Steger's (1971) fourth graders and college students recalled objects better than pictures, and pictures better than printed words. Kossuth et al. (1971) found superior recall of items presented as objects over items presented as written words.

Thus, items that elicit semantic processing are recalled better and often organized to a greater extent than items that may be more superficially processed. Possibilities for "dual encoding" provided by visual stimuli may also contribute to recall superiority (Lockard & Sidowski, 1961; May & Hutt, 1974). (See Reese, this volume, for a discussion of this issue.)

D. Providing the Category Name During Presentation

It has been suggested that the individual must discover the categorized nature of the list in order for organization to occur (Bower, 1972; Mandler, 1967). Presentation of the category name before or during item presentation might be expected to "prime" the use of organization by helping the child discover and use the category structure in the list. However, no such effect has been demonstrated with young children. Nelson (1969) used a pretraining procedure in which children 5 and 8 years of age were taught the names of the categories that would be used to construct the recall list. The results showed no effect of pretraining on the recall or organization of items. Williams and Goulet (1975) found no facilitation of recall or organization for 4-year-old children when categories were named prior to presentation or before recall.

The results of several other studies indicate that the effect of the category name may vary with the age of the individual. Rossi (1964) compared recall of typical category items with recall of a list on which one item from each category was replaced by the category name. Children 5, 8, and 11 years of age showed no overall effect of list type on clustering, but there was a tendency for the 11-year-olds to produce greater organization on the list containing category names. A similar interaction of age with condition was found by Kobasigawa and Middleton (1972), who reported that fifth-graders, but not younger children, showed greater recall and organization of a list after categories had been identified and labeled for them during presentation. Moely et al. (1969) and Shultz et al. (1973) also found that the effect of category labeling varied with the child's age or ability level.

Thus, the presence of the category name during presentation may affect the child's recall and use of organization within a particular age range. It may be necessary that the child be near the point in development at which categories would be discovered and used spontaneously in order for labeling to facilitate organization. The primary effect of providing labels may not be on the child's detection of categories, since 7-year-olds are able to detect categories without such cues (Moynahan, 1973); rather, labels may induce the child to generate a means of organization for recall. Worden (1974) found no effect of giving the category labels at the time recall began, when children had sorted items into categories during presentation. The sorting task apparently was sufficient to ensure discovery and use of category organization, so that the category labels served no additional purpose. The category name has a limited effect on recall relative to conditions that more directly control the child's use of organization. Several studies have reported that providing the category names during presentation or prior to recall is not as effective as a condition that forces the child to recall items in category sets (Cole, Gay, Glick, & Sharp, 1971; Lange, 1973; Scribner & Cole, 1972). (Kobasigawa, this volume, has discussed the use of category labels as cues for retrieval.)

E. Blocked Presentation of Related Items

In the traditional free recall task, items are presented in a random, sequential order, with category members occurring in nonadjacent positions in the list. Cofer, Bruce, and Reicher (1966) and others have shown that adults' recall and use of category organization can be increased by presenting all items from a given category in succession. Such "blocked" presentation has been shown to increase both organization of recall and amount recalled for retarded children (Gerjuoy & Alvarez, 1969; Gerjuoy & Spitz, 1966); for kindergarteners (Kobasigawa & Orr, 1973; Kobasigawa & Wilmhurst, 1973); and for children of elementary school grade levels (Cole, Frankel, & Sharp, 1971; Moely, 1968). Blocking may facilitate recall by increasing the likelihood that the child will discover the category structure of the list (Furth & Milgram, 1973; Hasher & Clifton, 1974). In addition, it may allow the child to rehearse items in category sets as presentation for recall. Blocked presentation, relative to a random order of presentation, typically increases the average number of items recalled from each category accessed in recall (Moely, 1968); affects the timing of responses during recall, such that category items recalled in sequence are given with short latencies between items (Kobasigawa & Orr, 1973); and produces a change in the serial position curve, such that children receiving blocked presentation show superior recall of items presented in the middle positions of a list (Cole, Frankel, & Sharp, 1971, Exp. 2).

Age comparisons made by Cole, Frankel, & Sharp (1971), Moely (1968), and Moely and Shapiro (1971) showed facilitation of recall and organization through blocking across a wide age range, with no differential effects at different ages. However, several other investigations have reported results consistent with the notion that blocking will have greater effects at higher developmental levels. Yoshimura, Moely, and Shapiro (1971) compared 4- and 9-year-olds on recall of multiple lists over several days, and found that blocking of sets of three related items, successively presented, increased organization only for the older group. Furth and Milgram (1973) found that grouping of related items during successive presentation increased recall and organization for children 9 and 12 years of age, but not for 4- and 6-year-olds. Similar developmental differences in the effects of blocking on recall were noted by Kobasigawa and Middleton (1972).

Blocking appears to be helpful to children as young as 3 or 4 years of age when presentation conditions are appropriate to the child's abilities. Use of small (two- or three-item) categories and use of simultaneous presentation of all items from a category aided 4- and 6-year-olds in the use of blocked presentation (Furth & Milgram, 1973). Similarly, use of small categories and/or simultaneous presentation may account for the positive effects of blocking shown with young children in studies by Moely (1968), Moely and Shapiro (1971), Kobasigawa and Orr (1973), and Kobasigawa and Wilmhurst (1973).

F. Learning to Learn

In the light of general findings that young children are not as likely to organize recall as older individuals, a number of investigators have attempted to induce greater use of organization in transfer to new lists following training procedures. Perhaps the simplest manipulation attempted has been that of presenting children with several lists in order to determine whether they would become more proficient in the use of organization through practice. Shapiro and Moely (1971) investigated learning to learn by children 9, 11, and 13 years of age, using lists of unrelated items that could be organized into subjective units. Free recall learning tasks were given to each child on each of four days. No clear effects of practice were found for either organization or recall. Recall scores showed a slight "warm-up" effect for early trials, but no consistent improvement across days. Moely and Shapiro (1971) investigated learning-to-learn effects in the recall of 3- to 7-year-old children, using lists composed of category pairs or of unrelated items. A general improvement in recall occurred over six lists, but there was no suggestion that this was dependent on increased organization of items. Yoshimura et al. (1971) found no systematic effects of practice on recall produced by 4- and 9-year-old children. Lange (1973) reported that 14-year-olds, but not 5- or 10-year-olds, showed some increase in recall and clustering over three free recall lists. It appears that simply providing practice with the recall task is not notably effective in facilitating the use of organization or in increasing recall, although some learning to learn may be possible at higher developmental levels.

G. Transfer of a Recall Strategy

There have been several investigations of possible transfer of an organizational technique induced by exposing the child to a constrained-recall procedure. In constrained recall, the child is required to recall items in category sets. The extent to which the child will maintain organization when constraining cues are dropped and the possibility of transfer of the organizational strategy to a new free recall task have been tested. Transfer is measured by comparing the free recall performance of children previously given constrained-recall trials with that of children who have received prior free recall trials. Williams and Goulet (1975) found that 4-year-old children recalled more items under constrained than under free recall conditions. However, the constrained-recall experience did not affect performance on subsequent free recall trials with either the same or a new list of items. Several studies have reported that children 7 to 10 years of age and above will show positive transfer of organizational strategies to additional trials with a list that previously was constrained; there is little evidence, however, for transfer of organizational strategies to a new list (Cole, Gay, Glick, & Sharp, 1971; Scribner & Cole, 1972).

Thus, the developmental level of the child is a determinant of the extent of transfer to be expected following constrained-recall trials. Nursery school children are not able to maintain the strategy of organization or to keep recall at a high level when cues are dropped, even with the same items. Elementary school children can maintain organization and recall facilitation for a list that was previously constrained. However, generalization of the organizational strategy to a new list is not successful, even for older children.

H. Training Organizational Skills

Given the young child's limited benefit from most of the manipulations described here, and his or her ability to infer that organization is a useful tool for recall (Moynahan, 1973; Wellman, Drozdal, Flavell, Salatas, & Ritter, 1975), several investigators have been concerned with the effects on recall of procedures that deliberately teach the child to organize. Moely et al. (1969) showed that teaching of an organizational strategy was effective with kindergarten and first-grade children, when carried out with the same items that were later to be recalled. Children's transfer of an acquired grouping strategy to new items has been examined in other studies. Moely and Jeffrey (1974) investigated the extent to which such transfer would occur with 6-year-olds. Children were told that grouping items by category was a useful technique for recall, and were given practice at grouping and recalling items in category sets on a preliminary list. Subsequently, a new, longer list was presented, using presentation methods in which sorting of items for study was not allowed. As expected, children given organization training showed higher recall than those who had received no suggestions about organization during practice trials. Clustering during recall was somewhat higher following such training, although the extent of the effect varied with the measure of organization employed.

Rosner (1971) examined the effect of instructions on the child's tendency to employ subjective organization in recall. Other studies have shown that provision of sentence connections between items increases recall and organization (Bencomo, Carroll, & Rogers, 1971; Kobasigawa & Wilmhurst, 1973). Rosner tested children from grades 1, 5, and 9 either under the usual free recall procedure or following one of two kinds of instruction. Chunking instructions, designed to encourage the use of subjective organization, consisted of telling the child to make up a link between pairs of test items. The experimenter demonstrated a sentence connection ("You can water the *daisy* with the *hose*"), and then asked the child to produce a sentence for another set of items. Another group of children received rehearsal instructions, in which they were told to repeat the name of each item twice as it was presented.

Rosner found evidence for differing effects of instructions across grades. For first graders, instructions did not affect the number of words recalled or the amount of subjective organization shown, relative to the control condition. The most notable effect of instructions occurred among fifth graders, for whom chunking instructions produced greater recall and organization than were shown in the control or rehearsal conditions. For ninth graders, both recall and organization were slightly increased with chunking instructions and decreased with rehearsal instructions relative to controls.

Both Moely and Jeffrey and Rosner found that children who had been instructed in the use of organization showed greater ability to sort items into sets in a sorting task given after recall was obtained. This improvement in sorting-task performance indicates that suggestions about organization do increase children's awareness of item relationships, even though the child may not be able to effectively employ the technique to organize recall. Application of a grouping technique to recall was easier for first graders when items were members of common conceptual categories (Moely & Jeffrey, 1974) than when items were unrelated pictures (Rosner, 1971). Additional studies to evaluate the strength and stability as well as the limitations of organization induced through teaching would be of interest.

V. CONCLUDING REMARKS

A. A Sketch of the Developmental Sequence

On the basis of the research just reviewed, it is possible to describe characteristics of organization in the child's recall at several developmental levels. It has been suggested in this chapter that changes in performance with age are a result of developmental changes both in semantic knowledge and in the ability to devise and carry out appropriate strategies for remembering.

Preschool children may demonstrate knowledge of similarity relations at a very early age, if the task is such that grouping is a relatively automatic process. Even in the traditional free recall task, young children will show some recall organization, which probably does not result from a deliberate attempt to prepare for recall, but may occur through a process like free association during the time of recall. The use of rhyme, syntactic ordering, and small (two-item) sets of related items as a basis for grouping are suggestive of a process like free association. The memory demonstrated by preschoolers appears to fit the Russian term *involuntary memory* (Smirnov & Zinchenko, 1969; Yendovitskaya, 1971), in that through examining or acting on the items to be recalled, the child retains some information. Instructions to remember do not affect the amount retained more than instructions to simply look at pictures, although an orienting task that engages the child's attention and interest in the materials may facilitate recall.

Smirnov and Zinchenko (1969) have noted that the young child's motivation for performing a task may be different from that of a more mature individual. The child may not be motivated to "do well" in the rather formally structured free recall task, but may excell in a "game" situation, or one in which memory is relevant to some personally involving practical activity. Perhaps the usual recall task is set up in a fashion that does not strongly engage the interest or effort of the young child. Several investigators (Buschke, 1974; Kobasigawa, 1974) have drawn attention to the young child's difficulty in systematically retrieving information during recall. Often preschoolers will spend only a few seconds attempting to recall; the experimenter's attempts to elicit further items meet with silence or irrelevant verbalizations. The effectiveness of constraining cues in increasing recall supports the notion that the young child stores more information than will typically be retrieved in free recall; with assistance in structuring retrieval, recall can be improved. Thus, performance factors related to motivation, efficiency in retrieval, and the ability to infer useful strategies for recall, in addition to less highly developed systems of semantic knowledge, may be responsible for the low recall and organization shown by young children.

At the kindergarten and first-grade levels, children continue to show little awareness of the usefulness of category organization as a tool for recall. Although they will often group items in recall (Appel et al., 1972; Kagan & Klein, 1973), they are less likely than the older child to adopt category organization as a deliberate study strategy (Moely et al., 1969; Neimark et al., 1971). Between the ages of 5 and 9, the child appears to suffer, in varying degrees, from a production deficiency for the use of category organization in recall. The strength of experimental manipulations needed to engage the child's abilities more fully varies with age, so that younger children require more directive "hints" or assistance in order to use category organization than are required by more mature individuals. It appears that the acquisition of broader and better-bounded semantic categories makes the child progressively more amenable to manipulations designed to aid category discovery. Nine-year-olds still differ from adults and older children in the manner in which they sort items in preparation for recall, forming smaller categories with less stability or commonality. Children 6 through 9 years of age may try out varied bases for organization, especially the use of complementary relations or story themes. In this age period, the child is becoming aware of the need to engage in preparatory activities to meet task demands, but he or she still may not be able to determine the most effective study strategies for a given task. As Smirnov and Zinchenko (1969) note, awareness of the requirement to remember material may lead the child into the use of ineffective strategies. An example is shown in 5- and 6-year-olds' attempts to reproduce the serial order of presentation in their recalls.

Children 10 to 11 years of age demonstrate new levels of attainment. They will often generate category organization as a way of dealing with the recall task, so that the discrepancy between knowledge and recall organization is not as great as was true of younger children. Their sorting in preparation for recall is closer to that used by the adult, and they return to the use of similarity as a basis for grouping in a more systematic and complete fashion than is shown by younger children. With increased knowledge of semantic categories, they are able to benefit from task manipulations (e.g., category name or blocking) designed to aid in the discovery of list categories. Fifth graders can employ subjective organization, when appropriately instructed, although they will still show a production deficiency for its use, which typically will be overcome within the next three or four years.

B. Reflections on Recall Research

A fairly consistent finding in the research reviewed in this chapter is the tendency for task manipulations to show an interaction with age level, such that older children are more able than younger children to profit by the presence of the category name, blocking of items in presentation, use of a recall strategy induced through constrained recall or with instructions, and possibly, practice with the task. It appears that a certain level of semantic development needs to be attained before the child can be induced to organize through these manipulations. Better ways of specifying the child's level of conceptual knowledge are needed, so that interactions of age with task may be understood more clearly. Most variations in instructions or methods of item presentation that have been used with children are based on findings in the adult research, so that it is reasonable that they should be more effective with older children, who are closer to the adult in capabilities and in awareness of their own memory processes. Rather than trying to shape the child to the adult model through teaching, it may be more useful, in terms of understanding development and assisting the child's learning in other situations, to design tasks so as to maximize the child's opportunity to use available skills. Interesting attempts to do this are the modifications used by Goldberg et al. (1974) and by Lange and Jackson (1974). Investigation of motivational variables involved in the production deficiency of young children would be of interest in further delineating young children's capabilities.

Methodological problems of two types are noted in this research. First, in investigations of recall differences due to list characteristics, such as cohesiveness or number of categories, it would be well to use more than one exemplar of each list type, to be sure that differences shown are not specific to the lists used or attributable to factors other than those of interest. Second, some of the reports, especially those published before 1970, were limited in information about the characteristics of recall. Statistics for amount recalled, as well as for organization, should be provided. It may be useful, for category lists, to also report component scores for recall, that is, the number of categories represented in recall and average within-category recall. As Colle (1972) suggested, until we have a better idea of the most appropriate way to measure organization, and of the relationship between organization and recall, it is best to report information that will provide a broad picture of the characteristics of recall. Finally, it should be noted that children will show considerable recall even when their use of secondary organization is very low (Rosner, 1974). Manipulations that affect recall performance do not always do so by changing the extent to which organization is used, indicating that other factors, including primary organization and rehearsal strategies, are also important determinants of the amount recalled. In general, however, there is a consistent tendency for recall of category items to be superior to that of unrelated items; and both organization and recall show increases with age and vary as a result of task changes. Further, children become more likely with age to infer that organization is a useful tool for recall, thus reflecting in their own cognitions and behavior the assumption on which semantic models of free recall performance are based.

REFERENCES

Anderson, J. R. FRAN: A simulation model of free recall. In G. H. Bower (Ed.), *The Psychology of learning and motivation* (Vol. 5). New York: Academic Press, 1972.

Appel, L. F., Cooper, R. G., McCarrell, N., Sims-Knight, J., Yussen, S. R., & Flavell, J. H. The development of the distinction between perceiving and memorizing. *Child Development,* 1972, *43,* 1365–1381.

Bach, M. J., & Underwood, B. J. Developmental changes in memory attributes. *Journal of Educational Psychology,* 1970, *61,* 292–296.

Bartlett, F. C. *Remembering: A study in experimental and social psychology.* Cambridge: Cambridge University Press, 1932.

Bencomo, A., Carroll, W. R., & Rogers, C. A. The role of object display and verbal mnemonic cues in free recall. Paper presented at the biennial meeting of the Society for Research in Child Development, Minneapolis, April 1971.

Bevan, W., & Steger, J. A. Free recall and abstractness of stimuli. *Science,* 1971, *172,* 597–599.

Bousfield, W. A. The occurrence of clustering in the recall of randomly arranged sequences. *Journal of General Psychology,* 1953, *49,* 229–240.

Bousfield, A. K., & Bousfield, W. A. Measurement of clustering and of sequential constancies in repeated free recall. *Psychological Reports,* 1966, *19,* 935–942.

Bousfield, W. A., Esterson, J., & Whitmarsh, G. A. A study of developmental changes in conceptual and perceptual associative clustering. *The Journal of Genetic Psychology,* 1958, *92,* 95–102.

Bousfield, W. A., & Wicklund, D. A. Rhyme as a determinant of clustering. *Psychonomic Science,* 1969, *16,* 183–184.

Bower, G. H. A selective review of organizational factors in memory. In E. Tulving & W. Donaldson (Eds.), *Organization of memory.* New York: Academic Press, 1972.

Bozinou, E., & Goulet, L. R. Acquisition and transfer of sorting mechanisms in discrimination learning and free recall by nursery school children. *Child Development,* 1974, *45,* 816–820.

Buschke, H. Components of verbal learning in children: Analysis by selective reminding. *Journal of Experimental Child Psychology,* 1974, *18,* 488–496.

Cofer, C. N., & Bruce, D. R. Form-class as the basis for clustering in the recall of nonassociated words. *Journal of Verbal Learning and Verbal Behavior,* 1965, *4,* 386–389.

Cofer, C. N., Bruce, D. R., & Reicher, G. M. Clustering in free recall as a function of certain methodological variables. *Journal of Experimental Psychology*, 1966, *71*, 858–866.

Cole, M., Frankel, F., & Sharp, D. Development of free recall learning in children. *Developmental Psychology*, 1971, *4*, 109–123.

Cole, M., Gay, J., Glick, J. A., & Sharp, D. W. *The cultural context of learning and thinking*. New York: Basic Books, 1971.

Colle, H. A. The reification of clustering. *Journal of Verbal Learning and Verbal Behavior*, 1972, *11*, 624–633.

Corsini, D. A. Memory: Interaction of stimulus and organismic factors. *Human Development*, 1971, *14*, 227–235.

Craik, F. I. M. A "levels of analysis" view of memory. In P. Pliner, L. Krames, & T. Alloway (Eds.), *Communication and affect: Language and thought*. New York: Academic Press, 1973.

Craik, F. I. M., & Lockhart, R. S. Levels of processing: A framework for memory research. *Journal of Verbal Learning and Verbal Behavior*, 1972, *11*, 671–684.

Dalrymple-Alford, E. C. Some further observations on the measurement of clustering in free recall. *British Journal of Psychology*, 1971, *62*, 327–334.

Deese, J. Influence of inter-item associative strength upon immediate free recall. *Psychological Reports*, 1959, *5*, 305–312.

Denney, N. W. Evidence for developmental changes in categorization criteria for children and adults. *Human Development*, 1974, *17*, 41–53.

Denney, N. W., & Ziobrowski, M. Developmental changes in clustering criteria. *Journal of Experimental Child Psychology*, 1972, *13*, 275–282.

Dietrich, D. M. The development of memory skills: Instructed forgetting and induced semantic category use. Paper presented at the biennial meeting of the Society for Research in Child Development, Denver, April 1975.

Dolinsky, R. Clustering and free recall with alternative organizational cues. *Journal of Experimental Psychology*, 1972, *95*, 159–163.

Eagle, M., & Leiter, E. Recall and recognition in intentional and incidental learning. *Journal of Experimental Psychology*, 1964, *68*, 58–63.

Entwistle, D. R., Forsyth, D. F., & Muuss, R. The syntactic-paradigmatic shift in children's word associations. *Journal of Verbal Learning and Verbal Behavior*, 1964, *3*, 19–29.

Ervin, S. M. Changes with age in the verbal determinants of word-association. *American Journal of Psychology*, 1961, *74*, 361–372.

Fagan, J. F., III. Measuring verbal recall. II: The ITR score expressed as a ratio. *Psychonomic Science*, 1968, *11*, 205.

Fagan, J. F., III. Free recall learning in normal and retarded children. *Journal of Experimental Child Psychology*, 1969, *8*, 9–19.

Fagan, J. F., III. Rehearsal and free recall in children of superior and average intelligence. *Psychonomic Science*, 1972, *28*, 352–354.

Flavell, J. H. Concept development. In P. H. Mussen (Ed.), *Carmichael's manual of child psychology* (Vol. 1). New York: Wiley, 1970.   (a)

Flavell, J. H. Developmental studies of mediated memory. In H. W. Reese & L. P. Lipsitt (Eds.), *Advances in child development and behavior* (Vol. 5). New York: Academic Press, 1970.   (b)

Flavell, J. H. Stage-related properties of cognitive development. *Cognitive Psychology*, 1971, *2*, 421–453.

Forrester, W. E., Effects of semantic and acoustic relatedness on free recall in a between-subjects design. *Psychological Reports*, 1972, *30*, 637–638.

Forrester, W. E., & King, D. J. Effects of semantic and acoustic relatedness on free recall and clustering. *Journal of Experimental Psychology*, 1971, *88*, 16–19.

Frender, R., & Doubilet, P. More on measures of category clustering in free recall—although probably not the last word. *Psychological Bulletin*, 1974, *81*, 64–66.

Furth, H. G. *Piaget and knowledge.* Englewood Cliffs, N.J.: Prentice-Hall, 1969.

Furth, H. G., & Milgram, N. A. Labeling and grouping effects in the recall of pictures by children. *Child Development,* 1973, *44,* 511–518.

Geis, M. F. Encoding dimensions in memory: Developmental similarities at two grade levels. *Developmental Psychology,* 1975, *11,* 396–397.

Gelfand, H. Organization in free recall learning: Output contiguity and interresponse times as a function of presentation structure. Unpublished doctoral dissertation, University of Michigan, 1971.

Gerjuoy, I. R., & Alvarez, J. M. Transfer of learning in associative clustering of retardates and normals. *American Journal of Mental Deficiency,* 1969, *73,* 733–738.

Gerjuoy, I. R., & Spitz, H. H. Associative clustering in free recall: Intellectual and developmental variables. *American Journal of Mental Deficiency,* 1966, *70,* 918–927.

Goldberg, S., Perlmutter, M., & Myers, N. Recall of related and unrelated lists by 2-year-olds. *Journal of Experimental Child Psychology,* 1974, *18,* 1–8.

Gorfein, D. S., Blair, C., & Rowland, C. The generality of free-recall: Subjective organization as an ability factor. *Psychonomic Science,* 1968, *11,* 279–280.

Hall, J. W., & Halperin, M. S. The development of memory-encoding processes in young children. *Developmental Psychology,* 1972, *6,* 181.

Halperin, M. S. Developmental changes in the recall and recognition of categorized word lists. *Child Development,* 1974, *45,* 144–151.

Hamill, B. W. A study of form-class clustering in free recall using overt suffixes. Paper presented at the meeting of the American Psychological Association, Montreal, August 1973.

Hasher, L., & Clifton, D. A developmental study of attribute encoding in free recall. *Journal of Experimental Child Psychology,* 1974, *17,* 332–346.

Heckelman, S. B., & Spear, N. E. Effect of interitem similarity on free learning by children. *Journal of Verbal Learning and Verbal Behavior,* 1967, *6,* 448–450.

Hess, J. L., & Simon, S. Extra-list intrusions in immediate free recall as a function of associative strength in children. *Psychological Reports,* 1964, *14,* 92.

Holroyd, R. G., & Holroyd, J. C. Associative clustering in a retroaction paradigm. *The Journal of General Psychology,* 1961, *64,* 101–104.

Horowitz, A. B. Effect of stimulus presentation modes on children's recall and clustering. *Psychonomic Science,* 1969, *14,* 297–298.

Horowitz, A. B., & Horowitz, V. A. The effects of task-specific instructions on the encoding activities of children in recall and recognition tasks. Paper presented at the biennial meeting of the Society for Research in Child Development, Denver, April 1975.

Horowitz, L. M., Lampel, A. K., & Takanishi, R. N. The child's memory for unitized scenes. *Journal of Experimental Child Psychology,* 1969, *8,* 375–388.

Jablonski, E. M. Free recall in children. *Psychological Bulletin,* 1974, *81,* 522–539.

Jenkins, J. J. Remember that old theory of memory? Well, forget it! *American Psychologist,* 1974, *29,* 785–795.

Johnson, N. F. Organization and the concept of a memory code. In A. W. Melton & E. Martin (Eds.), *Coding processes in human memory.* Washington, D.C.: Winston, 1972.

Kagan, J., & Klein, R. E. Cross-cultural perspectives on early development. *American Psychologist,* 1973, *28,* 947–961.

Kellas, G., McCauley, C., & McFarland, C. E., Jr. Developmental aspects of storage and retrieval. *Journal of Experimental Child Psychology,* 1975, *19,* 51–62.

Keppel, G. Verbal learning in children. *Psychological Bulletin,* 1964, *61,* 63–80.

Kintsch. W. *The representation of meaning in memory.* Hillsdale: N.J.: Lawrence Erlbaum Associates, 1974.

Kobasigawa, A. Utilization of retrieval cues by children in recall. *Child Development,* 1974, *45,* 127–134.

Kobasigawa, A., & Middleton, D. B. Free recall of categorized items by children at three grade levels. *Child Development,* 1972, *43,* 1067–1072.

Kobasigawa, A., & Orr, R. R. Free recall and retrieval speed of categorized items by kindergarten children. *Journal of Experimental Child Psychology,* 1973, *15,* 187–192.

Kobasigawa, A., & Wilmhurst, L. A. Verbal elaboration in young children's free-recall learning. *Perceptual and Motor Skills,* 1973, *36,* 1062.

Kossuth, G. L., Carroll, W. R., & Rogers, C. A. Free recall of words and objects. *Developmental Psychology,* 1971, *4,* 480.

Kroes, W. H., & Libby, W. L., Jr. Relative power of selected encoding categories for the organization of free recall in children. *The Journal of Genetic Psychology,* 1973, *122,* 9–15.

Lange, G. The development of conceptual and rote recall skills among school age children. *Journal of Experimental Child Psychology,* 1973, *15,* 394–406.

Lange, G. W., & Hultsch, D. F. The development of free classification and free recall in children. *Developmental Psychology,* 1970, *3,* 408.

Lange, G., & Jackson, P. Personal organization in children's free recall. *Child Development,* 1974, *45,* 1060–1067.

Laurence, M. W. Age differences in performance and subjective organization in the free recall learning of pictorial material. *Canadian Journal of Psychology,* 1966, *20,* 388–399.

Laurence, M. W. A developmental look at the usefulness of list categorization as an aid to free recall. *Canadian Journal of Psychology,* 1967, *21,* 153–165.

Laurence, M. W., & Trotter, M. Effect of acoustic factors and list organization in multitrial free recall learning of college age and elderly adults. *Developmental Psychology,* 1971, *5,* 202–210.

Liberty, C., & Ornstein, P. A. Age differences in organization and recall: The effects of training in categorization. *Journal of Experimental Child Psychology,* 1973, *15,* 169–186.

Lockard, J., & Sidowski, J. B. Learning in fourth and sixth graders as a function of sensory mode of stimulus presentation and overt or covert practice. *Journal of Educational Psychology,* 1961, *52,* 262–265.

Locke, J. L. Phonetic mediation in four-year-old children. *Psychonomic Science,* 1971, *23,* 409.

Mandler, G. Organization and memory. In K. W. Spence & J. T. Spence (Eds.), *The psychology of learning and motivation* (Vol. 1). New York: Academic Press, 1967.

Mandler, G., & Stephens, D. The development of free and constrained conceptualization and subsequent verbal memory. *Journal of Experimental Child Psychology,* 1967, *5,* 86–93.

Masur, E. F., McIntyre, C. W., & Flavell, J. H. Developmental changes in apportionment of study time among items in a multitrial free recall task. *Journal of Experimental Child Psychology,* 1973, *15,* 237–246.

May, R. B., & Hutt, C. Modality and sex differences in recall and recognition memory. *Child Development,* 1974, *45,* 228–231.

McCarson, C. S., & Daves, W. F. The development of free recall of object names as a function of overt verbalization and intracategory variation. *Developmental Psychology,* 1972, *6,* 178.

Meacham, J. A. The development of memory abilities in the individual and society. *Human Development,* 1972, *15,* 205–228.

Miller, G. A. The magical number seven plus or minus two: Some limits on our capacity for processing information. *Psychological Review,* 1956, *63,* 81–97.

Moely, B. E. Children's retention of conceptually related items under varying presentation and recall conditions. Unpublished doctoral dissertation, University of Minnesota, 1968.

Moely, B. E. Category use in children's free recall: A training study and some problems in studying organization. Paper presented at the meeting of the American Psychological Association, Montreal, August 1973.

Moely, B. E. Facilitation of young children's recall through the use of nonmeaningful recall cues. Unpublished manuscript, Tulane University, 1974 (ERIC Document Reproduction Service No. ED 100 482).

Moely, B. E., & Jeffrey, W. E. The effect of organization training on children's free recall of category items. *Child Development,* 1974, *45,* 135–143.

Moely, B. E., Olson, F. A., Halwes, T. G., & Flavell, J. H. Production deficiency in young children's clustered recall. *Developmental Psychology,* 1969, *1,* 26–34.

Moely, B. E., & Shapiro, S. I. Free recall and clustering at four age levels: Effects of learning to learn and presentation method. *Developmental Psychology,* 1971, *4,* 490.

Morrison, F. J., Holmes, D. L., & Haith, M. M. A developmental study of the effect of familiarity on short-term visual memory. *Journal of Experimental Child Psychology,* 1974, *18,* 412–425.

Moynahan, E. D. The development of knowledge concerning the effect of categorization upon free recall. *Child Development,* 1973, *44,* 238–246.

Murphy, M. D., & Brown, A. L. Incidental learning in preschool children as a function of level of cognitive analysis. *Journal of Experimental Child Psychology,* 1975, *19,* 509–523.

Neimark, E., Slotnick, N. S., & Ulrich, T. Development of memorization strategies. *Developmental Psychology,* 1971, *5,* 427–432.

Nelson, K. The organization of free recall by young children. *Journal of Experimental Child Psychology,* 1969, *8,* 284–295.

Nelson, K. Some evidence for the cognitive primacy of categorization and its functional basis. *Merrill-Palmer Quarterly,* 1973, *19,* 21–39.

Nelson, K. Concept, word, and sentence: Interrelations in acquisition and development. *Psychological Review,* 1974, *81,* 267–285.   (a)

Nelson, K. Variations in children's concepts by age and category. *Child Development,* 1974, *45,* 577–584.   (b)

Newman, M. A. A developmental investigation of the priority effect. *Developmental Psychology,* 1975, *11,* 106.

Newman, M. A., & Edmonston, L. P. Priority of recall of old items in free-recall learning of preschool children. *The Journal of General Psychology,* 1973, *88,* 185–189.

Northrop, S. K. The effects of organization training and list difficulty on children's free recall over varying delay intervals. Unpublished master's thesis, Tulane University, 1974.

Osborn, W. J. Associative clustering in organic and familial retardates. *American Journal of Mental Deficiency,* 1960, *65,* 351–357.

Pellegrino, J. W. A reply to Frender and Doubilet on the measurement of clustering. *Psychological Bulletin,* 1975, *82,* 66–67.

Piaget, J., & Inhelder, B. *Memory and intelligence.* New York: Basic Books, 1973.

Postman, L. A pragmatic view of organization theory. In E. Tulving & W. Donaldson (Eds.), *Organization of memory.* New York: Academic Press, 1972.

Robinson, J. A. Category clustering in free recall. *Journal of Psychology,* 1966, *62,* 279–285.

Roenker, D. L., Thompson, C. P., & Brown, S. C. Comparison of measures for the estimation of clustering in free recall. *Psychological Bulletin,* 1971, *76,* 45–48.

Rosch, E. H. On the internal structure of perceptual and semantic categories. In T. E. Moore (Ed.), *Cognitive development and the acquisition of language.* New York: Academic Press, 1973.

Rosner, S. R. The effects of rehearsal and chunking instructions on children's multitrial free recall. *Journal of Experimental Child Psychology,* 1971, *11,* 93–105.

Rosner, S. R. Effective list length and part-whole transfer in first graders' multitrial free recall. *Journal of Experimental Child Psychology,* 1974, *17,* 422–435.

Rossi, E. L. Associative clustering in normal and retarded children. *American Journal of Mental Deficiency,* 1963, *67,* 691–699.

Rossi, E. Development of classificatory behavior. *Child Development,* 1964, *35,* 137–142.

Rossi, E. L., & Rossi, S. I. Concept utilization, serial order and recall in nursery-school children. *Child Development,* 1965, *36,* 771–778.

Rossi, S. I., & Wittrock, M. C. Clustering versus serial ordering in recall by four-year-old children. *Child Development,* 1967, *38,* 1139–1142.

Rossi, S. I., & Wittrock, M. C. Developmental shifts in verbal recall between mental ages two and five. *Child Development,* 1971, *42,* 333–338.

Rumelhart, D. E., Lindsay, P. H., & Norman, D. A. A process model for long-term memory. In E. Tulving & W. Donaldson (Eds.), *Organization of memory.* New York: Academic Press, 1972.

Scribner, S., & Cole, M. Effects of constrained recall training on children's performance in a verbal memory task. *Child Development,* 1972, *43,* 845–857.

Shapiro, S. I., & Moely, B. E. Free recall, subjective organization, and learning-to-learn at three age levels. *Psychonomic Science,* 1971, *23,* 189–191.

Shuell, T. J. Clustering and organization in free recall. *Psychological Bulletin,* 1969, *72,* 353–374.

Shuell, T. J. On sense and nonsense in measuring organization in free recall—oops, pardon me, my assumptions are showing. *Psychological Bulletin,* 1975, *82,* 720–724.

Shultz, T. R., Charness, M., & Berman, S. Effects of age, social class, and suggestion to cluster on free recall. *Developmental Psychology,* 1973, *8,* 57–61.

Simon, S., & Hess, J. L. Supplementary report: Influence of inter-item associative strength upon immediate free recall in children. *Psychological Reports,* 1965, *16,* 451–455.

Smirnov, A. A., & Zinchenko, P. I. Problems in the psychology of memory. In M. Cole & I. Maltzman (Eds.), *A handbook of contemporary Soviet psychology.* New York: Basic Books, 1969.

Stacey, J. T., & Ross, B. M. Scheme and schema in children's memory of their own drawings. *Developmental Psychology,* 1975, *11,* 37–41.

Steinberg, E. R., & Anderson, R. C. Hierarchical semantic organization in 6-year-olds. *Journal of Experimental Child Psychology,* 1975, *19,* 544–553.

Steinmetz, J. I., & Battig, W. F. Clustering and priority of free recall of newly learned items in children. *Developmental Psychology,* 1969, *1,* 503–507.

Tenney, Y. J. The child's conception of organization and recall. *Journal of Experimental Child Psychology,* 1975, *19,* 100–114.

Thurm, A. T., & Glanzer, M. Free recall in children: Long-term store vs. short-term store. *Psychonomic Science,* 1971, *23,* 175–176.

Tillman, M. H. & Bradley, M. Note on form class clustering with children. *Psychological Reports,* 1969, *24,* 135–138.

Tomlinson-Keasey, C., Crawford, D. G., & Miser, A. L. Classification: An organizing operation for memory. *Developmental Psychology,* 1975, *11,* 409–410.

Tulving, E. Subjective organization in free recall of "unrelated" words. *Psychological Review,* 1962, *69,* 344–354.

Tulving, E. Intratrial and intertrial retention: Notes toward a theory of free recall verbal learning. *Psychological Review,* 1964, *71,* 219–237.

Tulving, E. Theoretical issues in free recall. In T. R. Dixon & D. L. Horton (Eds.), *Verbal behavior and general behavior theory.* Englewood Cliffs, N.J.: Prentice-Hall, 1968.

Tulving, E. Episodic and semantic memory. In E. Tulving & W. Donaldson (Eds.), *Organization of memory.* New York: Academic Press, 1972.

Tversky, B. Encoding processes in recognition and recall. *Cognitive Psychology,* 1973, *5,* 275–287.

Underwood, B. J. Attributes of memory. *Psychological Review,* 1969, *76,* 559–573.

Vaughan, M. E. Clustering, age, and incidental learning. *Journal of Experimental Child Psychology,* 1968, *6,* 323–334.

Wachs. T. D. Free recall learning in children as a function of chronological age, intelligence, and motivational orientation. *Child Development,* 1969, *40,* 577–589.

Wachs, T. D., & Gruen, G. E. The effects of chronological age, trials, and list characteristics upon children's category clustering. *Child Development,* 1971, *42,* 1217–1227.

Wellman, H. M., Drozdal, J. G., Flavell, J. H., Salatas, H., & Ritter, K. Metamemory development and its possible role in the selection of behavior. G. A. Hale (Chair), *The development of selective processes in cognition.* Symposium presented at the biennial meeting of the Society for Research in Child Development, Denver, April 1975.

Wicklund, D. A., Palermo, D. S., & Jenkins, J. J. Associative clustering in the recall of children as a function of verbal association strength. *Journal of Experimental Child Psychology*, 1965, *2*, 58–66.

Williams, K. G., & Goulet, L. R. The effects of cueing and constraint instructions on children's free recall performance. *Journal of Experimental Child Psychology*, 1975, *19*, 464–475.

Willner, A. E. Associative neighborhoods and developmental changes in the conceptual organization of recall. *Child Development*, 1967, *38*, 1127–1138.

Worden, P. E. The development of the category-recall function under three retrieval conditions. *Child Development*, 1974, *45*, 1054–1059.

Worden, P. E. Effects of sorting on subsequent recall of unrelated items: A developmental study. *Child Development*, 1975, *46*, 687–695.

Yendovitskaya, T. V. Development of memory. In A. V. Zaporozhets & D. B. Elkonin (Eds.), *The psychology of preschool children*. Cambridge, Mass.: M.I.T. Press, 1971.

Yoshimura, E. K., Moely, B. E., & Shapiro, S. I. The influence of age and presentation order upon children's free recall and learning to learn. *Psychonomic Science*, 1971, *23*, 261–263.

Yussen, S. R., Gagné, E., Gargiulo, R., & Kunen, S. The distinction between perceiving and memorizing in elementary school children. *Child Development*, 1974, *45*, 547–551.

Zupnick, J. J., & Forrester, W. E. Effects of semantic and acoustic relatedness on free recall in normal children and retardates. *Psychonomic Science*, 1972, *26*, 188–190.

Part II

THE ROLE OF MEMORY
IN COGNITIVE DEVELOPMENT

8

Cross-Cultural Studies of Memory and Cognition

Michael Cole
Sylvia Scribner
The Rockefeller University

I. INTRODUCTION

More than most topics in cognitive development, the relation between cultural experience and the development of memory is not the special province of psychology. While the experimental study of culture and memory has become popular only in recent years, there is an extensive body of observation and speculation, familiar to anthropologists, that antedates the origin of psychology as a science. A separate body of interesting theoretical work on this topic is to be found in philology.

Each of these three fields has developed its theories of the relationship between culture and memory from a distinctive data base, generated by its own specialized concerns. While broad agreement has been reached *within* each discipline on the general direction between "cultural development" and "memory development," *between* disciplines there is little agreement at the level of either theory or fact.

In this chapter, we will first present the major theoretical positions advanced in anthropology and philology, describing the questions and observations that motivated them. We will then turn to the theoretical contributions made by psychology and review the principal experimental studies conducted over the past forty years. Here we face a special problem: In contrast to the other two disciplines in which theory and fact, however limited and incomplete, speak to each other, psychological research presents a split personality. Many of the basic questions posed by psychological theories have never been subjected to empirical investigation, while many of the investigations have been conducted without reference to specific hypotheses about cultural influences on memory. Our review of the present "state of the art" has convinced us that there are striking discontinuities between the important psychological questions on culture and memory and the

239

evidence at hand. In our concluding section, therefore, we not only suggest the generalizations warranted by current evidence, but also indicate some of the untraveled roads that await exploration.

A. Theories in Anthropology

The earliest body of evidence concerning culture and memory was produced by post-Renaissance explorers, whose work provided an important source of ideas for early anthropologists (Hodgen, 1952). With surprising regularity, this literature refers to exceptional mnemonic powers in "savage" peoples. Since there was generally little admiration for native people to be found among the harbingers of colonialism, it is not surprising to find that the observation of impressive memory skills was, from the beginning, coupled with a point of view that downgraded these skills. Unlike contemporary theories, which treat remembering as a product of essentially nonmnemonic problem solving (Flavell, 1970), Levy-Bruhl, in his famous monographs on primitive mentality (1910, 1923), and other early theorists posited a trade-off between memory and other skills, implying that a "total reservoir" of mental energy could be channeled into different "faculties"; the less expended in "thinking," the more available for "memory." This idea was expressed quite clearly by W. H. R. Rivers (1903), who participated in the first combined psychological-anthropological expedition at the beginning of this century.

In modern anthropological writing, one still encounters the idea that native peoples possess remarkable powers of memory. Such references to superior memory capacities, however, are now accompanied by commonsense rationales for why this should be the case. A leading contemporary view provides an account in terms of the requirements of information retention in nonliterate societies. Lacking a writing system with which to record events, society must develop a living system for such information in the minds of individuals. This line of reasoning was made quite explicit in the work of Riesman (1956), who was influenced by McLuhan's (1962) writing on the effects of widespread literacy. Riesman suggested that members of literate culture "can afford to be careless with the spoken word, backstopped as we are by the written one [1956, p. 9]," while nonliterates, unable to store their experiences in print, must devote full attention to the spoken word.

While all social scientists may not link superior memory skills to the absence of a writing system, there seems to be rather broad agreement in anthropology that technologically advanced cultures place fewer demands for recall on their members; as a consequence, as "cultural development" proceeds, "memory" declines.

As far as we can determine, however, there has been no anthropological research explicitly attempting to relate specific cultural activities or institutions to remembering. The closest approximation to such a study is to be found in Gregory Bateson's (1936) classic ethnography of the Iatmul tribe in New Guinea. Bateson's attention had been attracted to the significance the Iatmul attached to family lineages and to the distinctive ceremonies they had evolved to keep alive interest in, and preservation of, detailed historical information on totemic relationships.

One practice seen among the Iatmul was the organization of "naming contests" that served as occasions on which men who had invested time and effort in memorizing totemic names could compete against each other. Those who produced the greatest number of totemic names were accorded high esteem by the community. Bateson compared the Iatmul with other South Pacific cultures. He concluded that each culture exerts a pressure toward the development of particular intellectual skills and that the Iatmul's involvement in totemism led to "hyperdevelopment" of memory.

When he returned from the field, Bateson became acquainted with Bartlett's monograph *Remembering* (1932), which included one of the earliest psychological studies of recall among nonliterate peoples. Bartlett distinguished several forms of remembering and hypothesized that nonliterate people engage in "rote recapitulation" more frequently than literate peoples. Looking back at his observations, Bateson found data clearly contradictory to this hypothesis: On different occasions, Iatmul memory experts narrated totemic names in different sequential orders, rather than in the single, fixed order that the rote recapitulation theory requires. He was unable, however, to specify just *how,* through what study and retrieval processes, Iatmul adults acheived their remarkable memory feats. The interconnection between cultural values or ceremonial activities and the psychological activities of individual members of the society remained unelucidated.

B. Philology: Memory Is the Mother of the Muses

A more comprehensive and refined specification of cultural phenomena that facilitates oral recall is to be found in the work of contemporary classical scholars whose investigations of literary forms in antiquity led them to intriguing conclusions about the "supports" for memory of complex verbal material in nonliterate societies.

The source of speculation about culture and memory within philology is almost totally a by-product of that discipline's efforts to understand the way in which two classics of world literature, the *Iliad* and the *Odyssey,* were constructed and transmitted. As in recent anthropology, the role of literacy is a central issue. Unlike anthropology, however, the data of philology generally are not derived from field observation but from a textual analysis of the primary documents themselves and of early Greek commentaries on Homer, especially Plato's critique in *The Republic* (Havelock, 1963).

In the 1930s, three lines of evidence converged with the conclusion that the Homeric epics were *oral* compositions, produced in a series of performances over a period that extended for a least a century. First, Carpenter (1933) demonstrated that the earliest writing in the Greek alphabet postdated by many years the time at which the Homeric epics were produced. Most important from the point of view of contemporary psychological analysis is the research of Milman Parry, who discovered that the epics are constructed on the basis of patterned combinations of set phrases and themes that have no parallel in demonstrably written verse. Not content to rest the argument solely on textual analysis, in the early 1930s Parry and his student Lord (1965) made an expedition to Serbo-Croatia, where they recorded many performing artists who still maintained an epic tradition. The singers they met often claimed that they sang their songs exactly as they had heard them from other singers. In fact, recordings demonstrated amply that the songs were changed a good deal. The singer-poet really composed as he performed. His songs were constrained in topic and meter by tradition, but their precise content varied with the singer's skill and interests, as well as the occasion and the mood of his audience.

Parry and Lord argued that such singer-poets had no concept of a fixed, original song, to be repeated verbatim. What the singer meant when he said that he sang the song exactly as he heard it was that he faithfully built his performance "or song in our sense, on the stable skeleton of narrative, which is the song in his sense" (Lord, 1965, p. 99). Parry and Lord observed the effects of the literacy that was spreading in Yugoslavia and concluded that only with literacy can one observe singers attempting to reproduce an exact original. In effect, then, it would seem that verbatim recall is a consequence of literacy!

Parry and Lord's work has been generalized by another philologist, Havelock (1963, 1971), in a manner quite germane to psychology. According to Havelock, the oral devices discovered by Parry evolved as a means of ensuring the transmission of Greek culture from generation to generation. Thus, the *Iliad* and the *Odyssey* represent oral encyclopedias of Greek culture. The elaborate metric, acoustic, and syntactic devices in the poems are intended as mnemonic aids to ensure that the critical elements of the narrative (and the culture) are reproduced in each retelling.

Havelock's work contains a clear theory of nonliterate memory. The first "memory resource" in nonliterate societies (and, we might add, literate societies as well) is the spoken language system, which allows the culture to maintain its basic identity through the stability of its vocabulary and syntax. This function can be carried out by the vernacular, which supplies children with their "cultural expectations" as they acquire the language.[1]

But, Havelock continued, the vernacular is not a suitable medium for preserving special statements of a culture's history and folkways. These require a specialized language with the characteristics identified by Parry in the epic poems. Narrative components are linked through mnemonic "elaborations" (to use Rohwer's, 1970, term) that lead from one sequence to another, with the stylistic formulas serving as reminders which ensure recall of the entire sequence.

Havelock went beyond Parry and Lord's concentration on the literary devices as aids to memory by pointing out the situational features of the epic recital that contribute to the reproduction of the material. Epic bards viewed themselves as entertainers rather than teachers, but both functions were inextricably combined in the service of remembering. Rhythm, supplemented during the performance by musical instruments, served as esthetically based reinforcement for the act of memorizing. The spread of literacy and the new genres that arose with it eroded both the epic language and the epic recital.

Unlike other scholars who accord a key role to literacy in changing techniques of recall, Havelock did not apply this change to all human activity but only to a relatively circumscribed part of life and to certain individuals who are the chroniclers of their time. This distinction is well worth keeping in mind as we review the psychological literature on culture and memory.

C. Psychological Theories in Search of Relevant Data

A number of statements have been made within psychology concerning culture and memory, but only two approaches have been elaborated theoretically. One seeks to specify the relationship between the development of cultural institutions and technology and the development of individual memory; the second is non-developmental and is concerned with the relationship between socially dominant interests in a particular culture at a given time and the way in which these regulate both the "matter" (content) and "manner" (process) of recall.

The developmental theory is attributable to the work of Vygotsky, writing in the latter 1920s (Vygotsky & Luria, 1930). In the only theoretical effort of its kind, Vygotsky sought to link processes governing the cognitive growth of individual children within society to the historical processes governing social change. His colleague, Leontiev, applied this general theory to the study of the development of memory, considered from both the historical and the ontogenetic points of view (Leontiev, 1960, chap. 5; see also Meacham, this volume).

---

[1] This idea of the role of language is very similar to that popularized by Luria, who maintains that the word provides the child with a condensed history of his own culture (cf. Luria, 1974).

The second theory is associated with the work of Bartlett (1932), who approached the study of memory from the perspective of a social psychologist interested in tracing the influence of socially determined values and attitudes on mental processes.

We will consider each of these theories in turn.

1. The Vygotsky-Leontiev Theory of Memory Development

Schematically, the Vygotsky-Leontiev theory posited an initial, "natural" stage of memory existing in the earliest period of prehistory that is akin to contemporary notions of involuntary recall; no special intention to remember or special activity is engaged in by people either to store information or to ensure its retrieval at a later, appropriate time. Experienced scenes and events are "imprinted in memory," but while such memories may be accurate, complete, and "indelibly imprinted," they may still not be recalled at the proper moment. They may be called up, however, if they enter into a natural relationship with the new situation via a "common link"—the presence in the new situation of a person or material object involved in the initial experience.

The first step in the movement of memory away from its natural "biological state" occurs when humans attempt to eliminate the chance aspects and begin to make deliberate use of naturally occurring components of the original situation to aid reproduction at a later time. That is, the *intention* to commit material to memory emerges. The second step consists in the invention of artificial "stimuli" to mediate retrieval of the desired information at the desired time. This inventive line of development proceeds along two paths—first, the individual creates *external* devices; then, at a later period of cultural development, he produces *internal* devices. In the beginning, external aids are simply particular things that are used as reminders of other things—a leaf of a tree, perhaps, or a notch in a stick in primitive societies, and among us, the canonical "string around the finger" that helps the absent-minded professor remember to carry his lecture notes with him to class. Such aids, wherever they are employed, are "primitive" in the sense that they are specific to one occasion and to the recall of one item of information.

The elaboration of external aids results in their becoming more generalized "props" to memory, useful on a number of occasions. Citing the observations of early anthropologists, Leontiev drew attention to various devices of this kind invented by primitive peoples: the Peruvian custom of tying knots in rope; the "herald's rods" of the Australian aborigines. Even these devices are restricted, since they can be used only for particular situations known in advance. For Leontiev, they have a double significance as examples not only of "externally aided primitive memory'' but as rudimentary sign systems that over the course of historical development evolve into the universally applicable sign systems of written languages. Man's attempt to improve his ''natural memory'' by technological means such as external devices culminates, paradoxically, in its ''replacement'' by notational systems!

The line of development of internally aided memory and its relationship to externally aided memory is not at all clear. A critical point of origin appears to be the production by the individual rememberer of some activity in which he engages for the specific purpose of remembering. Initially, the activity is some piece of behavior that is actually carried out, but this, in time, is superseded by a ''thought'' about the behavior, by *mental* activity. Mentally mediated memory, referred to by Leontiev as ''logical memory'' and considered a higher form of memory, has as a prerequisite the conversion of speech from an external to an internal function. Leontiev gives no clear reason as to why the internalization of speech should be associated with the advent of writing systems, but he strongly implies that this is the historical fact.

In summary, Leontiev's theory holds that primitive nonliterate man remembers primarily through unmediated natural processes and, on special occasions, with the help of low-order, external aids. Modern, literate man remembers primarily through the use of writing systems and internalized memory aids. The approach allows him to accord special memory prowess of one kind to nonliterate people but to claim that literate, more culturally advanced people will have a better memory of a different sort.

Leontiev's theory is not exclusively, or even primarily, a theory about culture and memory. Rather, his essay on the sociohistorical development of memory is part of a general attempt, participated in by his colleagues Vygotsky and Luria, to formulate a broad theory of intellectual development that includes both individual and social factors.

Thus, Leontiev found it completely natural to offer evidence from developmental studies carried out in Moscow as support for his general thesis about the historical stages of memory development. His major empirical work rests on a comparison of performance by children of different ages, some of whom are given external aids to recall and some of whom are not. The fact that 4-year-old children do not benefit from such aids is attributed to their dependence on ''natural'' memory; the usefulness of external aids to somewhat older children shows that they can use external mediators. Finally, the equality of performance with and without external aids among older schoolchildren reflects, in Leontiev's schema, their ability to use internal mediators, rendering external mediators superfluous.

The theory leads to the conclusion that various stages of memory development should be reached at earlier ages in societies with relatively higher levels of sociocultural development than in societies that are less developed. This implication of the theory has never been tested by the methods Leontiev advocated. As we shall see, however, crude, indirect evidence regarding this aspect of his theory can be gleaned from existing cross-cultural studies.

2. Bartlett's Social Schema Theory

The first psychological–experimental observations related to a theory of memory were put forward by Bartlett in his monograph *Remembering* (1932). Bartlett's general thesis was that recall will be effective insofar as material to be remembered fits preexisting mental schemas. Although he had heard stories of remarkable memory among South African tribal peoples, he was loath to attribute such recall to some new principle of memory, choosing instead to assume that "the lines of accurate and full recall are very largely, indeed, just as they are with us, a matter of social organization [1932, p. 248]."

Bartlett began his argument by noting that cultures are more than simple collections of people, but are collectivities with specialization of function transmitted in customs, institutions, and ideals. "Strong sentiments" form around these institutions to guide the group's selection of information from the environment. These socially determined psychological tendencies and the knowledge assimilated through their operation constitute schemas on which reconstructive recall can operate. Cultural differences in recall then reduce to differences in the persistent social tendencies that provide the schema into which information can fit. In content domains where such schemas have developed, the manner of recall can be "reconstructive"—involving generation of the required information from the general features of the schema (in a manner reminiscent of Parry's description of epic performers)—or the details can be read directly from the schema.

In addition, a "low-level type of recall' close to rote recapitulation operates in areas in which there are no persistent social tendencies and in which, consequently, the individual has no organizing schemas. Rote recall is likely to occur where the group has "plenty of time, in a sphere of relatively uncoordinated interests where everything that happens is about as interesting as everything else" (Bartlett, 1932, p. 266). Under these conditions, the "normal, temporal" schema will take over and events will be recalled in the order of their occurrence.

Bartlett was, in effect, asserting that the principles of recall are universal; only the specific social schemata and the occasions on which they are brought into play will differ from one group to another. This approach implies that cross-cultural studies of recall must carefully specify the way in which the materials and conditions of recall "fit" existing schemata.

Bartlett provided only preliminary evidence of an informal, experimental nature to support his assertions, and we have encountered only two studies that derive explicitly from his work. We will discuss these and the relevance of his theory to data collected within different theoretical frameworks in our review of experimental research.

II. EMPIRICAL DATA IN SEARCH OF A THEORY

When we turn our attention to the bulk of psychological data collected with cross-cultural comparisons explicitly in mind, we find only weak links between data and the theories we have just summarized. Not only is the general fit between theory and data minimal, but the data represent little more than pockets of research clustered around particular memory paradigms applied to one or two potentially relevant contrasts between cultures (for example, language, urbanization, education). Rather than pushing the data into existing theoretical molds, we will attempt to summarize research findings in their own terms, organizing them according to the nature of the tasks involved (as currently conceived in cognitive psychology) before returning to a reexamination of the theories.

A. Eidetic Imagery: A Model of Natural, Unmediated Recall?

At least since the work of Jaensch (1930), psychologists have speculated that the phenomenon of eidetic imagery may represent an early, relatively unmediated form of recall that is to be found in small children and pathologically or experientially "underdeveloped" adults. Leontiev, in the work described earlier, refers to work on eidetic imagery as evidence of a primary, "natural" memory process. Similar ideas can be found in several sources (for review, see Gray & Gummerman, 1975).

As attractive as the idea of negative correlations between eidetic imagery and age or acculturation[2] may be, the evidence after more than a decade of research can only be considered equivocal at best. Doob seemed to find support for this relation in his early work (1964), but by 1970 he concluded that while he was convinced that eidetic imagery was a real phenomenon, his work provided only "wisps of evidence . . . for the view that EI [eidetic imagery] incidence may be negatively correlated with age and acculturation [1970, pp. 228, 229]." He also suggests that theorists will have to go beyond the "kind of crude variables implicit in demographic factors" if they are to discover the processes mediating eidetic imagery.

---

[2] "Acculturation" as used by Doob (1960), and henceforth in this chapter, refers to increased urbanization, involvement in technological trades, formal education, and related experiences.

B. Visual Memory

Within the same theoretical orientation that generates interest in eidetic imagery and cultural experience, repeated sugestions are made that visual recall will be superior in nonliterate peoples, presumably because it represents retrieval of relatively unprocessed information that retains the major properties of the stimulus input. Yet we have been able to find only one study bearing directly on this hypothesis. Kleinfeld (1971) tested the ability of rural Eskimo and urban Caucasian children ranging in age from 9 to 16 to reproduce complex visual patterns in a paper and pencil test. Each of four items in the test could be scored on a scale of adequate reproduction from 0 to 5.

Reproductions made by subjects in the Eskimo sample were markedly superior to those of the Caucasian sample. Further, accuracy of visual recall increased with age for both groups. Kleinfeld attributed these results to a combination of ecological socializing, genetic, and linguistic factors, all of which led her to predict the superiority of the Eskimo sample.

In terms of more general theoretical approaches, Kleinfeld's data offer possible support for Leontiev's notion of two lines of development. Although she makes little of the fact, the performance of the Eskimo sample did not improve markedly as a function of age/education. The youngest group tested, 9- and 10-year-olds, achieved a total score of 16.7 out of a possible 20 points; the oldest group, 14- to 16-year-olds, a score of 17.7.[3] In contrast, the youngest Caucasian group scored 11.9, while the oldest scored 15.8, suggesting an increase in visual recall with age. Kleinfeld remarked that the Eskimo children's "unusual ability in visual memory" is accompanied by "weak verbal abstract skills." In Leontiev's terms, it is tempting to hypothesize that Kleinfeld found evidence of two lines of visual memory development, one acquired early as a result of socialization, the other a verbally mediated memory developed in school.

A great deal more work would be needed to put meat on this thin skeleton. It would help greatly, for example, to work with groups of rural Caucasian and urban Eskimo children to help deconfound the many independent variables that are linked in Kleinfeld's comparisons. It would also be most useful to find response measures that related theoretically to "direct" and "mediated" visual recall.

C. Memory for Location

In Kleinfeld's discussion of experiential factors that might promote visual recall among Eskimos, memory for location is discussed as a component of visual memory, but no test of memory for location was made. There are several sugges-

---

[3] Ceiling effects may have depressed age-related changes among the Eskimo children.

tions in recent work that the study of location as an attribute of visually presented material may be a fruitful area for comparative research. As Schulman (1973) has demonstrated, location is an attribute of most events. He shows that among American college students location recall and event (word) recognition are correlated. Underwood (1969) included location as one of the attributes that constitutes any learning event (see also Kail & Siegel, this volume).

Although anecdotal evidence suggests that young children have exceptional memory for the spatial location of objects (e.g., children beating their parents in games of "concentration"), there has been little systematic research on this topic. (See Siegel & White, 1975, for a review of developmental studies on children's representation of space.) Some evidence for a negative correlation between age/acculturation and memory for location is suggested by a recent study conducted by Meacham (1975), which has been extended and replicated in our laboratory.

Meacham (1975) presented six small objects randomly paired with eight drawings of "places" (a house, a corral, a cornfield) to Guatemalan children from an agricultural town near Guatemala City and American children from Buffalo, New York. The children ranged in age from 5 to 7. As each object was presented, the child was told, "I am going to hide the (object) in the (place)." The two experimental conditions were differentiated by the recall instruction: "What did I hide in the (place)" versus "Where did I hide the (object)?" Although the design was somewhat complex, the major results concern the relative recall of "place" or "object" after place and object were paired on a presentation trial. American children recalled more, overall, than the Guatemalan children, and the 7-year-olds recalled more than the 5-year-olds. Of greatest interest, however, was the fact that while the American children recalled place and object with equal efficiency, the Guatemalan children recalled place better than object.

We have conducted a replication of Meacham's basic procedure with educated and uneducated Vai (Liberian) children in collaboration with Elizabeth Hurlow-Hannah. The children ranged in age from 5 to 14; half the children at each age level attended school and the remainder were unschooled.

Each child was presented a set of eight photographs of familiar locations that were matched with eight line drawings of familiar objects in a procedure designed to repeat Meacham's as faithfully as possible. Half the children in each subgroup were asked for "object" recall before they were asked about the location of the object cards; the remainder were asked the two recall questions in the opposite order.

With one exception (7- to 9-year-old unschooled children), all groups performed better when asked about locations, consistent with the results obtained by Meacham in Guatemala. The extent of the superiority of location over object recall varied in a complex manner across the groups, however. We had expected to see an interaction between age and education such that educational experience would produce more rapid change toward equality in response to the two tasks, but the data do not support such an interpretation. Indeed, the largest difference in favor of location recall was observed among the educated 7- to 9-year-olds. Educated children at all ages performed better than their uneducated counterparts on both recall tasks.

Older children performed better than younger children only on location recall; and age, independent of education, did not contribute significantly to better object recall. These results indicate that memory for location and memory for things may follow different courses of development and may be contingent on different kinds of culturally determined experiences. So little work has been done on this issue that any generalizations about cultural influences appear premature.

D. Short-Term Spatio-Temporal Recall

A quite different kind of task that has received some attention in cross-cultural research derives from the work of Maccoby and Hagen (1965), which assesses memory for the location of a stimulus after brief, variable temporal delays. Wagner (1974) constructed sets of stimulus cards each of which contained a picture of an animal and a domestic object, from the popular Mexican game *lotteria*, similar in nature to American "bingo." A given set contained seven cards and a "probe" card depicting an animal (for half the subjects) or a domestic object (for the other half).

The basic task was for the subject to recall the position of the target items (animals or objects) after the cards had been presented in a linear array at two-second intervals. The probe trials were selected to test each of the seven possible positions in a random order. Since the cards were always laid out from the subject's left to his right, the position of the probe stimulus also determined the delay between presentation of a card and the test for recall of the card's position.

Wagner's first (1974) study was conducted on the Yucatan Peninsula with groups of Yucatec Mayan children and adults. In addition to age (subjects ranged from 7 to 9 through 22 to 35 years of age), Wagner investigated the influence of urbanization and educational experience on the development of recall performance. The rural subjects all came from a small town about 50 kilometers from Merida, the capital city; the urban subjects were all Meridians. The rural groups, except for the two youngest, had far fewer years of education than the age-matched urban groups.

The major result of this study is that the performance of urban and rural groups differed significantly only after educational levels diverged at age 13 to 16. Divergence in overall recall of the older groups was associated primarily with differences in recall of early (primacy) items from the stimulus array.

Wagner repeated this experiment in Morocco, where he was able to introduce two refinements on the Yucatecan work. First, he independently varied educational experience and rural versus urban upbringing by finding urban and rural samples matched for grade in school. He also included a group of young adult men who were attending a well-known Koranic school in a town near the one in which he obtained the rural subjects.

The major findings of Wagner's second study confirm the results of the first. Age-related increases in recall of early items of the list were observed only for the educated subjects, regardless of locale. The Koranic students, however, whose education consisted solely of memorizing the Koran and applying it to religious observances, performed in a manner closely resembling that of the *unschooled* subjects in the major groups. This is a finding of potential importance in disentangling the many factors that enter into the education effects observed in this and other studies.

These data are most compatible with theories that draw a parallel between individual and cultural development, assuming that exposure to formal schooling constitutes the requisite cultural change. Wagner used exactly this framework in his own interpretation. Referring to the work of Atkinson and Shiffrin (1968), Flavell (1970), and Hagen (1971), he attributed the population differences to differential development of higher mnemonic strategies—in this case, spontaneous, active rehearsal—in his various populations. Wagner ended his 1974 paper with the conclusion that

Higher mnemonic strategies in memory may do more than lag by several years (in un-educated subjects)—the present data suggest that without formal schooling, such skills may not develop at all [p. 395].

One other feature of Wagner's studies must be described before we turn to their theoretical interpretation. It will be recalled that each stimulus card contained two pictures, one of which was the target stimulus. Following the procedure used in several studies by Hagen and his associates, Wagner tested for recall of the nontarget stimuli following the seven trials of probed recall. Here the results in the two studies diverge somewhat. In the Yucatecan study, incidental recall was a curvilinear function of age, with the peak somewhat later for rural than urban subjects. In the Moroccan data, incidental recall either was unchanging as a function of age/education or increased slightly for the educated subjects, with no hint of decrease at older age/educational levels. For the Yucatecan data, Wagner found no systematic evidence that performance on the central and incidental tasks "trade off"; the pattern of central and incidental task performance correlations was not systematically related to any of his population variables.

We have carried out one further analysis of theoretical relevance on Wagner's (1974) data, calculating the difference between central and incidental task performance. According to Smirnov and Zinchenko (1969), the difference between performance on the two tasks should increase with increasing age. Using this measure (to which no statistics have been applied, since we have merely read the data from the graphs provided), we found that central recall was greater than incidental recall by a constant amount for the uneducated subjects, but the difference between the two tasks increased with age for the educated subjects.

While Hagen's notion of an attentional tradeoff is not supported by the data, the observation of a relatively greater difference between central and incidental recall for older, educated subjects supports that part of the Vygotsky–Leontiev theory which assumes that the difference between incidental and intentional recall should increase with development as a consequence of the increasingly diversified and spontaneously generated activities educated people bring to intentional memory tasks.

However, several aspects of the data are not consonant with Leontiev's notion of "two memories," one that relies more on "natural processes" and the other relying on generated, mental mediational processes. One might expect, in accord with this theory, that recency recall (widely referred to as "echoic memory") would be superior in the noneducated groups. In addition, one might expect absolute levels of incidental recall to be higher for the less educated subjects on the assumption that much of what they know is "picked up" rather than deliberately learned. Neither of these expectations is met.

Little support is provided for Bartlett's idea that rote recapitulation will tend to appear in the recall of the noneducated subjects; were such the case, we would clearly expect improved recall of early items in the list. But it is the educated subjects who show primacy effects.

Finally, a difficulty in current formulations of memory for location is apparent in these data. In the Meacham task, we saw evidence of relatively greater recall of location (as a place in the world) for children who were, presumably, less acculturated. In the Wagner studies, children were also asked to recall location—the physical location where they saw the stimulus card previously. This kind of location recall is poorer in the less acculturated subjects. Clearly, greater specificity is needed in defining what type of "location" is involved in a given task before comparative statements are warranted.

E. Recognition Memory

In recent years, several authors have suggested the utility of studying the development of memory using multiple tasks varying in the degree to which their successful performance requires the application of higher-order mnemonic processes. Brown, for example (cf. Brown, 1974), has made excellent use of this strategy in a series of studies investigating retardate and normal memory development. Among the tasks that do not seem to require the application of complex strategies and for which developmental differences are much reduced is recognition of simple pictorial stimuli.

Cross-cultural work on recognition memory has been very scanty, and with mixed results. Kagan and Klein (1973) reported a study in which young rural Guatemalan children "lag" their American counterparts in recognition performance at 5 to 8 years of age, but are equally proficient at 11 years. Excellent performance in all the older groups renders this result somewhat difficult to interpret.

Wagner (personal communication, 1975) conducted a study of continuous recognition memory for rug patterns using the same populations of Moroccan subjects as in his short-term memory task. Although at the time of this writing data from this study had not been analyzed completely, one preliminary finding is intriguing. Wagner compared educated and noneducated subjects not only in terms of their overall recognition scores but also in terms of their performance on different aspects of the task. Accurate performance on this task requires that the subject reject new (that is, previously unseen) stimuli and accept old (previously seen) stimuli. When performance is analyzed in this way, it appears that education does not exert a uniform effect, but rather, has a differential influence on rejections and acceptances. This suggests that separation of recognition performance into the components of response strategies (saying no or saying yes) and true memory scores will be necessary for a full interpretation of cross-cultural studies.

In our own work among the Kpelle (Cole, Gay, Glick, & Sharp, 1971), we did no systematic studies of recognition recall to compare with our studies of free recall. However, one pilot study on this topic suggests that Wagner's strategy of comparing recall and recognition within the same population may prove useful in future research.

The subjects in this study were 6- to 8-year-olds, 10- to 14-year-olds, and adult rural Kpelle. The two younger groups were equally divided between those who had attended school and those who had not. The 6- to 8-year-olds who were attending school were in the first or second grade. The grade level for the older children ranged from 2 to 4, with an average of about grade 3. None of the adults had attended school. Half of the subjects in the five resulting groups were presented to-be-recognized stimuli orally; the remainder were shown the objects named in the oral recognition group.

The target stimuli (names or objects) were 16 things, 2 each from 8 Kpelle categories such as root crops, sewing things, blacksmith's tools. These were read, or shown, one at a time. These items were then interspersed randomly among 24 filler items, 3 from each of the same 8 categories. Each subject was given 5 presentations of the target items and 5 recognition tests, each with a

TABLE 8-1
Recognition Scores as a Function of Age and Education

Age	Educated		Uneducated	
	Object	Word	Object	Word
6–8	52	72	63	59
10–14	55	65	65	52
Adult	—	—	80	41

different random ordering of the lists. Presentation and recognition trials were in the same modality (oral–oral or visual–visual).

Each subject's performance was scored using a standard correction for guessing (correct minus incorrect divided by total number of items). The recognition scores for each group are shown in Table 8-1.

A marked interaction between the kind of stimuli presented for recognition and the age/educational experience of the subject populations is apparent in the data presented in Table 8-1. Educated groups recognized words presented orally better than objects. Exactly the opposite relation held for uneducated children and adults.

In addition, the relationship between age and recognition seems to follow a different developmental course for words and objects. Recognition for objects seems to increase as a function of age, while recognition for spoken words decreases. The perplexing decline with development in recognition of words may represent a change in decision processes toward a stricter criterion and may be relatively uninfluenced by memory processes. Again, as suggested in Wagner's work, it appears that we need more sophisticated recognition studies if we are going to be able to separate memory and decision-making processes.

Finally, the relatively good performance of the uneducated adults when recognizing objects presents a strong contrast with the performance of such groups on the standard free recall task using similar stimulus materials. It is unfortunate, in view of this result, that we could not obtain suitable groups of educated adults for comparative purposes in this work.

Speaking more generally, the lack of systematic recognition-recall studies in the cross-cultural literature represents a major shortcoming in current scholarship on the development of memory. In both the Wagner study and our own small study, it appears that under some conditions, for some response measures, recognition of unacculturated peoples can exceed that of their educated counterparts. This kind of reversal deserves attention not only because it stands in contrast to most other results we have reviewed but because such reversal can be predicted by developmental theories such as Leontiev's if we assume that recognition is closer to natural, unmediated remembering than recall (an assumption very much in tune with recent developmental memory theory, e.g., Brown, 1974).

F. Free Recall

1. Early Studies

Beginning in the late 1960s, Cole and his colleagues, and later Scribner, undertook a rather extensive investigation of cultural differences in the development of free recall. The early studies in this series have been described in a number of publications (Cole & Gay, 1972; Cole et al., 1971) and will be described here only in sufficient detail to provide a framework for discussing later work. One list was "clusterable" because of the obvious division into easily identifiable semantic categories, and the other was "nonclusterable" because it was constructed so as to provide minimal groupings into semantic categories.

The experimental attack focused on the types of persons, verbal instructions, and material conditions that could reasonably be expected to affect the rate of learning and degree of clustering in free recall. The first variation involved the nature of the stimulus materials. One point on which many observers of African learning seem to agree is the presumed "concreteness" of African thought. Perhaps, then, if we showed the objects named by each of our stimulus words to our subjects, instead of reading them aloud, we would observe greatly augmented recall and clustering.

A second variation involved the nature of the lists. American evidence indicates that clusterable lists are easier to learn and are better recalled in general than lists whose components belong to disparate classes. If the Kpelle rely on rote memory rather than on the semantic organization of the list, they ought to recall both lists equally well.

Another variable that has been found to affect recall is the arrangement of items in a clusterable list. If the items are *not* randomly arranged as originally suggested, but rather, are presented with all items in a given class succeeding each other, clustering and recall are enhanced for American college students (Cofer, Bruce, & Reicher, 1966).

Kpelle subjects were selected from three age groups: 6 to 8, 10 to 14, and 18 to 50. Within the first two age groups, comparisons were made between unschooled children and children in the first grade and the second to fourth grades, respectively. The experiments did not include educated adult groups, since at that time it was very rare to find an educated tribal adult.

In general, Kpelle children do not know their ages. Moreover, grade in school very often does not correspond to years in school, because a student is likely to remain in the beginner's half of the first grade until his English comprehension is adequate to continue, and because children may begin school at widely differing ages. These factors complicate the already complex task of cross-cultural comparison.

The series of free recall experiments using the groups and procedures just outlined as well as several additional studies using procedures that are more or less standard in American studies of memory can be summarized in capsule form as follows:

1. As American children grow older, the number of words recalled and the rate at which the list is learned increase markedly (Jablonski, 1974). Older Liberian Kpelle subjects recall only slightly more than younger subjects, and educated subjects recall slightly more than uneducated subjects, but on the whole learning is very slow and the differences among groups are relatively small.

2. Clusterable lists are learned a little more easily by all groups.

3. American children begin to "cluster" their recall with repeated trials, but the Kpelle subjects show little or no semantic clustering.

4. The Kpelle groups all show better recall for objects than for spoken words, but so do the Americans.

The general picture to emerge from this set of standard experiments was that the memory performance of the Kpelle was poor, the developmental trends found in Western studies were all but lacking, and five to six years of formal education did little to help matters. No evidence was found for rote learning, but memory was certainly poor for these subjects in this situation.

2. Improving Retention by the Kpelle

Clearly, many interpretations are possible for the outcome of this experimental series. We felt that the proper object of this research was to find out what kinds of conditions are required for Kpelle subjects to show good memory skills in an experimental situation. Our guiding hypothesis was that something in the structure of free recall experiments as they are usually conducted failed to provide Kpelle subjects with the needed "reminders" of the material that had been presented.

We began our investigations with the vague notion that the performance of the Kpelle subjects would be improved if the categories latent in the clusterable list were somehow signaled by an object in the real world. Thus, we arranged a situation in which the objects shown to subjects were associated with chairs. Perhaps "concreteness" is not an attribute of the material to be learned, but the relationship of this material to some external recall cue.

The experimenter stood behind four chairs with the subject in front. A table behind the experimenter contained the objects to be remembered. These objects were held over chairs, one at a time, as the names were read, and then the subject was asked to recall the items (but not the chair with which they were associated).

The presentation of items followed a different pattern for each of three different groups of 10- to 14-year-old schoolchildren. For one group, items from a given category were held over one particular chair on each trial, so that each category was assigned one chair. For a second group, items were assigned at random to the four chairs, with the assignment remaining the same for each trial. For the third group, there was only one chair over which the items were held; the other three chairs were not used.

In all three groups, recall was much higher than any we had previously observed for this population, making it appear that the fact of having a "concrete reminder" is more critical for good recall than the particular form the reminder takes.[4] The next problem was to determine if this "reminder" notion could be extended to other kinds of cues besides physical ones.

In an initial attempt to use verbal cues, subjects were read the standard clusterable list and recall was measured under five conditions. For the groups cued when the list was introduced on each trial, the experimenter said, "I am going to tell you about several things. *These things will be clothes, tools, food, and utensils.* When I tell you these things, listen carefully." The list was then presented in the standard, oral fashion. For groups cued at the time of recall, the list of categories was repeated then. If no cuing occurred, the italicized sentence was omitted. The possibilities of cuing or not cuing, prior to presentation (input) or prior to recall (output), resulted in four experimental conditions. In addition, a group of subjects was tested for four trials with no cuing at input, but highly constrained cuing at the time of recall. After the list of items was presented to the subjects in this group, they were asked to recall the items by category. For instance, the experimenter would say, "Tell me all the clothes you remember." After the subject had named all the clothing items he could remember, the experimenter would repeat the procedure with each of the other categories. On the fifth trial, no cuing was given at all, and these subjects were told simply to remember as many of the items as they could.

Comparison of the first four groups indicated that simply naming the categories at time of input or output had little effect on recall or clustering; performance did not differ among groups and was comparable to that obtained in the standard, oral presentation situation.

The results from the fifth group whose recall was constrained to systematic retrieval by category were quite different. The number of words recalled on the first four trials was extremely high and, most important, remained high on the fifth trial, when recall was not constrained. Clustering was forced to be perfect for the first four trials with this group, but on trial 5 clustering, too, remained high and comparable to the performance of American schoolchildren. It appears that good recall and highly organized recall can be induced through sufficiently explicit verbal instruction and training.

The demonstration that there are ways of presenting material in the free recall

---

[4] In another experiment with similar groups of children but with a different experimenter, recall and clustering were higher when items were assigned to chairs by semantic category rather than randomly. We have no reliable data, therefore, on differences *among* the chairs procedures.

experiment that greatly enhance the Kpelle person's ability to remember items in our standard task, coupled with the new evidence that proper cuing at the time of recall can produce essentially perfect performance, suggests that the difficulty experienced by the Kpelle was one of retrieving material stored in memory. It could be said that the constrained-recall procedure taught the subject retrieval habits that carried over to the unconstrained-recall trial.

Having achieved such effects in our standard experimental situation, we next wanted to determine if Kpelle would routinely use efficient retrieval processes on their own in a more natural memory situation. One such situation in Kpelle land involves remembering stories.

The basic strategy we adopted was to provide a range of story contexts in which to present the twenty basic clusterable items. At one extreme, no context at all was provided (our basic oral presentation procedure was repeated); at the other extreme, items were embedded in a story context in which each item was meaningfully linked to a neighboring item, either in clusters or in a linear string. The stories were read by the experimenter, who wrote down the subject's responses in the standard manner. Then a tape recorder was turned on to record the subject's version of the story.

The upshot of this experiment was that the way in which the items to be recalled fit into the story almost perfectly determined the organization of recall. For clustered input, there was a very strong tendency to recall the items by category. For linear input, just the opposite relation held: Items were recalled more or less in the order in which they fit into the story, and category clustering was at a minimum.

3. A Production Deficiency Hypothesis

Results similar to those obtained among the Kpelle were also found among groups of slightly educated or noneducated Yucatec Mayans and members of the Vai tribe in Liberia who were, or were not, literate in their indigenous script (cf. Cole et al., 1971, p. 261ff). More recently, Sharp and Cole (1975) have replicated these basic relationships in studies among Yucatec Maya differing in age and educational experience, with age ranging from 7 to 9 up to mature adulthood. While the Mayan samples show some improvement with repeated trials, really marked improvement over trials and high levels of clustering are associated with secondary education. The appearance of marked clustering among noneducated adults if items are embedded in stories was also replicated in the Yucatan.

Recall studies among the Vai, recently conducted by Gologor (1975), also confirm and extend earlier findings. In one study, Gologor presented word lists for free recall that were constructed from functional rather than taxonomic categories—items were selected that could be organized around such prominent activities in the culture as tailoring or cooking. With these materials, Gologor found low levels of organization and little effect of a few years of education—

essentially the same results as those obtained with functional word lists among the Kpelle. Moreover, Gologor's Vai subjects showed the same relative lack of improvement on successive lists that had characterized the Kpelle data. The same negative conclusion with respect to semantic clustering held true when semantically related items were used to detect proactive inhibition in recall, or when semantic relations were manipulated to test for a "von Restorff" effect.

These studies underscore the fact that the way in which the Kpelle performed on our early memory tasks was determined not so much by unique features of their culture as by factors that might be common to many noneducated traditional peoples. Our interpretation of the early Kpelle studies had in fact taken this tack: We accounted for the results by a combination of Flavell's (1970) notion of a "production deficiency" and Bartlett's idea that recall is guided by available organizational schemas that are culturally determined. In standard free recall tasks, the subject must "produce" the schema latent in the material, and the tendency to look for and generate schemas to organize material varies from group to group. All of the modifications we introduced into the task shared the common feature of producing the structure for the subject, thus reducing differences attributable to production deficiencies. But the cultural saliency of the kinds of structure produced by the two principal experimental manipulations may have differed. In the case of explicit cuing of the categories, the structure was that of a classified word list without any context; we have no way of knowing how often and on what occasions classified lists are utilized by the Kpelle in the course of their daily activities. We do know, however, that listening to and recounting stories is a familiar and favored activity. Embedding material to be remembered in traditional story contexts thus provided a structure that made contact, in Bartlett's terms, with a preexisting organizational schema. Although the notion that more salient cultural *schemas* should have a facilitative effect on memory performance is intuitively appealing, there are no data to our knowledge that speak to this point. Most attempts to vary cultural familiarity have been concerned with the *context,* rather than the *organization,* of stimulus material, and indeed, there is little ethnographic work available to guide experimenters who would put this aspect of Bartlett's theory to the test.

It is possible, however, to test the production deficiency hypothesis for differences among cultural groups, or between educated and noneducated subjects within one culture. A study by Scribner (1974) explored the question of why uneducated Kpelle subjects failed to make use of semantic categories in the original free recall situation.

Her first experiment proceeded in two parts. First, subjects were required to classify and reclassify a set of objects until they reached a consistent way of classifying. Then they were asked to remember the objects they had been classifying. This procedure provided an opportunity for subjects to organize material according to their own preferred criteria and for the experimenter to find out if subjects *required* to produce their own structure prior to remembering would use that structure in recall. Two lists of 25 objects were prepared, one a clusterable list composed of five 5-item categories and one a "nonclusterable" list. The four adult populations involved in this study included high schoolers, cash crop farmers, rice farmers in a road village, and rice farmers living deep in the bush. The groups were selected to represent various degrees of education and involvement in modern economic institutions.

The initial sorting task was carried out somewhat more rapidly by the high schoolers than by the other populations, with bush adults slowest. The high schoolers also differed from the remaining populations in manifesting a strong tendency to sort the items by semantic category, while the remaining populations manifested a good deal of functional grouping.

The outstanding finding was that subjects in each of these populations *made use of their own groupings* to structure their recall. This common technique of using structure to guide recall is all the more interesting because different "structures" were involved for the different populations, especially for those at the extreme ends of acculturization. High schoolers relied almost exclusively on semantic category membership as the basis for grouping; the bush farmers made little use of this principle.

This does not mean, however, that the nature of the groupings had no effect on the amount of clustering in recall: While all recall cluster scores were greater than chance, in general they paralleled the scores for semantic grouping—clustering was highest for the high schoolers, followed closely by the cash workers and then by the two farming groups. Moreover, clustering was reduced markedly among all populations for the list that was put together out of unrelated items, although this list, too, had been given forced organization. It would appear, then, that organizing principles that may be used to group stimuli may differ in their efficiency as guides to their recall.

This study provided support for our hypothesis that Kpelle people will manifest organized recall if they are *required* to work on the material ahead of time and to reorder it. The question still remains: Do Kpelle spontaneously reorganize such material as an aid to memory? Based on Scribner's second study, it appears that the answer is "rarely." A free study situation was devised, patterned after that employed by Moely, Olsen, Hawes, and Flavell (1969), in their investigation of the development of memorizing techniques among American schoolchildren. The subjects included 40 villagers in traditional occupations. All subjects were given a 2-minute period to study 24 familiar objects selected from the materials used in the sorting study which we have just described. Half of the subjects were given broad instructions to do "anything they wanted to help them remember," and half were given additional instructions to carry the objects to another table "in any way that would help them remember." The "carry" instruction was introduced in the belief that forced handling of the material would encourage grouping activities.

Only 3 villagers out of 20 attempted to group the material in any way at all under the "no-carry" condition: The great majority left the items as the experimenter put them on the table and relied on various simple mnemonics, such as saying the names of the items, describing their uses, sometimes counting to help them remember. Only 3 of the 20 villagers who were required to bring the items to another table made any attempt to "reorder" them; most laid out the objects haphazardly or heaped them up; several tried to reconstitute the original order in which the experimenter had laid them out.

Surprisingly enough, few high schoolers attempted to organize the objects either, although we know from the sorting study that the semantic structure built into this object array had high salience for them. Just 11 out of 40 subjects spontaneously regrouped some or all of the objects by category, and 9 of these did so only under the "extra prodding" of the "carry instructions," which forced a breakup of the original order. Here there seems to be a genuine cultural difference, as Moely et al. (1969) found that American school children at the fifth-grade level spontaneously use categorical grouping of material as an aid to memory.

On the face of it, these studies seem to provide strong support for the view that formal education exerts a major influence on the development of higher-order mnemonic activities (although there are subsidiary results in Scribner's study indicating that involvement in the cash economy may exert a similar influence to a reduced degree). However, this line of work leaves several issues unresolved, even if we restrict ourselves to the "has attended school—has not attended school" dichotomy that seems to emerge in a wide range of studies.

One problem has to do with the number of years of schooling required to produce a difference in the standard tasks; the bulk of the evidence suggests that low levels of education (that is, one to four years) exert little influence. From some studies (Scribner, 1974; Sharp & Cole, 1975), it would appear that children or adults with five to six years of schooling perform somewhat better than those with one to three years, but secondary education is required to produce sharp qualitative changes in behavior. There is good justification for assuming that at the higher levels of education on this continuum, and perhaps at the intermediate levels as well, strong selection factors based on individual achievement and economic factors have been responsible for reducing the population sizes. No work has separated selection and experiential factors, thus making causal statements suspect.

We are also uncertain about how various sorting procedures designed to induce organization exert their effect at the time of recall. We have spoken as if various "structure-inducing" procedures exert their effects in psychologically equivalent ways. However, a study by Sharp and Cole (1975) calls this view into question. In all of the sorting-recall studies in the literature (e.g., Liberty & Ornstein, 1973; Moely et al., 1969; Scribner, 1974), several trials of sorting are followed by a single trial of recall. Sharp and Cole replicated the facilitative effects of object sorting with uneducated Mayan groups *using just a single sorting trial followed by recall.* In addition, they continued to present the list orally for four trials, asking for recall following each list presentation. They compared performance using this procedure with performance on the standard procedure of presenting five trials of oral free recall. On Trial 1, those who had just sorted the 20 objects into 4 categories recalled and clustered more than those who had been presented the objects orally in a random order. However, clustering dropped precipitously on Trial 2 for the group that had sorted, while recall improved slightly. The sort-recall curve then began to rise again, remaining slightly above the level of the control group tested with the standard procedure for oral free recall.

These results, obtained in two separate studies, are consistent with the view that recall and clustering on a single trial following physical sorting of objects are under the control of different processes than recall and clustering following categorization of successively presented verbal stimuli.

This possibility is worth exploring because of its implications for theories that posit dual memory processes of the natural-logical mediated memory scheme proposed by Leontiev. In this view, imposing categories on a randomly ordered set of stimuli presented sequentially may be considered to require mediational processes not demanded by a task in which recall categorization may be achieved by simple retention of an organization represented in a physical way.

G. Recall of Connected Materials: Remembering Stories

Considering the broad scope of the theories relating memory skills to features of culture, it is remarkable how limited a range of empirical techniques have been employed to test them. In all of the previous studies (with the possible exception of the list-within-story experiment by Cole et al., 1971), the subject's task was to recall a set of materials that were presented as isolated bits of information. While such tasks have proved useful, they do not provide an opportunity for observing culturally determined effects on the method and manner of recall in remembering situations that are more representative of those naturally encountered in daily life.

Some studies, however, have sought to test the specific culture-and-memory hypotheses by the use of more complex verbal materials. An early effort by Nadel (1937) was conceived as a direct test of Bartlett's theory that persistent social tendencies would be reflected in the content of story recall. For his subject population, Nadel used two groups of 16- to 18-year-old schoolboys from neighboring Nupe and Yoruba tribes in Nigeria. Ethnographic studies indicated that while these two tribes shared similar ecology, languages, and socioeconomic institutions, they differed in other spheres of life. The Yoruba religion posited a rationalized and elaborate hierarchy of dieties, while the Nupe beliefs centered on a magical concept of impersonal power; Yoruba art was highly developed, while the Nupe art was imageless, with emphasis on decoration; the Yoruba engaged in pantomine and drama, while the Nupe did not.

These and other differences were used to predict differences in the content of a recalled story designed to be familiar in form and general content to both the Yoruba and Nupe groups. Nadel reports that omissions and additions in recall were consistent with his analysis of the two cultures. The Yoruba emphasized the logical structure of the story, even elaborating on the logical links between episodes; the Nupe subjects were reported to be indifferent to the logic of the story, emphasizing instead circumstantial facts, details, and descriptive features while describing the events in the story one after the other "without endeavoring to establish, or to preserve, an inner cohesion in the narrative" (Nadel, 1937, p. 428).

Nadel was primarily concerned with showing the relevance of psychological data to anthropological analysis. He interpreted his findings as support for Bartlett's position regarding the influence of social tendencies. Nadel did not comment on the part of Bartlett's theory that predicts different manners of recall (rote or constructive). It appears from his description that the Nupe are giving what Bartlett would call a rote performance, while the Yoruba are constructing their stories. No reason for this is discernible from Nadel's analysis, nor does he suggest a sphere of Nupe life where constructive recall would be expected.

A second experiment supporting Bartlett's emphasis on social tendencies was conducted by Deregowski (1970). Deregowski took as his point of departure the observation by Doob (1960) and others that awareness of time increases with increasing "civilization." He presented a story containing eight quantitative elements, four of which referred to time, to two groups of Zambian subjects: a group of adult women living in a rural area with little or no schooling and a group of schoolboys living in the capital city, Lusaka. The schoolboys were about 13 years of age and had attended school for an average of six years. Deregowski hypothesized that the heavy emphasis on punctuality and dates in school would produce relatively greater recall of the temporal items among the schoolboys. This was, in general, what he found. The differences between the two populations were neglible for three of the four nontemporal concepts, and very marked in favor of the schoolboys for the temporal ones.[5]

---

[5] Lancy (1974) compared multitrial story recall with multitrial list recall among Kpelle boys aged 6–9 and 10–13. The story was an original one constructed in the manner of a traditional Kpelle folktale. It was read on three consecutive Sundays, and on each succeeding Friday the boys were asked to tell as much of the story as they could recall. After the last story recall, each boy was given three presentation-and-recall trials of a list of 16 nonrelated words. There were certain similarities in recall of the two types of materials: Older children had higher overall recall for both stories and lists; all children improved over trials on both stories and lists. However, there was no relationship between an individual child's performance on the story task and his performance on the word list task.

H. The Study of Memory in "Nonmnemonic" Tasks

Remembering was the goal of the subject's activity in all of the studies reviewed thus far. However, remembering enters into virtually every kind of task studied by cognitive psychologists. Differences in memory may be sources of differences in the performance of tasks where memory is not usually considered a crucial factor in performance.

Evidence consistent with this view comes from a study of factors associated with two- and three-dimensional perception of pictorial material. Deregowski (1969) was interested in the factors associated with the widespread observation that many sub-Saharan African children and adults fail to interpret line drawings with conventional depth cues as three dimensional. He reasoned that if those who respond to tests of two- versus three-dimensional picture perception as "two-dimensional responders" do not even attempt to interpret line drawings as three dimensional, they will not be confused by "impossible figures" such as the "two-pronged trident." In effect, they will fail to notice anything anomolous about the figure.

The language in which this hypothesis is phrased suggests that the effect itself is not, strictly speaking, perceptual, but the result of information processing that follows perceptual input. If this is so, Deregowski reasoned, there may be little difference between two- and three-dimensional "perceivers" if they are asked to draw the figures immediately after they see them. However, if they have to draw them from memory they will, in effect, be reproducing the figures from a representation that has had time to be assimilated to the subject's interpretation of what he saw. This expectation was neatly confirmed by Deregowski's study. Immediate reproduction produced no difference between the two groups, but three-dimensional perceivers experienced significantly more difficulty than did two-dimensional perceivers with the "two-pronged trident" when a 10-second delay was imposed prior to reproduction of the figure.

A quite different illustration of the role of memory in a "nonmnemonic" task comes from the work of Ciborowski and Cole (1973) on the influence of age and educational experience on concept identification. Using a modification of the procedures popularized by Bruner, Goodnow, and Austin (1956), Ciborowski and Cole asked subjects to classify a set of cards depicting two geometric forms varying in shape and color. For half of the subjects within any population group, the rule defining the correct set of cards represented the combination of a value from each dimension. For example, if conjunction were the rule for combining attributes, "red triangle" would be an example of a correct concept. If disjunction of attributes defined the correct exemplars, stimulus cards with red or triangular pictures would be correct.

A second class of problems involved the contrast between conjunctive and disjunctive rules. These problems, however, were all based on combinations of attributes *within* a particular dimension (e.g., red and red for conjunction, red or red for disjunction).

When this experiment was conducted in the United States, Ciborowski and Cole observed a striking difference in the pattern of solution between the two classes of problems. Combining attributes *across* dimensions in the traditional manner produced the well-documented superiority of conjunctive over disjunctive concepts. However, when the rule was applied *within* dimensions no such difference appeared. Further analyses showed that the finding of no difference between conjunctive and disjunctive problems in the within-dimension set was due to the tendency of subjects to reformulate the problems in terms of a simplifying rule (e.g., the disjunctive exemplar "red *or* red" could become "one red," and the conjunctive exemplar "red *and* red" could become "two red"). Moreover, the use of a simplifying rule increased with age.

When these procedures were replicated with groups of educated and uneducated Kpelle schoolchildren, there was no observable tendency for either group of Kpelle subjects to reformulate the nonstandard problems. Since earlier studies had shown the importance of the memory components of this task, Ciborowski and Cole replicated their basic procedures, allowing the Kpelle students to have visual access to all past instances. The result was not only to greatly speed the learning process but to change its structure as well. Kpelle students who were provided with a running memory of their past examples restructured their learning of the problems so that the pattern of errors corresponded to the pattern we had observed for the older American schoolchildren; that is, they invoked the simplifying rule for the *within*-dimensional problems and showed the customary conjunctive-disjunctive discrepancy on the *across*-dimension problems.

These results seem to support Leontiev's insistence that the mediation of recall via external aids restructures the process of memory itself, with the clear suggestion that when memory is affected in this way, the consequences will show up in complex intellectual tasks that require memory operations.

III. CONCLUSIONS

In the preceeding sections, we have tried to provide the reader with an overview of the "grand theories" relevant to interpreting cultural differences in memory performance and to examine existing data in the light of these theories. We said at the outset that the task was rendered difficult by the extreme variety of the theories and the paucity of data. It does not seem unfair to conclude that the lack of theoretical precision is well matched by the lack of theory-relevant data.

Considering the state of this area of inquiry, we see no point in totting up evidence in favor of one theoretical position over another. Rather, we would like to propose a framework, drawing on each of the theories that we have discussed, that is general enough to encompass the major empirical phenomena we have described and that can serve as a guideline to future research on this general topic.

Any such framework will have to encompass the three major memory phenomena summarized in this chapter:

1. The manifestation of normal, if not exceptional, recall of everyday events by nonliterate adults. Although these data have not been gathered systematically, our own experience, as well as the written records of anthropologists, urge it on us.

2. The existence in at least some nonliterate societies of special mnemonic devices for the transmission of esoteric knowledge. While these devices are presumably accessible to all members of the society, they are employed systematically by only a few. Philological analysis urged on us the conclusion that elaboration is the psychological key to this process.

3. The repeated demonstration of better recall in educated subjects within traditional societies on a variety of memory tasks derived from developmental-psychological and general cognitive research. We will consider a few exceptions to this generalization presently because they form a part of the overall argument.

A theoretical framework adequate for interpreting memory studies in contemporary societies must also take into account the fact that the "primitive" cultures that so intrigued early explorers are not the cultures that anthropologists or psychologists visit today. On what corner of the earth are there groups of people who have not, in the last few centuries, experienced explorers, anthropologists, psychologists, missionaries, or various other emissaries of industrialized nations? Radios, cigarettes, and coins are only a few of the "imported artifacts" that have irrevocably changed the way of life, the knowledge, and the "mental activities" of traditional peoples. It seems time to acknowledge that theories of historical development drawing on observations in the pre- or early colonial period cannot *in principle* be tested by any research methods applied in the societies where investigators now carry out their cross-cultural work. Such theories require elaboration in the light of twentieth-century conditions and careful studies of the social and cultural realities of our own time.

Within the limits of our available knowledge, we would like to suggest that analytic machinery developed to account for phenomena within the normal purview of cognitive psychology itself can be broadened to provide the necessary interpretative framework. Numerous developmentally oriented cognitive psychologists (Brown, 1974; Gollin, 1965; Klahr, 1973) have recently stressed the importance of assessing the cognitive demands of various tasks as they interact with the cognitive skills brought to them by various groups of subjects. Brown, for example, has stressed the difference between tasks that require the application of control processes (cf. Atkinson & Shiffrin, 1968) and those that permit relatively automatic readout of material. This has led her into a fruitful study of retardate memory, showing that (for example) the oft-observed differences in memory between retardate and normal children do not occur in recognition memory. The same strategy was followed in our own free recall work among the Kpelle, leading us to reach the conclusion that recall deficits are most likely to be found in situations where the materials are presented as isolated units, devoid of ready-made structuring devices or external cues for retrieval.

These examples, and others we could garner, all come from within the range of tasks normal for cognitive psychology. What if we were to apply this line of reasoning not only to psychological tasks but to the variety of tasks posed in different nonexperimental settings within our own culture as well as the recall situations encountered in the different cultural groups that provide the grist for the cross-cultural psychologist's mill?

Two major characteristics of most laboratory studies of memory set them off from nonlaboratory remembering situations in our own society and, we suspect, even more so in nonliterate societies. First, in all of the studies we have reviewed, and in all but a handful of the studies to be found in the psychological literature on memory, *remembering is the goal* of the subject's activity from the very outset of the experiment. By contrast, in most situations where the memory of nonliterate peoples has attracted the attention of anthropologists, the individuals whose recall seemed so remarkable were not engaged in committing things to memory for later retrieval. Rather, they were engaged in a variety of other activities (taking care of cows about to be sold, learning to make a rice farm, making medicines) that produced excellent recall as an incidental by-product.

The second distinguishing characteristic of nonlaboratory recall is related to the first in a way that is almost certainly nonaccidental; the situations in which the remembering (but not necessarily the retrieval) takes place are given structure and meaning by virtue of the "dominant social tendencies" that organize all mundane life. As we have repeatedly been led to remark in our review of the cross-cultural literature, population differences in recall such as those between educated and noneducated subjects appear most frequently in tasks in which the structure of the material to be remembered is not made explicit. Such tasks require the employment of specialized mnemonic activities that structure the material for retrieval purposes. The production of structure, whether by categorizing operations, serial ordering, or other activities, makes the memorizing task meaningful. Such meaning-inducing operations, however, are rarely required in everyday life.

The one possible exception to this broad classification occurs in those cases, well documented in both anthropology and philology, where individuals deliberately have to commit some large body of esoteric material to memory with the sure knowledge that they will have to reproduce it at a later time. Here, we would like to suggest, societies have provided a number of psychologically sound mnemonic devices that provide the structure lacking in the activity itself. This is surely what Parry, Lord, and Havelock have demonstrated in the case of

Homeric and Yugoslav epic poetry. More recently, Colby (1975; Colby & Cole, 1973) has been able to make a very strong case for the same principle operating in the folk stories of people as disparate as the Canadian Eskimo and the Ixil of northeast Guatemala. In all these cases, cultural education is ensured by the existence of culturally given, meaning-inducing devices.

If we accept the general proposition that laboratory studies differ from most nonlaboratory situations in the goals and structures of the activities that result in remembering, we are led to a reexamination of current cross-cultural research on memory development along two lines. First, we need to reexamine the psychological literature to determine the range of memory tasks that have been used to sample remembering in different societies. Second, we are led to a reexamination of the way in which demands on memory are distributed in different societies. Two kinds of distributions need to be considered: the conditions under which people have to engage in remembering as a task in and of itself, and the extent to which the activities that support remembering must be provided by the individual rememberer. Cultures may differ in the extent to which they require of their members deliberate, intentional memorization of information, and in the situations where deliberate memorization is required, cultures may differ with respect to the "supports for memory" they provide. In some cultures and with respect to certain domains of material, such supports may take the form of special literary devices (epic poems, for example). In other cultures, supports may be provided in the features of the situations in which information must be retrieved.

We have already remarked on the sparsity of experimental evidence, even as it relates to systematic studies using paradigms borrowed directly from currently popular cognitive research. Now we can see that the data are also woefully inadequate in the narrowness of the task demands that are represented by the paradigms currently in use.

There is not a single study in the literature of cross-cultural psychology in which remembering of some kind is not the explicit goal of the activity that the subject is asked to engage in. Furthermore, task demands have been varied in theoretically relevant ways within subject populations in only a handful of studies. And in the few cases where people have been presented with material of the sort that they might normally be expected to remember, such as stories, the analysis has changed in focus from concentration on the evaluation of memory skills to evaluation of cultural values via the differential recall of aspects of the story.

In our earlier work, we were led to the conclusion that cultural differences in cognitive skills, including remembering, reside more in the situations to which the skills are applied than in the existence of certain skills in one society and their absence in another. Here we are suggesting that the distribution of situations possessing different demand characteristics vis-à-vis memory may itself be the source of differences in memory performance in different groups. The ubiquitous, if ofttimes ambiguous, observation that formal education produces marked differences in performance on tasks that require the spontaneous production of mnemonic devices provides a good case in point. Schools represent the major cultural institution in technological societies where remembering as a distinct activity, occuring apart from the application of anything remembered, is engaged in repeatedly with a great variety of stimulus materials. If, for the moment, we consider religious and secular schools together, it is difficult to think of any other generally experienced setting in which members of technological societies engage in deliberate memorizing. Certainly "deliberate memorization" does not characterize the processes by which we learn our native language, the use of elementary tools or social customs. When we turn to societies that lack formal educational institutions, when can we find such activities? The answer, we believe, is *rarely*. Moreover, in cases where remembering for its own sake seems to take place, there are likely to be cultural devices ready to provide structure for the rememberer.

If the general thrust of these remarks is correct, it must lead to a rather marked shift in the way we organize the study of cultural variations in the development of memory. It may also lead to a more catholic view of cognitive development in which the skills induced in formal schools do not represent the only, or even the dominant, yardstick of the growth of the mind. It may even lead to a study of memory within our own culture that respects the richness and variety of remembering activities as they occur in the course of our daily activities and as they carry the imprint of the values and social tendencies imposed by our own culture.

ACKNOWLEDGMENTS

We wish to thank the Ford Foundation, Carnegie Corporation, and the National Institute of General Medical Sciences for support in the preparation of this paper.

REFERENCES

Atkinson, R. C., & Shiffrin, R. Human memory: A proposed system and its control processes. In J. T. Spence & G. Bower (Eds.), *The psychology of learning and motivation* (Vol. 2). New York: Academic Press, 1968.

Bartlett, F. C. *Remembering*. Cambridge: Cambridge University Press, 1932.

Bateson, G. *Naven* (1st Ed.). Stanford: Stanford University Press, 1936.

Brown, A. L. The role of strategic behavior in retardate memory. In N. R. Ellis (Ed.), *International review of research in mental retardation* (Vol. 7). New York: Academic Press, 1974.

Bruner, J. S., Goodnow, J., & Austin, G. A. *A study of thinking*. New York: Wiley, 1956.

Carpenter, R. The antiquity of the Greek alphabet. *American Journal of Archaelogy*, 1933, *37*, 8–29.

Ciborowski, T., & Cole, M. A developmental and cross-cultural study of the influences of rule structure and problem composition on the learning of conceptual classifications. *Journal of Experimental Child Psychology*, 1973, *15*, 193–215.

Cofer, C. N., Bruce, D. R., & Reicher, G. M. Clustering in free recall as a function of certain methodological variations. *Journal of Experimental Psychology*, 1966, *71*, 858–866.

Colby, B. N. Culture grammars: An anthropological approach to cognition may lead to theoretical models of microcultural processes. *Science*, 1975, *187*, 913–919.

Colby, B. N., & Cole, M. Culture, memory and narrative. In R. Horton & R. Finnegan (Eds.), *Modes of thought*. London: Faber & Faber, 1973.

Cole, M., & Gay, J. Culture and memory. *American Anthropologist*, 1972, *74*, 1066–1084.

Cole, M., Gay, J., Glick, J., & Sharp, D. *The cultural context of learning and thinking*. New York: Basic Books, 1971.

Deregowski, J. B. Perception of the two-pronged trident by two and three dimensional perceivers. *Journal of Experimental Psychology*, 1969, *82*, 9–13.

Deregowski, J. B. Effect of cultural value of time upon recall. *British Journal of Social and Clinical Psychology*, 1970, *9*, 37–41.

Doob, L. *Becoming more civilized: A psychological exploration*. New Haven, Conn.: Yale University Press, 1960.

Doob, L. Eidetic imagery among the Ibo. *Ethnology*, 1964, *3*, 357–363.

Doob, L. Correlates of eidetic imagery in Africa. *Journal of Psychology*, 1970, *76*, 223–230.

Flavell, J. H. Developmental studies of mediated memory. In H. W. Reese & L. P. Lipsitt (Eds.), *Advances in child development and behavior* (Vol. 5). New York: Academic Press, 1970.

Gollin, E. S. A developmental approach to learning and cognition. In Lipsitt, L. P., & Spiker, C. C. (Eds.), *Advances in child development and behavior* (Vol. 2). New York: Academic Press, 1965.

Gologor, E. Recall organization amongst West African adults. Paper delivered at the annual meeting of the Eastern Psychological Association, New York, 1975.

Gray, C. R., & Gummerman, K. The enigmatic eidetic image: A critical examination of methods, data, and theories. *Psychological Bulletin*, 1975, *82*, 383–407.

Hagen, J. W. Some thoughts on how children learn to remember. *Human Development*, 1971, *14*, 262–271.

Havelock, E. A. *Preface to Plato*. Cambridge, Mass.: Harvard University Press, 1963.

Havelock, E. A. *Prologue to Greek literacy*. Cincinnati: University of Cincinnati Press, 1971.

Hodgen, M. *Culture and history*. Viking Fund Publications in Anthropology, 1952 (No. 18).

Jablonski, E. M. Free recall in children. *Psychological Bulletin*, 1974, *81*, 522–539.

Jaensch, E. R. *Eidetic imagery*. London: Kegan, Paul, Trench, & Trubner, 1930.

Kagan, J., & Klein, R. C. Cross-cultural perspectives on early development. *American Psychologist*, 1973, *28*, 947–961.

Klahr, D. An information processing approach to the study of cognitive development. In A. Pick (Ed.), *Minnesota symposia on child psychology* (Vol. 7). Minneapolis: University of Minnesota Press, 1973.

Kleinfeld, J. Visual memory in village Eskimo and urban Caucasian children. *Arctic*, 1971, *24*, 132–137.

Lancy, D. F. Work, play and learning in a Kpelle town. Unpublished doctoral dissertation, University of Pittsburgh, 1974.

Leontiev, A. N. *The development of mind* (in Russian). Moscow: University of Moscow, 1960.

Levy-Bruhl, L. *How natives think* (in French, 1910). Translation, New York: Washington Square Press, 1966.

Levy-Bruhl, L. *Primitive mentality* (in French, 1923). Translation, Boston: Beacon Press, 1966.

Liberty, C., & Ornstein, P. A. Age differences in organization and recall: The effects of training and categorization. *Journal of Experimental Child Psychology*, 1973, *15*, 169–186.

Lord, A. B. *Singer of tales*. New York: Atheneum, 1965.

Luria, A. R. Speech and intellect among rural, urban and homeless children. *Soviet Psychology*, 1974, p. 7–39.

Maccoby, E. E., & Hagen, J. W. Effects of distraction upon central versus incidental recall: Developmental trends. *Journal of Experimental Child Psychology*, 1965, *2*, 280–289.

McLuhan, M. *The Gutenberg galaxy*. Toronto: University of Toronto Press, 1962.

Meacham, J. A. Patterns of memory abilities in two cultures. *Developmental Psychology*, 1975, *11*, 50–53.

Moely, B. E., Olson, F. A., Halwes, T. G., & Flavell, J. H. Production deficiency in young children's clustered recall. *Developmental Psychology*, 1969, *1*, 26–34.

Nadel, S. F. Experiments on culture psychology. *Africa*, 1937, *10*, 421–435.

Riesman, D. *The oral tradition, the written word and the screen image*. Yellow Springs, Ohio: Antioch Press, 1956.

Rivers, W. H. R. Observation on the senses of the Todas. *British Journal of Psychology*, 1903, *1*, 321–396.

Rohwer, W. D. Mental elaboration and proficient learning. In J. P. Hill (Ed.), *Minnesota symposia on child psychology* (Vol. 4). Minneapolis: University of Minnesota Press, 1970.

Schulman, A. I. Recognition memory and the recall of spatial location. *Memory & Cognition*, 1973, *1*, 256–260.

Scribner, S. Developmental aspects of categorized recall in a West African society. *Cognitive Psychology*, 1974, *6*, 475–494.

Sharp, D. W., & Cole, M. The influence of educational experience on the development of cognitive skills as measured in formal tests and experiments (Final report to Office of Education Grant OEG 1965). 1975.

Siegel, A. W., & White, S. H. The development of spatial representations of large-scale environments. In H. W. Reese (Ed.), *Advances in child development and behavior* (Vol. 10). New York: Academic Press, 1975.

Smirnov, A. A., & Zinchenko, P. I. Problems in the psychology of memory. In M. Cole & I. Maltzman (Eds.), *A handbook of contemporary Soviet psychology*. New York: Basic Books, 1969.

Underwood, B. J. Attributes of memory. *Psychological Review*, 1969, *76*, 559–573.

Vygotsky, L. S., & Luria, A. R. *Studies in the history of behavior* (in Russian). State Publishing House, Moscow, 1930.

Wagner. D. A. The development of short-term and incidental memory: A cross-cultural study. *Child Development*, 1974, *45*, 389–396.

9
Soviet Investigations of Memory Development

John A. Meacham

State University of New York at Buffalo

I. INTRODUCTION

At least two distinct advantages may derive from an increased familiarity with Soviet investigations of memory development. First, Soviet research can provide independent confirmation of the conclusions of non-Soviet researchers. Second, Soviet research may indicate additional and potentially significant directions for future research on memory development. Unfortunately, there exist certain obstacles to acquiring the necessary familiarity; among these are the time for translation and publication of Soviet research, differences in the use of statistics and style of reporting that make it difficult for the reader to evaluate research reports, and last, but certainly not least, the assumption that the reader is already familiar with the historical, philosophical, and theoretical contexts within which the research has been conducted. On the other hand, the task is made easier by the large number of translations of books and articles now available (for a partial bibliography, see Meacham & Spielman, 1973, and Misiak & Sexton, 1966, pp. 279–280), and it is now possible to consider Soviet research from a variety of sources. The situation with respect to Soviet research may indeed be similar to that of Piagetian research only a few years ago; when Soviet research is understood in its proper context, its impact on the direction of non-Soviet research may be considerable.

Among the leading contributors to Soviet research on memory have been Leont'ev (1931, 1932), Blonskii (1935), Zankov (1944, 1949, 1951/1957), Smirnov (1948, 1958), Istomina (1948/1975, 1953), and Zinchenko (1961; reviewed by Berlyne, 1964). Translations of articles on memory development occasionally

273

appear in the journal *Soviet Psychology* (Istomina's 1948/1975 article is particularly significant); Leont'ev's 1931 chapter is available in a more recent book (Leont'ev, 1959/1964); and a revised version of Smirnov's 1948 work is also available in a recent translation (Smirnov, 1966/1973; reviewed by Estes, 1974). In addition, there exist a number of reviews of Soviet research on memory and memory development, including those by Smirnov and Zinchenko (1969), Yendovitskaya (1964/1971), and Rahmani (1973, Chapter 5). Because these translations and reviews do exist, the primary purpose of the present chapter is to provide an indication of the historical, philosophical, and theoretical contexts within which Soviet research on memory can be understood. A second purpose is to provide an extension of certain themes of Soviet research on memory development and to indicate some potential implications for non-Soviet research.

Three major themes are emphasized in the present chapter: First, it is the interaction of the material to be remembered with the individual's activities that determines what can be remembered later. Consequently, a consideration of motives and the structure of the individual's activities is necessary. Second, the individual's activities depend on cultural and historical conditions, and so investigations of memory abilities must not neglect the changing social world of the developing individual. Third, Soviet theory is primarily a developmental theory, based on a dialectical model that emphasizes activity and change rather than stability and balance. This emphasis in Soviet theory is elaborated in the present chapter, and a dialectical model for the development of memory abilities in the individual is presented.

In translations from Russian to English, the terms *memory, memorization, recall,* and *remembering* often are used interchangeably, and the precise meaning must be established, if possible, from the context. This ambiguity of terms certainly exists in English as much as it does in Russian. For example, the term *memory* is used to refer somewhat loosely to the system of abilities by means of which the individual is able to remember (as in the title of this chapter). More precisely, a memory is a cognitive representation of a previously experienced event. The term is also used, inappropriately, to refer to a thing or place where memories are stored or to an abstract faculty possessed by an individual (Meacham, 1972b; Rozeboom, 1965). The appropriate use of this term—to claim to be remembering a memory—is to claim to know something without having just learned and without having just inferred. In other words, what is remembered must have been known previously, that is, learned or inferred in the past (see, e.g., Munsat, 1966). Continued attention to such distinctions is necessary, particularly in approaching a body of theory and research carried out within unfamiliar contexts. The historical, philosophical, and theoretical contexts of Soviet reserch will now be reviewed briefly in order to provide a framework within which memory research can be discussed later.

II. HISTORICAL, PHILOSOPHICAL, AND THEORETICAL CONTEXTS

A. The Unity of Consciousness and Behavior

The history of recent Soviet psychology can be considered to consist of three major periods (Payne, 1968; Riegel, 1973). During the first of these, lasting from the Russian Revolution until 1930, introspection and philosophical idealism were rejected in favor of more dialectical materialist psychologies. A dominant approach during this period was Kornilov's reactology, which was similar to behaviorism but also considered the subjective aspects of reactions and recognized socioeconomic influences on behavior. Reactology itself, however, was later to be criticized as overly mechanistic, reductionist, and insufficiently dialectical.

The period from 1930 to 1950, initiated with the publication of Lenin's *Philosophical Notebooks,* was dominated by an increasing emphasis on dialectics, particularly as applied to the sociohistorical nature of human development and the relationship of the mind to the external, material world. A major event during this period was the 1936 decree against mental testing and pedology, a biological approach to the study of child development. These were said to contribute little toward understanding the etiology of "backwardness" in children; further, they provided no recommendations for how one might help such children, thus relieving parents and educators of their responsibility to do so (Smirnov, 1957). Vygotskii (1934/1962) and Blonskii (1935) were among those who were criticized at this time, although in fact Vygotskii had contributed greatly toward the new emphases on the role of social and historical factors in the development of mental activities and on the active responsibility that adults must assume in the upbringing and education of children (pedagogy).

The major problem for psychology and philosophy during this period was to determine the nature of mind and its relationship to the external, material world. A solution to this problem, accepted by many Soviet psychologists, was presented by Rubinstein (Payne, 1968; Riegel, 1973; Rubinstein, 1955/1957). According to Rubinstein, it is a mistake to equate mind with consciousness. In doing so, idealists incorrectly assume that consciousness is the sole determinant of mental events; behaviorists, in avoiding consciousness, also avoid the problem of mind. Rubinstein's solution to the problem was to view mind as *activity* and to assert the unity—an interaction, not an identity—of consciousness and behavior. Thus consciousness, an advanced state of mind, is an active reflection of the material world, and behavior occurs within a structure of motives provided by consciousness (Payne, 1968, pp. 84–94). The development of consciousness consists in the acquisition of activities available in the social and historical milieu; as the individual's practical activities change, his mental activities also change. Both of these themes—the emphasis on the structure of activity and the importance given to the sociohistorical context in development—have played a major role in Soviet investigations of memory development.

During the third period, from 1950 to the present, Soviet psychologists have attempted a synthesis between the materialism of Pavlov and the sociohistorical dialectics of the second period. In response to the criticism that the principle of the unity of consciousness and behavior provided insufficient attention to the material world, particularly the relationship between the mind and the brain, Rubinstein proposed a theory of constitutive relationism. This theory asserts that mind is determined by its relationships to all material phenomena, and is thus at the same time both an active reflection of the external world and a higher nervous activity.

Soviet theory is not inconsistent with that of Piaget, particularly in its emphases on the activity of the individual, the accommodation of mind to the external world, the dependence of behavior on an internal organization—and on development (see Wozniak, 1975, for further discussion). Piaget's theory, however, gives less consideration than does Soviet theory to the effects of sociohistorical conditions and views society as merely a supportive context rather than an active force in the development of the individual (Meacham & Riegel, in press). Soviet theory is also consistent with Riegel's (1975a, b) dialectical theory of development, which, like Rubinstein's theory, considers interactions occurring among major developmental progressions—biological, cultural-historical, and psychological. In summary, the development of Soviet psychological theory expresses a continuing concern with the dialectical relationship of consciousness to both the biological and the cultural-historical worlds.

B. Activities, Actions, and Operations

The emphasis in Soviet psychology on activity as the nature of mind means that it is possible to study the development of consciousness by studying the individual's activities. Consequently, considerable attention has been given to the structure of activities, defined as neither behaviors nor physiological processes, but rather, as processes that transform objects into subjective forms and make objective the more subjective aspects of personality (compare assimilation and accommodation in Piaget's theory). Thus, activities structure the relationship of the individual to his material and social world, and it is through his activities that the individual is able to understand or give meaning to this external world. Activities may be identified by their specific motives, for example, to play or to work. They depend for their development on social interactions, and develop initially as interpsychological processes occurring between two persons, only later becoming individual psychological processes (Leont'ev, 1972/1974–1975). At each stage in development, a particular activity can be characterized as a "leading" activity, not because it is most frequent, but rather, because it is within the context of this activity that mental processes are reorganized and new activities are differentiated. The sequence of leading activities depends on the specific social and historical conditions of the developing child (Elkonin, 1971/1972, p. 236; Leont'ev, 1959/1964, p. 173). The sequence described by Soviet psychologists is a familiar one: In infancy and early childhood, the activities consist of direct emotional communication and manipulation of objects; in childhood, role playing and learning in school; in adolescence, intimate personal relations and career activities (Elkonin, 1971/1972, pp. 240–250; Kussmann, in press).

Activities serve to motivate specific *actions*[1] (acts), which are processes structured and directed by conscious goals (Leont'ev, 1959/1964, p. 176; 1972/1974–1975, p. 23). For example, in order to do well in school the child may attempt to understand a particular book. The same motive can instigate attempts to reach other goals, and the particular action can also be subordinated to other motives. An action can be converted into an activity, if the outcome of the action acquires sufficient significance independent of that of the original motive. For example, comprehension of the text of a book may lead to the development of motives to master a particular content area, such as history or psychology.

Actions are carried out subject to the limiting conditions of each psychological task; because of these conditions, different *operations* or means of action are employed (Leont'ev, 1959/1964, p. 180; 1972/1974–1975, p. 26). An action can be performed by various operations, depending on the conditions of the task, and a particular operation can facilitate numerous actions. An operation is acquired first as an independent, goal-directed action, and only in a second step can this new action become an operation by being subordinated as a means of accomplishing some other action. This process has been demonstrated by Neverovich (Lisina & Neverovich, 1964/1971, p. 350), who taught children to hammer nails into a board. He directed the children's attention to the movement of their hands by providing practice trials with no nails; thus, the children learned swinging of the hammer as an independent action. Later, when nails were provided, the children were better able to subordinate hammering to the goal of driving the nails. Similarly, actions such as rehearsing or categorizing can be subordinated as operations to facilitate the action of remembering (Meacham,

[1] Activities and actions were not distinguished in Meacham (1972b). The activities considered in that article (organizing, labeling, rehearsal, etc.) should have been termed *actions,* or *operations* when employed to facilitate remembering, in order to be consistent with the present chapter.

1972b, p. 216). Skill or proficiency at remembering then depends on sufficient practice of the appropriate operations or remembering abilities.

Because actions can be a source of new activities and also be subordinated to become operations, it is important to consider the stages by which stable, external actions can become mental actions. Gal'perin (1959/1969, pp. 256–264) has outlined a sequence that emphasizes the role of speech in internalization. Initially, the child performs the action only with external, material support. Later, although he can accompany the action with audible speech, the speech and action remain unrelated. In a third stage, external speech becomes a means of reflecting on the external action and can also serve as an independent plane of action. In the fourth stage, the child is able to anticipate and guide his own actions with audible speech; finally, abbreviated, internal speech is used for this purpose. Gal'perin's theory has not gone without criticism. For example, Kabanova-Meller agrees that the theory is adequate for describing the child's transition from external actions to mental actions, but points out that no mention is made of other mental actions that can be formed through abstraction, generalization, and perception of logical relations (Rahmani, 1966, p. 159, 1973, p. 275).

Thus Soviet developmental theory has provided a general framework for the investigation of the development of cognitive abilities. The structure of memory abilities can be analyzed in terms of the subordination of actions, as operations, to facilitate the performing of other goal-directed actions in a means-end relationship. The development of operations and actions takes place within a context of leading activities, which in turn are determined by the social and historical conditions of the developing child.

III. THE DEVELOPMENT OF MEMORY ABILITIES

A. Overview

Soviet and non-Soviet research on memory abilities differ in a number of ways. First, Soviet research is more likely to consider the problems of remembering in various practical settings, such as working a telephone switchboard or remembering the results of a scientific investigation. Research with children is directed toward increasing performance in educational settings and focuses on the comprehension and memorization of prose material. This no doubt reflects the emphasis, stemming from the 1930s, on the responsibility that parents and educators have in training their children. Second, remembering as a mental process can be understood only by considering the activities of the individual. Consequently, remembering is not studied in isolation from the study of other psychological processes. Relative to non-Soviet research, a greater portion of Soviet research has been directed toward the role of motivation in remembering, and the relationship between remembering (as an action or operation) and other psychological processes such as comprehension and problem solving. Third, Soviet psychologists, perhaps owing to their closer ties to philosophy, rely more on observation and the coherence of explanations than on control and prediction as means of verifying theories of psychological development (see Pepper, 1942, pp. 47–51). Finally, questions regarding the development of psychological processes, although often viewed as being of secondary importance in the United States, are the primary questions for Soviet psychological theory. This reflects the dialectical foundation of Soviet psychology.

A distinction is made in Soviet research between involuntary and voluntary memorization. Involuntary memorization can result either from goal-oriented actions other than memorizing, such as classifying, or from chance orientations toward the materials. Only in the latter case is the process termed *incidental learning*.[2] Involuntary memorization is far more important in Soviet than in non-Soviet research, and a major effort has been made to discover the principles that govern its occurrence. Voluntary memorization occurs when remembering is the conscious goal of an action (Smirnov, 1966/1973, p. 26; Smirnov & Zinchenko, 1969, p. 456). Investigations of both involuntary and voluntary remembering will now be reviewed; the problem of development will be considered in the following section.

B. Involuntary Memorization

Involuntary memorization can be understood by considering the position occupied by the material to be remembered within the structure of the individual's activity. In particular, material that is a part of the goal of an action is remembered best, and material that is related to the means (operations) for achieving the goal or to the conditions that define the task is remembered less well. Unrelated background material is remembered least (incidental learning), unless it is novel material (Smirnov, 1966/1973, pp. 70–80; Smirnov & Zinchenko, 1969, p. 461).

1. Investigations with Adults

An experiment conducted by Leont'ev and Rozanova (1951/1957) is often cited to support these principles of involuntary memorization (cited in Smirnov & Zinchenko, 1969, p. 460; Smirnov, 1966/1973, p. 75; and Bocharova, 1968/1969). In this investigation, adults were shown a four-by-four array of cards, on

---

[2]Smirnov thus considers both Type I (no instructions to learn) and Type II (materials not covered by the learning instructions) incidental learning (Postman, 1964) as instances of involuntary memorization, but excludes Type II for which the materials bear no relation to the task.

each of which a common word was printed. As each card was illuminated, subjects were required to say the words aloud and remove six cards. In one condition, the experimenter pointed to the cards to be removed. In a second condition, subjects were told to remove the cards with words beginning with the letter *s*. Following fifteen minutes of conversation, subjects were asked to recall the words and to point to the positions of cards that had been removed. Recall of the words was poor in both conditions, but in the second condition (involving the letter *s*) subjects were able to point to an average of 5.5 of the 6 positions from which they had removed cards. These results were explained by the fact that in the second condition the positions of the six key cards were related to the goal of the subject's action, that is, removing the cards.

However, these specific results were not obtained in an attempted replication study (Meacham, 1972a). This failure to replicate the results of Leont'ev and Rozanova suggests that those findings may not be generalizable across such variables as subject population, testing circumstances, or perhaps the set that the subject brings to the experimental situation. An observation by Zeigarnik (1971/1972–1973) suggests that the discrepancy may be due to differences in subjects' motivation to strive to recall the words and positions. Zeigarnik reported that the differential recall of unfinished versus completed tasks varies according to whether subjects are asked "What kind of tasks did you do?" or told "The experiment was done to test your memory . . . enumerate the tasks you carried out [p. 63]."

In Meacham's (1972a) attempted replication, significantly more words and initial letters were recalled in the second condition (in which subjects removed *s* words) than in the first condition (in which subjects removed cards to which the experimenter had pointed). Thus, the study does provide support for the general conclusion that recall is dependent on the actions of the subject. The number of words recalled was also significantly greater in the second than in a third condition, in which subjects removed cards illuminated by a light differing slightly in hue from that which illuminated the remaining cards. Thus, the critical aspect was not whether the subject or the experimenter made the decision regarding which cards were to be removed, but rather, the actions surrounding identification by the subject of words starting with the letter *s*.

2. Investigations with Children

The principles relating involuntary memorization to the structure of activity are also illustrated in various investigations with children. Zinchenko (cited in Smirnov, 1966/1973, p. 71; Smirnov & Zinchenko, 1969, p. 453) asked children and adults to arrange cards showing both numbers and pictures of objects. Subjects for whom categorizing of objects was the goal-oriented action were able to recall many of the objects but few of the numbers; subjects who arranged the cards according to the numbers recalled many numbers but few objects. The recall of objects and numbers when these were not related to the goal, that is, when they were background stimuli, was observed to decrease with age, a finding consistent with non-Soviet studies of incidental learning (see Hagen & Hale, 1973, for a review). The greater recall by younger children of background or incidental material is interpreted as reflecting the greater time required to become involved with the task.

Although material that forms part of an operation is not remembered as well as information related to the goals of an action, involuntary memorization of such material can be accurate when the operation is not yet well developed. In this case, the performance of the operation has the nature of a goal-directed action (Section IIB). For example, in a study by Zinchenko (cited in Smirnov, 1966/ 1973, p. 73; Smirnov & Zinchenko, 1969, p. 459) first- and third-grade children and college students were asked (1) to solve arithmetic problems; (2) to invent and solve problems when given only the arithmetic operations to be used; or (3) to invent and solve problems when given the arithmetic operations and the numbers (presumably the same numbers as provided in the first condition). For the older children, involuntary memorization of the numbers was greater in the second condition. Although solving the arithmetic problems in the first and third conditions presumably made use of well-practiced operations, thinking of numbers functioned as a specific goal-directed action. Nevertheless, the numbers provided in the first and third conditions were evidently not the same as those generated by subjects in the second condition. Thus, it can be argued that the latter group of subjects did not actually recall numbers that had been used earlier, but instead merely generated during the recall test a new set of numbers similar to those they had invented earlier, and so their high "recall" scores were an artifact. The principles of involuntary memorization are better illustrated by the results for the first-grade children, who recalled more numbers in all three conditions than did the older children or adults. For these younger children, not only thinking of numbers but also solution of the problems using the arithmetic operations of addition and subtraction apparently functioned as a goal-directed action.

The influence of motives on involuntary memorization was demonstrated in a study by Zinchenko (cited in Smirnov & Zinchenko, 1969, p. 462), who asked preschoolers, second-grade children, and fifth-grade children to provide associations to words either in the context of play activity or in an academic, testing context. It is important to note that the leading activities are different for preschoolers as opposed to older children, for example, role playing versus learning. Involuntary memorization of the words was greater for preschoolers when the motive was play, and providing associations was the goal of the action that they carried out. For the older children, involuntary memorization was greater when the motive was learning and the goal was thinking up words; under play conditions, providing associations was only a means of winning, and so recall was somewhat less.

Thus, involuntary memorization depends on developmental changes in leading activities or motives, on the extent to which various operations are well developed and thus can be carried out without being conscious goal-directed actions, and on the place that the material to be remembered occupies in the means-end structure of the individual's activities. How does the integration of the material to be remembered with the goal of an action facilitate involuntary memorization? It is essential to regard the activities of the individual not as mere attentional or associative processes, but rather, as processes by which the individual assimilates and gives meaning to the objects with which he interacts (Meacham, 1972b, p. 207). Smirnov's (1966/1973) conclusion that "depth of understanding and intellectual activity connected with it are the most important conditions for the productivity of involuntary memorization [p. 92]" is consistent with the levels-of-processing model of Craik and Lockhart (1972), according to which retention depends on the extent to which information is processed, rather than where it is stored. Smirnov's conclusion is also in agreement with studies showing the dependence of recall on comprehension processes, for example, meanings of words, rather than on responses involved in the performance of orienting tasks, for example, checking for the presence of certain letters (Hyde & Jenkins, 1973; Jenkins, 1974).

C. Voluntary Memorization

Voluntary memorization occurs when the goal of the individual's action is memorization; other actions are then subordinated as operations for the purpose of achieving this goal. Memorizing as a goal has been differentiated to a greater extent in Soviet than in non-Soviet research. For example, Smirnov (1966/1973, p. 29) has distinguished mnemonic goals along dimensions of completeness (whole content versus gist or facts), exactness (of content, form of expression, etc.), importance of the sequence of the material, and duration over which the material is to be remembered. These mnemonic goals in turn depend on a number of factors, including the nature of the material to be remembered and the requirements of the memorization task and the conditions under which it must be carried out. Young children are less able than older children and adults to differentiate mnemonic goals, and so the operations employed are not always appropriate (Smirnov, 1966/1973, p. 46; cf. Kreutzer, Leonard, & Flavell, 1975).

Voluntary memorization is influenced also by the motives and the operations or memory abilities of the individual. The dependence of voluntary memorization on motives has been shown by Istomina (1948/1975, 1953), who compared children's recall in three situations: on laboratory tasks, within a context of play activity ("store"), and in the course of practical activity (preparation for an exhibit). Recall was particularly poor for preschool children on laboratory tasks, because the mnemonic goal failed to correspond with their leading activities or motives. Within the context of play and practical activity, however, these children were better able to understand the mnemonic goal. This goal derives its meaning from its relationship to the motives for the children's role-playing activities. The presence of a meaningful goal facilitates the choice of appropriate operations for attaining the mnemonic goal (Istomina, 1948/1975). More generally, mnemonic goals are first isolated and recognized during the preschool years, in particular when it is necessary for the child to recall. It is the failure to be able to recall that leads to the isolation of mnemonic goals during the presentation and memorization of material. The goal of remembering emerges before the child has the means to facilitate this goal (Istomina, 1948/1975). Mnemonic operations or abilities are developed as goal-directed actions, which are later subordinated to the goal of remembering in games, learning situations, social interactions, and other situations (Smirnov & Zinchenko, 1969, p. 476). The relationship of operations to the mnemonic goal is illustrated in a study carried out to teach memorization techniques (Smirnov, Istomina, Mal'tseva, & Samokhvalova, 1969/1971–1972). Each technique was first taught as an independent action; in a second stage of training, this action was introduced as an operation to facilitate remembering. Four-, 5-, and 6-year-old children were taught to use pictures in remembering words. The first step, teaching an independent action, was accomplished by having the children match pictures to words. The second step, teaching a remembering operation, involved first having the child indicate which pictures had been matched to the words to be remembered. Finally, the child was taught to use the pictures as a means of remembering the words. These children were able to substantially outperform a control group in remembering, both immediately following training and a year later. This same two-step action-operation training procedure was also successfully employed to teach 8- to 14-year-olds conceptual classification of words and context analysis of texts.

Points in the developmental sequence at which the child does not spontaneously use remembering operations that are, however, within his capacity have been termed *production deficiencies;* that is, the child is able to produce the remembering operation only with the assistance of the experimenter (Flavell, 1970). Production deficiencies in children have been identified for various operations, including serial rehearsal and categorizing during memorization and using category names during remembering. In the terms of Soviet theory, production deficiencies occur when an action has not yet been sufficiently practiced and then subordinated to the goal of remembering. In this case, involuntary memorization may occur if the action is induced by means of an adult's guidance, but voluntary memorization is not yet possible (Meacham, 1972b, pp. 213–217). Reese (1975) has noted that this Soviet model for the subordination of operations to goal-directed actions also provides an explanation for development within Craik and Lockhart's (1972) depth-of-processing model, described earlier. Briefly, as newer actions become subordinated as operations, a hierarchy of operations emerges, ordered in levels of complexity.

To summarize, voluntary memorization depends on recognition of a mnemonic goal (cf. Appel, Cooper, McCarrel, Sims-Knight, Yussen, & Flavell, 1972) and the availability and subordination of the appropriate operations. The factors essential to the development of voluntary memorization were summarized nicely almost 30 years ago by Istomina (1948/1975):

> We have assumed that the emergence of voluntary memory from earlier forms [i.e., involuntary memorization] takes place as a result of the differentiation of a specific type of act, the purpose of which is to remember or recall something from among the child's activity. Consequently, this transformation requires, first, that there be motives capable of making such mnemonic goals meaningful. Second, it requires that these goals have some concrete reality, i.e., that remembering be conscious and intentional and that the operations of remembering and recall be discrete, conscious acts. Third and last, this hypothesis requires that a child have at his disposal some means for carrying out the voluntary acts of retention [i.e., memorization] and recall [p. 8].

1. Comparison of Involuntary and Voluntary Memorization

Under appropriate conditions, recall following involuntary memorization can be greater than recall following voluntary memorization, particularly for preschool children. This was illustrated in an investigation by Zinchenko (cited in Smirnov & Zinchenko, 1969, p. 468, and Smirnov, 1966/1973, p. 83[3]), in which children and adults either (1) classsified pictures of objects and were then tested for involuntary memorization; (2) were asked to memorize pictures; or (3) were asked to memorize the pictures using classification as a means. In general, recall was as good in the involuntary memorization condition as in the two voluntary conditions. For preschool children, however, recall was substantially greater in the involuntary memorization condition. Thus, for young children, carrying out an appropriate action can have greater effect on recall than having a conscious mnemonic goal. In such a case, the goal may not be understood, or otherwise fails to lead to or perhaps interferes with the appropriate actions. The presence of an intention to remember does not directly affect recall (this role is played by actions), but in older children and adults, may have an indirect effect by influencing the choice of particular actions or strategies engaged in for the purpose of remembering (Meacham, 1972b, p. 214; Smirnov & Zinchenko, 1959/1969, p. 466).

Smirnov (1966/1973, pp. 84–93) has investigated the conditions that affect the strength of recall following involuntary memorization. Children were required to interact with words and sentences by means of various actions, including copy-

---

[3] The data shown in Smirnov's text are approximately like those in Smirnov and Zinchenko's chapter, collapsed across some age groups.

ing, forming associations, checking for spelling errors, and evaluating meanings, and their recall was then compared with recall following voluntary memorization. In general, actions that led to "depth of penetration into the meaning of the material" and greater "intellectual activity" produced a greater amount of involuntary memorization. When compared to voluntary memorization, involuntary memorization facilitated remembering to a greater effect in second graders than in older students.

A similar investigation has been conducted recently with preschoolers by Murphy and Brown (1975). Involuntary memorization following actions designed to produce comprehension (categorization; rating of items as pleasant or unpleasant) was found to be greater than recall in a baseline voluntary memorization condition; no differences from baseline recall were found following actions that instigated lesser degrees of semantic analysis (identification of sounds and colors). Children's recall is increased more by appropriate organization of the child's activities than by emphasis on the importance of memorization without providing the means by which this may be accomplished.

2. Memorization of Prose Materials

The emphasis in Soviet psychology on practical applications has led to several studies of the process of memorization and comprehension of prose materials, particularly in educational settings (e.g., Smirnov, 1966/1973, Chap. 6). These studies are basically descriptive, but the theoretical framework is the same as that presented already. Among the operations used to facilitate memorization of texts are, for example, breaking the material into groups according to its meaning and distinguishing the main thoughts. These abilities must be acquired and practiced as independent actions before they can be used to facilitate voluntary memorization. Korman (cited in Yendovitskaya, 1964/1971) analyzed young children's reproduction of connected verbal material and found that even preschoolers could remember events that were essential to the main action of a story. Christie and Schumacher (1975) obtained similar results in replicating Korman's study with American children. Kindergarten, second-, and fifth-grade children all were able to recall more information relevant to the logical sequence of a story than irrelevant information; in addition, a greater portion of the relevant than of the irrelevant information was recalled in its original order. Their findings are consistent with those of Korman and suggest that young children's abilities to reproduce prose materials are greater than had previously been thought. These results also are consistent with the finding that children, as well as adults, incorrectly recognize as familiar new sentences based on premises found in sentences actually presented earlier; thus, children acquire and remember semantic information in a manner similar to adults (see Paris and Lindauer, this volume).

Although the differences between Soviet and non-Soviet research noted at the beginning of this section still remain, Soviet research can be seen to cover a range of phenomena—involuntary and voluntary memorization, memorization of isolated words, numbers, and objects and of textual material, and training of memory abilities in young children—similar to that covered by non-Soviet researchers. Soviet researchers have viewed all of these within a framework that emphasizes the motivational context, for example, play or work, within which memorization and remembering occur, and encourages analysis in terms of means-end relationships constructed among various operations or abilities and the action of remembering.

IV. THE CULTURAL-HISTORICAL CONTEXT OF DEVELOPMENT

A. Developmental Theorists: Blonskii, Vygotskii

Among the theories advanced to explain the development of the memory abilities described in the preceding section have been those of Blonskii and Vygotskii. Blonskii (1935; cited in Smirnov, 1966/1973, pp. 15–20; Rahmani, in press) regarded memory as primarily a biological phenomenon with four stages or levels of development: motoric (habits), affective, image or pictorial, and verbal–logical. This descriptive sequence is reflected in recent studies of habituation in infancy, recognition memory for familiar perceptual events (for example, faces), and recall abilities that depend on the development of symbolic or representational abilities. At the higher stages, memory was considered a means for the transmission of social experience; this theme was later to be greatly elaborated by Vygotskii. Nevertheless, Blonskii was criticized during the 1930s as a biologically oriented pedologist.

Vygotskii (1929; reviewed in Rahmani, 1973, pp. 38–45; Smirnov, 1966/ 1973, pp. 20–23) considered the development of higher mental processes to consist in the merging of biological maturation with the historical sequence of human cultural development. The latter sequence provides symbols that are analogous psychologically to tools and thus can facilitate mental activity. These symbols are acquired initially as external stimuli, employed in social interactions. Thus, in the case of memory abilities, the child initially is able to remember only by "natural or primitive" methods of association. Later, "at a certain level of the internal development of the organism" (Vygotskii, 1929, p. 423), the child is able to acquire cultural methods of remembering such as tying knots in string or tearing bits of paper. This external activity subsequently can become internal activity.

Vygotskii's theory also was criticized during the 1930s, primarily for contrasting too sharply natural and cultural mental processes (Leont'ev & Luria, 1968,

p. 342). Vygotskii's emphasis on biological determinants is clear: "Cultural development does not create anything over and above that which potentially exists in the natural development of the child's behavior [1929, p. 416]." Further, Vygotskii did not emphasize sufficiently that the child's mental development depends on the interaction of subject and object, that is, the interaction of the child with social objects, as opposed to the interaction of the consciousness of the child with that of an adult (Rahmani, 1973, p. 47). In the 1930s (Section II. A), these points were critical with regard to the increasing emphasis on practical activity (education, training, etc.) in the development of mental processes. In summary, although Vygotskii's efforts led to increased awareness of the importance of cultural and historical factors in human development, these effects were quickly overtaken and criticized within the political and educational context of the 1930s (see Section II. A).

B. Internalization of Cultural Activities

Leont'ev (1972/1974–1975) has extended Vygotskii's theory, attempting to eliminate the earlier problems by emphasizing that children can acquire cultural activities only through social interactions carried out in an external form, for example, as actions or as external speech. Thus, consciousness is not a condition of development, but rather, is produced through social development. Leont'ev's theory also differs from Vygotskii's in attributing greater significance to the role of social activities, developed in the course of history, than to biological factors (Rahmani, 1975). Rubinstein, however, criticized both Leont'ev and Gal'perin for suggesting that mental actions are merely the internalization of external actions (Rahmani, 1973, p. 275). For Rubinstein, it is more appropriate to say that internalization is a result of the "transformation of the mental component of a material act into a mental phenomenon existing independently . . . in other words, the transformation of one form of activity into another" (Rahmani, in press). More recently, Leont'ev (1972/1974–1975, p. 21) has indicated that internalization, by which external actions are transformed into internal actions, is made possible by the similarity of structure of internal and external activity. This clarification by Leont'ev shows some accommodation with Rubinstein's position.

Leont'ev's emphasis on the importance of the cultural–historical context for development in the individual has only a few parallels in contemporary non-Soviet theory. For example, Berger and Luckmann (1966) emphasize that "the relationship between man, the producer, and the social world, his product, is and remains a dialectical one [p. 57]." "This dialectic is given in the human condition and manifests itself anew in each human individual. For the individual, of course, it unfolds itself in *an already structured socio-historical situation* [p. 165; emphasis added]." Similarly, Keniston (1971) argues that we must examine how changes in historical conditions have in turn changed human development; he suggests that the relationship between these two developmental progressions may be much closer than was believed earlier. Buck-Morss (1975) argues that even Piagetian formal operations may reflect particular social and economic structures. The point, for our understanding of the development of memory abilities, is that development in the individual must reflect the cultural and historical conditions within which the individual develops. As Elkonin (1971/ 1972, p. 237) notes, even objects with which the child acts, although they have definite physical properties, must be considered as social objects, for the means of interacting with those objects have evolved within a social context.

Evidence is accumulating to support Leont'ev's theory of internalization, and to demonstrate the significance of the cultural–historical context for development.[4] Kreutzer et al. (1975, p. 51), for example, found that kindergarteners were more likely to indicate that they would use external means of memorizing, such as writing a telephone number, than internal means, such as rehearsing. These children also reported a readiness to rely on other people to facilitate their own remembering. Older children, on the other hand, were more likely to use internal than external means. (See Flavell and Wellman, this volume.)

The impact of environment and culture on the differential development of memory abilities has been shown in numerous investigations of memory abilities among children in various African and Latin American countries (See Cole and Scribner, this volume, for a review of these studies.) Meacham (1975b), for example, compared the recall abilities of American children with those of children living in a rural village in Guatemala. The ability to recall objects and the ability to recall, independently, the locations of the objects were assessed. The experimenter placed six objects at various pictured locations; the objects and places were then covered, and the experimenter asked the children to recall either (1) the locations in which specific objects were hidden or (2) the objects hidden in specific locations. Different patterns of recall were found in the two cultures: The Guatemalan children were relatively better at recalling the locations of objects than the objects at specific locations, while the children from the United States recalled locations and objects equally well. These data are not consistent with theories that recall abilities are determined by maturation; rather, differences in performance are associated with differences in the social context within which the children develop. It is critical that such data be based on patterns of memory abilities, rather than differences in level of performance between the two cultures. The latter finding (performance was in fact higher in the United States than in Guatemala) is open to a great variety of alternative interpretations, such as linguistic and motivational differences in the procedures. For the present

---

[4]Leont'ev's theory is illustrated nicely by Luria's (1971) investigations in Central Asia during the 1930s, a time of radical changes in social and economic structure. Luria did not study memory abilities, however, but rather, changes in syllogistic reasoning.

data, however, differences in patterns of memory abilities can be attributed to factors intrinsic to each culture, if it can be assumed that procedural variations affect each aspect of the pattern (that is, objects, places) to the same extent.

A more recent demonstration of the need to attend to the historical context of memory development is the observation that 3- and 5-year-olds tested after 1969, the year in which broadcasting of "Sesame Street" was initiated, benefit more from the use of pictorial elaboration in learning paired associates than to children tested previously (Reese, 1974). These various studies certainly have not yet provided the data necessary for a comprehensive theory of the interaction of cultural-historical with individual development; more thorough analyses are needed to understand the ways that memory activities are shaped by the contexts within which they occur.

V. A DIALECTICAL MODEL OF MEMORY DEVELOPMENT

The value of dialectics for understanding problems of memory development has been illustrated by Soviet theories of the internalization of cultural activities (Section IV), and by Leont'ev's model for the subordination of operations to goal-directed actions such as remembering (Section III). Applications of Leont'ev's model, in explaining the development of levels of processing and in conceptualizing the problem of production deficiencies, were also discussed. Nevertheless, up to this point the dialectic model leaves unanswered questions regarding the origins of actions that are later to be subordinated as operations, and the nature of the social contexts that promote such subordination in the course of development.

The impetus for elaboration of a dialectical model is again found within Soviet psychology. Leont'ev (1959/1964) states as a "first and most general principle" of mental development that:

Changes do not occur independently of one another but [are] intrinsically connected with one another. In other words, they do not represent independent lines of development of the various processes (perception, memory, thinking, etc.). . . . For example, the development of memory creates an associated series of changes, but *the need for them is not determined by the relationships occurring within the development of memory itself* but by relationships depending on the place which memory occupies in the child's activity at the given level of its development [p. 184, emphasis added].

This view appears to be consistent with Wohlwill's (1973) reciprocal interaction model of developmental stages, in which "development in two or more domains proceeds . . . such that progress in one initially follows, and subsequently overtakes that in the other(s) [p. 209]." In other words, development in one domain, such as representational abilities, may facilitate development in another, such as remembering. For example, Wohlwill argues from the effectiveness, in teaching conservation, of certain experimental conditions that do not include conservation items that "observed changes in response may occur . . . in a purely indirect fashion, that is, as a result of changes in other areas to which they are functionally linked [p. 322]."

A dialectical model of memory, one that emphasizes continuing development and the interdependence of development in different domains, can now be proposed (Meacham, 1975a). At any time in the course of development, there exist interactions of the individual's actions in each of many psychological domains with the activities provided by the cultural-historical context. As a first step in a dialectical cycle, the interaction leads to the acquisition of a new, independent, goal-directed action in one of the psychological domains. As a second step, the original context of development is changed, both as a result of the acquisition of the new action and as a result of the subordination of this action as an operation in other domains. Thus, through the acquisition and the reorganization of actions by the individual there arise possibilities for new activities in the cultural-historical context, and so for further development in the individual. The individual develops within a cultural-historical context, but also contributes to that context through his own actions; as the context is changed by the individual, the potential for continuing development of the individual arises.

In addition to this emphasis on continuing development and on the interdependence of development within the individual and the development of the culture, this dialectical model of memory also emphasizes that it is appropriate to search in practical contexts and psychological domains other than those of remembering, such as comprehension and classification, for the origins of actions to be used as operations in remembering. In other words, the development of memory abilities may not be susceptible to understanding by investigation of only this narrow domain. For example, the complete development of verbal means of facilitating remembering may depend on the prior acquisition of writing and role-taking skills as means of communicating over extended durations of time with persons other than oneself. Similarly, processes of semantic integration in remembering (see Paris and Lindauer, this volume) certainly depend on the prior acquisition by the child of logical concepts involving time, space, and causality.

Further, not only must the impact on remembering of developments in other domains be considered, but within this dialectical model it is also appropriate to consider the impact of changes in remembering operations on developments in diverse domains such as perception and problem solving. McLaughlin (1963), for example, suggests that the development of Piagetian operations can be expressed as a function of increasing memory span. Smirnov's (1966/1973) text, for example, includes a chapter on the effects of memorization on the comprehension of prose material. As a third example, Meacham and Leiman (1975) have been investigating prospective remembering, that is, the remembering of memories that have implications for actions to be performed in the future, such as stopping at the store or keeping an appointment. Prospective remembering, which involves memories from the past but not necessarily about the past, can be distinguished from retrospective remembering, which is the recall of memories about the past. Prospective remembering is an important aspect of those behaviors that we refer to as planned, and prospective remembering abilities ought to bear on one's self-concept as an efficient, reliable, and well-organized person. Munsat (1966), for example, suggests that "if a person makes memory claims about what he did in the past, and they are frequently wrong, we say his memory is unreliable. If a person . . . forgets to do things he said he would do and is in general 'forgetful,' it is *he* that we brand as unreliable [p. 18]." Indeed, adults reflecting on their own or their children's memory lapses often appear more concerned with instances of forgetting to carry out actions than with the forgetting of information about the past. As a further example, Flavell and Wellman (this volume), in discussing possible relationships between metamemory and memory abilities, suggest both that awareness of the remembering requirements of a situation, for example, of the need to plan ahead, can lead to the acquisition of new memory abilities, and that engaging in certain remembering actions might lead to increased knowledge, that is, metamemory, of those actions and their outcomes. To summarize, not only does the development of memory abilities depend on developments in other domains, but the development of memory abilities may also lead to changes in logical or conceptual abilities, comprehension, self-concept, and knowledge of one's planning abilities.

The dialectical model that is proposed here is consistent with the views of Kvale (1975) and Reese (1975), who have also offered dialectical formulations. Kvale (1975) notes that research that is conducted outside of a dialectical framework fails to consider that memories are remembered within various contexts, including those provided by the life history of the individual and of the society. Reese (1975), discussing the implications of a dialectical approach, also points to the changing nature of memories as the environmental conditions of the individual change, or as the structures employed in reconstruction of memories develop, as in Piaget's discussion of memory and intelligence (see Liben, this volume). Kvale and Reese, however, as well as Piaget's investigations, focus on changes in memories as they are remembered, while the dialectical model being advanced here has focused on developmental changes in memory abilities.

In conclusion, the dialectical model emphasizes, consistent with the emphases in Soviet developmental theory, the interdependence of developments within different domains of activity. In particular, attention is given to the interaction of the individual with the cultural–historical context, and to the interactions within the individual of developments in various psychological domains. A dialectical perspective makes clear that through his own actions the individual can change the social context for his future development. Further, the origins of actions that will later serve as operations in remembering may lie as easily in various psychological domains as in memory per se. This model can be contrasted with that of Piaget, for example, who gives relatively less emphasis to the impact of the individual's actions on the social context. That is, in the dialectical model the individual not only knows by means of his actions, but these actions also change the context for development within which the individual is situated, thus creating the potential for continuing development. This cultural-historical context for development continues to develop in its own right, and the development of the individual must be considered as it interacts with this moving background.

VI. CONCLUSION

Soviet investigations of memory development have been found to differ from non-Soviet research in several aspects, including emphases on remembering in practical rather than laboratory contexts, on the motivational and cultural-historical contexts of remembering, on description rather than hypothesis testing, and on development as a basic problem to be investigated. Soviet psychologists, of course, have their own perspective on non-Soviet psychology, and find a failure to consider sufficiently the role of conscious mental activity in remembering, as well as a failure to analyze qualitatively the processes by which remembering is accomplished, as opposed to what and how much is remembered (Smirnov, 1966/1973, pp. 3–11). Such criticisms do not consider more recent information-processing approaches to memory, which do emphasize the activity of the individual in transforming material to be remembered, and also focus on the processes by which remembering is accomplished rather than on the products of those processes. Nevertheless, information-processing models are *not* basically developmental, and so the task faced by non-Soviet developmental psychologists is to consider how such models might be useful in explaining developmental changes (see, e.g., Reese, 1973). Soviet psychologists, starting from a dialectical, developmental foundation, have made greater progress in understanding development, and for several decades have been investigating qualitative changes in processes of remembering. The Soviet developmental perspective includes not only changes in the individual but also changes in the cultural–historical context, and the interaction of these two developmental progressions. Soviet psychologists have also considered more broadly the motivational context of remembering, and the relationship of remembering to other psychological processes. In conclusion, it is hoped that greater understanding of the development of memory abilities can come through increased dialectical interactions between Soviet and non-Soviet developmental psychologists.

ACKNOWLEDGMENTS

The author wishes to thank Barbara Goldman and Ann Keller, whose contributions are reflected in this chapter. In addition, the suggestions of Michael Cole were quite helpful.

REFERENCES

Appel, L. F., Cooper, R. G., McCarrell, N., Sims-Knight, J., Yussen, S. R., & Flavell, J. H. The development of the distinction between perceiving and memorizing. *Child Development*, 1972, *43*, 1365–1381.

Berger, P. L., & Luckmann, T. *The social construction of reality*. New York: Doubleday, 1966.

Berlyne, D. E. Haply I may remember and haply may forget (Review of P. I. Zinchenko, *Involuntary remembering*). *Contemporary Psychology*, 1964, *9*, 323–324.

Blonskii, P. O. [*Memory and thinking*]. Moscow, 1935. In P. P. Blonskii, [*Selected psychological works*]. Moscow: Izd. Prosveshchenie, 1964.

Bocharova, S. P. Influence of the information value of objects on the level of involuntary memorization. *Soviet Psychology*, 1969, *7*, 28–36 (*Voprosy Psikhologii*, 1968, *14*, 86–95).

Buck-Morss, S. Socio-economic bias in Piaget's theory and its implications for the cross-culture controversy. *Human Development*, 1975, *18*, 35–49.

Christie, D. J., & Schumacher, G. M. Developmental trends in the abstraction and recall of relevant versus irrelevant thematic information from connected verbal materials. *Child Development*, 1975, *46*, 598–602.

Craik, F. I. M., & Lockhart, R. S. Levels of processing: A framework for memory research. *Journal of Verbal Learning and Verbal Behavior*, 1972, *11*, 671–684.

Elkonin, D. B. Toward the problem of stages in the mental development of the child. *Soviet Psychology*, 1972, *10*, 225–251 (*Voprosy Psikhologii*, 1971, *4*, 6–20).

Estes, W. K. Memory—East and West (review of A. A. Smirnov, *Problems of the psychology of memory*). *Contemporary Psychology*, 1974, *19*, 179–182.

Flavell, J. H. Developmental studies of mediated memory. In H. W. Reese and L. P. Lipsitt (Eds.), *Advances in child development and behavior* (Vol 5). New York: Academic Press, 1970.

Gal'perin, P. Y. Stages in the development of mental acts. In M. Cole & I. Maltzman (Eds.), *A handbook of contemporary Soviet psychology*. New York: Basic Books, 1969. (Originally published, 1959.)

Hagen, J. W., & Hale, G. W. The development of attention in children. In A. D. Pick (Ed.), *Minnesota symposia on child psychology* (Vol. 7). Minneapolis: University of Minnesota Press, 1973.

Hyde, T. S., & Jenkins, J. J. Recall for words as a function of semantic, graphic, and syntactic orienting tasks. *Journal of Verbal Learning and Verbal Behavior*, 1973, *12*, 471–480.

Istomina, Z. M. The development of voluntary memory in preschool-age children. *Soviet Psychology*, 1975, *13*(4), 5–64 (originally published, 1948).

Istomina, Z. M. [The development of voluntary memory in preschool children]. *Doshkolnoe Vospitanie*, 1953, *4*, 31–39.

Jenkins, J. J. Remember that old theory of memory? Well, forget it! *American Psychologist*, 1974, *29*, 785–795.

Keniston, K. Psychological development and historical change. *Journal of Interdisciplinary History*, 1971, *2*, 330–345.

Kreutzer, M. A., Leonard, C., & Flavell, J. H. An interview study of children's knowledge about memory. *Monographs of the Society for Research in Child Development*, 1975, *40*(1, Serial No. 159).

Kussmann, T. The Soviet concept of development and the problem of activity. In K. F. Riegel & J. A. Meacham (Eds.), *The developing individual in a changing world*, Vol. 1: *Historical and cultural issues*. The Hague: Mouton, 1976.

Kvale, S. Memory and dialectics: Some reflections on Ebbinghaus and Mao Tse-tung. *Human Development*, 1975, *18*, 205–222.

Leont'ev, A. N. [*Development of memory*]. Moscow: Uchpedgiz, 1931.

Leont'ev, A. N. Studies on the cultural development of the child: III. The development of voluntary attention in the child. *Journal of Genetic Psychology*, 1932, *40*, 52–83.

Leont'ev, A. N. *Problems of mental development.* Washington, D.C.: Joint Publications Research Service, 1964. (Originally published, 1959.)

Leont'ev, A. N. The problem of activity in psychology. *Soviet Psychology,* 1974–1975, *13,* 4–33 (*Voprosy Filosofii,* 1972, *9,* 95–108).

Leont'ev, A. N., & Luria, A. R. The psychological ideas of L. S. Vygotsky. In B. Wolman (Ed.), *Historical roots of contemporary psychology.* New York: Harper & Row, 1968.

Leont'ev, A. N., & Rozanova, T. V. The formation of associative connections: An experimental investigation. In B. Simon (Ed.), *Psychology in the Soviet Union.* London: Routledge & Kegan Paul, 1957 (*Sovetskaya Pedagogika,* 1951, *10,* 60–77).

Lisina, M. I., & Neverovich, Ya. Z. Development of movement and formation of motor habits. In A. V. Zaporozhets & D. B. Elkonin (Eds.), *The psychology of preschool children* (trans. J. Shybut and S. Simon). Cambridge, Mass.: M.I.T. Press, 1971. (Originally published, 1964.)

Luria, A. R. Toward the problem of the historical nature of psychological processes. *International Journal of Psychology,* 1971, *6,* 259–272.

McLaughlin, G. H. Psycho-logic: A possible alternative to Piaget's formulation. *British Journal of Educational Psychology,* 1963, *33,* 61–67.

Meacham, J. A. Activity and involuntary memory: A failure to replicate. *Psychonomic Science,* 1972, *26,* 197–198.   (a)

Meacham, J. A. The development of memory abilities in the individual and society. *Human Development,* 1972, *15,* 205–228.   (b)

Meacham, J. A. Dialectics, cognitive development, and history. Paper presented at an interdisciplinary conference on Dialectics: Paradigm for the Social Sciences, York University, Glendon College, Toronto, August 1975, also presented at the meeting of the American Psychological Association, Chicago, September 1975.   (a)

Meacham, J. A. Patterns of memory abilities in two cultures. *Developmental Psychology,* 1975, *11,* 50–63.   (b)

Meacham, J. A., & Leiman, B. Remembering to perform future actions. Paper presented at the meeting of the American Psychological Association, Chicago, September 1975.

Meacham, J. A., & Riegel, K. F. Dialectical perspectives on Piaget's theory. In G. Steiner (Ed.), Vol. 7, Piaget's developmental and cognitive theory within an extended context, *The Psychology of the 20th Century.* Zürich: Kindler, in press.

Meacham, J. A., & Spielman, K. S. Dialectics and development: Soviet preschool psychology (review of A. V. Zaporozhets and D. B. Elkonin, (Eds.) *The psychology of preschool children*) *Human Development,* 1973, *16,* 243–247.

Misiak, H., & Sexton, V. S. *History of psychology: An overview.* New York: Grune & Stratton, 1966.

Munsat, S. *The concept of memory.* New York: Random House, 1966.

Murphy, M. D., & Brown, A. L. Incidental learning in preschool children as a function of level of cognitive analysis. *Journal of Experimental Child Psychology,* 1975, *19,* 509–523.

Payne, T. R. S. *L. Rubinstein and the philosophical foundations of Soviet psychology.* New York: Humanities Press, 1968.

Pepper, S. C. *World hypotheses.* Berkeley: University of California Press, 1942.

Postman, L. Short-term memory and incidental learning. In A. W. Melton (Ed.), *Categories of human learning.* New York: Academic Press, 1964.

Rahmani, L. Studies on the mental development of the child. In N. O'Connor (Ed.), *Present-day Russian psychology.* New York: Pergamon, 1966.

Rahmani, L. *Soviet psychology: Philosophical, theoretical, and experimental issues.* New York: International Universities Press, 1973.

Rahmani, L. Philosophy and psychology in the Soviet Union. In K. F. Riegel & J. A. Meacham (Eds.), *The developing individual in a changing world,* Vol. 1: *Historical and cultural issues.* The Hague: Mouton, 1976.

Reese, H. W. Models of memory and models of development. *Human Development,* 1973, *16,* 397–416.

Reese, H. W. Cohort, age, and imagery in children's paired-associate learning. *Child Development,* 1974, *45,* 1176–1180.

Reese, H. W. Information processing and the development of memory. Paper presented at the biennial meeting of the Society for Research in Child Development, Denver, April 1975.

Riegel, K. F. Developmental psychology and society: Some historical and ethical considerations. In J. R. Nesselroade & H. W. Reese (Eds.), *Life-span developmental psychology: Methodological issues.* New York: Academic Press, 1973.

Riegel, K. F. Adult life crises: A dialectic interpretation of development. In N. Datan & L. H. Ginsberg (Eds.), *Life-span developmental psychology: Normative life crises.* New York: Academic Press, 1975.   (a)

Riegel, K. F. From traits and equilibrium toward developmental dialectics. In W. J. Arnold & J. K. Cole (Eds.), *1974–1975 Nebraska Symposium on Motivation.* Lincoln: University of Nebraska Press, 1975.   (b)

Rozeboom, W. W. The concept of "memory." *Psychological Record,* 1965, *15,* 329–368.

Rubinstein, S. L. Questions of psychological theory. In B. Simon (Ed.), *Psychology in the Soviet Union.* Stanford: Stanford University Press, 1957 (*Voprosy Psikhologii,* 1955, *1,* 6–18).

Smirnov, A. A. [*The psychology of memorization*]. Moscow: Izd. Akad. Pedag. Nauk RSFSR, 1948.

Smirnov, A. A. Child psychology. In B. Simon (Ed.), *Psychology in the Soviet Union.* Stanford: Stanford University Press, 1957.

Smirnov, A. A. (Ed.). [*Problems of the psychology of memory*]. Moscow: Izd. Akad. Pedag. Nauk RSFSR, 1958.

Smirnov, A. A. *Problems of the psychology of memory* (trans. S. A. Corson). New York: Plenum Press, 1973. (Originally published 1966.)

Smirnov, A. A., Istomina, Z. M., Mal'tseva, K. P., & Samokhvalova, V. I. The development of logical memorization techniques in the preschool and young child. *Soviet Psychology,* 1971–1972, *10,* 178–195 (*Voprosy Psikhologii,* 1969, *5,* 90–101).

Smirnov, A. A., & Zinchenko, P. I. Problems in the psychology of memory. In M. Cole & I. Maltzman (Eds.), *A handbook of contemporary Soviet psychology.* New York: Basic Books, 1969.

Vygotskii, L. S. II. The problem of the cultural behavior of the child. *Journal of Genetic Psychology,* 1929, *36,* 415–434.

Vygotskii, L. S. *Thought and language* (ed. and trans. E. Hanfmann and G. Vakar). Cambridge, Mass.: M.I.T. Press, 1962. (Originally published, 1934.)

Wohlwill, J. F. *The study of behavioral development.* New York: Academic Press, 1973.

Wozniak, R. H. Dialecticism and structuralism: The philosophical foundation of Soviet and Piagetian cognitive developmental theory. In K. F. Riegel & G. C. Rosenwald (Eds.), *Structure and transformation: Developmental and historical aspects.* New York: Wiley, 1975.

Yendovitskaya, T. V. Development of memory. In A. V. Zaporozhets & D. B. Elkonin (Eds.), *The psychology of preschool children* (trans. J. Shybut and S. Simon). Cambridge, Mass.: M.I.T. Press, 1971. (Originally published, 1964.)

Zankov, L. V. [*A schoolchild's memory*]. Moscow: Uchpedgiz, 1944.

Zankov, L. V. [*Memory*]. Moscow: Uchpedgiz, 1949.

Zankov, L. V. The theory of memory. In B. Simon (Ed.), *Psychology in the Soviet Union.* Stanford: Stanford University Press, 1957 (*Sovetskaya Pedagogika,* 1951, *6,* 59–80).

Zeigarnik, B. V. Personality and the pathology of activity. *Soviet Psychology,* 1972–1973, *11,* 4–89. (Originally published, 1971.)

Zinchenko, P. I. [*Involuntary memorization*]. Moscow: Izd. Akad. Pedag. Nauk RSFSR, 1961.

10

Memory in the Context of Cognitive Development: The Piagetian Approach

Lynn S. Liben

The Pennsylvania State University

I. INTRODUCTION: IMPLICATIONS OF A CONSTRUCTIVE EPISTEMOLOGY FOR MEMORY

One of the fundamental characteristics of Piaget's theory is its highly constructive nature. In explaining the child's acquisition of knowledge, Piaget (1970) explicitly rejects the assumption that a prestructured reality is imposed on, and absorbed by, an essentially passive organism. Instead, Piaget proposes that knowledge is constructed by the child through the continual interaction of the intelligence and the environment. As the child's intellectual structure develops, there are qualitative changes in the way in which the world is known.

Just as Piaget denies that the child acquires knowledge passively by absorbing a preexisting reality, Piaget and Inhelde (1973) similarly reject the notion of a passive memory. In particular, they reject the classic associationistic view of memory in which it is hypothesized that (1) the strength of a particular memory is dependent on repetition and reinforcement of associations in the environment and (2) the deterioration of that memory occurs over time as a function of disuse or interference. Piaget and Inhelder (1973) suggest instead that memories are integrally tied to the child's operative schemes.[1]

---

[1] The word *scheme* (from the French *schème*) is used to refer to "that which can be repeated and generalized in an action" (Piaget, 1970, p. 705). To maintain consistency, even "direct" quotations from *Memory and Intelligence* (Piaget and Inhelder, 1973) have been modified to conform to this translation.

The impact of the intelligence on memory is most evident in the concept of memory in the "broad" or "wide" sense. Memory in the broad sense involves the conservation of the schemes of intelligence in general, but schemes that are focused specifically on the past rather than on the present reality. Memory in the strict sense, by contrast, is concerned with the highly specific rather than the generalizable, bearing on "situations, processes or objects as are singular and recognized or recalled as such" (Piaget & Inhelder, 1973, p. 5). It is not, however, possible to dissect memory in the strict sense from the more general conservation of schemes. Instead, particular past experiences are embedded in, and reconstructed through, the generalizing schemes.

If, as Piaget and Inhelder (1973) suggest, even specific memories are influenced by the child's general cognitive structure, and if this intellectual structure changes qualitatively with development, then there should also be qualitative differences in the way that events are remembered by children at different developmental levels. This view has two testable implications. First, there should be cross-age differences in the way that an "identical" stimulus is remembered. Second, there should be longitudinal changes in the way in which a child remembers a particular event, changes which reflect that child's developing operative schemes. The research paradigm used to test these implications is described in the next section, as are the findings from studies using this paradigm.

II. EMPIRICAL EVIDENCE FOR THE OPERATIVE APPROACH TO MEMORY

A. Genevan Research

To test the two implications just discussed—that children at different stages remember stimuli differently and that memories change in accordance with changes in operative levels—Piaget and Inhelder (1973) used the following paradigm. Children of different ages were shown a picture or event, and were then tested for recall (using reproduction and/or reconstruction and/or recognition tasks) after one or more relatively short intervals (for example, one day and/or one week) and again after a long interval (for example, six or more months).

In one such study, for example, children 3 to 8 years old were shown an array of seriated sticks and were asked to reproduce it from memory one week and again eight months later. Both cross-sectional and longitudinal findings supported the hypothesized relation between memory and intelligence. That is, children of different ages drew reproductions which paralleled their levels of development. Thus, most of the youngest children (3- and 4-year-olds) failed to reproduce the seriated order at one week, and instead drew lines of equal length or irregular hatches. Somewhat older children (5-year-olds) more typically reproduced the sticks as a series of uncoordinated pairs (for example, alternating small and large sticks); as uncoordinated triplets (for example, two groups of three sticks); or as seriated along the top but neither aligned nor seriated along the base. Still older children were able to reproduce the array in seriated order. These age differences in memory correspond to the age differences found when children are asked to construct seriated arrays without first being shown a seriated model.

The longitudinal data on memory change were also consistent with the proposed relationship between operative level and memory. Of the children shown the seriated array who were available for retesting eight months later, 26% showed memory stability, while 74% produced more highly seriated drawings after eight months than they had after only one week. These changes occurred both within the unseriated categories (for example, from pairs of small and large sticks to subsets of seriated triplets) and across categories (that is, from unseriated to fully seriated arrays). Such improvements parallel the operative progress typically displayed by children of this age over the course of several months. Piaget and Inhelder interpret these memory improvements as strong evidence against the classic associationist approach to memory in which all memories are assumed to deteriorate over time. The legitimacy of this interpretation is discussed later in this chapter.

Many different stimuli were used in the Genevan work, including (1) stimuli in which a single dimension is relevant, as a seriated array; (2) stimuli in which two dimensions msut be coordinated, as in multiplicative matrices; (3) events in which cause and effect must be linked, as in transmitted motion; and (4) stimuli involving spatial configurations and transformations, as in a stimulus showing horizontal liquid in a tipped container. While the incidence of "long-term memory improvements" was not as high with these stimuli as it had been with the seriated array, the general patterns of results were comparable: Some children reproduced the stimulus more accurately after the longer retention interval than they had after the short retention interval.

It should be noted that the operative interpretation of memory does not predict memory improvement for all stimuli. For memory improvement to occur, the stimulus must tap the child's developing operative schemes. Thus, memory for arbitrary components of stimuli (for example, colors of sticks) would not be expected to improve over time. Similarly, memories would not be expected to improve if the stimulus taps "two or more schemes [that] are in active conflict because of nonsynchronous development (Inhelder, 1969, p. 349), as, for example, when a stimulus shows numerical, but not spatial, equivalence of two rows of objects.

B. Replications of Genevan Work

1. Overview

The studies prompted by the Genevan work on memory have been directed toward answering two major questions. The first is whether the empirical results described by Piaget and Inhelder—particularly those showing long-term memory improvement—are replicable. The second question is whether or not Piaget and Inhelder's theoretical interpretations of these empirical data are justified. The findings bearing on the first of these questions are reviewed in the present section (II.B); the issues and evidence related to the second question are discussed in the following section (III).

2. Cross-Sectional Evidence

As noted earlier, cross-sectional evidence on the relationship between operativity and memory can be obtained by testing children at different developmental stages for their memories of identical stimuli. Only two of the replication studies have included a sufficiently wide age range of children to provide such data.

In one of these studies, Furth, Ross, and Youniss (1974) showed kindergarten, first-, second-, and fourth-grade children four pictures. One picture concerned the concept of horizontality: A partially filled glass was shown tipped at a 45° angle ("glass"). A second picture concerned verticality, but included an operative error: A chimney on a house was shown at right angles to the oblique roof ("house"). A third stimulus involved a spatial transformation: Four positions of the movement of a falling, turning stick were shown in relation to the table from which it fell ("stick"). The fourth picture showed an imperfect numerical progression: Five squares were arranged contiguously, each having a progressively higher number of dots with one interruption in the sequence ("dots"). Sketches of the stimuli and chronological ages of the children from this and other studies are shown in Table 10-1. Half the children were asked to draw the stimuli during presentation ("copy" condition), while the others were asked to reproduce them immediately after viewing ("immediate" condition). All children were asked for reproductions again after two hours, two weeks, six months, and one year.

Furth et al. (1974) used a three-category system to classify drawings from all sessions. *Unmodified* drawings were those that preserved correctly the "important characteristics of the original"; *relevant* drawings "indicated at least one relevant characteristic, but modified other characteristics"; and *nonrelevant* drawings "lacked all relevant characteristics of the original and consequently demonstrated absence of a specific memory for the original event [p. 66]." For example, for the glass stimulus, reproductions were classified as unmodified if

TABLE 10-1
Summary of Major Variables in Long-Term Memory Investigations

Author	Stimulus	Grade (Age)	Recall Time[a] Memory Task	Operative Assessment
ALTEMEYER FULTON & BERNEY (1969)	SERIATED: RANDOM:	K	1w, 6m REPRODUCTION	
CROWLEY (1975)	STIMULUS III: STIMULUS IIB (PRESERIATED): NONSERIATION: A FACE	(5-0 TO 5-8)	1w, 4m 4m REPRODUCTION	PRETEST + POSTTEST POSTTEST
DAHLEM (1968)	SERIATED:	K(5-9)	i, 6m 1w, 6m RECONSTRUCTION	
DAHLEM (1969)	SERIATED: CONTROL: NO STIMULUS	K	i, 1w(TWICE), 6m i, 1w 6m 1w, 6m 6m RECONSTRUCTION	
FINKEL & CROWLEY (1973)	SERIATED: PRESERIATED IIB: PRESERIATED IIA:	K	1d, 1w, 5m 1w, 5m 5m REPRODUCTION + RECOGNITION	
FURTH, ROSS & YOUNISS (1974)	ALL SUBJECTS: STICK: GLASS: DOTS: HOUSE:	K(5-9) 1(6-9) 2(7-9) 4(9-10)	c, 2h, 2w, 6m, 1y i, 2h, 2w, 6m, 1y REPRODUCTION	
LIBEN (1974)	HORIZONTAL GROUP: NONHORIZONTAL GROUP:	5(10-8)	1w, 6m REPRODUCTION AT 1w REPRODUCTION + RECOGNITION AT 6m	PRETEST + POSTTEST POSTTEST
LIBEN (1975b)	ALL SUBJECTS: SERIATION, HORIZONTALITY, VERTICALITY: (SEE FIGURE 1)	K(5-3) 4(9-3)	1w, 5m PARTIAL REPRODUCTION 1w REPRODUCTION + RECOGNITION 5m	PRETEST + POSTTEST POSTTEST

(continued)

TABLE 10-1　(continued)

Author	Stimulus	Grade (Age)	Recall Time[a] Memory Task	Operative Assessment
MURRAY & BAUSELL (1970, 1971)	ALL SUBJECTS: CONSERVATION: AMOUNT: LENGTH: NUMBER: SERIATION: HORIZONTALITY:	1 (6-7) 2 (7-9)	i, 1w, 5m REPRODUCTION + RECOGNITION	PRETEST
SAMUELS (1974)	VIDEOTAPE: CONSERVATION (C) NONCONSERVATION (NC)	(3-7 TO 7-4)	i, 1d, 5m VERBAL "RECALL" AND "REASONS"	PRETEST + POSTTEST

Note:　Separate lines represent between-subject variables, unless otherwise noted.
[a] c=copy, i=immediate, h=hour, d=day, w=week, m=month, y=year

liquid was shown in a tilted glass and was within 15° of the horizontal; reproductions were classified as nonrelevant if there was no tilt and/or no liquid; and reproductions were classified as relevant if liquid was shown in a tilted glass but was at an incorrect angle (for example, parallel to the bottom of the glass). Categorization of drawings from the stick stimulus was similar in that operatively correct drawings were called unmodified, incorrect drawings were called relevant, and drawings which failed to reproduce the crucial operative component (that is, omitted the fall of the stick) were called nonrelevant. With the operatively primitive stimuli, the opposite held. That is, operatively incorrect drawings were called unmodified (as in the reproduction of the erroneously tilted chimney), while operatively correct drawings were classified as modified (the chimney shown on the true vertical). In interpreting the results of this study, it should be remembered that drawings with the same category label (for example, ''unmodified'') fall into different operative levels depending on the stimulus. For example, while an ''unmodified'' reproduction of the glass picture is both an accurate reproduction and an operatively advanced drawing, an ''unmodified'' reproduction of the house picture is mnemonically accurate but operatively primitive.

Collapsing responses over all sessions, older children produced more unmodified and fewer nonrelevant drawings than did younger children on the glass, stick, and dot stimuli. For the house stimulus, the number of relevant drawings increased with age. These findings fit satisfactorily with the Piagetian position in that with increasing age, drawings increasingly conformed to high-level operative concepts. In cases in which stimuli were operatively correct, unmodified reproductions became more common, while when stimuli were operatively incorrect (as in the house stimulus), relevant modifications became increasingly common.

Performance in the first session ("copy" or "immediate") provided mixed support for the Genevan position. As expected, the number of unmodified drawings of the glass increased developmentally. Comparable increases were not, however, found for the other stimuli. Furthermore, a surprisingly large number of children of all ages produced unmodified drawings in the first session, even though the younger children presumably lacked the operative schemes necessary for an advanced assimilation of these memory stimuli. Particularly surprising was the high percentage of children who reproduced the stick drawing without modification, since the stick drawing was presumed to tap an extremely advanced operative concept. One likely explanation of this finding is that extra information was given during presentation of the stick stimulus: "To facilitate this second task, the drawing of the stick was initially presented with both concrete demonstration and the verbal explanation" (Furth et al., 1974, p. 64).

The cross-sectional findings from a second investigation that included children across a wide operative range (Liben, 1975b) were generally consistent with expectations of the operative theory of memory. Kindergarten and fourth-grade children were shown six pictures, two each related to concepts of seriation, horizontality, and verticality (see Figure 10-1). One week and again five months after these pictures were shown, the children were asked to complete pictures from which the operative components (that is, the nails, blocks, bottle, bowl, cable, and flags) were omitted.

Since seriation schemes should be transitional in kindergarten children, it was hypothesized that the kindergarten children would reproduce seriation stimuli at mixed operative levels, and would show memory improvements for these stimuli over the five-month interval. At the same time, schemes related to Euclidean concepts should be very primitive in kindergarten children. Thus, it was hypothesized that the kindergarten children's reproductions of the horizontality and verticality stimuli would be operatively poor, with few memory improvements occurring during the subsequent five-month retention interval. For the fourth-grade children, in contrast, seriation schemes should have been firmly established prior to the beginning of the study, and thus it was expected that the older children's reproductions of the seriation stimuli would be consistently advanced. On the other hand, since fourth-grade children's Euclidean concepts should be transitional, their reproductions of the horizontality and verticality stimuli were expected to be at mixed developmental levels and to show improvement over the retention interval.

The findings from this study generally supported these hypotheses. That is,

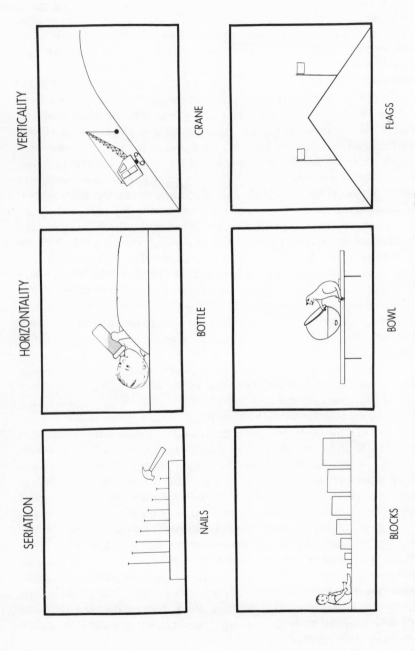

FIGURE 10-1 Seriation, horizontality, and verticality stimuli used in memory task by Liben (1975b). (Copyright 1975 by The American Psychological Association. Reproduced by permission.)

the reproductions of the seriation stimuli drawn by kindergarten children varied from low to high operative levels, while those drawn by the fourth-grade children were, with few exceptions, at the highest operative level. Similarly, most of the high-level reproductions of the Euclidean stimuli were drawn by the fourth-grade children. In addition, the cross-sectional differences in memory change were consistent with the operative approach: Long-term improvements in reproducing the seriation stimuli were found in the kindergarten group, whereas improvements in reproducing the horizontality stimuli were found in the fourth-grade group. Although a comparable number of long-term improvements in reproducing the verticality stimuli was evident in the two age groups, the patterns of improvement were different. For the easier of the two verticality stimuli (the Flags stimulus shown in Figure 10-1), the fourth-grade group could not display more improvement because of a ceiling effect at the one-week recall session. For the more difficult of the stimuli (Crane), the improvements into the most advanced operative level were found almost entirely among the fourth-grade children.

Thus, both studies which included children across wide developmental levels found cross-age differences that are generally consistent with the operative interpretation of memory. Most research on memory from the Piagetian perspective has focused on longitudinal change within individual children, and it is this work that is reviewed in the following section.

3. Longitudinal Evidence

In the first attempt to replicate Piaget and Inhelder's findings on changes in long-term memory, Altemeyer, Fulton, and Berney (1969) showed each of 100 kindergarten children an array of different-sized sticks, and asked the children to reproduce the array one week and six months later. The sticks were arranged either in a fully seriated array or in an unorganized, random array (shown in Table 10-1).

The longitudinal data from this study were interpreted by Altemeyer et al. (1969) as a successful replication of earlier Genevan findings. Analyses of individual and group change showed that drawings tended to be more highly seriated after six months than after one week. This improvement was attributable largely to children who had produced completely unpatterned, unordered drawings at one week, but patterned, ordered drawings at six months. A tendency toward increased seriation over time was apparent among children who had seen the random array as well as among children who had seen the seriated array. Although memory regressions were also found, they occurred only about half as often as progressions and generally represented smaller shifts than did the improvements. For these reasons, Altemeyer et al. (1969) considered the regressions to be relatively insignificant in comparison with the improvements.

Dahlem (1968) also studied kindergarten children's memories for a seriated array. Kindergarten children were asked to reconstruct the array either immediately after viewing the stimulus or one week later. Approximately one-third of the children who had been tested at one week were then asked to reconstruct the arrays again six months later.

Differences between the two groups' first constructions suggested that memory deteriorates over short intervals: Perfect reconstructions were produced more often in the group tested immediately after stimulus presentation than in the group tested one week later. Over the six-month interval, however, memory improvements were noted: Of children who had imperfect reconstructions at the one-week session, slightly over half showed improvement by six months, while only about 10% deteriorated. Of children who had perfect reconstructions at one week, none showed memory deterioration by six months. Dahlem (1968) concluded that "results agreed with Piaget's finding of improved memory over a six-month period [p. 331]."

In a later study, Dahlem (1969) attempted to replicate and extend her earlier work using the same stimulus and reconstruction task. The number and spacing of recall sessions were varied among four groups of kindergarten children. In one group, children were asked to reconstruct the stimulus after six months only; in a second group, after one week and six months; in a third group, immediately after viewing, after one week, and after six months; and in a fourth group, immediately, twice successfully after one week, and again after six months.

As in the earlier study (Dahlem, 1968), children who reconstructed the stimulus accurately during the first recall session (either immediately or one week after viewing the stimulus) also tended to reproduce the stimulus correctly at the later recall session. Furthermore, the number of perfect reproductions increased by the later recall session. Contrary to expectations, however, improvements and deteriorations (other than to, or from, perfect performance) were equally common over the six-month interval. In addition, there was no evidence for memory loss between immediate and one-week sessions, a finding that was inconsistent with Dahlem's earlier results. Other than noting the apparent lack of generality of her earlier findings, Dahlem (1969) offered no explanation of the discrepancies in the two studies, and indeed none is apparent.

Murray and Bausell (1970) studied first- and second-grade children's recall of stimuli related to conservation, seriation, and horizontality. Children were given booklets that showed initial correspondence between three pairs of items: two identical beakers, equally full; two sticks of equal length, aligned spatially; and two numerically equal rows of circles and cups, also aligned spatially. Shown beneath each pair of items was an appropriate conservation transformation: Water was poured into two new beakers, one tall and narrow, one short and wide; one stick had been moved to the right of the other; and one row of objects had been spread out. Also included in the booklet were seriation and horizontality problems. In the former, children were asked to copy a seriated array; in the latter they were asked to draw the waterline in a tilted bottle that was shown directly under a partly filled upright bottle (see Table 10-1).

Children first answered questions about the equivalence of each of the transformed pairs in the conservation stimuli, and then completed the seriation and horizontality tasks. This was followed by a memory task in which children were asked to draw the jars into which the liquid had been poured, the sticks after one had been moved, the balls and cups after one had been moved, the row of sticks, and the tilted jar and water level. This reproduction task was followed by a recognition task in which four or five alternatives were provided for each of the five problems.

Data on immediate memory and the relation between memory and operative schemes were described in the published report of this work (Murray & Bausell, 1970). Longitudinal data were collected subsequently and reported by Murray and Bausell (1971). For the longitudinal investigation, the transformed stimuli were re-presented to the children one week after the initial conceptual and memory tasks had been given. Reproduction and recognition tasks were then repeated one week and six months later.

Reproductions were scored as correct if they were "correct in all critical aspects, i.e., (1) jars differed in width and height, (2) equal sticks and dark stick to the right, (3) correct number of circles and cups and longer row of cups, (4) correct number of sticks and seriated in correct direction, and (5) correct height and level of water" (Murray & Bausell, 1970, p. 335).

The incidence and direction of long-term memory changes are shown in Table 10-2. Since Murray and Bausell (1971) did not present data from the one-week session in relation to earlier or later memory performance, or in relation to operative level, only immediate and six-month data are included in Table 10-2. As may be seen in this table, the number of long-term memory improvements is very small, and is far exceeded by the number of memory regressions.

Although these data appear to be strong evidence against the Genevan position, there are several aspects of the study that make its findings tentative. First, the memory stimuli themselves had several unusual characteristics. For example, children were not actually shown a correctly filled tipped jar for the horizontality task prior to the immediate memory task, and hence, had only their own drawings to remember. (A correct drawing was given, incidentally, as part of the conservation of liquid task.) The stimuli used in the conservation of liquid task were also potentially confusing in that the size relation between the two sets of beakers was unrealistic. In addition, the reproduction task was unusual in that it required the child to draw the set of beakers, but not the water level in the beakers.

Two additional aspects of this study may have led to a spuriously large number of regressions in performance. First, recognition tasks were included in all memory sessions. By the later session children may have mistakenly reproduced

TABLE 10-2
Relationship Between Children's Immediate and Five-Month Recall (N = 81)[a]

Immediate Recall	Five-month recall									
	Amount		Length		Number		Seriation		Horizontality	
	R	W	R	W	R	W	R	W	R	W
	Reproduction									
Right (R)	12	37	6	44	0	25	19	43	0	5
Wrong (W)	3	29	3	28	1	55	5	14	2	74
	Recognition									
Right (R)	56	17	14	52	4	25	72	4	40	21
Wrong (W)	3	5	7	8	7	45	5	0	11	9

[a] From Murray and Bausell (1971).

inaccurate recognition alternatives rather than the original stimuli. Second, the scoring criteria included not only operative components of the stimuli (for example, sticks of equal length, an equal number of circles and cups, size order, horizontal water level) but also highly figurative aspects (for example, the dark stick to the right, correct absolute number of balls and cups, correct number of sticks, correct height of liquid). The high number of deteriorations may have resulted from memory loss for the relatively arbitrary components of the stimuli, rather than for components tied to operative schemes. Thus, while the extremely low incidence of improvements appears to be negative evidence, several aspects of the study suggest that these results should not be weighed too heavily in the evaluation of the Piagetian position.

In a later study, Finkel and Crowley (1973) investigated kindergarten children's retention of stimuli related to concepts of seriation. In one group, children were shown a fully seriated array of ten sticks (Stimulus III) comparable to that used by Piaget and Inhelder (1973). In two other groups, children were shown arrays comparable to those produced by children who do not yet understand seriation. In one of these stimuli (IIA), large and small sticks were alternated; in the other (IIB), there were three small, four medium, and three large sticks (see Table 10-1). These two "preseriation" stimuli were included to determine whether drawings consistently become more seriated over time regardless of the degree of seriation shown in the original stimulus.

Recall schedules were varied to evaluate the effects of repeated testing. One group of children was given reproduction and recognition tasks one day, one week, and five months after viewing the stimulus; another group was given these tasks after one week and five months; and a third group was tested at five months only.

Drawings made by children in all groups were scored according to a nine-category system. Drawings in the lowest categories contained no evidence of seriation (for example, no sticks; equal-sized sticks; randomly arranged sticks), while those in the highest category were perfectly seriated. Those in the middle categories showed ordered arrangements of some kind (e.g., alternating large and small sticks; different-length sticks positioned to create a seriated top but an uneven bottom).

The data on memory change are presented in Table 10-3, in which progress and deterioration refer to increased and decreased degrees of seriation, respectively. For all stimuli, performance on the recognition task was better and more stable than performance on the reproduction task. As predicted, some children's drawings were more seriated after long intervals. This improvement is substantial, however, only when compared to an expectation of zero improvements. When contrasted with the number of regressions, the improvement is unimpressive.

As is also evident from Table 10-3, the patterns of change differed markedly across the three stimuli. Only in Stimulus IIB were there significantly more

TABLE 10-3

Percentages of Children Showing Increased, Stable, or Decreased Seriation in Reproductions
(Recognition Data in Parentheses)[a]

Stimulus	Time interval								
	1 day to 1 week			1 week to 5 months			1 day to 5 months		
	Increased	Stable	Decreased	Increased	Stable	Decreased	Increased	Stable	Decreased
Alternating small and large sticks (IIA)	17 (13)	61 (83)	25 (04)	32 (18)	50 (61)	18 (21)	18 (18)	73 (73)	9 (09)
Small, medium, and large sticks (IIB)	50 (13)	41 (79)	9 (08)	40 (26)	22 (57)	38 (17)	59 (24)	23 (67)	18 (09)
Fully seriated array (III)	32 (03)	54 (86)	14 (11)	20 (02)	43 (91)	37 (07)	33 (00)	37 (100)	30 (00)

[a] Condensed from Finkel & Crowley (1973).

long-term improvements than regressions (between one day and five months). It appears, however, that at least some of this effect is a consequence of repeated testing, since half the children shown Stimulus IIB performed better after one week than they had after one day. It is unlikely that so many children would have shown significant operative growth during so short an interval, thus implicating repeated-testing effects.

A comparison of performance across groups with different testing schedules indicates that repeated testing did affect performance, in interaction with the stimulus. Specifically, for children shown the fully seriated array, more frequent testing led to significantly higher seriation in both reproduction and recognition tasks. For children shown alternating small and large sticks, repeated testing tended to decrease the likelihood of change. Finally, for children shown the small, medium, and large sticks, repeated testing led to a decrease in accuracy with respect to the reproduction of the stimulus itself, but tended to increase the degree of seriation in the reproductions. It is, unfortunately, unclear what is actually responsible for the repeated-testing effects in this study, since each recall session included a recognition task as well as a reproduction task. Thus, the repeated-testing effects may have resulted either from seeing the recognition task alternatives or from repeating the reproduction task per se. In either case, the findings on long-term change in this study cannot be considered conclusive.

Furth et al. (1974) obtained longitudinal data on memory for stimuli related to spatial and numerical concepts, as well as the cross-sectional data described earlier. Over the year during which this study was conducted, there was a decrease in the number of unmodified drawings and an increase in the number of nonrelevant drawings at all ages (explanations of unmodified, nonrelevant, and relevant categories are given on pages 300, 302). While some changes occurred relatively early in the study, the greatest shift occurred between the two-week and six-month recall sessions.

Different patterns of results were evident across the stimuli. Such differences were expected since stimuli varied both in content and in whether or not they were operatively correct. With the two operatively advanced and correct stimuli (glass and stick), some long-term memory improvements were found, generally among older children. However, even for these stimuli the most common pattern of change was regression, particularly by the six-month and one-year sessions.

For the arbitrarily interrupted number series shown in the dots stimulus, children generally produced unmodified drawings in the early (immediate through two-week) sessions, but modified their drawings by the later recall sessions. In the older grades, the modifications were generally relevant, thereby rectifying the arbitrary gap in number. In the kindergarten children, the modifications were generally toward the nonrelevant category, indicating that the children forgot the ordering altogether.

For the house stimulus (with the chimney that was operatively incorrect), the number of relevant modifications increased over the year, thus increasing the number of operatively correct drawings. Such modifications were generally found in the older children, while nonrelevant changes (no chimney shown at all) were found in the younger children's six-month and one-year reproductions.

Furth et al. (1974) interpreted their data as supportive of the Genevan position. Although younger children made operatively correct drawings after short periods, their long-term reproductions were incorrect (nonrelevant changes), thus reflecting their operative inadequacies. While the older children also showed a decrease in the number of unmodified drawings over time, their modifications at the later sessions tended to fall into the higher-level relevant classification, rather than the lower-level nonrelevant classification. It should be noted, however, that while Furth et al. (1974) have interpreted nonrelevant drawings as operatively poor, Liben (1974, 1975b) has argued that such drawings should be regarded as unscorable because they do not provide sufficient information about operative level. If such reproductions are eliminated from the study by Furth et al. (1974), the incidence of long-term improvements is reduced.

In addition to a relatively low incidence of long-term improvements, there were also "massive regressions" (p. 70), that is, children whose reproductions were mnemonically and operatively accurate at the early recall sessions but whose later reproductions were operatively poor. Furth et al. (1974) suggest that these regressions are indicative of children's transitional operative levels, and of a fading dominance of figurative memory over time. The viability of this interpretation is discussed in the concluding section of this chapter.

In an investigation of long-term memory for a stimulus related to horizontality, Liben (1974) showed fifth-grade children a picture of a half-filled, tipped bottle. In the picture shown to half the children, the liquid was horizontal, while in the picture shown to the remaining children, the liquid was not horizontal (as shown in Table 10-1). The former stimulus was included to replicate Piaget and Inhelder's (1973) work; the latter stimulus was used to determine whether memories would shift toward higher operative levels over time, regardless of whether the operative level depicted in the stimulus was advanced or primitive. Reproduction tasks were given after one week and six months, and a recognition task was given following the six-month reproduction task.

As in the studies reviewed earlier, improvements in long-term memory were found. The number of improvements was significant when compared with the number of improvements expected under the hypothesis that all memories either remain stable or deteriorate over time. The number of improvements was not, however, significantly greater than the number of regressions. The long-term memory changes that occurred were toward more advanced levels of horizontality regardless of whether the correct or incorrect picture had been seen initially. Although many errors were made on the recognition task, recognition performance exceeded reproduction performance as expected.

As described earlier in the discussion of cross-sectional data (pages 303–305),

Liben (1975b) also examined memory for pictures related to concepts of seriation, horizontality, and verticality in kindergarten and fourth-grade children. The patterns of longitudinal memory change from one week to five months in the two age groups did correspond to operative differences: Improvements for kindergarten children were found largely in the seriation stimuli and in the easier of the verticality stimuli (Flags), while improvements for the fourth-grade children were concentrated in the Euclidean stimuli. Again, while there were significant numbers of memory improvements when contrasted to a null hypothesis of zero improvements, there were not significantly more improvements than regressions. Again, as in earlier studies, responses on the recognition task were superior to reproduction responses.

Samuels (1974) studied long-term memory for an episode that demonstrated either conservation or nonconservation reasoning. Children ranging in age from 3 to 7 were shown a videotape in which a boy and a girl were playing with toy cars. The two children first lined up their cars in one-to-one correspondence, after which the girl spread her cars out, saying that she now had more cars. In the videotape depicting conservation reasoning, the boy responded, "No you don't. You just spread them out but we still have the same number." In the tape that showed nonconservation reasoning, he responded: "That's not fair. You do have more cars than I do now."

One day, one week, and five months later, each child was asked to describe what had happened on the tape. One dependent variable, "recall," concerned what the child thought he or she had seen or heard. A second variable, "reasons," concerned the child's explanations of the event and responses to the experimenter's questions about what had *really* happened.

In the one-day and one-week sessions, almost all children recalled the reasoning—conservation or nonconservation—that they had actually seen. By the five-month session, very few children recalled enough of the event to permit scoring. The few responses that could be scored again corresponded to the actual event. Thus, no long-term memory improvements were evident in this study.

One possible explanation of the unusually good correspondence between the event witnessed and the child's recall is that the recall measure was exclusively verbal. It is possible, therefore, that children were able to mimic the reasoning they had heard by assimilating the event "at nothing other than a verbal level" (Piaget, quoted by Duckworth, 1964, p. 3).

Samuels (1974) suggests that a truer indication of the child's understanding may be found in his or her explanation of the event, that is, in the "reasons" measure. Changes were found over time in the types of explanations given by the children. Specifically, there was an increase between one day and five months in the number of children who explained that one child on the tape had more cars because of having taken more. The shift toward these "take" reasons may be interpreted as support for the position that memories reflect operatively advancing schemes, since the "take" reason provides an explanation of how one child can have had more cars, without denying conservation. Thus, although the results from the recall measure did not show operative advance, the results from the "reasons" measure may be interpreted as consistent with the operative theory.

Crowley (1975) studied 5-year-old children's memories for pictures related to seriation using one of two seriation stimuli: a fully seriated array of sticks (Stimulus III) or a "preseriated" array consisting of three small, four medium, and three large sticks (Stimulus IIB). Another group of children was shown a picture unrelated to seriation (a face). This stimulus was included to determine whether memories would improve even for a stimulus that was not directly tied to developing operative schemes.

Children were asked to reproduce the picture they had seen either after one week and four months or after four months only. Reproductions were scored according to the level of seriation, as in the earlier study by Finkel and Crowley (1973). Children who had seen the fully seriated array produced more highly seriated drawings at the one-week recall session than did children who had seen the preseriated array, although in neither group were typical reproductions fully seriated. By the four-month session, children's reproductions were equally advanced in both stimulus groups. The patterns of memory change, then, differed. Of children who were shown the fully seriated stimulus, 26% drew more advanced reproductions after four months than they had after one week, but 50% drew *less* advanced drawings at the later recall session. Of children who were shown the preseriated stimulus, 54% drew more advanced drawings at the later session, while only 12% drew less advanced drawings. No long-term memory changes were found in reproductions of the face picture.

Thus, although some long-term improvements were found with the fully seriated array, the incidence of memory regressions was greater. As in the earlier study by Finkel and Crowley (1973), more improvement was found among children who had been shown the preseriated Stimulus IIB than among those who had been shown the fully seriated array. Crowley (1975), like Furth et al. (1974), suggests that these patterns of change may be explained by strong figurative memories at the early session, but weak figurative memories at the later recall session. Under this interpretation, the one-week drawings by children who were shown the fully seriated stimulus are assumed to be artificially inflated, leaving little opportunity for improvement and much opportunity for regression. In contrast, the one-week drawings by children shown the preseriated stimulus would be operatively immature even if they were figuratively correct, and thus leave more opportunity to show operative progress and less opportunity to demonstrate operative regression. The viability of this explanation is discussed in the last section of this chapter.

4. Summary and Conclusions

Studies that have used the Genevan research paradigm have generally replicated the phenomena observed by Piaget and Inhelder (1973). Cross-sectional studies have shown that the ways in which children remember stimuli vary with age, and that these variations generally parallel age differences in operative schemes which have been documented elsewhere in Piagetian work.

Similarly, the longitudinal replication studies have generally found some children who reproduced stimuli more accurately after a long retention interval than they had after a short retention interval. The incidence of long-term improvements found in the replications, however, has been smaller than the incidence reported by Piaget and Inhelder (1973). These quantitative differences may result from the fact that the children were from different populations and/or that they were at different chronological or developmental levels. Another factor that may have contributed to the generally smaller incidence of improvements in replications is the use of shorter retention intervals. For example, in the Genevan study in which a seriated array served as the stimulus, the long-term retention interval was eight months, whereas in the replications using this stimulus, retention intervals ranged from only four to six months (see Table 10-1).

While the number of long-term improvements found in the replications has been small, the number has generally been significant when contrasted to zero improvements. Piaget and Inhelder (1973) propose that this is the contrast that should be used to evaluate the operative theory, since other theories cannot accommodate memory improvements. According to Piaget and Inhelder (1973), other mnemonic theories posit either that transformations in memory "necessarily result in mnemonic distortions or memory losses [p. 383]," as in classic associationism, or that "no memories can ever be lost or modified [p. 383–384]," as in Freudian theory.

This interpretation is, however, open to criticism, since other theories can, in fact, account for improvement in performance at later recall sessions. For example, Tulving (1974) posits that performance on a memory task can improve over a retention interval, since "changes in the retrieval environment, which we know is at least partly determined by the person's informational intake and mental activity, can become more appropriate for retrieval as well as less appropriate [p. 80]." While Tulving's view is unlike the Genevan view in that the memory trace is presumed to remain identical over time (it is the *access* to that trace which changes), both views can accommodate improvements in performance. Since few contemporary theorists hold that memories necessarily deteriorate over time, evidence that there are significantly more than zero memory improvements cannot be taken as support for only the operative approach. (A more detailed comparison between the operative approach to memory and other classic and contemporary mnemonic theories may be found in Liben, 1977.)

A second reason for questioning the validity of contrasting the number of observed memory improvements to zero is that this contrast assumes perfect measurement of memory, that is, that performance on the memory task reflects only the true value of memory, but no component of random error. It is probable, however, that variations in environmental, physiological, and motivational factors affect the child's performance on recall tasks, even without changes in underlying memory. Since these and other unidentified factors would occasionally favor performance at the later recall session, apparent "memory improvements" would be found. Unfortunately, measures of test-retest reliability have not been made in these memory studies, and thus the role of imperfect test reliability is unknown.

Another approach that may be used to evaluate the role of nonoperative factors in producing memory change is to examine the number of memory regressions. Since "operative knowing is held to be stable and developing in one direction" (Furth et al., 1974, p. 70), operatively induced changes should be consistently upward. As is evident from the preceding review, however, most studies have found at least as many memory regressions as progressions. If such regressions are attributed to momentary fluctuations in performance common in children at transitional levels (see Furth et al., 1974), it seems parsimonious (although not logically necessary) to explain progressions similarly.

The operative theory of memory cannot, therefore, be accepted simply on the basis that improvements in performance on recall tasks are found. It is also necessary to show that these improvements occur for the reasons postulated by Piaget, that is, because of the child's operative growth. In the next section, evidence bearing on the operative interpretation of long-term memory improvements is discussed.

III. AN EVALUATION OF THE OPERATIVE INTERPRETATION OF MEMORY IMPROVEMENT

A. Overview

In evaluating the operative interpretation of memory improvement, it is necessary to establish that the improvements in performance are not occurring as a result of factors unrelated to operativity. For example, performance could improve at a later session as a result of experiences gained from repeated testing (for example, practice in completing the task), or from improvements in skills unrelated to operativity per se (for example, improvement in motoric skills needed for drawing). The possible role of nonoperative factors in enhancing performance is discussed in Section III.B.

The proposition that memory improvements reflect operative growth would be strengthened not only by eliminating alternative explanations of improvements but also by showing that those children whose memories improved over time are children whose operative levels have also advanced during the retention interval. Studies in which both memory and operativity are measured within the same children provide relevant data. Findings from such studies are discussed in Section III.C.

A third area in which the operative interpretation of memory improvement must be evaluated concerns whether the observed changes in performance on recall tasks are justifiably considered to be *mnemonic* changes. A discussion of evidence related to this issue is presented in Section III.D.

B. Changes in Performance: Nonoperative Factors

1. Effects of Repeated Testing

One possible nonoperative explanation of improved performance at later recall sessions is that children have had additional practice on the memory task. Practice in retrieving stored information, practice in drawing the stimulus, and greater familiarity with the experimental situation are examples of by-products of the retest paradigm that may lead to an improvement in performance without an underlying improvement in memory. To examine the effects of repeated testing, investigators have varied the number of recall sessions across groups of children. If repeated testing has no effect on performance, then reproductions produced at the final recall session should be comparable across groups that have participated in different numbers of earlier recall sessions.

In one such investigation, Dahlem (1969) found no differences in the degree to which six-month reconstructions were seriated as a function of the number of prior memory tests (see Table 10-1 for testing schedules). In another study in which recall schedules were varied, Crowley (1975) found that repeated testing did improve the likelihood that the stimulus was remembered. However, given that the child remembered the stimulus at all, four-month reproductions were at comparable operative levels in the two groups, regardless of the inclusion or omission of an earlier recall session. Data from the remaining study in which testing schedules were varied (Finkel & Crowley, 1973) showed that repeated testing did affect performance on the memory task, in interaction with the type of stimulus. It is difficult to evaluate the meaning of this finding, however, since a recognition task was included in each recall session. Thus, the repeated-testing effect may have resulted from repeated participation in the reproduction task itself, or from exposure to the various recognition alternatives.

Additional research on the effects of repeated testing, both with and without recognition tasks, is needed to clarify these findings. If it is the use of recognition tasks that is responsible for the repeated testing effects, future memory research may continue to use the test-retest paradigm if recognition tasks are omitted from early recall sessions. In this case, however, findings from studies that included early recognition tasks (e.g., Finkel & Crowley, 1973; Murray & Bausell, 1970; several studies by Piaget & Inhelder, 1973) would be of questionable value.

If, on the other hand, it is found that participation in any early recall session influences later memory performance, it would be necessary to modify the test-retest paradigm. For example, short- versus long-term memory might be studied by testing different children after different intervals, that is, using between- rather than within-subjects designs. Another means of overcoming a repeated-testing effect would be to identify the specific aspects of retesting that lead to improvements in performance, and modify experience accordingly. For example, if the child's performance is found to be better at the second session because the child is more comfortable with the experimenter at the second meeting, the memory task might always be preceded by an extended interaction between the child and the experimenter.

Altemeyer et al. (1969) studied the potential impact of one specific aspect of the retest paradigm with a seriated array as the memory stimulus. They hypothesized that mentioning the size of the sticks at the one-week session might alert the child to the relevance of size order, and this, in turn, might lead the child to restructure his or her memory with respect to size. To test this hypothesis, two different sets of instructions were used at the one-week recall session. In one, "size" was specifically mentioned; in the second, all reference to size was avoided. No differences between the two groups' reproductions or changes in reproductions were found, leading to the rejection of the hypothesis.

2. Changes in Nonoperative Skills

Another possible explanation of improvements in performance by later recall sessions is that certain nonoperative skills tapped by the memory task are more advanced by the second recall session. Adams (1973), for example, suggested that apparent "memory improvements" would occur if children were able to understand the experimenter's demands better at the later recall session, and thus if children were made aware of the relevant aspects of the stimulus array prior to the memory task, their performance would not show the usual long-term improvements. To test this hypothesis, kindergarten children in an experimental group were given a discrimination training task in which seriation was the relevant dimension. Children in a control group were given discrimination training using geometric forms. All children were then given a standard long-term memory task in which a seriated array was used as the stimulus. Contrary to Adams' hypothesis, the patterns of memory change between one week and six months were comparable in the experimental and control groups, suggesting that improvements in performance cannot ordinarily be attributed to increased understanding of the task demands.

Improvement in drawing skills has also been suggested as a nonoperative factor that could account for better performance at later recall sessions (Piaget & Inhelder, 1973). If the child is more skilled at graphic representation in the later session, reproductions could be more accurate on the later task even though the child's memory (for example, mental image) of the stimulus is identical at both sessions.

The finding that memory improvements are also found in studies using recognition tasks argues against this hypothesis. However, since there are typically fewer memory changes with recognition tasks, and since results from recognition tasks may be suspect for reasons discussed earlier, this evidence is not conclusive. A stronger case against the hypothesized effect of improving graphic skills is derived from studies in which children are asked to copy stimuli that are in full view. If the child's operative level is near that tapped by the stimulus, the child is often able to produce an operatively correct copy, although unable to produce an operatively correct reproduction. Piaget and Inhelder (1973) found, for example, that although 3-year-old children could neither copy nor reproduce a seriated stimulus correctly, 4-year-old children could copy but not reproduce the stimulus accurately. Similarly, when kindergarten children were asked to copy a seriated stimulus that was in full view, approximately 80% were able to pattern their drawings (Altemeyer et al., 1969; Liben, 1975a). If children have the graphic skills required to pattern their drawings when a model is present, they must possess the graphic skills necessary to pattern their drawings when the model is absent as well.

3. Summary

The evidence related to nonoperative causes of memory improvements is unfortunately very limited. Of the three studies designed to evaluate the effects of repeated testing, only one found a significant testing effect. Since this study was also the only one that included a recognition task in the initial testing sessions, it is unclear whether it was the exposure to the recognition alternatives or repeated testing per se that affected later performance. Additional research is needed to evaluate these alternatives, particularly since there have been so few studies addressed to this issue, and since the relevant studies have been concerned exclusively with seriation.

If future work establishes that repeated testing affects performance only if recognition tasks are included, the continued use of the test–retest paradigm would be justified, provided that recognition tasks are omitted from early recall sessions. If, on the other hand, future work demonstrates an effect of repeated testing per se, additional research will be necessary to determine which aspects of the testing experience are responsible for the effect. If these aspects are not inextricably bound to the act of recall, it should be possible to compensate for them. If, however, it is the very act of recall that affects later performance, it would be inappropriate to continue to use within-subject, repeated-measure designs.

Another potential explanation of improvements in performance is that the child becomes increasingly skilled at meeting the nonoperative demands of the task. Although the empirical evidence suggests that progress in two areas—comprehension of task demands and drawing skills—cannot explain memory improvements, it remains possible that future research will implicate the role of other nonoperative skills in producing improvements.

To strengthen the operative explanation of long-term memory improvements, however, it is necessary to demonstrate not only that advances in nonoperative skills *cannot* account for improvements in performance on memory tasks, but also that progress in operative schemes *can* account for improvements on the memory tasks. Evidence relating operative level and memory within subjects is reviewed in the following section.

C. The Relationship Between Memory and Operative Level: Within-Subject Analyses

1. Introduction

As reviewed earlier, the finding invoked to demonstrate the relationship between operative level and memory has generally been that the errors made by children in reproducing stimuli are similar to the errors made by children of the same age on anticipatory tasks. However, given the variability in operational levels at any given age, this evidence cannot be considered conclusive. The evidence presented for the relationship between memory change and operative change has also had a circular quality. When a particular child's later reproduction is conceptually more advanced than that child's earlier reproduction, the change is attributed to underlying operative progress. When another child's memory does not improve during the same time interval, it is presumed that there has not been significant underlying operative growth.

Within-subject data on operativity and memory are needed to substantiate the relationship between the two. Piaget and Inhelder (1973) did not consistently obtain such data. More usually they simply inferred the child's operative level from age, as in the case of memory for double serial correspondences: "After six months, the distribution of memory types varied with age and hence, probably, with the operational level" (Piaget & Inhelder, 1973, p. 150). In other studies, they did assess conceptual understanding, but at the conclusion of the memory task only. For example, in the study of memory for horizontality of liquid, children were asked questions about drawings that showed liquid in impossible positions. The relationship between operative level and memory was then demonstrated by illustration with selected children's protocols. In the study of seriation memory, operativity was assessed prior to the memory task. Piaget and Inhelder (1973) reported a generally good correspondence between the two measures. Exceptions were noted, however, such that some children's reproductions were correct, but their anticipatory seriations were not. This discrepancy was attributed largely to the fact that most of these children were "taught at a private school where particular attention was paid to drawing" (Piaget & Inhelder, 1973, p. 37).

Thus, in Piaget and Inhelder's work, relationships between operativity and memory either were inferred from age or were documented by case studies, while discrepancies were explained on idiosyncratic bases. In addition to a lack of systematic evidence for the relationship between operativity and memory at any given point in time, the Genevan studies do not provide information on whether mnemonic and operative *changes* occurred in parallel. The task of systematically analyzing the relationship between memory and operativity therefore fell to later investigators. The findings from this later work are reviewed in the following section.

2. Empirical Evidence

a. Pretest or posttest assessment.   In order to study the relationship between memory and cognitive structure, Dahlem (1969) gave all children a "transfer task" following the six-month seriation reconstruction task. For this task, the largest of ten equilateral triangles was glued at the far left of the bottom of a piece of cardboard, the smallest at the far right, with the sixth and seventh triangles glued in their correct positions. Children were asked to complete the triangle picture. Dahlem found that while the relationship between the children's performance on the memory task and their performance on the transfer task was significant, perfect prediction was not possible: Of the 40 children who had reconstructed the memory stimulus without error, 12 did not order the triangles in the transfer task perfectly. On the other hand, of the 89 children who had performed imperfectly on the memory task, 8 performed perfectly on the transfer task. It is possible that these mismatches resulted from relatively superficial differences between the two tasks rather than from differences in the underlying mechanisms. For example, the memory and transfer tasks used different materials (sticks versus triangles), and provided different degrees of initial seriation (four triangles, but no sticks, were glued in place at the beginning of the task).

Murray and Bausell (1970) also examined the relationship between memory and conceptual level. As described earlier (pages 306–309), first- and second-grade children were given conservation, seriation, and horizontality problems prior to tests of immediate memory. Among the conservation stimuli, the evidence for a relation between operative level and memory was mixed: Performance on the conservation of number task was significantly associated with recall of the number stimulus, but performance on the conservation of amount and length tasks was not significantly associated with recall of the related memory stimuli. Conceptual performance on the seriation task was significantly related to reproduction, but not to recognition. On the horizontality task, very few children either anticipated or remembered the water level as horizontal, so that no meaningful information about the relation between conceptual level and memory was obtained with this task.

The findings from this study, then, provide only scattered evidence for the relationship between conceptual level and memory. It should be noted again, however, that the criteria used for classifying reproductions as correct included highly figurative components of the stimuli (for example, in the conservation of length problem the dark stick had to be displaced to the right), and this factor may have attenuated the correspondence between memory and operative level.

Although Murray and Bausell (1970) assessed operative level prior to giving the memory tasks, other researchers (e.g., Finkel & Crowley, 1973) have assumed that such pretest assessment would interfere with performance on subsequent memory tasks. More recently, several studies have obtained within-subject data on operative and mnemonic change, and have, in addition, examined the effects of pretest operative assessment on memory and posttest operative performance. Data from these studies are reviewed below.

b. Pretest and posttest assessment. Liben (1974) used a within-subject design in the study of long-term memory for horizontality described earlier (page 312). Fifth-grade children in one group were given an operative assessment task both prior to and following the memory task, while children in a second group were given the assessment task following the memory task only. The data showed no significant differences between the two groups' final mnemonic and final operative performance. This finding is contrary to the assumption that operative assessment necessarily interferes with memory, and helps justify the use of within-subject designs to study the relation between operativity and memory.

The findings concerning the relationship between operative level and memory were mixed. Supporting the operative position was the finding that there were significant correlations between performance on the operative assessment tasks and the memory task at both the beginning and the end of the study. The operative position was weakened, however, by the findings that these correlations were low and that changes in memory and operative level did not occur in parallel.

One possible explanation of the failure to find a strong relationship between operative level and memory in this study is the choice of stimulus for the memory task. Although Piaget and Inhelder (1973) and subsequent investigators (Furth et al., 1974; Murray & Bausell, 1970) have used pictures of partly filled, tipped containers as memory stimuli, recent work has shown that the horizontality of liquid is not always understood even by adolescents and adults (e.g., Harris, Hanley, & Best, 1975; Liben, 1975c; Thomas, Jamison, & Hummel, 1973), and thus, the progression of the horizontality concept may be developmentally uneven. Other possible explanations for the weakness of the relationship found by Liben (1974) include the highly abbreviated assessment procedure and the relatively uninteresting nature of the stimulus. These problems were minimized in a subsequent study (Liben, 1975b) by using an extensive operative assessment and interesting pictorial stimuli related to seriation, verticality, and horizontality concepts (see Figure 10-1). As in the earlier study, children in one group were assessed both before and after the memory task, while children in a second group were assessed after the memory task only.

A comparison of the two groups' reproductions indicated that memory was not significantly affected by initial operative assessment in either kindergarten or fourth grade. A comparison of the two groups' performance on the final operative assessment task revealed only one area of effect: Specifically, kindergarten boys' final scores on spatial tasks were higher in the group given the operative pretest.

The within-subject data from this study again provided only weak support for the operative approach. That is, there were significant but quantitatively small associations between performance on the operative assessment tasks and the related memory tasks, and in addition, the change data on the two measures did not correspond. This was true regardless of the criteria used to define change (that is, large or small shifts).

Crowley (1975) also included operative assessment tasks in her study of long-term memory for seriation stimuli described earlier (page 314). Half the children were tested for their understanding of seriation prior to the memory tasks, while all children were so tested following the memory task. The two groups did not differ on either later memory or conceptual assessment tasks, again providing justification for using the within-subject design.

In support of the hypothesized relationship between operative level and memory was the finding that children's performance on the seriation pretest did not differ significantly from performance on the one-week reproduction task. (This was true for both stimuli shown in Table 10-1.) Similarly, the developmental levels of children's performance on the seriation posttest did not differ significantly from the levels shown in their four-month reproductions. However, as in the other studies in which intrasubject data were collected, changes in operative level and memory were not parallel over the four-month period.

In studying long-term memory for conservation or nonconservation reasoning, Samuels (1974) collected data on operative level and memory within subjects. One week prior to showing the videotapes described earlier (pages 313–314), children were tested for their understanding of conservation of number. (Since all children were given this pretest, data concerning the effects of pretesting are not available from this study.)

As described earlier, most scorable "recalls" at all memory sessions matched the conservation or nonconservation reasoning, as witnessed. Thus, no relationship could be found between operative level and memory, or between operative change and memory change. There was, however, a significant relationship between the child's operative stage and the "reasons" measure at the one-day recall session: When shown the nonconservation tapes, children who were at the highest level of conservation on the pretest were significantly more likely than children at lower levels to explain that one child had more cars because of having "taken" more cars. The number of "take" reasons did increase by the five-month session, as might be expected under the operative theory. However, these increases occurred indiscriminately among children who saw conservation or nonconservation tapes, among children at various levels of conceptual understanding of conservation, and among children who did, or did not, progress operatively. Thus, Samuels' within-subject data provided little support for the Genevan position.

3. Summary and Conclusions

In summary, the within-subject data provide limited support for the hypothesis that memories and operative levels are related. Significant associations have been found between performance on memory tasks and performance on operative assessment tasks. These relationships have not, however, been strong, with occasional disconfirmations occurring (for example, children who reproduce stimuli accurately despite poor performance on the operative assessment task). In addition, there has been virtually no support for the hypothesis that changes in memory and operativity occur in parallel.

While these data may indicate that the operative interpretation of memory is inadequate, they may also result from methodological problems. For example, although the same fundamental processes may underlie both mnemonic and anticipatory tasks, children's attention and interest may be engaged differentially by the two tasks. Furthermore, the very precautions that have been taken to reduce intertask confusion (for example, use of figuratively different materials, different experimenters) may have inadvertently reduced intertask comparability, particularly for children in conceptually transitional stages (see Flavell, 1971; Flavell & Wohlwill, 1969). In addition, failure to find a significant relationship between changes in memory and changes in operative level may result largely from the fact that change scores compound two measurement errors (e.g., see Nunnally, 1973).

Another explanation of the poor relationship between memory and operative level, and between memory change and operative change, is that there is a strong figurative influence on the child's early reproduction which dissipates by the later recall session. While this hypothesis can account for otherwise troublesome data, it also represents theoretical difficulties that are discussed in the concluding section (IV) of this chapter.

D. The Role of Authentic Memory

1. Introduction

Another critical question in the evaluation of the operative approach to memory is whether the phenomena noted by Piaget and Inhelder (1973) are truly memory phenomena. This question was asked in its extreme form by Altemeyer et al. (1969) as "Is memory involved at all? [p. 853]." The answer to this form of the question must be "yes," since with rare exceptions children match the content of stimuli, a feat that would be impossible on the basis of chance. It is possible, however, that the *operative* components of the child's reproductions (e.g., the seriation of the sticks, the horizontality of the liquid) are not dependent on recall of the original stimulus, but are instead formulated *de novo* on the basis of the child's existing strategies and knowledge, both of which become increasingly advanced over time.

2. Empirical Evidence

a. Primitive stimuli.   One approach that has been used to evaluate whether the child's reproductions actually reflect the stimulus per se, and become increasingly like that stimulus over time, is to use stimuli that are operatively primitive in the memory task. The findings from these studies implicate the role of general response strategies in that children seeing operatively primitive stimuli generally show changes in their reproductions toward higher operative levels. For example, Altemeyer et al. (1969) found that children's reproductions became increasingly seriated over time, regardless of whether a fully seriated array or a random array of sticks was used as the stimulus. Similarly, Liben (1974) found that even children who were shown a primitive, nonhorizontal stimulus produced increasingly more advanced drawings (with respect to horizontality) over time. It should be noted, however, that when extremely primitive stimuli are used (as in the studies by Altemeyer et al., 1969, and Liben, 1974), there is little opportunity for operative deterioration and much room for operative progress.

Although these results suggest that the *direction* of change is generally toward higher operative levels regardless of the operative level of the stimulus, it is also true that the operative levels of reproductions are influenced by the stimulus. For example, although Liben (1974) found that changes in reproductions followed a similar direction among children who saw primitive and advanced horizontality stimuli, the absolute levels of reproductions differed in the two groups. At both one-week and six-month recall sessions, children shown the correct stimulus most commonly reproduced the liquid as horizontal, whereas children shown the primitive stimulus most commonly reproduced the liquid as parallel to the base of the tipped bottle.

b. Omission of mnemonic stimuli. The role of changing response strategies in producing memory improvements has also been investigated with tasks that activate response strategies in the absence of memory stimuli. For example, Dahlem (1969) included control subjects who were not shown a seriated stimulus in the original session, but were instead shown pairs of pictures and asked to indicate which of the two they preferred. At varying time intervals thereafter (six months only; one week and six months; immediately, one week, and six months), these children were given the materials needed to construct the seriated stimulus shown to children in experimental groups, and were instructed to "make a stick picture" (Dahlem, 1969, p. 101). The control children typically used the sticks as crayons or building blocks, with only two children making perfectly seriated arrays at the six-month session. On this basis, Dahlem (1969) concluded that the perfect reproductions made by children in the experimental groups were based on authentic memory rather than on general response strategies.

Altemeyer et al. (1969) used a related approach by giving kindergarten through second-grade children a "spontaneous drawing task." Children were told that the experimenter was "thinking about some sticks" (p. 854), and were asked to draw a picture like the one the experimenter was thinking about. These investigators reasoned that if older children are more likely than younger children to apply seriation schemes spontaneously in a memory task, they should be more likely to produce patterned drawings in this task as well. No support for this hypothesis was found. In fact, very few seriated drawings were produced by children of any age.

The vagueness of the hint used by Altemeyer et al. (1969) left so much of the drawing to the child's imagination that other age differences in completing the task may have obscured any age differences in the spontaneous tendency to seriate (Liben, 1975a). To test this hypothesis, Liben (1975a) gave kindergarten through third-grade children the task used by Altemeyer et al. (1969), but examined drawings for other age-related changes. As before, few seriated drawings were found. However, other age differences were evident: In the unseriated drawings of younger children the sticks were usually arranged randomly, whereas in the unseriated drawings of older children the sticks were incorporated into objects such as tepees, log cabins, and campfires. To determine if more information could eliminate these confounding age differences and thereby uncover age differences in the tendency to seriate, children in a second group were given a more informative hint in which the different sizes and upright position of the sticks were mentioned. With this hint, older children did produce seriated drawings significantly more often than did younger children.

The findings from this study indicate that changing response strategies may, in part, account for the apparent improvements in long-term memory found in other investigations. The results of all three studies demonstrate the role of "authentic" memory as well. First, simply giving vague information about the stimulus (as in Altemeyer et al., 1969) or providing the stimulus materials (as in Dahlem, 1969) did not lead children to make drawings or constructions like those produced in memory studies. Second, even in the study in which a developmental trend toward increasing seriation was found (Liben, 1975a), the patterns of response were still not entirely like those typically produced in memory tasks. For example, with comparable groups of kindergarten children, more than twice as many perfectly seriated drawings were produced by children who were given the memory task (Liben, 1975b) than by children who were given the highly informative hint (Liben, 1975a).

3. Summary and Conclusions

The findings from both types of studies just reviewed suggest that the operative components of reproductions are influenced both by the operative level depicted in the stimulus and by the child's response strategies. While there is little question that the former is reasonably conceptualized as mnemonic, it has been suggested that the latter is not (e.g., Altemeyer et al., 1969; Carey, 1971). However, insofar as response strategies are considered to be part of the reconstructive process used at the time of retrieval, changes in strategies are justifiably interpreted as part of the memory process (Liben, 1977). Operativity is thus shown to influence memory during the retrieval process, an interpretation consistent with Piaget and Inhelder's (1973) assertion that schemes influence the memory at the time of recall as well as during memory fixation and retention.

IV. CONCLUSIONS

The evidence reviewed earlier in this chapter shows that the empirical findings reported by Piaget and Inhelder (1973) are replicable. Studies that included children of different ages have shown that the developmental levels of reproductions and the patterns of memory change correspond to the differing cognitive levels of the age groups tested. Furthermore, in almost all investigations in which memory was studied longitudinally, some long-term memory improvements were found.

Although the phenomena themselves are replicable, the Genevan interpretation of these phenomena cannot be accepted uncritically. While longitudinal studies have consistently shown some improvements in long-term memory, the number of these improvements is generally significant only if contrasted to zero. As discussed earlier, this comparison may be criticized both because it fails to account for random error and because it implies that the only viable alternative theory of memory is classic associationism, an alternative endorsed by few contemporary theorists (Kausler, 1970).

The operative theory cannot, then, be confirmed simply by the existence of long-term memory improvements. To support the operative explanation, it is necessary to show both that nonoperative mechanisms do not account for the memory improvements and that operative growth is linked with memory growth.

Research findings related to the first of these issues suggest that improvements in auxiliary skills (for example, drawing ability) cannot explain the observed improvements. The evidence also suggests that repeated testing does not in itself affect performance, although exposure to alternatives in recognition tasks may. Additional research is needed to determine whether by-products of the retest paradigm enhance performance at the later recall sessions, and/or whether there are developments in essentially extraneous skills that can account for the improvements in reproductions.

To evaluate the proposal that memory improvement occurs as a function of operative growth, the relationship between operative level and memory has been examined within individual children. The results from studies using within-subject designs support the Piagetian position insofar as scores on operative tasks and memory tasks have generally been significantly related at single points in time. However, the Genevan position is undermined by the fact that performance on the two measures has been only weakly related, has occasionally been strikingly asynchronous (for example, children with poor performance on the operative task and perfect performance on the reproduction tasks), and has not changed in parallel over the long-term retention interval.

There are several possible explanations for the negative findings, in addition to the obvious possibility that the operative theory of memory is incorrect. One alternative is that random error accounts for the observed inconsistencies. If the measures used are not highly reliable, then the correspondence between memory and operativity would be poor, spurious memory regressions would occur, and change scores would be virtually meaningless. If, however, the negative findings are attributed to measurement error, it is reasonable to suppose that memory improvements are attributable to the same cause as well. Before findings on long-term memory can be evaluated meaningfully, the test–retest reliability of both memory and assessment tasks must be assessed.

Another possible explanation of the failure to find a closer relationship between performance on memory tasks and performance on operative tasks is that the procedures used in the two tasks have not been comparable. Investigators who have used within-subject designs have intentionally attempted to differentiate the operative and memory tasks, usually by using different experimenters and by using figuratively different materials. While these tasks have been presumed to be operatively equivalent, such equivalences have not been established empirically, and it is possible that the very procedures employed to reduce intertask confusion have reduced intertask comparability. Batteries of figuratively different but operatively equivalent tasks should be developed for studies using within-subject designs.

A third explanation of the negative findings—the high incidence of regressions, the imperfect match between operative level and memory and between operative change and memory change—is that children's early reproductions are largely figurative, and only later fall under operative control (Crowley, 1975; Furth et al., 1974; Liben, 1974). If children's reproductions are artificially inflated at the early recall session, the relationship between performance on operative tasks and performance on memory tasks would be attenuated. Furthermore, if figurative memory fades by the later recall session and the child's operative level remains immature, long-term memory would regress. Such regressions could occur even if the child had progressed operatively during the retention interval, provided that the child's final operative level remained inferior to that depicted by the original memory stimulus.

There are, however, two major problems with this explanation. The first is that unless there is a way to determine when a particular reproduction is "figurative" or "operative," the explanation is untestable. The second difficulty is that this explanation seems to dilute the very operative explanation of memory it is trying to save, since it suggests that operativity may not affect memory for weeks or even months after the stimulus was viewed. This description seems foreign to the highly integrated nature of the operative and figurative processes proposed by Piaget (Piaget, 1970; Piaget & Inhelder, 1971). Without the integration of the operative and figurative processes, the operative conception of memory loses its distinctiveness, and the fading figurative memory becomes fundamentally like the deteriorating memory trace of associationism. Thus, while this explanation can account for the empirical data, it does not do so satisfactorily within the context of operative theory.

In summary, findings from group analyses have generally been compatible with the operative theory of memory, but those from finer, within-subject analyses have revealed inconsistencies. Possible explanations of these inconsistencies have been suggested. Future work must evaluate these and other explanations not only with respect to their empirical testability and validity, but also with respect to their fit with fundamental concepts in Piagetian theory.

Whether the operative theory of memory is ultimately accepted or rejected, it is likely to have an important impact on the study of memory development. Other developmental psychologists who have studied memory have typically been concerned with memory capacity or with the development of skills used in encoding and decoding information, rather than with the changing forms in which information is stored. At the same time, psychologists who have been concerned with changes in the ways information is coded over time (for example, Gestalt psychologists: see Riley, 1962; Bartlett, 1932) have generally ignored developmental change. Piaget and Inhelder (1973) have combined these approaches and have thus provided a uniquely developmental perspective from which memory can be viewed.

ACKNOWLEDGMENT

Preparation of this chapter was partially supported by a grant from the University of Rochester, Rochester, New York.

REFERENCES

Adams, W. Effect of pretraining on long-term memory improvement. *Developmental Psychology*, 1973, *9*, 433.

Altemeyer, R., Fulton, D., & Berney, K. Long-term memory improvement: Confirmation of a finding by Piaget. *Child Development*, 1969, *40*, 845–857.

Bartlett, F. *Remembering: A study in experimental and social psychology*. Cambridge: Cambridge University Press, 1932.

Carey. P. An information-processing interpretation of Piaget's memory experiments. Paper presented at the biennial meeting of the Society for Research in Child Development, Minneapolis, 1971.

Crowley, C. The development of the concept of seriation and its role in short- and long-term memory of fully seriated and preseriation arrays. Unpublished doctoral dissertation, University of Washington, 1975.

Dahlem, N. Reconstructive memory in kindergarten children revisited. *Psychonomic Science*, 1969, *17*, 101–102.

Dahlem, N. Reconstructive memory in children revisited. *Psychonomic Science*, 1969, *17*, 101–102.

Duckworth, E. Piaget rediscovered. In R. Ripple & V. Rockcastle (Eds.), *Piaget rediscovered*. Ithaca, N.Y.: Cornell University Press, 1964.

Finkel, D., & Crowley, C. Improvement in children's long-term memory for seriated sticks: Change in memory storage or coding rules? Paper presented at the biennial meeting of the Society for Research in Child Development, Philadelphia, 1973.

Flavell, J. Stage-related properties of cognitive development. *Cognitive Psychology*, 1971, *2*, 421–453.

Flavell, J., & Wohlwill, J. Formal and functional aspects of cognitive development. In D. Elkind & J. Flavell (Eds.), *Studies in cognitive development*. New York: Oxford University Press, 1969.

Furth, H., Ross, B., & Youniss, J. Operative understanding in children's immediate and long-term reproductions of drawings. *Child Development*, 1974, *45*, 63–70.

Harris, L. J., Hanley, C., & Best, C. T. Conservation of horizontality: Sex differences in sixth-graders and college students. Paper presented at the biennial meeting of the Society for Research in Child Development, Denver, 1975.

Inhelder, B. Memory and intelligence in the child. In D. Elkind & J. Flavell (Eds.), *Studies in cognitive development*. New York: Oxford University Press, 1969.

Kausler, D. Retention—Forgetting as a nomological network for developmental research. In L. Goulet & P. Baltes (Eds.), *Life-span developmental psychology*. New York: Academic Press, 1970.

Liben, L. Operative understanding of horizontality and its relation to long-term memory. *Child Development*, 1974, *45*, 416–424.

Liben, L. Evidence for developmental differences in spontaneous seriation and its implications for past research on long-term memory improvement. *Developmental Psychology,* 1975, *11,* 121–125. (a)

Liben, L. Long-term memory for pictures related to seriation, horizontality, and verticality concepts. *Developmental Psychology,* 1975, *11,* 795–806. (b)

Liben, L. Adolescents' Euclidean concepts: Effects of sex, cognitive style, and intellectual abilities. Paper presented at the annual meeting of the American Psychological Association, Chicago, 1975. (c).

Liben, L. Memory from a cognitive-developmental perspective: A theoretical and empirical review. In W. Overton & J. Gallagher (Eds.), *Knowledge and development, Volume 1: Advances in research and theory.* New York: Plenum, 1977.

Murray, F., & Bausell, R. Memory and conservation. *Psychonomic Science,* 1970, *21,* 334–335.

Murray, F., & Bausell, R. Memory and conservation. Paper presented at the biennial meeting of the Society for Research in Child Development, Minneapolis, 1971.

Nunnally, J. Research strategies and measurement methods for investigating human development. In J. Nesselroade & H. Reese (Eds.), *Life-span developmental psychology.* New York: Academic Press, 1973.

Piaget, J. Piaget's theory. In P. Mussen (Ed.), *Carmichael's manual of child psychology.* New York: Wiley, 1970.

Piaget, J., & Inhelder, B. *Mental imagery in the child.* New York: Basic Books, 1971.

Piaget, J., & Inhelder, B. *Memory and intelligence.* New York: Basic Books, 1973.

Riley, D. Memory for form. In L. Postman (Ed.), *Psychology in the making.* New York: Knopf, 1962.

Samuels, M. Children's long-term memory for events. Unpublished doctoral dissertation, Cornell University, 1974.

Thomas, H., Jamison, W., & Hummel, D. Observation is insufficient for discovering that the surface of still water is invariantly horizontal. *Science,* 1973, *181,* 173–174.

Tulving, E. Cue-dependent forgetting. *American Scientist,* 1974, *62,* 74–82.

11

The Role of Memory as a System in Making Transitive Inferences

Tom Trabasso

Institute of Child Development
University of Minnesota

I. INTRODUCTION

If you read a sentence like:

(1)   The preoperational child *does not* make a transitive inference. *A* is greater than *C (A > C)*, given the information that *A > B* and *B > C*

would you interpret this to mean that a child under seven years of age either (1a) *cannot* or (1b) *may not* make such inferences? The semantic interpretation of (1) given in (1a) or (1b) is important because the first inference, (1a), implies that the child does not have the ability to reason logically and is an assertion about competence. Implicit in the second inference (1b), is the recognition that the demands of a task and performance factors may obscure or prevent the manifestation of the child's reasoning (as well as other cognitive) abilities.

The central objective of this chapter is to convince you that (1a) is an incorrect inference and to provide an interpretation consistent with (1b) but much richer in its theoretical content and implications. The subject of the chapter is a case history of a single test item that operationally defines the textbook sentence (1). The case begins by asking you to be a willing subject on the item and to submit your own behavior to analysis while answering the question. Various diagnoses of your performance follow, and the case is developed as my colleagues and I have come to understand it.

A. An Example of a Transitive Reasoning Test Item

Suppose you were taking an "intelligence" test and you came across the following item (adapted from Burt, 1919):

(1) Edith is fairer than Suzanne.
(2) Edith is darker than Lili.
(3) Who is the darkest?

Now we ask three "textbook" psychologists, each representing a different tradition, to analyze or interpret your performance. The first, a psychometrician, is interested in intelligence testing per se; the second, a developmental psychologist, adheres to a Piagetian view; the third, a cognitive psychologist, is concerned with human information processing. These three persons are, of course, fictitious, but their views are not. At the risk of caricaturing them, we now turn to their respective interpretations of your answer.

1. A Psychometric Interpretation

Of first concern to the psychometrician would be whether you "succeed" or "fail" on the item. He interprets the task as being a test of "reasoning" ability. The item, he asserts, requires you to draw an inference from premises. By definition, if A, B, C form a transitive order, then it follows that $A > C$, given $A > B$, $B > C$. The item provides an "operational definition" of the reasoning ability it purports to measure.

Burt (1919) found that it is not until about age 11 that children reach about a 50% success rate on the item. Likewise, the item "discriminates" between persons who differ in reasoning ability. Performance on the item is correlated with age, correlates with other items in the test, correlates with performance on standard IQ tests, correlates with grades in school, and is, therefore, a "valid" predictor of intelligence.

A key assumption of our fictional mental tester lies in his operational definition. By this, the item may be *described* as having a logical structure that reflects the formal logical structure of an ordered syllogism. It is further assumed that this description of the test item structure corresponds to that of the thinking involved in the solution of the problem. The latter assumption, we shall see, is false.

2. A Piagetian View

The second psychologist comes from a tradition that shares some assumptions with the first. In particular, he notes that the formal logical structure contained in the item corresponds to that for making a transitive inference. He is also concerned with the age of the person, since performance on a transitive inference task is determined by the development of certain grouping structures (see Flavell,

1963). Since this item is "abstract" or entirely verbal, then it should not be performed "correctly" until the person is in a stage of formal operations. Citing Piaget (1921, 1970), he might point out to you that reasoning abilities associated with formal operational thought are critical to a full understanding of measuring, making comparisons, and ordering events. In particular, "failures" to respond correctly are of diagnostic interest (cf. Smedslund, 1969), since they tell you about the "absence" of certain mental abilities, operations, or structures. An incorrect answer for an item would indicate a failure on the child's part to appreciate reversible, asymmetric relations (that is, since $A > B$, then $B < A$) and possibly a failure to "coordinate" relations (that is, $A > C$ if one uses B as a middle term to relate them; cf. Piaget, 1970).

As with the psychometrician, the Piagetian places much faith in the assumed correspondence between the formal description of the item and mental operations. Neither psychologist has an explicit model of the psychological processes involved in the solution of the problem; both rely instead on a presumed set of logical operations inherent in the structure of the test item itself.

In order to guard against errors in diagnosis, some workers in the Piagetian tradition (Smedslund, 1969; Youniss & Furth, 1973) have made explicit criteria that must be satisfied if a person's response is to be judged as indicating "true transitivity." For example, you might be asked to justify your answer or to solve other "control" items that would reflect whether or not you were using "pseudotransitive" solutions. This attempt to measure "pure" cases of reasoning is critical if one is trying to determine when such operations are acquired and the sequence of emergence among different kinds of logical structures. However, one must recognize that the theory is assumed to be true and that the central emphasis is on logical operations (and a particular logic at that); psychological processes, including those involving what have been traditionally called perception, memory, and language, play a minimal role, since the interest is in measurement of an assumed structure.

3. An Information-Processing Position

Our third analysis of performance is given by the cognitive psychologist. He believes intelligence to be the ability of an individual to adapt to different environments (Simon, 1969), and his analysis of how you deal with the task follows from his view of intelligence. He begins as did the first two psychologists: He looks at the test and asks himself, What demands does it place on the person? He recognizes that an inferential component is required. That is, you must work out, in some way, that Suzanne is darker than Lili from the information that Suzanne is darker than Edith and Edith is darker than Lili. He notes that the information in the premises is not in a form that allows you to deduce the answer directly. Since the premises are sentences, they must be interpreted semantically and held in working memory. The question must also be interpreted and then used to scan the information in the premises. Since the question involves a comparative term, *darker,* that does not agree or is not congruent (Clark, 1969a) with one of the premises, you must achieve congruence by transforming the first premise from "Edith is fairer than Suzanne" to "Suzanne is darker than Edith." Still, holding in memory the transformed premise, you could now form an ordered series, coordinating Suzanne, Edith, and Lili on a scale of darkness. Then, from this internal representation of a linear order, you could literally "read off" the first name in the list, Suzanne.

According to the cognitive psychologist, you have not performed a transitive inference per se; that is, you did not follow a logical algorithm to deduce the answer, nor did you necessarily "coordinate" A with C via the middle term B. Rather, you coded the problem linguistically using a set of symbols including names and ordered relations. Once encoded, you had to retain the information from the premises and the question in working memory and operate on these encodings. You may also have recognized that you would have to "decode" this information later to fit the requirements of the task. Of particular interest to our information-processing psychologist is the way in which you encoded the information—*how you interpreted the premises semantically and how you represented the interpretation internally.* This representation is critical, since the internal description of the problem space, when operated on, may or may not lead to the solution of the problem as stated by the experimenter. He notes that you "transformed" one premise and that this is a general characteristic of internal representations; that is, they are capable of being recoded or transformed. The linear order of Suzanne, Edith, and Lili may be represented by different symbol systems: as a list, as a spatial array, or as a set of categories, "dark," "medium," and "fair." Of central concern to him is that you *were able to construct a representation of the task and that you operated on that representation in order to draw the inference.*

Having constructed a representation of Suzanne, Edith, and Lili as a linear order, you could then scan this order and match the comparative label in the question to that which matches it (cf. Clark, 1969a), that is, "darker" and "darkest." If the label of the question and that of the scale match, then you terminate your processing by stating, "Suzanne."

Note that several processes are described, all of which fall under the general rubric of memory as understood by cognitive psychologists: encoding, representing, recoding, transforming, ordering, listing, scanning, matching, and retrieving, to name a few. The selection of these process descriptions was deliberate, for each of them is a part of cognition in general; each is a part of what we mean by memory as a general information-processing system; and each of them has its own logic in the sense that they are orderly processes and we can describe their contents and rules of operation. None of them, however, can be conveniently summarized by an algorithm of formal logic: $A > B, B > C, \therefore A > C$.

Thus, the third psychologist takes issue with the first two. He says he is more concerned with what you do or how you solve the problem. He has no a priori commitment to measuring your performance relative to others or to an assumed set of logical structures. He wants you to "tell" him what your mental operations are or at least allow him to infer them and to test these inferences by means of critical experiments.

In the remainder of the chapter, I shall present and discuss evidence that my colleagues and I have found favoring the position of the information-processing psychologist. First, the relationship between performance on inferential tests and memory as retention or retrieval of the premises is established. Then the nature of what is coded in a transitive reasoning task is examined. Following this, a model for the construction of an internal representation of the elements in the syllogism is presented. Finally, the implications of this research for developmental psychology and mental testing are discussed.

II. IS MEMORY RELATED TO REASONING?

Memory, in the narrow sense of retention of the premises, would seem to be a necessary but not sufficient condition for answering an inference question. In most studies done on transitive reasoning (see Smedslund, 1969), the premises are not present for the child to examine throughout the test as they were in the item just described. Rather, each premise is demonstrated by a physical comparison and then removed. Consequently, failure to retain the information from either premise may prevent the construction of a representation or the carrying out of the necessary operations that lead to an inference.

This problem led Bryant and Trabasso (1971) to reexamine the issue of transitive reasoning by children in the "preoperational" stage, 4 to 7 years of age. Their procedures, which formed the basis for much of the research to be discussed here, were devised to answer a simple question: Is a child's ability to retrieve information about the premises related to his answers on inferential questions? The answer from the initial Bryant and Trabasso experiment and from several studies conducted subsequently (reviewed by Trabasso, 1975) is a consistent "yes."

A. The Bryant and Trabasso Study

Bryant and Trabasso (1971) had children learn color codes to relate differences in length between adjacent pairs of sticks in a series of five sticks. Thus, the children, 4 to 7 years of age, learned to make pairwise discriminations on the basis of color for four pairs: (1, 2), (2, 3), (3, 4), and (4, 5). On a given training trial, they were shown a pair of sticks that did not differ in length when viewed, but differed in color, and were asked one of two possible comparative questions:

"Which is longer?" or "Which is shorter?" The child made a choice and then was told the correct relation, for example, "Red is longer than Blue" or "Blue is shorter than Red." In one kind of feedback condition, the children could see the actual lengths of the sticks; in another, the relation was only stated verbally. Training continued until the child made six correct consecutive choices to each pair of sticks in a random series of all adjacent pairs. A test sequence followed in which the child was asked either of the two comparative questions on all ten possible pairs of sticks. The child received feedback as to the correctness of the answer during the test phase. Thus, information was obtained on retention of the four pairs in training (the premises), and on inference pairs of two kinds: those involving the end anchors of the series (1 or 5) and those involving the intermediate pair (2, 4). It is important to note that sticks 2 and 4 were both "longer" and "shorter" throughout training, whereas sticks 1 and 5 were always "shorter" or "longer." (For a similar problem, see Youniss and Murray, 1970, who along with Bryant and Trabasso, adopted these five-term series problems to satisy diagnostic criteria raised by Smedslund, 1969.)

The performance of these preoperational children was well above chance expectations, ranging from 78 to 92% correct on four critical, inferential tests involving pair (2, 4). More than half of the 25 children in each of the three age group—4-, 5-, and 6-year-olds—showed perfect performance on the inference tests. Furthermore, performance was quite similar for the two types of feedback, indicating that the children could comprehend comparative information in the absence of concrete references other than color codes.

The test data and correlations can be better understood in a larger context that includes data from the replications of this initial study. Trabasso (1975) described some 29 different groups of children, adolescents, and adults, comprising some 379 subjects in all, who were trained and tested with these procedures. The correlation between the mean percent correct in retrieval of the critical premises (2, 3) and (3, 4) with mean proportion correct answers on the inference question (2, 4) was very high and positive ($r = .80$, $p < .01$).

For children and mentally retarded subjects in the 4- to 7-year-old age range, the data in terms of proportion correct responses in the test series are given in Table 11-1.

The data in Table 11-1 have been arranged according to accuracy of performance on five kinds of pairs tested. We note first that overall performance was substantially above chance levels and that performance was exceptionally high when both end pairs were present. Second, children were only slightly less accurate on tests involving the long anchor, followed by tests for the short anchor. This effect is perfectly consistent with those found by Clark (1969a) and others on adults and reflects the well-known *lexical marking* effect. Presumably, "long," which is used neutrally, is unmarked, of positive polarity, more frequent, and therefore, more available than "short." The term *long* occurs more frequently in English usage than does *short*. Further, *long* can be used both to

TABLE 11-1
Summary Test Data for 16 Conditions Involving Children
4–7 Years of Age[a]

Type of test pair	Mean percent correct	N^b
Both anchors (1, 5)	95.8	1228
Long anchor (2, 5) (3, 5) (4, 5)	94.2	3684
Short anchor (1, 2) (1, 3) (1, 4)	92.9	3684
Premise (2, 3) (3, 4)	87.0	2456
Inference (2, 4)	84.3	1228

[a] These data are from 16 different conditions (five from Bryant and Trabasso, 1971; three from an unpublished study on retraining by Bryant and Trabasso but described by Trabasso, 1975; two from Lutkus and Trabasso, 1974; two from Riley and Trabasso, 1974; four from Trabasso, 1975, which replicated the original Bryant and Trabasso study).
[b] N is the number of tests times the number of children; there were a total of 307 children.

name and to describe a portion of the length scale. For example, you can say that a stick is nine inches long or ask, "How long is it?" You do not describe a stick as nine inches short and describe its length. Nor would you ask, "How short is it?" unless you were comparing the stick to some other standard length or an anticipated length. Long tends to be positive in valence or preferred; short tends to be negative in valence and not preferred. All of these factors play a role in the onset of usage of *long* versus *short* and in their relative ease of processing.

In Table 11-1, performance on the premises is only slightly better than performance on the inference tests. Thus, the substantial effect of the Bryant-Trabasso training and test procedures is noted for inferences that involve end anchors and for those that do not.

B. Other Evidence for the Relationship Between Premise Retention and Inferential Performance

Another way to show that ability to perform inferences is related to retention of the premises is to vary the degree of training the children receive. Increases in performance on the inference tests associated with training have been demonstrated in four studies.

The first study involved the 4-year-old children in the original experiment by Bryant and Trabasso (1971) and is reported by Trabasso (1975). Of the original 20 children who scored 78% correct on inferences after being trained in the visual feedback condition, 17 were retested twice following retraining. As before, *no* feedback occurred on test trials. The percentage of correct responses on the inference pair (2, 4) increased to 84 and 93% on the respective tests.

Stetson (1974) had 7-, 9-, and 11-year-old children read stories involving transitive relations among various persons or things. An example of one of her stories involving transitive orders was:

One day, Jane was playing in the yard.
She saw four friends from school.
The friends were different sizes.
Fred was bigger than Becky.
Becky was bigger than Victor,
and Victor was bigger than Cindy.

After hearing a story, the children were asked if they had heard or recognized a sentence in the story. Recognition tests included sentences in the paragraph and sentences that were either appropriate or inappropriate inferences from those included in the paragraph.

The stories were repeated for the child until he correctly recognized the premises from the passage. Stetson found that the performance on inferred relations increased with age. On inference tests after the first presentation of the premises, the respective percentage correct was 80, 94, and 96% for the three age levels.

Younger children required more trials to reach the criterion of two consecutive correct recognitions on true and false premises. However, when all children met the criterion correct recognition of inferences was independent of age. Here the percentage correct on inference tests was 95, 97, and 97% for the 7-, 9- and 11-year-olds, respectively. Furthermore, for the children who had perfect recognition of the premises, the proportion of inferences recognized correctly was .87; for those showing chance recognition, it was .63. These conditional probabilities reflect the dependence of inferences on retention of the premises.

Harris (1975) reported two experiments in which 4-year-old children made appropriate transitive inferences when problems associated with retention of premise information were minimized. He presented each of 20 4-year-old children with three items of information:

(1) $A = B$
(2) $B > C$
(3) $C = D$

and then asked about the relationship between A and D. The relationships for (1) and (3) were stated verbally, for example, ''The red stick is the same size as the black stick; the green stick is the same size as the white stick.'' However, relation (2) was displayed visually with an 8-inch black stick and a 4-inch white stick so that the middle terms were available to the child throughout the task. The child was then asked, ''Are the red *(A)* and the green *(D)* sticks the same size?'' If the child answered ''no,'' he was asked which was bigger.

On the critical test involving A and D, the children were correct on 94% of the tests; 15 of the 20 children responded without error. The inference that $A > D$

could be made only if the children "coordinated" the A and D relations via B and C, since A and D had been labeled "equal" in the premises. The child could infer that A > D only by identifying A and D with the middle terms in the series via some understanding of equality and inequality relations.

In a second experiment, Harris required 4- and 5-year-old children to learn the premises to a criterion before he tested an inference. Problems involving four terms were presented verbally in stories similar to the following:

(1) Peter is the same size as David.
(2) David is bigger than you.
(3) You are the same size as John.

The child restated the premises following presentation of the story; the experimenter repeated the "story" if the child failed to recall one or more relations. Children at both age levels could recall the story accurately in all details after approximately two repetitions. When asked the inference question, "Is Peter bigger than John?" 73 and 77% of the children in the respective age groups were correct.

Bryant (1973) described an unpublished study by Perkins and himself in which a trial-by-trial presentation and test procedure was used with 5-year-olds. Each child heard a story about brothers and sisters in a family and how, on different occasions, brother-sister pairs were met and it was found that one brother (or sister) was taller than the other, following the structure A > B, B > C, C > D, and D > E. For example:

On Monday we went to the house and met Jane and Tom. Jane was taller than Tom. The next day, we returned and found Susan and Tom together. Tom was taller than Susan. On Wednesday, we paid another visit and saw Susan and Bill. Susan was taller than Bill. Later, that same day, Bill and Mary were walking together. Bill was taller than Mary.

Perkins and Bryant then asked the child comparative questions on the four adjacent pairs and the critical inference pair, B and D, (Tom and Bill). Note that these persons were always labeled "taller" and that end anchoring and labeling per se could not play a role because the problem included five terms.

Perkins and Bryant found that these 5-year-old children could make the BD inference as soon as they were able to recall the BC and CD comparisons consistently. Unfortunately, Bryant (1973) provided no numerical data to support his claims.

Thus, four recent studies that manipulated the degree of retention of the premises also produced substantial increases in the degree to which inferences were correctly made. In fact, in two studies age differences were eliminated, since the children were nearly perfect in recalling the premises and in making inferences. Retrieval of the critical information in the premises goes hand in hand with the child's performance on inferential tests. These data, however, do not tell us what was encoded, stored, or retrieved, and we now turn to these questions.

III. WHAT IS ENCODED FROM THE PREMISES?

In order for a child to make an inference that Tom is taller than Bill from the information that Tom is taller than Susan and Susan is taller than Bill, it is not sufficient that he merely recall the premises. This appears to be true empirically. In the studies summarized in the previous section, the level of performance on the inference tests was, on average, below that for recall of the premises.

It should be obvious that rote repetition of the premises, as was used in the Stetson, Harris, and Perkins and Bryant studies, is not a test of whether the child understands them. Rather, the procedure of asking the child to make comparisons between pairs of sticks in *both directions* during the learning of the premises would seem to promote understanding of the contrastive relationship being stated between the elements on a dimension. Forcing a child to make choices in both directions may aid an understanding of the *reversible, asymmetrical relations* focused on by Piaget (1970). Responding to assertions of the relationship or hearing them listed in only one direction, on the other hand, may promote only the encoding of the premise as a string of words or in a reduced form. This assertion is supported by the fact that the inferential performance in studies using the Bryant and Trabasso (1971) procedure is much nearer to that for recall of the premises than was found in those studies that did not state both comparative relations *within* a premise. Thus, *how the child understands the premise determines how he encodes its relationship in memory.* We wish to argue that an ordered set *(A, B)* is a critical encoding and that the content or representation in memory becomes a focal issue rather than recall of the premises per se. We also suggest, as have Bransford and Johnson (1973), that memory and the making of inferences entail comprehension processes or greater depth of processing than mere recital of the premises. Without comprehension of the relationships entailed in the premises, there can be no meaningful recall or inferences.

Bryant and Trabasso (1971) had departed unwittingly from traditional procedures in which the comparative terms are not contrasted within the premises. Their training procedure employed the use of *both comparative terms.* On some trials the comparison was "longer" and on other trials it was "shorter," allowing *contrastive* comparisons. Others (Clark, 1969b; Piaget, 1970) have noted that children may use a *nominal* labeling strategy to code the relations. If they do this, the comparative form is "reduced"; that is, "Red is longer than Blue" becomes "Red is long." Such a reduction will cause problems in acquiring the set of premises, since contradictions will occur. If the child encodes "Red is longer than Blue" as (1) "Red is long" and infers (2) "Blue is not longer," then when he is told "Blue is longer than Green" he may note the contradiction between (3) "Blue is longer" with (2). While noting such a contradiction may lead to altering one's codes, the problem may be avoided if the child is forced, by the task demands, to form an *ordered* set (Red, Blue) or if he is required to make the comparisons contrastively.

Riley and Trabasso (1974) investigated the possibility that the manner in which the premises are encoded may influence performance on the transitive inference task. For one group of 4-year-old children, the comparatives were used contrastively over trials; for a second group, only one comparative term was used throughout training, both groups being trained to the same criterion that Bryant and Trabasso (1971) used. The acquisition data are telling: For the contrastive group, 20 out of 23 children reached the criterion; for the group trained with only a single comparative, 7 out of 20 children were able to succeed in reaching the training criterion on the relationships in the premises. Of the seven children who reached criterion, six were trained with the comparative "longer," while only a single child learned the premises with the comparative "shorter."

The contrastive comparison of shorter and longer for two objects, A and B, apparently promoted the ordering of A and B into a set (A, B) on the dimension underlying the relation. That is, if A is longer than B and B is shorter than A, then on a scale of length the pair is ordered A, then B, or A, B. Such a representation is "reversible," since from it one can "read" $A > B$ and $B < A$, given the scale and knowledge of the ordering. In order to make correct and consistent discriminative choices in questions such as "Which is longer, A or B?" and "Which is shorter, A or B?" the child has to have arrived at this kind of knowledge. In contrast, if only asked, "Which is longer, A or B?" the child may learn only to choose A and not learn anything about the contrastive relations between A and B. It is possible that the child learns two conditional discriminations:

Given "Which is longer?" choose A.
Given "Which is shorter?" choose B.

However, this kind of learning will not lead to correct answers on the inference tests. In the five-term series, "Which is longer, B or D?" cannot be answered, since B and D are "correct" in conditional discriminations equally often to "longer" and "shorter" questions. The inferential test data are clearly above chance and argue against this interpretation. Finally, it would appear that the use of two contrastive questions within the premise offset a tendency on the part of children to "reduce" a comparative to a nominal. In training, nominal coding could not lead to learning the discriminations, and one can assume that such codes are abandoned early in training.

These results attest to the fact that a task demand or structure can control how the child represents or encodes some aspect. In this case, the encoding may or may not lead to success. Traditional procedures appear to promote failure in logic because they produce codes that lead to logical contradiction.

IV. HOW IS A REPRESENTATION OF THE
TRANSITIVE SERIES CONSTRUCTED?

We discussed in the previous section ways in which the double-comparative procedure may have promoted the construction of a representation in memory of the premises as reversible, ordered pairs. This may be only part of the story of how the task becomes represented in memory.

In all the studies conducted using the Bryant and Trabasso (1971) paradigm, a *serial position curve* is obtained in the learning of the premises in training. That is, the end pairs, (1, 2) or (4, 5) are learned to criterion first, followed by the middle premises (2, 3) and (3, 4). When one plots the trial of last error or errors on trials to criterion as a function of the position of the pairs in the series, (1, 2), (2, 3), (3, 4), and (4, 5), one finds the typical inverted "serial position curve." Apparently, children were trying to map the color codes onto an underlying dimension of length. Bower (1971) has reviewed a considerable number of paired-associates experiments where human adults were required to learn to pair names to locations in a linear, spatial array or on a continuum or to other names on a continuum. The common finding is that the acquisition of the associates results in a serial position curve.

The analogy here is striking. Instead of learning to map single names onto a continuum, the children are being asked to construct a continuum from partially ordered pairs. However, if they recognize that there is an underlying dimension, they can use this dimension to help order the members in the series.

Following the lead of Wishner, Shipley, and Hurvich (1957) and Feigenbaum and Simon (1962), Riley and Trabasso (1974) speculated that children were employing an "ends-inward" strategy in learning the set of pairs and that this strategy could lead to the construction of a linear order or serial list of the pairs. That is, the strategy is to first isolate the end anchor members of the dimension. If feedback is visual, one can detect the shortest or longest member of the array by noting the absolute tallest or shortest member of the set. However, when the feedback is verbal, then the isolation of the end anchors requires more trials, since one must find that member which is only tall or only short. This isolation may require twice as many trials with verbal as opposed to visual feedback, since it involves a process of elimination, that is, finding the members that have both comparative functions.

After isolating the ends, the child could begin ordering the pairs. He first orders the end pairs (1, 2) and (4, 5). Then he orders (2, 3) and (3, 4). At this point, he would, if successful, have a list of ordered pairs, (1, 2), (2, 3), (3, 4), and (4, 5). The next step would be to integrate the pairs into subcategories of "short" and "long" elements. This could be done at first by considering (1, 2) as short, (4, 5) as long, and (2, 3), (3, 4) as medium pairs. One level of integration would be to join (1, 2) and (2, 3) into a "short" set (1, 2, 3) or (3, 4) and (4, 5) into a "long" set (3, 4, 5), preserving order within. A final integration would be to join the remaining subsets into a linear order (1, 2, 3, 4, 5).

From a mnemonic point of view, there are several good reasons why a person would create a linear ordering of the members of the series. First, the list structure (1, 2, 3, 4, 5), is a more efficient representation than the listing of the pairs (1, 2), (2, 3), (3, 4), (4, 5). Second, the list structure (1, 2, 3, 4, 5), carries all the information of the original training on the pairwise relations and maps that information onto a common underlying dimension. A dimension of size, such as "big–little," might underlie all dimensions of comparison (Wales & Campbell, 1970). The child, then, could use his understanding or knowledge of physical dimensionality to comprehend comparative terms and to make comparisons. The linear order (1, 2, 3, 4, 5) allows one to make a *direct* comparison between any member of the series, whereas storage of the separate premises requires coordination at the time of testing of two pairs or more. That is, the linear representation of the problem is constructed to handle all the demands of the task. Finally, the list structure can be easily transformed into a spatial array, promoting the use of imagery in a working, short-term memory, or into external representations involving distance and spatial order. The pervasive serial position curves obtained in training are strong evidence that the children were trying to construct a representation of the information contained in the premises that corresponded to an internal, psychophysical scale (Bower, 1971).

A. What Is the Nature of the Representation?

If the child constructs, during the training trials, a representation of the information in the task that has the properties of a linear order, how might he use this to answer inferential questions? In particular, are there testable consequences of assuming that the child has integrated the information from the premises as opposed to having stored in memory the separate premises?

Trabasso, Riley, and Wilson (1975) derived two such consequences by altering the original Bryant and Trabasso (1971) paradigm slightly. They added a sixth member to the series, thus creating five pairs in training and 15 possible tests. In addition, they obtained choice reaction time measures during training and testing by concealing the sticks behind hinged Plexiglas windows and covering the windows with a guillotine door. To start a trial, a comparative question was posed, for example, "Which is longer, Red or Blue?" and after completing the question, the door was raised, starting a clock. The child indicated his choice by pressing one of the two windows, thus stopping the clock.

If the child is attempting the "ends-inward" strategy, then pair (3, 4) should be the most difficult to learn. Trabasso et al. (1975) found this to be the case for 6- and 9-year-olds, as well as for college students. Moreover, when they calculated the serial position data in terms of the proportion of trials to criterion per pair relative to the total number of trials to criterion for the whole series, presented in Table 11-2, the three resulting sets of proportions were virtually identical.

In Table 11-2, note that children required relatively more trials to learn pair (3, 4), that the distributions tend to be symmetrical, and that the effect is independent of age. The latter finding suggests a common basis of performance in this task for individuals of different ages.

The test series included tests of 15 pairs. Excluding the nine end anchor tests, six tests are of interest: three tests on original premises (2, 3), (3, 4), and (4, 5); two inference tests involving a distance of one member apart—(2, 4) and (3, 5); and one test involving a distance of two members apart—(2, 5). If the child stored five separate premises in memory and coordinated them at the time of testing, the time to draw an inference should increase as the distance between members increases. Test (2, 5) requires coordination of three pairs; test (2, 4) or (3, 5) requires coordination of two pairs; test (2, 3) or (3, 4) or (4, 5) requires no coordination at all, since these were training pairs and may be retrieved directly.

The linear representation implies an opposite prediction, namely, that *the farther apart the two members are in the order, the faster the decision time*. There are a variety of process models that predict this result, all of which assume that the information has been integrated into a serial order. To illustrate one such model, suppose that the child represents the colored sticks as an ordered list (1, 2, 3, 4, 5, 6). When a question on the relationship between a pair of sticks is posed, he begins by scanning the list from the end mentioned in the question. If "longer," then he starts with 6; if "shorter," he starts with 1. Suppose the question is on the relationship between Stick 2 and Stick 4. If the question contains "shorter?" then he must scan two members, 1 and 2, to find 2, and he can terminate at this point. If the question contains "longer," he will scan three members 6, 5, and 4, to find 4. On average 2½ members are scanned. For a

TABLE 11-2
Relative Difficulty of Each Premise in a 6-Term Series
Problem: Proportion of Errors Relative to Total Errors[a]

Age level	Pair				
	(1, 2)	(2, 3)	(3, 4)	(4, 5)	(5, 6)
6 years	11	24	28	26	11
9 years	18	23	28	23	12
College	11	18	26	24	12
Mean	13	22	28	24	12

[a] Data from Trabasso, Riley, and Wilson (1975).

question on Sticks 2 and 3, however, the respective number of members scanned are two and four, or an average of three members. Hence, more members are scanned to answer a question on the relationship between a premise (Sticks 2 and 3) than on the relationship of an inference pair whose distance is one member apart (Sticks 2 and 4). In a similar manner, a question on Sticks 2 and 5 would require two and two members to be scanned, respectively, or an average of two. Thus, the relationship between Sticks 2 and 5 would require less scanning and therefore less time than that for 2 and 4 and that for 2 and 3, despite the fact that training occurred only on 2 and 3. Since the distance between 2 and 5 is greater than that between 2 and 4, which, in turn, is greater than that between 2 and 3, this particular model predicts that the greater the distance, the faster the decision time, an outcome opposite to that predicted by the separate-pairs model.

Trabasso et al. (1975) compared two training conditions that varied the kind of feedback in training (visual or verbal) and added a third, control condition as a "converging operation." This condition consisted of presenting the person with a physical display of 6 colored sticks, ordered in a row according to length, asking him all 15 possible test questions, and recording the decision times.

The decision time data conclusively supported the idea that the subjects, regardless of age, had integrated the information into and used a linear ordering of the sticks to answer inferential questions. For all nine conditions, excluding all end anchor items, the reaction times decreased with increasing distance on inferential tests. Moreover, the inferential decision times were *faster* than those for answering questions on the original training pairs for all but one condition.

Trabasso (1975) converted the decision times for inferences to ratios by dividing each time by the decision time for the premises. This is analogous to creating Weber fractions in psychophysics, viz.:

$$\Delta I = (I - P)/P$$

where ΔI is a change in inference time, I, relative to a baseline time for premises, P. Note that $\Delta I = (I/P) - 1$, so that Trabasso's ratios represent the variable part of a Weber fraction. When thus converted, the ratios decreased linearly with a slope of .06, independent of age of the subjects and the kind of training condition. When all the information was in memory at the time of testing, the subjects appear to be using a common, internal psychophysical scale (see Moyer & Landauer, 1967). Regardless of the nature of the input, the judgments on ordinal comparisons yielded similar reductions in relative decision time as a function of distance in the series. These converging data suggest that children and adults were employing common operations on common, internal, representations.

The error data showed similar effects; namely, the percentage of correct responses increased with distance. Accuracy of responding on the tests is summarized in Table 11-3, which lists the rank order of the tests in terms of decision time and gives the proportion of correct answers for groups of tests. The rank order is derived from the 12 conditions studied by Trabasso et al. (1975).

The test data show the same end anchor and lexical marking effects observed in Table 11-1: Children responded most rapidly on anchor tests, and the long-anchor questions were answered more quickly than the short-anchor questions. In addition, there was a consistent interaction between the comparative term used in the question and the anchor that was present in the test pair. If the codes match, that is, if the comparatives are the same for the question and for the pair in the test, the reaction time is faster than when the codes mismatch (see also Clark, 1969a, for similar findings for adults).

B. Process Models for Accessing the Representation

A central problem in cognitive psychology is the problem of describing internal representations. As dealt with here, we assume that the information in the task, partial orderings of members comprising a series, becomes represented on a dimension as a linear order. The next question is how this representation is accessed or used in response to task demands such as the test questions. The success of the models in predicting data depends on both the structural and the process assumptions.

Consider the rank order of the reaction times observed for the 15 tests in the series presented in Table 11-3. How well can we account for these times and by what assumptions about processes?

Suppose we adopt the process model that was discussed earlier when the reaction time predictions were motivated. In this model, the person searches inward from either end until he finds at least one member of the test pair. For example, given the question "Which is longer?" and a presentation of (5, 6), *only one member of the list* needs to be searched if the search is self-terminating; if the question was "Which is shorter?" five members would be searched for the same pair. The average number of searches is 3.0 for the (5, 6) pair. One can apply this model to all 15 pairs and assume that the reaction time to answer the question is inversely proportional to the number of members searched. If one does this, the predicted order of the reaction times to that listed previously correlates .59 with the observed ranks.

While this may seem high, it is not a very good fit. Trabasso and Riley (1975), by assuming lexical marking or end anchor effects, report two models that yield rank order correlations of .96. The search model just presented makes no assumption about end anchor effects. The two models follow Bower (1971) and

TABLE 11-3
Proportion of Correct Response for Tests in 6-Term
Problems[a]

Rank	Test	Percent correct
1	both anchors (1, 6)	95.7
2	long anchor a. (3, 6) b. (5, 6) c. (2, 6) d. (4, 6)	95.3
3	short anchor a. (1, 5) b. (1, 4) c. (1, 2) d. (1, 3)	93.3
4	inference, distance = 2 (2, 5)	94.3
5	inference, distance = 1 a. (3, 5) b. (2, 4)	91.2
6	original training pairs, distance = 0 a. (4, 5) b. (2, 3) c. (3, 4)	90.6

[a] Data from Trabasso, Riley, and Wilson (1975).

account for two facts: the serial position effects in training (see Table 11-2) and the rank order of the reaction times for the 15 test pairs in Table 11-3.

In deriving the linear ordering of the six terms in the series, the child may not only seriate the terms but also associate category names with the locations in the orders. These codes could range from something like "very long" to "very short," or each location could have two associations that vary in strength, "long" or "short." An individual could use this mapping to make comparisons of length and justify a decision on grounds of "logical necessity"; that is, if Red is more strongly associated with "long" than is Blue, he could answer "Red" to the question "Which is longer?" and justify by a decision rule:

If $V(R) > V(B)$, choose R,

where $V(\ \ )$ denotes the relative associative strengths to "long" of Red (R) and Blue (B). From this argument, it would appear that the use of logical justifications as evidence for "true transitivity" is misleading, since the logic does not involve using a middle term. Only if a child asserted the full rule—"Red is larger because it is the case that Red is larger than Blue and Blue is larger than Green"—would one have confidence that something like a logical inference was made. This logical justification is an unlikely event, and we have not found it stated by adults or children in any of our tasks.

Various writers have argued that the representation of a three-term series problem entails spatial imagery (DeSoto, London, & Handel, 1965; Huttenlocher, 1968). Trabasso and Riley (1975) interpreted this as follows: The person represents the information as an internal display having spatial properties, analogous to the display conditions that Trabasso et al. (1975) used. A person first locates each member in the array via a discrimination process, notes their relative locations, assigns the appropriate label, and chooses the member that is the subject of the relation. For example, given "Which is longer: Red or Blue?" the person first locates the ordinal position of Red and of Blue, outputting something like Red = 2 and Blue = 4. Since the number 1 anchors the short end and 4 > 2, then Blue is longer than Red, and the person responds, "Blue." The resemblance to a spatial strategy is that the process depends on locating the members in an ordered, spatial array, and distance between the members plays a major role here.

Another method an individual could use involves the associative strengths of the locations in the linear order with the comparative labels. It is assumed that these strengths are built up in training, with 1 and 6 having the strongest respective associations with the ends of the scale, "short" and "long." From the ordinal locations of the colors, associations of length are generated and that color is selected which is stronger on that dimensional label. As in the preceding example, the person notes that Red has so many relative units of "shortness" and Blue has so many relative units of "shortness." The decision rule is: Choose that color which has the greater relative units.

The associative strength model can be interpreted as a generalization model: As the locations of the colors in the linear order are acquired in training, the color-dimensional name association becomes associated maximally with that location but generalizes to other locations. Assuming a generalization gradient over the colors, one can obtain a confusion matrix of each location with every other for each kind of length. From this gradient, an individual generates appropriate dimensional codes for each color, compares their relative strengths (using something like Luce's 1959 choice axiom), and selects the color with the greatest relative strength for the comparative term used in the question. From a knowledge of the strengths, one can obtain the probabilities of locating each of the 15 pairs of color codes relative to all other pairs. On the assumption that the probability of locating the codes for a pair of colors is related monotonically to the speed of responding, the rank order of the reaction times is predicted. Trabasso and Riley (1975) built into their strength parameters the lexical marking effect by giving the long anchor (Stick 6) a stronger association with the "long" code than the short anchor (Stick 1) had with the "short" code. When they did this, they predicted the rank order extremely well: The correlation was .96, virtually perfect.

There is an isomorphic relation between a generalization model and a spatial model. Recall that in the spatial model the person first locates the colors in the array so that the ease of comparing ordinal positions depends directly on how "discriminable" each color location is from every other color location in the array. In Murdock's (1960) model, the relative discriminability of a color's location is found by summing its distance from all the other colors and then forming a ratio of its summed distance to the sum of all the distances in the array to get its relative discriminability. Once the relative discriminability for a given color is known, the relative discriminability or ease of finding *a pair of colors* in the array can be indexed by summing their respective relative discriminabilities. Assuming that speed and ease of discrimination are related, one obtains exactly the same rank order of reaction times as was found by the generalization model.

The point of Trabasso and Riley's (1975) modeling is that one cannot decide which process is operating on the basis of the test data. Both models have inherent linear orders but radically different process assumptions. Both have logical decision rules. To make matters worse, one can think of two more alternative models that may yield close to the same predictions, although we have not formulated their assumptions explicitly and derived quantitative predictions as Trabasso and Riley (1975) did for the association generalization and spatial distance models.[1]

While constructing a linear order during training, the child might achieve two subcategories that have, in turn, linear orders within. For example, in the six-term problem the child may have derived a "short" set (1, 2, 3) and a "long" set (4, 5, 6) but also knows that the members are ordered on the dimension within each set. This gives a hierarchical structure, shown in Figure 11-1. If the child classified the terms into "long" and "short" subsets, then he can use this information to make decisions and the decision times will decrease with distance between terms in the series. To illustrate, test (2, 5) involves a comparison across categories, and the child can easily determine the long(er) or short(er) member. Tests (2, 3) and (4, 5) would involve comparisons within categories, and consequently, a more careful search of the ordinal relations. Further, test (3, 4) may also be slow because the category "boundary" is uncertain or varies across the group of children. In any event, the subcategorization representation and its

---

[1] These alternatives are mentioned here because they seem plausible and have been put forward to the author at various colloquia presentations on some of the work described here or have arisen in discussions with colleagues. In particular, we have benefited from comments by Brendan McGonigle at the University of Edinburgh and Richard Shiffrin at Indiana University, who independently suggested a "subcategorizing" strategy, and Charles Collyer and Ron Kinchla at Princeton, who proposed that what gets acquired in training is a set of "magnitudes." None of these colleagues, however, is responsible for our interpretation of their ideas here.

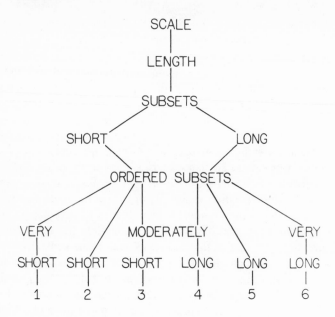

SCALE

|

LENGTH

|

SUBSETS

SHORT   LONG

ORDERED SUBSETS

VERY   MODERATELY   VERY

SHORT   SHORT   SHORT   LONG   LONG   LONG

1   2   3   4   5   6

FIGURE 11-1   A possible hierarchical representation of the levels of integration of the pairwise, ordinal relations expressed in a six-term series problem on the scale of length.

search allow one to predict the decision times to be faster as a function of distance between items.[2]

Another possible representation is one that contains sufficient information to generate a linear order but has more general storage possibilities, since individual "magnitudes" are assigned to the members in the series. This is analogous to our

[2] This analysis bears on de Boysson-Bardies and O'Regan's (1973) "labeling" strategy, and permits a reinterpretation. They suggested that in the Bryant and Trabasso (1971) study each pair presented during training is learned as a conditional discrimination so that, given a pair, the child can choose the longer or the shorter member. Second, the child labels each member within a pair as "long" or "short." As a result, Sticks 2, 3, and 4 are assigned inconsistent labels across the four pairs in training but 1 and 5 would retain the consistent labels, "long" and "short," respectively. Then 2 and 4 may lose their "inconsistent" labels and become associated with the end labels. Thus, 2 and 4 could be compared using labels that de Boysson-Bardies and O'Regan (1973) claim are not "genuine" inferences from a Piagetian perspective.

Harris' (1975) experiments discredit a simple end-labeling strategy for four-term series problems. However, the development of the linear ordering of the terms via ordered pairs and subcategorized triples closely resembles the de Boysson-Bardies and O'Regan description. However, labeling the ends and joining adjacent members into an ordered subset or set can occur only if the child knows that the relationships are transitive and can be so ordered onto an underlying dimensional scale. Further, the creation of ordered pairs entails an appreciation of asymmetrical, ordered relationships, and the construction of the ordinal series constitutes "coordination" of terms, both of which are not supposed to be done by children in the 4- to 7-year-old range. The very alternative model that de Boysson-Bardies and O'Regan (1973) propose and dismiss as irrelevant to Piaget would seem to meet at least two of the ability criteria he himself set (Piaget, 1970).

stored knowledge about animal sizes. We probably do not order all the animals we know on some single scale, but we probably do store lexical codes (small, large, huge, etc.) with each animal's name. We may, in an abstract form, store some averaged absolute size with prototypic animals, for example, "dog" is two feet tall, on average. Moyer (1973) asked people to compare the sizes of two animals from information stored in memory, and their speed in doing so was inversely proportional to the difference in magnitudes or average sizes of the animals being compared. Moyer (1973) claimed that his subjects used images to make the comparisons, and coined the phrase "internal psychophysics."[3]

The idea that magnitudes are discerned or generated from the comparisons is appealing when referring to real-life experiences (for example, animals, cars, buildings). However, in the experiments on transitive reasoning these magnitudes would have to be generated from (1) absolute lengths in varied locations and contextual arrangements; (2) stated relative comparisons; (3) distance in linear arrays; or (4) relative locations in serial order. It seems unlikely that the subjects across these conditions would adopt the same strategy of generating magnitudes. Rather, from a set of magnitudes, such as absolute lengths, one could derive a linear order for solution to the problem, forgetting the magnitudes per se once the order was derived. One way to test this argument would be to train subjects to make quantitative comparisons on members whose differences in magnitudes vary across tasks, and see if the differences in magnitudes for pairs sharing the same ordinal positions correspond to differences in decision times or error rates. If not—that is, if the times were independent of the absolute magnitude differences but the same for pairs of the same ordinal values—one would have evidence that once the linear ordering is derived, the original information becomes discarded, an idea not different from Craik and Lockhart's (1972) depth-of-processing and memory relationship. Only those transformations that remain after processing is completed are stored, while temporary representations during processing are lost.

In the foregoing section, we discussed a variety of ways in which one may construct and operate on the ordinal information contained in transitive inference tasks where the basic inputs are pairwise comparisons among adjacent members on a scale. It is by no means clear which of the several alternatives provides the best description of the data, and as Trabasso and Riley (1975) have shown, two of the models provide extremely accurate predictions of the serial position data in training and the rank order of the 15 decision times in testing. As is often the case, the existing data cannot be used to decide among the alternatives, and one has to resort to other ways of assessment. One way is to let the child tell us more about what he or she knows. Riley (1975) has done this in an experiment that attempted to make overt the internal representation that the child is using.

---

[3]It is worth noting that Moyer (1973), in his instructions, had inadvertently given the subjects a linear order by listing the six animals that were to be compared in order of size. This serial list, rather than size magnitudes or imagery, may have been the representation used in making comparisons.

C. Can One Externalize the Internal Representation?

So far, we have had to infer the nature of the way in which the person represented the task environment via observed outcomes involving either the relative difficulty in acquiring the premises or the speed in answering questions about the members in a series. Riley (1975, 1976) sought to externalize how the child might represent the series by allowing him to use an external mnemonic consisting of the members in the series. She investigated the relative ease with which 7- to 9-year-old children could acquire the comparative relations and make inferred comparisons for each of four dimensions: niceness, happiness, heaviness, and tallness. These comparative terms varied in how closely they resembled physical dimensions. Wales and Campbell (1970), Bower (1971), and Trabasso et al. (1975) all had conjectured that children would use a common, underlying scale or dimension to represent different comparatives. Would they "map" the linguistic codes onto a common linear order and use this representation to make comparative relations and inferences? This was the central question of the thesis.

In one of Riley's three experiments, children learned comparative relations for a set of six faces of children. No obvious physical clues in the pictures could be used by the children to create a dimension or make comparisons on any of the four comparatives. The faces were named with common boys' and girls' names. The reaction time procedure was the same as that used by Trabasso et al. (1975), and pairs of faces appeared in the test apparatus rather than colored sticks as before.

Four independent groups of children in the display condition answered all possible pairwise comparative questions, with each group having a different comparative. Children in one of two training groups were given partial orderings via adjacent members in the series, replicating and extending the Trabasso et al. (1975) reaction time study on length discussed earlier, and served as a control. A second group was given an external memory aid, the six faces, to use any way the children wished during training on pairwise relations among the faces. Then both groups underwent testing without any aids present.

The first result of interest was in training, where the children with the memory aid had 84 percent fewer errors compared to the group without memory aid. For the control group, which had *no* pictures to use as a memory aid, mean errors to criterion were 3.45, 7.57, 8.38, 6.38, and 3.57 for the five pairs, (1, 2), (2, 3), (3, 4), (4, 5), and (5, 6), respectively, yielding the well-known serial position effect. With the external mnemonic, the errors to criterion in training averaged .76, 1.19, 1.40, 1.19, and .97 for the same respective positions. The savings in training were very striking.

In order to provide converging evidence and data on whether the children could use a scale, Riley (1975, 1976) studied a third group of children. An array of six faces was displayed in a horizontal order. The pairwise comparisons were stated by the experimenter on adjacent members, from left to right, and then the child was asked all 15 possible test questions without feedback, using the same reaction time apparatus. Since the six faces were present during testing, they provided another external display of the linear order and reduced memory load. We shall refer to this condition as Display.

In testing, the three groups showed the decrease in reaction time as the distance or number of inferential steps increased between members in the series. The mean times are given in Table 11-4.

Of central interest, however, is the way in which the children in the memory-aid condition used the six pictures during training to construct an external representation of the series from the premise information. When the children reached criterion, they showed two kinds of constructions: one was a linear order (1, 2, 3, 4, 5, 6) with the six faces laid out, in a row, left to right in the correct order; the second was a subcategorization of the series with two groupings of three faces, each grouping being ordered as either (1, 2, 3) or (4, 5, 6), in either vertical or irregular arrays. Forty-one of the 48 children tested used the linear order representation; the remaining 7 children used the subcategory strategy.

Thus, when constrained to the use of the six members in the series, children created external mnemonics that proved to be extremely efficient and that resembled two of the representations in Figure 11-1 that Riley and Trabasso (1974) assumed to take place during the construction of the linear order. It remains to be seen what younger children would do under similar circumstances and when duplicates of the six faces are available. That is, given two Toms, two Freds, two Mikes, two Pauls, two Georges, and two Steves, would the children form five ordered pairs or linear arrays?

D. Can One Force a Child to Use a Nonlinear Representation?

Riley (1975, 1976) investigated another kind of external display condition in an effort to force 7- to 9-year-old children to separate the premises in memory and to prohibit their integration in a linear order. In the first of three conditions, a linear display of six faces, similar to that of Trabasso et al. (1975), was used as a

TABLE 11-4

Average Decision Times for Critical Test Questions Following Two Kinds of Training or Under Conditions of a Linear Display[a]

Condition	Premise (2, 3) (3, 4) (4, 5)	Inference 1 (2, 4) (3, 5)	Inference 2 (2, 5)
Display	2.03	1.89	1.71
Memory aid	2.10	1.98	1.74
Control	2.13	2.04	1.94

[a] Data from Riley (1975).

converging operation on the assumed, internal linear order. The key assumption here is that the distance between the members in the internal linear order corresponds to their spatial distances in the external display. For the 15 possible tests on pairs of the 6 members, the rank order of the reaction times was identical to that found by Trabasso et al. (1975), presented in Table 11-3.

Different displays were used in two other conditions, and all 15 test questions were posed. In one, the display was arranged as a series of *vertically ordered pairs:*

1, 2
2, 3
3, 4
4, 5
5, 6

In the other, the display was arranged as a *random series of ordered pairs:*

4, 5
1, 2
3, 4
5, 6
2, 3

Note that the horizontal linear order display used in the first condition and the vertical ordered-pair display contain space and distance information that is correlated with the serial order of the terms. In the horizontal display, the linear order is left-to-right in spatial orientation; in the vertical display, the linear order is top-down except for the last pair (5, 6), which is ordered left to right. In the random series, the vertical pairs are randomized but the pairs themselves are ordered *within,* left to right.

For each kind of display, what should be the expected pattern of decision times for the tests, excluding the end anchor items? If the child uses the spatial information in the left-to-right linear display, and orders the series, we would expect that the decision times would decrease as the distance between the members increases. However, for the other two conditions in which separate pairs are maintained, one would expect faster times for the premises, since these are ordered horizontally, but longer times for inferences *unless* the child uses the vertical spatial information or imposes a re-ordering on the random pairs.

Riley (1975, 1976) carried out the tests in two ways: first with the displays present and then with the displays absent. The latter tests require some representation of the pairs in memory. The decision times for both testing phases for each display condition are presented in Figure 11-2 as a function of the distance between terms in the series. All tests involving end anchor items are excluded as before.

When the display was present (left-hand panel), the pattern of decision times was similar for the conditions in which pairs were separated: RT (Inference 1) >

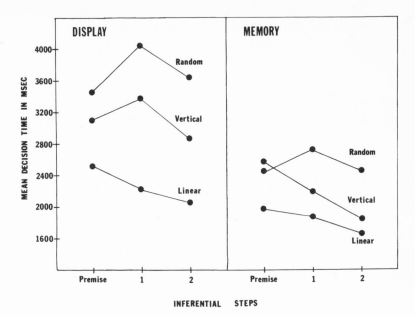

FIGURE 11-2   Average decision time to answer questions on premises or make inferences in three display conditions. The random and vertical arrays contained separated pairs, ordered within. (Data from Riley, 1975).

RT (Inference 2) = RT (Premise). The times for the linear display, by comparison, decline as a function of distance between the members of the series. The result of interest is that inferences of greater distance (Size 2) are made faster than those of shorter distance (Size 1) in all conditions. This result indicates that the children were constructing an order in the random display as well as using the spatial order information in the vertical display. We note that these data are also similar to the pattern found for 6-year-old children who received verbal feedback in training in the Trabasso et al. (1975) study. The similarity suggests that the representation of the problem for these children was as follows:

$$1, 2$$
$$2, 3$$
$$3, 4$$
$$4, 5$$
$$5, 6$$

of an *ordered series of ordered pairs*. This representation preserves the original information but also is a kind of integration of the series into a linear order.

Based on the data presented in the right-hand panel of Figure 11-2, it would appear that when the information from the pairs was in memory, the nature of the representation changed for the children who had the vertically ordered pairs. When tested in the absence of the display, the pattern of their decision times now

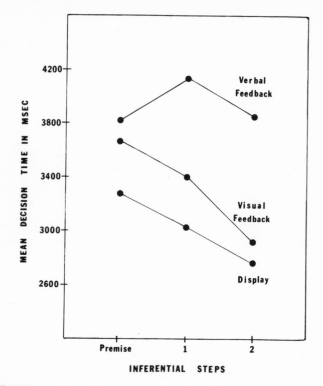

FIGURE 11-3 Average decision time for 6-year-old children to answer questions or make infer-ences in two training conditions with verbal or visual feedback and in the presence of a physical display of the series. (Data from Trabasso, Riley, & Wilson, 1975).

closely resembles that for the horizontal, linear display group. Apparently, these children integrated the pairs into a linear order despite Riley's efforts to keep them separate. The data from children who were tested via the random pairs remain qualitatively the same. All groups improved in overall reaction time.

It is worth noting that when the displays were present during the first testing phase, several children complained about the random ordered-pairs displays and asked to have them removed, saying that they had "got the idea" and that the displays *interfered* with their answering the questions. We can interpret these complaints to mean that the children actively tried to construct a linear order that was incompatible with the random display. In fact, testing without the displays was more accurate and faster than when the displays were present.

Riley's (1975, 1976) attempt to keep the pairs physically separate in mem-ory apparently failed, since the children preferred to construct a representation that efficiently summarized the ordinal information contained in the displays. The failure to find that the decision time was longer for inferences requiring more coordination is most damaging to the idea that the children stored the individual premises separately in memory. The close correspondence of the performance by

6-year-olds in the Trabasso et al. (1975) study to the present data can be seen by comparing Figure 11-3, in which the data from the former experiment are presented, with Figure 11-2.

The data in Figure 11-3 are from the 6-year-old children studied by Trabasso et al. (1975) in three conditions. The decision times are those found in testing for the premises (2, 3), (3, 4), and (4, 5), and the inferences of Step 1 (2, 4) and (3, 5), and Step 2, (2, 5), after the children had received different kinds of feedback in training. When the relationships were stated only verbally in pairwise training on the premises, the data in testing on the premises and the inferences correspond qualitatively to those Riley (1975) found for the vertically ordered pairs and the randomly ordered pairs in Figure 11-2. However, when the feedback had been both verbal and visual, the data correspond to those for the linear display condition, which represents an integrated series. Thus, the one deviant case reported by Trabasso et al. (1975) may now be interpreted as reflecting the 6-year-old child's organization of the pair comparisons into an ordered set. The pairs are linearly ordered both within and between, but are not fully integrated into a single linear order of six members. This is strong evidence that 6-year-olds can coordinate information under rather demanding conditions and that nonlinear representations are difficult to come by.

V. DEVELOPMENTAL IMPLICATIONS AND DIFFERENCES

For the most part, the discussion has glossed over developmental *differences* and has focused on developmental *similarities*. There was a good reason for such a "gloss," since the children, while slower or less accurate than adults, were qualitatively very similar to adults in the strategies used and representations achieved for the transitivity tasks. Children and adults show the following effects:

1. *Lexical marking effects,* involving faster and more accurate responses to questions and items involving terms that are unmarked or of positive polarity (longer, happier, etc.);

2. *Congruence effects,* involving an interaction between the comparative term used in the question and the comparative term used to code the members in the test pair; responses are more accurate and faster when the codes match;

3. *End anchor effects* in training and testing, involving similarly shaped serial position acquisition curves for the premises and faster and more accurate responding;

4. *Decision time and distance effects* in testing for pairs not involving end anchors where the greater the distance or inference level, the faster the time, indicating that the information from the premises was integrated or ordered; the

percentage reduction in slope for the inferential decision time was identical for different ages and input conditions;

5. *Serial position effects* in training where the relative number of errors was the same for all age groups studied, suggesting common "ends-inward" construction of a linear order or mapping of the ordinal pairwise relations onto a dimensional scale.

The developmental differences seem to be restricted to difficulty in training and verbal feedback. These differences also seem to be mnemonic rather than logical or semantic in nature.

Consider comparisons of the two kinds of feedback studied. A summary of three experiments that permit direct contrasts of the effect of visual versus linguistic feedback in training on overall test performance is presented in Table 11-5.

When the feedback was visual and provided a context in which to interpret the relationship expressed in the premise with physical referents via absolute lengths, the overall success rate on the test series was independent of age and average 94.8%. This rate is comparable to the 95% correct that Trabasso et al. (1975) found when the subjects had a physical display of the sticks directly in front of them during the test series. People do as well with the quantities represented in memory as they do with the information perceived directly.[4]

In Table 11-5, the developmental difference appears in the overall proportion of correct responses under conditions where the feedback is verbal. The one exception seems to be in the original Bryant and Trabasso (1971) study, where the 4-year-old children performed as well after training with verbal feedback as when the feedback had been visual. Their finding for 4-year-olds does not seem reliable, since Riley and Trabasso (1974) found that 4-year-olds did better in a subsequent visual feedback training and test series than they had done in initial testing following verbal feedback. The proportions of the latter were well below Bryant and Trabasso's (1971) comparable verbal feedback condition (70 versus 84% on the critical inference tests). Trabasso (1975) found that 5-year-old children performed nearly as well as Bryant and Trabasso's (1971) children after training with verbal feedback, but his 4-year-olds were not nearly as accurate.

The question is, Why the difference? Trabasso (1975) systematically ruled out a confound in the Bryant and Trabasso (1971) study that had a correlation

---

[4]One criticism by Youniss and Furth (1973) of the original Bryant and Trabasso (1971) study was that the children could use the absolute size information to compare Stick 2 with Stick 4, and the visual feedback results suggest that this may be the case. However, the similarity of the findings on test decision times when the feedback was relational clearly rules out such a possibility. Furthermore, the Youniss-Furth assertion that the children might use absolute length information to make comparative judgments is another variant of the stored-magnitude hypothesis, and all the criticisms advanced previously against this apply. Even if true, the children would be performing a difficult intellectual feat worthy of study. They would have to abstract, from varying positions and contexts, the exact magnitudes of five or six colors over the training series.

TABLE 11-5
Overall Percent Correct on Tests for Three Comparable Studies
Contrasting Age and Feedback Variables

Study	Subjects' age	Feedback	
		Visual	Linguistic
Bryant & Trabasso (1971)	4	92	92
	5	96	94
Trabasso (1975)	4	94	69
	5	96	86
Trabasso, Riley, and Wilson	6	95	80
(1975)	9	95	87
	college	96	97

between relative spatial location of the sticks in the testing apparatus. In their experiments, the end anchors were physically closer to the edges of the test box, although the left and right positions of the sticks had been randomized. Trabasso (1975) found that this spatial correlation did not increase performance.

Besides the fact that Bryant and Trabasso's (1971) children were British and came from working-class families (as contrasted with American, middle-class children in the related studies showing lower performance following verbal feedback), the Bryant and Trabasso children were also in school, while the American children, for the most part, were not. On this point, Riley (1975) found a "schooling" effect on 4- to 6-year-old children's abilities to map linguistic codes onto external, physical linear displays. She used arrays of six faces in a horizontal row and first stated the relationship between adjacent members in the series. The relationships were "heavier," "taller," "nicer," or "happier," and both affirmative and negative equative relations were used. For example, "Fred is nicer than Mike, Mike is not as nice as Fred, Mike is nicer than George, George is not as nice as Mike" would be the way in which the linear array of six faces would be described, with the experimenter pointing out each pair as the relations were described. Then, using the reaction time apparatus, all 15 possible pairs were tested on their relationships.

Riley (1975) compared two age groups, namely, children who were not in school and who were 4½ to 5½ years of age, and those who had completed kindergarten and were 5½ to 6½ years of age. Approximately 40% of the preschool children did not perform the task above chance levels; the vast majority of the schoolchildren did so. However, for the children in both age groups who did perform above chance, there were no differences in the decision times and the patterns of times over the tests. Thus, qualitatively, those who succeeded at all in understanding the instruction resembled each other. Riley made an interesting observation: There was no correlation with the one-year range and performance.

Note that the variation in age within and between the two groups was alike, yet the age variation *within* failed to correlate with performance. The only other variable correlated with the age difference *between* the groups was school. Schooling, which entails learning how to follow instructions from strangers, may be a potent factor in performance and may affect conclusions on what young children can do.

The developmental differences with verbal feedback are more striking in the studies in which six terms rather than five were used and in which decision times were recorded (Trabasso et al., 1975). Clearly, the six-term task demands more of working memory in training and, as Riley (1975) has shown, if one can provide an external mnemonic, then the average error rate for 7- to 9-year-olds decreases 44% in tests, and the number of trials required to reach criterion is reduced by 84%. Thus, the use of an external, spatial mnemonic aid—the set of six faces—leads to more efficient acquisition and test performance.

Riley's (1975) demonstration that relational terms can be comprehended, acquired, and used to make inferences when the child is simply allowed to use an external coding system points to the locus of the developmental problem. One could argue that "comprehension" is better when the child has visual feedback, since he can relate the verbal comparisons directly to visual referents. Thus, a semantic interpretation of the abstract, comparative relations is facilitated by visual feedback, and the younger children may not have the internal resources or stored knowledge necessary to make such a semantic interpretation. Riley's (1975) study, however, did *not* involve any visual feedback on the relations. Rather, in her study she gave the children an external symbol system to manipulate spatially and instructed them to construct an external representation of the series that, in turn, could be stored internally as a linear order. Her results suggest that the holding of the information in working memory via symbols is a critical limitation for the younger child. When one frees his working memory from this demand, he can demonstrate abilities to understand linguistic relations and transitive relations and to integrate information.

A. Should We Believe the Textbooks?

In this concluding section, we would like to return to the questions and views stated at the outset. When a child does not do something, one cannot, it would seem, conclude that he cannot do it or that he lacks some ability, logical or otherwise, to do it. The message of the research is that the systems involved in solving problems, such as making transitive inferences, are not amenable to simple categorization as logic, memory, or language. Rather, one can find elements of all of these in transitive reasoning. We have emphasized memory processes here, since the task demands—coding the relationships, holding them in working memory, integrating the members from the ends inward, and coming up with a representation of the information in the task that contained the original premises and permitted inferences—are demands that one would regard as memorial in character. However, interpreting the premises semantically and coding are also linguistic in charater; the decision rules are logical in nature. The systematic ways in which the children go about solving the task possess a logic of their own, at least at a descriptive level. Any attempt to reduce the analysis to exclusively memory or logic would seem to be both futile and misleading, given what we know about human information processing.

With respect to our textbook psychologists, a naive reliance on operational definitions of abilities and correlations with equally undefined external criteria such as IQ tests or school grades, while having some limited practical value, leaves one without any interpretations other than superficial ones. The studies discussed earlier indicate that what is being measured is not reasoning ability per se. Nor is it memory per se or language per se. It is a set of processes that is not independent of the task demands, and as we have shown, the median age at which children can pass this item may range from 4 to 11, depending on how we structure the task. The children over this range perform as well as adults, then in what sense are such tests a measure of intelligence?

B. A Final Note on Defenders of Piaget

The relevance of this research for Piagetian theory is a matter of some controversy. We have already alluded to two papers that have criticized the original Bryant and Trabasso (1971) study, namely the de Boysson-Bardies and O'Regan (1973) and Youniss and Furth (1973) studies. The essence of the first paper is that since one can think of an alternative solution to the transitivity test that does not involve the use of the middle term, such as labeling the ends of the series and associating the members near the ends with these labels, then the study does not bear on Piaget at all. The second paper, by Youniss and Furth (1973), makes essentially the same claim but for different reasons. Their argument is that Bryant and Trabasso (1971) did not carry out a series of experiments that (1) manipulated memory via frequency of pairs or time; (2) manipulated the inequality-equality relations among the terms; or (3) ran various controls such as pairings without middle terms.

Our strong demonstration of the correlation between retrieval of the premises and performance on inference tests and the related studies that manipulated the number of trials in training clearly implicate memory at least in terms of the traditional variable of frequency of experience (Bryant & Trabasso, 1971; Harris, 1975; Stetson, 1974). Further, Harris (1975) found that variation in the equality and inequality relations led to the same high degree of success in making inferences by 4- and 5-year-old children that Bryant and Trabasso (1971) found.

The omission of the middle term appears to be critical, for one does not apparently find the children making transitive inferences unless *all* adjacent, pairwise comparisons are made in testing. Bryant and Martin (personal communication, Bryant, 1975) have found that 4- and 5-year-old children conclude that $B < D$, given $A > B$ and $D > E$. That is, they code B as short and D as long when the critical middle term, C, is omitted. In their studies, Bryant and Martin trained the children to make pairwise relational choices on colored rods for pairs (A, B) and (D, E) in a five-term series. On a critical (B, D) test, 82% of the choices were D over B to the question "Longer?" and 82% of the choices were B over D to the question "Shorter?" Children, in the absence of a linking middle term, relate a member to its end anchor in an oppositional way rather than categorizing it with the end anchor scale value.

The point of alternative experimental requirements seems to be that one *must rule out* alternative explanations before one can conclude that transitive reasoning is involved! While the Youniss and Furth (1973) criticisms of the Bryant and Trabasso (1971) study apply with equal force to every single study ever done on transitive reasoning by children, different interpreters of Piaget have different criteria as to what constitutes transitive reasoning. Youniss and Furth (1973) seem to have an implicit process model in mind that involves the use of the middle term as a coordinating event in integrating the information. Theirs is but one of many such process models, and our earlier discussion suggests that it is the ends as well as the middle that are critical to construction of linear orders or making transitive inferences.

Several persons of a Piagetian persuasion have indicated to us that their purposes are different from ours. They are interested in the epistemological question, What does a child *know about* transitivity. That is, if we gave a set of paired relations that were not transitive, such as:

(1)   John likes Bill.
(2)   Bill likes Fred.
(3)   Fred likes George.

would the children treat them as transitive? Our guess is "yes"—and so do adults, if one is to believe the "balance theory" put forth by social psychologists (see Heider, 1958).

Another question might be, Would the children construct a linear order from:

(1)   John is taller than Bill.
(2)   Bill is taller than Fred.
(3)   Fred is taller than George.
(4)   George is taller than John.

which is a transitive but nonlinear order?

There are further questions about a person's knowledge and understanding or use of transitive or nontransitive relations, and they are certainly of general interest. However, on the older questions of age, sequence of operations, and sources of difficulty indicated, we believe that our research provides strong evidence that Piaget and Inhelder (1967) are not correct. The age and performance correlation disappears when one makes sure that the child understands and can remember the information critical to making inferences. If so, there seems to be no clear sequence in emergence of such abilities. The logic model, while a reasonable description of task structures and task dependency, does not seem to be a very good psychological model. For the most part, we have found that children can, in fact, reason like adults. Adults, in turn, seem to employ reasoning strategies like children.

ACKNOWLEDGMENTS

This paper was written while the author was a Visiting Research Professor at the University of Edinburgh, Edinburgh, Scotland, in spring 1975 while on leave from Princeton University. He thanks David Vowles for providing support facilities, and the members of his department, notably Margaret Donaldson Salter and Brendan McGonigle, for their hospitality and intellectual stimulation during the visit. The research was supported by U.S. Public Health Service, National Institutes of Health Grants MH 19223 and MH 29365.

REFERENCES

Bower, G. H. Adaptation-level coding of stimuli and serial position effects. In M. H. Appley (Ed.), *Adaptation-level theory*. New York: Academic Press, 1971.

Bransford, J. D., & Johnson, M. K. Considerations of some problems of comprehension. In W. G. Chase (Ed.), *Visual information processing*. New York: Academic Press, 1973.

Bryant, P. E. What the young child has to learn about logic. In R. Hinde & J. Hinde (Eds.), *Constraints on learning*. New York: Academic Press, 1973.

Bryant, P. E., & Trabasso, T. Transitive inferences and memory in young children. *Nature*, 1971, *232*, 456–458.

Burt, C. The development of reasoning in school children. *Journal of Experimental Pedagogy*, 1919, *5*, 68–77.

Clark, H. H. Linguistic processes in deductive reasoning. *Psychological Review*, 1969, *76*, 387–404. (a)

Clark, H. H. The influence of language on solving three-term series problems. *Journal of Experimental Psychology*, 1969, *82*, 205–215. (b)

Craik, F. I. M., & Lockhart, R. S. Levels of processing: A framework for memory research. *Journal of Verbal Learning and Verbal Behavior*, 1972, *11*, 671–684.

de Boysson-Bardies, B., & O'Regan, K. What children know in spite of what they do. *Nature*, 1973, *246*, 531–534.

DeSoto, C. B., London, M., & Handel, S. Social reasoning and spatial paralogic. *Journal of Personality and Social Psychology*, 1965, *2*, 513–521.

Feigenbaum, E. A., & Simon, H. A. A theory of the serial position effect. *British Journal of Psychology*, 1962, *53*, 307–320.

Flavell, J. H. *The developmental psychology of Jean Piaget*. New York: Van Nostrand-Reinhold, 1963.

Ginsburg, H., & Opper, S. *Piaget's theory of intellectual development: An introduction.* Englewood Cliffs, N.J.: Prentice-Hall, 1969.

Harris, P. Transitive inferences by four-year-old children. Presented at the biennial meeting of the Society for Research in Child Development, Denver, 1975.

Heider, F. *The psychology of interpersonal relations.* New York: Wiley, 1958.

Huttenlocher, J. Constructing spatial images: A strategy in reasoning. *Psychological Review,* 1968, *75,* 550–560.

Luce, R. D. *Individual choice behavior.* New York: Wiley, 1959.

Lutkus, A., & Trabasso, T. Transitive inferences by preoperational, retarded adolescents. *American Journal of Mental Deficiency,* 1974, *78,* 599–606.

Moyer, R. S. Comparing objects in memory: Evidence suggesting an internal psychophysics. *Perception & Psychophysics,* 1973, *13,* 180–184.

Moyer, R. S., & Landauer, T. K. Time required for judgments of numerical inequality. *Nature,* 1967, *215,* 1519–1520.

Murdock, B. B. The distinctiveness of stimuli. *Psychological Review,* 1960, *67,* 16–31.

Piaget, J. Une forme verbal de la comparison chez l'enfant. *Archives de Psychologie,* 1921, 141–172.

Piaget, J. *Genetic epistemology* (Translated by Eleanor Duckworth). New York: Columbia University Press, 1970.

Piaget, J., & Inhelder, B. Genèse des structures logiques élémentaires (2nd Ed.). Paris: Delachaux et Niestlé, 1967.

Riley, C. A. Representation and use of comparative information and inference making by young children. Unpublished doctoral dissertation, Princeton University, 1975.

Riley, C. A. The representation of comparative relations and the transitive inference task. *Journal of Experimental Child Psychology,* 1976, in press.

Riley, C. A., & Trabasso, T. Comparatives, logical structures, and encoding in a transitive inference task. *Journal of Experimental Child Psychology,* 1974, *17,* 187–203.

Simon, H. A. *The sciences of the artificial.* Cambridge, Mass.: M.I.T. Press, 1969.

Smedslund, J. Psychological diagnostics. *Psychological Bulletin,* 1969, *71,* 237–248.

Stetson, P. C. Verbal transitivity in children. Unpublished doctoral dissertation, University of Delaware, 1974.

Trabasso, T. Representation, memory and reasoning: How do we make transitive inferences? In A. D. Pick (Ed.), *Minnesota Symposia on child psychology* (Vol. 9). Minneapolis: University of Minnesota Press, 1975.

Trabasso, T., & Riley, C. A. The construction and use of representations involving linear order. In R. L. Solso (Ed.), *Information processing and cognition: The Loyola Symposium.* Hillsdale, N.J.: Lawrence Erlbaum Associates, 1975.

Trabasso, T., Riley, C. A., & Wilson, E. G. The representation of linear order and spatial strategies in reasoning: A developmental study. In R. Falmagne (Ed.), *Reasoning: Representation and process in children and adults.* Hillsdale, N.J.: Lawrence Erlbaum Associates, 1975.

Wales, R. J., & Campbell, R. N. On the development of comparison and the comparison of development. In G. B. Flores d'Arcais & W. J. M. Levelt (Eds.), *Advances in psycholinguistics.* Amsterdam: North-Holland Publ., 1970.

Wishner, J., Shipley, T. E., & Hurvich, M. S. The serial-position curve as a function of organization. *American Journal of Psychology,* 1957, *70,* 258–262.

Youniss, J., & Furth, H. G. Reasoning and Piaget: A comment on Bryant and Trabasso. *Nature,* 1973, *244,* 314–315.

Youniss, J., & Murray, J. Transitive inference with nontransitive solutions controlled. *Developmental Psychology,* 1970, *2,* 169–175.

12
Memory and Metamemory Development in Educable Retarded Children

Joseph C. Campione
Ann L. Brown
University of Illinois

I. GENERAL BACKGROUND

A. Introduction and Brief History

This chapter differs from the others in this volume in a number of respects, the main one being that it is concerned with a particular subject population rather than a specific process area. That is, the treatment deals with individual differences in memory performance, rather than with a thorough description of the development of particular aspects of memory development (e.g., storage, retrieval, acquisition strategies). As such, less detail about the specific processes will be presented, and the reader is referred to other chapters for more detailed analyses of particular subareas.

The efficiency of memory in the retarded has long been of both theoretical and practical interest. Dating back to at least Galton (1887) and Binet (1904), memory deficiencies have been seen as one index or property of retarded individuals. This notion is inherent in the inclusion of memory items, such as digit span, on standardized intelligence tests. While the relationship between memory and intelligence has been presumed for many years, it is only within the past 15 years that much in the way of theoretical analysis has been forthcoming. Further, with the renewed interest in general memory functioning (witness this volume) and the development of information-processing approaches, the depth of theoretical analysis within the area of retardation has increased significantly during the past decade.

Given that the retarded manifest deficiencies in a number of memory tasks, a conclusion that is reasonable given the many demonstrations of normal-retardate differences, the theoretical and practical question concerns a specification of the area(s) and process(es) that are implicated. It is in this context that progress has been made recently; however, we are still far from being able to put forth a coherent comparative-theoretical picture.

In attempting to provide a general perspective on the theoretical development in the area, we will make use of the distinction between the structural features of a memory system and its associated control processes (Atkinson & Shiffrin, 1968). From our perspective, it is possible to discern a cycle whereby theoretical speculation concerning memory deficits in retarded individuals originally involved structural limitations, with a subsequent emphasis on the role of control processes (or strategies). In some more recent approaches, both structural features and control processes are considered. Here, sources of individual differences are sought within a theoretical framework, with the question of whether the obtained differences are to be explained in terms of structure or control becoming an empirical matter. Before developing this framework in more detail, however, we would like to indicate some of the limitations of the review.

B. Population to Be Considered

The set of all retarded individuals is an extremely heterogeneous one, and any attempt to deal with the entire range of IQs would require more space than is available here. As a consequence, we will in general restrict our attention to the performance of moderately and mildly retarded individuals (IQ = 50) with no known organic impairment, that is, those individuals who could be characterized as being on the lower end of the normal distribution of intelligence scores.

In addition to this restriction, within that population no attempt will be made to ferret out effects due specifically to CA, MA, or IQ. While there are good reasons for attempting such a separation, our approach here is essentially to adopt the position espoused by Ellis (1970) and make inferences on the basis of equal-CA comparisons. That is, retarded individuals of a given CA are characterized by having both a lower MA and a lower IQ than nonretarded individuals of the same CA. Performance differences between groups matched on CA do reflect areas of retardate deficiencies. While subsequent determinations can presumably refine our knowledge by identifying MA or IQ as the major variable, such findings do not violate the initial conclusion that we have identified an area of retardate inefficiency.

II. CONTROL PROCESSES versus STRUCTURAL DIFFERENCES

A. Statement and Difficulties

The distinction between control processes and structural features, proposed by Atkinson and Shiffrin (1968) and emphasized in the retardate area by Fisher and Zeaman (1973), is a deceptively simple one. Structural features are invariant components of the system, akin to the hardware of a computer. As such, these aspects are unmodifiable, and adapted for reference to retarded individuals, refer to areas of functioning where training would be ineffective. If, for example, retardate inferiority on a number of short-term memory tasks could be attributed to an enhanced rate of spontaneous decay of information, and if training could not overcome that deficiency, then rate of decay would reflect a structural difference between retarded and nonretarded persons. Such differences, if found, would serve to define retardation in terms of basic psychological processes. "Since individual differences in intelligence are highly stable traits in our retardate population, only stable parameters, those representing structural features, are meaningfully relatable to intelligence" (Fisher & Zeaman, 1973, p. 251).

Control processes, however, are seen as optional strategies that an individual brings to bear on memory tasks. Any control process can be used, or not used, at the choice of the memorizer. As such, the implication is that the use of control processes is trainable; that is, they are not an invariant part of the memory system. While structural features are essentially constants, the choice of control processes can vary widely. Within this context, one extremely impressive property of the mature memorizer is the array of control processes that can flexibly be brought to bear on a wide variety of memory tasks. Some factors that may underlie this ability, and a discussion of their role in retardate performance, will be discussed toward the end of this chapter.

The essential difference between structural and control failures lies in their susceptibility to training: Control deficiencies are, by definition, trainable, while structural features are not. This distinction, of course, is the same as that between production and mediation deficiencies (Flavell, 1970). Empirically, the question of whether a retardate deficiency reflects structural or control features rests on the effectiveness of training procedures. If the deficiency responds to training, control failures are implicated; if training is unsuccessful, the inference is that a structural difference is involved. It is at this point that one difficulty clearly emerges, as a failure of training may result from an inappropriately designed training procedure. In principle, the inference that a structural feature is responsible for performance differences is possible only when all possible training procedures have been tried without success. Obviously, such a state of affairs will never be obtained, and the structural/control distinction rests on the relative ease of training aspects of performance.

There are also a number of more substantive problems involved in the distinction. First, as Newell (1972) has pointed out in a more general context, what we regard as structure and what we regard as process is very much a function of the theoretical viewpoint we adopt. Second, and especially troublesome for a developmental psychologist, if the structure of intelligence changes developmentally, then some structural limitations are, or at least can be, temporary. What is untrainable at one point in time may evolve quite naturally subsequently. This is most clearly true in the case of structures underlying "cognitive competence" in the Piagetian sense. It is also possible to distinguish another type of structural limitation, which may or may not change developmentally. This type is illustrated by the notion of a channel capacity. While cognitive competency-type structures undergo ontogenetic changes and should result in different memories at different points in development (Brown, 1975; Piaget & Inhelder, 1973), it is not so clear that channel capacity-type structural features undergo such growth. These different structural properties are also distinguished by the fact that one (competency) may vary qualitatively, whereas the second (capacity) varies only quantitatively.

In this chapter, we are equating structural features with untrainable determinants of performance and control processes with trainable aspects. Also, the references to structural features usually involve the capacity, rather than competency, referent.

B. Early Approaches

1. "Gross" Structural Differences

If we assume, as Fisher and Zeaman (1973) do, that intelligence is conceived as a relatively stable trait, it is obviously tempting to infer that some stable mechanism must be responsible for reduced levels of performance in a variety of tasks. As such, the theoretical aim is to isolate those stable mechanisms, and it is this outlook that seems to have influenced most early theorists, whose major hypotheses involved sources of structural limitations. In many cases, while the theories were not physiological in nature, possible neurophysiological mechanisms were suggested or described. Examples of such theories include those of Lewin (1935), Spitz (1963), and Ellis (1963), among others.

Of these, Ellis's stimulus trace theory has received the closest experimental scrutiny. Essentially, Ellis hypothesized that the retarded are characterized as having a diminished, or more rapidly fading, stimulus trace, with the result that they should perform more poorly than equal-CA normals in a wide variety of tasks that involve short-term memory. Specifically, the prediction was that IQ and retention interval should interact, with the rate of retention loss being greater for the retarded. As can be seen, the postulation of a single structural limitation can be used to predict a large number of more specific differences.

2. Problems with the Structural Theories

Theories of this type have encountered a number of difficulties, and their proponents have advanced different positions more recently (e.g., Ellis, 1970; Spitz, 1966, 1970). As will be described in more detail later, the difficulties these theories encountered stem from a failure to separate out the effects of the memorizer's activity during and following presentation of the material to be remembered. That is, short-term memory performance can be affected by structural limitations, but performance can also be determined by what the individual does with the material. Using Ellis's 1963 position as a basis, two nonindependent sources of difficulties can be described briefly.

a. *Rate of forgetting.* As Belmont and Butterfield (1969) have pointed out, no strong evidence supports the prediction of an interaction between intelligence and retention interval. Differences in performance between retarded and nonretarded individuals tend to remain relatively constant, rather than increasing, as the retention interval increases. Restricting attention to the relatively few cases where the predicted interaction has been obtained, there was no attempt to control the subject's strategic behavior in any way, and the types of tasks investigated in those studies appear to be of the episodic-strategic[1] variety (Brown, 1975), where adequate performance seems to require the use of task-appropriate strategies. In any event, the data either fail to support the notion of differential rates of forgetting, or can be interpreted in terms of differing degrees of strategic intervention.

b. *Modifiability of performance.* If the factor(s) responsible for poor performance are structural, training should produce little or no improvement. However, as we shall illustrate, training effects with the retarded are typically extremely large. Thus, the problem encountered by the retarded cannot be due *solely* to structural factors. It should be noted, however, that if training does not completely eliminate comparative differences, the possibility of structural differences remains.

---

[1] Tasks assessing episodic memory generally involve situations where, for example, the material to be remembered is relatively meaningless and exact reproduction of the input is required. The contrast is with paradigms assessing semantic memory, where, for example, the material is more meaningful and recall of the substance or gist of the information, rather than exact reproduction, is required.

C. Summary and Organization

While early theories emphasized structural differences, the research findings have not been confirmatory. We know of no structural differences that have been demonstrated clearly, and, as will be reviewed in the next section, there is abundant evidence for control deficiencies. In fact, various types of training components have been included in much of the recent research, and the emphasis has been on an individual's activity as he is trying to memorize a set of items. In reviewing this research, Brown (1974) has argued that one main problem with the retarded is their failure to employ various types of strategies—strategies that they use effectively when explicitly instructed to do so.

We will first review some of the major findings in the strategy training area. In reviewing these studies, we will consider the immediate outcomes of training, along with the more general effects, that is, what happens when the experimenter stops instructing the individual to carry out the strategy. To anticipate the outcome, the conclusion is that moderately and mildly retarded children and adolescents are unlikely to spontaneously adopt mnemonic strategies suitable to the task at hand. Specific training of a strategy is effective; however, the beneficial effects are typically limited to the specific task on which the training was conducted.

Given that there is a retardate deficit in the spontaneous production of mnemonic strategies and that the effects of training are limited to the specific training context, it is reasonable to ask why this might be true. In Section III.D we will describe some "more general" factors that are hypothesized to underlie the use of control processes. Finally, having noted that the trend has been from an emphasis on structural features to an emphasis on control processes, we will look at a number of more recent formulations, theories that allow the inclusion of both control and structural parameters.

III. INTERACTION OF TASK DEMANDS AND SUBJECTS' ACTIVITY

As already mentioned, with the advent of information-processing models and with the subject regarded as a more active participant in the memory situation, the emphasis in research changed correspondingly, and during the past several years the subject's activity has become of major importance. More detailed theoretical analyses of specific tasks have been made in terms of the kinds of control processes required for effective performance, and impaired performance has been interpreted, at least in part, as being due to a failure in spontaneous utilization of such control processes; support for that conjecture has been sought via training experiments of one type or another.

A. Task Demands

The kinds of tasks that have typically been employed in experimental work with the retarded require a variety of different control processes. That this feature of the tasks is important is highlighted by the fact that there are other types of tasks that do not appear to require strategies for effective performance. In the latter tasks, there appears to be no marked developmental trend within the nonretarded population (Brown, 1974, 1975). For example, in one particular task, involving judgment of relative recency, developmental differences appear only when some strategic component is involved (Brown, 1973a; Brown, Campione, & Gilliard, 1974). Of more relevance here, in a number of experiments reported by Brown (1972a, 1973b) retarded children performed extremely well on a number of recognition memory tasks. The subjects in these experiments also participated in another experiment (Brown, 1972b), where the task required the use of a rehearsal strategy. In the rehearsal experiment, their performance was very poor. While the data base is not overwhelming, the conclusion is that developmental or comparative differences are obtained only when some kind of strategic intervention is required. This conclusion is consistent with the hypothesis that comparative differences are attributable to varying control, rather than structural, features.

The majority of research, however, has involved three types of tasks that do require mnemonic strategies and are developmentally sensitive, namely rehearsal, organization, and elaboration. Within each, we will mention the spontaneous use of the strategy, its susceptibility to training, and the available information on transfer or generalization.

B. Maintenance and Generalization

While the term *transfer* has been used quite generically in the literature, we would like to make a distinction between *maintenance* and *generalization* of a trained strategy. The distinction depends on the extent to which the training and transfer situations differ. If the tasks used in both phases of experimentation are the same, we prefer to use the term *maintenance* (a synonym might be *strategy retention*), reserving *generalization* for use when the transfer task differs from that of training.[2] While both terms imply use of the trained strategy beyond the precise training period, the effects may be qualitatively different. For example, in a series of experiments on discrimination learning (Campione & Brown, 1974)

[2]While we will not deal with this aspect, generalization may also require some modification of the trained strategy. A simple case is one in which recombining the component activities in some way may be necessary to meet the new task demands.

it has been found that maintenance is readily achieved, whereas generalization is much less likely to occur. In the retardation area, it is possible to demonstrate that trained strategies can be maintained over time and over some minor changes in the stimulus material, for example, new pictures, but there are few data indicating that the strategy will transfer to another problem type or across bigger changes in stimulus type, for example, from pictures to numbers. In our view, most transfer work with the retarded in the memory area has investigated maintenance rather than generalization.

C. Specific Skills and Activities

While the number of activities individuals can and do use in memory situations is enormous, we will concern ourselves with only three here. The three are different in kind and of optimum use in different situations. Generally, the subject is required to learn and remember relatively meaningless material or arbitrary associations. Rehearsal seems best suited to tasks where the amount of information to be remembered is relatively small, and where exact reproduction is required (e.g., remembering a telephone number). Organizational strategies are best suited to tasks where there is some inherent order to the material to be remembered, or where the individual can impose his own order (subjective organization). Elaborative strategies are particularly useful in the case where a number of associations between unrelated items are to be learned, and where the subject is provided sufficient time to elaborate on the material in order to create a more meaningful context in which to embed the items. In the case of organization and elaboration, the aim is either to use the meaning inherent in the material or to seek out and create meaning in order to render the material more memorable.

Obviously, the strategies are not mutually exclusive, and in some cases a combination of, say, elaboration and rehearsal would result in superior performance than would either used alone. The point is that different strategies are effective in different situations, and the mature memorizer is able to evaluate the task demands accurately enough to come up with an appropriate choice. Brown (1974) has argued that the retarded not only do not do this well but seem to be deficient in the intent to use any strategy or, borrowing from Miller, Galanter, and Pribram (1960), in the "plan to use a plan." Evidence in keeping with this conclusion will be reviewed in the next section (III.C1). The question of whether the failure to employ the strategies is due to an inability to use them is the topic of Section III.C2. Finally, the aim of training is ultimately to bring an individual to the point where he can generalize the use of the trained strategy to other tasks having the same type of demands, or at least to maintain the strategy in the same task at a later time. An evaluation of transfer effects is the aim of Section III.C3.

I. Spontaneous Use of Activities

a. *Rehearsal.* In the retardation area, the use of rehearsal has received more attention than has any other mnemonic strategy. In general (with some exceptions to be discussed later), the data on spontaneous use are consistent in showing that retarded adolescents do not spontaneously rehearse efficiently in a number of situations where it would be appropriate. The evidence comes from a variety of sources employing both direct and indirect measures. A series of experiments by Ellis (1970) provides some indirect evidence. The task Ellis used consists of presenting a series of items, such as single-digit numbers or letters of the alphabet, followed by a probe item. The probe consists of a re-presentation of one of the items viewed, and the subject's task is to indicate the position that item had occupied in the series. Variables that are presumed to be sensitive to rehearsal activity produce different patterns of results in retarded and nonretarded adolescents and adults.[3] More specifically, college students accurately recall items from both the initial and terminal positions in the series ("primacy" and "recency" effects). Retardates and college students do not differ in their ability to recall items presented late in the series, but college students show a marked superiority in recall of items presented early in a series, a difference attributed to the retardates' failure to rehearse. Also, increasing the temporal spacing between successive items, thus allowing more time for rehearsal, has a beneficial effect on college students, but has no effect on the performance of the retarded (Ellis, 1970, Study 1). In taking a different stance than in 1963, Ellis (1970) states that "we favor an 'RS (rehearsal strategy) deficiency hypothesis' to account for the retardate-normal differences rather than an SM (secondary memory) deficit. It would appear that the retardate does not rehearse, even under spaced conditions, therefore his memory for items exceeding the limited capacity of PM (primary memory) is poor [p. 10]."

Further evidence comes from the work of Belmont and Butterfield (1969, 1971), who have modified the Ellis task by allowing subjects to go through the set of items at their own rate. The assumption is that the pattern of pauses exhibited by the subjects will reflect the basic acquisition strategies being employed. College students show stable pause patterns indicating use of a "cumulative rehearsal, fast finish" strategy, whereas the pause patterns of adolescent retardates are essentially flat, leading to the inference that no active acquisition strategy was being used.

Finally, a series of experiments in our laboratory (Brown, 1972a; Brown, Campione, Bray, & Wilcox, 1973) are also consistent with the notion that the

---

[3] As a general point, the clearest examples of strategic differences stem from experiments in which the strategic individual should differ from a nonstrategic one in his pattern of performance in addition to simple accuracy level. In such a case, an interaction between the population variable and some manipulated independent variable should emerge.

retarded are deficient in the spontaneous production of efficient rehearsal strategies. Again, the main evidence stems from an interaction between population and an independent variable. In the experiments, a total pool of 16 pictures was used, consisting of two exemplars of one category, four of each of two categories, and six of a fourth category. The task is one in which the subject sees a series of four pictures, one from each of the four categories, and is then questioned about the state of one of the categories, for example, "What was the last animal you saw?" Theoretically, rehearsing subjects should be uninfluenced by the number of states variable, as they can simply refer to the set of items being rehearsed and determine which one is, say, an animal. The other possible states of that variable need not be considered. For nonrehearsing subjects, however, the items would not be available in the rehearsal buffer, and the subject would be assumed to search through the set of animals and determine which one occurred most recently. This search should be more difficult and should take more time as the number of items increases. Thus, for nonrehearsers performance should decline, and latency should increase, as the number of states of the probed variable increases. That is, accuracy should be highest and latency of response should be shortest when the probed category contains the fewest (two) exemplars. Adolescent retardates show this "nonrehearsal" pattern, whereas nonretarded junior high school subjects' performance (accuracy and latency) is independent of the number-of-states variable.

While the results of these sets of experiments are consistent with each other, the conclusion that retarded adolescents *never* rehearse is obviously incorrect. There are data indicating rehearsal use in highly selected retarded subjects (Glidden, 1972), and in the experiments described in the preceding paragraph a number of untrained retarded subjects were designated as spontaneous rehearsers (Brown, 1974; Brown et al., 1973). Even given these data, however, it is clear that retarded adolescents are much less likely to employ an efficient rehearsal strategy than are their equal-CA nonretarded counterparts.

b. *Organization.* When required to remember a supraspan amount of information, one option is to try to deal with the material in terms of chunks (Miller, 1956) rather than individual items. Such attempts require an individual to transform the input in some way, and the most popular method of investigating the use of organizational strategies in retardate memory has involved free recall of organized lists. A number of reviews of the literature are available elsewhere (e.g., Goulet, 1968), and we will simply indicate some of the general conclusions. When categorized lists are presented for free recall, retardates tend to recall fewer items and show less clustering than do nonretarded subjects matched for CA. Also, the correlations between amount recalled and clustering scores tend to be higher for nonretarded than for retarded subjects. Inferences about the use of organizational strategies based purely on measures of organization, or "clustering scores," however, are somewhat suspect, as the patterns differ somewhat as a function of the clustering measure employed (see Spitz, 1966, for one example). Also, some clustering measures are not independent of the amount recalled (Murphy & Campione, 1974).

Stronger evidence for an "organizational deficiency" hypothesis can be obtained from other studies, some of which will be reviewed in the training section. One other experiment that provides some relevant evidence has been reported by Jensen and Fredericksen (1973), who included both random and organized free recall lists, and obtained a population × list type interaction. For the lower-IQ individuals, the difference between random and categorized lists was less pronounced than the corresponding difference for higher-IQ individuals. Changing from a random to an organizable list facilitated the performance of the brighter individuals more, the result expected if they are presumed more likely to employ organizational strategies.

c. *Elaboration.* While various forms of mnemonic elaboration have been described and studied, the vast majority of such research has been concerned with learning of paired associates. The developmental course of elaborative strategies within the nonretarded population has been described by Rohwer (1973), and a review of the retardate research has been presented recently by Borkowski and Wanschura (1974). It is difficult to separate studies on spontaneous use of elaboration from training studies, as inferences about spontaneous use are made from comparisons of individuals who are instructed in the use of elaboration versus those who are not so instructed. If instructions to use elaboration result in better performance, the conclusion is that subjects do not tend to elaborate unless instructed to do so. While the relevant experiments will be described in the next section, we can anticipate the results here and note that instructions to elaborate, or the provision by the experimenter of an elaborative context, either verbal or visual, always results in improved performance, thus suggesting a lack of spontaneous use.

2. Susceptibility to Training

In the three areas mentioned, the general conclusion is that retarded children do not spontaneously employ appropriate mnemonic strategies. The question of whether each failure is due to structural limitations or simply to failure to employ a usable strategy (alternatively, a mediational deficiency or a production deficiency) is answerable in terms of the effects of specific training.

a. *Rehearsal.* Training retarded adolescents to rehearse results in improved levels of performance and in patterns of performance similar to those of equal-CA comparative groups (Belmont & Butterfield, 1971; Brown et al., 1973; Butterfield, Wambold, & Belmont, 1973). The designs employed by Belmont and Butterfield (1971) and Brown et al. (1973) were similar in that both included untrained and rehearsal-trained retardates, along with noninstructed and "rehearsal-prevented" groups of nonretarded subjects. In both experiments, retardates trained to rehearse performed significantly better than untrained retardates, and the general patterns generated by those given training were the same as those of the "free strategy" nonretarded. Also, in both experiments nonretarded individuals prevented from rehearsing showed patterns characteristic of the untrained retarded subjects. This overall picture is consistent with the idea that the original retardate deficiency was due (at least in part) to a rehearsal deficiency. Retardates trained to rehearse show both improved performance levels and specific effects characteristic of equal-CA nonretarded individuals; conversely, the nonretarded subjects prevented from rehearsing show reduced performance and patterns characteristic of untrained retardates.

While both of the aforementioned studies showed clear effects due to rehearsal training, the most ambitious training study involving rehearsal has been reported by Butterfield et al. (1973). The work involved a more detailed analysis of the strategic requirements involved in their short-term memory paradigm, specifically, the adoption of a particular acquisition strategy essentially requiring the use of a specific (corresponding) retrieval plan. The acquisition strategy trained in the Butterfield et al. research was, in their terms, a "3–3" strategy. Individuals are exposed to an array of 6 items in a self-paced task. The 3–3 (active–passive) strategy consists of having the subject pause after the third item and actively rehearse the initial 3 items. Following this, the subject is taught to expose the last three items passively and call for the probe immediately. The logic of the acquisition strategy, of course, is that if the time period is short enough, the last three items will still be in short-term memory at the time of test; thus, no active attempt at maintenance would be required. This is the "cumulative rehearsal, fast finish" strategy often adopted by adults (Pinkus & Laughery, 1970).

Having adopted such an acquisition strategy, efficient performance now requires that the individual respond to the probe item by searching through the last three items initially; if the target item is not located, the subject can then refer to the initial set of three (actively rehearsed) items. If the order of search is reversed, and if the target item is not in the set of three rehearsed items, the second set of three (passively viewed) items will have faded from memory, and performance will obviously be poor. The use of a passive viewing of the last three items is based on the assumption that the contents of primary memory will not have time to fade if the probe comes quickly enough. If, however, the subject himself imposes a retention interval by searching through the initial trio of items first, the main rationale for having used such an acquisition strategy is violated.

The data from Butterfield et al. indicated that training the 3–3 acquisition strategy did not guarantee that individuals would spontaneously adopt the corresponding retrieval schemes. In fact, performance was much higher on the initial trio of items than on the second set. When training of the appropriate retrieval was added to the program, performance improved, with the amount of improvement being related to the extent to which the actual sequencing of the various acquisition–retrieval components was specifically and explicitly trained, a point to which we shall return later.

The results of these experiments are clear enough. Training in rehearsal results in dramatic improvements. In the Butterfield et al. (1973) research, trained retardates were eventually performing at the same level as untrained college students. It may still be the case, however, that there are some structural limitations on the use of rehearsal. In our own research, we have found that the maximum number of items our subjects could rehearse concurrently was three (Brown et al., 1973). Having them add a fourth item to this rehearsal set resulted in a dramatic impairment in performance. (It should be noted that in this research the rate of stimulus presentation was experimenter-determined, not subject-determined.) McBane (1972), in a study designed to determine the amount of rehearsal obtainable, has also argued that level of cognitive development limits the maximum number of items rehearsable. However, the issues concerning structural limitations on rehearsal are complex and depend, to some extent, on the nature of the task and the investigator's definition of rehearsal. For instance, Turnbull (1974) has shown that retarded adolescents can rehearse as many as seven items cumulatively when within-trial prompting is allowed, with the amount of prompting necessary decreasing after extensive training. Ferguson and Bray (in press) have shown that four items can be successfully rehearsed without prompting for first graders when the child is required to repeat the entire set of items in order several times rather than repeat them cumulatively. They also demonstrated that there are fewer rehearsal errors with digits than with picture names. Thus, a more complete understanding of limitations on rehearsal will await a more detailed analysis of task-related variables such as the type of rehearsal required, the type of training used, and the nature of the materials.

b. *Organization.* In a number of experiments, retarded adolescents and adults have been induced to make use of the organization inherent in a categorized list. Two successful methods, employed in an experiment by Gerjuoy and Spitz (1966), have been called presented clustering (blocked input) and requested clustering (constrained recall). In the presented-clustering situation, the presentation list is blocked by category; that is, all the instances of each category are presented together within the list. In the case of requested clustering, the items are presented in a random order, but the individual is instructed to recall by category, for example, "Tell me all the animals." In one case, the list is presented in an already organized form, whereas in the other the organization is "pointed out" after the initial viewing. The two methods were equally effective in the Gerjuoy and Spitz experiment, and resulted in significantly better recall than a control group given random presentation and no instructions to recall by category.

The results from this and other experiments (Bilsky & Evans, 1970; Gerjuoy, Winters, Pullen, & Spitz, 1969) indicate that retarded individuals can make effective use of organization when the organizational principles are somehow made salient. Again, the conclusion is that it is the failure to spontaneously employ organizational strategies, rather than an inability to use them, that is the main problem.

c. *Elaboration.* In a number of experiments, either providing individuals with verbal or visual elaborations or instructing them in the use of such elaborations results in a clear improvement in performance, allowing the obvious inference that the use of mediational strategies is well within their capabilities. This research has been reviewed recently by Borkowski and Wanschura (1974), and they have concluded that mildly and moderately retarded individuals can successfully employ elaborative strategies. The retarded make efficient use of mediators provided by an experimenter and, when trained, can provide some form of mediator (or elaboration) of their own, although the quality of these mediators might not be as good as that of those provided by their normal peers. As Borkowski and Wanschura (1974) conclude, "apparently, there is little evidence to support a mediation *control deficiency* in the retarded. . . . However, most mediational findings indicate a limited *production deficiency,* especially with lower functioning retarded children [p. 49]."

3. The Problem of Transfer

In many of the earlier training studies, the intent was to demonstrate that training would effectively improve performance. With the success of such demonstrations, the obvious next question concerned the magnitude or power of the training procedures, and investigators have turned their attention more to the longer-range effects of training, with the interest being in whether the training would have any effects beyond the original training situation. In terms of the distinction introduced earlier, we would argue that the vast majority of the studies have been concerned with *maintenance* rather than *generalization.* That is, the format of the transfer task is the same as that employed during training.

a. *Rehearsal.* The results of a number of studies (Brown, Campione, & Murphy, 1974; Kellas, Ashcraft, & Johnson, 1973; Turnbull, 1974) indicate that long-lasting effects of rehearsal training can be obtained. In the Brown et al. study, the one with the longest retention interval, 8 out of 10 retarded adolescents given extensive rehearsal training (12 days) continued to rehearse effectively 6 months later. Those 8 individuals showed patterns of performance clearly indicating rehearsal, and maintained their advantage over an untrained control group. However, the trained and untrained subjects were then given a generalization test using the probe technique employed by Ellis and by Belmont and Butterfield. In this (unpublished) experiment, the overall level of the trained group was exactly the same as that of the control group. Thus, there was clear evidence of maintenance of the trained strategy over a six-month interval, but no evidence of generalization.

b. *Organization.* A number of studies in the clustering literature have looked at maintenance. Here, individuals are induced to make use of the organization available in a categorized list, and are then given a transfer task involving recall of another categorizable list. For example, Bilsky and Evans (1970) presented items blocked by category on a first list, and followed that with a transfer list in which items from a common category were distributed randomly throughout the list. While Bilsky and Evans found evidence of maintenance when the same materials were employed in both phases, no such evidence was available in another study where new materials were introduced on transfer (Bilsky, Evans, & Gilbert, 1972). While evidence of maintenance on new lists has been reported by Nye, McManis, and Haugen (1972), the amount of training was extensive, and maintenance was much more pronounced with old, as opposed to new, items.

c. *Elaboration.* The picture here is not dissimilar to that in the rehearsal and organization areas. Evidence for maintenance has been obtained by some investigators (e.g., Turnure & Thurlow, 1973), but not by others (e.g., Jensen & Rohwer, 1963; Milgram, 1967). One factor determining the type of outcome is the amount of practice, or the number of different lists employed during training, with maintenance being more likely when two or more lists are used during training.

In an experiment by Ross, Ross, and Downing (1973), there was also evidence of generalization of an elaborative strategy. After extensive training on the use of elaborative techniques in game settings in the classroom, individuals were given a paired-associates task. The performance of the trained subjects was significantly better than that of an untrained control group given the same amount of (classroom) practice with the game settings, but without any training in elaboration. Also, the individuals who had received training showed dramatically more evidence of the use of elaborative, or mediational, strategies on the paired-associate task.

4. Summary

The evidence from these areas seems quite consistent. Moderately retarded children show a deficiency in the use of a variety of mnemonic strategies. The deficiencies appear to be of the production type, as training results in marked improvement in performance. Maintenance can be achieved if there is a sufficient amount of training, but there is almost no evidence showing impressive generalization effects.

D. General Skills and Activities

While it is true that a failure to be strategic results in poor performance on a variety of tasks (Brown, 1974), the results of maintenance and generalization tests indicate that *(1)* training specific skills will not result in real remediation effects and *(2)* more general factors must underlie both the lack of spontaneous use of strategies and the failure to show generalization of training. A search for these factors would then be of both applied and theoretical interest.

In this section, we shall enumerate what some of the general factors might be, and summarize what data are available. In some cases, there is either little data available on retarded individuals and/or a lack of comparative studies. Given these gaps in the retardation literature, we will borrow somewhat from the general developmental literature.

1. The Problem of Transfer

Transfer itself is obviously a general factor, as it is independent of specific tasks, that is, involved in all the areas we have considered here. In fact, a case can be made that transfer failures are the source of many of the specific production deficiencies which have been indentified. If it is assumed that at least some of the activities of which strategies are composed are available to individuals prior to training, then failure to employ them spontaneously can be regarded as a failure of generalization. Further, if this is an accurate assessment, it should not be surprising that training studies do not result in generalization, since an inability to generalize would be the factor making the training necessary in the first place.

Adopting this bias, one way of indicating some other general factors is to consider what an individual must do in order to generalize effectively. Figure 12-1 presents an oversimplified summary of some of the steps involved. The first step indicated is to evaluate the task and determine whether any strategic intervention will be required. The main determinant here is most likely the perceived difficulty of the task, and some factors that would influence this decision include the extent to which exact reproduction of the material will be required (Brown, 1975) and the extent to which subjects are aware of their own capacity limitations (Brown, 1977). At this point, the subject may decide to, or have no choice but to, act passively, or to search for an appropriate way of dealing with the specific task. Given the latter option, the subject must evaluate the exact task demands in more detail in an attempt to choose the appropriate strategy. This choice can be determined by such factors as the meaningfulness of the material, the amount of information to be retained, and the retention interval. Again at this point, the subject can decide to use some particular strategy(ies) or may decide that none of his available strategies would be useful given the particular task at hand, or he may set into motion an inappropriate strategy that happens to be the only (or dominant) one in his repertoire.

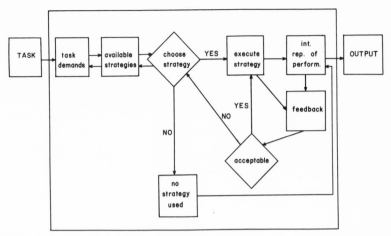

FIGURE 12-1   An illustration of some of the possible components that could be involved in applying a strategy.

Assuming that a strategy has been chosen, the subject must monitor both the execution of the strategy and its effectiveness. That is, strategies can be carried out either well or poorly, and they can lead to either high or low levels of performance. Considering level of performance, there are at least two sources of information—an individual's estimate of his performance and the feedback provided by the experimenter. The memorizer must also make an implicit comparison between the level of performance obtained with the chosen strategy and that which would be obtained without the strategy. For example, if the amount of cognitive strain (Bruner, Greenfield, & Olver, 1966) generated by the strategy is too great, or if execution of the strategy itself requires an excessive amount of M-space (Pascual-Leone, 1970), its use may actually interfere with performance. Once all this information is collected, the individual can decide whether to maintain or abandon his chosen approach to the problem.

While it may be reasonable to assume that the mature memorizer carries out many of these steps automatically, it is likely that for persons of a lower developmental level each step "require(s) especially intensive conscious control" (Smirnov & Zinchenko, 1969, p. 469). Thus, a failure to produce or generalize a strategy could be due to a breakdown in any combination of the many phases of the overall process. In the ensuing sections, we will present data indicating that the retarded child seems to have difficulty with each area; consequently, it is not surprising that little spontaneous production or generalization has been demonstrated. The strategy is to summarize what we know about the performance of retarded children with regard to some of the processes indicated in Figure 12-1. Specifically, topics to be discussed include estimating task difficulty, monitoring the use of a strategy, adjusting the strategy to task demands, and making use of implicit and explicit information and feedback.

2. Metamemorial Factors

Metamemorial factors involve the individual's awareness of his own memory processes, including his ability to estimate task difficulty and to evaluate the current strength or durability of his memory representations. The point of departure is a series of studies by Flavell and his associates (see Flavell & Wellman, this volume). In the context of retardation, it is at least arguable that one factor underlying production deficiencies stems from a failure on the part of the retarded child to realize that the task is difficult and thus requires the use of goal-directed mnemonic activities. Individuals would not attempt to rehearse or organize, for example, if they believed they could do well without resorting to such devices.

Except for some recent work in our laboratory, there has been no research aimed at assessing metamemorial efficiency in retarded children. Given the evidence that retarded children tend to be deficient in the use of strategic intervention, our hypothesis was that they would also perform poorly on such tasks as predicting their own recall and assessing their recall readiness. If such problems were encountered, it seemed possible that training metamnemonic ability might result in increased strategy usage.

At this point, there is the question of what to train and how to go about it. We decided on a pair of approaches, the first (Brown, Campione, & Murphy, 1976) involving direct training of an aspect of metamemorial functioning: span estimation. The second avenue of research (Brown & Barclay, 1976) can be placed into context by considering an apparent disagreement between Butterfield and Belmont (in press) and Brown (1974). Butterfield and Belmont have argued that attempts to train specific skills should be abandoned in favor of training more general factors (for example, executive control—see later discussion), whereas Brown has indicated that some training of specific skills should take place initially, as it would be difficult to train an individual to monitor or control his set of strategic activities if that set were empty. Given the consideration that it would be difficult to monitor a nonexistent strategy, the study by Brown and Barclay (1976) involved the training of specific memorization routines in a recall readiness situation (see Flavell & Wellman, this volume) where the memorizer is required to continue the use of the trained strategy until he is satisfied that he has learned the material and is ready to recall it. Thus, this experiment investigated the extent to which the training of appropriate memory strategies would lead to effective metamnemonic behavior. From this perspective, the experiments can be seen to differ in one important respect. In the Brown et al. (1976) study, the problem of metamemory is contacted directly and training is specifically on metamemorial functioning. In the Brown and Barclay work, the treatment of metamemorial functioning is more indirect. Strategies are trained, and the individual's monitoring of them is then observed.

The studies also differ in one other interesting way. The span estimation task requires the individual to estimate his or her performance prior to performing on the task, while in the recall readiness paradigm the task is to estimate degree of learning while performing on the task. In this case, more complex processing seems to be required, as concurrently applying a task-relevant mnemonic and monitoring its success or failure appears to involve a complex coordination of introspective and overt behavior, a coordination that is late developing in both nonretarded and retarded populations.

a. *Estimating task difficulty.* The initial study (Brown et al., 1976) addressed the simpler and presumably more basic component—span estimation. If the individual cannot determine when a problem is difficult, he would not be expected to produce deliberate memorization strategies. Two groups of naive educable children (MAs = 6 and 8, IQs = 69 and 72, respectively) were shown an array of ten pictures and asked to predict how many they would be able to recall. This prediction was then compared with their (subsequently determined) actual recall. Individuals whose estimates were within two items (±2) of their actual recall were termed realistic estimators; those whose guesses were more than two items in error were termed unrealistic estimators. Only 31% of the older children and 21% of the younger ones could be classed as realistic, with the remainder overestimating their performance levels (most predicted that they could recall all ten). All unrealistic estimators were then given a series of ten training trials on which they were required to estimate their performance and then to recall. For half the participants at each MA level, those in the feedback condition, explicit feedback was given reminding them of their prediction and indicating visually and orally the number of items they had actually recalled. This feedback was given following each estimation-recall series. The remaining children predicted and recalled, but no explicit feedback was provided.[4] After training was completed, three posttests were given, the first one day after training, the second two weeks after training, and the third approximately one year after the original posttests.

The data of major interest are shown in Figures 12-2 and 12-3. Figure 12-2 gives the proportion of realistic estimators separately for the two MA levels on the pretest and on each of the subsequent posttests. In general, the younger children show improvement on the first posttest (one day after training), but are back to baseline levels following two weeks. For the older children, the initial improvement is more dramatic and is better maintained over time. Even one year later, the proportion of realistic estimators (.56) is considerably larger than it was prior to training (.31).

In Figure 12-3, the data of only the originally unrealistic estimators are con-

---

[4]Subsequent testing indicated that the individuals in the no-feedback groups could report the number of items they recalled. Thus, they did have the information concerning recall available to them; it simply was not emphasized.

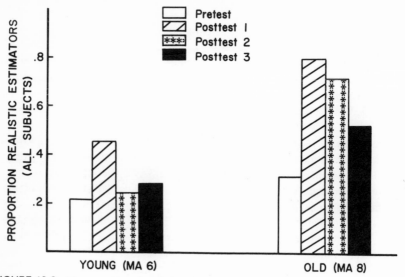

FIGURE 12-2   The proportion of realistic estimators as a function of mental age and test phase.

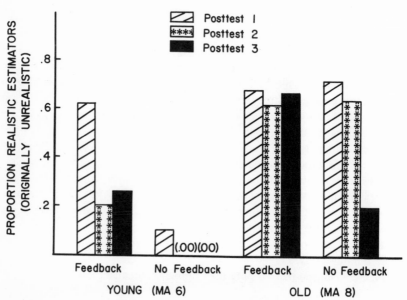

FIGURE 12-3   The proportion of realistic estimators considering only those who were originally unrealistic, as a function of mental age, feedback condition, and test phase.

sidered; further, the results are broken down in terms of both MA level and the feedback variable. (Students classed as realistic initially remained so throughout the experiment.) Considering the first posttest, of the originally unrealistic children, 65% of the older individuals became realistic independent of the feedback condition. Of the younger trainees, 62% of those given feedback became realistic, whereas only 9% of those not given feedback improved to the point of being realistic. Looking at the data from Posttest 2, the older individuals remained unchanged; 60% were still realistic, and there was no effect of the feedback variable. However, for the younger children only 18% of those given feedback remained realistic, and none in the no-feedback group could be classed as realistic. Thus, considering only the first two posttests for the older children, training, with or without explicit feedback, is sufficient to bring about realistic estimation, and the effect is somewhat durable. The pattern obtained with the younger students contrasts sharply: There is significant improvement on the first posttest only when explicit feedback is provided during training, and even in this case the effects are not durable, as the proportion of realistic estimators drops from .62 on posttest 1 to .18 on posttest 2. The effect of providing explicit feedback for the older children is illustrated only on the final posttest. The proportion of realistic estimators remains unchanged in the feedback condition, whereas for those not given feedback during training only 20% remain realistic approximately one year after training.

In addition to assessing maintenance, a number of generalization probes were administered. On each posttest, individuals' span estimations were obtained through the seriated method used by other investigators (Flavell, Friedrichs, & Hoyt, 1970; Markman, 1973; Yussen & Levy, 1975). With this procedure, individuals are shown a series of cards, the first containing one picture, the second two (novel) pictures, and so on to a total of ten cards. The cards are presented sequentially, and the person's task is to say whether or not he would be able to remember the set of items. (This task was administered on the pretests, but was never presented during the training phase of the experiment.) Responders were initially classed as consistent or inconsistent. Consistent individuals responded "yes" to all sets up to a given point, then "no" for all larger sets; inconsistency refers to a series of responses in which the first "no" (for example, at set size 5) is followed by at least one subsequent "yes" (for example, at set size 7).[5] The consistent responders were then classed as realistic if their estimate was within two units of their actual recall and unrealistic otherwise. A second generalization test, given only after Posttest 2, involved estimating the number of digits out of a set of ten that could be recalled. The procedure here was the same

---

[5] The procedure employed here differed from that of other experimenters. They stopped the assessment when the first "no" response was given, with the consequence that no inconsistent responders could be identified.

as in the original portion of the experiment, with the exception that digits, rather than pictures, were used.

Briefly, the originally realistic estimators remained realistic on the generalization tests; the individuals who became realistic only following training, however, did not. Considering the seriated tests, the data are shown in Figure 12-4. As can be seen, there is no evidence for generalization, with two sources of evidence leading to this conclusion. First, there is a sharp difference between performance on the ten-item sets and the seriated sets, and second, there is no change from the pretest level.

A similar conclusion is reached if we consider the data from the number generalization test. Restricting attention to the originally unrealistic estimators, only 8 out of 49 can be classed as realistic on the number task. Thus, in neither case is there any evidence for generalization, although the conditions for obtaining it would appear to be optimal (Campione & Brown, 1974). The same basic judgment was required in training and in both generalization tasks. Further, in one task (numbers) the problem format remained the same, and in the other the type of stimuli remained the same.

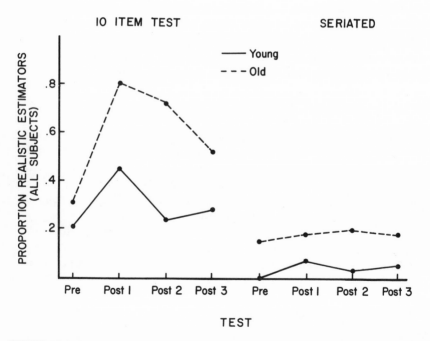

FIGURE 12-4 The proportion of realistic estimators on the training (10-item test) and generalization (seriated) tasks as a function of mental age and test phase.

b. *Monitoring strategy usage.*   In a second experiment using comparable subjects[6] (IQ = 70; MA groups of 6 and 8 years), Brown and Barclay (1976) investigated both recall readiness and the effects of training mnemonic skills on recall readiness. In the initial phase of the experiment, each individual's span of ordered recall was determined. For the remainder of the experiment, each subject was presented on each trial with a number of items equal to 1.5 times his own span. Thus, if a particular individual's span were four, he would be presented six items to remember. The apparatus consisted of a 2 × 6 array of windows, each with a separate shutter. The subject would press a window when he was ready, and the picture would appear and remain on until he pressed another window, at which time the first picture would disappear and the picture in the pressed window would appear. Each person was to study the items as long as he wanted in whatever order he wanted, and to signal the experimenter when he was ready to recall all the items in order.

During the baseline, or pretraining, portion of the experiment, each participant was given three trials, on each of which he was told to study the items until he was sure he could recall all of them *in order.* During this phase, average recall was only approximately 57% correct, and 60 out of 66 subjects failed to have even one trial on which they recalled perfectly. Only 1 out of 27 and 5 out of 39 older subjects had at least one perfect trial.

Following baseline, individuals at each MA level were divided into three separate groups: anticipation, rehearsal, and label. Anticipation and rehearsal involve a self-testing component, while labeling does not. As such, the label condition essentially serves as a control group. All individuals were required to go through the list once, labeling each item. This labeling trial was followed by a series of three more trials on which the procedures differed between the groups. Those in the anticipation group were trained to try to anticipate the next item before exposing it. The rehearsal subjects were trained to rehearse the items in sets of three (as nearly as possible; that is, if their list length was five, they would rehearse the first three, then the remaining two). Finally, the label group were told to go through the list three more times, labeling each item. All groups were further encouraged to continue with the instructed activity until they were sure they could recall all the items in the proper order. Training consisted of three trials (lists) per day for two days.

Following training, four posttests were given, a prompted posttest in which individuals were instructed to continue the trained strategy one day after training,

---

[6] In this experiment, some of the subjects had participated in the span estimation study previously described, whereas others were naive with regard to memory experiments. There was no difference between naive and sophisticated individuals in either this experiment or a number of others not reported here, a finding that may bear on the extent of generalization that can be expected.

and three unprompted posttests given one day, approximately two weeks, and approximately one year later. The main results are shown in Figure 12-5, which gives the percentage of correct recall. The break in the curve between posttests 3 and 4 indicates that not all individuals were retested on the final posttest; however, 21 out of 27 younger subjects and 35 out of 39 older ones were tested at that time. As can be seen, both younger and older retardates in the anticipation and rehearsal groups perform signficantly better on the prompted posttest (posttest 1) than on the pretest. In addition, if we consider the anticipation and rehearsal groups, 13 out of 18 younger subjects recalled perfectly on at least one trial, compared with 0 out of 18 on the pretest; the corresponding figures for the older subjects are 24 out of 26 on posttest 1 compared with 2 out of 26 on the pretest. Thus, training the useful mnemonic strategies resulted in both enhanced performance (percent recall data) and improved monitoring (data on number of perfect recalls).

The MA 6 and MA 8 groups differ considerably on the last three (unprompted) posttests. For the younger group, performance on posttests 2, 3, and 4 is not significantly different from the pretraining level (see Figure 12-5), whereas for the older group performance on all posttests differs significantly from the pretraining level. Thus, as in the previous experiment, training facilitates performance, with the effect being somewhat durable for the older retardates but transitory for the younger ones.

Regarding monitoring of strategy usage, one other aspect of the data is worthy of mention. The experimenter attempted to identify an individual's activity during the posttest study periods as either labeling, anticipating, rehearsing, other,

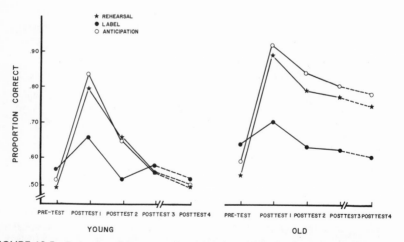

FIGURE 12-5 Proportion of correct recall as a function of mental age, training condition, and test phase. (Adapted from Brown & Barclay, 1976.)

or none. While the results are somewhat suspect, as no reliability data were collected on the classifications, the pattern is provocative. Of the 27 younger retardates, 20 on Posttest 2 and 18 on Posttest 3 were observed to continue executing their trained strategy. The interesting point is that, while two-thirds of the subjects continued in the trained activity, a corresponding increment in accuracy was absent. One interpretation of this outcome is that the reduced level of performance reflects a failure in memory monitoring. While the trained activity was maintained, individuals failed to assess their memory strength adequately, and hence terminated the activity before the items were sufficiently well learned. This did not happen with the older (MA = 8) group, and the suggestion is that for the older retardates training in strategy usage results in adequate metamemorial functioning, whereas with the younger children such is not the case unless explicit prompting is maintained.

c. *Summary.* The results of these initial experiments indicate that mildly retarded children have problems estimating their own performance, both prior to and during the time they are performing on some task. It also seems clear that, for the younger children, information about their performance needs to be explicit before it will have any effect, and that continual prompting may be necessary to maintain performance. Also, in both experiments a clear developmental trend was found regarding the durability of training effects. Whereas training had a relatively durable effect with the older subjects, the effects with the younger ones were extremely short-lived.

One final noteworthy outcome is that there was little evidence of generalization in the Brown et al. (1976) study, even when the test procedure assessed only minimal generalization effects. Regarding the hypothesis that training more general factors, such as metamemory, would result in more general improvement, these data can only be regarded as discouraging.

3. Executive Control

Butterfield and Belmont (in press) have also advanced the view that research efforts should be increasingly concerned with general determinants of performance, rather than with investigations of specific skills and strategies. They have emphasized the role of executive control, which refers to "the means whereby we select, sequence, evaluate, revise or abandon these operations (control processes)." In terms of Figure 12-1, they are concerned with the memorizer's ability to evaluate the specific task demands, to choose an appropriate strategy for a particular problem, and then to monitor the execution and effectiveness of that approach. In the reported research, Butterfield and Belmont were concerned primarily with "within-strategy changes" as a function of task difficulty. That is, they do not specifically deal with the factors involved in the initial choice of a strategy, but are concerned with the efficiency with which individuals abandon a strategy when it is no longer necessary and subsequently reinstate it when its use again becomes necessary.

The basic procedure consists of presenting a number of lists of items for recall and observing the amount of time required for selection of a stable strategy. Later one list is re-presented for a number of successive trials, at which time an individual no longer needs to work actively on the items. Finally, new lists are introduced, and the individual must again begin using his chosen strategy to deal with the information. Only nonretarded individuals were tested, and the data indicate that younger children, as compared with older children and adults, took longer to *(1)* select a strategy initially; *(2)* abandon it when it was no longer necessary; and *(3)* reinstate it when its use was again required.

While Butterfield and Belmont argue that attempts to train the executive function are preferable to attempts to train specific strategies, some data they present can be taken to indicate the reverse of that suggestion, or at least to indicate that the choice of which training strategy to use depends on the developmental level of the subject. The same data also seem to reinforce the importance of metamemorial functioning. If we look at the data from some of the younger (CA = 10) children in their research, it is not really clear that there is evidence for stable use of a strategy.[7] Even if it is granted that the younger children did select a particular strategy, there remains the problem of accounting for variations in performance level (79, 65, and 45% recall on the initial, presumably rehearsed, set of items for adults, 12-year-olds, and 10-year-olds, respectively). If the pause pattern data are to be interpreted as indicating strategy selection and stabilization, and if the strategies are taken to be the same for all individuals, the reason for the recall differences is not clear. One suggestion, consistent with the Brown and Barclay data, is that the younger children may execute the strategy, but may not monitor its usage adequately (may not accurately assess their recall readiness), with the result that they terminate their activity prior to learning the items. Supportive of this suggestion is the fact that the amount of study time increased with the age of the subjects.

In a subsequent experiment, Butterfield and Belmont (in press, Experiment 7) reported an experiment in which a specific strategy was trained in 10-year-olds. Following training, executive control of that strategy was investigated. Compared to untrained 10-year-olds in the earlier study, the result was more rapid abandonment of the trained strategy with repeated lists and more rapid reinstatement when a series of new lists was introduced. One interpretation is that, for individuals above some developmental level, training the strategy also results in effective executive control of that strategy.

[7]If it is the case that these subjects do not generate a strategy, it seems clear that training should involve the strategy in conjunction with the executive function, rather than simply executive function; otherwise, the executive would have nothing to control.

4. Use of Information

In this section, we will deal with two types of information use. The first is essentially an instructional variable: An experimenter provides information about the way in which a subject should attempt to deal with the problem at hand. The second concerns the use of feedback provided after a subject has responded. In both cases, the data do not necessarily indicate that the problems are specific to retardate, or even that they are more pronounced within the retardate population. That is, possible interactions between IQ and the relevant independent variables have not been investigated extensively. However, within these areas clear developmental trends are evident, and the retardate data available appear consistent with the assertion that retarded children do not use available information effectively.

a. *Prompt explicitness.* Rohwer (1973) has summarized a number of developmental studies investigating the use of elaborative techniques. His general conclusion is that the younger the child, the more explicitly he must be prompted before he will show signs of using elaboration as an aid to learning. One contribution of Rohwer's analysis is the demonstration that it is possible to vary systematically the degree of prompting involved in training experiments. In the retardate research, the main variable has been presence versus absence of training, with little attention paid to the minimal amount of prompting necessary to effect a change in behavior. While Rohwer does present some data that can be interpreted as indicating that lower-IQ children may require more explicit prompting than their higher-IQ counterparts, there has been little systematic attempt to use the various levels of prompt to describe the rate of development of particular activities and compare that rate in the retarded and nonretarded populations. The only exception to this is a series of studies conducted by Bray and his students. Bray (1973) showed that retarded adolescents were able to eliminate interference from irrelevant information in memory when a cue to forget was given in a directed-forgetting paradigm.[8] These studies used several days of pretraining in which the significance of the forget cue was carefully explained and reviewed. Subsequently, Hyatt (1976) found that normal and retarded adolescents show substantial interference from the information to be forgotten when the significance of the cue to forget is not explained. When a verbal explanation was provided, performance increased for both normal and retarded adolescents, but interference was still present for the retarded group. Goodman (1976)

[8] The procedure in these experiments is to present a series of digits. Each digit is presented on a colored background, with a change in background color serving as a cue that the previous items will not be tested and should be forgotten. For example, if the series were 3 4 8 6 1 2 and if the first three items were presented on a red background the last three on a blue background, the subject would be tested only on the last three items. Specifically, the color change on the fourth item would serve as the cue that the first three items would not be tested.

showed that a pretraining procedure in which a verbal explanation and trial-by-trial review is given is the minimal degree of instruction necessary for retarded adolescents to eliminate interference from information to be forgotten. This research is relevant to questions regarding the relative rates of development of spontaneous production, with the conclusion being that development is slower within the retarded population; that is, the minimal degree of prompting necessary to affect performance decreases more slowly for retarded, as compared to nonretarded, children. Also of obvious interest is the question of ultimate level of development. In the nonretarded population, Rohwer has presented some data indicating that instructions to learn the material are sufficient to induce elaboration; however, in some cases instructions to learn seem never to be sufficient, and stronger prompting is necessary at all age levels tested.

In addition to the work on directed forgetting, there is other, more indirect, evidence regarding the importance of prompt explicitness within the retarded population. Instructions to learn do not tend to arouse the use of appropriate learning and memory strategies, a fact that is obvious from the need for explicit training procedures. Also, in reviewing the results of a number of training studies involving retarded children, Butterfield and Belmont (in press) compared studies involving explicit instructions and implicit training procedures. Implicit manipulations generally consist of the experimenter's restructuring the problem format to highlight the type of strategy that would be most beneficial. Across the studies, explicit manipulations resulted in an average increase in performance of 64%, while the corresponding figure for implicit manipulations was only 34%. Thus, the explicit procedures effected twice as great an improvement in performance as the implicit ones. The comparison is obviously a gross one, as the different studies involved different tasks, and persons of varying levels of retardation. Nonetheless, the result can be regarded as suggestive, and it is a problem for future research to decide whether more adequately controlled studies can establish a pattern indicating a retardate deficiency, that is, whether an IQ × explicit/implicit interaction would be obtained.

Some of the best evidence regarding the importance of prompt explicitness within the retarded population was reported in the Butterfield et al. (1973) research described earlier (Section III.C2a). One of the major findings concerned the fact that retarded individuals in their experiments required explicit training in each individual component activity and in the sequencing and integration of these activities. The comparative question of interest is whether nonretarded children trained in the particular acquisition strategy would spontaneously adopt the corresponding retrieval strategy, that is, whether acquisition training would lead to efficient retrieval, or whether both steps would have to be trained explicitly.

Finally, degree of prompting remains important even after "successful" training has been completed. With young nonretarded children, the trained strategy ceases to be produced when the experimenter stops instructing the subject to employ it (e.g., Keeney, Cannizzo, & Flavell, 1967). Similarly, the results of many maintenance studies with the retarded lead to the conclusion that explicit prompting must be maintained in order to guarantee continued use of the trained strategy effectively (see the Brown & Barclay study described in the metamemory section for an illustration of both the continuing need for prompting and some developmental trends).

b. *Use of feedback.*   Again, what little comparative data exist indicate that retarded children require more complete feedback about their performance than do nonretarded children. For example, Spence (1966) investigated performance on a verbal discrimination task where individuals were required to learn which member of each of a number of pairs of words is correct. Some children were given feedback only on correct choices ("right"), others only on incorrect choices ("wrong"), and a final group following each choice. Whereas all subjects performed relatively poorly when given feedback following correct choices only, the nonretarded children performed equally well under the two conditions involving feedback following an incorrect choice. For the retarded children, however, only feedback following *each* choice resulted in improved performance. Thus, the data suggest that more explicit feedback is required by the retarded.

E. Summary

In a variety of areas, it seems clear that retarded children do not tend to choose a mnemonic activity appropriate to the task at hand, with the result that their performance, in terms of both patterns and levels (Brown, 1975), differs from that of an equal-CA nonretarded child. Part of the problem stems from a general tendency to fail to be strategic rather than from an inappropriate choice of activity. This conclusion is of course subject to the caveat that we may not have employed experimental procedures sensitive to the right activities, that is, that subjects can be strategic but do not employ the activities we set out to measure (see Wellman, Ritter, & Flavell, 1975).

Even when the activities are trained specifically, generalization occurs only rarely, although maintenance can be achieved relatively easily through extended training. In the previous section, we presented a summary of some of the steps necessary to achieve generalization (estimate memory capacity, evaluate task demands, choose an activity, monitor its execution, monitor performance level, estimate performance level given other approaches), and delineated a number of "general" factors that are involved. While the amount of research, both in the general developmental area and more specifically in retardation, is sparse, it seems reasonable to proffer the tentative conclusion that the retarded child experiences special difficulties in these areas. Questions about the effects of training general factors and the extent to which improved metamemorial functioning, for example, will result in more strategic approaches to memory situations remain open, and appear to represent a possibly profitable area for future research.

Before concluding this section, one further point should be made. In each of the areas we have considered, performance can be dramatically improved through the use of explicit training procedures. As such, the differences manifested by the retarded are seen to be of the production type, and the initial conclusion is that comparative differences are due to the use of control processes, rather than being associated with structural features. This statement, however, is considerably oversimplified. If training retarded children results in improved performance, it is next reasonable to ask whether their performance is now equal to that of an untrained nonretarded child matched for CA. If not, structural differences may still be implicated. If there is still a difference, one approach (e.g., Butterfield et al., 1973) is to employ more explicit training procedures with the retarded in an attempt to improve performance to the point where no comparative difference remains. Even if this attempt is successful, however, there remain some further questions. Would comparable training result in enhanced performance with nonretarded equal-CA groups? If it would, would the magnitude of individual differences between the populations be reduced, or would both groups improve equally, so that individual differences would continue to be of the same magnitude as they were prior to training? The lack of research designed to answer these questions makes it impossible to draw any firm conclusions about the possible role of structural features.

IV. STRUCTURAL FEATURES REVISITED

In the preceding discussion, the emphasis has been on the role of control processes and the differential development of their use within the retarded and nonretarded populations. This should not be taken to imply that the retarded do not differ structurally from the nonretarded, rather that we do not feel that clear structural differences have been identified. As already suggested, training may improve performance in the retarded groups, but the result of providing training for nonretarded groups may be to reinstate clear comparative differences. Thus, even in the research we have already considered, the possibility of structural differences remains. In fact, we would guess that structural differences do exist, and can suggest two additional reasons why they have not yet been found. First, it may be that a more general and powerful theoretical framework is necessary to guide the research. Second, it may be the case that we have simply not looked at the kinds of tasks where structural differences would be most likely to be observed.

A. The Role of Theory

Considering the first point, the need for theory, it seems reasonable to assume that both structural and control features are involved in most of the research we have considered. A separation of their effects would require a theory that incorporates both and allows the development of inferential rules relating performance to specific theoretical processes, components, or parameters. Generally, theories in retardation have not been of sufficient scope or detail to allow such a treatment. There are a few exceptions to this theme, and we will describe them briefly, attempting to highlight both the strengths and weaknesses of each approach.

1. The Fisher–Zeaman Attention–Retention Theory

The attention-retention theory proposed by Fisher and Zeaman (1973) does provide a general framework, adapted from Atkinson and Shiffrin (1968), in which to view the structural control issue. While the theory is presented in quantitative form, the approach can best be described as semiquantitative. Although performance can be modeled in terms of parameters reflecting either control processes or structural features, the attempts to apply and test the theory do not involve precise parameter estimation techniques. Instead the attempt is to indicate that the general levels and patterns of performance manifested by retarded individuals can be generated from the theory. Since the parameter estimation procedures are somewhat imprecise, possible small but reliable variations between either *(1)* retarded and nonretarded children or *(2)* retarded groups of different developmental levels would not be detected.

Keeping in mind this reservation, it is the case that the main contribution of the theory has been to indicate areas where structural differences have *not* been found. That is, most of the parameters either do not mirror developmental differences (for example, learning rate) or do not remain constant across training attempts (for example, initial attention parameter). One exception to this pattern is that the number of items that an individual can rehearse effectively may vary with developmental level (McBane, 1972). This trend was found within the retarded population, and data on nonretarded children would be necessary before any strong conclusions could be reached. Again, the point is that if there are structural differences between groups of subjects at different developmental levels, it is possible that these differences should be found both between and within populations. A retardate deficiency would manifest itself in terms of the differential rate of improvement and/or differing asymptotic levels.

2. The Sperber, Greenfield, and House Theory

Also working in the Connecticut laboratory, Sperber, Greenfield, and House (1973) have proceeded in a somewhat different way. The theory they have developed is of more restricted scope than that of Fisher and Zeaman, and parameter estimation techniques are somewhat more precise. In the initial experiment (Sperber et al., 1973), retarded subjects (MA = 1–8; IQ = 56) were trained on a number of discrimination learning problems concurrently, and the major variable was the spacing of training trials. Each problem was presented 16 times, with 8 different problems receiving 1, 2, 4, or 8 trials per day. Thus, the 16 trials were either spaced widely (1 trial per day) or relatively massed (8 trials per day). Within any day, repeated trials on a given problem were blocked.

Let us consider performance on Trial 9 of each problem, noting that this trial always occurs at least one day following Trial 8. For example, in the case where a child receives 4 trials per day, Trial 9 would be the first trial on Day 3; in the 2 trials per day condition, Trial 9 would be the first trial of Day 5; etc. The finding is that the effect of spacing is nonmonotonic, with performance better in the 2 per day and 4 per day, as compared to the 1 per day and 8 per day, conditions. To account for this outcome, Sperber et al. outlined a four-state Markov model in which each problem could be either learned (L, in long-term memory), in short-term memory (S), familiar (F), or uncoded (U). If an item is in either L or S, an individual should respond correctly; if it is either of the last two states, he is forced to guess. The theory involves two transition matrices, which are shown in Table 12-1. Matrix (a), applied on each training trial, reflects changes due to

TABLE 12-1
The Transition Matrices Employed by Sperber, Greenfield, and House (1973)[a]

	L_{n+1}	S_{n+1}	F_{n+1}	U_{n+1}		L_{n+1}	S_{n+1}	F_{n+1}	U_{n+1}
L_n	1	0	0	0	L_n	.92	0	.08	0
S_n	0	1	0	0	S_n	0	0	.80	.20
F_n	.65	.35	0	0	F_n	0	0	.80	.20
U_n	.08	.92	0	0	U_n	0	0	0	1
	Matrix (a)					Matrix (b)			

[a] Matrix (a) is the acquisition matrix, whereas Matrix (b) is the forgetting matrix. The entries are those used in the final data simulation.

learning, while Matrix *(b)*, applied on between-days retention intervals, indicates the forgetting dynamics. All items are assumed to be in the U state at the outset of learning, and the entries in each matrix give the probabilities of the various allowable moves between the four states. One major assumption, indicated in Matrix *(a)*, is that an item cannot move directly from state S to state L. For our purposes, the critical state is F. As Sperber et al. (1973) points out, "our conception of the familiar state is one of partial knowledge. The subject may recognize that the stimuli have appeared before and he may remember his response, but he does not know the correct solution [p. 192]." The parameter f denotes the probability of familiarity loss over a 24-hour period; that is, a problem can move either from S to F or from F to U. Given the assumption that an item can move from F to L, but cannot move from S to L, the inclusion of the f parameter allowing familiarity loss both helps (when an item moves from S to F) and hurts (when an item moves from F to U). Essentially, in the 1 trial per day condition items do not have much chance to become learned; in Conditions 2 and 4, items may either get learned or end the day in S. The retention interval imposed between days "allows" them to move back to the F state, from where they can be learned. In the 8 trials per day condition, the items get "locked" into S, from which they cannot escape. Learning is most likely to take place when items are in the F state, but successive presentations are likely to send the item into S. Once this happens, a retention interval is necessary for learning, as the item can move back to the F state, where such learning is possible. Viewed anthropomorphically, if the item is in S at any point in time, an individual responds correctly, and given that he knows the answer, he makes no further attempt to learn the item. If, however, he is in the F state, he recognizes the problem as old, does not know the answer, and (realizing the need for additional processing?) makes an attempt to encode the item.

In a second experiment employing a different procedure wherein each problem consisted of two training trials and a test trial, Sperber (1974) varied the spacing between the training trials, either 0 or 4 interpolated trials, and the retention interval imposed between the second training trial and the test trial, 0 interpolated trials, 8 interpolated trials, or 24 hours. He included two groups of retarded children, with the two groups differing in terms of both MA (6–5 versus 10–0) and IQ (43 versus 63). Briefly, with adult subjects (Peterson, Hillner, & Saltzman, 1962), massed training leads to better performance than does spaced training if the retention interval is relatively short, whereas the reverse is true for longer retention intervals. Sperber obtained this crossover effect with his more intelligent subjects but not with the lower-functioning ones. Further, the differing performance could be explained theoretically in terms of variation of the parameter f, with the brighter subjects showing less rapid loss of familiarity.

While the research is still at an early stage of development, it does indicate nicely how a detailed and precise theoretical framework can function to indicate the locus of developmental differences in some memory situations. One next step would be to apply the analysis to other situations to determine how general the processes are. That is, if rate of familiarization loss does covary with developmental level, what other types of empirical manifestations might be expected?

Also, the question remains, assuming that the f difference is a real one, of whether the variation is structural or of the control variety. For example, to posit a control explanation, assume that it is reasonable for an individual to spend more time or processing effort whenever he makes an error on a (recognized) repeating problem but does not do so if he is correct. That is, if on Trial 2 he is correct, he "leaves well enough alone." As the spacing interval increases, the likelihood that the item is no longer in STM increases and the subject is more likely to make an error. Consequently, he is more likely to spend effort attempting to learn the item (subject it to deeper processing or attempt to transfer it to LTM), effort that pays off when the next presentation is long delayed. For the younger or less bright individual, the occurrence of such an error may not elicit additional processing, and the crossover would not be obtained. If such were the case, the type of training experiment to be undertaken would be obvious, and the relationship of such an experiment to the metamemory area equally straightforward, as the additional processing would presumably be done as a result of the subject's awareness that the strength of his memory representation was not as high as it could be. This control explanation would also lead to the expectation that performance on Trial 3, 24-hour retention interval items, would be better if Trial 2 resulted in an error, as compared with a correct response, for the more intelligent subjects but not for the less bright ones. In any event, one virtue of the theoretical treatment is that it does indicate where in the overall sequence some training or intervention procedure would be required. That is, while the theory is complex, it does specify the locus of developmental differences quite clearly.

B. Areas of Investigation

Another possible reason why structural differences may not be evidenced in this review concerns the kind of phenomena and processes considered. The bulk of the research has been conducted in situations where subjects are given ample time to encode incoming stimulation, and theoretical interest has centered on the type of encoding and the organization and maintenance of that information in STM and LTM. In other words, the emphasis has been on what an individual does with the material once it has been recognized and identified.

What is missing in this analysis, of course, is a treatment of iconic memory phenomena or of situations in which speed, rather than accuracy, of processing is the major variable of interest. For example, in a series of experiments investigating individual differences related to verbal intelligence in the college population, Hunt and his associates (Hunt, Frost, & Lunneborg, 1973; Hunt, Lunneborg, &

Lewis, 1975) have argued that high-verbal-ability adults are more rapid processors in terms of both obtaining access to LTM and manipulating items in STM. As an example of speed of accessing LTM, Hunt et al. (1975) report an experiment using the Posner, Boies, Eichelman, and Taylor (1969) procedure where subjects are required to make same–different judgments to pairs of letters alike in terms of physical (AA) or name (Aa) properties. The difference between conditions in terms of speed of responding is taken as a measure of the amount of time required to retrieve the letter's name from LTM. The finding that the name identity/physical identity difference is greater for the low-verbal-ability adults is taken as evidence for slower access to LTM for these subjects.

In addition, Hunt et al. (1975) indicate differences between high- and low-verbal-ability subjects in terms of rate of scanning items in STM, with one example stemming from differences in the slope of the function relating positive ("yes") reaction times to number of items in a Sternberg (1966) type of task.[9] The amount of time needed to scan an array of items increases more rapidly with increasing set size for low- as opposed to high-verbal-ability adults. Hunt (1977) also suggests that some classifications of retarded individuals are characterized by slower scan rates than nonretarded subjects, and Harris and Fleer (1974) have presented data consistent with this notion. They have also found different scanning rates in cultural–familial and brain-injured samples of retarded individuals. While these differences are obviously impressive, it is not clear that the differences are of the structural variety, as no attempts to modify the slopes have been reported. Also, the participants in the experiments do not appear to be as highly practiced as those in the earlier (noncomparative) work. Thus, employing more highly practiced subjects (and retarded children may require more practice before, for example, attention is optimal) may result in an elimination of the differences.

C. Summary

The approaches described in the preceding sections provide different ways of assessing the hypothesis that structural features differentiate individuals of varying developmental levels. The Fisher–Zeaman theory incorporates the structural-control distinction, and is aimed at a wide variety of phenomena. There are two main ways in which structural features are investigated. First, the semiquantitative theorizing allows an assessment of change in parameter values over a broad developmental spectrum. Second, the question of whether training results in changing parameter values is also addressed.

[9] In the Sternberg procedure, the individual is given a series of N items to remember. Then a probe item is presented, and the task is to determine if that item is, or is not, a member of the original set. The number of items (N) in the memory set is the major variable, and interest centers on the shape of the function relating response speed to set size.

In the Sperber research, a more restricted situation is investigated, and parameter estimation techniques are somewhat more precise. While developmental differences within the retardate population are shown clearly, the question of whether these differences can be reduced or eliminated through training remains an open and interesting question. Similarly, the work reported by Hunt does not include any attempts to manipulate performance through training or instruction. Any inference that the differences obtained are structural would be based on a belief that the phenomena under investigation are sufficiently basic so that they are not mediated by strategic intervention. In the research with college students, the use of converging operations reinforces the notion that the various speed differences are real, but this does not necessarily imply that they are not modifiable.

V. CONCLUSIONS

Differences in memory performance between retarded and nonretarded children may be due to structural differences and/or differences in the use of control processes. While the vast majority of the research reported in the past decade has been concerned with control processes, there appears to be some renewed interest in locating structural determinants of performance differences. In general, the search appears directed more toward finding capacity limitations than toward finding limitations reflecting varying levels of cognitive competence. Further, regarding structural differences, there appear to be at least two types. The simplest (and most elusive) is one that is purely IQ related. Children of varying IQs manifest, for example, different values of some theoretical parameter, and this value remains unchanged throughout development. A second case is one where the parameter values change with development, but the rate of change and/or asymptotic levels vary with IQ.

Despite the renewed interest in the role of structural features in retardate memory, little can be said at the present time. While a number of candidates for structural differences have been identified, more research is necessary before any firm conclusions can be reached with regard to either (1) whether the differences are in fact structural, that is (apparently), impervious to training or (2) which type of structural difference is involved.

Regarding the role of control processes, we are on stronger ground. When memory tasks require the use of strategies for efficient performance, retarded individuals are less likely to employ them than are their nonretarded counterparts. That the differences do not reflect purely structural limitations is seen from the results of training studies. Even when training results in enhanced performance, there are problems in terms of maintenance and generalization of the strategy. Extended training on a specific task does enhance maintenance, but does not appear to influence generalization. It may also be the case that the research has not been carried out in such a way as to maximize generalization. For example, there has been little attempt to communicate to the subject the reasons why the strategy may be useful, that is, to explain the nature of the task and the reason why the strategy may help. Instead, it is generally the case that the experimenter simply tells the subject what to do and leaves the subject to infer why he should do it.

Within the context of generalization, we indicated a number of more general factors that might underlie the many production deficiencies that have been identified. While it is again true that little research has been done in this area, the findings to date indicate that these areas are ones in which the retarded child performs exceptionally poorly. The implicit assumption is that training of such general factors will have a more widespread effect than training specific skills, or at least that the two types of training in conjunction will have such effects. While such a hypothesis cannot be evaluated at present, it is certainly possible that the problem of generalization may again limit the effectiveness of such training.

ACKNOWLEDGMENTS

Research from our laboratory and preparation of this manuscript were supported by PHS Grants HD-05951 and HD-06864 from the National Institute of Child Health and Human Development. The authors would like to express their special gratitude to Wilma Noynaert, assistant director of special education for the Peoria Public Schools, without whose continual support the research would not have been possible. Thanks are also due William Jordan, principal, and the teachers of the Von Steuben School, and Lee Nugent, principal, and the staff of the Hines School, both of Peoria, Illinois, for their continual cooperation and encouragement. Finally, the authors would also like to thank Robert Kail and John Hagen for their comments on an earlier version of this paper, and would particularly like to thank Norman Bray for his time, effort, and suggestions.

REFERENCES

Atkinson, R. C., & Shiffrin, R. M. Human memory: A proposed system and its control processes. In K. W. Spence & J. T. Spence (Eds.), *The Psychology of Learning and Motivation* (Vol. 2). New York: Academic Press, 1968.

Belmont, J. M., & Butterfield, E. C. The relations of short-term memory to development and intelligence. In L. C. Lipsitt & H. W. Reese (Eds.), *Advances in child development and behavior* (Vol. 4). New York: Academic Press, 1969.

Belmont, J. M., & Butterfield, E. C. Learning strategies as determinants of memory deficiencies. *Cognitive Psychology*, 1971, *2*, 411–420.

Bilsky, L., & Evans, R. A. Use of associative clustering techniques in the study of reading disability: Effects of list organization. *American Journal of Mental Deficiency*, 1970, *74*, 771–776.

Bilsky, L., Evans, R. A., & Gilbert, L. Generalization of association tendencies in mentally retarded adolescents: Effects of novel stimuli. *American Journal of Mental Deficiency*, 1972, *77*, 77–84.

Binet, A. Les frontières anthrompometriques des anormaux. *Bulletin de la Societé libre pour l'étude psychologique de l'enfant*, 1904, 430–438.

Borkowski, J. G., & Wanschura, P. B. Mediational processes in the retarded. In N. R. Ellis (Ed.), *International review of research in mental retardation* (Vol. 7). New York: Academic Press, 1974.

Bray, N. W. Controlled forgetting in the retarded. *Cognitive Psychology, 1973, 5,* 288–309.

Brown, A. L. Development, schooling and the acquisition of knowledge about knowledge. In R. C. Anderson, R. J. Spiro, & W. E. Montague (Eds.), *Schooling and the acquisition of knowledge.* Hillsdale, N.J.: Lawrence Erlbaum Associates, 1977, in press.

Brown, A. L. A rehearsal deficit in retardates' continuous short term memory: Keeping track of variables that have few or many states. *Psychonomic Science, 1972, 29,* 373–376. (a)

Brown, A. L. Context and recency cues in the recognition memory of retarded children and adolescents. *American Journal of Mental Deficiency, 1972, 77,* 54–58. (b)

Brown, A. L. Mnemonic elaboration and recency judgments in children. *Cognitive Psychology, 1973, 5,* 233–248. (a)

Brown, A. L. Temporal and contextual cues as discriminative attributes in retardates' recognition memory. *Journal of Experimental Psychology, 1973, 98,* 1–13. (b)

Brown, A. L. The role of strategic behavior in retardate memory. In N. R. Ellis (Ed.), *International review of research in mental retardation* (Vol. 7). New York: Academic Press, 1974.

Brown, A. L. The development of memory: Knowing, knowing about knowing, and knowing how to know. In H. W. Reese (Ed.), *Advances in child development and behavior* (Vol. 10). New York: Academic Press, 1975.

Brown, A. L., & Barclay, C. R. The effects of training specific mnemonics on the metamnemonic efficiency of retarded children. *Child Development, 1976, 47,* 71–80.

Brown, A. L., Campione, J. C., Bray, N. W., & Wilcox, B. L. Keeping track of changing variables: Effects of rehearsal training and rehearsal prevention in normal and retarded adolescents. *Journal of Experimental Psychology, 1973, 101,* 123–131.

Brown, A. L., Campione, J. C., & Gilliard, D. M. Recency judgments in children: A production deficiency in the use of redundant background cues. *Developmental Psychology, 1974, 10,* 303.

Brown, A. L., Campione, J. C., & Murphy, M. D. Keeping track of changing variables: Long-term retention of a trained rehearsal strategy by retarded adolescents. *American Journal of Mental Deficiency, 1974, 78,* 446–453.

Brown, A. L., Campione, J. C., & Murphy, M. D. Maintenance and generalization of trained metamnemonic awareness by educable retarded children: Span estimation. Unpublished manuscript, University of Illinois, 1976.

Bruner, J. S., Greenfield, P. M., & Olver, R. R. *Studies in cognitive growth.* New York: Wiley, 1966.

Butterfield, E. C., & Belmont, J. M. Assessing and improving the cognitive functions of mentally retarded people. In I. Bailer & M. Steinlicht (Eds.), *Psychological Issues in Mental Retardation.* Chicago: Aldine, in press.

Butterfield, E. C., Wambold, C. & Belmont, J. M. On the theory and practice of improving short-term memory. *American Journal of Mental Deficiency, 1973, 77,* 654–669.

Campione, J. C., & Brown, A. L. The effects of contextual changes and degree of component mastery on transfer of training. In H. W. Reese (Ed.), *Advances in child development and behavior* (Vol. 9). New York: Academic Press, 1974.

Ellis, N. R. The stimulus trace and behavioral inadequacy. In N. R. Ellis (Ed.), *Handbook of mental deficiency.* New York: McGraw-Hill, 1963.

Ellis, N. R. Memory processes in retardates and normals. In N. R. Ellis (Ed.), *International review of research in mental retardation* (Vol. 4). New York: Academic Press, 1970.

Fisher, M. A., & Zeaman, D. An attention-retention theory of retardate discrimination learning. In N. R. Ellis (Ed.), *International review of research in mental retardation* (Vol. 6). Academic Press, 1973.

Flavell, J. H. Developmental studies of mediated memory. In H. W. Reese & L. P. Lipsitt (Eds.), *Advances in child development and behavior* (Vol. 5). New York: Academic Press, 1970.

Flavell, J. H., Friedrichs, A. G., & Hoyt, J. D. Developmental changes in memorization processes. *Cognitive Psychology*, 1970, *1*, 324–340.

Galton, F. Supplementary notes on "prehension" in idiots. *Mind*, 1887, *12*, 79–82.

Gerjuoy, I. R., & Spitz, H. Associative clustering in free recall: Intellectual and developmental variables. *American Journal of Mental Deficiency*, 1966, *70*, 918–927.

Gerjuoy, I. R., Winters, J. J., Pullen, M., & Spitz, H. Subjective organization by retardates and normals during forced recall of visual stimuli. *American Journal of Mental Deficiency*, 1969, *73*, 791–797.

Glidden, L. M. Meaningfulness, serial position and retention interval in recognition short-term memory. *Journal of Experimental Child Psychology*, 1972, *13*, 154–164.

Goodman, M. A. Directed forgetting strategies in mentally retarded adolescents. Unpublished master's thesis, University of Cincinnati, 1976.

Goulet, L. R. Verbal learning and memory research with retardates: An attempt to assess developmental trends. In N. R. Ellis (Ed.), *International review of research in mental retardation* (Vol. 3). New York: Academic Press, 1968.

Harris, G. J., & Fleer, R. E. High speed memory scanning in mental retardates: Evidence for a central processing deficit. *Journal of Experimental Child Psychology*, 1974, *17*, 452–459.

Hunt, E., Frost, N., & Lunneborg, C. Individual differences in cognition: A new approach to intelligence. In G. Bower (Ed.), *The psychology of learning and motivation* (Vol. 8). New York: Academic Press, 1973.

Hunt, E., Lunneborg, C., & Lewis, J. What does it mean to be high verbal? *Cognitive Psychology*, 1975, *7*, 194–227.

Hunt, E. We know who knows, but why? In R. C. Anderson, R. J. Spiro, & W. E. Montague (Eds.), *Schooling and the acquisition of knowledge*. Hillsdale, N.J.: Lawrence Erlbaum Associates, 1977, in press.

Hyatt, T. Directed forgetting in retarded and normal adolescents: The effect of pretraining information. Unpublished master's thesis, University of Cincinnati, 1976.

Jensen, A. R., & Frederiksen, J. Free recall of categorized and uncategorized lists: A test of the Jensen hypothesis. *Journal of Educational Psychology*, 1973, *3*, 304–314.

Jensen, A. R., & Rohwer, W. D. The effects of verbal mediation on the learning and retention of paired associates by retarded adults. *American Journal of Mental Deficiency*, 1963, *68*, 80–84.

Keeney, T. J., Cannizzo, S. R., & Flavell, J. H. Spontaneous and induced verbal rehearsal in a recall task. *Child Development*, 1967, *38*, 953–966.

Kellas, G., Ashcraft, M., & Johnson, N. Rehearsal processes in the short-term memory performance of mildly retarded adolescents. *American Journal of Mental Deficiency*, 1973, *77*, 670–679.

Lewin, K. A. *A dynamic theory of personality*. New York: McGraw-Hill, 1935.

Markman, E. M. Factors affecting the young child's ability to monitor his memory. Unpublished doctoral dissertation, University of Pennsylvania, 1973.

McBane, B. Short-term memory capacity and parallel processing. Unpublished doctoral dissertation, University of Connecticut, 1972.

Milgram, N. A. Verbal context versus visual compound in paired-associate learning in children. *Journal of Experimental Child Psychology*, 1967, *5*, 597–603.

Miller, G. A. The magical number series, plus or minus two: Some limits on our capacity for processing information. *Psychological Review*, 1956, *63*, 81–97.

Miller, G. A., Galanter, E., & Pribram, K. H. *Plans and the structure of behavior*. New York: Holt, 1960.

Murphy, M. D., & Campione, J. C. Measures of clustering in free recall. Unpublished manuscript, University of Illinois, 1974.

Newell, A. A note on process-structure distinctions in developmental psychology. In S. Farnham-Diggory (Ed.), *Information processing in children*. New York: Academic Press, 1972.

Nye, W. C., McMannis, D. L., & Haugen, D. M. Training and transfer of categorization by retarded adults. *American Journal of Mental Deficiency*, 1972, *77*, 199–207.

Pascual-Leone, J. A mathematical model for the transition rule in Piaget's developmental stages. *Acta Psychologica*, 1970, *32*, 301–345.

Peterson, L. R., Hillner, K., & Saltzman, D. Supplementary report: Time between pairings and short-term retention. *Journal of Experimental Psychology*, 1962, *64*, 550–551.

Piaget, J., & Inhelder, B. *Memory and intelligence*. New York: Basic Books, 1973.

Pinkus, A. L., & Laughery, K. R. Recoding and grouping processes in short-term memory: Effects of subject-paced presentation. *Journal of Experimental Psychology*, 1970, *85*, 335–341.

Posner, M. I., Boies, S. J., Eichelman, W. H., & Taylor, R. L. Retention of visual and name codes of single letters. *Journal of Experimental Psychology Monograph*, 1969, *79*, 1–16.

Rohwer, W. D., Jr. Elaboration and learning in childhood and adolescence. In H. W. Reese (Ed.), *Advances in child development and behavior* (Vol. 8). New York: Academic Press, 1973.

Ross, D. M., Ross, S. A., & Downing, M. L. Intentional training vs. observational learning of mediational strategies in EMR children. *American Journal of Mental Deficiency*, 1973, *78*, 292–299.

Smirnov, A. A., & Zinchenko, P. I. Problems in the psychology of memory. In M. Cole & L. Maltzman (Eds.), *A handbook of contemporary Soviet psychology*. New York: Basic Books, 1969.

Spence, J. T. Verbal-discrimination performance as a function of instructions and verbal-reinforcement combination in normal and retarded children. *Child Development*, 1966, *37*, 269–281.

Sperber, R. D., Greenfield, D. B., & House, B. J. A nonmonotonic effect of distribution of trials in retardate learning and memory. *Journal of Experimental Psychology*, 1973, *99*, 186–198.

Sperber, R. D. Developmental changes in effects of spacing of trials in retardate-discrimination learning and memory. *Journal of Experimental Psychology*, 1974, *103*, 204–210.

Spitz, H. H. Field theory in mental ı rdation. In N. R. Ellis (Ed.), *Handbook of mental deficiency*. New York: McGraw-Hill, 1963.

Spitz, H. H. The role of input organization in the learning and memory of mental retardates. In N. H. Ellis (Ed.), *International review of research in mental retardation* (Vol. 2). New York: Academic Press, 1966.

Spitz, H. H. Consolidating facts into the schematized learning and memory system of educable retardates. In N. R. Ellis (Ed.), *International review of research in mental retardation* (Vol. 6). New York: Academic Press, 1970.

Sternberg, S. High speed scanning in human memory. *Science*, 1966, *153*, 652–654.

Turnbull, A. P. Teaching retarded persons to rehearse through cumulative overt labeling. *American Journal of Mental Deficiency*, 1974, *79*, 331–337.

Turnure, J. E., & Thurlow, M. L. Verbal elaboration and the promotion of transfer of training in educable mentally retarded children. *Journal of Experimental Child Psychology*, 1973, *15*, 137–148.

Wellman, H. M., Ritter, K., & Flavell, J. H. Deliberate memory behavior in the delayed reactions of very young children. *Developmental Psychology*, 1975, *11*, 780–787.

Yussen, S. R., & Levy, V. M., Jr. Developmental changes in predicting one's own span of short-term memory. *Journal of Experimental Psychology*, 1975, *19*, 502–508.

13
Memory Development and Educational Processes

William D. Rohwer, Jr.
Frank N. Dempster
University of California, Berkeley

I. MEMORY DEVELOPMENT IN PSYCHOLOGY AND EDUCATION

In recent years, criticism of public education has been frequent and intense, resulting in repeated demands for improvements in schooling. Far from objecting, educators often join with their critics in valuing the goal of improvement, so that many teachers and administrators are responsive to ideas that promise help in improving educational effectiveness. While this attitude should be conducive to productive exchanges between educators and psychologists, our impression is that research on memory and its development has contributed little, if at all, to efforts for educational improvement.

Of the many possible reasons for this gap between research and practice, one deserves special attention.[1] The fact is that educators may not appreciate the central importance of memory for attaining intellectual competence. Indeed, some give the impression that they regard memory proficiency as antithetical to academic excellence, feeling that memorization interferes with the operation of more laudable, higher mental processes. Such misconceptions about psychological perspectives on memory must be dispelled if work on memory development is to constitute a positive contribution to educational practice.

The task of clarifying conceptions of memory and conveying them to educators, of course, falls entirely to psychologists, who may or may not be

---

[1] For a more sociopolitically minded discussion of the impact of research on educational policy, see Cohen and Garet (1975).

prepared for effective communication with members of the educational community. If not, they will be unable to help in narrowing the present gap between research and practice. Students of memory development may be neither aware of the specific ways that their work might contribute to education, nor skillful at relating it explicitly to particular educational issues. The problem is not irrelevance. In principle, the success or failure of virtually any instructional effort in school depends heavily on the same structures and processes of memory that psychologists analyze in the laboratory. But the relationship between such analyses and the practice of education are not self-evident; they must be intentionally constructed or, at the least, illuminated by the psychologist. So the need is for an approach that will assist students of memory development to exploit the inherent commonality between their concerns and those of educators, and to discern in their research the potential for effective contributions to the resolution of educational issues.

II. RESEARCH AS A RESOURCE FOR EDUCATIONAL PRACTICE

In considering possible approaches to the goal of contributing to educational practice, one quickly confronts a major decision: whether to address problems of instructional theory and research directly or instead to maintain an emphasis on the psychology of memory development per se. The first of these options, the direct approach, is exemplified in efforts such as those of Atkinson (1973), Gagné and Briggs (1974), and Suppes (1973), to construct and verify theories and models of instruction that include memory among their several components. In an allied approach, one can select empirical generalizations initially established under laboratory conditions and ascertain their validity for actual instructional materials presented to students in naturally occurring school settings (cf. Surber & Anderson, 1975).

Direct approaches have a strong appeal: Their potential for resulting in educational contributions is immediately evident. Theoretical terms and constructs can be readily identified with concrete aspects of instructional practice. Empirical research, however experimental it may be, is usually conducted with school-like materials in classroom settings. Thus, educators can easily appreciate the relevance of the psychologist's work.

Despite these advantages, the cost of adopting a direct approach to educational problems may prove too high for many students of memory development. Work on instructional theory and research differs in substantial ways from that involved in explicating the development of memory. To pursue the direct approach, one must master the essentials of a distinctive field of inquiry, allocate time and energy accordingly, and perhaps even relegate problems of memory development to the status of secondary issues.

Assuming that most investigators would prefer to maintain the primacy of their commitment to inquire into the development of memory, we will devote this chapter to presenting and illustrating an alternative to the direct approach. The alternative is for researchers to use conceptual and empirical analyses of memory development as resources for viewing and for anticipating the consequences of educational practices. In this *resource* approach, investigators can work in ways that are indigenous to their normal activities. They can begin by using theoretical distinctions to delimit and characterize the domains of educational tasks and objectives to which their work might be pertinent. For example, if their research is addressed to problems of memory for sequential information, they can use the distinction between response and associative learning (the learning of items *versus* the learning of relationships among them) to limit subsequent pronouncements to educational tasks where items are well known to students and the objective is to remember their order.

After delimiting a domain, investigators can next exploit relevant theoretical propositions and experimental analyses to specify factors responsible for variations in memory of the designated variety. In the case of serial memory, they might emphasize, as a function of age or developmental level, how inducing the rehearsal of item order affects memory for the initial, medial, and terminal portions of sequences (Hagen & Kingsley, 1968). They might also emphasize the potentially damaging effects of demanding overt repetition of item names on the student's memory for sequences, suggesting the inadvisability of instituting or continuing such an instructional practice.

Thus, in the resource approach researchers capitalize on the theoretical distinctions, propositions, and empirical information that are their stock in trade. They use these resources to specify relevant domains of educational activity, and to identify factors within these domains that can affect the quality of student achievement. Through this approach, investigators can provide educators with ways of viewing the memory demands of educational tasks analytically, and of estimating for different kinds of students the likely consequences of alternative instructional practices.

In the remainder of the chapter, we will offer two lengthy illustrations of the resource approach. The starting point for the first is a theoretical distinction of a structural character, that between short- and long-term memory, while the touchstone for the second illustration is the process distinction between storage and retrieval aspects of memory.

III. SHORT- AND LONG-TERM MEMORY

Before illustrating how the distinction between short- and long-term memory may be used as an educational resource, a few preliminary comments are in order. Theoretically, short- and long-term memory are hypothetical constructs that share primary responsibility for the storage or representation of information. But, as the labels suggest, each has a different storage function; short-term memory represents information on a temporary basis and long-term memory represents information on a permanent basis. Moreover, since the contents of short-term memory are transitory, information can be continuously added and deleted in order to meet changing task demands. For example, in attempting to solve a problem it is often necessary to store and discard one partial result after another, while simultaneously coordinating these changes with the resources of long-term memory. Given these functions, it is clear why short-term memory is commonly referred to as the system's "working memory." By contrast, long-term memory plays a passive role in information processing; its primary importance arises from the fact that it represents the products of the individual's experience. These products range from the particular, such as individual letter codes, to the general, including strategies for processing and transforming new information.[2]

Together, short- and long-term memory form the nucleus of the information-processing system, and when understood should have considerable potential for helping educators create favorable learning environments. In the remainder of this section, we will explore this potential by considering each of the storage systems separately, short-term memory and then long-term memory.

A. Short-Term Memory

According to information processing theories, the single most important aspect of short-term memory is its limited storage capacity (representational capacity). This limitation is usually described in terms of a fixed number of slots (for example, Atkinson & Shiffrin, 1968), or storage registers (Conrad, 1965), each of which is capable of accommodating a single unit of information at any one moment. Alternatively, STM may be viewed in terms suggesting a fluid system, having as its hallmark a fixed amount of energy or space capable of being allocated as the storage process demands (Pascual-Leone, 1970). But, here again the important point is that short-term memory can sustain simultaneously only a limited number of internal units, and on this, despite different sets of structural descriptions, there is little disagreement.

The notion of limited capacity might provide a resource of considerable educational value in implying the possibility of severe constraints on the ability of individuals to profit from instruction. But the utility of the implication depends on the success of research in verifying the claim and in quantifying the limits. Thus, the resource potential of the construct of short-term memory is, in turn, contingent on the resource value of relevant empirical work. Hence, as is typical

---

[2] The reader who is used to thinking in Piagetian terms may wish to think of these as figurative and operative schemes, respectively.

in the resource approach, we must first appraise a selection of available research, much of which pertains to the issue of developmental trends, before focusing directly on the question of the educational value that might stem from the implications of limited capacity.

I. Research on Capacity Limits

Unfortunately, attempts to measure the representational capacity of short-term memory have met with numerous difficulties. Traditionally, estimates have been derived from the immediate memory span, that is, the number of discrete units that can be reproduced in correct serial order after a single presentation. The attraction of this procedure lies mainly in the face validity of its requirement that an individual maintain and coordinate simultaneously several units of information for a very brief period. However, as numerous investigators have pointed out, the memory span is not a pure measure of short-term memory, since performance may reflect long-term memory as well. Miller (1956), for example, noted that individuals may organize or group nominally independent units into familiar chunks on the basis of information already stored in long-term memory. Because each chunk may contain more information than is contained in any of the nominal units, there need not be a one-to-one correspondence between storage capacity and memory span.

Additional problems are involved in determining capacity values for individuals who differ in age. Foremost among these is the fact that children are able to call upon a growing amount of information in long-term memory as they grow older. Thus, even though digit span increases throughout childhood, from about three digits at age 3 to about seven at age 16 (Jacobs, 1887; Starr, 1923; Terman & Merrill, 1937), it is unwarranted to conclude that representational storage capacity varies accordingly. Alternatively, these differences may be due to the fact that as children grow older they acquire an increasing amount of information about digits and about how they may be encoded into larger and larger chunks. According to one proponent of this view (Simon, 1972, 1974), the increase in digit span reflects the older child's ability "to call on a growing repertoire of familiar chunks so that a fixed number of chunks designates a steadily growing amount of information [1972, pp. 97]."

Although this hypothesis has not yet received a critical test, it is consistent with the effects of different material on the length of the memory span. As several studies have shown, age differences in digit span are noticeably greater than those observed with less frequently encountered arrangements, such as consonants and unrelated words (Baumeister, 1974; Dempster, 1976). In the study by Dempster, for example, a deliberate effort was made to construct series that would be difficult to chunk and to compare them, in terms of performance, with more familiar material, including digits. While digit span increased in accordance with previous findings, age differences on less frequently encountered series were negligible, with 12-year-olds recalling only about one-third more of a word than 7-year-olds. Although these results appear to contradict the notion that capacity increases with age, more systematic studies on digit span will have to be conducted before any conclusions can be considered more than tentative.

In view of these limitations, other means of estimating capacity have been developed in recent years. Several of these, though little more than simple variations on the conventional memory span test, appear to hold considerable promise for illuminating this problem area. However, since they have received little use in a developmental context they will not be considered here (the interested reader is referred to Crowder, 1969, and Frank & Rabinovitch, 1974, for a discussion of the merits of one of these variations—the running memory span). Instead, we will focus our attention on tasks that represent a significant departure from memory span methodology having been developed in order to test a neo-Piagetian model of intellectual development (Pascual-Leone, 1970). But, before we do so, a brief introduction to the model is in order.

According to this model, the progressive competencies described by Piaget are governed largely by developmental changes in capacity, which is assumed to increase in linear fashion from one unit at age 3 to seven units by age 15. What sets this model apart from others of similar persuasion (that is, Biggs, 1971; McLaughlin, 1963) is the fact that Pascual-Leone derived capacity values primarily on the basis of a Piagetian task analysis, while all other models have been predicated on digit span norms. Accordingly, in Pascual-Leone's model, each value is associated with a particular Piagetian substage and thus is securely linked to general changes in intellectual performance.

The first task used to evaluate the model was the compound-stimulus visual information task developed by Pascual-Leone (1970). In this task, children aged 5, 7, 9, and 11 were taught a different response (for example, raise hand, clap hands) to each of several different visual cues (for example, square shape, red color). After having learned to respond to the entire series without error, they were presented with several compound stimuli (for example, red square) systematically varied with regard to the number of cues in the compound. Each compound was exposed for five seconds, and the individual's task was to "decode the message" by producing every response that was appropriate. The results show that the number of correct responses that children were capable of producing increased, from 2 at age 5 to 5 at age 11, in accordance with the model. According to Pascual-Leone, a child ceases to output responses when the number of previously made responses that he must keep in mind exceeds his available capacity. Hence, younger children's failure to produce as many responses as older children is attributed to their more limited representational capacity.

Similar congruence with Pascual-Leone's theory has been obtained using a number ordering task (Case, 1972), in what is perhaps the most frequently cited test of the model. In this experiment, children were exposed to a series of numbers presented successively and, except for the last, always in ascending order of magnitude—for example, 3, 9, 18, 11. The object was to place the final number in its correct position within the ordinal series. A pronounced age effect was evident: The majority of 6-year-olds succeeded only when the total number of series constituents did not exceed 2, the majority of 8-year-olds when the total did not exceed 3, and most 10-year-olds, when the total equaled four or fewer.

Like digit spans, however, the results of both experiments must be interpreted with caution, and do not necessarily support the contention that capacity increases with age. Rather, the age differences might reflect the child's repertoire of mnemonic strategies, which, as it grows, enables him to construct increasingly larger chunks. In addition to this possibility, the nature and complexity of the tasks suggests sources of bias related to aspects of cognitive functioning not required in the memory span task. For example, the compound-stimulus task, in addition to its simple memory demands, imposes stringent demands on the child's learning and decoding skills. Since proficiency in these skills may be expected to vary as a function of experience, children who appear to be deficient in representational capacity, may, in fact, be deficient in the necessary skills.

A similar interpretation may be offered for Case's experiment. Since the number-ordering task requires children to order numbers in terms of their natural sequence, age differences may be attributed to different levels of cognitive proficiency. In an attempt to preclude this interpretation, Case required all children to pass several practice trials prior to the administration of the test series. Even so, since older children would be more likely to have overlearned ordering skills, it cannot be assumed that all children were equally proficient. If not, the storage demands imposed by ordering may have varied as a function of age, with older children having more capacity available for remembering numbers than younger children.

One bit of evidence consistent with this interpretation is the normative relationship found between neo-Piagetian tasks on the one hand, and tasks that do not place prominent demands on the child's transformational skills (digit span) on the other. On neo-Piagetian tasks children under the age of 9 score about 2 ½ units less than they do on digit span. By the time the child is 11, however, this difference is reduced and, according to Pascual-Leone's model, should disappear entirely by age 16. It appears then that with increasing experience, the child is able to execute transformations with less and less drain on capacity, so that in time he is able to perform them using about as much capacity as he would for forward recall. In view of this, tasks used to assess Pascual-Leone's model or tasks bearing a similar normative relationship with them, such as backward digit span (Jensen & Figueroa, 1975), do not appear to offer unequivocal measures of capacity.

Pending further developments that can resolve this dispute, students of memory remain divided on "what is perhaps the basic developmental issue about

STM'' (Simon, 1972, p. 10). Nevertheless, available research provides strong endorsement for three theoretical propositions. The first is that short-term memory has a sharply limited representational capacity in even the most proficient of learners. Second, whether or not basic capacity increases with advancing age, the functional limits it imposes are substantially more severe for younger than for older persons. Finally, unless circumvented, these limits can prevent successful performance on any intellectual task that demands an even momentary representation of more units than short-term memory can sustain. Given the preceding appraisal, we can address the question of the resource potential for education constituted by the assumption of structural limits on the representational capacity of short-term memory.

2. Capacity Limits and Education

Limited capacity has at least two kinds of implications for educational practice, one diagnostic, the other prescriptive. The diagnostic implications develop from the notion that school assignments may vary in terms of the demands they impose on short-term memory. Accordingly, educators have a resource that allows them to anticipate what one source of school difficulty is likely to be. Teachers would be well advised, for example, to consider the possibility of short-term memory failure whenever they present a great deal of new material orally, as they might in a social studies or science lesson. If failure does occur, information intended for the student's long-term memory may not be acquired. Although these failures may be of little immediate consequence, when multiplied over a long period of time their cumulative effects may be a major source of intellectual improficiency.[3]

A second class of school activity that might make stringent demands on representational capacity is problem solving. Many problem-oriented tasks appear to require the individual to store some information, or details of the problem, while simultaneously processing other information. As a result, the functional limits imposed on short-term memory may be a critical factor in the student's chances for success. Some support for this contention is found in recent studies showing a high correlation between digit span and two problem-solving tasks, mental arithmetic (Whimbey, Fischhof, & Silikowitz, 1969) and syllogistic reasoning (Whimbey & Ryan, 1969). This correlation gains significance from

[3] The relationship between intellectual ability and capacity is made evident by the fact that digit span correlates highly with a host of psychometric measures of cognitive ability. Most notably, digit span correlates about .67 with the WISC full-scale IQ (excluding digit span) and .93 with the WAIS vocabulary subtest, after correction for attenuation (Jensen, 1964). In addition, digit span is substantially loaded on the general intelligence factor ("g") common to all tests in the WAIS battery and a factor labelled "efficiency of short-term memory." This last factor, it is worthwhile to note, emerged as the largest and statistically most reliable factor in a recent study of intelligence, accounting for 25% of the variance (Hunt, Frost & Lunneborg, 1973).

the fact that digit span does not correlate well with other measures of memory performance, such as serial learning and free recall, presumably because these tasks do not strain representational capacity (Whimbey et al., 1969).

The general prescriptive implication is that schooling should be arranged to make the most of the representational capacity available in every student. One approach is to design instruction in such a way that the individual's capacity is exceeded as infrequently as possible. In order to do so effectively, it will be necessary to analyze intellectual tasks in terms of the demands they place on short-term memory, an effort that has already begun (Case, 1975; Farnham-Diggory & Gregg, 1975; Perfetti & Hogaboam, 1975; Resnick, 1975; Simon, 1975). An especially promising application of task analysis, described by Case (1975), involves the concept of "hierarchy span." Once a complicated skill is broken down into its components, an instructional sequence is designed in which each successively higher-level skill requires the simultaneous representation of a minimal number (or narrow span) of subordinate skills. This is contrasted with an instructional hierarchy having wide span, one where many subordinate skills must be integrated at each successively higher level. The major difference between the two lies in the number of internal units that need to be represented simultaneously. In the case of a sequence characterized by narrow span the student is never asked to deal with more than a minimal number of internal units, whereas in the case of one characterized by wide span the student's representational capacity is more likely to be overloaded.

Although this instructional concept has not been formally evaluated in terms of performance variables, one recent training study has encouraging implications (Case, 1974a). In this study, Piagetian tasks requiring the control of variables were subjected to task analysis and the representational demands of each subskill estimated. On the basis of this information, it was predicted that normally intelligent 8-year-olds could be taught to perform well on the tasks, even though mastery is not ordinarily achieved until the period of formal operations, some four years away. The instructional sequence was designed to provide them with the opportunity to acquire, one by one, all of the subskills necessary to set up a general procedure for verification. In the final step of the sequence, the children were taught to evaluate each of the variables separately, thus having to integrate no more than a minimal number of subskills at any one time. The results were fairly dramatic: The instructed group learned the subordinate skills, performed well on the criterion tasks, and retained this ability over a two-month period. By comparison, a control group performed poorly, rarely labeling the uncontrolled variables and generally failing to note their confounding effects.

This example of the first prescriptive approach illustrates its foremost characteristic—the tailoring of instructional presentation to the learner's capabilities. By contrast, a second prescriptive approach entails attempts to prompt or modify the learner so that his functional representational capacity, relative to nominal units, increases to match more strenuous task demands. As the structural locus of such manipulations is in long-term memory, we come to the next part of this initial illustration of the resource approach to educational relevance.

B. Long-Term Memory

The objective of attempts to influence long-term memory is that of increasing the organizational and grouping proficiency of students. Several methods for accomplishing this objective are suggested by research involving overload conditions, best exemplified by procedures in which span or supraspan lists are presented only once, and at fairly rapid rates. The methods include *(1)* arranging the material to be remembered into subgroups (imposed grouping); *(2)* instructions designed to foster the use of a particular grouping technique; and *(3)* task-related practice. We will examine each of these procedures in turn.

1. Imposed Grouping

Experimental analyses of imposed grouping have been numerous, especially with college students. Almost invariably, immediate recall is facilitated when digit or letter strings are partitioned into subgroups by the experimenter. Although numerous methods of grouping have been employed, including rhythmical (Adams, 1915) and spatial (Mayzner & Gabriel, 1963), temporal grouping, in which pauses are introduced between predefined chunks, has been used most frequently and generally has produced the greatest facilitation of recall (Bower & Springston, 1970; Ryan, 1969). Accordingly, we will focus our attention primarily on research involving temporal groups.

The most salient feature of this method of grouping is that more time is available between items from different subsets than between items from the same subset. This enables individuals to recode segments on the basis of information stored in long-term memory, without having to be concerned simultaneously with processing new items. For example, given sufficient time, the individual may recode nominally separate numbers (for example, 3, 6, 5) into a single number code (for example, 365), or nominally separate letters (for example, B, A, L) into a meaningful unit (for example, ball). These groupings may be so well unitized, in fact, that latencies to respond during a probe test are often longer when the stimulus is outside the chunk containing the item to-be-recalled than when it is inside the predefined chunk (Wilkes & Kennedy, 1970). In short, this technique facilitates recall by providing an opportunity for individuals to organize information into a form that reduces the load on short-term memory.

This line of research not only suggests a practical technique for improving short-term memory, but also specifies several conditions that qualify its effectiveness. For example, it appears that pauses must have certain characteristics in order to improve recall. Patterns of division that are irregular or that contain groups of five or more lead to little or no improvement. Conversely, regular patterns and small group sizes (especially groups of three) improve performance the most (Ryan, 1969). A further qualifying factor is that temporal grouping improves memory for order information more than for identity information.[4] Thus, the educational utility of this resource is clearest when conditions warrant the retention of sequential information, as might be the case, for example, in spelling.

Temporal grouping has also been employed in investigations with children, although more often (Harris & Burke, 1972; McCarver, 1972) than not (Frank & Rabinovitch, 1974) in combination with spatial grouping. On the whole, these studies indicate that the effectiveness of grouping depends on the age of the child, with college students benefiting the most and young children the least. Furthermore, they indicate that grouping does not facilitate recall for children below the age of 8. Thus, it appears that a child must attain a certain age before grouping will be effective.

The importance of these studies lies, on the one hand, in their implications for theory, and on the other, in their implications for education. With regard to theory, they strengthen the widely held presupposition that very young children do not engage as frequently as do their older counterparts in spontaneous organizing activities. With respect to education, these findings may be used as a resource enabling the educator to anticipate how children of different ages are likely to respond to chunking opportunities afforded by temporal grouping. Accordingly, the educator would be well advised to consider alternative means of improving short-term memory in the primary grades.

The research we have so far considered raises the question—an important one for educators—of whether experience with grouped input will transfer to ungrouped input. That is, might such experience encourage the individual to adopt a grouping strategy even when information is no longer externally grouped? If the answer is positive, the potential of this resource for education will be heightened.

Although data relevant to this question are largely lacking, one study of spatial grouping is encouraging despite a small treatment effect. Spitz (1966) presented children between 8 and 9 years old with both grouped and ungrouped digits, offering the grouped numbers in pairs whenever possible. Although grouping was not very facilitative, children achieved higher memory spans for ungrouped digits when they were preceded by a grouped series than when they were preceded by another ungrouped series. Moreover, when ungrouped presentation followed group presentation, performance in the two conditions was nearly equivalent.

---

[4] However, it should be noted that experimental designs may have precluded large effects on item recall.

In viewing the results of this study, the question that comes to mind is why grouping did not have a larger facilitative effect. One possible reason is that the children were too young to benefit substantially and that if they had been a year or two older the effect would have been more dramatic. Another possibility is that the conditions of grouping (by twos and with no temporal pauses between subsets) were not maximally effective. As already noted, temporal grouping in subsets of three generally produces the greatest improvement. Whatever the explanation, however, little transfer was obtained and a more definitive resolution of the question must await further research.

2. Grouping Instructions

In this section, we discuss instructions designed to encourage the use of a particular grouping strategy. Since research has focused on two principal types of grouping, we will limit our discussion accordingly. The first involves instructions to group stimuli into subsets of a specific size, and may be used in conjunction with groups imposed by the experimenter (McCarver, 1972). The second is more elaborate and involves instructions in the use of a recoding scheme, accompanied by a period of training.

Wickelgren (1964, 1967), in several investigations of the first type, instructed college students to organize digits by rehearsing them in nonoverlapping groups of a designated size. He found that instructions to group in threes were optimal and instructions to group in sets of smaller size were least effective. Moreover, his findings agree with those obtained in studies of imposed grouping (Ryan, 1969) in that the major effect of group size was on recall of order information. This is explained by assuming that the individual has a limited number of serial position concepts—beginning, middle, and end—that may be used as organizational aids. When the number of items within a group gets too high, these concepts prove inadequate. However, when there are just three items in a group the concepts can be used appropriately and recall is facilitated.

The major implication of this research for education is that there appear to be limits on the amount of information that an individual can effectively group together. However, several areas of ignorance limit its usefulness. First, Wickelgren, like Ryan (1969), used lists containing digits, with no digit repeated in a list. Thus, little can be concluded about the effects of grouping instructions on memory for identity information. In order to assess these effects more decisively, lists designed to reduce the possibility of successful guessing are required. Second, little is known about the relative effectiveness of various group sizes for children. Not only would such knowledge be useful educationally, but it would also be of theoretical interest to know if developmental changes in memory span are accompanied by changes in optimal group size.

There are several reports in the literature of studies involving a second type of grouping instruction. One of these is Miller's (1956) description of the now classic experiment involving a procedure for recoding strings of binary digits into successively richer chunks of information. With it, college students were able to achieve moderate increases in recall for binary digits after a brief period of instruction and study. After an extended period of study, Smith, the experimenter, increased his own span dramatically, from 12 to 40 digits. In another experiment, Slak (1970) provided college students with a code for grouping decimal digits into phonemic sequences so that each digit triplet was represented by a consonant-vowel-consonant triplet. After about 20–30 hours of study, memory spans improved from approximately 9 to 13 digits. This improvement, though not as impressive as the one described by Miller, is noteworthy, since it involved material frequently encountered in natural settings.

These two studies are important in that they demonstrate how information stored in long-term memory can increase the amount of information that an individual can manipulate effectively in short-term memory. Moreover, they show that effective coding strategies can be devised and transferred from one individual to another. However, the educational utility of the research is limited by the fact that only specialized strategies were investigated and no children were sampled. Until research encompasses more generalizable coding strategies and involves children, the potential of this area for education will remain very much underexploited.

3. Practice

The effect of practice on memory span has been assessed by providing individuals with intensive experience with digit sequences. Martin and Fernberger (1929) administered digit series to two university students during 50 sessions over a period of 4 months. During this period spans increased regularly, culminating in a 47% gain for one individual and a 36% improvement for the other. In addition to measures of span, introspective reports were obtained during each session. From these, it was concluded that the individuals attempted to organize the digits into increasingly larger groups as practice progressed. Eventually, they became proficient in grouping by fives, but by the end of practice were not yet able to group by sixes. These reports, though perhaps of limited scientific value, suggest that their improved memory span was due to methods of grouping that enabled them to construct increasingly larger chunks.

Similar improvement in digit span was obtained in a study of very young children with a mean age of just over 5 (Gates & Taylor, 1925). In this experiment, children received 78 consecutive school days of practice, with each session lasting about 20 minutes. Their performance, like that of the college students, increased regularly, progressing from an initial mean of 4.3 digits to a final level of 6.4 digits—a percentage gain of 48%. By comparison, a matched control group gained on the average only .73 digits, or 17%, during the same period. Thus, in contrast to grouping imposed by the experimenter, massive task-related practice appears to be an effective technique for improving the short-term memories of very young children.

In order to investigate the nature of the improvement made by the practice group, Gates and Taylor conducted two follow-up experiments. In the first, the children were retested several months later. This time, the group that had received the practice performed no better than the control group. In fact, their digit spans returned to normal—just a little over five digits. In the second experiment, small samples of children from both groups received three weeks of intensive practice beginning a few months after the posttest. Both groups improved equally, reinforcing the conclusion that the 78 days of practice had produced little in the way of permanent improvement in digit span.

Together, these studies provide strong evidence that massive amounts of practice can lead to significant improvements in digit span. In a limited sense, therefore, they are consistent with teaching methods that stress the positive effects of repetition, such as those that are based on the learning principles of Thorndike. However, much still remains to be understood about the long-term effectiveness of practice and possible developmental differences. Until these issues are resolved, the practical implications of research on practice for increasing the efficiency of short-term memory will not be fully realized.

In summary, this brief review suggests several methods for enhancing an individual's functional representational capacity; that is, the study of memory and its development has produced a resource of practical value to educators. In order to capitalize on this resource, the educator might structure the learning environment in one or all of the following ways, depending on his specific instructional objectives: First, he might arrange and present information so as to encourage the discovery and use of organizational processes. Second, he might provide instruction enabling the student to acquire and use particular organizational strategies. And third, he might provide the student with sheer repetition or practice on some particular skill or task.

In this section, we chose to highlight research involving span or supraspan lists of items in order to illustrate how the concept of long-term memory could be used as an educational resource. This research is characterized by procedures that place few or no transformational demands on the individual. However, we hasten to add that research also suggests ways that students can be taught strategies that reduce storage demands in problem-solving situations (Case, 1974b; Simon, 1975; Whimbey & Ryan, 1969). Whimbey and Ryan, for example, have shown that college students can be taught, in just a few hours, how to use Venn diagrams to improve their ability to solve syllogistic reasoning problems. The students were taught to use the diagrams to represent the premises of a problem and then to draw the correct conclusion. Before training, the students' scores on an aurally administered syllogistic-reasoning task were found to be highly related to digit span. However, after training, scores on the two tasks did not show a relationship, which implies that training enabled the students to deal with the problems in a way that no longer strained short-term memory. Indeed, questioning of the students following training tended to indicate that the diagram patterns corresponding to various premise patterns were stored in long-term memory, and that all students had to do when premises were presented was to visualize the patterns. This study demonstrates that the resource value of the distinction between short- and long-term memory is not limited to tasks requiring only reproductive memory, but applies to problem-solving situations as well.

In closing, we wish to emphasize how little is known about the conditions likely to promote efficient utilization of representational capacity on a permanent basis. To date, research has been instructive mainly in showing that enduring gains are more difficult to achieve than temporary gains. Young children, especially, appear to lack spontaneous access to long-term memory and the ability to monitor and coordinate several strategies simultaneously. As a result, they tend to abandon their newly acquired skills whenever the task demands change (lack of transfer) or unless specifically prompted to use them. Accordingly, it may be worthwhile to concentrate more of our research efforts on the problem of the durability and transferability of capacity-conserving techniques. Until we have a better understanding of the processes involved in the effective utilization of information available in long-term memory, the distinction between it and short-term memory will be a limited educational resource.

IV. STORAGE AND RETRIEVAL

For a second illustration of ways that the psychological study of memory development may be viewed as a resource for educational contributions, we have elected to explore the potential of the distinction between storage and retrieval. Patently, we have already made some use of these concepts in the preceding section. But our focus there was on two kinds of memory structures or systems, and our concern with storage and retrieval was limited to performance conditions that severely tax the capacities of short-term memory. By contrast, our focus here is on storage and retrieval processes, and our discussion presupposes task conditions that are much more relaxed in the capacity demands imposed on short-term memory. Our reference is to tasks that permit repeated exposure to information, or that allow relative leisure during periods of study and testing, so that the number of informational units that must be stored or retrieved concurrently falls short of the limits of simultaneous representational capacity.

The psychological study of memory under such conditions has been considerably enhanced by the apparently simple idea of distinguishing between storage, a person's mental representation of information in long-term memory, and retrieval, the processes of returning to that information. Our present concern with the storage-retrieval distinction, however, is how it might be viewed as a useful resource for education. We begin by considering the utility of the distinction as a framework for making observations and for establishing valid presuppositions about the significance of memory performance. Then we will explore the fruit of psychological research on storage and retrieval processes in an effort to highlight its potential as a resource for education.

As an observational framework, the storage-retrieval distinction has led investigators to think of memory events as being comprised of two separable components, and to identify each component with a distinctive locus. They identify storage events with occasions when learners have opportunities to study material and retrieval events with occasions when learners provide evidence of what they have acquired. Operationally, storage and retrieval correspond roughly with study and test trials, respectively. But the correspondence is by no means exact; self-testing may occur during study trials, and test trials may offer opportunities for study. Nevertheless, the division is useful in calling full attention to the potential functions of each type of occasion.

The main import of the storage-retrieval distinction for educational observation lies in directing the viewer's attention to both of the loci involved in memory performance. The distinction is germane to instructional practice in that students are characteristically asked to commit material to memory and to retrieve it in response to some kind of subsequent test. But the fruits of observation will be sparse indeed unless educators distinguish and give full attention to each kind of occasion. Their diagnoses might founder if test conditions are regarded as immutable or are ignored as potential sources of difficulty. In evaluating the effectiveness of instruction, teachers might be misled if they overlook or neglect to separate the events and possible consequences of storage occasions from those of retrieval. In short, for observational purposes, the storage-retrieval distinction may serve as a resource in offering the educator guidance in where to look for the sources of memory phenomena in students.

Beyond its observational utility, the distinction between storage and retrieval is the source of two major presuppositions that may have as much potential value for education as they have for the psychology of memory. Both presuppositions focus on beliefs about the relationship between memory and performance. Stated coarsely, the first is that the performance of students on a retention test reveals much more about the efficacy of their study activities than about their retrieval abilities. This proposition applies mainly to instances in which an instructor is inclined to make inferences about retrieval efficiency from performance under constant conditions of testing. A teacher might wish to use test outcomes to decide whether some topics are more retrievable than others or to classify students with reference to their relative degrees of retrieval proficiency. Contrary to these aims, the first presupposition implies that performance under constant conditions of testing can reveal little about comparative retrievability or relative retrieval ability; instead, what it offers is an index of storage effectiveness. According to this proposition, for example, it would be a mistake to infer that a student is poor at retrieval solely from the fact that he or she does not remember the major mineral resource of Zaïre, even though it had been presented in the social studies lesson of the previous day. A more supportable interpretation would be that the student had acquired little from the lesson.

In a sense, the second presupposition represents the other side of the coin, since it asserts that what students can remember under any particular set of test conditions indicates only what they can retrieve under those conditions, not what they have available in memory. This proposition supports the belief that much more may be in a student's memory than can be revealed by any single condition of testing. For example, an instructor who takes the proposition seriously would not be at all surprised that the same student who draws a blank when asked to list the mineral resources of Zaïre might perform perfectly if asked to name them for the Congo. In this proposition, it can be seen that the distinction between storage and retrieval yields a related distinction: that between the availability and the accessibility of information in memory. Information can indeed be available—stored in memory—but resistant to retrieval, inaccessible, under some conditions of testing. Thus, to determine what a student remembers, or to diagnose apparent memory failure, an instructor is well advised to use multiple means of testing.

As critical as these presuppositions might be for guiding the thinking of instructors, they by no means exhaust the resources that students of memory development can offer education in connection with the storage-retrieval distinction. Just as the distinction can provide educators with direction in their observations and a perspective for viewing student performance, it has given psychologists a wedge for constructing and verifying detailed conceptions of the processes and conditions that determine remembering. These achievments, in turn, form additional resources that, as we shall see next, might be exploited for understanding and designing educational practice.

When trying to discern potential educational contributions in the products of research on memory development, the psychologist should be mindful of the possibility that educators might regard his wheat as being nothing but chaff. To the psychologist, the greatest value of an experimental manipulation often lies in its power for resolving a theoretical point, while its value to the educator may reside mainly in the way the manipulation affects performance. The enhancement of acquisition through imagery instructions may be important to the psychologist for indicating that mental information can be represented imaginally (Paivio, 1971), whereas the enhancement itself might be more noteworthy for the educator. Thus, as we discuss a selection of the available research on storage and retrieval processes, we will emphasize the aspects that might successfully be offered for educational use.

One approach to this objective is to comb available research on memory development for answers to a series of five questions:

1. What storage and retrieval processes characterize those who perform memory tasks proficiently?
2. What conditions are optimal for efficient processing in such persons?

3. What is the scope of developmental and individual differences in processing proficiency?
4. What are the specific sources of such differences?
5. What can be done to compensate effectively for sources of improficiency?

Fortunately, within some limited task domains students of memory development have produced information sufficient to provide at least provisional answers to these questions.

We describe and qualify some of the answers, with reference to both storage and retrieval, for a limited set of tasks. That is, we will confine our treatment to tasks that *(1)* involve the acquisition of information about items already familiar to the learner and *(2)* require retention of discrete items, in contrast to prose or other forms of connected discourse. Within these boundaries, we first discuss processes presumed to be responsible for storage and then those related to retrieval.

A. Research on Processes and Conditions of Storage

A person may wish or be asked to remember at least two different kinds of information about a collection of familiar items such as objects, pictures, or words. The first type of information can be exemplified with reference to the free recall paradigm, in which the person must encode, or represent in storage, information sufficient to identify the constituents of the collection and to discriminate them from all other items the individual already knows. Thus, one class of storage processes that has received attention concerns the encoding of single-item identify information. In other paradigms, serial and paired-associate learning, for example, the person must encode not only item identify information but also information about relationships among items. For successful serial performance, one needs to encode information about sequential order, while for paired-associate performance one needs to encode information about the way the collection is divided into subgroups. Even in free recall performance, which ostensibly demands only the storage of item identity information, the person may encode interitem information as well. Hence, we shall also attend to a second major class of storage processes, those responsible for the successful encoding of relational information.

1. Encoding of Item Identity Information

In the resource approach we are taking, the first question to be addressed is, What storage processes characterize those who are proficient at encoding item identity information? If we presume that college students generally qualify as proficient, recent research suggests some persuasive, though not conclusive, answers. Apparently, a defining characteristic of proficient performers is that they encode semantic information about each item (Elias & Perfetti, 1973; Hyde & Jenkins, 1973). Ordinarily, more encoding emphasis is given to the meaning of items than to their formal or physical features such as sound, shape, or size, and when this tendency is impeded performance suffers.

A complete answer is not yet available to the second question in our approach to educational utility; that is, the optimal conditions for efficient processing have not been isolated. Nevertheless, indications are that for college students conditions that facilitate semantic encoding include direct instructions to remember the items encountered or, in the absence of an intent to remember, instructions that orient the learner to the meanings of the items, as in suggesting that synonyms be produced for each one.

Research to date offers at least tentative answers to the third and fourth questions, those relating to the scope and sources of individual and developmental differences. Although little, if anything, is known as yet about individual differences in the retention of item identity information, it varies dramatically with chronological age, being much higher for college students than for children (Hasher & Clifton, 1974). Evidence provided by Bach and Underwood (1970) and by Ghatala (1970) suggests that a major source of the developmental discrepancy lies in age-related differences in the learner's propensity for encoding items semantically. (In this volume, chapters by Kail and Siegel and by Moely provide detailed descriptions of this evidence.) For encoding in young children, it may be that item features such as sound, shape, form, and size may be more decisive than meaning. If so, the study of memory development has produced a resource worth offering to education. The teacher can use this resource to understand, for example, the informal observation that primary school children often regard a numeral written in a large hand as signifying a larger quantity than one written smaller. In general, this line of research offers a resource allowing the educator to form an accurate expectation about what children of various ages are likely to remember about items because of differences in their encoding propensities.

An answer to the final question, how improficiency can be compensated, might constitute an even more significant resource for education than the answers to the previous questions. Suppose the teacher or curriculum maker wishes to assist children in achieving more effective encoding. Does psychological research suggest any ways of compensating for sources of encoding improficiency? Two such suggestions may be adduced from work to date. One derives from the research with college students mentioned previously (Elias & Perfetti, 1973; Hyde & Jenkins, 1973) and is mainly promising for identifying conditions that should be avoided if the instructional aim is to encourage semantic encoding. For example, instructing college students to attend to the spelling or pronunciation of words typically diminishes retention. Thus, in school the teacher might be well advised to abandon the not uncommon practice of requiring students to respond to the acoustic and graphic features of words when it is their utility as conveyors of meaning that is to be remembered.

A second suggestion comes from studies with children that have included a manipulation of task instructions. Clearly, even though simple instructions to learn are effective in activating semantic encoding in college students, they do not have this consequence in young children. Other instructions, however, have shown some promise of producing the desired result. Dempster and Rohwer (1974), for example, report that directions to imagine the referents of nouns, or to construct sentences containing the nouns, substantially enhance memory for item identity. Thus, it appears that certain measures under the control of the instructor have the potential of enhancing memory for item identity in learners who do not have a strong propensity for semantic encoding.

2. Encoding of Relational Information

At least two varieties of relational information are subject to encoding: information about order or sequence, on the one hand, and information about group membership, on the other. For each variety, we will appraise the potential of relevant psychological research and theory as an educational resource.

The problem of identifying the processes responsible for item order memory in proficient performers is by no means entirely resolved. Nevertheless, available research suggests that such memory is supported by subject activities that preserve order through time by reiterating all of the previous items in a series as each new one is presented (Palmer & Ornstein, 1971). Apparently, a learner may accomplish this by merely rehearsing, from the beginning, an item sequence each time an item is added. A more elaborate device that seems to serve the same function is the construction of a narrative that incorporates each item and that is extended to include new items as they are presented (Levin & Rohwer, 1968). The effects of both devices appear to lie mainly in improving the storage of information about early and middle portions of sequences. One condition that facilitates such activities in proficient memorizers is a low rate of encountering items in the sequence, allowing sufficient time for either cumulative rehearsal or construction of a narrative. In the case of the latter activity, it may be useful as well to encourage it through direct instructions, even for college students, suggesting that the construction of narratives may not be characteristic of proficient learners when given only standard instructions (Bower & Clark, 1969).

There is little question that the retention of sequential information improves considerably as a function of age (Hagen & Kingsley, 1968; Jensen & Rohwer, 1965). Furthermore, the locus of this age-related performance difference seems to be principally in memory for information about the early and middle components of sequences, consistent with the diagnosis that younger learners are less prone than older ones to engage in either cumulative rehearsal or narrative construction. As before, the potential educational utility of this analysis lies mainly in informing teachers that the younger students are, the less likely they will be to invoke, without assistance, effective strategies for storing sequential information.

Knowing this, a teacher of younger students will wish to offer aid that will successfully enhance the encoding of order information. Research to date suggests some straightforward means by which this might be done. The simplest method of demonstrable effectiveness is that of inducing young children to engage overtly in cumulative rehearsal of sequences as each successive item is presented (Keeney, Cannizzo, & Flavell, 1967; Kingsley & Hagen, 1969). An alternative, inducing learners to construct narratives that incorporate items in sequence, has only provisional value, since to date it has received so little in the way of experimental verification. It appears that college students profit from narrative instructions (Bower & Clark, 1969), and that the performance of children is facilitated by the presentation of items in a narrative context (Levin & Rohwer, 1968), but little is known about possible developmental differences in the effects of inducing narrative activity. Finally, empirical research (Hagen & Kingsley, 1968) seems to indicate the exercise of caution in encouraging children, especially those older than 10 or 11, to say aloud the names of the discrete items in a sequence, for the result may be diminished recall of early items.

Whether or not a task demands memory for interitem relationships, it appears that the encoding of such information tends to facilitate performance (cf. Tulving & Donaldson, 1972). In psychological research, two varieties of group membership encoding have been explored extensively. We will touch briefly on one of these, the organization of an item collection in terms of previously learned relationships, and emphasize the second—the extemporaneous construction of relations.

If the items in a collection can be systematically classified into known categories, their memorability may be increased by the encoding of each with reference to its appropriate category. Such encoding appears to be characteristic of college students. Their performance on free recall tasks is relatively efficient and usually exhibits clustering, the contiguous recall of category members regardless of the order in which they are encountered during study. Marked developmental differences in free recall of categorizable lists have been observed repeatedly, and correlated differences in clustering suggest that the source of the trend lies in an age-related propensity for relational encoding. (see Moely, this volume). The probability of such encoding can be increased by enhancing the salience of the category structure in a list; for example, during study, category members can be presented in blocks rather than randomly. Thus, the resources offered by this line of psychological investigation consist of information about *(1)* age-related tendencies to encode relationally and *(2)* means for structuring materials so as to increase such encoding among the improficient.

Many collections of items do not lend themselves to encoding with reference to known categories, either because the items are relatively unrelated or because the categories have not been learned. Nevertheless, older children are vastly more proficient than younger children, whether performance is indexed by a test of cued recall (Jensen & Rohwer, 1965) or of free recall (Laurence, 1966; Rosner, 1971). Here too, the capability of the more proficient learner may be regarded as residing in a propensity for relational encoding.

In the case of collections of unrelated items, however, rather than discerning the applicability of previously learned categories, the learner must construct relationships extemporaneously. Rohwer (1973) has advanced the hypothesis that extemporaneous relationships result from the activation of a storage process called *elaboration,* the generation of an event that jointly implicates two or more items that are initially disparate. In college students, elaboration is reflected in self-reports of the construction of stories or interacting images that subdivide a collection of items into internally coherent subgroups (Bugelski, 1962; Montague & Wearing, 1967; Runquist & Farley, 1964).

For some older learners, indications are that elaboration occurs readily, provided only that memory instructions are given and the rate of presentation allows enough time for the generation of events. Under the same conditions, however, other older learners show little evidence that they customarily engage in elaboration when confronted with memorization tasks (Rohwer, 1976). Similarly, most younger subjects, especially children between the ages of 4 and 13, exhibit little if any propensity to elaborate relations while studying items in preparation for either a cued or a free recall memory test (Rohwer, 1973). Thus, available evidence favors the presumption that both developmental and individual differences abound in the effectiveness with which information about group membership is stored.

As an educational resource, the utility of research on this point would be increased substantially by a more precise identification of the characteristics that distinguish individuals who are inclined to elaborate from those who are not so disposed. Evidence suggests that age is some guide in that the tendency toward self-activated elaboration appears to emerge during adolescence. But age must be regarded as a very coarse index indeed, since the probability of self-activation sometimes varies with social class membership (Rohwer & Bean, 1973), and because of pronounced individual differences in elaborative propensity even among late adolescents from relatively wealthy family backgrounds (Rohwer, 1976).

A review of the relevant research yields both positive and negative answers to the question of what can be done to compensate for the disinclination of many students to activate elaboration on their own. Positive answers pertain when the question is confined to cases where special instructional provisions can be implemented each time students are requested to learn and remember information about group membership. Elaboration can be encouraged in a number of ways, through either task instructions or the prestructuring of materials (e.g., Prestianni & Zacks, 1974; see Rohwer, 1970, 1973; Rosner, 1971). Moreover, the effectiveness of these methods appears to be general across wide ranges of age, social classes, and ethnicity (Kee & Rohwer, 1973; Rohwer, Ammon, Suzuki, & Levin, 1971; Rohwer & Bean, 1973; Rohwer, Kee, & Guy, 1975).

By contrast, when it comes to the matter of effecting a permanent increase in the probability of self-activated elaboration, psychological research has only meagre resources to offer education. Little, if anything, is known about the conditions responsible for the development of elaborative propensity in those characterized by self-activation. Furthermore, attempts to enhance self-activation through training have achieved mixed results (Milgram, 1967; Rohwer & Ammon, 1971a, b; Yuille & Catchpole, 1973, 1974). Pending further progress, the educational potential of research on memory for information about group membership is confined largely to the functions of supporting veridical expectations about learner capabilities and providing guidance in the choice of conditions that effectively activate relational encoding.

B. Information About Retrieval Processes and Conditions

In comparison with advances of psychological research in the area of storage processes, such efforts have hardly begun to penetrate the mysteries of retrieval (the research available is reviewed by Kobasigawa, this volume). Because of this, substantial additional research will have to be accomplished in order to constitute an educational resource of estimable magnitude. Still, limited resource that it is, our present knowledge of retrieval processes may offer educators some guidance in understanding and attempting to improve student performance.

As matters now stand, it appears that effective retrieval depends primarily on successful storage, ready access to appropriate retrieval cues, and a propensity to use such cues to return to information previously stored in memory. As we have seen, successful storage by proficient memorizers stems from their tendency to encode item identity information semantically, sequential information cumulatively, and group membership information relationally. It remains to consider here how such persons gain possession of retrieval cues and use them in effecting accurate recall. Accordingly, for purposes of the present discussion, we will assume that information to be recalled has already been stored effectively.

Though students of memory are far from a general consensus, the weight of present thought and evidence favors the proposition that the utility of a cue for retrieving an item to be remembered depends on prior storage of relational information about the cue and the item. Tulving and Thomson (1973) have advanced and elaborated this proposition in the form of the principle of encoding specificity: A cue will serve retrieval only if it has been encoded in relation to the item to be remembered. Thus, an item encoded in sequential relation with another can serve a retrieval function in a serial task, while one item semantically related to another can be an effective retrieval cue in a group membership task.

Only a few studies have been conducted in accordance with the methods required for determining the extent of developmental differences in the self-production of retrieval cues. One requirement is to ensure that persons at all age levels sampled achieve equivalent degrees of storage prior to the retrieval test. Another is the manipulation of test conditions so as to provide a comparison between cued and free recall. One study of this kind (Kobasigawa, 1974) revealed large age differences in the tendency to produce appropriate retrieval cues. The same study also produced results strongly suggesting age differences of similar magnitude in the propensity to use retrieval cues when provided by the experimenter. Finally, such age differences in performance were reduced dramatically by imposing conditions tantamount to forcing the use of provided cues. Conditions of strong constraint substantially facilitated performance in younger children, an effect that decreased as a function of age. The educational value of these tentative interpretations lies mainly in suggesting that the younger the student, the less inclined he or she is either to produce or to use cues of potential effectiveness in aiding recall.

One other product of research on retrieval deserves mention for its possible value as an educational resource. A series of studies on the effects of providing cues at testing indicates that such a practice may be hazardous in the absence of knowledge about the relationship of a cue to an item in storage. In particular, presentation of cues that have been inadequately stored in relation to other items can actually diminish recall (Roediger, 1973; Roth & Rohwer, 1974; Rundus, 1973). The educational import of such findings is that the teacher's ability to enhance students' memory performance hinges on careful appraisal of the character of storage, and the exploitation of such diagnoses in constructing conditions for retrieval.

Though far from comprehensive, this brief review of research on retrieval carries a message for students of memory development who are committed to enhancing the value of their work as an educational resource. In this problem area, our ignorance is vast about the basic processes responsible for retrieval, about conditions that enhance retrieval, about developmental and individual differences in retrieval processes, and about conditions that might compensate for as yet unidentified improficiencies. A reduction in any and all of these unknowns would greatly increase the potential of research as a resource for education.

V. SUMMARY COMMENTS

In this chapter, we have introduced an approach that may enable students of memory to make a contribution to the educational process while working in ways indigenous to their normal activities. In the resource approach, as we refer to it, the investigator uses the products of theoretical and empirical analyses as resources for viewing educational practices and for anticipating their consequences. This approach was contrasted with research strategies that tend to focus directly on educational problems.

To illustrate the resource approach, we have discussed two theoretical distinctions made by students of memory. The first is of a structural character, that between short- and long-term memory, while the second is the process distinction between storage and retrieval. In our discussion of research pertaining to each distinction, we have tried to emphasize the aspects that may currently be offered for educational use. However, we have also noted areas of ignorance and uncertainty that greatly limit its resource value. The highlighting of such gaps may be useful to students of memory development in directing their continuing research. The closing of the gaps, in turn, would substantially increase the educational value of their efforts.

In closing, we hasten to emphasize that the distinctions we chose for purposes of illustration are far from eccentric. The resource approach to educational contributions can be exemplified just as readily with reference to many other research products. In particular, we have in mind the work presented in the preceding chapters of this volume, and we hope the resource approach will prove useful and applicable to a large share of it.

ACKNOWLEDGMENTS

In preparing this chapter, our work was supported by a fellowship from the Van Leer Jerusalem Foundation, by Grant HD-03869 from the National Institutes of Health, and by a fellowship from USPHS Training Grant TO1 GMO120-11.

REFERENCES

Adams, H. F. A note on the effect of rhythm on memory. *Psychological Review,* 1915, *22,* 289–298.

Atkinson, R. C. Ingredients for a theory of instruction. In M. C. Wittrock (Ed.), *Changing education: alternatives from educational research.* Englewood Cliffs, N.J.: Prentice-Hall, 1973.

Atkinson, R. C., & Shiffrin, R. M. Human Memory: A proposed system and its control processes. In K. W. Spence & J. T. Spence (Eds.), *The psychology of learning and motivation: Advances in research and theory* (Vol. 2) New York: Academic Press, 1968.

Bach, M. J., & Underwood, B. J. Developmental changes in memory attributes. *Journal of Educational Psychology*, 1970, *61*, 292–296.

Baumeister, A. A. Serial memory span thresholds of normal and mentally retarded children. *Journal of Educational Psychology*, 1974, *66*, 889–894.

Biggs, J. B. *Information and human learning*. Glenview, Ill.: Scott, Foresman, 1971.

Bower, G. H., & Clark, M. C. Narrative stories as mediators for serial learning. *Psychonomic Science*, 1969, *14*, 181–182.

Bower, G. H., & Springston, T. Pauses as recoding points in letter series. *Journal of Experimental Psychology*, 1970, *83*, 421–430.

Bugelski, B. R. Presentation time, total time, and mediation in paired-associate learning. *Journal of Experimental Psychology*, 1962, *63*, 409–412.

Case, R. Validation of a neo-Piagetian mental capacity construct. *Journal of Experimental Child Psychology*, 1972, *14*, 287–302.

Case, R. Structures and Strictures: Some functional limitations on the course of cognitive growth. *Cognitive Psychology*, 1974, *6*, 544–573.   (a)

Case, R. Mental strategies, mental capacity, and instruction: A neo-Piagetian investigation. *Journal of Experimental Child Psychology*, 1974, *18*, 382–397.   (b)

Case, R. Gearing the demands of instruction to the developmental capacities of the learner. *Review of Educational Research*, 1975, *45*, 59–87.

Cohen, D. K., & Garet, M. S. Reforming educational policy with applied research. *Harvard Educational Review*, 1975, *45*, 17–43.

Conrad, R. Order error in immediate recall of sequences. *Journal of Verbal Learning and Verbal Behavior*, 1965, *4*, 161–169.

Crowder, R. G. Behavioral strategies in immediate memory. *Journal of Verbal Learning and Verbal Behavior*, 1969, *8*, 524–528.

Dempster, F. N. Short-term storage capacity and chunking: A developmental study. Unpublished doctoral dissertation, University of California, Berkeley, 1976.

Dempster, F. N., & Rohwer, W. D., Jr. Component analysis of the elaborative encoding effect in paired-associate learning. *Journal of Experimental Psychology*, 1974, *103*, 400–408.

Elias, C. S., & Perfetti, C. A. Encoding task and recognition memory: The importance of semantic encoding. *Journal of Experimental Psychology*, 1973, *99*, 151–156.

Farnham-Diggory, S., & Gregg, L. W. Short-term memory function in young readers. *Journal of Experimental Child Psychology*, 1975, *19*, 279–298.

Frank, H. S., & Rabinovitch, M. S. Auditory short-term memory: Developmental changes in rehearsal. *Child Development*, 1974, *45*, 397–407.

Gagné, R. M., & Briggs, L. J. *Principles of instructional design*. New York: Holt, Rinehart and Winston, 1974.

Gates, A. I., & Taylor, G. A. An experimental study of the nature of improvement resulting from practice in a mental function. *Journal of Educational Psychology*, 1925, *16*, 583–592.

Ghatala, E. S. Encoding verbal units in memory: Changes in memory attributes as a function of age, instructions and retention interval (Tech. Rep. No. 134). Madison: University of Wisconsin, Wisconsin Research and Development Center for Cognitive Learning, 1970.

Hagen, J. W., & Kingsley, P. R. Labelling effects in short-term memory. *Child Development*, 1968, *39*, 113–121.

Harris, G. J., & Burke, D. The effects of grouping on short-term serial recall of digits by children: Developmental trends. *Child Development*, 1972, *43*, 710–716.

Hasher, L., & Clifton, D. A developmental study of attribute encoding in free recall. *Journal of Experimental Child Psychology*, 1974, *17*, 332–346.

Hunt, E., Frost, N., & Lunneborg, C. Individual differences in cognition: A new approach to intelligence. In Gordon H. Bower (Ed.), *The psychology of learning and motivation* (Vol. 7). New York: Academic Press, 1973.

Hyde, T. S., & Jenkins, J. J. Recall for words as a function of semantic, graphic, and syntactic orienting tasks. *Journal of Verbal Learning and Verbal Behavior,* 1973, *12,* 471–480.

Jacobs, J. Experiments on prehension. *Mind,* 1887, *12,* 75–79.

Jensen, A. R. Individual differences in learning: Interference factor (Cooperative Research Project No. 1867, U.S. Office of Education). Berkeley: University of California, 1964.

Jensen, A. R., & Figueroa, R. A. Forward and backward digit span interaction with race and IQ: Predictions from Jensen's theory. *Journal of Educational Psychology,* 1975, *67,* 882–893.

Jensen, A. R., & Rohwer, W. D., Jr. Syntactical mediation of serial and paired-associate learning as a function of age. *Child Development,* 1965, *36,* 601–608.

Kee, D. W., & Rohwer, W. D., Jr. Noun-pair learning in four ethnic groups: Conditions of presentation and response. *Journal of Educational Psychology,* 1973, *65,* 226–232.

Keeney, T. J., Cannizzo, S. R., & Flavell, J. H. Spontaneous and induced verbal rehearsal in a recall task. *Child Development,* 1967, *38,* 953–966.

Kingsley, P. R., & Hagen, J. W. Induced versus spontaneous rehearsal in short-term memory in nursery school children. *Developmental Psychology,* 1969, *1,* 40–46.

Kobasigawa, A. Utilization of retrieval cues by children in recall. *Child Development,* 1974, *45,* 127–134.

Laurence, M. W. Age differences in performance and subjective organization in the free-recall learning of pictorial material. *Canadian Journal of Psychology,* 1966, *20,* 388–399.

Levin, J. R., & Rohwer, W. D., Jr. Verbal organization and the facilitation of serial learning. *Journal of Educational Psychology,* 1968, *59,* 186–190.

Mayzner, M. S., & Gabriel, R. F. Information "chunking" and short-term retention. *Journal of Psychology,* 1963, *56,* 161–164.

Martin, P. R., & Fernberger, S. W. Improvement in memory span. *American Journal of Psychology,* 1929, *41,* 91–94.

McCarver, R. B. A developmental study of the effect of organizational cues on short-term memory. *Child Development,* 1972, *43,* 1317–1325.

McLaughlin, G. H. Psycho-logic: A possible alternative to Piaget's formulation. *British Journal of Educational Psychology,* 1963, *33,* 61–67.

Milgram, N. A. Retention of mediation set in paired-associate learning of normal children and retardates. *Journal of Experimental Child Psychology,* 1967, *5,* 341–349.

Miller, G. A. The magical number seven, plus or minus two: Some limits on our capacity for processing information. *Psychological Review,* 1956, *63,* 81–97.

Montague, W. E., & Wearing, A. J. The complexity of natural language mediators and its relation to paired-associate learning. *Psychonomic Science,* 1967, *7,* 135–136.

Paivio, A. *Imagery and verbal processes.* New York: Holt, Rinehart and Winston, 1971.

Palmer, S. E., & Ornstein, P. A. The role of rehearsal strategy in serial-probed recall. *Journal of Experimental Psychology,* 1971, *88,* 60–66.

Pascual-Leone, J. A mathematical model for the transition rule in Piaget's developmental stages. *Acta Psychologica,* 1970, *63,* 301–345.

Perfetti, C. A., & Hogaboam, T. Relationship between single word decoding and reading comprehension skill. *Journal of Educational Psychology,* 1975, *67,* 461–469.

Prestianni, F. L., & Zacks, R. T. The effects of learning instructions and cueing on free recall. *Memory & Cognition,* 1974, *2,* 194–200.

Resnick, L. B. "What should we teach? Information processing approaches to task analysis for instruction." Paper presented at the annual meeting of the American Educational Research Association, Washington, D. C., April 1975.

Roediger, H. L. Inhibition in recall from cueing with recall targets. *Journal of Verbal Learning and Verbal Behavior,* 1973, *12,* 644–657.

Rohwer, W. D., Jr. Images and pictures in children's learning: Research results and educational implications. *Psychological Bulletin,* 1970, *73,* 393–403.

Rohwer, W. D., Jr. Elaboration and learning in childhood and adolescence. In H. W. Reese (Ed.), *Advances in child development and behavior* (Vol. 8). New York: Academic Press, 1973.

Rohwer, W. D., Jr. An introduction to research on individual and developmental differences in learning. In W. K. Estes (Ed.), *Handbook of learning and cognitive processes,* Vol. 3: *Approaches to human learning and motivation.* Hillsdale, N.J.: Lawrence Erlbaum Associates, 1976.

Rohwer, W. D., Jr., & Ammon, M. S. Elaboration training and learning efficiency in children. *Journal of Educational Psychology,* 1971, *62,* 376–383. (a)

Rohwer, W. D., Jr., & Ammon, P. R. The assessment and improvement of learning and language skills in four and five year old culturally disadvantaged children (Final report on OEO Contract No. B99-4776). Berkeley: University of California, 1971. (b)

Rohwer, W. D., Jr., Ammon, M. S., Suzuki, N., & Levin, J. R. Population differences and learning proficiency. *Journal of Educational Psychology,* 1971, *62,* 1–14.

Rohwer, W. D., Jr., & Bean, J. P. Sentence effects and noun-pair learning: A developmental interaction during adolescence. *Journal of Experimental Child Psychology,* 1973, *15,* 521–533.

Rohwer, W. D., Jr., Kee, D. W., & Guy, K. C. Developmental changes in the effects of presentation media on noun-pair learning. *Journal of Experimental Child Psychology,* 1975, *19,* 137–152.

Rosner, S. R. The effect of rehearsal and chunking instructions on children's multitrial free recall. *Journal of Experimental Child Psychology,* 1971, *11,* 93–105.

Roth, J. E., & Rohwer, W. D., Jr. The effects of elaborative prompts and retrieval cues in children's free recall learning. Paper presented at the annual meeting of the Western Psychological Association, San Francisco, 1974.

Rundus, D. Negative effects of using list items as recall cues. *Journal of Verbal Learning and Verbal Behavior,* 1973, *12,* 43–50.

Runquist, W. N., & Farley, F. H. The use of mediators in the learning of verbal paired associates. *Journal of Verbal Learning and Verbal Behavior,* 1964, *3,* 280–285.

Ryan, J. Grouping and short-term memory: Different means and patterns of grouping. *Quarterly Journal of Experimental Psychology,* 1969, *21,* 137–147.

Simon, H. A. On the development of the processor. In S. Farnham-Diggory (Ed.), *Information processing in children.* New York: Academic Press, 1972.

Simon, H. A. How big is a chunk? *Science,* 1974, *183,* 482–488.

Simon, H. A. The functional equivalence of problem solving skills. *Cognitive Psychology,* 1975, *7,* 268–288.

Slak, S. Phonemic recoding of digital information. *Journal of Experimental Psychology,* 1970, *86,* 398–406.

Spitz, H. H. The role of input organization in the learning and memory of mental retardates. In N. R. Ellis (Ed.), *International review of research in mental retardation* (Vol. 2). New York: Academic Press, 1966.

Starr, A. S. The diagnostic value of the audito-vocal digit memory span. *Psychological Clinic,* 1923, *15,* 61–84.

Suppes, P. Facts and fantasies of education. In M. C. Wittrock (Ed.), *Changing education: Alternatives from educational research.* Englewood Cliffs, N.J.: Prentice-Hall, 1973.

Surber, J. R., & Anderson, R. C. Delay-retention effect in natural classroom settings. *Journal of Educational Psychology,* 1975, *67,* 170–173.

Terman, L. M., & Merrill, M. A. *Measuring intelligence.* Boston: Houghton Mifflin, 1937.

Tulving, E., & Donaldson, W., (Eds.). *Organization of memory.* New York: Academic Press, 1972.

Tulving, E., & Thomson, D. M. Encoding specificity and retrieval processes in episodic memory. *Psychological Review,* 1973, *80,* 352–373.

Whimbey, A., Fischhof, V., & Silikowitz, R. Memory span: A forgotten capacity. *Journal of Educational Psychology,* 1969, *60,* 56–58.

Whimbey, A. E., & Ryan, S. F. Role of short-term memory and training in solving reasoning problems mentally. *Journal of Educational Psychology,* 1969, *60,* 361–364.

Wickelgren, W. A. Size of rehearsal group and short-term memory. *Journal of Experimental Psychology,* 1964, *68,* 413–419.

Wickelgren, W. A. Rehearsal grouping and hierarchical organization of series position cues in short-term memory. *Quarterly Journal of Experimental Psychology,* 1967, *19,* 97–102.

Wilkes, A. L., & Kennedy, R. A. The relative assessibility of list items within different pause-defined groups, *Journal of Verbal Learning and Verbal Behavior,* 1970, *9,* 197–201.

Yuille, J. C., & Catchpole, M. J. Associative learning and imagery training in children. *Journal of Experimental Child Psychology.* 1973, *16,* 403–412.

Yuille, J. C., & Catchpole, M. J. The effects of delay and imagery training on the recall **and** recognition of object pairs. *Journal of Experimental Child Psychology,* 1974, *17,* 474–481.

14
The Instructional Approach to Developmental Cognitive Research

John M. Belmont
Earl C. Butterfield

University of Kansas

I. INTRODUCTION

A new approach has appeared in developmental cognitive research, an approach that cuts across substantive and theoretical concerns. At the most abstract level, it is a change in the experimenter's attitudes toward the children he tests in the laboratory. We see it in modifications of standard methods and measures, as well as in the invention of altogether new procedures. We see it in the very criteria by which research is being judged to be worthwhile. But we see it most clearly in the kinds of things experimenters are telling their subjects to do, so we call it the instructional approach.

We will examine the instructional approach from three viewpoints. We aim first to pick up its introduction from Europe in the early 1960s and trace its American evolution from that time. This developmental outline shows that the approach was inspired and informed by theoretical issues, and that some of the approach's major methodologic requirements could be seen in the very ideas from which it arose. Against this backdrop, our second aim is to examine the approach's methodologic requirements, which we place under the rubrics "Direct Measurement," "Task Analysis," and "Standards of Evaluation." Finally, we will consider a variety of applications within the instructional approach to show where it is in the mid-1970s. It is time to examine the approach at its best and draw lines at its limits.

An approach to research is an intangible thing. It is a constellation of laboratory activities and ways of interpreting experimental results that must be considered in aggregate to give force to the intuition that there is something new and important afoot. As an introduction to what we mean by the instructional approach, consider two hypothetical studies. The first we call inferential, the second instructional.

A. An Inferential Study

Children in three age groups are required to memorize a list containing 16 words that fall naturally and evenly into 4 categories. For some children, the words in each category are distributed randomly throughout the list. For other children, the words are blocked by category. The instructions are standard for free recall and do not mention categorizability or any other attribute of the materials, save that the words are names of things. The experimental question is whether and to what degree children of different ages will take advantage of the blocked condition, which is an unannounced provision of potentially useful information. Let us say that on the average the youngest children's recall is relatively poor, and they do not benefit from blocking, while the oldest children recall much better, and do benefit from blocking. And the middle children fall in between on both counts. Whether or not this interaction of age × blocking would actually obtain is unimportant for present purposes. What is important is that the study has the familiar, hard-nosed flavor characteristic of much of our literature. And so we would not be surprised to see a maturational deficiency inferred from the observed interaction: Young children do not (or some might say cannot) make use of information-processing facilitators inherent in the task at hand. Older children, by contrast, have cognitive abilities sufficient to enable them to benefit from implicit aids to organizational processing.

B. An Instructional Study

Now consider doing an alternative to the inferential study, perhaps adopting somewhat the same procedures as were used in Moely and Jeffrey's (1974) categorized list experiment. Some of the children in each age × blocking subgroup are treated as previously. The others in each subgroup are told how to process categorizable words. The experimenter demonstrates an appropriate solution for a shorter but similar word list. He explains in simple terms his understanding of the input and output processes required for category-cued free recall, and he enjoins the children to follow his lead. The children are then required to learn test lists, with occasional reminders about how to memorize and recall categorizable words. Moreover, every few trials the experimenter asks the children to explain how they have been processing the list. Hypothetical results could well be that the age × blocking interaction for the uninstructed subgroups is the same as in the inferential study. But the results are quite different for the children who were specially instructed and whose intertrial reports confirmed that they had been using a sound categorization strategy: The age × blocking interaction is altered because the youngest and the oldest both benefit largely from the blocked condition. The instructional effect is thus very large, and leads to a conclusion which must exactly contradict the earlier one. The instructional method shows that all children, regardless of age, can make use of information-processing facilitators inherent in the task at hand.

The second study is not as neat as the first. For one thing, it would require much effort to report the procedures well enough to permit exact replication. The instructional ingredients are many, and the effective ones are unknown. The most salient is, however, the particular strategy given to the children, and its effectiveness clearly depends on a host of variables. Principal among these are the quality of the experimenter's knowledge about mature information-processing strategies for the laboratory task in question, and the precise character of his translation of this knowledge into explicit instructions. Then there are motivational factors, and the degree to which the children actually comply with instructions. In the example, these things were neither quantified nor varied systematically, and so their relative contributions elude us. These are but a few of the problems encountered in the instructional approach, and we have no intention of minimizing the difficulties of coping with them. Indeed, it is precisely because the approach is both problematic and promising that we analyze it here.

II. THE DEVELOPMENT OF THE INSTRUCTIONAL APPROACH

Pointing, touching, handling; naming, labeling, vocalizing; categorizing, chunking, rehearsing, elaborating; defining problems and problem solutions; identifying logical, temporal, or causal relations; applying rules or strategies: Over the past 15 years a growing number of cognitive psychologists have been instructing their laboratory subjects to do these things. Some investigators have known ahead of time that the activities produce good results, and they have used them to help their subjects. Others have deliberately elicited actions inimical to good performance, and they have made theoretical progress out of their subjects' losses. Still others, through gross ignorance of critical interrelationships between tasks and cognitive strategies, have created unintended mismatches, or even failed outright to affect performance. But enough archival dust has settled for us to see that in capable hands instruction on how or what to think can be a potent and subtle tool for cognitive research.

The tool has evolved largely within developmental cognitive psychology, which was once little more than a parody of the literature on adults. It is now a hardy experimental science, in some respects better developed than its parent discipline. This evolution probably did not arise out of, but it certainly is reflected in, developmentalists' embrace of cognitive instruction. They have applied it as an analytic method to a wide range of problems in memory, perception, cognitive style, and problem solving. Key turning points in this evolution are foreshadowed in the American literature as far back as 1932, but its major applications really began developing here only in the early 1960s. We will briefly consider two of these, the Piagetian and the mediational.

A. Cognitive Instruction in Piagetian Research

This application is technically the more difficult of the two, and it is also the better known. It is American psychology's confrontation with Piaget's notion that the development of children's thinking is limited by a succession of stages. The cognitive instruction studies resulting from this confrontation dealt with a large variety of Piagetian concepts, but especially the conservations. The work was meant to show that children who do not spontaneously conserve can be led to do so by instructional intervention, and it seems to have been motivated by a wish to disprove Piagetian structuralisms. The idea of doing so owes largely to Flavell's (1963) popularization of Piaget's work, in which (pp. 370-379) Flavell reviewed the Swedish, French, Canadian, and finally American training studies, reacting to them with what he called a creeping sense of disbelief. He was struck by the early instructional studies' almost total failure to achieve even small changes in children's cognitive performance, and this "apparent recalcitrance of preoperational structures to deliberately engineered, short-order reorganization" seemed to confirm "a deep developmental reality about these structures" (Flavell, 1963, p. 377).

Whether read as pure Flavell or as interpreted Piaget, this idea was, we think, the main impetus to the American movement, which was really excited not simply by the assumption that infantile structures are unshakable, but rather, by the fact that early interventionists had failed to shake them. Kuhn (1974) regards this motivation to destroy an assumption as being the least "noble" of three alternatives, the other two being to understand the "precise capacities, and perhaps mechanisms" of thought and to accelerate growth. Can these be distinguished from the antistructuralist drive? We think so, and by our reading, the first American Piagetian studies, reported between 1960 and 1965, show almost no evidence for either of the two alternatives. If there was any wish to understand mechanisms, it was the mechanisms of change, not the mechanisms of thought per se. Indeed, these studies were designed to determine the laboratory conditions required to change children from preoperational to operational thought. **But** while the focus was on change, it was not on accelerating growth. The instructional methods were brief; the target behaviors—particular conservations—were narrow; and the criterion for success was no more than reliable improvement, regardless of absolute size. Accelerated growth does not fit that picture, but a pure-hearted antistructuralism does.

The Piagetian instructionalists were irritated by structural pessimisms like Flavell's, and nobly or not, they simply chipped away until the idea of rigid organizational limitations on cognition could no longer stand. All they needed was to disprove the idea *in principle,* and this required only that instruction (however brief) about any cognitive activity (however narrow) result in significant improvements (however small). Their basic method remained unchanged, but the way they applied it changed continuously until success was at hand. The instructionalists now appear to have succeeded for conservation in young children, and also for much more heady thinking, such as scientific inference and experimental design in 10-year-olds (Siegler, Liebert, & Liebert, 1973; Siegler & Liebert, 1975).

Kuhn (1974) is dissatisfied with this antistructuralist work because it has not shown long-term effects on cognitive growth. Starting where Brainerd and Allen (1971) left off, Kuhn's analysis covers a wide range of research problems in considerable depth. We will return to her ideas. For now, we acknowledge that she has produced a document of great value to anybody who wishes to understand cognitive instruction experiments within or beyond the Piagetian realm.

B. Cognitive Instruction in Mediational Research

Except for one important cross-exchange, the Piagetian interventionist movement evolved independently of the other big branch of cognitive instruction research. But both branches evolved against a similar environmental problem, which we know by observing the similarities in their ultimate forms. The problem was developmental structuralism.

The second branch, which is focused on verbal control of behavior (verbal mediation), clearly comes out of the Russian systems of Luria and Vigotsky. Its hardiest American roots were well defined in Kuenne's (1946) precursory two-stage description of children's verbal self-control, in the first stage of which the child "is able to make differential verbal responses . . . but this does not control or influence his . . . behavior [p. 488]."

At its very inception, this idea had an ambiguity that went uncorrected through several revisions over the course of 20 years. It ended up being the driving force of the instructional movement. The ambiguity is in the neutral descriptive "does not control." Are the verbal responses similar to older children's, but the nervous system not developed sufficiently to make use of them? Or perhaps the system is ripe but the responses are inappropriate? Or is it that they are in fact appropriate, but the child does not make them in the mediation situation, even though he does make them in other situations?

Kendler, Kendler, and Wells (1960) clarified the issue a little. They spoke of "a stage in which verbal responses, though available, do not readily mediate between . . . stimuli and . . . responses" (Kendler et al., 1960, p. 87). Here the ambiguity is diminished by the qualifier "readily," which weakly implies that the appropriate verbal responses, even if made, are nonetheless ineffective as mediators. In this form, the idea reached Reese (1962), whose term *mediational deficiency hypothesis* entered the standard research lexicon. It was not until two years later, however, in a paper by Kendler (1964) and one by Maccoby (1964), that the ambiguity was resolved.

Kendler developed the mediational deficiency hypothesis as a Lurian three-stage model of development in discrimination learning. In the first stage, the child's discriminative choices are not changed by his making verbal mediation responses, and in fact he does not make them spontaneously. At this point, then, a structural deficiency is accepted as responsible for immaturity of thought. Later, the child still does not make mediational responses spontaneously, but when forced to do so by explicit instructions he automatically exhibits *qualities* of thought characteristic of children in the third stage, who differ from those in the second only in the spontaneity of their verbal mediation. In the experiments from which Kendler adduced evidence in support of this scheme, the instructed verbal mediator had, if anything, a detrimental effect on second-stage children's learning rate on the theoretically crucial optional reversal shift. Thus, for quantitative aspects of performance, the instructed behavior had either no effect or an undesirable one. However, Kendler was akin to the Piagetians in not requiring that children learn things more rapidly or more thoroughly than prior to instructions, but merely that they perceive or respond to the task more maturely. This qualitative emphasis is, we think, the principal reason for the failure of Kendler's hypothesis to excite mediation instructionalists as strongly as Maccoby's more open-ended formulation.

Following a careful analysis of work on mediational deficiencies, Maccoby suggested that young children may possess the mediator but not produce it unless "experimental situations are arranged so that the relevant verbalizations will be elicited [1964, p. 215]." There was absolutely no implication of structural or stagewise development in this production deficiency hypothesis, and it was forthright even to the point of supplying the conditions for testing it: The method would be *elicitation;* the thing to elicit was *relevant* verbalizations; and the goal was wonderfully indefinite, thus opening the door to a variety of quantitative approaches and to experimental tasks other than discrimination learning.

Now, given such a flexible challenge, anybody could set up situations that would elicit verbalizations from young children. But relevant ones? That question has been the key to instructional cognitive psychology from the mid-1960s down to the present. As we shall show in our discussion of task analysis, the question's procedural implications, when followed to their extremes, radically alter our most cherished views of children's thinking. This has happened recently, but only as a result of developments that began in 1966, when almost nobody in developmental psychology knew anything about what constituted a relevant verbalization for any laboratory task.[1] To find out, researchers used both of the ways that Atkinson and Shiffrin (1968) later independently suggested for adult psychology: Either intuit the relevant verbalization or discover it by experimentation. Intuition was used by Silverman (1966), for example, and by Marsh and Sherman (1966). They forced children to verbalize the "relevant dimensions" for discrimination learning problems, even though they had no certain knowledge that people who perform well on the task actually verbalize that way.

The alternative to guessing about such things was to research them. It was hit upon by Flavell, the same Flavell who so eloquently developed the structural position for the Piagetians. This time, however, he evidently felt more hopeful about the potential of instructional intervention to surmount difficulties encountered by the earlier movement, and he recognized exactly what was missing from Maccoby's formulation, to which he was responding directly. In a developmental memory experiment, Flavell, Beach, and Chinsky (1966) simply arranged to watch the children's lips as they performed the task. The procedure neither interfered with nor even required knowledge about the children's recall accuracy. This masterstroke legitimized and largely established *direct measurement* of task-related activity as the basis for creating instructions to produce quantitative gains in children's information processing. We think direct measurement is fast becoming the foremost technique of developmental cognitive psychology.[2]

Flavell and his colleagues combined cognitive instruction and direct measurement of task-related activities in a research strategy that they pursued far enough to grasp some of the important implications of both techniques. Flavell (1970)

---

[1] Spiker (1960) is unique in, and completely unheralded for, his early efforts to improve children's paired-associates learning by instructing them to use systematic, professionally developed mnemonics. The technique was to link the associated items using interactive imagery.

[2] The reader may well boggle at the suggestion that simple measurement could ever be a radical departure from established scientific tradition. If so, let him recall that just prior to Flavell, Beach, and Chinsky's work, Kendler, Kendler, and Learnard (1962) deliberately rejected active measurement of mediational processes in favor of the indirect inferential techniques that long dominated and are still commonly used in mediational research.

It should also be noted that Flavell et al. (1966) unknowingly repeated part of what Marjorie Pyles (1932) had accomplished much earlier. She used a multiple-choice discrimination learning task with three-dimensional nonsense and familiar forms, and a sophisticated experimental design reminiscent of Flavell's first follow-up study (Keeney, Cannizzo, & Flavell, 1967). Pyles recorded spontaneous verbalizations, and she instructed nonverbalizers with a highly successful stimulus-naming routine. Her one decisive mistake, which the later group easily avoided, was in reporting her work to an unreceptive 1932 audience. Pyles's isolated inventions led nowhere.

put these together in his landmark development of the production deficiency hypothesis. We interpret his conclusions as follows: First, one cannot fix an age range within which children make the transition from mediational nonproducers to producers; the age of transition depends on the particular experimental conditions and the particular mediator in question. The second point, closely related to the first, is that dichotomizing children as producers and nonproducers is inaccurate and misleading. Over a wide age range, children are producers or nonproducers depending on conditions and instructions. It is therefore much more accurate and informative to measure the child's "production threshold" for a particular kind of mediator. The production threshold is the level of situational and instructional support required to elicit the mediator, and this threshold decreases with age [cf. Rohwer's (1973) thorough development of this idea vis-à-vis semantic elaboration in paired-associate learning]. Third, the mediators that children *and adults* produce with minimal explicit instruction are not likely to be optimal in any particular task. Flavell could therefore correctly speak of children's mediational inefficiencies, but we must add in view of the adults' inefficiencies that the concept of inefficiency itself is very much a matter of judgment requiring the setting of standards that may be arbitrary. Finally, we have a preview of the theme that Flavell and Wellman (this volume) and others in and out of developmental psychology are now vigorously developing: Mnemonic mediation is most readily understandable as a particular example of the creative efforts that people expend as a matter of course in dealing with new problems of any sort. Freely emitted mnemonic mediators seem to be theoretically important in this scheme only to the extent that they can be related to the growing child's interaction with his own cognitive processes. Thus, the child's creative proclivities and his self-knowledge have come into central focus, and this is very much a part of the instructional approach.

C. Conclusion

Both the Piagetian and the mediational instruction movements evolved in reaction to structural views of children's cognitive immaturities. Piaget's stages were interpreted as fixed limitations on general conceptual operations, while the mediational deficiency hypothesis was interpreted as saying that good information processing may be prevented by inadequacies in the young child's cognitive apparatus. In each case, the instructionists hoped to discredit the structural idea by showing that youngsters can be induced to perform at levels ordinarily (that is, in standard testing situations) achieved only by older children.

The job was and still is, frankly, harder for the Piagetians because they have no good means of measuring the processes by which conservation is achieved. This is not a criticism of these researchers' ingenuity or persistence, for of both they have ample. The problem is that conservation, much like recognition memory, is a swift exercise, unaccompanied by reliably measurable thinking. It has thus never been possible to base "how to conserve" instructions on firm measurement, and the cognitive training has necessarily proceeded—largely on intuitive grounds—by example and implication.

As Kuhn (1974) reports, some of the Piagetian instructors thought that the young children's failure resulted from being misled by perceptual, semantic, or informational aspects of conservation tests. Accordingly, they forced children to attend to relevant task dimensions, hoping that the supposedly latent conservation inferences would automatically reveal themselves. There is an element of magical thinking in this method very similar to that found in some of the early mediation approaches. We are reminded of McKee and Riley's (1962), Silverman's (1966), and Marsh and Sherman's (1966) inexplicable use of instructed labeling to facilitate verbal and auditory discrimination, and Flavell, Beach, and Chinsky's (1966) use of labeling to "prime" rehearsal in the memory task. This naive hopefulness is also found in a variety of recent developmental studies which are neither Piagetian nor mediational. These instructional methods are intended "to focus attention" on stimuli, stimulus attributes, or other task elements in list learning, rule learning, and so forth (see, e.g., Johnson, Warner, & Lee, 1970; Balling & Myers, 1971; Wheeler & Dusek, 1973; Dusek, Kermis, & Mergler, 1975). Such approaches say to the child "pay attention," but as Denny (1973) observed, such instruction results in children's doing almost nothing else. Denny concluded that to improve thinking of any sort the child's attention must be drawn to the stimulus array, yes, but also to the thinking itself. Sure enough, the most notable successes have been carded by Piagetians who focused on verbal rules or on constituent processes that logically underlie conservation (reversability, identity, synthesis, compensation, multiple classification, and numeric relations, to name a few). Likewise, Seggie (1970) and Siegler et al. (1973, 1975) succeeded in teaching logical relations and scientific inference and design by training logically implicated subprocesses of cognition.

Instructional researchers in the mediation camp also met with success when they attended to the mediational processes, and their success came easier and more dramatically than the Piagetian achievements. This was so because good performers tend to do mediation tasks slowly and with much measurable activity. The measurability of the relevant activity permitted the mediation instructors to do two crucial things: They could base their instructional routines on task-related activity actually observed in successful people, and they could monitor directly their young children's use of the instructed activity, rather than relying solely on inference from criterion task performance. Success in using measurement in these two ways requires close attention to individual differences in cognitive activity and individual differences in criterion task performance, so the instructional movement has inevitably turned developmental cognitive psychology away from its traditional nomothetic orientation (cf. Butterfield & Dickerson, 1976).

We have tried to show in this little history that the instructional approach embraces a philosophy which questions research methods and basic concepts that psychologists have long used to rationalize conclusions about children's cognitive deficiencies. The philosophy was perfectly captured by Hall, Salvi, Seggev, and Caldwell (1970) in a warning to the investigator who makes structural interpretations of his young subjects' failures on the experimental task:

> When capacity limitations are implied or stages hypothesized, . . . he must investigate and rule out alternative explanations. A more plausible solution to employ when a task proves too difficult for a group of subjects is to continue searching for other possible training conditions rather than using labels (such as maturation) as explanations. One strategy for looking at these other possibilities is to employ a detailed analysis of the criterion task [p. 427].

Only in that crucial matter of criterion task analysis does there appear to be an important difference in the Piagetian and mediational applications. The mediational instructionalists, precisely because their tasks were more readily analyzed, have enjoyed a measure of success that still largely eludes the Piagetians. For this reason alone, our study of contemporary methods of cognitive instruction will be directed primarily toward the mediational literature.

III. AN ANALYSIS OF THE INSTRUCTIONAL APPROACH

A. Definitions

Methodology requires definitions. Hard-and-fast distinctions have a way of falling apart under microscopic analysis, but we are nevertheless bound to try to define instruction, which we hold to be a method separate from, but importantly adjunct to, those of traditional laboratory science. By *instruction* we mean calculated models, suggestions, rules, or injunctions that have a known influence on the way a child thinks about the materials with which he must work in the laboratory task. The definition rules out instructions and demonstrations that simply define the criterion task's information-processing requirements, and it rules out variables relating to the materials, such as choices, arrangements, modes, and rates or rhythms of presentation. We recognize that task instructions and arrangements of materials do influence a child's thinking, as this is precisely what they are intended to do. But the thinking they influence concerns grasping the task requirements. By contrast, cognitive instruction is directed at solutions to meet those requirements.

To see how these distinctions work in practice, consider the first free recall study described on page 438. The blocking of items by category is a hint to the child that paying attention to the categories might help subsequent recall. But the hint inheres in the materials, and as it happens the child can catch it or miss it. That chanciness is what distinguishes the manipulation of materials from instruction per se. Instruction, like that given to the children in the second free recall study, is not a matter of opening up options, but rather, of closing them. It is an active procedure that channels the person's thinking, and it requires corroboration independent of criterion task performance. This and a couple of other requirements must be clear if the instructional approach is to be fully understood.

B. Methodologic Requirements

Methods of cognitive instruction must follow these three principles:

1. *Direct Measurement.* The experimenter observes as directly as possible how a person is thinking while performing the criterion task.
2. *Task Analysis.* He knows as accurately as possible how a person should be thinking while performing the criterion task.
3. *Standards of Evaluation.* He specifies what or how well a person must do to permit the conclusion that the instruction worked successfully.

We have adhered rather closely to these principles in some of our own studies of memory in normal, deaf, and retarded children and adults that we will be reviewing throughout this discussion, but for the following reasons we make no claim to the principles themselves: In a nonexhaustive literature search we have turned up 114 titles, the prime selection criterion for which was that they should either have considered or actually used cognitive instruction. In 32 of these papers, 42 different people gave something more than lip service to task analysis, and in 27 papers 38 different people (a good number of whom were Piagetians) discussed or made at least some effort to establish standards of evaluation. Similarly, in 35 papers 42 different people either discussed, or thought that their work would have benefited by using, or actually did use, some measure of the subject's activity independent of his criterion task performance.

1. Direct Measurement

For three excellent reasons, instructional researchers who ignore direct measurement almost surely miss the boat. First, direct measurement can reveal the general character and variability of cognitive activities used by good task performers. This information may not stand alone as an optimal basis for inventing instructional routines, but it is far better than guessing. Second, measurement of the instructed activities can tell whether and to what extent the children actually follow the instructions. This information is necessary for clear inferences about whether or not the instructions work. After all, if children ignore or misinterpret instructions intended to induce particular kinds of cognition, one can hardly conclude that the instructed cognition itself would be ineffective for them. Third (the other side of the same coin), measurement can reveal which people are inclined to generate useful activity without instruction. Such pretest information is essential to judging the efficacy of the instructed activities, for it separates children who actually require help from those who are already well on the way to successful spontaneous production.

Acknowledging thus the central role of direct activity measurement in the instructional approach, we should now take a close look at measurement itself. All measures are inferences about underlying processes, and they are indirect to the degree of their removal from the processes. This removal can be logical or temporal. The temporal distance of a measure from its object processes is the disparity between the time at which the processing occurs and the time at which it is measured. We may speak of concurrent measurement when temporal distance is zero.

The logical distance of a measure from its object processes is indexed by the number of rationally acceptable alternative explanations of variability in the measure. Magnetic tape recording for monitoring audible speech is not far removed logically from its object because there is rarely any question about the source of what is heard at playback. In contrast, IQ for measuring the quality of thought is logically far removed from its object exactly because variation in IQ may be explained in so many ways. The principle of direct measurement requires minimizing logical distance, which is not necessarily correlated with temporal distance. Both must be small.

Consider, as an example of the two kinds of removals, the serial position curve of free recall errors as a measure of input processing. In many developmental studies, the shape of the curve relating recall errors to item input position has been taken to reflect thinking that might have gone on during item input. The typical task analysis holds that successful recall of the earliest list items depends on the child's rehearsing those items at some time during list presentation. On this basis, it has been inferred that children who recall early items poorly must not have been rehearsing those items as much as the more successful children had. The serial position curve is thus a measure of input activity, but it is temporally and logically removed from the activity. It is taken after the fact, and it is responsive to many different, equally reasonable alternative interpretations regarding input and output behaviors. It could, therefore, never be as satisfying or as informative as a measure of item rehearsal taken during list learning.

We have adopted such a measure of input activity (Belmont & Butterfield, 1969). It is the amount of time a person spends as he works his way through a serial list, and so it is certainly concurrent with learning processes, though its logical removal from item rehearsal is greater than zero. Our findings with this input measure agreed with the most general form of the inferences from recall errors. The measure also showed, however, that age-related differences in recall of short lists correlated not only with the amount but also with the form of the activity devoted to early list items (Belmont & Butterfield, 1971b). We found, too, that younger children are generally slower to settle on whatever mnemonic method they do choose, and their method is generally less reliable, even after that choice is made (Butterfield & Belmont, 1977). These observations could not have been made, not even guessed at, from the serial position curves or any other analysis of recall errors.

Direct concurrent measurement can expose sizable qualitative and quantitative individual differences in thinking unobservable by more remote methods, but instructionists have differed greatly in how much use they make of it. The range is as follows: (1) no activity measurement; (2) postexperimental questioning to eliminate failures to follow instructions; (3) introspections or other measures of subject-generated activity before or after the fact; (4) recording of ongoing subject-generated activity. We have chosen five studies to illustrate these procedures. The first, by Kobasigawa and Middleton (1972), is virtually a random choice from among many nonmeasurement studies. We chose the studies by Taylor, Josberger, and Knowlton (1972), Milgram (1968), MacMillan (1972), and Turnure, Buium, and Thurlow (1976) because they share a common problem area (sentence elaboration in paired-associates learning) and thereby make for clarifying contrasts in the comparison of their subject activity measures. By the time we have made our way from Kobasigawa and Middleton, through the others, to the Turnure et al. study, we hope to have sufficiently illustrated both the use and the necessity of direct measurement.

Kobasigawa and Middleton wanted to account for young children's poor free recall of categorizable materials. The experimental question was whether grouping or category labeling would induce the younger children to adopt organizational strategies thought to facilitate recall. They used six pictures of common objects from each of four categories arranged in four rows for simultaneous presentation. For half the children in each of three grades (K, 3, 5), the exemplars were grouped by category, by row. For the other children, they were randomly dispersed among the rows. Each of these subgroups was further divided so that half the children were directed to the items' categorizability. The tester pointed out the various items in a category, for example, ''These are all animals, these are all . . .,'' and so on. The other children were not treated to this hint. Every child studied the display for two minutes, followed by (tape-recorded) oral free recall. Two more identical trials completed the recall testing, after which each child was given a random arrangement of the 24 pictures and asked to group the pictures that ''go together.'' Finally, each child was asked to pick out the six items from each named category, which all children did perfectly.

No direct measures of organizational strategies were employed. The recall results alone were reported, and these were combined over the three trials. Kindergarteners showed no significant differences for either grouping or category labeling (hint). Grouping was significant for third graders and marginally so for fifth graders; hint was significant only for fifth graders. These statistics notwithstanding, neither grouping nor hint helped performance much at any grade. The single largest effect was the *simple* difference at grade 5 between ungrouped-without hint (15.7 items correct) and grouped-with hint (18.9 items correct). This difference of about three items is 20% of the lower score, and thus we may say that the combined effect was a 20% gain in recall accuracy. The *main* effects at Grade 5 were much smaller: Grouping yielded a step from 16.5 to 17.8 items, a one-item absolute difference worth only a 7.9% gain, and the significant hint effect was from 16.2 to 18.1, two items, worth an 11.5% gain. The significant grouping effect at Grade 3 was also about two items, from 14.2 to 16.5, a 17% gain. By contrast, the nonsignificant hint effect for kindergarten-ers was 9.5 to 10.5 items, a one-item, or 10.7%, gain.

These differences between treatment groups are small, but they could nevertheless have resulted from a variety of possibly informative individual differences in study period activity. Unfortunately, in this research there was no measure of how the children were processing the items during the two-minute study intervals, so the best that Kobasigawa and Middleton could hope for was to infer the study behavior by looking at the remote and indirect measure of item organization during recall. Large effects on this measure accrued to grouping for kindergarteners, but none to hint. However, hint, not grouping, yielded improvement in recall accuracy for kindergarteners. This is precisely the sort of quandary that leads to protracted conjecture, but very little positive increase in knowledge. Moreover, there is an alternative approach to analyzing recall accuracy data (cf. Balling & Myers, 1971) that Kobasigawa and Middleton did not take, but that might have forced them to revise their conclusion that the hint effect "was clearly limited to Grade 5": True, the hint induced only a one-item average gain at the kindergarten level (9.5 versus 10.5 items correct on the average), but 60 children received the hint at that grade. Perhaps 50 of them averaged 9.5 items recalled, thereby showing no advantage over their 60 no-hint peers, while 10 others, who caught the hint and adopted an organizational strategy based on the categories, might have averaged 15.5 correct, a whopping six-item, 63% gain. The overall hint group average would have been the actually observed 10.5 items correct, but the conclusion would be that some 5-year-old children benefit tremendously from the hint, while others benefit not at all. We raise this possibility simply to make this point: The group difference is the statistical best estimate of effect, certainly, but to the extent that it masks highly variable results, the best estimate may be very poor indeed. Experimental inductions of new ways of thinking are directed at individual children, not groups of children arbitrarily leveled on age. The effects should therefore be evaluated by looking for individual differences, preferably in the activity itself, but failing that, at least in the criterion task performance or other indirect indexes of the activity.

Although we obviously hold direct measurement of subject-produced activity in high esteem, we should note that its success in the instructional approach depends entirely on how it is used in any particular application. The last four studies of paired-associates learning to be discussed here are arranged to illustrate a progression from relatively weak to relatively strong applications.

Taylor et al. (1972) instructed subgroups of 12-year-old retarded children (MA ≈ 8.8) to use imagery elaboration, sentence elaboration, or simple repetition in paired-associates learning of common objects. The study began with standard PA instructions for a single trial with an eight-pair list. Mean recall was 1.58 items (20%) correct. The three instructional conditions were then imposed on separate groups, the tester giving an example for one pair and the child producing a similar (covert) activity on the next. Three practice trials followed, with a subsequent interview to determine that the child was following instructions. Then came one trial on a 12-pair test list (List 2) followed by one trial on another test list composed of 8 stimuli, each accompanied by two response items (List 3). Finally came the delayed, direct measure: "To obtain subjective validation of the instructional treatments," all children were asked to describe what they had been doing as they learned the last two lists.

The criterion task performance clearly showed that imagery and sentence instructions were superior to simple repetition and uninstructed pretest strategies (whatever they may have been): 77 and 71% versus 24 and 20% correct recall, respectively, for List 2; 66 and 62% versus 9 and 20% for List 3. In neither case was the difference favoring imagery over sentence elaboration statistically significant, and even if it had been, the postexperimental inquiry did not provide sufficiently precise information to understand the difference in terms of study activity. The interview information was like this: "Two subjects admitted not using the specified elaboration strategy [data excluded and not reported]. However, other subjects did mention that they were unable to generate verbal contexts or images for specific pairs. Each child was asked to give his verbal context or describe his image for at least three of the pairs from List 2 and two of the triplets from List 3" (Taylor et al., 1972, p. 72-73).

Such information is directly related to the child's study activity, and it is independent of his criterion task performance. However, it is so far removed from the pair-by-pair elaborations that it can do little more than exclude individuals who admit outright failure to follow instructions, and whet the appetite for measures that can reasonably be related to task performance. It might have happened, for example, that the children who turned in 77% recall under imagery instructions on List 2 failed to recall many pairs for which they had made an interactive image, whereas those who managed 71% recall under sentence elaboration actually recalled 100% of the pairs for which they had made a sentence. Such a result would cast a very different light on the relative efficacy of the two treatments suggested by the obtained trend favoring imagery. Or consider this alternative: What if all sentence-instructed children had produced sentences for every pair? Then the individual differences analysis might have shown that the group's 71% had actually resulted from nearly perfect recall by some children and mediocre recall by others, with a qualitative analysis showing large differences between the types of sentences produced by these proficiency subgroups. The point is that understanding *group* differences (or spurious similarities!) in criterion task performance will come only in a carefully balanced analysis of *individual differences* in criterion task performance matched off against *individual differences* in a satisfactory independent measure of study activities.

Taylor et al. did in fact go on to test 5 additional children under each elaboration treatment, using an 18-pair list on which each child described his elaboration for each pair. It is unclear whether the description was taken during or after list presentation, but in either case Taylor et al. made no effort to relate recall accuracy (preferaby pair by pair) to the subsequent qualitative analysis of the reported elaborations.

We are reminded at this point of Newell's (1973) excellent prescriptions for scientific psychology: Find out what strategies people are actually using, and never average over strategies. Lest one suppose that Newell's prescriptions are easy to follow, however, we now consider the Milgram and MacMillan studies, which were well intentioned but ran into difficulties.

Milgram (1968) tried to teach young children to use the sentence elaboration technique for PA learning. There were two groups of retarded children (MA 5 or 8) and two of normal children (MA 4 or 7). Three lists containing 4 or 6 pairs of common objects were each presented for a maximum of 18 trials or two perfectly anticipated consecutive trials. Each of the four groups was divided into a control subgroup which received no instruction, and a treatment subgroup to which graded instruction was given within subjects. For the treated children, the tester went through the List 1 pairs before administering the learning trials on List 1, saying an elaborative sentence for each pair, with sentence quality varying systematically across pairs. Before learning List 2, the child was required to formulate an elaborative sentence of his own for each pair. Prior to List 3, he was simply reminded about remembering sentences "and thinking about how the pictures can go together in the sentence." Thus, the instructional method was to give some good models, then elicit elaboration, and then trim down the elicitation to a mere reminder. The question for the third list was whether or not the instructed elaboration method would transfer to fresh materials.

Looking only at trials to criterion, Milgram concluded that the treatment effect (control vs. treatment) was very strong for tester-provided sentences, diminished somewhat for sentences generated by children, and then fell almost to nil for the transfer list. The task turned out to be so easy for the treatment groups, however, that interpretation of these findings is very difficult. The treated children started off near the ceiling and thereafter dropped only a little, while the controls improved steadily across lists, and thereby came within range of the treated children on the last list. The ceiling effect thus largely accounts for the drop in treatment efficacy over trials, and it also vitiates the analysis of retarded versus normal children's relative mediational deficiencies. This is a pity because the experimental methods were otherwise well conceived.

The study's major strength resides in Milgram's attempt to relate learning speed to the quality of sentences generated by the treatment subjects before learning List 2. He classified the sentences after the fashion of Martin's scheme (see Martin, Boersma, & Bulgarella, 1968), but unfortunately the effort was futile. Milgram found no correlation between learning rate and sentence quality. The ceiling effect probably contributed to this failure, but the low correlation between study activity and performance would not have been surprising even if there had been variability in learning, simply because there was no check, and hence no guarantee that during learning the children actually used the sentences they had generated prior to learning.

This distant-measure criticism might also have fallen on MacMillan's (1972) study, which was similar to Milgram's in many ways, including its failure to record activity after the first trial. MacMillan also used two nine-item training lists, followed by a transfer list, with normal and retarded children (MA = 8). Unlike Milgram's study, however, the tester-provided and child-generated conditions were administered between subjects, each condition spanning the first two lists. Considering that children who made their own elaborations had no models to work from, the effect was astounding. To come to a criterion of one perfectly anticipated trial, on the average the uninstructed controls made 34 errors, while both of the treated groups made only 2 errors. Thus, in effect the treatments yielded one-trial learning, and so, as it happened, MacMillan's subsequent qualitative analysis à la Milgram was done on direct measurements that were (unlike Milgram's) concurrent with the learning activity because all of the learning was done during the measurement period. The irony in this inadvertent technical upgrading is that the conditions from which it arose also defeated its purpose: When learning is complete in one trial, there are no longer any errors to explain.

The remedy for all of these difficulties came in Turnure et al.'s (1976) altogether fascinating comparison of six conditions, including tester-supplied versus child-produced elaborative sentences. Turnure et al. used two devices that did away with the problem of ceiling effects: They studied very young children (MA = 5), and used a very long list. As for guaranteeing concurrent measurement, they used a single learning trial followed by a single anticipation trial, and the children did all of their sentence elaboration aloud.

The list was 21 pairs of pictured objects, the stimulus items of which comprised three exemplars from each of 7 categories. The response items were conceptually unrelated to the stimuli. The pairs were shown one at a time, and the children (like MacMillan's) either repeated elaborative sentences spoken by the tester for each pair, or made up their own sentences without benefit of previous models. On the single anticipation trial that followed, the sentence repetition group averaged 8.4 correct (40%). The sentence production group averaged 3.5 correct (17%), leaving 276 errors, which is an ample supply to classify and relate to the quality of the concurrently measured elaborative sentences. In spite of having obtained data appropriate for this job, however, Turnure et al. have not yet reported the analysis. Nevertheless, this is the first time in this line of instructional research that the problem and the methods have coincided sufficiently to permit good analytic work to be done on the relationships between recall accuracy and child-generated input activity.

In view of the analytic power of the Turnure et al. method, the paralyzing weaknesses in the preceding studies' methods, and the total absence of appropriate measures in the first study, it is hard to exaggerate the quality of Turnure et al.'s technical advances. There is one point, however, that needs clarification, and this is an inevitable question about direct measurement: Did the measures capture all of the relevant processing? Were the Turnure et al. sentence-production children doing mnemonically effective things besides making up overt sentences, things that the qualitative analysis of the sentences themselves would not reflect? This reduces to questioning the direct measure's ability to capture the full range of task-relevant activity, and it is a valid question for all of the studies in this line. It is, however, probably more important for the earlier studies than for this one, because the children in the Turnure et al. study were all through repeating or making up sentences before they were given any inkling that theirs was in fact a learning task. Thus, during the study trial there was at least no reason for them to have *tried* to do anything but what the tester had requested explicitly and then measured directly and concurrently. We should add that this problem is not strictly one of logical or temporal removal of the measure. The problem is, rather, whether or not the researcher has chosen to measure the right thing in the first place, and this is an empirical issue resolvable in the data. The measure either accounts for most of the variability in subsequent recall, or fails to do so. As noted, Turnure et al. have not told us which.

The foregoing studies were chosen for this discussion of direct measurement because they used cognitive instruction to attack a common problem, and they used basically the same task and the same activity measure for a single purpose. As it turned out, they also faced similar problems of data interpretation, so they stood as rich illustrations of the principle of concurrent measurement, and of the inextricability of this principle from other methodological concerns: uninterpretable group differences, ceiling effects, and choices of measures and other matters of task analysis.

In citing these very similar studies, we have not illustrated the range of concurrent measures that other researchers have used in conjunction with cognitive instructions to elicit overt activity. These we will discuss separately later on. There are also measures that focus on spontaneous activity, and these tend to be somewhat less obtrusive than the elicited measures, even though they are as a rule somewhat more logically distant from the target processes. Farnham–

Diggory and Gregg's (1975) recording of eye movements to measure children's object classification strategies is a particularly fine example outside of the verbal learning literature. One does well to read their comments on the importance of direct measurement for describing the development of metacognition. Other unobtrusive concurrent measures include recordings of spontaneous overt verbalizations, study time in self-paced learning, recall latency, and item output order, all of which input and output measures are independent of recall accuracy (Belmont & Butterfield, 1971b; Butterfield & Belmont, 1971, 1972; Flavell, Friedrichs, & Hoyt, 1970; Kellas, Ashcraft, Johnson, & Needham, 1973b; Kellas, McCauley, & McFarland, 1975).

We hope that this discussion and partial listing of direct concurrent measures has conveyed both the importance and the practicality of inventing open windows to the child's thought. Without them, we think there is little hope of advancing beyond vague understandings of cognitive development. With them, the possibility of accounting for age-related changes in criterion task performance can be realized, provided only that the investigator chooses to focus his measures on the right processes. This provision is the subject of the following discussion of task analysis.

2. Task Analysis

If one wishes to understand the instructional approach, and especially if one intends to adopt instructional methods for any of the many purposes to which they are suited, then he must acknowledge and come to grips with three facts about laboratory tasks and the strategies with which individuals may perform them.

The first fact is that no sort of information-processing strategy can be depended on to have an equal or even unidirectional effect across tasks. Consider, for example, that naming the stimulus materials can reduce mediator effectiveness in discrimination learning (Cook & Smothergill, 1971), can facilitate rule learning (Balling & Myers, 1971; Dusek et al., 1975; Wheeler & Dusek, 1973), can interfere with verbal learning by older children (Belmont & Butterfield, 1971a; Brown, Campione, Bray, & Wilcox, 1973; Leicht & Johnson, 1970), and can facilitate verbal learning by younger children (Rosner, 1971). The second fact is that on some tasks people can perform comparably using very different strategies. The example par excellence is visual imagery and sentence elaboration, both of which can be effective for paired-associate learning. The third fact is that there can be large differences both among and within individuals in the strategies they select to cope with any particular task (see, e.g., Battig, 1975; Butterfield & Belmont, 1971).

Many instructional researchers do not understand their tasks in terms of these facts. Many do not know how their instructions relate to the task requirements, or how much effect could be expected from using devices like labeling, rehearsal, chunking, elaboration, and imagery. The process of understanding these things with reference to a particular task is what we mean by task analysis. It is a confrontation with individual differences, on the one hand, and regularities in relationships between strategies and task demands, on the other. It is essential to the instructional approach, and it can be a complicated problem in its own right (Glaser & Resnick, 1972).

Atkinson and Shiffrin (1968) have noted that for some tasks the analysis can be done in the armchair, while others require a laboratory approach. In either case, the ideal result is an accurate, detailed understanding of how task performance is influenced by the strategies people apply to the task, and some idea of optimum strategies as well. A good example of the lengths to which the laboratory exercise can be taken is our own analysis of a short-term memory task. The analysis began with the development of unobtrusive strategy measures. Pause times and recall times were collected for an automated task in which an individual paced himself through each of a number of different lists to be memorized. The first job was to establish the validity of these measures of input and output processes for variants of a single task. We began doing this by asking adults to make posttask reports about what they had been thinking as they paced themselves through and subsequently recalled the lists. In most cases, an individual's report correlated beautifully with his average distribution of input pause times across serial positions. We also found that output times were systematically related to the input pause time curves and to the person's report about how he had recalled the lists. To put a finer point to the input/output relationships, we shifted from the observational to the instructional method. We had individuals recall the lists in various ways (serial recall, backward recall, circular recall) and found good correspondence between these recall requirements and the subject-generated input pause patterns (Butterfield, Belmont, & Peltzman, 1971; Kellas & Butterfield, 1971). Going the other way, we instructed individuals to use a number of input strategies that we had distilled from the variety seen in the observational studies. The result was highly regular corresponding output patterns exactly similar to those seen in the observational work (Butterfield & Belmont, 1971).

This task analysis also gave us three important collateral findings: (1) Individuals easily adopted the instructed strategies; (2) Interindividual variability was smaller under instructional than under free strategy conditions; and (3) recall accuracy was higher under instructional than under free strategy conditions. We knew, therefore, that we were telling our subjects to do something comfortable and more effective on the average than what they had spontaneously elected to do.

Selecting among a variety of appropriate coordinated input/output strategies, we settled on the one described by Butterfield et al. (1973) to train retarded adolescents how to perform the position probe version of the task. This version involved a series of six-item lists. The person paced himself through the lists, seeing a probe item after each list. His recall response was to indicate the position in the list where the probe had occurred.

Figure 14-1 is a flow diagram of the coordinated input/retrieval strategy we trained the retarded adolescents to use. The first three steps are input, and they specify that the initial list items are rehearsed as a chunk (Steps 1 and 2), while the terminal items are only briefly attended to (Step 3) and thus held in short-term storage (STS). Following the probe exposure (Step 4), STS is activated (Step 5). If the item is there, its position is ascertained by a search (Step 7), and the response is made (Step 8). If the probe is not located in STS, then LTS is called up and searched (Step 6; Step 7) and the response made (Step 8). We were confident that *anybody* whose thoughts were put together according to this blueprint would recall very well. Moreover, we knew that in the process he would spend less time than he would on any other equally effective strategy. Information of this kind is exactly what investigators need when their instructional manipulations turn out to be unsatisfactory (Belmont & Butterfield, 1971a; Ha-

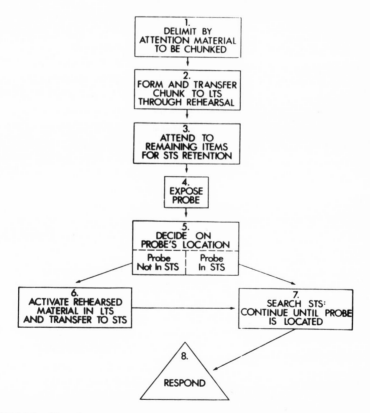

FIGURE 14-1   Flow diagram analysis of position probe memory task used by Butterfield, Wambold, and Belmont (1973) as basis for instructing retarded adolescents.

gen, Hargrave, & Ross, 1973), when they obtain widely different performance by using a variety of instructions (Hohn & Martin, 1970), or when they want to specify the conditions under which some particular instructions are likely to be effective (Flavell et al., 1966).

It should make no difference how task analysis is accomplished. Whether it is done in or out of the laboratory, all that matters is how well it predicts a child's performance on the task in question, given knowledge about how he is thinking as he does the task. In practice, however, successful task analysis does seem to rest on experimental confirmation, as may be seen in the outstanding jobs done by Resnick and Glaser (1974) in their approach to problem solving, and Rohwer (1973), Turnure et al., (1975), and Craik & Tulving (1975) in their analyses of semantic elaboration.

We are particularly impressed by the semantic elaboration work because it has confirmed and refined what we learned in our analysis of the serial memory task. Our idea was that "if a plan is given to the child, he will perform as if he had invented the strategy himself" (Butterfield & Belmont, 1977). The counterpart to this is Rohwer's (1973) notion that "the underlying elaboration process is . . . common to virtually all persons (except infants . . .); what varies across persons is the type of prompt necessary to activate the process [p. 9]." Both statements maintain the distinction between the child as information processor and the methods by which his processes are controlled. In so doing they portray children's, indeed all people's, information processing as being responsive to instructions in the most fundamental sense imaginable. Our conviction on this point comes directly from the instructional approach we have taken, and it is the approach, not the particular cognitive domain, that forces the conclusion. Consider the striking similarities of interpretation in Resnick and Glaser's instructional work on problem solving and our work on memory:

> In each of the studies . . . the subjects demonstrated unequivocally that they could competently perform each of the routines necessary for solving the presented problems. Not only did they pass pretests on the component routines; but in every instance, direct prompting of the transformation routine was sufficient to promote full solution of the task if the child had not "invented" the solution himself. Yet many did not invent. The routines were available but not accessible when needed [Resnick & Glaser, 1974, p. 55].

> Clearly, the retarded subjects' passive (primary) memory capacity is not greatly impaired, for if it were they could not have rehearsed the 3 letters accurately. Clearly, too, they can rehearse, and having rehearsed, they can recall accurately even after doing an interfering task that seems at least as disruptive as attending passively to 3 letters. Yet, . . . they recalled accurately only when they were also instructed to use a retrieval strategy appropriate to the instructed learning strategy. These retarded subjects did not lack the memory processes. . . . What they did lack was spontaneous access to the processes and coordination among them [Butterfield, Wambold, & Belmont, 1973, p. 668].

By our lights, the problem of being able to make full use of mature processes but failing to call upon them when appropriate is the most extreme form of the production deficiency idea because it reaffirms that the important aspects of cognitive structure are laid down early and remain unchanged. The implications of this position are easiest to understand in terms of a simple analogy adopted by Newell (1973) and many other contemporary psychologists: computer programming. We will expand the analogy here because it embodies the essence of task analysis. It makes it very easy to grasp recent advances in developmental cognitive psychology, and it gives good perspective to the perennial problem of structure and process.

There are four principal elements in the computer-programming business: The computer, the programmer, the job he must accomplish with his program, and the program itself. Computers come equipped with a structure that is divided into two parts: internal programs and physical structure (hardware), of which the computer programmer has almost no practical understanding and over which he has no control.

Some of the internal programs are designed to translate the programmer's commands (for example, Fortran statements) into commands that the computing hardware will respond to. The programmer's job is to provide statements that the translator will accept as valid, in a sequence (user program) that will get the job done. This implies that the programmer has a functional listing of acceptable commands, and that he understands the job's information-processing requirements well enough to develop a workable program. In fact, except in the most elementary applications, the programmer does not at the outset fully understand the information-processing demands of his job, but may come to understand them as he develops the program. He writes a series of approximations until the computer's output is certifiably correct in the arithmetic sense, and is in a format that lends itself to easy reading. In the process, he also drives for brevity. Long programs are time-consuming and expensive to execute, and they may eat up so much of the computer's memory that it cannot handle the numbers the program is written to process.

The end product of the programmer's activity, the user program, is a series of computer-compatible statements. It does not reflect the intentions, plans, false starts, and happy discoveries by which the programmer finally comes to meet the task's information-processing requirements. Furthermore, the program is difficult to read and understand unless we know its language and have a good idea of what it was written to do.

As for the computer, it neither knows nor cares what the program is for. It does not care who the programmer was nor what he had in mind in struggling through his program development. If the computer can read the program and has enough capacity to hold it and the information it is written to process, this is sufficient, *so long as the program is sufficient.*

And what if the program is not sufficient? Consider the point when the latest version of a program gives the correct answer about half the time. The programmer has four options: He can assume that the program is correct but the computer's limits have been exceeded. Or he can redefine his goal, declaring intermittant success sufficient. Or he can quit. Or he can assume that all is well with the computer, acknowledge his failure to reach the job's information-processing goal, and resume his programming.

To nail down the analogy, we note that the cognitive development laboratory situation—for example, in a noninstructional multiple-list free recall experiment—looks rather like a final orals in computer programing at which the candidate is required to write a program without benefit of pencil and paper, and with very little idea of the functional value of the commands he manages to dream up. The experimenter supplies some materials and gives free recall instructions, then the child roughs in a program, tries it out on his brain, reads out some miserably bad results, then waits for another list, and so on until it is time to leave. While working on the lists, the child might refine his program a little, but unless the experimenter knows the brain's structure and can see the current version of the child's program and knows precisely how the child has interpreted the task's information-processing requirements, he cannot know whether the brain's structure, the child's program, the child's interpretation of the task, or a combination of these is responsible for the deficient output. All the experimenter knows is that the recall performance is poor.

What the experimenter does then determines his stamp as a researcher. If he tries to develop programs that work well for that task (task-specific strategies), then he is adopting the instructional approach. His main problem is the same as that of the children participating in his experiment. He has no list of commands acceptable to the brain, and he does not know its storage limits. He would be no better off than the children, were it not for these compensations: Unlike the children, he need not invent a good strategy in only 45 minutes. Moreover, he can be privy to hundreds of people's best efforts, and he can fashion model strategies that combine the best features of those efforts. Still, his ignorance of brain structure and function will require him to set arbitrary standards of success. To begin with, he might choose normal adult performance as his standard, and then set out to discover what kinds of strategies adults use to reach this standard. Along the way, he will instruct people to employ various strategies to check their usefulness.

As Resnick and Glaser (1974) describe it, the aim of this method

is not to investigate the question of instructability as such; rather, the instructability of particular hypothesized processes is assumed, and these processes are taught. If the instruction . . . is successful, and if the instructed individual behaves in ways similar to individuals who have become good problem-solvers on their own, then presumptive evidence will exist in favor of the reality of the processes we have hypothesized [p. 62].

The investigator may thus conclude that he thoroughly understands the task's information-processing demands when his instructions or other means of transmitting the strategy bring children up to adult levels of performance in every measurable respect. He has not thereby shown, however, that he understands uninstructed children's cognitive processing. For this purpose, he must continue the analysis until he has produced immature performance by having mature people mimic what he understands to be childlike processes (Belmont & Butterfield, 1971a; Brown et al., 1973; Hagen, Meacham, & Mesibov, 1970). When the adults' processing and performance are childlike in every measurable particular, the researcher knows where the children are beginning as well as where they will eventually arrive.

Having documented the children's deficient programs and the adults' efficient ones, what does the researcher not know? He does not know how adults program themselves, nor what is lacking in the children's programing that prevents their arriving at mature strategies. The processes involved in strategy invention are what Flavell (1970), Butterfield et al. (1973), Butterfield and Belmont (1977), Greeno and Bjork (1973), and others have called the "executive" functions of cognition. These functions are the means by which people manage simultaneously to be programers and processors. The executive is currently almost a total mystery, and we are sure it will be the object of a great deal of research in cognitive development, much of which will be done within the instructional approach, and much of which will adopt the computer analogy as a frame of reference. This will come easily because the computer programer is so clearly serving· the executive functions as he develops programs for particular information-processing tasks.

Within the instructional approach, experimenters can also serve as the executive for individuals in their experiments, as can be seen very clearly in recent studies by Craik and Tulving (1975) and Turnure et al. (1976). To us, this work evokes the cold corners of computerdom, where the machines simply read, translate, and execute instructions. It shows that people, too, can process information using highly particular programs to meet complex task demands without knowing what those demands are, without regard for the travails of developing the programs, and without regard even for the programs themselves.

In both studies, the criterion task was concealed from the subject until after he had processed task materials using a program he had not designed. The method was to ask him questions meant to elicit mnemonically effective verbal elaborations of materials for which recall was later unexpectedly tested. Craik and Tulving instructed adults to answer yes or no to a different question for each list item ("Tell me if it rhymes with 'bite 'im' "). While they were not warned that memory would be tested, their item recall varied with the quality of the questions in exactly the same measure as for a group who knew the test was coming.

Banking on children's normal eagerness to play and to please, Turnure et al. posed evocative questions about 21 pairs of pictured objects, the items of each pair being exhibited side by side ("What is the DUCK doing in the OVEN?"). The children responded quite innocently, but by the way created idiosyncratic bases for astoundingly good recall on the single anticipation trial that followed. Five-year-olds given one particular question-answering program recalled an average of 76% (16 items) on the unannounced test. This compares with 40% (8 items) for children required to repeat experimenter-supplied elaborative sentences, 17% (4 items) for children who made up their own elaborative sentences, and 8% (2 items) for children who simply labeled the pictures. The gain from 2 to 16 items correct is 700%, amounting to 74% of the total possible, an excellent gain by any standard, and particularly impressive in view of the age of the children, the length of the list, and the fact that recall was tested without warning.

Along with Craik and Tulving, Turnure et al. (1976) show that the successful individual need not analyze the task's information-processing requirements if the experimenter does it for him. He need not execute the strategy on his own if the experimenter leads him through it. He need not even realize the relationship of his strategy to his performance if the experimenter has already determined it. But what happens when the experimenter is not there to make these executive decisions? For better or worse, the person makes them for himself on the basis of some sort of microcosmic task analysis in view of his understanding of his own cognitive processes. Instructional researchers and their young subjects are thus evidently engaged in the same enterprise. Is it important who makes the executive decisions, so long as they are made well?

3. Standards of Evaluation

We have called this approach instructional because its most striking aspect is the use of instructions on how or what to think. From the discussion of task analysis, it should be clear that the really important distinction of the approach is not the instructional researcher's particular method, but rather, that he leads children to use particular cognitive programs. We have seen that explicit instruction in the details of a program is not the only, or even necessarily the most successful, way to do this. Indeed, for some applications (for example, Piagetian studies) it may be impossible to instruct the child directly. With the exception of instructions meant solely to externalize measurable activity, however, some effort to change children's thinking is always there, and the question we are posing now is how the researcher knows when he has succeeded, by whatever method. The answer will depend on the experiment's purpose, but it will be cast according to one or more of three criteria: size, durability, or transferability of the instructional effects.

The size of an instructional effect may be gauged in a variety of ways, depending on the scale characteristics of the dependent variable.

When the emphasis is on *qualitative* changes in criterion performance (for example, nonconserving to conserving responses), one measure is the proportion of people who change from one to the other qualitative category. If the proportion is large relative to some contrast or control conditions, then at least the instructions are proven effective. Lest the investigator be criticized for having shown children today what they would do spontaneously tomorrow, however, he might wish to go beyond noting the proportion of children who change, adding to this criterion of success an assessment of the relative difficulty of the change. One approach is to look at the age at which the target performance is normally achieved without instruction. If it is known that the beginning performance and the one achieved following instruction are characteristic of children at widely different ages, the effect is more impressive than if the two performances are characteristic of children at closely adjoining ages. Thus, it may be satisfying to show that 85% of all nonconserving 5-year-olds can be trained in a couple of sessions to conserve as 7-year-olds do, but it would be more compelling to show that 25% of all nonconserving 5-year-olds can be taught in only two years to solve the pendulum problem, which is normally solved without instruction around the age of puberty. The scientific returns from demonstrating such a large effect would easily justify the laboratory effort.

For *quantitative* measures, the size of an instructional effect may be judged against a scale of standards ranging from statistically significant improvement to the theoretically maximum possible improvement. Each step in this range provides a greater challenge and a correspondingly greater scientific payoff.

The statistical test is the most common, but it is unconvincing. For one thing, it denies the concept of standards even while appearing to be rigorously evaluative because any reliable improvement will do, regardless of size. Furthermore, a small, reliable group improvement can result by many children improving slightly or by a few improving dramatically, so interpretation of the effect will in any case go beyond the statistical test. Regardless of the group average gain, the question must always be asked, How many children improve and by how much?

The first worthy step on the scale of size standards is achieved by raising children at one age to criterion performance characteristic of children at a higher age. If this increase represented, for example, a 2-year gain for 8-year-olds (that is, to the 10-year level), the result would perhaps not be very exciting, but it would be entirely creditable if the instructed strategy were characteristic of 10-year-olds. Then the performance increment would be consistent with the task analysis. A less fortunate outcome would be a 2-year increase resulting from instructing 8-year-olds to use a strategy typical of children much older than 10 years of age. We will return to the implications of such a failure.

The next-highest standard is adult performance, and the considerations here are the same as for the previous standard. If the 8-year-old child is instructed with a typical adult strategy, and he thereupon achieves adult-level criterion performance, the procedure is clearly successful. If, however, he is taught to use a super-adult strategy, yet manages to rise only to the adult level, the investigator is bound to explain the failure.

Beyond the adult standard, there is only the theoretically maximum possible performance, which may be established in two ways. One way is simply to choose the ceiling of the measurement scale. The other way is to choose the best performance ever observed on the criterion task. The scale ceiling is purely anomalous, a will-o'-the-wisp. The argument in its favor is that perfect performance cannot be bettered and so instructions that bring performance to the ceiling are, for that particular task, perfect. The difficulty with this view is that the ceiling is a scale limit. It is not a limit on the psychological dimension that we assume the scale is reflecting. To the extent that the underlying dimension exceeds the portion reflected by the scale, therefore, the scale itself should be expanded. The easiest expansion is usually to increase the amount of information the child must deal with. If one accepts the obvious implication that the scale ceiling is arbitrary, and that it is always lower than possible, then it follows that instructions themselves must also always be imperfect. Task difficulty can always be increased beyond the point where any particular strategy works perfectly.

The process of manipulating list length or otherwise diddling with task difficulty is akin to locating a psychophysical threshold. The closest that developmental psychology usually comes to threshold setting is with procedures like the digit span test, in which "threshold" means something like "capacity." Aside from this example, the concept of a threshold for information processing, and manipulating tasks to assess it in individuals, are still foreign to most cognitive researchers. The threshold premise is nevertheless a good one: Assess the threshold under each instructional condition by varying the task until the individual is located midway between the scale limits, at the 75% mark, or at any other point that is far enough away from the limits to permit the assumption of fair measurement. Belmont (1972) used this technique in a short-term retention study to clarify the age × retention interval interaction, a theoretically important datum that had long been obscured by measurement problems.

Other than the ceiling, there is only one maximum possible performance standard for evaluating instructional effects: the best performance ever observed on the task in question. If instructions have not previously been used with the task, then this will be the best performance ever turned in by an uninstructed individual. If task analysis has been done, however, the best uninstructed performance will have been found to be well below that obtainable by instructions. The best illustration of this point that we have seen is Wallace, Turner, and Perkins's (1957) demonstration with interactive imagery instructions. They reported that normal adults instructed to use interactive imagery to learn noun pairs began falling below the ceiling only when the number of pairs studied reached 500, and performance was still above 90% for 700 pairs. These remarkable results were achieved despite the fact that subjects saw each pair only once. The arbitrary one-day session length precluded testing beyond 700 pairs, but results like these suggest that the standard of maximum possible performance would be a very severe test of instructional routines for young children.

No study has ever adopted the standard of maximum possible performance. The most rigorous standard we know of is our use of uninstructed adult performance to judge retarded adolescents' responses to an instructed strategy for a 6-item memory task (Butterfield et al., 1973). We stopped refining the instructed strategy when the retarded subjects' average recall accuracy was 114% that of uninstructed normal adults, and 94% that of normal adults who had been given less complete instructions than the final routine administered to the retarded subjects. Longer lists would have raised the ceiling, and hence would have permitted a finer comparison between instructed subjects at the two ability levels.

Before leaving size standards, we must examine a problem left dangling earlier. The problem is what to do when an instructed strategy agrees with task analyses, and looks like strategies actually observed in older children, but does not bring younger children all the way up to the target performance level. This is the moment when the faint of heart defect to the structuralist camp, blaming the instructional failure on inadequacies in young children's brains. Mowbray and Luria's (1973) appeal to ''memory capacity'' to explain kindergarten children's too-small improvement in a stimulus-labeling condition is a case in point. Brown (1974) has explained the philosophical absurdity of reacting with such structural interpretations, and we can do no better than to add this point of simple faith: When instructions fail, the problem is not with the child but with the instructions or the task analysis on which they are based. The only worthy response is to improve the instructional routine until it works according to whatever standard has been adopted. When we devise instructions that do work, we may then look at what we went through to fashion them. Each step in refining the instructions may be viewed as an inadequacy in the child's self-programing, and those inadequacies may then become the targets of training in their own right.

The durability of instructional effects has been hailed by Piagetians and others as an important standard of evaluation. The argument is that the longer a child holds onto an activity without further training, the more surely he must have understood it when last instructed. This criterion is obviously irrelevant to any study that is concerned solely with children's programmability. It is just as obviously necessary for studies of trainability, but it is not trivial. The fact is that children can be trained to use effective strategies, but, once trained, they frequently revert to their immature strategies when no longer explicitly constrained to play the instructor's programs (Brown, Campione, & Murphy, 1974; Butterfield & Belmont, 1972; Flavell, 1970; Hagen et al., 1973; Wanschura & Borkowski, 1975). What the instructor knows about and how he interprets such a regression will depend largely on the quality of his direct measures.

Three examples make the point. Brown et al. (1974) retested a group of retarded adolescents six months after training half of them to use a rehearsal strategy for a keeping-track task. By observing overt rehearsal of the trained retardates during the follow-up test, Brown et al. defined two subgroups—those who did and those who did not rehearse. The rehearsers recalled very accurately, whereas the nonrehearsers performed identically to the untrained control group. Had the follow-up data been averaged across these two subgroups of trained retardates, the comparison between the trained and untrained groups might well have been uninterpretable.

Brown et al. did not look back to see if the trained retardates who later abondoned the strategy were in any way separable in the original learning data. Wanschura and Borkowski (1975) and Butterfield and Belmont (1972) did look back at pretest and training data for the retarded individuals in their studies. Neither study's pretest data showed individual differences between the retardates who later maintained the trained strategy and those who did not. Wanschura and Borkowski's training procedures were so good relative to the task difficulty that their trained individuals, including those who did and those who did not later maintain the strategy, were very near the ceiling, leaving too little variability to predict strategy maintenance from the training data. We were more fortunate. We divided the children according to whether their posttest pause time curves showed strategy maintenance. Looking back at the training data, it was clear that all children had followed rehearsal instructions during training, but only those who maintained the strategy at posttest had actually improved their criterion performance during training, and this improvement was nearly maximal. Evidently, training in this study resulted in all-or-none benefits, and it is not surprising that strategy maintenance was seen only in children who originally enjoyed those benefits. The implication is that *durability* becomes an interesting measure of instructional effects only if it is viewed in conjunction with direct measures of activity independent of criterion performance, and only when these measures are used to expose and classify individual differences.

The last standard we are considering is *transfer of instructed activity* to new situations, by far the most highly debated standard for the instructional approach. Borkowski and Wanschura (1974) and Brown (1974) have addressed the issue in the literature on mental retardation; Kuhn (1974) has done likewise for the Piagetians; and Denny (1973) has examined the areas of cognitive style, cognitive tempo, and cognitive strategy (constraint seeking vs. hypothesis testing). These people have written intelligently and at length about transfer, and they have done so from very different perspectives, yet out of their work emerges one common theme: Unless a child exhibits activity akin to the trained activity in some situation other than the training task, he has done nothing but parrot the instructor. Borkowski and Wanschura called this parroting "rote mediation," Denny called it "task-specific response set," and Kuhn called it "specific rote-learned responses." It was generally agreed that even if the parroting is seen long after the instructions are given, durability does not necessarily mean that the child has grasped what the instruction was all about. He has not necessarily exhibited what Kellas et al. (1973a) called "cognitive understanding" or Denny's "comprehension of the essential nature of the behaviors being trained." Transfer is thus seen as the *sine qua non* of Kuhn's "genuine structural change" or Denny's "true changes along an information processing dimension" or "real acquisition of generalized cognitive functions."

Words like *genuine, real,* and *true* always signal problems for behavioral research. Their use to rationalize failures of transfer is an important event in the evolution of the instructional approach, for it shows how the approach depends on thorough task analysis, and it shows the need to appreciate how each facet of the approach relates to theory.

It would be lovely if informed guessing or loose reasoning could provide the task analysis required for tests of transfer. Unfortunately, the task-analytic requirements are much too specific and detailed. The investigator who would demonstrate transfer must thoroughly understand both the task he uses during training and the one he uses to test transfer. By definition, training and transfer tasks are not identical, but they are similar in the sense that performing both must require processes taught during training. They are different in that they also depend on other processes. If they did not, the test would not be for transfer but for durability. Since the tasks are not identical, both must be analyzed to demonstrate that they share the instructed processes. Even certain knowledge that the two tasks share some processes does not guarantee, however, that a failure on the transfer task depends on a failure to transfer the shared processes. The child might very well understand that the transfer task requires use of his newly learned processes, but fail to engage the unshared processes on the second task that were not trained on the first. Without knowing precisely where his performance broke down, the investigator can hardly interpret a failure on the transfer test.

We know of no transfer test that has employed two well-analyzed tasks. Until such tests are made, it will remain premature to conclude that performance changes that meet the size or durability requirements could be any more *genuine*, for failing the transfer criterion may say only that the investigator's understanding of his tasks is incomplete or his activity measures are insufficient.

We believe that the size and transfer standards address different levels of theory. The size standard is required to ensure the adequacy of instructors' comprehension of particular cognitive tactics. It is relevant to the level of theory that specifies cognitive processes. The transfer standard is relevant to the level of theory that specifies how people select amongst and invoke combinations of cognitive tactics. In the arena of memory theory, the size standard tests our understanding of control processes, while the transfer standard tests our understanding of executive functions. Consider the fact that transfer tests are given only to people who require instruction on the training task. The fact that training is successful, which it must be before the investigator tests for transfer, says that the people who are tested never did lack the appropriate control processes. They simply failed to invoke them without training. Assuming that they were suitably motivated, it seems the individuals' failure on the original task was in the business of assessing its cognitive requirements. This we identify as an executive shortcoming. Observing that training and transfer tasks come from the same class of cognitive problem, and assuming that the executive is no less important on the second task than on the first, the most reasonable prediction is that the instructed child would not transfer unless he were trained in matters of executive decision making. We have seen no reports of attempts to do this.

Nobody yet knows how to train executive functions. We suspect that this is partly because instructional investigators have failed to appreciate the aspect of cognitive theory to which transfer tests properly relate, namely, theory about executive functioning. The belief that transfer speaks to lower levels of theory, such as the specification of cognitive tactics, seems fundamentally mistaken, yet that seems to have been the belief of many who have tussled with the meaning of their failures to promote transfer.

IV. VARIETIES OF INSTRUCTIONAL APPLICATIONS

Process-oriented instructions are being applied to an increasingly wide range of tasks. In this concluding section, we will classify the applications and illustrate each class with examples from the literature. The classification is based on three reasons for using process-oriented instructions: (1) to provide direct measures of cognitive activity; (2) to change criterion task performance; and (3) to regulate one sort of cognitive activity so as to analyze another.

A. Establishing Direct Measures

Instructions have often been used to provide direct measures of task-related activity. The measures have been temporally removed from the activity or concurrent with it. They have required complete externalization of thought or simply provided a scaled indicator for the child to manipulate. The delayed measures include introspections or overt demonstrations by the child to show what he had previously been doing covertly. For Hohn and Martin (1970), this method reduced to having children indicate which of a number of listed alternative paired-associate learning strategies they had previously been using. In addition to such straightforward measurement applications, Rohwer (1973) has advocated introspective methods for testing the effectiveness of mediational prompts, thus using instructions both to change and to measure. Similarly, Sabo and Hagen (1973) asked children various questions about their previous attention to stimuli and their rehearsal techniques in a picture recognition and recall task. In this category of delayed measures we also find Shackleton's (1974) particularly well-controlled self-paced multiple-list learning study, in which he periodically required children to repeat aloud their immediately preceding covert learning strategies. Shackleton related these after-the-fact demonstrations to interitem pause times measured concurrently during the preceding covert trials, thus giving himself independent converging measures.

Instructional methods for obtaining concurrent activity measures are more varied than the delayed ones. If the researcher is confident that his young subjects understand what is meant by rehearsal—or any other covert activity—then he can adopt Kroll and Kellicut's (1972) method of having the person press a button whenever he uses that activity. Or one may assume that children ordinarily work with internal speech, and that speech, being easily externalized, can hence provide a direct view of task-relevant thought. That was the basis on which Keeney, Cannizzo, and Flavell (1967), Beaudechon (1973), Cuvo (1975), Fagan (1972), Kellas et al. (1975), Ornstein, Naus, and Liberty (1975), and others have instructed children to do their thinking aloud in problem solving, free recall learning, and paired-associates learning. Similarly, when Kobasigawa (1974) handed category cue cards to children during recall of categorized lists, and suggested that the children look at the cards if they thought it would aid recall, he assumed that a child's manipulation of the cards reflects internal recall processes that occur when the cards are not at hand. This is analogous to the Neimark, Slotnick, and Ulrich (1971) procedure of laying out stimulus cards in front of the child during a study period and suggesting that he can move them around if he thinks it will help him learn.

The choice of a measure will of course depend on the target activity. Moreover, the decision to try to take a concurrent measure instead of a delayed one must in part reflect a judgment about process contamination. There is always a chance that a measure based on instruction will alter the activity it is intended to reveal, and some of the most popular measures are susceptible. For example, Kellas et al. (1975) found that the Rundus (1971) technique of having people do their thinking aloud influences the amount of time children spend memorizing lists. What is worse, the influence increases with age, as Shackleton (1974) also found. Along similar lines, Phillips and Levine (1975) showed that introspecting about hypotheses improves children's discrimination learning compared to inferring hypotheses with probe techniques, and Neimark (1975), in the best study to date of children's free recall strategies, showed that thinking changes and performance improves following directed questioning à la Piaget.

Such measurement effects are unintended, and will always be small compared to closely reasoned deliberate instructions. Nevertheless, if the purpose is to measure thinking under some particular set of conditions that, for important theoretical or practical reasons, must not be altered, it may be necessary to obtain the direct measure postexperimentally or following an uncontaminated test period. Such delayed measures cannot capture changes in thinking during the uncontaminated period, but they can log the child's asymptotic activity, and for many purposes this is sufficient. Clearly, these are matters for prudent evaluation in the particular experimental context. Using obtrusive measures is chancy, but we think the potential gains warrant the effort, especially when a study is designed not merely to monitor a child's thinking but to change it in order to obtain theoretically important changes in criterion task performance.

B. Changing Criterion Task Performance

Using instructions to obtain direct measures of underlying processes is atheoretical. Most instructional experiments have been done to clarify theory, and practically all of these tried to alter criterion task performance. Recall the production deficiency work. It was designed to expose inadequacies in structural explanations by using instructions to promote performance. The production deficiency hypothesis is the general form of many task-specific hypotheses, which in aggregate have motivated most of the efforts to change performance by instruction. Some of these hypotheses have focused on processes revealed by task analysis. The more detailed that analysis, the more specific the instructed activities have been, and some have focused very narrowly indeed (e.g., Butterfield et al., 1973). But the most heavily cited instructional work has not been based on detailed task analyses. For example, the Keeney et al. (1967) and Moely, Olson, Halwes, and Flavell (1969) manipulations were not highly analyzed for task propriety, and the resulting performance increases were not large. This is also true of current instructional efforts to resolve the debate over verbal versus imagery elaboration in paired-associate learning. Even though there is a developmental problem underlying this work—the age-related shift in imagery effectiveness reviewed by Reese (1970) and Rohwer (1970)—which says that task analysis is needed, none has been performed. Instead, there has been a continuous refinement of designs for evaluating the relative, rather than the absolute, effectiveness of various syntactic factors involved in verbal elaborations, and various tactual and manipulative factors involved in imagery. Representative examples of the two sorts of study are Hughes and Walsh (1971) and Wolff and Levin (1972). Their work, like most other on imagery and verbal elaboration, relies on directional hypothesis testing without regard for other possible standards of evaluation. The observed performance changes have been small and educationally inconsequential. The question of whether young children can actually make good use of imagery has therefore not been answered, and will not be until somebody does for imagery what Turnure et al. (1975) have done for semantic elaboration, in which there is no longer any question regarding young children's excellent capabilities.

Not all of the performance change work has been designed to enhance performance. Attempts to reduce children's and adults' scores by instructed activity have been motivated by a wish to put the cap on process explanations of developmental phenomena. The idea is to have mature people emulate hypothesized immature activity to see whether their criterion performance drops to the level of children who are being modeled. Success would add much validity to our understanding of what young children are up to.

Examples of this reversal technique are the Belmont and Butterfield (1971a) and Brown et al. (1973) requirement that mature people simply label (rather than rehearse) materials to be learned, and Leicht and Johnson's (1970) similar attempt to eliminate other organizational activity. The reversal technique has also been used to clarify dichotomous qualitative aspects of cognition, including analytic versus relational responding on tests of conceptual style, and constraint seeking versus hypothesis testing on tests of information reduction (Twenty Questions). Denny's (1973) review of this work suggests that reversal is much harder to achieve here than in the quantitative realms in which we have been working. This may be so because the experimenters have not yet specified instructible processes for each element of the qualitative dichotomy, thus leaving an individual much freer to decline to play an immature role. We hasten to acknowledge, however, that it is not easy to induce older children and adults to think in a childlike way, even when the instructed activity can be shown to correspond quite closely to measured activity in younger children. This is another example of the most important difficulty (and gnawing frustration) in the instructional approach. Though successful reversal tests of developmental hypotheses can be as theoretically important as successful performance enhancement tests, failures to meet reasonable standards of evaluation are no more theoretically interpretable for the one than for the other. In both cases, even the most liberal standards can be so strict that highly reliable effects in the right direction may still fall short of the desired goal. If the goal is to emulate immature performance, then both old and young children must turn in identical on-scale performances under the instructional condition. We have not seen this goal reached.

C. Analytic Regulation of Activity

Instructional regulation to aid process analysis generally looks like a subtraction procedure. Task performance is visualized as requiring a series of cognitive steps. The instructions are meant to regulate some of these so as to permit the study of those remaining. Some of this work is inferential. Performance changes are taken as evidence of process variability. Other applications look directly at the uncontrolled processes. Illustrations of these various techniques are found in Balling and Myers (1971), Conrad (1972), Kobasigawa (1974), and some of our own applications.

Balling and Myers wanted to see whether children's double-alternation failures resulted from information-processing deficiencies or from mnemonic or attentional deficiencies. They arranged to display the child's past choices, and forced the child to label those choices to eliminate the mnemonic and attentional components of the task. As it turned out, Balling and Myers found that nursery school children substantially improved their performance when both factors were eliminated, whereas kindergarten children required only the mnemonic aid. The instruction-based subtraction method thus showed that attentional processes mature in the brief age span covered in the study, but information processing itself does not. Dusek et al. (1975) similarly used the controlled-attention approach to study the problem of test anxiety.

Conrad was concerned with the mnemonic effects of naming the stimuli versus vocalizing the names, a point not fully appreciated in much short-term memory theorizing. Conrad's solution was to require either the subject or the experimenter to do the actual naming aloud, and thus to show that naming is an effective mnemonic aid, while vocalizing can best be viewed as an attention-altering variable.

Unlike Balling and Myers, and Conrad, who depended on criterion task scores to infer process variation, Kobasigawa looked directly at the target activity while regulating others. The study was on free recall of categorized lists and aimed to see how the use of categorical information during recall develops with age. In order to hold storage strategy constant across age, and to be sure that categories and exemplars were stored together during learning, Kobasigawa led all children through a highly formalized study trial in which the child systematically paired each item with its corresponding category. This done, three different recall tests were administered: standard free recall, free recall with a deck of category cue cards in hand for ad lib review, and recall directed explicitly by cue cards. Under the directed-recall condition, young children managed to perform precisely as well as older children, whereas on the other two tasks there were clear age progressions, and highly interesting age-related changes in intersubject variability of recall activity. Aside from these relevations about individual differences, Kobasigawa's discussion is worth studying for itself as a model of analytic balance and brevity.

We used activity regulation to study some executive functions of cognition. Regulation was done in two steps, the first of which was just the opposite of Kobasigawa's: We controlled recall activity, leaving study activity free to vary. In the second procedure, both recall and study activity were regulated, but materials were varied to test the children's practical knowledge about and executive deployment of a particular memory control process called "echo" memory.

By our view, *executive functions* can be studied by observing whether "the subject spontaneously changes a control process or sequence of control processes as a reasonable response to an objective change in an information processing task" (Butterfield & Belmont, 1977). We started by instructing 10-year-olds and 17-year-olds to recall each of a series of 8-word lists by recalling the last 3 words of each list before recalling the first 5. This circular recall requirement was meant to reflect a normal adult approach to free recall, and we expected that the mature individuals, given completely self-paced study, would divide each list, spending a long time studying the first 5 words but very little time on the last 3 (which would be recalled immediately).

Twenty people at each age were given 10 lists under the circular recall requirement. Instructions on circular recall were not repeated beyond the third list. Each list contained 8 different words (80 words total), and we recorded the time (to .04 sec.) that each person devoted to each word as he paced himself through each list. We use the term *study time pattern* to refer to the graph of his study times plotted against the serial positions of the words in the list.

Unlike Moely et al. (1969), who reported seeing no interesting changes in study activity over trials, we found large systematic changes in study time patterns in the early lists, followed by increasing similarity—both within and between subjects—on later lists. We note in particular that these effects were seen within subjects. The group average study time pattern, especially for the older group, became remarkably stable early in the series. By the fourth list, the 17-year-olds' group average pattern took on a shape that remained largely unchanged through List 10. The 10-year-olds' average pattern took on the same shape around List 8 and stayed the same thereafter. Figure 14-2a shows how the median raw study time patterns looked on List 10, where the dominant activity pattern for both groups conformed to the theoretically required increase to Position 5, though the youngsters spent much less time overall. To compare the List 10 distributions independent of total time, we converted each individual's eight study times to normal scores based on his own pattern's mean and standard deviation. Adding a constant 4.0 to the resulting z's to bring them all positive, and taking the median once again over subjects within groups, we see in Figure

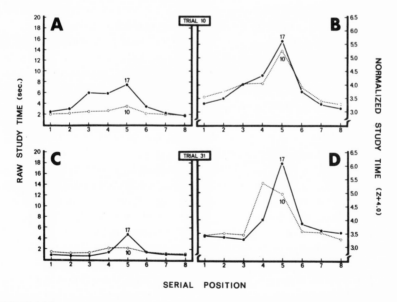

SERIAL   POSITION

FIGURE 14-2   (a) Trial 10 median ad lib study time patterns for children (10) and youth (17) under instructions to recall last three words of list followed by first five; (b) same data normalized to show similarity of forms independent of level; (c) study time patterns later on (Trial 31) for a highly overlearned list in which novel words unexpectedly appear at Positions 4 and 5; (d) same data normalized to show dissimilarity of children's and youths' responses to novel words.

14-2b the very close correspondence of average normalized study time patterns. By regulating output, we thus showed clearly that children as young as age 10 understand the corresponding input requirements, but they invest an order of magnitude less time executing them. Needless to say, their recall accuracy suffers accordingly.

Without prior announcement, the words seen on List 10 were repeated in the same order on the eight succeeding trials. As one may expect, all individuals' study time patterns quickly became low and flat as they mastered the list. Starting on Trial 19, they were hit with seven new and different lists, the question being whether or not they would reinstate the time patterns they had previously invented. Finally, a single list was repeated for 12 trials, the sixth of which (Trial 31) was a crucial exception.

The reader will have guessed that all patterns again became low and flat during the second series of repeated lists. They remained thus going into Trial 31, all save two of whose words were the usual ones for the repeated list. The two novel words came at Serial Positions 4 and 5, and the question was whether or not individuals would use echo memory in response to this change in a highly overlearned list. A simple view suggests that the subject would not bother to pause at Position 4 (the first novel word) because he could pause at Position 5 (the second novel word) without fear of forgetting the new words, and then form all five (three old plus two new) words into a retrievable group, as he had so often done before on changing lists.

The group median raw study time patterns for Trial 31 are shown in Figure 14-2c, in which it appears that the older subjects took roughly the simple view, reserving most of their study for Postion 5, while the younger ones certainly did not. Figure 14-2d shows the median normalized curves, which statistically clarify the group patterns. To assess the reliability of the group differences in normalized times, we ran two tests. First, ranking the increases from Position 3 to Position 4 for all 40 individuals, then tabulating the number of 10-year-olds and 17-year-olds who fell above and below the median of the combined distribution, we found 13 of the youngsters above the median versus only 7 of the 17-year-olds. The Fisher exact test for this median split yielded $p = .056$. We then considered Serial Positions 3, 4, and 5 by analysis of variance, for which the age $\times$ position interaction netted $F(2, 76) = 9.56, p < .001$. Thus, it seems that the younger children had distributed their study time much more evenly over the two novel words than the 17-year-olds. This reluctance by the youngsters to use echo memory in the service of constructing rehearsable groups stands in astonishing contrast to their fine use of echo on the terminal test items throughout the study, but it corresponds very nicely to our earlier observation that terminal nonrehearsal is developmentally less advanced than nonrehearsal used to form a chunk for study (Belmont & Butterfield, 1971b).

Before accepting the conclusion about deficient executive processing that seems to emerge from the Trial 31 data, we decided to put the two age groups to a much cleaner test. The main reason for this was that many of the 10-year-olds were giving even the changing lists so little attention that the scale floor was all there was betweem them and terra firma. New samples of ten 10-year-olds and ten adults were therefore given an identical sequence of changing and repeated lists, but this time they were given exacting instruction not only on the circular recall requirement but on a suitable input strategy as well. All subjects were trained to build up and thoroughly rehearse the grouping of five initial words and then dash through the last three. Instruction was continued if necessary up through List 7, but not repeated thereafter. The experimental question was whether the 10-year-olds, having practiced a highly active, mature strategy for many lists, would still opt to pause when they encountered the first new word of Trial 31.

Figure 14-3a and b shows the two groups' median raw and normalized study time patterns for Trial 10. The study strategy instructions were clearly successful in equalizing the two groups' patterns and their effort in executing the strategy. Figure 14-3c and d shows the median raw and normalized patterns for Trial 31. For the normalized patterns, the median split for the jump from Position 3 to Position 4 was significant this time (Fisher exact $p = .012$), with 8 out of 10

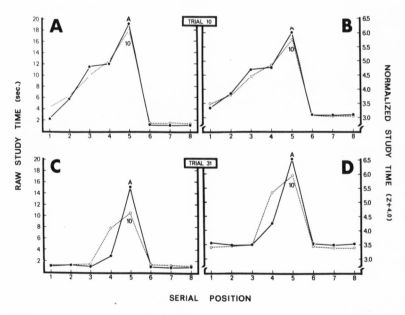

FIGURE 14-3 (a) Trial 10 median study time patterns for children (10) and adults (A) under instructions to systematically rehearse first five words but not last three as preparation to recall last three followed by first five; (b) same data normalized (note similarity with Figure 14-2b); (c) study time patterns later on (Trial 31) for a highly overlearned list in which novel words unexpectedly appear at Positions 4 and 5; (d) same data normalized (note similarity with Figure 14-2d).

youngsters falling above the median, compared with 2 out of 10 adults. For Serial Positions 3, 4, and 5, the analysis of variance again yielded a significant age × position interaction, $F(2, 36) = 12.52$, $p < .001$. In spite of having adopted and used the adultlike strategy on many changing lists, and having managed to enter Trial 31 with fine flat patterns appropriate for repeated lists, the 10-year-olds made very much the same immature decisions that their peers who were not instructed on input had earlier shown on Trial 31. This time, however, there was no question about floor effects. Explicit process regulation thus gave an undistorted magnification of executive decision making in children who ordinarily use very little processing at all. No methods seem better suited for such a complex problem than the concurrent process regulation and measurement offered by the instructional approach.

V. SUMMARY

A trend toward the use of cognitive instructions has grown up in developmental cognitive psychology. In the past twenty years, both Piagetian and general experimental approaches to development have increasingly used direct instructions to study cognitive development. Successful use of instructional methods requires first the directest possible measurement of processes that account for performance. The general principle is for the scientist to maximally reduce both the temporal and the logical distance between the processes under study and the procedures by which they are measured. A second requisite of the instructional method is careful analysis of the processes underlying task performance. Some sorts of cognitive performances (for example, episodic memory activities) are more readily amenable to process analysis than are other performances (for example, the conservation of volume). The former situations have produced more complete examples of the effectiveness of instruction as a research tool, though instruction has been informative for the less analyzed skills as well. The third requirement of the instructional method is new conventions concerning when an experiment has been effective. The standard of statistically significant group effects is inadequate. The magnitude of the instructional effect scaled in terms of uninstructed developmental milestones is a more important standard, and it requires attention to the size of instructional effects obtained from each participant in instructional experiments. The durability of instructional effects and their generalizability are also important, but these must be evaluated in terms of a thorough understanding of the processes underlying performance on the criterion tasks. This chapter illustrated the instructional approach and its requirements with developmental research in a wide range of behavioral domains.

ACKNOWLEDGMENTS

A product of the Ralph L. Smith Mental Retardation Research Center and the Department of Pediatrics, University of Kansas College of Health Sciences and Hospital, this chapter was prepared, and the new research reported in it conducted under the auspices of HEW grants HD-00026, HD-08911, HD-00870, and HD-02528. Data collection, analysis, and graphics were done by Rick Bentzinger, Mary E. Nelson, and Carole Byrd, with indispensable bibliographic work by Pamela Behl and computer program development and execution by Lee Hubbell. The manuscript was typed ever so patiently by Pamela Behl, and criticized ever so keenly by Michael Karchmer and John Borkowski. To all of these people many thanks.

REFERENCES

Atkinson, R. C., & Shiffrin, R. M. Human memory: A proposed system and its control processes. In K. Spence & J. Spence (Eds.), *The psychology of learning and motivation* (Vol. 2). New York: Academic Press, 1968.

Balling, J. D., & Myers, N. A. Memory and attention in children's double-alternation learning. *Journal of Experimental Child Psychology,* 1971, *11,* 448–460.

Battig, W. F. Within-individual differences in "cognitive" processes. In R. L. Solso (Ed.), *Information processing and cognition.* Hillsdale, N.J.: Lawrence Erlbaum Associates, 1975.

Beaudechon, J. Nature and instrumental function of private speech in problem solving situations. *Merrill-Palmer Quarterly,* 1973, *19,* 117–135.

Belmont, J. M. Relations of age and intelligence to short-term color memory. *Child Development,* 1972, *43,* 19–29.

Belmont, J. M., & Butterfield, E. C. The relations of short-term memory to development and intelligence. In L. Lipsitt & H. Reese (Eds.), *Advances in child development and behavior* (Vol. 4). New York: Academic Press, 1969.

Belmont, J. M., & Butterfield, E. C. Learning strategies as determinants of memory deficiencies. *Cognitive Psychology,* 1971, *2,* 411–420. (a)

Belmont, J. M., & Butterfield, E. C. What the development of short-term memory is. *Human Development,* 1971, *14,* 236–248. (b)

Borkowski, J. G., & Wanschura, P. B. Mediational processes in the retarded. In N. R. Ellis (Ed.), *International review of research in mental retardation* (Vol. 7). New York: Academic Press, 1974.

Brainerd, C. J., & Allen, T. W. Experimental inductions of the conservation of "first-order" quantitative invariants. *Psychological Bulletin,* 1971, *75,* 128–144.

Brown, A. L. The role of strategic behavior in retardate memory. In N. R. Ellis (Ed.), *International review of research in mental retardation* (Vol. 7). New York: Academic Press, 1974.

Brown, A. L., Campione, J. C., Bray, N. W., & Wilcox, B. L. Keeping track of changing variables: Effects of rehearsal training and rehearsal prevention in normal and retarded adolescents. *Journal of Experimental Psychology,* 1973, *101,* 123–131.

Brown, A. L., Campione, J. C., & Murphy, M. D. Keeping track of changing variables: Long-term retention of a trained rehearsal strategy by retarded adolescents. *American Journal of Mental Deficiency,* 1974, *78,* 446–453.

Butterfield, E. C., & Belmont, J. M. Relations of storage and retrieval strategies as short-term memory processes. *Journal of Experimental Psychology,* 1971, *89,* 319–328.

Butterfield, E. C., & Belmont, J. M. The role of verbal processes in short-term memory. In R. L. Schiefelbusch (Ed.), *Language research with the mentally retarded.* Baltimore: University Park Press, 1972.

Butterfield, E. C., & Belmont, J. Assessing and improving the executive cognitive functions of mentally retarded people. In I. Bialer & M. Sternlicht (Eds.), Psychological issues in mental retardation. New York: Psychological Dimensions, Inc, 1977.

Butterfield, E. C., Belmont, J. M., & Peltzman, D. J. Effects of recall requirement on acquisition strategy. *Journal of Experimental Psychology*, 1971, *90*, 347–348.

Butterfield, E. C., & Dickerson, D. J. Cognitive theory and mental development. In N. R. Ellis (Ed.), *International review of research in mental retardation* (Vol. 8). New York: Academic Press, 1976.

Butterfield, E. C., Wambold, C., & Belmont, J. M. On the theory and practice of improving short-term memory. *American Journal of Mental Deficiency*, 1973, *77*, 654–669.

Conrad, R. The developmental role of vocalizing in short-term memory. *Journal of Verbal Learning and Verbal Behavior*, 1972, *11*, 521–533.

Cook, H., & Smothergill, D. Verbal mediation and satiation in young children. *Child Development*, 1971, *42*, 1805–1812.

Craik, F. I. M., & Tulving, E. Depth of processing and the retention of words in episodic memory. *Journal of Experimental Psychology: General*, 1975, *104*, 268–294.

Cuvo, A. J. Developmental differences in rehearsal and free recall. *Journal of Experimental Child Psychology*, 1975, *19*, 265–278.

Denney, D. R. Modification of children's information processing behaviors through learning: A review of the literature. *Child Study Journal Monographs*, 1973, *3*(Whole No. 1).

Dusek, J. B., Kermis, M. D., & Mergler, N. L. Information processing in low- and high-test anxious children as a function of grade level and verbal labelling. *Developmental Psychology*, 1975, *11*, 651–652.

Fagan, J. F. Rehearsal and free recall in children of superior and average intelligence. *Psychonomic Science*, 1972, *28*, 352–354.

Farnham-Diggory, S., & Gregg, L. W. Color, form, and function as dimensions of natural classification: Developmental changes in eye movements, reaction time, and response strategies. *Child Development*, 1975, *46*, 101–114.

Flavell, J. H. *The developmental psychology of Jean Piaget*. Princeton, N.J.: Van Nostrand, 1963.

Flavell, J. H. Developmental studies of mediated memory. In H. Reese & L. Lipsitt (Eds.), *Advances in child development and behavior* (Vol. 5). New York: Academic Press, 1970.

Flavell, J. H., Beach, D. R., & Chinsky, J. M. Spontaneous verbal rehearsal in a memory task as a function of age. *Child Development*, 1966, *37*, 283–299.

Flavell, J. H., Friedrichs, A. G., & Hoyt, J. D. Developmental changes in memorization processes. *Cognitive Psychology*, 1970, *1*, 324–340.

Glaser, R., & Resnick, L. B. Instructional psychology. *Annual Review of Psychology*, 1972, *23*, 207–276.

Greeno, J. G., & Bjork, R. A. Mathematical learning theory and the new "mental forestry." *Annual Review of Psychology*, 1973, *24*, 81–116.

Hagen, J. W., Meacham, J. A., & Mesibov, G. Verbal labeling, rehearsal, and short-term memory. *Cognitive Psychology*, 1970, *1*, 47–58.

Hagen, J. W., Hargrave, S., & Ross, W. Prompting and rehearsal in short-term memory. *Child Development*, 1973, *44*, 201–204.

Hall, V. C., Salvi, R., Seggev, L., & Caldwell, E. Cognitive synthesis, conservation, and task analysis. *Developmental Psychology*, 1970, *2*, 423–428.

Hohn, R. L., & Martin, C. J. Mediational styles: An individual difference variable in children's learning ability. *Psychonomic Science*, 1970, *18*, 348–349.

Hughes, S. E. D., & Walsh, J. F. Effects of syntactical mediation, age, and modes of representation on paired-associate learning. *Child Development*, 1971, *42*, 1827–1836.

Johnson, P. J., Warner, M. S., & Lee, D. R. Effects of enforced attention and stimulus phasing upon rule learning in children. *Journal of Experimental Child Psychology*, 1970, *9*, 388–399.

Keeney, T. J., Cannizzo, S. R., & Flavell, J. H. Spontaneous and induced verbal rehearsal in a recall task. *Child Development*, 1967, *38*, 953–966.

Kellas, G., Ashcraft, M. H., & Johnson, N. S. Rehearsal processes in the short-term memory performance of mildly retarded adolescents. *American Journal of Mental Deficiency*, 1973, *77*, 670–679. (a)

Kellas, G., Ashcraft, M. H., Johnson, N. S., & Needham, S. Temporal aspects of storage and retrieval in free recall of categorized lists. *Journal of Verbal Learning and Verbal Behavior*, 1973, *12*, 499–511. (b)

Kellas, G., & Butterfield, E. C. The effect of response requirement and type of material on acquisition and retention performance in short-term memory. *Journal of Experimental Psychology*, 1971, *88*, 50–56.

Kellas, G., McCauley, C., & McFarland, C. E. Developmental aspects of storage and retrieval. *Journal of Experimental Child Psychology*, 1975, *19*, 51–62.

Kendler, T. S. Verbalization and optional reversal shifts among kindergarten children. *Journal of Verbal Learning and Verbal Behavior*, 1964, *3*, 428–436.

Kendler, T. S., Kendler, H. H., & Learnard, B. Mediated responses to size and brightness as a function of age. *American Journal of Psychology*, 1962, *75*, 471–486.

Kendler, T. S., Kendler, H. H., & Wells, D. Reversal and nonreversal shifts in nursery school children. *Journal of Comparative and Physiological Psychology*, 1960, *53*, 83–88.

Kobasigawa, A. Utilization of retrieval cues by children in recall. *Child Development*, 1974, *45*, 127–134.

Kobasigawa, A., & Middleton, D. B. Free recall of categorized items by children at three grade levels. *Child Development*, 1972, *43*, 1067–1072.

Kroll, N. E. A., & Kellicut, M. H. Short-term recall as a function of covert rehearsal and of intervening task. *Journal of Verbal Learning and Verbal Behavior*, 1972, *11*, 196–204.

Kuenne, M. K. Experimental investigation of the relation of language to transposition behavior in young children. *Journal of Experimental Psychology*, 1946, *36*, 471–490.

Kuhn, D. Inducing development experimentally: Comments on a research paradigm. *Developmental Psychology*, 1974, *10*, 590–600.

Leicht, K. L., & Johnson, R. P. Effects of rehearsal instructions on recall and organization in free learning of retardates. *American Journal of Mental Deficiency*, 1970, *75*, 163–167.

Maccoby, E. E. Developmental psychology. In P. Farnsworth (Ed.) *Annual review of psychology*. Palo Alto, Calif.: Annual Reviews, 1964.

MacMillian, D. L. Paired-associate learning as a function of explicitness of mediational set by EMR and nonretarded children. *American Journal of Mental Deficiency*, 1972, *76*, 686–691.

Marsh, G., & Sherman, M. Verbal mediation of transposition as a function of age level. *Journal of Experimental Child Psychology*, 1966, *4*, 90–98.

Martin, C. J., Boersma, F. J., & Bulgarella, R. Verbalization of associative strategies by normal and retarded children. *Journal of General Psychology*, 1968, 209–218.

McKee, J. P., & Riley, D. A. Auditory transposition in six-year-old children. *Child Development*, 1962, *33*, 469–476.

Milgram, N. A. The effects of MA and IQ on verbal mediation in paired associate learning. *Journal of Genetic Psychology*, 1968, *113*, 129–143.

Moely, B. E., & Jeffrey, W. E. The effect of organization training on children's free recall of category items. *Child Development*, 1974, *45*, 135–143.

Moely, B. E., Olson, F. A., Halwes, T. G., & Flavell, J. H. Production deficiency in young children's clustered recall. *Developmental Psychology*, 1969, *1*, 26–34.

Mowbray, C. T., & Luria, Z. Effects of labeling on children's visual imagery. *Developmental Psychology*, 1973, *9*, 1–8.

Neimark, E. D. The natural history of spontaneous mnemonic activities under conditions of minimal experimental constraint. Unpublished manuscript, Rutgers, The State University, Douglass College, 1975.

Neimark, E., Slotnick, N. S., & Ulrich, T. Development of memorization strategies. *Developmental Psychology*, 1971, *5*, 427–432.

Newell, A. You can't play 20 questions with nature and win: Projective comments on the papers of this symposium. In W. Chase (Ed.), *Visual information processing*. New York: Academic Press, 1973.

Ornstein, P. A., Naus, M. J., & Liberty, C. Rehearsal and organizational processes in children's memory. *Child Development*, 1975, *46*, 818–830.

Phillips, S., & Levine, M. Probing for hypotheses with adults and children: Blank trials and introtacts. *Journal of Experimental Psychology: General*, 1975, *104*, 327–354.

Pyles, M. Verbalization as a factor in learning. *Child Development*, 1932, *3*, 108–113.

Reese, H. W. Verbal mediation as a function of age level. *Psychological Bulletin*, 1962, *59*, 502–509.

Reese, H. W. Imagery and contextual meaning. *Psychological Bulletin*, 1970, *73*, 404–414.

Resnick, L. B., & Glaser, R. Problem-solving and intelligence. Paper presented at a conference at the Learning Research and Development Center, University of Pittsburgh, March, 1974. Revised version appeared in L. B. Resnick (Ed.), *The nature of intelligence*, Hillsdale, N.J.: Lawrence Erlbaum Associates, 1976.

Rohwer, W. D. Images and pictures in children's learning: Research results and educational implications. *Psychological Bulletin*, 1970, *73*, 393–403.

Rohwer, W. D. Elaboration and learning in childhood and adolescence. In Hayne W. Reese (Ed.), *Advances in child development and behavior* (Vol. 8). New York: Academic Press, 1973.

Rosner, S. R. The effects of rehearsal and chunking instructions on children's multitrial free recall. *Journal of Experimental Child Psychology*, 1971, *11*, 93–105.

Rundus, D. Analysis of rehearsal processes in free recall. *Journal of Experimental Psychology*, 1971, *89*, 63–77.

Sabo, R. A., & Hagen, J. W. Color cues and rehearsal in short-term memory. *Child Development*, 1973, *44*, 77–82.

Seggie, J. L. The utilization by children and adults of binary propositional thinking in concept learning. *Journal of Experimental Child Psychology*, 1970, *10*, 235–247.

Shackleton, P. D. The effects of age and recall requirement on short-term memory rehearsal strategies. Unpublished doctoral dissertation, University of Kansas, 1974.

Siegler, R. S., & Liebert, R. M. Acquisition of formal scientific reasoning by 10- and 13-year olds: Designing a factorial experiment. *Developmental Psychology*, 1975, *11*, 401–402.

Siegler, R. S., Liebert, D. E., & Liebert, R. M. Inhelder and Piaget's pendulum problem: Teaching preadolescents to act as scientists. *Developmental Psychology*, 1973, *9*, 97–101.

Silverman, I. W. Effects of verbalization on reversal shifts in children: Additional data. *Journal of Experimental Child Psychology*, 1966, *4*, 1–8.

Spiker, C. C. Associative transfer in verbal paired-associate learning. *Child Development*, 1960, *31*, 73–87.

Taylor, A. M., Josberger, M., & Knowlton, J. Q. Mental elaboration and learning in EMR children. *American Journal of Mental Deficiency*, 1972, *77*, 69–76.

Turnure, J., Buium, N., & Thurlow, M. The effectiveness of interrogatives for promoting verbal elaboration productivity in young children. *Child Development*, 1976, *47*, 851–855.

Wallace, W. H., Turner, S. H., & Perkins, C. C. Preliminary studies of human information storage (DA Project No. 3-99-12-023, SC Proj. No. 1320 for the U.S. Army Signal Engineering

Laboratories, Fort Monmouth, N.J.). Philadelphia: University of Pennsylvania, Institute for Cooperative Research, 1957.

Wanschura, P. B., & Borkowski, J. G. Long-term transfer of a mediational strategy by moderately retarded children. *American Journal of Mental Deficiency,* 1975, *80,* 323–333.

Wheeler, R. J., & Dusek, J. B. The effects of attentional and cognitive factors on children's incidental learning. *Child Development,* 1973, *44,* 253–258.

Wolff, P., & Levin, J. R. The role of overt activity in children's imagery production. *Child Development,* 1972, *43,* 537–547.

Author Index

Numbers in *italics* refer to pages on which the complete references are listed.

A

Aaron, D. L., 82, *86*
Ackerman, B. P., 133, 138, *168*
Acredelo, L. P., 8, 9, *30*, 74, *85*
Adams, H. F., 416, *431*
Adams, J. A. 158, *166*
Adams, J. F., 135, 136, 143, 153, *168*
Adams, W., 318, *330*
Aiello, N., 55, *58*
Alexander, R. A., 137, *173*
Allen, T. W., 441, *477*
Allik, J. P., 66, 73, 74, *87*, 95, 96, *109, 111*
Altemeyer, R., 49, *58*, 305, 318, 319, 325, 326, 327, *330*
Alvarez, J. M., 206, 210, 224, *232*
Ammon, M. S., 132, 136, 141, 144, *173*, 429, *431, 434*
Ammon, P. R., 429, *434*
Anderson, J. R., 128, *166*, 205, *230*
Anderson, R. C., 36, 46, *58*, 214, *235*, 408, *434*
Angell, J. R., 115, *166*
Anglin, J. M., 79, *85*
Appel, L. F., 7, 8, *30*, 137, *166*, 196, *200*, 219, 220, 228, *230*, 284, *293*
Aristotle, 115, *166*
Ashcraft, M. H., 103, *110*, 380, *405*, 455, 466, *479*
Atkeson, B., 50, *59*

B

Atkinson, R. C., 4, *30*, 89, 90, 91, *109*, 117, 128, 146, 165, *166, 173*, 251, 266, *269*, 368, 369, 397, *403*, 408, 410, *431*, 443, 456, *477*
Attneave, F., 128, *166*
Austin, G. A., 264, *269*

Bach, M. J., 212, *230*, 425, *432*
Ball, S., 137, *166*
Balling, J. D., 445, 450, 455, 471, *477*
Barber, T. X., 121, *166*
Barclay, C. R., 384, 389, 390, *404*
Barclay, J. R., 38, 40, 41, 46, 50, 52, *58*
Barker, W. J., 145, *175*
Baron, C. R., 182, 184, *200*
Barron, R. W., 70, *86*
Bartlett, F. C., 35, 36, 43, 44, *58*, 203, *230*, 241, 244, 246, *269*, 330, *330*
Bartz, W. H., 137, *172*
Bateson, G., 241, *269*
Battig, W. F., 126, *171*, 208, *235*, 455, *477*
Baumeister, A. A., 411, *432*
Bausell, R., 306, 307, 308, 318, 321, 322, 323, *331*
Beach, D. R., 26, *31*, 90, 94, *109*, 443, 445, 458, *478*
Bean, J. P., 428, 429, *434*

483

Subject Index